STUDIES IN
CONTEMPORARY
JEWRY

The publication of *Studies in Contemporary Jewry* was
made possible through the generous assistance of
the Samuel and Althea Stroum Philanthropic Fund,
Seattle, Washington.

INSTITUTE OF CONTEMPORARY JEWRY
THE HEBREW UNIVERSITY
OF JERUSALEM

STUDIES IN CONTEMPORARY JEWRY

I

———— 1984 ————

Edited by Jonathan Frankel

Published for the Institute by
INDIANA UNIVERSITY PRESS • BLOOMINGTON

The preparation of the book review sections was made possible by the aid of the Joseph M. and Bertha Levine Bibliographical Center in Contemporary Jewry.

Copyright © 1984 by Indiana University Press

All rights reserved

No part of this book may be reproduced or utilized in any form or by any means, electronic or mechanical, including photocopying and recording, or by any information storage and retrieval system, without permission in writing from the publisher. The Association of American University Presses' Resolution on Permissions constitutes the only exception to this prohibition.

Manufactured in the United States of America

ISBN 0-253-39511-9

ISSN 0740-8625

STUDIES IN CONTEMPORARY JEWRY

Editors: Jonathan Frankel,
Peter Medding, Ezra Mendelsohn

Institute Editorial Board:

Michel Abitbol, Mordecai Altshuler, Haim Avni, Yehuda Bauer, Moshe Davis, Sergio DellaPergola, Sidra Ezrahi, Moshe Goodman, Yisrael Gutman, Menahem Kaufman, Israel Kolatt, Abraham Margaliot, Dalia Ofer, Gideon Shimoni, U. O. Schmelz, Pnina Morag-Talmon, Geoffrey Wigoder

Managing Editor: Eli Lederhendler

International Advisory and Review Board:

Chimen Abramsky (University College, London); Abraham Ascher (City University of New York); Arnold Band (University of California, Los Angeles); Doris Bensimon (Unversité de la Sorbonne Nouvelle); Bernard Blumenkrantz (Centre National de la Recherche Scientifique); Lucjan Dobroszycki (YIVO Institute for Jewish Research); Solomon Encel (University of New South Wales); Henry Feingold (City University of New York); Martin Gilbert, Oxford University; Zvi Gitelman (University of Michigan); S. Julius Gould (University of Nottingham); Ben Halpern (Brandeis University); Irving Howe (City University of New York); Paula Hyman (Jewish Theological Seminary of America); Lionel Kochan (University of Warwick); David Landes (Harvard University); Seymour Martin Lipset (Stanford University); Heinz-Dietrich Löwe (Albert-Ludwigs-Universität, Freiburg); Arthur Mendel (University of Michigan); Michael Meyer (Hebrew Union College - Jewish Institute of Religion, Cincinnati); Alan Mintz (University of Maryland); George Mosse (University of Wisconsin); Gerard Nahan (Centre Universitaire d'Études Juives, Paris); Gyorgy Ranki (Hungarian Academy of Sciences); F. Raphael (Université des Sciences Humaines de Strasbourg); Jehuda Reinharz (Brandeis University); Monika Richarz (Technische Universität, Berlin); Joseph Rothschild (Columbia University); Ismar Schorsch (Jewish Theological Seminary of America); Marshall Sklare (Brandeis University); Michael Walzer (Princeton University); Bernard Wasserstein (Brandeis University); Ruth Wisse (McGill University).

Contents

Editorial Note — xv

Symposium: *Ostjuden* in Central and Western Europe

Steven E. Aschheim, The East European Jew and
   German Jewish Identity — 3
David Weinberg, "Heureux comme Dieu en France":
   East European Jews in Paris, 1881–1914 — 26
Jehuda Reinharz, East European Jews in the
   Weltanschauung of German Zionists, 1882–1914 — 55
Paul Mendes-Flohr, *Fin-de-Siècle* Orientalism, the
   Ostjuden and the Aesthetics of Jewish
   Self-Affirmation — 96
Jack Wertheimer, Jewish Lobbyists and the German
   Citizenship Law of 1914: A Documentary
   Account — 140
A. Goren, Judah L. Magnes' Trip to Przedborz — 163
Trude Maurer, The East European Jew in the Weimar
   Press: Stereotype and Attempted Rebuttal — 176

Essays

Yehuda Bauer, The Place of the Holocaust in
   Contemporary History — 201
Victor Karady, Jewish Enrollment Patterns in
   Classical Secondary Education in Old Regime
   and Inter-war Hungary — 225

Mordecai Altshuler, The Jewish Anti-Fascist Committee in the USSR in Light of New Documentation	253
Sergio DellaPergola, On the Differential Frequency of Western Migration to Israel	292
Ezra Mendelsohn, Recent Work on the Jews in Inter-war East Central Europe: A Survey	316

Review Essays

Lloyd P. Gartner, Metropolis and Periphery in American Jewry	341
Michael Brown, The Emerging Colossus of the North: Three Recent Books on Canadian Jewry	347
Gershon Bacon, The Jewish Question in Pre-World War II Poland	355
Benjamin Pinkus, On Dissidents and Refuseniks	359
Sidra DeKoven Ezrahi, Aharon Appelfeld: The Search for a Language	366
Dov Levin, The Holocaust in Lithuania and Latvia	381
Uriel Tal, The Nazi Legal System and the Jews in Germany	386

Books in Review

Irving Abella and Harold Troper, *None Is Too Many* / Michael Brown	347
Shmuel Almog, *Ẓiyonut vehistoriah* / Yoav Peled	399
Yitzhak Alperovitz (ed.), *Sefer Gorzd* / Dov Levin	381
Mordecai Altshuler, *Hayevsekẓiah bivrit hamo'aẓot, 1918–1930: bein leumiut vekomunizm* / Matityahu Mintz	401
Aharon Appelfeld, *Mikhvat haor* / Sidra Ezrahi	366
Aharon Appelfeld, *Tor hapelaot* / Sidra Ezrahi	366
Robert Attal and Yosef Tobi, *Yehudei hamizraḥ uẓefon afrikah: bibliografiah mu'eret 5734–5736 (1974–1976)* / Alfred A. Greenbaum	404

Contents

Shlomo Avineri, *The Making of Modern Zionism: The Intellectual Origins of the Jewish State* / Ben Halpern	405
Mark Azbel, *Refusenik: Trapped in the Soviet Union* / Benjamin Pinkus	359
Kenneth Ray Bain, *The March to Zion* / Menahem Kaufman	562
Yehuda Bauer, *American Jewry and the Holocaust: The American Jewish Joint Distribution Committee, 1939–1945* / Stephen J. Whitfield	408
Myron Berman, *Richmond's Jewry, 1769–1976* / Lloyd P. Gartner	341
R. Bilski, et al. (eds.), *Can Planning Replace Politics? The Israeli Experience* / Michael Keren	410
Max Birnbaum, *Staat und Synagoge 1918–1938; Eine Geschichte des Preussischen Landesverbandes jüdischer Gemeinden* / Abraham Margaliot	412
Janet Blatter and Sybil Milton, *Art of the Holocaust* / Ziva Amishai-Maisels	512
John W. Boyer, *Political Radicalism in Late Imperial Vienna. Origins of the Christian Social Movement, 1848–1897* / Robert Wistrich	416
Randolph L. Braham, *The Politics of Genocide. The Holocaust in Hungary (2 vols.)* / Yeshayahu Jellinek	419
Arthur A. Cohen, *The Tremendum: A Theological Interpretation of the Holocaust* / Emil Fackenheim	422
Gary B. Cohen, *The Politics of Ethnic Survival: Germans in Prague, 1861–1914* / Hillel J. Kieval	424
Stuart A. Cohen, *English Zionists and British Jews: The Communal Politics of Anglo-Jewry, 1895–1920* / Gideon Shimoni	427
Scott Cummings (ed.), *Self-Help in Urban America* / Paul Ritterband	430
Norman Davies, *God's Playground—A History of Poland (2 vols)* / Paul Glikson	485
Moshe Davis (ed.), *Zionism in Transition* / Milton R. Konvitz	432

Shlomo Deshen and Walter P. Zenner (eds.), *Jewish Societies in the Middle East—Community, Culture and Authority* / Pnina Morag-Talmon ... 433

Leonard Dinnerstein, *America and the Survivors of the Holocaust* / Melvin I. Urofsky ... 436

Ulrich Dunker, *Der Reischsbund jüdischer Frontsoldaten 1919–1938* / Donald L. Niewyk ... 439

A. Roy Eckardt with Alice Eckardt, *Long Night's Journey into Day* / Emil Fackenheim ... 422

Daniel J. Elazar (ed.), *Kinship and Consent: The Jewish Political Tradition and Its Contemporary Uses* / Michael Walzer ... 441

M. Eliav (ed.), *Sefer ha'aliyah harishonah* / Yossi Goldstein ... 442

Sidra Ezrahi, *By Words Alone: The Holocaust in Literature* / Alvin H. Rosenfeld ... 445

Egal Feldman, *The Dreyfus Affair and the American Conscience, 1895–1906* / Jonathan D. Sarna ... 447

Geoffrey Field, *Evangelist of Race: The Germanic Vision of Houston Stewart Chamberlain* / Robert A. Pois ... 448

Gerald Fleming, *Hitler und die Endlösung* / Yehuda Bauer ... 450

Maurice Friedman, *Martin Buber's Life and Work: The Early Years, 1878–1923* / Bernard Susser ... 451

Lloyd P. Gartner, *History of the Jews of Cleveland (1836–1945)* / Steven G. Hertzberg ... 453

Martin Gilbert, *Atlas of the Holocaust* / Yehuda Bauer ... 454

Günther Ginzel (ed.), *Auschwitz als Herausforderung für Juden und Christen* / Emil Fackenheim ... 422

Frank Golczewski, *Polnische-Jüdische Beziehungen 1881–1922* / Gershon Bacon ... 355

Morris Goldman (ed.), *Society in Israel 1980—Statistical Highlights* / U. O. Schmelz ... 455

Sherry Gorelick, *City College and the Jewish Poor: Education in New York 1880–1924* / Jeffrey S. Gurock ... 457

Arthur Goren (ed. and intro.), *Dissenter in Zion* / Ben Halpern ... 458

Moshe R. Gottlieb, *American Anti-Nazi Resistance, 1933–1941* / Evyatar Friesel ... 460

Contents

Alfred Abraham Greenbaum, *Jewish Scholarship and Scholarly Institutions in Soviet Russia 1918–1953* / Alexander Orbach	462
Evgenia Guinzbourg, *Sous le ciel de kolyma* / Benjamin Pinkus	359
Jeffrey S. Gurock, *When Harlem Was Jewish* / Deborah Dash Moore	464
Fruma Gurvitch, *Zikhronot shel rofah: im yehudei lita biyemei shoah* / Dov Levin	381
Zeev Hadari and Zeev Tzahor, *Oniot o medinah? Korot oniot hama'apilim "Pan York" u-"Pan Crescent"* / Dalia Ofer	465
Janet R. Hadda, *Yankev Glatshteyn* / David G. Roskies	468
Arthur Hertzberg, *Being Jewish in America: The Modern Experience* / Ben Halpern	405
Colin Holmes, *Anti-Semitism in British Society 1876–1939* / Ernest Krausz	471
Alfred Jospe (ed. and intro.), *Studies in Jewish Thought: An Anthology of German Jewish Scholarship* / Michael A. Meyer	472
Nathan M. Kaganoff (ed.), *Guide to America-Holy Land Studies 1620–1948 (2 vols.)* / Alfred A. Greenbaum	473
Nathan M. Kaganoff and Melvin I. Urofsky (eds.), *"Turn to the South": Essays on Southern Jewry* / Lloyd P. Gartner	341
Yehoshua Kaniel, *Hemshekh utemurah: hayishuv hayashan vehayishuv heḥadash bitkufat ha'aliyah harishonah vehashniyah* / Yossi Salmon	474
Marion A. Kaplan, *Die jüdische Frauenbewegung in Deutschland: Organisation und Ziele des jüdischen Frauenbundes 1904–1938* / Shulamit Volkov	478
Nathaniel Katzburg, *Hungary and the Jews: Policy and Legislation, 1920–1943* / Yeshayahu Jelinek	419
Yosef Kermish and Israel Bialostotski (eds.), *'Itonut hamaḥteret hayehudit begeto varshah* / Yisrael Gutman	481
Lev Kopelev, *The Education of a True Believer* / Benjamin Pinkus	359
Pawel Korzec, *Juifs en Pologne* / Gershon Bacon	355

Eduard Kuznetsov, *Mordovskii mirofan* [*Lettres de mordovie*] / Benjamin Pinkus	359
Shulamit Laskov, *Ha-Biluim* / Yossi Goldstein	442
Anny Latour, *The Jewish Resistance in France (1940–1944)* / Robert O. Paxton	483
R. F. Leslie (ed.), *The History of Poland since 1863* / Paul Glikson	485
Rosemarie Leuschen-Seppel, *Sozialdemokratie und Antisemitismus im Kaiserreich* / Abraham Ascher	490
Ladislav Lipscher, *Die Juden im Slowakischen Staat 1939–1945* / Livia Rotkirchen	491
Laurence D. Loeb, *Outcaste: Jewish Life in Southern Iran* / Amnon Netzer	493
Heinz-Dietrich Löwe, *Antisemitismus und reaktionäre Utopie—Russischer Konservatismus im Kampf gegen den Wandel von Staat und Gesellschaft 1890–1917* / Marc Raeff	496
Michael Marrus and Robert O. Paxton, *Vichy France and the Jews* / Richard Cohen	500
Ezra Mendelsohn, *Zionism in Poland: The Formative Years, 1915–1926* / Gershon David Hundert	503
Gabrielle Michalski, *Der Antisemitismus im deutschen akademischen Leben in der Zeit nach dem I Weltkrieg* / Donald L. Niewcyk	506
Deborah Dash Moore, *At Home in America: Second Generation New York Jews* / Lloyd P. Gartner	341
Deborah Dash Moore, *B'nai B'rith and the Challenge of Ethnic Leadership* / Eli Lederhendler	506
George Mosse, *Masses and Man: Nationalist and Fascist Perceptions of Reality* / Eugen Weber	508
Shlomo Netzer, *Maavak yehudei polin al zekhuyoteihem haezraḥiyot vehaleumiyot (1918–1922)* / Gershon Bacon	355
Donald L. Niewyk, *The Jews in Weimar Germany* / Marion A. Kaplan	509
Miriam Novitch, et al., *Spiritual Resistance: Art From Concentration Camps, 1940–1945* / Ziva Amishai-Maisels	512

Contents

Yisrael Oppenheim, *Tnu'at heḥaluẓ befolin (1917–1929)* / Ezra Mendelsohn	515
Esther L. Panitz, *The Alien in Their Midst: Images of Jews in English Literature* / Anita Norich	517
Leonard Prager, *Yiddish Literary and Linguistic Periodicals and Miscellanies: A Selective Annotated Bibliography* / Khone Shmeruk and Agnes Romer-Segal	519
Jehuda Reinharz (ed.), *Dokumente zur Geschichte des deutschen Zionismus 1882–1933* / Abraham Margaliot	523
Paul Ritterband (ed.), *Modern Jewish Fertility* / U. O. Schmelz	527
Dov Sadan, *Toyern un tirn: Eseyen un etyudn* / Janet Hadda	528
Gertrude Schneider, *Journey into Terror: The Story of the Riga Ghetto* / Dov Levin	381
Anita Shapira, *Berl: Biografia* / Jonathan Frankel	530
R. Shapira, et al., *Ḥulẓah k'ḥulah veẓavaron lavan* / David Mittelberg	533
Gideon Shimoni, *Jews and Zionism: The South African Experience (1910–1967)* / Dennis Diamond	535
Marshall Sklare (ed.), *Understanding American Jewry* / Sergio DellaPergola	538
Yehuda Slutzky, *Ha'itonut hayehudit-rusit bameah haesrim* / Steven J. Zipperstein	541
Roderick Stackelberg, *Idealism Debased: From Völkisch Ideology to National Socialism* / Geoff Eley	544
Herbert A. Strauss (ed.), *Jewish Immigrants of the Nazi Period in the U.S.A.* / Alfred A. Greenbaum	547
Walter Strauss (ed.), *Signs of Life: Jews From Württemburg. Reports for the Period after 1933* / Abraham Margaliot	549
Victor Teboul, *Mythe et images du Juif au Quebec* / Michael Brown	347
Shabbetai Tevet, *Kinat David: ḥayei David Ben-Gurion (vol. 2)* / Anita Shapira	550
Yosef Tobi, et al., *Toldot hayehudim be-arẓot ha-islam (vol. 2)* / Norman A. Stillman	553

Zeev Tzahor, *Baderekh lehanhagat hayishuv* / Henry Near	555
David Vital, *Zionism: The Formative Years* / Ben Halpern	558
Joseph Walk (ed.), *Das Sonderrecht für die Juden im NS-Staat* / Uriel Tal	386
Morton Weinfeld, et al. (eds.), *The Canadian Jewish Mosaic* / Michael Brown	347
Stephen J. Whitfield, *Into the Dark: Hannah Arendt and Totalitarianism* / Mitchell Cohen	560
Evan Wilson, *Decision on Palestine* / Menahem Kaufman	562
Y. Zilberscheid and A. Pielkov (eds.), *Tel-ḥai: kibbuẓ hakhsharah befolin* / Yisrael Oppenheim	567
Gebhard Zwerenz, *Kurt Tucholsky: Biographie eines guten Deutschen* / Istvan Deak	569
Partial List of Recently Completed Doctoral Dissertations	573
Paul Glikson: In Memoriam	583

Editorial Note

The last two decades have witnessed the rapid growth of modern Jewish studies in Israel, the United States, and, to a lesser but not insignificant extent, elsewhere. Various factors have been at work here. The expansion of higher education generally as well as the very high percentage of Jewish youth at universities in the West have been of key importance. In Israel, for example, there are now five universities, and a number of colleges, where in 1960 there was only the Hebrew University. And this transformation was part of the general trend characteristic of higher education in the United States, Great Britain, France, and other Western countries during the 1960's.

Such objective developments would, nonetheless, hardly have been sufficient in themselves to produce the mushrooming of modern Jewish studies at the universities. If one is looking for a single factor which was of decisive importance it is surely to be found at the more subjective level of historical awareness. The impact exerted on the public consciousness by the Holocaust, on the one hand, and by the establishment of the Jewish state, on the other, has only increased with the passage of time. These two phenomena are so totally out of the ordinary run of things even when set against the unusual history of the Jewish people that they naturally tend to produce in the beholder a sense of bewilderment, of wonder, of mystery. And these sentiments, in turn, lead many to seek further understanding through knowledge and analysis.

However, the scholarly infrastructure called upon to sustain and give direction to this demand has not built itself up at a rate to match that of the institutional expansion. The signs of this uneven development are to be seen at every turn. Hundreds of books a year are published in this field but relatively few are adequately reviewed. Doctoral dissertations appear in large numbers but are nowhere listed together. There are many monographs but few first class textbooks to synthesize their findings for the student. And most of the books which are published confine themselves within the boundaries of the single sovereign state even though modern Jewish history has been marked above all, perhaps—in contradiction to the expectations of the Enlightenment—by its international or transnational character.

None of this is said in any way to denigrate the genuinely major achievements of innumerable individual scholars, institutions and periodical publications but only to explain what we see as the particular function of this new venture, *Studies in Contemporary Jewry*. The goal which we have set ourselves is to fill, however partially, some of the gaps in the infrastructure. We hope to provide a forum for scholars (Jews and non-Jews) who work in the field of contemporary Jewish studies but live in different countries and belong to different disciplines. It was this consideration—together, of course, with the normal criteria of scholarly quality—which has largely dictated the selection of the monographic and review articles in this, the first, issue. Again, an extensive section of the *Studies* has been set aside for the review of books in a wide range of languages. And a list of recently completed doctorates is likewise included and planned as another permanent item.

The theme of the symposium, "*Ostjuden* in Central and Western Europe," was selected in part because it is now one hundred years since the mass migration from Eastern Europe began, ushering in a new era in the history of the Jewish people. Indeed, 1881 must surely stand as one of the key turning-points—perhaps the most decisive—in the shaping of the modern Jewish destiny. However, this theme was also chosen because until very recently it had been left largely neglected by historians. The essays collected here raise fundamental questions. Did the influx of the Jews from Eastern Europe contribute significantly to modern anti-Semitism or only provide it with one more theme among the many always available? Did they significantly influence and strengthen Zionism and Jewish national consciousness in Germany and Austria or, again, was their role marginal, that of the outsider regarded with condescension or with romanticism, but not as an equal?

It behooves a new periodic publication to view itself with much hope but with a modesty even greater. The success of such ventures has to be measured in terms of decades rather than single issues. And the ability to sustain an enterprise of this kind depends not only on internal but also on external factors (institutional, financial). But we are much encouraged by the initial response from our colleagues in the Institute of Contemporary Jewry (which under the leadership of Moshe Davis has made this entire project possible); in Israel generally; and in many countries abroad. The most generous support of the Samuel and Althea Stroum Philanthropic Fund has likewise been of the utmost importance.

If authors of new books in the field ensure that we are sent copies we on our part will make every effort to have them reviewed. And we would also like to reach a position where students who complete doctorates on relevant themes supply us as a matter of course with the information required for inclusion in our listing. (Doctorates omitted from our partial list dating from 1981 can be included in the next issue.) Again, it should be emphasized that we welcome unsolicited manuscripts which will be subject to normal review procedures. Thus, while the failure of this project would be ours alone, its success will be that of an entire community of scholars in many disciplines and many countries.

J. F.

Symposium
Ostjuden in Central and Western Europe

The East European Jew and German Jewish Identity[1]

Steven E. Aschheim
(HEBREW UNIVERSITY)

The modern German Jew, like other West European Jews, was a new and distinctive creation, the product of eighteenth century Enlightenment thought and nineteenth century emancipatory practice.[2] This, by now, is a historical commonplace. Less familiar is the proposition that the very notion of the *Ostjude* was similarly the outcome of the modernization of Jewish life and consciousness.[3] East European Jews were held to be loud, coarse and dirty. They were regarded as immoral, culturally backward creatures of ugly and anachronistic ghettos. This view was formulated and propagated largely by West European, and especially German, Jews as a symbolic construct by which they could distinguish themselves from their less fortunate, unenlightened and unemancipated East European brethren.

Such an attitude was encouraged by the implicit dictates of assimilation. Assimilation was not merely the attempt to blend into new social and cultural environments. It was also purposeful, even programmatic, dissociation from traditional Jewish national and cultural moorings. Political equality demanded a new kind of Jew, one whose identity was indissolubly a product of the society that was emancipating him. This marks the birth of the specifically German or English or French Jew. In their eagerness to prove their fitness for equal rights it was necessary for these "new" Jews to demonstrate their differences from the traditional Jews of the ghetto. At least in part, the German Jew was recognizable in terms of what he was not. The "modern" Jew was a new and distinctive creation—but so too was his mirror opposite, his dialectical antithesis, the *Ostjude,* who was made to embody all those negative traditional traits which German Jews had supposedly overcome. The emergent stereotype of the *Ostjude* was as much the product of Enlightenment thinking as was German Jewry's own self-image. Both ideas had their origins in the drive to modernity; both conceptions were the outcome of the breakdown of traditional Jewish self-understanding and signalled the rise of new modes of cultural perception. One fashioned the other.

This was an entirely new development. Before the penetration of Enlightenment thinking, Jews did not divide themselves (nor were they divided by others) into radically antithetical "Eastern" and "Western" components. Of course, local and regional differences between Jews had always existed but in the pre-emancipation era they were of little structural significance when compared with the overall similarities: Jews everywhere were bound by a common socio-political condition and linked by a shared system of beliefs and attachments.[4] Political events and ideological change had created an unprecedented situation. From about the 1780's on, Jewish historical development was characterized by a profound fragmentation. On the one hand, Enlightenment and emancipation in the West; on the other, the continuation of political disenfranchisement and traditional Jewish culture in Eastern Europe. These were the terms of discourse employed by and about European Jews well into the twentieth century. It was a polarity which produced a new dialectic in the fabric of Jewish life.

Central to this polarity was the ghetto—both as myth and reality. The idea of the "ghetto Jew" is crucial to any discussion of the disposition of modern Jewish history. It stands at the very center of the relationship between the Eastern Jew and German Jewish identity. By the second half of the nineteenth century the ghetto had become virtually synonymous with the *Ostjude*. It was this conjunction which provided the stereotype with its ongoing resonance. By their mere existence, unemancipated Eastern Jewry kept the historical memory of the ghetto Jew alive in Germany and elsewhere in Central and Western Europe.[5] But this exclusive identification was relatively new. At the beginning of the century Jews in Germany were still commonly regarded as ghetto Jews. Goethe's description of the ghetto as he remembered it from his youth in the 1750's referred to the Jewish quarter in Frankfurt, not to an obscure village in Eastern Europe. His shocked reaction to the dirt, the throngs of people, the ceaseless haggling and the ugly German Jewish dialect[6] reflects well the overall Enlightenment perception of the ghetto.

Contemporary discussions were not limited to a definition of the ghetto as an area in which Jews were forced to live by law. The conception was far broader than that. The ghetto referred to the simple fact of Jewish physical concentration regardless of its coercive or voluntary origins and, even more pointedly, to the perception of the separatist culture generated by such concentration. Ghetto became a kind of ontological and epistemological category: increasingly it connoted a certain mode of being, a state of mind. This was a viewpoint by no means limited to opponents of the Jews. Rather the rejection of the ghetto coincided with a progressive political outlook. To this day the phrase "ghetto" conjures up images of isolation, compulsion, narrowness, a form of life dependent upon mutual distrust and antagonism. A medieval remnant, for the liberal minds of the day it highlighted the distinction between progress and reaction, Enlightenment and superstition, even beauty and ugliness.[7]

To a large degree, then, Jewish modernization was conditional upon rejection of the ghetto and the fact that this demand came from progressive forces made the same exercise easier for German Jewry. Indeed, this project of de-ghettoization was enthusiastically undertaken. From 1800–1850 German Jews applied the critique of the ghetto to themselves as well as to other Jews; only when German Jewry was sufficiently confident that its own ghetto inheritance had been overcome did the stereotype of the *Ostjude* assume its full meaning. Acculturation had to be relatively complete before the synonymity of the Eastern Jew with the ghetto could be made definitive.

What was the substance of German Jewish acculturation? Jews did not integrate into some abstract *Volk* but into the middle class[8]; assimilation was a form of *embourgeoisement* and Jews spent much time and energy internalizing the economic, ethical and aesthetic standards of that class. But these standards were mediated in a particular way. As George L. Mosse has demonstrated, the Jewish struggle for emancipation occurred when the peculiarly German ideal of *Bildung* was at its height. Jews eagerly accepted the ideal and, long after the non-Jewish German middle class had deserted its tenets of rationality, tenaciously clung to it.[9] The notion of *Bildung* centered on the theme of self-improvement in the form of an integrated conception of "rationality" and "refinement." A highly non-political idea, *Bildung* was about the self-cultivation of the "cultured" personality.[10] From that point on— even when events appeared to radically belie this outlook—German Jews maintained their belief in the primacy of culture and reason.

Bildung thus determined the pattern of Jewish acculturation and became the criterion by which traditional Jewish life and culture was judged. Under its exacting standards it appeared that almost all old Jewish habits and modes of sociability had to be discarded. Little illustrates this better than the attitude of the early reformers towards *jüdisch-deutsch* (Yiddish). This, of course, was the pre-emancipation language of both Eastern European and German Jewry. Enlighteners everywhere opposed this "jargon" as an impediment to local linguistic integration. In Germany, however, the attack was particularly marked given the derivation of Yiddish from German. Elsewhere Yiddish sounded merely strange; in Germany it was the familiarity that bred contempt. This circumstance encouraged an almost demonic perception of the language. Thus, in 1782 Moses Mendelssohn, who as a youth had himself used the language, declared that Yiddish had "contributed not a little to the immorality of the common man; and I expect a very good effect on my brothers from the increasing use of the pure German idiom."[11] The "jargon" symbolized all the negative Jewish qualities of the past, the very antithesis of *Bildung*. More and more the traditional ghetto Jew—the language he spoke, the manners he displayed—became identical with *Unbildung,* the counter-example of what the new German Jew had to become. (Mendelssohn's remarks are typical of that faith in culture which held that immorality could be countered by the correct use of language, that purity of expression would somehow create an ethical personality.)

The modernization of the Jewish self was obviously not limited to the linguistic realm: a generalized middle class gentility became the norm for Jewish behavior.[12] Jewish reformers stressed manners, politeness, refinement and contrasted these modes with the crudity and boorishness of traditional Jewish life. The editor of *Sulamith* distinguished the common from the noble person in terms of the criterion of aesthetic sensibility.[13] This was not a random choice for it stressed those qualities—feelings for the beautiful in art and nature—which were absent in the ghetto Jew. Assimilation also entailed a change of dress; traditional external badges of distinction had to be removed. That is why the dress of the *Ostjuden,* the caftan and the sidelocks, came to be regarded both as an embarrassment to the German Jew and a deliberate provocation to the non-Jew.[14]

But the process was still more subtle. Acculturation applied also to a nuanced modulation of tone, a lowering of the decibel level. Writing in 1844, Anton Reé argued that political freedoms and religious reform had not led to any real emancipation.[15] The gulf dividing Jews from non-Jews, he declared, was *social* in nature and could be bridged only by a fundamental reshaping of Jewish manners and mannerisms. Reé explicitly incorporated "gentility" as an essential Jewish aim: *"Es ist doch gar zu ungentil, ein Jude zu sein!"*[16] In polite society Jewish characteristics were a source of shame—Reé's diagnosis and solution to the problem of Jewish integration reads like a manual of etiquette, an exercise in impression management. His work is a sustained plea to German Jews to finally cast off all traces of the ghetto past. Manner of speech becomes the key to social acceptance and by "dialect" Reé meant not only the "jargon" itself but also the tone, manner and particular gesticulations Jews used even when speaking German. The entire *Gestalt* of the ghetto Jew was to be removed.

Nineteenth-century German Jews, then, internalized the general distaste for the ghetto in a particularly urgent and intense way. By the time the westward mass migrations of Eastern Jews began in the 1880's, German Jews were confident that they had succeeded in their own project of de-ghettoization. By then it seemed clear that it was the unemancipated *Ostjude* who most closely fitted the category of the "ghetto Jew." Locked in narrow Talmudic worlds, eternal *shnorers,* boorish and dirty, still speaking the despised "jargon," the *Ostjuden* symbolized *Unbildung,* the incarnation of the Jewish past which German Jews had not only rejected but already transcended.

It must be remembered that we are talking here about myths and images, about the symbolic role Eastern Jews played in German Jewish identity. East European Jews were usually perceived as an undifferentiated mass. This was a misleading and often quite distorted picture: the reality was far more complex and differentiated. But stereotypes are never constructed as refined instruments of social understanding. They serve other, less disinterested, purposes. Yet, for all that, myths do carry a core of reality and there was sufficient substance in both the circumstances and culture of Eastern Jewry to give the stereotype plausibility. It was a stereotype which played an important function in the self-understanding of German Jews. The *Ostjuden,* geographically bordering Germany and always infiltrating its space and consciousness, became the living reminder to German Jewry of its own recently rejected past and an ubiquitous threat to assimilationist aspirations. At the same time, the Eastern Jew was a convenient foil upon which German Jews could externalize and displace "negative" Jewish characteristics. This dual function of the ghetto Jew—threat and foil—became very clear during the 1880's.

Yet the identification of the Eastern Jew as the ghetto Jew had begun considerably before that date. If German Jewry during the first part of the nineteenth century applied the rationalist critique of the ghetto to itself, it always reserved a special animus for the Jews of Eastern Europe and especially Poland. Often the critique was aimed at the debilitating influence of Polish Jewish teachers who, as a result of their migrations from 1600–1800, had become the dominant influence in German Jewish education. Polish Jewish teachers, one Jewish educational theorist proclaimed in 1812, imported not only sloppy language but also a flawed, backward culture into Germany.[17] While German Jews were straining towards the light, towards science and rationality, these men still purveyed Talmudic sophistry or, even worse, Kabbalistic superstition. German *Bildung* was explicitly juxtaposed to Polish Talmudic barbarism[18] or the degenerate fanaticism of Hasidism.[19]

In this manner, if assimilation did not proceed apace, Polish Jewry could be blamed. Even that proto-nationalist, committed Jew, Heinrich Graetz expressed this distaste in words hardly distinguishable from those of the Jew-haters. Polish Jews, he wrote, delighted in deception and cheating: "Against members of their own race cunning could not be well employed, because they were sharp-witted; but the non-Jewish world with which they came into contact experienced to its disadvantage the superiority of the Talmudical spirit of the Polish Jews." They had a love of "twisting, distorting, ingenious quibbling, and a foregone antipathy to what did not lie within their field of vision." Their manner of thinking led to a "crabbed dogmatism that defied all logic."[20] This was clearly a post-Enlightenment perception, one that percolated its way through German Jewry.

By the mid-nineteenth century few German Jews would have disagreed with the appraisal of Galician Jewry made by *Der Israelit*—that they were sunk in the lowest ethical and spiritual depths, lived in terrible filth and poverty and were ruled by ignorance and superstition.[21] All this, of course, contrasted with the German Jews who were making steady progress and advancing towards the light. This light put the darkness of Polish Jewry into an even more bleak focus. But the main reason for the constant comparison was the reassurance that German Jews had progressed to a point where little connected them with their unenlightened ghetto brethren across the border.

For all that, there were clear limits to the extent of Jewish denationalization. The young Abraham Geiger's "spiritualization" of Judaism, his rigid division of Jews belonging to "civilized" and "uncivilized" nations, his insistence that what "goes on among the Jews living in the uncivilized countries. . . . is of trifling importance only,"[22] never really triumphed. Beneath the rhetoric of Jewish dissociation, a stubborn sense of Jewish collective responsibility (if not solidarity) persisted. Traditional forms of mutual aid continued to operate as a real social force. What was new was the rationale for the continuing relationship. German Jews justified their concern for Eastern Jews in terms of the same Enlightenment concerns which had provided the grounds for denationalization in the first place. *Aufklärung* was both the basis for dissociation and justification for mutual aid. Surely German Jews could apply the same modern goals to their Eastern brethren as they did to themselves? Old traditions of mutual aid could realize new ends: providing Jews everywhere with the same rights would ensure one's own emancipation and assimilation and thereby reduce the reality of Jewish national solidarity. In this manner, both the imperative of integration and the demands of Jewish conscience seemed to be satisfied. It was a program which orthodox[23] as well as liberal Jews could find acceptable.

The new Jewish mission was to remake Jews in the image of German *Bildung*. Barbarism had to be combatted by Enlightenment and what better version of this was there than the German model? This advocacy of *Deutschtum* was not simply German nationalism camouflaged in Enlightenment dress. We should not forget that the idea of *Bildung* was always part of the humanist heritage—German Jews were therefore not indulging in a crude cognitive colonialism. Their arguments must be seen in the correct historical context: they were formulated at a time when German cultural superiority seemed self-evident. Nowhere was this peculiar combination of mission and distaste better expressed than in the numerous works of Karl Emil Franzos (1848–1904). Although forgotten today, his works were extremely popular in his own time. Actually, he did little more than articulate the post-Enlightenment perception of the ghetto in palatable literary form. His writings were more the crystallization than the creation of this attitude. Yet on the eve of the great westward migrations, with the appearance in 1876 of his *Aus Halbasien,* he captured a widely diffused sensibility which was to color future liberal Jewish confrontations with their mobile Eastern brethren.

In the stories of Franzos all the defects of the ghetto and the ghetto Jew are catalogued. Written in the didactic mode, there is no attempt to hide the distaste for the religious fanaticism, the treatment of women, the dirt, the superstition. At the same time this didacticism is couched in terms of an obvious commitment: the elevation of those pitiful creatures of the ghetto into a condition of *Bildung*. Franzos was explicit on this: Germanization was not a matter of political control but a cultural ideal. *Deutschtum* was the standard by which the nations could measure their own cultural progress.[24] Moreover, if the Eastern Jews were obviously backward this was a product of the even greater backwardness of their hosts. This is the context of Franzos's famous formulation *half-Asia*. Half-Asia (Galicia, Romania, Southern Russia, Bukovina) was not merely a geographical designation but a condition of the mind. It referred to a strange amalgam of European culture and Asian barbarism, Western industriousness and Eastern indolence. *Ostjuden* were half-Asian because they lived within these cultural and political boundaries. They were products of the society in which they lived. It was as part of this analysis that Franzos formulated his much-quoted, ambivalent dictum, "Every country gets the Jews it deserves" *("Denn-Jedes*

Land hat die Juden, die es verdient").[25] This, better than any other pithy statement, summed up the German *(Bildung)* idea of Eastern Europe and its Jews.

By the 1880's, a century of historical development had created two radically juxtaposed Jewish cultures. Some saw the gap as unbridgeable and the ghetto as a kind of anthropological curiosity:

> Whoever desires to experience an ethnological sensation need not venture to the far corners of the world. For that, a day's journey from Berlin will suffice. One need only cross the Russian border to find an almost unknown human type full of mystery and wonder. . . . to look with astonishment at these people with their dirty caftans, the exotic faces which, like ghostly apparitions from times long past, still haunt the modern present. . . .[26]

This, of course, was an extreme formulation. Nevertheless, when Eastern Jewish refugees streamed into the cities of Western Europe, the cultural distance seemed so large that only the philanthropic and paternalist modes appeared possible. The major expression of Jewish commonality was not in the sharing of a great historical tradition but in the provision of social welfare. Middle class German Jews, by and large, related to *Ostjuden* on the basis of responsibility rather than of genuine feelings of solidarity, more out of compassion than out of a sense of identification. The breakdown of traditional Jewish society had led to the collapse of even the pretense of equality in Jewish relationships.

The German Jewish response to the post-1881 problem of the Eastern Jews' persecution and mass migration was, then, grounded in an old ambivalence. German Jews approached the issue in terms of categories inherited from the nineteenth-century experience. Protective and dissociative modes operated side by side in uneasy alliance. German Jews undertook massive charitable work for the driven *Ostjuden*—while seeking the most efficacious (and humane) ways to prevent their mass settlement in Germany (an attitude always closely related to the general German antipathy to such settlement). Despite the gulf, perhaps because of it, German Jewish philanthropy attained a level of unprecedented magnanimity. Indeed, to outsiders the reflex of responsibility must have seemed so great, the material aid so large, that special justification seemed to be called for. There was, Franzos admitted, a special relationship between Eastern and Western Jews but this was based upon an essentially "denationalized" Judaism:

> We are no longer a uniform People . . . the Jew who lives in the civilized countries is today a German, a Frenchman of the Jewish faith and thank

God that this is so! We are now only a community of faith *(Glaubensgenossenschaft)* dispersed in all lands of the world! We feel Jewish only through our faith, not our nationality: we sacrifice our money, our energy to save our unfortunate brothers in faith. . . .[27]

But the notion of a common faith was more of a legitimizing formula than a reflection of the actual behavior and beliefs of most liberal German Jews. Many liberals, like Franzos, were quite indifferent to matters of faith and were, indeed, obstinately attached to the anticlericalism of the Enlightenment. The truth was that older habits and traditions of Jewish mutual concern remained alive. And it was the *family* which was a more accurate—if less invoked—model for describing and justifying the East-West relationship. This, at least, grasped the emotional and existential dimension. At the same time it did not threaten the sense of Germanness for, as Dr. Hugo Ganz put it, members of the same family could belong to different nations. But Ganz also alluded to an important unconscious source of the Western Jewish tie to the Eastern Jew: the caftan Jews, he declared, were simply "the images of our own fathers." This was not an ideological legitimation but rather an admission of a (not particularly desirable) psychological fact. Families, according to Ganz, contained inequalities whereby some members had "worked themselves into the brightness, while others had to remain in the shadows of wretchedness." Western members had to help their Eastern brothers become more like themselves.[28]

The analogy of the family did seem apt. A common "father" accounted for inherited responsibilities and explained the ambivalence. At the same time it did not threaten the structure of Jewish denationalization or undermine the sense of Western cultural superiority. Equal family membership was predicated upon the overcoming of a common, debilitating past. This was the source of both the rejection and the responsibility.

Ironically, the rise of the anti-Semitic movement in general and agitation over the presence of Eastern Jews in particular seemed to strengthen both the responsibility and the rejection. The representative bodies of liberal German Jewry such as the *Centralverein deutscher Staatsbürger jüdischen Glaubens* (Central Union of German Citizens of the Jewish Faith, CV) and the *Verband der deutschen Juden* protested discriminatory actions against the *Ostjuden* aware that there was a potentially thin line between the mistreatment of foreign Jews and the fate of German Jewry itself. At the same time the sense of personal and cultural estrangement from the growing numbers of resident Eastern Jews increased. Many assimilationists blamed the continuation of anti-Semitism and the failure of German Jewish integration upon this presence.[29] Even those Jews less extreme in their outlook viewed the Eastern Jews (both within and outside Germany) in negative and very undifferentiated, simplistic ways.

The German Jewish stereotype of the *Ostjude* must be regarded as a significant limit of the Jewish liberal-rationalist consciousness. As Peter Gay has pointed out, German Jews energetically rejected collective derogatory generalizations. Many consequently eliminated distasteful and prejudicial expressions like "goy" from their vocabulary. Yet when it came to the Eastern Jews this standard collapsed and the distaste represented "the triumph of uninterpreted experience over cherished principles."[30] The *Ostjuden* in Germany seemed again to be reconstructing precisely the transcended past and to embody the principle of a threatening Jewish *Sonderleben*. The need to critically distance oneself from all this became more important than self-proclaimed humanist principles. Indeed, given Eastern Jewish insistence on special Jewish characteristics, the dissociation could be rationalized in terms of those principles themselves.

More than ever, the specifically German Jewish sense of identity was based upon the explicit differences which divided the German from the East European Jew. For Ernst Lissauer (author of the famous "Hate Song against England") this juxtaposition was crucial to his own sense of Jewish self-definition. "Once," he relates, "as I stood with some fellow Jewish students outside my Berlin school, a man with a Jewish caftan and side-locks came from Friedrich Street station and asked us, 'Are there no Jews in Berlin?' And instinctively I answered to myself, 'No,' for he meant something else by the word than I did."[31] Lissauer was not indulging in an exercise of Jewish self-denial but a new and to him fundamental differentiation—the world was divided into cultured German and uncultured Eastern Jews. The famous novelist Jakob Wassermann (1873–1934) graphically described the gulf thus:

> When I saw a Polish or a Galician Jew I would speak to him, try to peer into his soul, to learn how he thought and lived. And I might be moved or amazed, or be filled with pity and sadness; but I could feel no sense of brotherhood or even of kinship. He was totally alien to me, alien in every utterance, in every breath, and when he failed to arouse my sympathy for him as a human being he even repelled me.

As with Lissauer, this was not a question of Jewish self-denial but Jewishness defined in its German mode. Wassermann drew a basic distinction between a "Jewish" Jew and a German Jew: "Are those not two distinct species, almost two distinct races, or at least two distinct modes of life and thought?"[32] At times the encounter did lead to a total denial of Jewish identity. When Theodor Lessing, who was raised unaware of his Jewish origins, was told by his classmates that he was a Jew, he was deeply shocked. Upon returning home he asked his mother what a Jew "really" was. Lessing, in his autobiography, describes her response: "Once," Lessing reports, "on the street, my mother pointed to a man in a caftan and said, 'There goes a Jew.' I then concluded that we were not really Jews."[33]

For some intellectuals, the post-1881 migration induced near hysteria and fear of the Eastern Jewish presence bordered on the paranoiac. These anxieties often appeared in general non-Jewish journals. Thus Max Marcuse's 1912 attack against the *Ostjuden* appeared, significantly, in *The Journal of Sexual Science* as part of a wider analysis of the prospect of Jewish-Christian intermarriage in Germany. Marcuse vehemently opposed all "racial" claims against intermarriage and saw the amalgamation of Jews and Christians through marriage as desirable. But it was not only anti-Semites who were slowing down the process. The process of intermarriage could reach its completion only if the *Ostjuden* could be legally prevented from entering the country *(Grenzsperrung)*: "These Jews are a disaster for us. . . . they constantly create new barriers, bring in old ghetto air, and are the greatest danger to the prosperity and harmony of the nations."[34]

But the attitudes of Marcuse and other out-and-out assimilationists[35] were extreme and untypical. The majority of German Jews attempted to fuse their Jewish heritage with their *Deutschtum* rather than exorcise it entirely. It was this acceptance of Jewishness, regardless how mild its cultural or religious expression, that accounted for the continuing liberal German Jewish sense of responsibility for the *Ostjuden*. A nagging sense of commitment remained. Moreover, a degree of nostalgia and sentimentality—a recent analyst has termed this *Schmalz Judaism*[36]—was always an antidote, however ineffective, to the dissociative drive. A certain admiration for the immersion of the Polish Jew in the tradition, for his spirit in the face of adversity, even for some of the endearing qualities of the despised *schnorrer* was never entirely absent. The rougher edges of the disdain were softened, humanized by a wide recognition of the Eastern Jewish sense of humor, by an admiration for their wit and gall *(huzpah)*. Sigmund Freud was quite open about this in his *Jokes and Their Relation to the Unconscious* (1905).[37]

For liberal German Jews prior to World War I, however, the relationship could not be conceived in more positive terms than those described above. German Jews felt like Germans and their culture was German culture. They did indeed possess very little which was akin to the "Jewish" culture that characterized life in the East European Jewish world. The liberal Western Jewish relationship to the *Ostjude* was always contained within the strictly delineated limits of the prevailing ideology of Jewish denationalization. Ideas of an equal East-West partnership were no part of this scheme and the notion that the East European Jew serve as any kind of a cultural model for Western Jews was viewed as palpably absurd. We must look outside the liberal mainstream if we are to grasp the more positive role which the East European Jew was to play in the evolution and disposition of twentieth century German Jewish identity.

Any Western Jewish attempt to recapture lost roots in the post-Enlightenment era was bound to bring with it a reappraisal of Jewish life in Eastern Europe. Whether negatively or positively conceived, all agreed that the *Ostjude* was the archetype of Jewishness, the living link in a continuous historical chain of tradition. In that sense, the celebration of the Eastern Jew was always a potential—albeit usually unrealized—element in Western Jewish self-understanding, the positive side of an inbuilt ambivalence. Characteristically, the basic ingredients of later glorifications of the Eastern Jew were outlined, as early as 1822, by that great German Jewish rebel Heinrich Heine. Along with his negative perceptions, Heine voiced the essence of what, years later, was to become the German Jewish "cult" of the *Ostjuden*. After an encounter with the Jews in a Polish village, he wrote of "the nausea I felt at the sight of these ragged creatures." They lived in "pigsties. . . . jabbered, prayed and haggled." They had degenerated into

> revolting superstition. . . . Yet in spite of the barbarous fur cap which covers his head, and the still more barbarous notions which fill it, I esteem the Polish Jew more highly than his German counterpart, even though the latter wear a beaver on his head and carry Jean Paul in it. As a result of rigorous isolation, the character of the Polish Jew acquired a oneness. . . . The inner man did not degenerate into a haphazard conglomeration of feelings. . . . The Polish Jew, with his dirty fur cap, vermin-infested beard, smell of garlic, and his jabber is certainly preferable to many other Jews I know who shine with the magnificence of gilt-edged government bonds.[38]

These remarks presciently anticipated future representations of the *Ostjude* as symbol of premodern, unfragmented wholeness (although these often lacked Heine's qualifying realism). Moreover, Heine foreshadowed the tendency to base the elevation of the Eastern Jew upon a critique of the Western Jew. The cult of the *Ostjude* always proceeded from a comparative East-West analysis. In this way, the Eastern Jew could become a foil for the shallow, imitative, assimilating Jew of the West. Beginning with Heine this evaluation was usually linked to anti-bourgeois sentiments.

Such attitudes, of course, could not become normative for German

Jewry. For emancipation was, as we have seen, integrally linked with the process of *embourgeoisement*. From about the middle of the nineteenth century on, once German Jews had securely transcended life in their own ghettos, a move towards their rehabilitation did take place. The popular paintings of the artist Moritz Oppenheim, for instance, depicted the ghetto as a refuge of sanctity and spirituality in an otherwise hostile, uncivilized world. In Oppenheim's pictures the ghetto itself underwent *embourgeoisement:* its dwellers embodied solid middle class virtues. No longer the locus of backwardness, this *Gemütlichkeit* was also reflected in a new genre of memoirs and stories. Here the German ghettos were evoked with considerably more warmth and sympathy than the early Haskalah literature would have allowed. Leopold Kompert and Aaron Bernstein associated the Bohemian and Posen ghettos of their youth with happy times and positive qualities. Such a reevaluation was possible precisely because it referred to the past, which had been overcome and which therefore allowed for a certain nostalgia. The ghettos of Eastern Europe, on the other hand, could not provide materials for a positive and useable Jewish past because they were not merely literary memories but immediate realities and it was there that most of the conventional evils of ghetto life were deflected. (For more details, see *Brothers and Strangers*, pp. 247–27 and the perceptive essay by Ismar Schorsch, "Art as Social History: Oppenheim and the German Jewish Vision of Emancipation," in *Moritz Oppenheim: The First Jewish Painter* [Israel Museum, Jerusalem, 1983]. The rehabilitation was real enough but should be seen in perspective. As Schorsch himself has impressively demonstrated in his [as yet unpublished] paper, "The Sefardi Mystique in the Mind of Nineteenth-Century German Jewry" [presented at the International Conference on Germans and Jews, Clark University, October 1983], the nineteenth century German-Jewish search for a legitimate and useable Jewish past overwhelmingly resorted to the Sefardi rather than the Ashkenazi model.) The positive counter-myth of the *Ostjude*—as a more widespread rather than individual attitude—was thus possible only under different, later conditions: the rise of the Zionist movement, *fin-de-siècle* German neo-romanticism, and conscious Jewish "post-assimilationism."

More than any other factor it was from the Zionist movement that the impetus towards a radical revision of the Western Jewish perception of the *Ostjude* developed. To be sure, the German Zionists were a small minority of Germany Jewry.[39] But they were exceedingly vocal and acted as the ideological gadflies of German Jewish life. Zionism, of course, threatened the liberal consensus because it asserted that the Jews, contrary to the premises of Enlightenment and emancipation, were indeed one nation. It was upon this simple proposition that they advocated a radically reformed relationship between the Eastern and the Western Jew. The national movement, it was proclaimed, would transform the *Ostjude* from the passive object of philanthropy into the natural and equal historical partner of his Western brother.

Once the national dimension of Jewish existence was accepted it seemed to follow automatically that the relationship of East and West had to be reconsidered fundamentally. Well before Herzl, the "communist rabbi" Moses Hess (1812–1875) understood that this could take place only on the basis of radical self-criticism. The formulation of a Western Zionist identity presupposed a period of secularization and was born with the critique of many assimilationist assumptions and the recovery of a Jewish commitment after a period of estrangement.[40] Hess's *Rome and Jerusalem* (1862) was far ahead of its time and found almost no echo, yet it marked the beginning of a Zionist intellectual tradition. Western Jews were mercilessly castigated, their denial of Jewish nationality characterized as cowardly and self-defeating ("It is the modern Jew who is the contemptible one . . ."). Hess combined the critique of the Western Jew with a search for more authentic models. The contrast with the more honest, self-respecting Jews of the Eastern ghettos is quite clear. Whereas Western Judaism was shallow, in the East the "kernel" of Jewishness had been preserved. All that was required was the secularization of such forms into the living idea of Jewish nationalism.[41] (Hess understood that in the West Zionism would have to take the form of a post-emancipationist reassertion of national identity while in the East a modernization of that same identity was necessary.)

This reclamation of the national dimension, then, entailed Western Zionists in a repudiation—at least in theory—of nineteenth-century liberal attitudes towards the Eastern Jews. Like Heine before him, Herzl noted that the Russian Jews possessed an inner unity lost to their Western counterparts. They were not torn by the temptations of assimilation and were "simple and unbroken." Yet they were on a cultural level quite the equal of the West Europeans. "National" Jews, they were also part of modern culture: "And yet they are ghetto Jews, the only ghetto Jews that still exist."[42]

Over the years this glorification of the Eastern Jew became a quite conscious Zionist "counter-myth" set against prevailing liberal definitions of Jewish identity. The image of the *Ostjude* as embodiment of Jewish authenticity, exemplar of the spiritual, unfragmented Jewish self, was diametrically opposed to the normative Franzosian idea of the ghetto and the ghetto Jew. The Western Jew, Max Nordau declared in the flush of his initial Zionist enthusiasm, was "an inner cripple" and contrasted his "poisoned" soul with the ghetto Jew who, despite all the poverty and persecution, maintained his integrity and "in the moral sense . . . lived a full life."[43]

This is all correct but it is important to note yet another side of the matter: the founders of Western Zionism and the first generation of German Zionism never entirely overcame the same liberal cultural biases characteristic of the assimilationist Jews whose position they were criticizing. Few doubted that the relationship was to proceed in terms of a Western elite and a compliant Eastern mass.[44] The familiar patronizing airs were everywhere apparent.[45] Furthermore, Zionists held that *Galut* (exile) was an unnatural state. In this context, the Eastern ghetto retained its paradigmatic status as a "pathological" form of life. Herzl's explicitly West European formulation of the problem referred basically to Eastern Europe. (It was a perspective with which not only Nordau but all the early leaders of German Zionism such as Max Bodenheimer, Adolf Friedemann and Franz Oppenheimer would have concurred). "Zionism," declared Herzl, "is a kind of new Jewish care for the sick. We have stepped in as volunteer nurses, and we want to cure the patients—the poor, sick Jewish people—by means of a healthful way of life in our own ancestral soil."[46] Often, Zionism was portrayed as a kind of safety valve for bourgeois German Jewry, a convenient mechanism for removing the ubiquitous threat of invading masses of *Ostjuden* from German territory.[47]

The newly established "national" sense of identity must therefore be seen in a somewhat qualified light. Membership entailed different rights and obligations for Eastern and Western Jews. German Zionists defined their responsibilities in terms of an older liberal philanthropy but applied this now to "national" ends for their Eastern brethren. They refused to universalize the Herzlian analysis and apply it to their own political situation in Germany. Zionism referred to "unfree" Jews. As Adolf Friedemann put it: "West Europeans will mainly provide the organizers for colonization. . . . naturally we are not about to initiate a mass emigration of German, French and English Jews."[48] So, too, Franz Oppenheimer, for instance, could regard Zionism—physical settlement on the land in Palestine—as a means of abolishing the physical degeneration and oppression of the ghetto.[49] He distinguished himself from liberal Jews because, as he put it, he regarded himself as an "ethnic Jew," proud of his Jewish past and present identity. But this had to be clearly differentiated from the "national" consciousness of the Eastern Jews.[49]

The early Zionists, then, "discovered" the Eastern Jews in specific and partial terms. Their Zionism was certainly an expression of their pride in being Jewish and openly affirming it. But it was not regarded as in any way antithetical to strongly held feelings of German identity, nor was there any fundamental attempt to indict the presuppositions of the emancipation. On the contrary, the fruits of those historical phenomena were now to be given to the deprived Eastern Jews. This was not mere national philanthropy. Zionism did indeed pave the way for a closer sense of East-West Jewish interdependence.

But the idea that Zionism demanded personal commitment and implied Jewish cultural totality only emerged with the second generation of German Zionism. This radicalized younger generation scandalized their Zionist elders with their belief that *Deutschtum* and *Judentum* were incompatible and that authentic Zionism involved an act of "uprooting" *(Entwurzelung)* from diaspora life. Zionism was, they proclaimed, also an internal and spiritual revolution: the call for Jewish renaissance was now transposed from the external and the political to the existential and cultural planes.[50] In this context the "counter-myth" of the Eastern Jew played a central, defining role. Once again the representation of the *Ostjude* was designed to give the German Jew a new and different picture of himself.

The radical Jewish revival can only be understood as part of a wider neo-romantic German mood.[51] This, of course, explicitly went against the grain of German Jewish traditional middle class rationalism. Overtly "romantic" in emphasis it proposed an alternative to the prevailing positivism. It revived what "rationalism" had repressed. The new emphasis on "myth" and a revised conception of the role of the "unconscious" and the "irrational" in culture facilitated a new appreciation of elements in Jewish life which had previously been castigated. Martin Buber's transvaluation of the Hasid is perhaps the most dramatic example of this change.[52] But the mood also created a greater receptivity to other aspects of Eastern Jewish culture and identity as well.[53]

Like many other German youth these radical Zionists sought meaningful "rooted" communities capable of regenerating the authentic *Volksgeist*. But unlike their Zionist elders they argued that genuine incorporation into the German *Volk* was both impossible and undesirable. On the basis of their *Volkisch* assumptions[54] they had to find their own people, establish their own national framework. They discovered it in the Eastern ghettos and linked themselves to it through Buber's "community of blood." *Ostjuden*, unlike Western Jews, they argued, were a "real" *Volk*. In the East was an authentic entity (not a pale adjunct to a foreign culture) replete with its own living, unique forms. Perhaps Buber's Hasid—vibrant, rooted in community and spiritual values—was the unconscious Jewish answer to the peasant, the ideal figure of the German *Volkish* movement. In any case, for these Zionists the Eastern Jews became a kind of surrogate for the German nation, an alternative framework of identification.

Of course, this celebration of the ghetto tells us more about the ideological predicament and proclivities of these German Jews than it illuminates the realities of ghetto culture. *Ostjuden,* once again, were a convenient foil by which to express convictions about German Jews. As we have seen, beginning with Heine, the positive representation of the ghetto Jew was always related to a critique of the assimilating Jewish bourgeoisie. This was certainly true for the Zionists but it also applied to non-Zionist intellectuals (such as Frank Rosenzweig[55] and, later in the 1920's, Alfred Döblin[56]). Indeed, Franz Kafka, who provided the most famous articulation of this mood, can only be called a Zionist in the loosest sense. His discovery of Eastern Jews classically illustrates the major impulses behind the intellectual search for a post-liberal Jewish identity. Like many of his German contemporaries (Gershom Scholem[57] is the most well-known but by no means the only instance) Kafka's Jewish return was to a large extent predicated upon conflict with his parents. Judaism, *Ostjuden* and Zionism became interesting only because of his father's frivolous dismissal of such matters: "Had you shown interest in them, these things might, for that very reason, have become suspect in my eyes."[58]

Kafka's passionate involvement with the Yiddish theater[59] personalized this relationship. At least in ideological terms personal contact was an imperative of the cult. Speaking of the Eastern Jewish refugees, Buber put it thus:

> [W]e shall perceive them, all of them, not merely as our brothers and sisters; rather. . . . every one of us will feel: these people are part of myself. It is not together with them that I am suffering; *I* am suffering these tribulations. My soul is not by the side of my people; my people *is* my soul.[60]

The problem with this exhortation was that such personal relations were very much the exception rather than the rule. Theory and practice (where the old cultural differences always manifested themselves) seldom merged. Even the theory reflected confusion, for the paradox of the German Zionist revolt against German culture was the fact that it was couched in deeply German neo-romantic terms.[61] The difficulties of establishing personal ties and a cultural community along East-West lines remained unresolved. The glorification of the *Ostjude* was both a challenge to and a demonstration of the tenacity of German cultural assumptions even amongst the most radically committed Jews.

Yet there were also built-in ideological limits to this counter-myth. Because they advocated the creation of the new Jew in Palestine, the younger Zionists could not, by definition, endorse an "empirical" acceptance of East European Jewish life as it was. As Hans Kohn (later to become a renowned historian of nationalism) put it: "We want to revolutionize Jewry, not just Western Jewry, but *above all* Eastern Jewry."[62]

It was precisely this rejection, the ultimate dismissal of ghetto life which prompted a small minority of Zionists to withdraw from Zionism in the name of East European Jewry. This was a case where Zionism spawned its own dialectic. Influenced by the Zionist opposition to assimilation and its romantic affirmation of living Jewishness, these intellectuals came to the conclusion that only in the Eastern ghettos did—and could—real Jewish culture exist. A tiny movement, it is nevertheless worth noting, for it constituted the most extreme affirmatory option for East-West Jewish relations. Men like Nathan Birnbaum (1864–1937) and Fritz Mordecai Kaufmann (1888–1921)—the former from an increasingly Orthodox viewpoint and the latter from a socialist perspective—sought to reconcile modernity with the ghetto and to affirm what both Zionist and assimilationist denied: that really authentic Jewish identity was the Judaism of Eastern Europe.

With these thinkers the inversion of the stereotype of the *Ostjude* and his putative role in Western Jewish self-definition reached its zenith. Both regarded Yiddish not as a bastardized German but as an autonomous and valuable expression of unique Jewish cultural values. Both accepted the liberal accusation that *Kulturjuden* were to be found exclusively in the ghettos of Eastern Europe. Unlike the liberals, however, they saw this as a virtue, not a defect. Both took issue with Zionists who sought to create a "mythical" culture of the future while destroying the vibrant national life of the present. Not Eastern Jewry but assimilated, deracinated Western Jewry was the danger and for Western Jews interested in reestablishing their Jewish identity only a total, even sensual, identification with the goals, rhythms and pulsating reality of Eastern Jewish life would render this possible.[63]

Critics labeled these ideas as absurd exercises in "backward assimilation." Kaufmann, wrote one irate Zionist, proposed "nothing less than the assimilation of West European Jewry to Eastern Europe.... trying to create an *Ostjude* out of a 'goy'."[64] That critic was probably unaware that a few—quite eccentric and radically unrepresentative—attempts at such conscious cultural demodernization had indeed been attempted. Self-ghettoization, of course, involved changes in language, dress, manners, religious belief. Both Ahron Marcus (1843–1916)[65] and Jiri Langer (1894–1943)[66]—German and Czech respectively—undertook independent but remarkably similar journeys. In the full anthropological sense of the word both went "native" by leaving their familiar bourgeois world and totally immersing themselves in the life of the Eastern ghettos. They "became" *Ostjuden.* Upon their reappearance in Western society both experienced a kind of culture shock in reverse, a shock shared by their liberal Jewish counterparts. The sight of these Western Jews dressed as archetypal ghetto Jews was the source of both shame and bewilderment and, for our purposes, neatly sums up the outer range of symbolic possibilities which the *Ostjude* could play in German Jewish self-definition.

From the Enlightenment on, the *Ostjuden* were a vital ingredient in German Jewish self-definition. At one extreme, they acted as the living reminder to German Jewry of its own recently rejected past and an ever-present threat to integrationist aspirations. *Ostjudentum* served as a convenient foil upon which assimilationist German Jews could displace characteristics labeled both negative and "Jewish." In the middle of the spectrum was the consistently ambivalent approach to the Eastern Jews—the dissociative commingling with the protective mode. At the other extreme, lay the celebration of the Eastern Jew. The cult was a "counter" movement whose psychological function was an inverted mirror of the myth of the ghetto Jew it so vehemently opposed. For if the creation of the German Jew was dependent upon a negative image of the *Ostjude,* then the recreation of the German Jew was obviously dependent upon the positive symbolic reconstruction of that despised ghetto neighbor. Such German Jewish representations revealed the "Rorschach" nature of the *Ostjuden:* both the negative and the positive stereotypes tell us more about the nature of German Jewish self-understanding than they illuminate the realities of Eastern Jewry. From Franzos to Buber there is a massive symbolic change in content—but not in underlying function: both are didactic, both employ archetypal (if not stereotypical) language, both address and mirror the world of German Jewry and *its* needs.

Much of modern Jewish history was conditioned by the rift between unemancipated Eastern and emancipated Western Jewry. The existence of the ghetto, both as myth and reality, profoundly influenced the fate and disposition of German Jews in particular. The *Ostjude* and the "German Jew" were archetypal representations of the dichotomy, the main participants in an unprecedented confrontation marked always by tension, often by intolerance and at times also creativity. Mirror opposites, they remained psychologically bound to each other. Idealized or despised, *Ostjuden* retained their symbolic resonance because they seemed to live their lives in a distinctively Jewish mode: this "totality" gave to them an *Ur* quality lost to German Jewry. They satisfied perfectly the requirements of both myth and counter-myth making. Their power as cultural symbols made them essential ingredients of German

Jewish self-definition. Their changing image always reflected the complex and often contradictory face of German Jewry itself.

Notes

1. This essay is based on my book, *Brothers and Strangers: The East European Jew in German and German Jewish Consciousness 1800–1923* (Madison: The University of Wisconsin Press; © 1982 by the Board of Regents of the University of Wisconsin System). It is an attempt to synthesize and provide a general overview of certain aspects of my book. Given constraints of space I have here only been able to sketch the broad outlines of a very complex development in somewhat crude fashion. For a more developed treatment of all these questions (and some not touched upon in the present essay) the book is indispensable.

2. See Michael Meyer, *The Origins of the Modern Jew* (Detroit, 1967) and Jacob Katz, *Out of the Ghetto: The Social Background of Emancipation* (New York, 1978).

3. The expression *"Ostjude"* only became widespread in the early twentieth century. Nevertheless all the characteristics had been delineated early on and different pejorative names were used until the generic, stereotypical description *"Ostjude"* was generally applied.

4. For an excellent outline of Jewish traditional life and society see Jacob Katz, *Tradition and Crisis: Jewish Society at the End of the Middle Ages* (New York, 1971).

5. I explore the significance of this factor for the development of anti-Semitism in an essay called "Caftan and Cravat: The *Ostjude* as a Cultural Symbol in the Development of German Anti-Semitism" in S. Drescher, D. Sabean, A. Sharlin eds., *Political Symbolism in Modern Europe* (New Brunswick, 1982).

6. See Wilhelm Stoffers, *Juden und Ghetto in der deutschen Literatur bis zum Ausgang des Weltkrieges* (Graz, 1939), p. 69.

7. For a sample of these many negative perceptions—a perception apparently shared by the author—see generally Stoffers, *Juden und Ghetto*.

8. See Jacob Toury, *Soziale und politische Geschichte der Juden in Deutschland 1847–1871* (Düsseldorf, 1967); also "Die Enstehung der Judenassimilation in Deutschland und deren Ideologie" in Jacob Katz, *Emancipation and Assimilation: Studies in Modern Jewish History* (Farnborough, 1972), p. 226.

9. George L. Mosse, "Thoughts on the German-Jewish Dialogue" (paper delivered at the 1979 Association of Jewish Studies Conference), pp. 5–9.

10. See the works of W. H. Bruford: *Culture and Society in Classical Weimar, 1775–1806* (Cambridge, 1962) and *The German Tradition of Self-Cultivation: "Bildung" from Humboldt to Thomas Mann* (Cambridge, 1975).

11. Mendelsohn to Klein, 29 August 1782 in Moses Mendelssohn, *Gesammelte Schriften* V, ed. Dr. G. B. Mendelssohn (Leipzig, 1844) pp. 604–5.

12. Although his historical analysis is somewhat undifferentiated John M. Cuddihy's *The Ordeal of Civility: Marx, Freud, Levi-Strauss and the Jewish*

Struggle with Modernity (New York, 1974) correctly emphasizes the importance of etiquette in the assimilatory process.

13. "Einige ideen über Erziehung und öffentlichen Untèrricht," *Sulamith* I (1806)46–47.

14. See, for example, Abraham Geiger's attempt to dissuade *Ostjuden* from wearing this garb in *Abraham Geiger's nachgelassene Schriften,* ed. Ludwig Geiger (Berlin, 1875–78), p. 298.

15. See his *Die Sprachverhältnisse der heutigen Juden im Interesse der Gegenwart und mit besonderer Rücksicht auf Volkserziehung* (Hamburg, 1844).

16. Ibid., p. 40.

17. Emanuel Wohlwill, "Bemerkungen über Sprache und Sprachunterricht als Beförderungs mittel der allgemeinen Bildung," *Sulamith* VII (1812)87–89.

18. David Friedländer's, *Über die Verbesserung der Israeliten im Königreich Pohlen: Ein von der Regierung daselbst im Jahr 1816 abgefordetes Gutachten* (Berlin, 1819) is the classic expression of this as well as a general exposition of enlightened German Jewish attitudes towards Polish Jews that was to last into the next century.

19. Most of the leading reformers and theoreticians of German Jewry shared this attitude, amongst them Leopold Zunz, Abraham Geiger and Markus Jost. For a typical statement see "Der sogenannte Chassidismus," *Der Israelit* VII, no. 22 (May 1866).

20. Heinrich Graetz, *History of the Jews: From the Chmielnicki Persecution of the Jews in Poland to the Period of Emancipation in Central Europe.* Vol. 5 (Philadelphia, 1895), pp. 5–6, 206.

21. "Galizische Zustände," *Der Israelit* VII, no. 12 (22 March 1846), p. 93.

22. See Geiger's letter to Dernberg, 3 August 1840 in *Abraham Geiger and Liberal Judaism,* compiled by Max Wiener (Philadelphia, 1962), pp. 87–88.

23. See "Emancipation," *Der Israelit* 11, no. 1 (January 1861).

24. See the foreword to Franzos, *Aus Halb-Asien,* vol. I (Stuttgart and Berlin, 1914), pp. xvii–xviii. This had already reached its fifth edition by that year.

25. Ibid., p. xxv.

26. See Jakob Fromer's introduction to Solomon Maimon's *Lebensgeschichte* (Munich, 1911), pp. 7–8. This is particularly interesting in that Fromer was, like his subject Maimon, a transplanted modernized *Ostjude*. It is worth noting that many key creators of the stereotype, including Franzos, were themselves of Eastern Jewish origin.

27. See Karl Emil Franzos, "Die Kolonisationfrage," *Allgemeine Zeitung des Judentums* LV (November 1891), especially pp. 555 and 567.

28. See "Das ostjüdische Problem," *Allgemeine Zeitung des Judentums* LV, no. 42 (6 November 1891).

29. See, for instance, Eugen Ehrlich, *Die Aufgaben der Sozialpolitik im österreichischen Osten* (Czernowitz, 1909); Moritz Friedländer, "Politische Strömungen im heutigen Judentum," *Zeitschrift für Politik* (1911), pp. 169 ff.

30. P. Gay, "At Home in America," *The American Scholar* XLVI, no. 1 (Winter 1976–77), p. 42. See also his *Freud, Jews and Other Germans: Masters and Victims in Modernist Culture* (New York, 1978).

31. Ernst Lissauer, "Deutschtum und Judentum," *Der Kunstwart* XXV, no. 13 (April 1912), p. 7. This differentiation still exerts an unexpected cultural influence. Commenting on the casting of the recent extremely popular televi-

sion production *Holocaust*, its writer Gerald Green explained: "I wanted a real German family, the equivalent of American Jews who think of themselves first as Americans. We didn't want *Fiddler on the Roof* Jews, although they were prime victims of the Holocaust. We were afraid they would vitiate what we were trying to do—appeal to a broad audience." See *Time* (April 17, 1978), p. 61.

32. Jakob Wassermann, *My Life as German and Jew*, English translation S. N. Brainin (New York, 1933), pp. 196–197, 197–198.

33. Theodor Lessing, *Einmal und nie wieder* (Gütersloh, 1969), p. 112.

34. Max Marcuse, "Über die christlich-jüdische Mischehe," *Sexualprobleme: Zeitschrift für Sexualwissenschaft und Sexualpolitik* (1912), See esp. pp. 702, 713, 745–49.

35. Similar ideas can be found in, amongst others, Friedrich Blach, *Die Juden in Deutschland* (Berlin, 1911), see especially pp. 20–21, 42; Fritz Mauthner in Werner Sombart, (ed.), *Judentaufen* (Munich, 1912) pp. 74–77.

36. For his use of the term see Henry Wassermann, "Jews and Judaism in the Gartenlaube," *Leo Baeck Institute Yearbook* XXIII (1978) p. 52.

37. See the James Strachey translation of this work (New York, 1963), especially pp. 80–81, 111.

38. Heine to Christian August Keller, 1 September 1822. See Hugo Bieber (ed.), *Heinrich Heine: Jüdisches Manifest* (New York, 1946) pp. 11–12. Heine later published his "Memoir on Poland" in *Der Gesellschafter* (January 1823). The translation here is from F. Ewen (ed.), *The Poetry and Prose of Heinrich Heine* (New York, 1948) pp. 690–91.

39. For membership figures see Table 3 in Stephen Poppel, *Zionism in Germany 1897–1933: The Shaping of a Jewish Identity* (Philadelphia, 1977) pp. 176–77.

40. The preconditions for modern Jewish national self-consciousness are discussed by Jacob Katz, "The Jewish National Movement: A Sociological Analysis" in his *Emancipation and Assimilation*, op. cit. See especially p. 137.

41. See *Rome and Jerusalem*, translated by M. J. Bloom (New York, 1958), especially the "Fifth Letter" and pp. 34, 37.

42. See "The Basel Congress" (1897) in Theodor Herzl, *Zionist Writings*, vol. 1, *1896–1898* (New York, 1973), pp. 152–54.

43. See the famed address to the First Zionist Congress: in Arthur Hertzberg (ed.), *The Zionist Idea: A Historical Analysis and Reader* (New York, 1975), pp. 235–41.

44. See, for instance, Nordau's *Zionistische Schriften* (Cologne and Leipzig, 1909) pp. 311, 317; Herzl, "The Solution of the Jewish Question," in his *Zionist Writings* I, 25–26. On the attitudes of Franz Oppenheimer and Adolf Friedemann see Kurt Blumenfeld, *Erlebte Judenfrage: Ein vierteljahrhundert deutscher Zionismus* (Stuttgart, 1962) pp. 52, 59.

45. See, e.g., Nordau's "Achad Ha'am über Altneuland," *Die Welt* VII, no. 11 (13 March 1903).

46. "The Family Affliction" (1899) in Herzl, *Zionist Writings* vol. 2, *1898–1904* (New York, 1975), p. 45.

47. M. Nordau, "Der Zionismus und seine Gegner" (1898), *Zionistische Schriften*, pp. 117ff.

48. Adolf Friedemann, *Was will der Zionismus?* (Berlin, 1903) p. 17 (quoted in Poppel, *Zionism. . .* , p. 27).

49. See his "Die Aufbau einer Jüdischen Genossenschäftsiedlung in

Palästina" in his *Erlebtes, Erstrebtes, Erreichtes: Lebenserinnerungen* (Düsseldorf, 1964) pp. 281–96.

50. This mood is well evoked in "Der XIV Delegiertentag im Leipzig am 14 und 15 Juni 1914," *Jüdische Rundschau*, no. 25 (June 1914) pp. 268–69.

51. See George L. Mosse, *The Crisis of German Ideology: Intellectual Origins of the Third Reich* (New York), esp. Chapter 3. Of course other currents from the wider Zionist movement also fed into this mood.

52. I have tried to document this as well as the reasons behind Buber's popularity for German intellectuals in Chapter 6 of *Brothers and Strangers*.

53. See *Vom Judentum* (Leipzig, 1913), especially the contributions by Robert Weltsch, Max Brod, Gustav Landauer and Moses Calvary.

54. George Mosse has analysed these assumptions in his pioneering "The Influence of the Volkish Idea on German Jewry" in his *Germans and Jews: The Right, the Left and the Search for a 'Third Force' in pre-Nazi Germany* (New York, 1971).

55. See N. Glatzer (ed.), *Frank Rosenzweig: His Life and Thought* (New York, 1961), esp. pp. 37–38, 73–74, 80.

56. See his *Reise in Polen* (Olten, 1968) and also the *Nachwort* by Walter Muschg in this new reprint.

57. See his *From Berlin to Jerusalem: Memories of My Youth* (New York, 1980), especially pp. 44, 83–84. Chapter 5 generally is relevant.

58. Franz Kafka, *Letter to his Father* (New York, 1965) p. 85.

59. See Evelyn Torton Beck, *Franz Kafka and the Yiddish Theater* (Madison, 1971).

60. See Buber, *On Judaism,* ed. N. Glatzer (New York, 1967) p. 20.

61. This was very apparent in the experimental East-West co-operative the Berlin *Jüdische Volksheim*. See Scholem's comments in *From Berlin*, p. 78 and generally pp. 76–80; Georg Lubinski, "Erinnerungen an das jüdische Volksheim in Berlin," *Der junge Jude* (July–August 1930), p. 135.

62. In *Vom Judentum*, op. cit., p. 17.

63. I have distilled these ideas from the relevant essays in N. Birnbaum, *Ausgewählte Schriften zur Jüdischen Frage* (Czernowitz, 1910) and Fritz Mordecai Kaufmann, *Gesammelte Schriften* (Berlin, 1923).

64. See George Strauss, "Das jüdische Lied im Blau-Weiss und das Blau-Weiss Liederbuch." *Blau-Weiss Blätter: Führerzeitung* II, nos. 1, 2 (October, November 1920), esp. pp. 20, 22–23, 25.

65. See Marcus Markus, *Ahron Marcus: Die Lebensgeschichte eines Chossid* (Basel, 1966).

66. See Jiri Langer, *Nine Gates to the Chassidic Mysteries* (New York, 1976) and especially the foreword by his brother Frantisek Langer.

"Heureux comme Dieu en France": East European Jewish Immigrants in Paris, 1881–1914

David Weinberg
(BOWLING GREEN STATE UNIVERSITY)

Among the hundreds of thousands of East European Jews who migrated westward in the period 1881–1914, a relatively small number chose to remain on the European continent. Of those who came to France, the overwhelming majority found their way to Paris, where a sizeable Jewish community already existed.[1] Yet Jewish immigration to France in the pre-war period paled beside the massive influx of Polish, Russian, and Romanian Jews to the United States and to England. No more than forty thousand immigrant Jews arrived in France before World War I compared to over two million who journeyed to America and over one hundred thousand who settled in England.

Nevertheless, the experience of East European Jews in Paris at the turn of the century had a distinctiveness that set it apart from immigrant experiences in cities such as New York and London. In part it had to do with the nature of the host country, which was subject to the political and ideological strife that would culminate in the infamous Dreyfus Affair. In part it had to do with the native Jewish community which, even more than its American and British counterparts, responded to East European immigrants with a hostility born of the deep-seated mythology of emancipation that equated Jewish ideals with the assimilationist vision of the French Revolution. And finally there were the immigrants themselves, drawn by the magnetic appeal of the "City of Lights" as a center of culture and political activism, or too poor—or lacking the initiative—to continue on to the United States (the *"goldene medine"*). It was the interplay among these three elements that defined the nature and extent of immigrant absorption and acceptance, a goal which even the staunchest defender of Old World traditions ardently desired. Whatever their anxieties about the world left behind, most East European Jews in Paris before World War I secretly dreamed of becoming "heureux comme Dieu en France," ("happy as God in France") as the old adage went.

What was the exact scope of East European Jewish immigration to Paris in the period between 1881 and 1914? It is difficult to gain an accurate count of Jewish immigrants in the pre-war era. Many entered France illegally, others were transients who moved on to America or returned to Eastern Europe. Even those who settled in the French capital often remained "invisible," refusing to register with government agencies or ignored by inept French officials.

Not that individuals were lacking in France quick to provide what they regarded as accurate statistics on Jewish immigrants. Both anti-Semites and immigrant leaders tended to exaggerate the number of new arrivals albeit for different reasons. Thus while the notorious anti-Jewish polemicist, Edouard Drumont, claimed that there were between four and five hundred thousand Jews in France in 1886 (comprised of rich bankers and increasingly of Polish "swindlers and criminals"), the editor of the *Yidish-frantsoyzisher kalendar* published in 1910 spoke of at least sixty thousand Jewish immigrants, the overwhelming majority of what he believed to be an increasingly powerful French Jewish community.[2]

An extrapolation from the often conflicting and sketchy figures reveals that there were no more than a few thousand East European Jews in the French capital before 1881 out of a total Paris Jewish population of about twenty thousand. The majority were itinerant peddlers, petty tradesmen, intellectuals, and students.[3] By 1891, Jews fleeing pogroms and economic hardship in the Russian Pale had boosted the East European population to six or seven thousand out of a total Paris Jewish population of approximately forty thousand. By 1900, Russian Jews had been joined by Romanian and Galician refugees as well as by individuals who had come to the World's Fair and had decided to remain.[4] The immigrant population swelled from between ten and twelve thousand in 1900 to about twenty thousand in 1906 as a result of the failure of the Russian revolution of 1905, the passage of the restrictive Aliens Act in Great Britain the same year, and the refusal of American Jewish relief agencies to accept more immigrants. Continued migration ensured that by the eve of World War I, there were twenty-five to thirty-five thousand East Europeans in the French capital, almost two-fifths of the total Paris Jewish population.[5]

The immigrant community at the turn of the century represented a variegated weave of disparate elements. Foreign travellers and French journalists searching for Jewish exotica in the streets of Paris found

Russian and Romanian youths living in the Latin Quarter and in Montmartre; petty tradesmen and semi-skilled laborers from Russian *shtetlekh* settled close to Jewish-owned *ateliers* in the so-called "Pletzl" adjoining the Place des Vosges in the Marais; and Jewish intellectuals intermingled with other aspiring artists in the cafes and workshops of Montparnasse.[6] If one looked closely, one could detect a rough socioeconomic differentiation between the Right and Left banks of the city with workers and artisans settling in the poorer quarters of the fourth and eighteenth *arrondissements* and the children of middle class Russians and Romanians living among French students and intellectuals in the fifth, sixth, and thirteenth *arrondissements*. Though immigrant Jews in Paris in the pre-war period often settled together in distinct areas of the city, they were not numerous enough to develop isolated Jewish ghettos. In the "Pletzl," East Europeans mingled with older immigrants from Alsace-Lorraine who had not yet succeeded in moving to wealthier districts of the city. Areas such as Belleville and Montmartre which would later become predominantly Jewish were shared with Germans and Italians. There is even some indication of immigrant Jewish settlement in the eastern and southern suburbs of Paris.[7] Although it is difficult to assess accurately, it appears that chain migratory patterns played a role in immigrant settlement in Paris, with former residents of East European cities such as Kovno settling together in the French capital. Undoubtedly, many who came and eventually settled in Paris had originally intended to go on to the United States. Lacking money and too weary from the long journey from Eastern Europe that often took them through two or three countries and many provincial cities, they could go no further and resigned themselves to remaining on the European continent.[8]

Yet there were many Jewish immigrants who consciously chose to settle in Paris. In this, they differed markedly from Italian and Polish immigrants who often were contracted by private industry to work in France, the former settling in agricultural areas in the Midi and in the South, the latter settling in mining areas in the North. Indeed, Jewish migrants seemed more like tourists than migrants, flocking to Paris to partake of its culture and its freedom. Even the most remote *shtetl* in the Pale knew of Paris. A study conducted by a Paris Yiddish paper of the Jewish press in Eastern Europe during the period discovered numerous articles about Paris fashions, medical experiments at the Sorbonne, and literary and musical events in the French capital.[9] Paris seemed to hold special attraction to Jews from larger urban centers such as Warsaw, Vilna, and Cracow, politically active communities such as Suwalki and Bialystok, and areas of pogroms such as Odessa and Kiev. As one immigrant militant wrote about the French capital:

"Just the word, 'Paris,' conjured up a fantasy for us, like a story from A Thousand and One Nights: a city of magic, of splendor."[10]

Despite the enthusiasm with which most East European immigrants greeted their arrival in Paris at the turn of the century, the French government and most Frenchmen remained reserved and often hostile toward what they perceived as "the alien invasion." For most of the nineteenth century, France had paid little attention to immigration. There were some efforts by private companies to recruit foreign workers especially for the mines of the North but government played little role. Nor were there any direct attempts to monitor individuals who arrived in France on their own. Though aliens could not vote, serve in the army or government, or head a union, they had not been forced to register in order to remain in France or to work. Because borders were open, foreign workers had moved relatively freely in and out of the country, especially those coming from the contiguous countries of Belgium, Spain, and Italy. In a period of economic growth and expansion, Frenchmen had seen little threat from the relatively small numbers of transient laborers from neighboring nations. The few East European immigrants who had arrived before the 1880's were hardly noticed. When they were referred to by government leaders or journalists, they were viewed as either living symbols of France's munificence toward political and religious refugees or as cultural exotica.[11]

By late in the century, the mood had changed. Benign neglect now gave way to deep concern as the new wave of immigration brought huge numbers of East and Southern Europeans who were widely regarded as "unassimilable." By 1911, there were one million immigrants, nearly 3 percent of the French population.[12] It was a different France that the immigrant encountered at the turn of the century—deeply scarred by the embarrassing defeat at the hands of the Prussians in 1871, subject to severe periodic economic crisis and rapidly being outstripped industrially by Germany and America, beset by political corruption and scandal, and faced with an alarming decline in native fertility. Fears and anxieties were exacerbated by the outbreak of the Dreyfus Affair which directly linked "the alien invasion" with the collapse of national values and ideals. In 1889 and again in 1893, the French government passed laws controlling alien residence and increasing police surveillance and control.

For the first time, French officials and academics entered into a serious investigation of immigration. The conclusions arrived at were by no means clear. For all those who were convinced that foreigners lay at the root of their nation's woes, there were others who recognized that an economically troubled France faced with a declining birthrate desperately needed cheap manual labor. A wistful sadness seemed to pervade the discussion. Unlike the United States, a "young" nation populated mainly by immigrants, France was an "old" country with deeply rooted traditions. The prospect of a culturally pluralistic society seemed to inspire not optimism, but fear of a profound decay in French society which would lead inevitably to the bastardization of French culture.[13] Such sentiments fed traditional xenophobic attitudes born of inexperience with migration, a centralized political system, and cultural chauvinism.[14] It seemed that France could not live with foreigners in its midst or live without them.

There was less ambivalence, however, in French attitudes toward the new Jewish immigrants. The Jew arriving from Poland and Russia after 1881 spoke a totally alien language, practiced a different religion, and cared little for manual labor. As a refugee, he did not benefit from mutual agreements between France and his native country and thus could not be repatriated easily. Despite his small numbers, he was often highly visible in the Jewish sections of Paris and in the so-called "Jewish trades" of textiles and clothing that grew up rapidly in the central and eastern *arrondissements* of the French capital. The migrations of East European Jews through France and their encampment in Paris streets further fed anti-Semitic sentiments.[15] In papers such as Edouard Drumont's *Libre Parole,* the French reading public was treated to lurid descriptions of the Jewish menace in France which was said to sap the nation's economic strength and to destroy its cultural heritage and physical well-being. Frenchmen spoke openly of the "Wandering Jew" while as late as 1910 and again in 1911, Jewish immigrants were accused of spreading cholera throughout the city.[16]

Images of caftaned peddlers rejected by their homelands now mingled in Frenchmen's minds with traditional stereotypes of an all-powerful international Jewish bourgeoisie and its archetypical French family, the Rothschilds. East European and French Jews were said to be joined in a conspiracy to destroy Gallic strength and to betray France to her mortal enemies. Contradictory images of capitalists and revolutionary socialists, of criminals and captains of industry, blended together to create a vision of the Jew as the harbinger of hated modernity, both the cause and the symbol of French biological and cultural debilitation. As Drumont wrote in his tract, *Les Juifs contre la France,* at the height of the Dreyfus fever in 1899, "It is French society's state of dissolution which alone has allowed Jews to carry out their abominable work . . . which will permit them, if there is no awakening, to transform France into a new Poland and to deliver her over to foreigners."[17]

Anti-foreigner and anti-Semitic attitudes were not limited to right-wing extremists fearful of change and seeking convenient scapegoats for the ills of France. As studies by Edward Silberner and Robert Wistrich have shown, xenophobic and anti-Jewish sentiments were deeply rooted in the French socialist tradition.[18] From the days of Pierre-Joseph Proudhon and Emil Toussenel, the Jew had been associated with capitalist exploitation and financial corruption. The French Left joined with the French Right in attacking the Rothschilds and other banking families as parasites preying upon the *menu peuple* of French society. Similarly, the French Left shared the average Frenchman's concern over the influx of East European Jews after 1881. Trade unions periodically denounced Jewish immigrants as scabs and strike-breakers and rejected immigrant attempts to form separate language sections.[19] Even liberal intellectuals were frightened by the appearance of Polish and Russian Jews with their strange customs and traditions. As Paula Hyman notes in her work on French Jewry, in 1907 both *L'Humanité,* the Socialist daily, and the League of the Rights of Man attacked the existence of four public schools in Paris which, because of the high number of immigrant Jewish students, did not meet on Saturday and provided kosher food. *L'Humanité* in a ringing attack noted that "the particularist developments of these races" only perpetuated racial hatreds and demanded that the school administration seek "to facilitate their fusion, even from childhood."[20]

Such attitudes rested on the intellectual heritage of the Enlightenment and the French Revolution, a view of society that emphasized the power of education and reason to destroy religious superstition and defined quality not in terms of individual freedom but as the sharing in the heritage of *la patrie.*[21] From this point of view, those who chose to retain Old World traditions were perceived not only as ignorant but also dangerous to society. The only solution lay in the rapid and total assimilation of the foreigners who unfortunately had already settled in France.

By far the most avid supporters of the assimilationist ideal were the leaders of the native Jewish community. For most French Jews, Jewish identity was closely linked to the post-revolutionary French experience. By emancipating Jewry from centuries of oppression and obscurantism, France was said to have earned the right to share in the responsibility of bearing the messianic ideals of justice and brotherhood to the world. The intertwining of French ideals with the tenets of Judaism led to the creation of a new theology, one which supposedly would appeal to both religious and non-religious Jews. Thus the men of the French Revolution, much like God at Sinai, were said to have given the world a new Decalogue which, if followed, would lead to a world of contentment and happiness. In return, the Jews were obligated, much in the same manner in which they thanked God and pledged to follow his Law, to give thanks to those who had freed them from the slavery of superstition and to accede to society's demand for assimilation.[22] From this perspective, East European immigrants in Paris seemed unpleasant reminders of a world happily left behind. Often sharing in the Enlightenment's anticlericalism, French Jews saw the East European Jewish identity as a mirror image of Catholicism with its strange rituals and its demand for total loyalty. In sum, the natives looked upon immigrants at the end of the century with both sympathy and revulsion. Though obligated toward their poor "fossilized" co-religionists, they tried desperately to prevent the latter from becoming too visible, lest they compromise the position of French Jewry.[23]

Such conflicting attitudes found their uncertain resolution in the policy of French Jewish relief agencies such as the Alliance Israélite Universelle which called upon Russian Jews to remain in their homeland and to struggle for their rights much as French Jews had done a century before.[24] When Jewish refugees from Russia found themselves stranded in the border city of Brody in 1882, the Alliance reluctantly agreed to settle 502 of them in Paris but insisted upon choosing only those who were skilled and who could not "under any circumstances" return to Russia.[25] When forced to take in refugees, the Alliance placed special emphasis upon placing foreign students. By providing them money for food, housing, and tuition, it hoped that the young men and women who had been exposed to French culture would have a beneficial effect upon their "backward" co-religionists.[26] If all else failed, there was at least a chance that many of them would eventually return to their families in Eastern Europe. Although they expressed compassion for their fellow Jews, French Jewish relief organizations were quick to point out that their defense of Russian Jewry reflected their adherence to the liberal values of France as much as Jewish solidarity. Not surprisingly, the French Jewish community actively supported the creation of a relief committee soon after the outbreak of pogroms chaired by Victor Hugo and comprised largely of non-Jewish dignitaries.[27]

Problems arose after the signing of the Franco-Russian Alliance in 1894. The 1890's witnessed a new rise in emigration from Russia which was to be surpassed in the years 1903–6. The Alliance could no longer hope for a solution of the Jewish problem in Russia yet it could not actively support emigration for fear of embarrassing the Tsar. The results were intense pressure upon American Jews to accept more immigrants and the assignment to the German Jewish Hilfsverein of the major responsibility for dealing with emigration from Russia.[28] In many cases, immigrants planning to leave Russia were induced to emigrate to America by Alliance agents who provided them with glowing accounts of life in the United States and lurid tales of anti-Semitism in France.[29]

Despite the intense efforts of French Jewry to limit immigration, Russian, Romanian, and Galician Jews came in hundreds and then thousands to Paris throughout the 1890's and 1900's as the pogroms, restrictive decrees and economic hardships sent more and more people fleeing westward. The French government refused to retreat from its traditional policy of granting political asylum to refugees but did little to aid Jews upon their arrival. As a result, the French Jewish community was forced to assume major responsibility for the care and sustenance of the new arrivals. The massive influx necessitated the creation of soup kitchens, boarding houses, crêches, make-shift hospitals, and temporary schools.[30] In 1892, the Comité de Bienfaisance, the major Jewish philanthropic organization in Paris, serviced over seventeen thousand people daily, the overwhelming majority of whom were Russian and Polish Jews. By 1897, the figure had risen to twenty thousand and rose markedly in 1903 after the Kishinev pogrom, and again in 1905–06 after the collapse of the revolution of 1905. According to the Comité in its report of 1904, over two-thirds of the Jewish poor in Paris were immigrants from Russia.[31] The sheer number of arrivals overwhelmed the native Jewish community. The archives of the Alliance contain numerous letters from frantic Jewish officials in cities on the main railroad line such as Lyon and Dijon complaining of immigrants reduced to beggary and thievery because of the inability of these small Jewish communities to handle the massive influx.[32]

Tragically, one of the largest waves of East European migration to France coincided with the outbreak of the Dreyfus Affair. As Michael Marrus has pointed out, anti-Dreyfus hysteria only exacerbated native Jewish fears and reinforced hostility toward the Jewish immigrants. In a period of national division, the maintenance of a separate cultural identity, it was felt, could only contribute to the disruption of the social order. The immigrants' flamboyant behavior and language offended the bourgeois sensibility of native Jews; their espousal of radical political ideas fed anti-Semitic stereotypes at a time when French Jewish leaders were convinced that no government official would dare to support a proposal offered by even a "respectable" Jewish organization.[33] If there was sympathy on the part of native Jews for what Marrus has aptly called " a community of suffering," there was often disgust as well. Maxime du Camp, writing in his work on native Jewish charitable organizations in Paris published before the Dreyfus Affair, reflected visceral French Jewish attitudes when he spoke of the immigrant poor in the following manner:

> The neglect of their health, to say the least, is a clear indication of their indifference to matters of propriety. Their dull and uncombed hair, their

hands which bear rings but have only accidental contact with soap, their feet squeezed into worn-out shoes, their tattered clothing; in short, their external demeanor denotes less misery than lack of self-respect.[34]

There was some change in native Jewish attitudes after 1905. Though French Jews continued to press for the complete integration of immigrants into French society, they became more solicitous and far less critical of the new arrivals. The shift in attitude stemmed from a number of factors. The end of the Dreyfus Affair brought a noticeable tapering off of anti-Semitic hysteria. At the same time, the failed Russian revolution of 1905 brought a different type of Jewish immigrant to Paris, more self-reliant, more skilled, and less aloof from Western culture. Finally, the separation of Church and State in 1906 meant a decline in the power of the *Consistoire,* the central religious body of French Jewry and its quasi-official spokesman. No longer could French Jewish leaders call upon the government to break up unauthorized religious services or political demonstrations led by East European Jews or force immigrants to join the *Consistoire* or one of its auxiliary agencies as a means of controlling their activities. Persuasion now had to replace coercion.[35]

An important indication of the transformation in French Jewish attitudes toward the immigrants was the expansion of the Comité de Bienfaisance facility on the rue Rodier in Montmartre. From 1905 to the outbreak of World War I, the Comité significantly increased its subsidies for rents, loans, and charitable aid and established numerous community kitchens. At the same time, the purchase of tickets to the United States declined, reflecting both the continued opposition of American Jewish relief agencies to further immigration and the decision of many immigrants to remain in Paris. During the same period, the *Consistoire* made serious efforts to enroll immigrant children in the supplementary schools and the three elementary public schools which it maintained. As an indication of the growing rapprochement between native and East European Jews, the *Consistoire* in 1911 invited representatives of two immigrant religious groups to participate in the Butchers and Mikveh Commissions of Paris.[36]

Yet tensions remained. Despite their increased tolerance of the East Europeans, French Jews continued to define the immigrant experience in terms that reflected their own image of France. Like French Jews, immigrants were seen as in search of the promised land, their arrival in France a reenactment of the emancipation of French Jews almost a century before. The frequent refusal of the new arrivals to accept its mythology and authority unnerved many in the French Jewish establishment. Ironically, the increased involvement of immigrants in Paris Jewish life often led them to be critical rather than supportive of communal activity. In particular, they attacked what they regarded as the paternalism of the relief agencies. As one exasperated immigrant noted in a hyperbolic letter to *Die moderne Zeit* in 1908, the bureaucracy and inefficiency of the Comité de Bienfaisance made him feel as though he were back in Russia![37]

In retrospect, such criticisms should not obscure the growing rapprochement between the natives and immigrants that was evident in the period before 1914. The very sharpness of the immigrant critique reflected the strong desire of many East European Jews to remain in Paris and their growing self-confidence as participants in Jewish community life. Similarly, if the attitudes of French Jews often smacked of paternalism, at least some among them recognized the richness of East European Jewish religious and cultural life and hoped that immigrants would help to revivify a moribund French Judiasm. The emergence of a small coterie of young Jewish intellectuals in Paris at the turn of the century was due in part to the injection into France of a vibrant new Jewish commitment. Critical of what they perceived as the vapidness of French Jewish communal institutions and aroused by the experiences of anti-Semitism to assert their Jewish identity, individuals such as André Spire, Edmond Fleg, and Bernard Lazare found inspiration and direction in the newly arrived East European Jewish settlement in Paris.[38]

But how responsive was the newly emerging immigrant community to the assimilationist pressures of both French society and native Jewry? It is a difficult question to answer given the fledgling nature of the community and the short time span under study. One must not forget that for the first generation of new arrivals the simple struggle to survive often overrode ideological and cultural concerns. East European immigrants in Paris at the turn of the century were also hindered by the fact that they lived in a cultural limbo, feeling increasingly distant from their homelands yet not tied to France. So too, the emergence "from slavery to freedom" was a mixed blessing for new arrivals. If it was true that the Russian Jew in Paris would no longer experience collective or state-imposed persecution, it was also true that he was now desperately on his own with none to blame for his inevitable failings except himself. Even if he felt self-assured enough to think positively about his future in France, he could not honestly emulate the behavior of native Jews whom he felt were too bourgeois and lacked knowledge of Jewish culture. Clearly in order to survive against the relentless pull of the dominant French society which threatened to destroy traditional values it would be necessary for East European immigrants to establish an environment which, though facilitating their entry into French society, would shield them from the psychological and emotional trauma stemming from their removal from the security of the *shetl*.

How successful were they in creating a precarious balance between the Russian Pale and the City of Lights? One can offer some tentative conclusions by evaluating four indices of assimilation that are often used in immigrant studies: organizational life, dispersion within the economy, political activity, and language and culture.

ORGANIZATIONAL LIFE

On the surface, the organizations created by East European Jews in Paris before World War I seemed to reflect their alienation from French society and their deep nostalgia for the "old country" *(alte heym)*. It was an understandable response given the traumatic events surrounding their departure from Russia and Poland—the flight itself and the disruption of a tightly-knit family and community structure. For many Jews, the migration from East to West meant not only physical dislocation but also a profound transformation in the manner in which the Jew looked at himself in society. It would take time for the immigrants in Paris to see themselves as "emancipated," as potentially active and equal participants in the dominant society.

This was certainly true of the Russian Jewish revolutionaries who settled in Paris at the end of the nineteenth century. The myriad of organizations created by Bundists, anarchists, Social Revolutionaries and then later Mensheviks and Bolsheviks served as a life-line to Russia, preparing future leaders for the inevitable overthrow of Tsarism.[39] Jewish radicals, who made up a high proportion of the Russian immigrant colony in the French capital in this period, generally had little contact with the French working class movement. Despite their respect for the French revolutionary tradition, they generally considered the French Left as too bourgeois, too respectable, and fundamentally naive.[40] While the French socialist groups and trade unions were bureaucratically well organized, the Russian revolutionary movements in Paris were held together by charismatic leaders. These militant figures shuttled back and forth between radical communities living in exile, rousing the faithful to action and keeping alive the dream of an eventual return to Russia. The most notable of these individuals was Peter Lavrov, who lived in Paris from 1870 until his death in 1900. Although himself a Russian (not a Jew), Lavrov became a father figure to many young radical Jewish students and intellectuals, and the audiences in his small apartment on the rue Saint-Jacques in the Latin Quarter were much prized. It was said that the crowds at his funeral on 25 January 1900 rivalled those which had participated in the demonstrations during the time of the Commune.[41]

Yet the magnetic appeal of French society as well as the simple need to confront the day-to-day reality of earning a living in Paris slowly led would-be Jewish revolutionaries away from the dreams of a Russian utopia and toward problems closer to their newly adopted home. Of particular significance were the attempts to create Jewish trade unions in Paris. By far the most successful union of Jewish workers before World War I was the *syndicat des casquettiers* (Hatmakers' Union) led by Solomon Lozovsky who lived in Paris from 1909 until his return to Russia in 1917. Unionization came slowly especially in the "Jewish" textile and garment trades, where workers dreamed of becoming entrepreneurs and the majority of employees were women who had little experience with trade unions. Though immigrants were involved in numerous strikes against Jewish *patrons,* their uncertain legal status and relative inexperience doomed most of their efforts to failure.[42]

Nevertheless, by 1914 the Jewish trade union movement encompassed the majority of immigrant hatters, tailors, bakers, bottlemakers, shoemakers, and waiters in Paris. Thanks to the efforts of Lozovsky and more militant activists who arrived in the French capital after 1905, a *Commission intersyndicale* of the major Jewish trade unions was created in 1911 to counter anti-Semitic attacks upon immigrant workers. By the eve of World War I, there were said to be over twenty thousand unionized immigrant workers. As the years went by meetings of Jewish working class groups were characterized more and more by intensive debates over wages and working hours and less by calls for revolution in Russia. In their growing emphasis upon domestic concerns, immigrant trade unions inculcated patterns of behavior and attitudes that would later aid in the integration of immigrants into the French working class movement in the inter-war period.

One of the major concerns of many immigrants upon their arrival in Paris was the maintenance of religious observance. Religious tradition served not only as a tie to Eastern Europe but also as a secure anchor in the strange and seemingly formless environment of the French capital. Even Jewish militants who espoused revolution often found security in religious activity. Still others joined religious groups in order to qualify for assistance from French Jewish agencies which were more favorable to traditional immigrants.

With the exception of a few wealthier Russian Jews, most religious immigrants shunned the consistorial synagogues.[43] Instead, they chose to establish their own *shtiblekh,* store-front or loft prayer rooms which were used by congregants coming from one *shtetl,* town or region in Eastern Europe. In 1900 there were five separate *shtiblekh* in Montmartre and seven in the "Pletzl" area.⁴⁴ After an intensive fund-raising campaign launched in 1911, immigrants succeeded in constructing their own synagogue on the rue Pavée in the "Pletzl" in 1914.

Throughout the pre-war period, efforts were made to create a federation of the various immigrant religious groups. The closest immigrants came to establishing a united religious community was the appointment of Judah Lubetski as Chief Rabbi of the "Pletzl" in 1887. Like many of the immigrant rabbis who settled in Paris, Lubetski had originally journeyed to the French capital in order to collect money for his East European yeshiva but was urged to remain. During his tenure as the unofficial religious spokesman for the immigrant community, Lubetski managed to gain some recognition from the French Jewish establishment. Thus he was appointed to the Paris *bet din* (religious law court) in 1904 though he was in continual conflict with the *Consistoire* over what he considered their religious laxity, particularly on the issue of granting divorces. Within the immigrant community itself, Lubetski faced severe competition from a never-ending stream of itinerant preachers and reputed "miracle rabbis" who drifted in and out of Paris before 1914.⁴⁵

By far the most active organizations in the immigrant community were the *landsmanshaftn,* mutual-aid societies that were created to provide basic social and economic services unavailable to aliens in France. Like the *shtiblekh* with which they were often in competition, *landsmanshaftn,* as their named implied, were organized according to geographical origin and thus reinforced ties to the *alte heym.* Indeed, the very provincialism of the mutual-aid societies proved comforting to the new arrival, a place of refuge from the ideological and religious quarrels within the immigrant community and an escape from the often hostile world of French society.

The first *landsmanshaft* in Paris, the *Société de secours mutuel des israélites polonais de la loi rabbinique,* was founded in 1856 as a burial society. Numbering only ten when the first great wave of immigrants began in the 1880's, there were over fifty separate societies by the outbreak of World War I. Some, such as the *Krakover landsleyt,* were organized according to geographical origin, others such as *Moderne Shnayder* brought together immigrants in the same trade; still others like the *Association des travailleurs originaires de Roumanie,* which also included *patrons* and students, combined both principles. So successful were the *landsmanshaftn* that Jewish working class groups began to form their own mutual-aid societies to counter what they felt was the reactionary and sentimental nature of the immigrant clubs.

There were at least three attempts to create a federation of societies before World War I—a fledgling effort by Rabbi Israel Salanter in 1880, a religious-based organization supported by Lubetski in 1902, and the Zionist Federation of Societies in 1913. Hindered by the parochialism of most *landsmanshaftn*, they met with complete failure.[46]

In a paradoxical sense, the proliferation of groups and *groupuscules* in the immigrant community and the failure to bring about coordination among revolutionary, religious, and mutual-aid circles illustrated the immigrants' unconscious acceptance of the liberal values of the new society. The multiplicity of groups reflected the desire of many immigrants to share in the free social atmosphere of Paris life and to gain some individual status in an environment which denied them the right to run for office or direct French organizations. Organizational affiliation was voluntary and even charismatic figures such as Lavrov and Lubetski, each in his very different sphere, were unable to enforce unity and control. The very idea of forming a federation of organizations rather than imposing centralized control reflected an awareness even among more traditional immigrant leaders of the influence of voluntarism and pluralism upon East European Jews in Paris. Contemporaneous observers looked at the chaos of organizational life among East European Jews in Paris before World War I and decried it as a sign of apathy and spiritual malaise. With hindsight, one can see it as a natural response of new arrivals to a new and more open society.

ECONOMIC LIFE

As in New York, immigrant business and labor centered on the so-called "Jewish" trades. It is estimated that nearly two-thirds of the immigrant work force in Paris before World War I were employed in clothing and textiles.[47] Immigrants often went to work for employers or with employees who came from the same region or city in Eastern Europe. Yiddish newspapers of the period frequently wrote of unscrupulous *patrons* who would wait at the Gare de l'Est to greet arrivals from Poland and Russia with a friendly Yiddish word, an offer of room and board, working papers, and employment at miserably low wages.[48]

In general, the "Jewish" trades provided newly arrived immigrants with semi-skilled jobs that either paralleled the work experiences of the Russian Pale or were relatively easy to learn. Entrance into the "Jewish" trades was also facilitated by the fact that textiles and clothing workshops needed a flexible work force that could work at varying times of the year. Some new immigrants were even able to start their own small *ateliers* with sewing machines that they purchased on credit. In a few cases, such as the capmakers, immigrants brought the particular skill with them. In others, such as the furrier trade, they responded to changes in fashion-conscious Paris and to an increase in demand. In still others, such as ready-made men's clothing, they created a demand for a new product where none had existed previously.[49]

Despite the readily available employment, the situation of most immigrant workers was desperate. In general, the more qualified workers went to the United States where they quickly found employment. Jews coming to France were not only less skilled but also were faced with an economy that was far less diversified than the American. Unprotected by government legislation, at the mercy of unprincipled employers who played upon their sense of Jewish solidarity, and unwilling to join unions, they faced a grim existence. Most barely eked out a living. During the so-called "dead season" in the clothing trades, many immigrants were forced to resort to peddling and other odd jobs to survive. According to newspaper reports, hundreds of unemployed East European Jews roamed the streets of the "Pletzl," in some cases committing suicide by jumping off the Bastille monument.[50] Beggary was common, penniless immigrants going from house to house in search of food and clothing. The long hours or work meant that many children were left alone for most of the day and night, a situation that led to petty thievery and juvenile delinquency.[51] According to an article published in the *Revue de Paris* in 1912 and cited in *Der Yid in Pariz,* the typical Jewish worker in the French capital could not even provide basic subsistence to his family.[52]

Typical of the plight of newly arrived immigrants was the uncertain existence of the *façonnier* or home-laborer. Under a crude form of the putting-out system, the *façonnier* worked in the privacy of his home through an unofficial agreement with the employer. Subject only to a verbal agreement, he was totally unprotected. Forced to live on subsistence pay, his home and his place of work generally was a single room in one of the ramshackle hotels in the Jewish areas of Paris. The cramped quarters, the poor lighting, the feverish attempt to produce as much as possible in the shortest amount of time led to countless accidents and numerous deaths. Despite the blatant exploitation of home laborers by *patrons,* attempts to organize *façonniers* were unsuccessful. As long as the new immigrant dreamed of one day establishing his own *atelier* and becoming a *patron,* he remained uninterested in unionization.[53]

The situation began to change for the better after 1905 with the arrival of immigrants fleeing military service and later the collapse of the revolution in Russia. Far more experienced in trade-union activity and with little hope of returning to Russia in the near future, they were largely responsible for the important gains which the Jewish workers made in the period before 1914. At the same time, one can discern in the first decade of the century a rough socio-economic division between older and newer arrivals from Eastern Europe, the former already beginning to join the ranks of the bourgeoisie as masters and subcontractors in the "Jewish" trades.[54]

Similarly, there were signs of a horizontal socio-economic differentiation among East European Jews in Paris as small numbers of immigrants began to leave the security of the textile and clothing trades and to venture into new fields. Thus, in 1910 Arthur Ruppin discovered that of sixteen thousand Jewish immigrants in Paris, almost 30 percent were not in the "Jewish" trades.[55] Yet few immigrants before World War I escaped entirely from the East European Jewish milieu. Those who forsook the "Jewish" trades often took up trades such as furniture-making and jewelry that had already been developed in Eastern Europe; others simply introduced new services such as dry goods stores to Jewish neighborhoods in the French capital. It would not be until after World War I, and even more noticeably after World War II, that immigrants would begin to be truly dispersed within the French economy. As Charlotte Rolland's study of Belleville Jews demonstrates, it would be only the second and third generations who would find new economic roles as middle-range retailers and professionals.[56]

POLITICAL ACTIVITY

The restricted nature of French municipal politics and the lack of a strong ethnic population in Paris at the turn of the century prevented the development of an immigrant Jewish power base so familiar to New York City political life in the early twentieth century. As we have seen, Russian Jewish revolutionaries displayed little interest in French politics. Tracked down by the French police who often worked closely with the Russian secret police, Jewish militants were closely monitored at the Russian embassy in Paris.[57] Other elements in the immigrant community shared the militants' apathy toward French politics. Too busy eking out a living, fearful of becoming too visible, and confused by a language they could barely understand, most immigrants left politics to "real" Frenchmen. It is an indication of their indifference and powerlessness that in 1900, anti-Semitic candidates were elected in heavily Jewish areas, including the editor of *Libre Parole* in Montmartre.[58]

What did occasion immigrant response was the plight of the Jews in Russia. Yiddish papers and observers of the period refer to numerous demonstrations sponsored by immigrant groups in Paris to protest against persecution in Russia.[59] We know that there was a great deal of discussion and activity during the tense days of the Beilis trial with immigrant leaders calling upon the French government to exert pressure on its Russian ally to free the innocent man. Even the generally separatist Bund participated in a meeting with the French socialists and the League for Human Rights against Tsarist persecution of the Jews.[60] Though such efforts reflect an activist posture on the part of many immigrants in Paris, they had little impact upon French political life. The techniques of demonstration and public protest clearly reflected a growing accommodation to Western political life yet the issues discussed and debated pointed to the past rather than to the future.

More significant was the response of East European Jews to the Dreyfus Affair. Here was an issue that challenged the very survival of the young immigrant community in France. Not only were immigrants threatened by roving mobs which sought out *"métèques"* in the Jewish quarters of Paris but the very justification for immigration and acculturation seemed to be placed in question by the anti-Dreyfusard movement. Unlike native Jews who for the most part dismissed the Affair as an aberration and chose to be silent, East European Jews could not afford to remain passive.

There is little question that the events surrounding the Dreyfus trial were followed with great interest by Jewish immigrants in Paris. Few copies of immigrant newspapers of the period survive but there is a fascinating collection (in the Ochs Collection on the Dreyfus Affair housed in the Bibliothèque de la ville de Paris) of Yiddish tracts which were disseminated among immigrants in Paris. A number of pamphlets present a detailed account of the trial; others praise Emile Zola as a "righteous gentile" defending the blameless Jew. There is even a political parody of the Scroll of Esther called "Megiles Dreyfus" with a French and English text and exegeses in Hebrew and Yiddish. Like the Purim story of old, immigrant Jews in Paris never lost hope that, in the end, justice would triumph over evil.

By far the most famous document which reflects immigrant interest in the Dreyfus Affair is a brochure entitled *Le Proletariat juif* published in 1898.[61] Unlike other immigrant writings, the tract seeks to go beyond the trial to examine the wave of anti-Jewish hysteria sweeping through *fin-de-siècle* France. In essence, it attempts to counter the anti-Semitic stereotype of the rich and greedy Jew by pointing out that the majority of Jews in France were hard-working and poor laborers. As loyal residents of France and committed Jews, the tract concludes, the Jewish proletariat had an obligation to stand up and to defend Dreyfus.

Much has been made of *Le Proletariat juif*. Although it would be difficult to show that its publication signalled a new chapter in Jewish-socialist relations in France, there is no doubt that the authors of the brochure were intensely concerned about the nature of French society and were seeking to ingratiate themselves with the French Left. It is also true that the tract attempted to capitalize on the growing interest in the plight of the Jewish worker on the part of the Parisian reading public.[62] But how representative were the attitudes contained in the document? Who were its authors and who were its readers?

Despite its title, it would appear that the authors were Jewish anarchists with few ties to the Jewish working class. The pamphlet was signed by "The Jewish Socialist Workers Group in Paris," an unknown group that was created expressly for the publication in order to circumvent the stipulations of the anti-terrorist law of 1894.[63] There is some reason to believe that it was ghost-written by Bernard Lazare, the radical French Jewish writer who took an active interest in the plight of the immigrant masses in Paris and whose ideas are clearly reflected in the language and phraseology of the tract.[64] It is unlikely that *Le Proletariat juif* was read by many immigrants in Paris and improbable that it was ever seriously considered by elements within the French Left. The authors themselves had rather high hopes. They planned to publish five hundred thousand copies of the tract. They even called a meeting in Montmartre in September 1899 to publicize their ideas. But little came of their publishing plans and few immigrants attended their meeting. Most East European Jews in Paris at the end of the century seemed uncomfortable with the linkage of a "Jewish" issue with what they perceived as narrow French party politics. The fact that *Le Proletariat juif* is often apologetic in tone, and stilted in its presentation demonstrates that even the most courageous immigrants in Paris felt uncomfortable in confronting French politics.

Though Paris played an extremely important role in the development of political Zionism, Zionist ideology had only minimal impact upon the immigrant Jews in the French capital. Few immigrants were aware of Theodor Herzl and of his tract, *The Jewish State*, written in 1896 on the rue Cambon. Only a small number came into contact with Max Nordau who lived and worked for most of his life in Paris and who was honorary president of the most important immigrant Zionist group of the period, *Mebasseret Zion*. Though sympathetic to East European Jews, both Herzl and Nordau cared little for the insignificant community which was only in the process of formation. Their major interests lay with French political officials and Jewish notables.[65] At the same time most of the immigrants in Paris had little time to worry about the utopian dreams of a small group of Central European bourgeois intellectuals. They had chosen migration to the West as their solution to the "Jewish problem" in Russia and even the Dreyfus Affair could not disillusion them.

Zionist influence among immigrants in Paris resulted largely from the tireless activities of Alexander Marmorek, a Russian Jewish bacteriologist at the Institut Louis Pasteur, who helped found the *Université populaire juive* in 1902.[66] Though Marmorek maintained a full program of Jewish studies including Hebrew language and Zionist theory at his informal school situated on the rue Jarente in the Marais, it was the French language program that attracted the most students. Marmorek and his associates often found themselves forced to defend their emphasis upon Jewish topics to an audience largely interested in integrating themselves into French society. In its brochures, the *UPJ* stressed the moral obligation of immigrants to study Jewish culture in order to defend themselves against anti-Semitic attack. Denying charges of exclusivism, Marmorek justified his emphasis upon Jewish subjects by noting that any organization appealing to immigrants had to create a milieu in which they could feel comfortable.[67] The *UPJ* also faced criticism from more militant Zionist movements such as the Poalei Zion branch organized in 1904 which stressed practical Zionism and called upon East European immigrants in Paris to establish a French Jewish colony in Palestine.[68] Marmorek, an ardent supporter of Herzl, could only respond that efforts to colonize Palestine were premature and that, in the meantime, the immigrants would do well to learn the ways of their newly adopted country.[69]

Ironically, the call for the establishment of a Jewish homeland found greatest support among native-born Jews and especially young Jewish intellectuals like Bernard Lazare who were attracted to the Zionists' call for national liberation. Political Zionism also appealed to some Jewish notables like Chief Rabbi Zadok Kahn who saw a Jewish homeland as a potential solution to the Jewish refugee problem. Indeed, the *Fédération des Sionistes de France,* though organized by Marmorek, mostly attracted native French Jews who were also the most visible element at a tribute organized in memory of Herzl in 1904.[70]

The relative lack of success of Zionist movements in the East European Jewish community in pre-war Paris suggests that, for better or worse, immigrants generally had decided to seek their fortunes within the borders of France. Even in the midst of the Dreyfus Affair, they clung to those aspects of French political ideology and behavior that reinforced their fervent belief in the underlying justice and humanity of their adopted country. They could hardly be expected to understand the intricacies of French political behavior. Very often, it was one individual such as Emile Zola who was seen to embody the ideals that had originally drawn them to France. Though their political concerns often centered on the "old country," their behavior, whether in public protest in demonstrations or in private discussions in cafes or in Yiddish newspapers, increasingly reflected their acceptance of Western political technique and discourse. As elsewhere, however, it would take participation in World War I to provide the immigrants with the confidence to take active part and be accepted in the political arena.

LANGUAGE AND CULTURE

For most of the period between 1881 and 1914, immigrants in Paris were far too caught up in the struggle for economic survival to give serious thought to the issue of developing a cultural life. It was not until the first decade of the new century, with the influx of better educated and articulate elements, that there was any serious discussion of establishing permanent cultural and educational institutions within the immigrant community. East European Jewish intellectuals in Paris generally agreed that immigrants should avoid the polarities of total assimilation and ghettoization. New cultural forms would have to be created that reflected the mingling of the two worlds which their lives embraced.

In seeking to develop a cultural life for the immigrant community in Paris, the writers and journalists were influenced by numerous factors. On the one hand, they still retained strong ties to Poland and Russia and were unimpressed by what they perceived as the vacuous cultural and religious life of French Jewry. No matter what the attraction of France, there could never be any question of abandoning the cultural forms born of centuries of creative expression in Russia and Poland. On the other, they were well aware that migration to the West necessitated a transformation in the ideology and value system of East European Jewry. Emerging from isolation and persecution, the immigrants now had to interact with the larger world around them. The crossfertilization of ideas and attitudes would inevitably lead to a dynamic new democratic culture forged by the masses rather than by an intellectual elite. If Italian and Polish immigrants could develop a synthesis of their own traditions and the cultural creativity of France, one Yiddish writer observed, why couldn't Jewish immigrants whose sophistication far outstripped other recent arrivals create a new culture of their own?[71] In so doing, they would bring new meaning to the familiar adage that every man has two homelands: France and his own.[72]

Most intellectuals in Paris agreed that the basic tool for the creation of the new culture would be Yiddish; the vehicles for its development and dissemination would be the newspaper and the theater. Though there were some who voiced concern over the maintenance of a German-based "jargon" in a Latin country, most immigrants saw Yiddish as a necessary link to the Jewish heritage they had left behind in body but not in spirit. Hopes for developing a distinctive Paris Yiddish culture in Paris were bolstered by the presence of writers such as Sholem Asch who settled in Paris on a semi-permanent basis and Sholem Aleichem who visited the French capital periodically.[73] But the physical presence of Yiddish writers was hardly sufficient to ensure a diversified cultural life. In part, the problem lay with the small number of immigrants and the lack of a critical core of committed Yiddishists; in part, it lay with the magnetic pull of French culture. Even the most avid supporters of cultural revival were forced to admit that what drew creative Jewish intellectuals such as Sholem Asch and Sholem Aleichem to Paris was not the small community of Yiddish speakers but the Latin Quarter and Montparnasse.

Despite the many obstacles, intellectuals pursued their dream with great fervor. An important component of their vision was the Yiddish newspaper, at once a living embodiment of the culture in development and a vehicle for its dissemination to the immigrant masses. In the period between 1881 and 1914, close to a dozen Yiddish papers appeared in Paris. Some of the more noteworthy were *Der Agitator,* a Bundist paper devoted largely to news about Russia; *Die Wahrheit,* a Zionist journal with close ties to the Hovevei Zion movement; *Der Nayer Zhurnal,* founded by Sholem Asch and Abraham Reisen in 1913 and published simultaneously in New York, Warsaw, and Paris; and *Der Yid in Pariz,* the most successful of the newspapers, undoubtedly because of its sensationalistic character. Lacking capital and direction, faced with a fickle audience, and run by untrained writers and editors, few lasted more than a couple of months.[74] Most of the papers had a highly ideological orientation, whether revolutionary or Zionistic, and thus could only attract a small though committed readership. Struggling papers such as Sholem Asch's *Der Nayer Zhurnal* tried their best to lift the cultural level of the new immigrant but the daily grind of earning a living led most readers of Yiddish to seek out material that entertained rather than provoked them. Like the editors of Yiddish newspapers in New York City at the turn of the century, immigrant journalists in Paris were faced with what Irving Howe aptly describes as the problem of how "to combine kindergarten and university."[75]

A similar problem faced the Paris Yiddish theater. Traveling troupes first came to the French capital in 1885. By the early 1890's, there were perhaps a half dozen amateur groups performing on a regular basis.[76] Audiences were very mixed: fans passionately devoted to a local Yiddish star, immigrant families with children looking for cheap entertainment, even French-born Jews who were drawn to the theater by the exotic nature of the productions. The typical production contained all the ingredients of a modern soap opera—unrequited love, adultery, divorce, suicide—though playwrights made sure that traditional morality won out in the end.[77]

While borrowing heavily from the *shund-teyater* ("trash theater") popular in Warsaw, London, and New York, Yiddish impresarios tried valiantly to present serious issues to the Paris immigrant audience. In 1902, for example, a Worker's Theater was organized to offer plays depicting realistic portrayals of the Jewish laborer. In the end, however, even the most ambitious productions contained goodly doses of escapism and a nostalgia for Eastern Europe. As one Jewish journal published in Paris and London described Yiddish theater in the French capital shortly after World War I:

> The people who came there are looking for the resurrection of a life that has disappeared. . . . They want, if even only for a night, to be transported there, to their dear land, where life seems so beautiful despite all the past miseries and the bloody nightmarish existence.[78]

In retrospect, the efforts by a few valiant immigrant intellectuals to develop a distinctive Paris Yiddish culture in the period before World War I would seem to have been doomed from the beginning. How could a culture be nurtured within a community that had yet to ensure its own continuity, among immigrants who could not yet be confident about their own future in France? How could it survive without a leisure class to enjoy it, or at least a sizeable number of people with enough economic security to rise above the concerns of the struggle for existence? It was one thing for a vibrant Yiddish life to flower in countries such as Russia and the United States whose dominant culture was viewed as either inferior or unsophisticated. It was quite another to develop autonomous cultural patterns and institutions in France whose rich and deeply-rooted culture had so attracted immigrant Jews to Paris in the first place.

The standard measurements of assimilation thus leave us with conflicting results. There are significant signs of a gradual accommodation to life in Paris before World War I but the precarious nature of daily life and the strangeness of the new environment led most immigrants to cling to their own traditions and attitudes. For as many factors that one can cite favoring the assimilation of East European Jews—the fact that they had nowhere to return; the fact that at least at the beginning of the period, they were ignored in a society that was apathetic toward immigrants; the fact that they were youthful and urban and thus less bound to tradition—there are an equal number of factors which obstructed their gradual incorporation into French society: the growing xenophobia of Frenchmen which was channeled into anti-Semitism during the Dreyfus Affair; the apathy and occasionally the hostility of the native Jewish community; the linguistic and religious differences that set immigrant Jews apart from other immigrants and from Frenchmen; the economic isolation of immigrants concentrated in the so-called "Jewish" trades or at least in Jewish areas of settlement.

On a fundamental level, assimilation to French life among East European immigrants before World War I was a process that took place at the level of daily life, in the intimate experiences of individuals that lie beneath the social, economic, and political forces shaping society and that elude the historian. In the absence of survivors of the period, we can only catch glimpses of this world from written sources, most notably the use of language. Thus one notes the significant number of name changes that reflect the desperate desire to be accepted: Petrovich becomes Pierre, Koenıg—Leroy, Shvarts—Lenoir.[79] Similarly, there is the development of hybrid terms that unconsciously reveal the blending of old and new worlds: "Makht attention" (Pay attention); "à la gelt" (working for piece-rate); "poirekougel" (pear-pie). So too, one finds malapropisms or deliberate mispronunciations of place names, signs of endearment which demonstrate the immigrant's growing familiarity with and affection for his newly adopted city: Boulevard de Sebastopol becomes "Boulevard de Shabbes-tepl" (pot for shabbat); rue de Rivoli—"Rivelegass"; Place des Vosges—"Place des Vurst" (Sausage Square).[80]

It is in the language of a highly verbal people that the subtle pull of French society upon immigrant Jewish life in Paris before 1914 is revealed. Many of the tendencies toward acculturation already evident before World War I would be reinforced with the massive immigration of Jews from Eastern Europe to the French capital in the 1920's and 1930's and would accelerate with second generation integration. Yet the experiences of the pre-war immigrants in the French capital were more than the awkward first steps in an inexorable process of assimilation. Given the horrifying events of World War II which would scar the European Jewish experience forever, the history of immigrant Jews in Paris between 1881 and 1914 seems like a moment frozen in time—an age of innocence and hopefulness where, for all its frustrations and travails, it was still possible to dream of becoming "happy as God in France."

Notes

1. Throughout the thirty year period under study, there was sporadic immigrant settlement in such provincial cities as Lyon, Nancy, and Strasbourg but no community outside of Paris had more than a few hundred East European Jews.
2. Drumont cited in Robert Byrnes, *Antisemitism in Modern France*, (Bloomington, 1950) I, p. 93; Wolf Speiser, *Yidish-frantsoyzisher kalendar* (Paris, 1910) p. 45. An article in *Die moderne Zeit* (1 January 1909) boasted that there were 100,000 immigrant Jews in France. S. Fridman (Zosa Szajkowski) in his *Etyudn tsu der geshikhte fun ayngevandertn yidishn yishev in frankraykh*, Volume I (Paris, 1937) p. 24, cites a similar figure for 1914.
3. For information on East European Jews in Paris before 1880: *ibid.*, pp. 11–15.
4. For information on East European Jews who came to the World's Fair and remained in Paris, see the Comité de Bienfaisance, *Assemblée générale, 18 mars 1901*, p. 12 and Sh. Bromberg, *Di Yidishe velt oysshtelung in pariz* (London, 1900) pp. 21, 25.
5. David Weinberg, *A Community on Trial* (Chicago, 1977) p. 3.
6. For an example of a French journalist's perceptions of immigrant Jewish settlement in Paris, see Charles Fegdal, *Le Ghetto parisien* (no place or date given).
7. *L'Univers israélite* (9 March 1900).
8. Many Jews from Romania appear to have come via the port of Odessa to Marseilles. From there, they journeyed by train to Paris with temporary stops in Avignon, Lyon, and Dijon. Jews from Russia, Poland and Galicia often travelled to Paris via Breslau, Berlin, Cologne, and southern Germany. For information on the travels of one group of Romanian Jews, see *L'Univers israélite*, (1 September 1892). For information on the itinerary of Russian immigrants, see Käthe Schirmacher, *La spécialization du travail par nationalité à Paris* (Paris, 1908) *passim*. An interesting insight into the plight of immigrants too tired to travel further is found in a letter from a husband traveling to France to his wife in Russia published in *Jüdische nachrichten* (7 August 1907).
9. *Jüdische nachrichten* (3 May 1907). See also Bromberg, *ibid.*, pp. 5–6.
10. Yisroel Belchatowski, *Fun a lebn vos iz nishto mer* (Tel Aviv, 1973) p. 105.
11. See, for example, the discussion of French attitudes toward immigrants in Jean Mesnaud de Saint-Paul, *De l'immigration étrangère en France considerée au point de vue économique* (Paris, 1902) p. 16.
12. For detailed figures on foreigners in France before World War I, see Albert Blanc, *L'Immigration en France et le travail national* (Lyon, 1901) pp. 33–39; J. Bercovici, *Contrôle sanitaire des immigrants en France* (Paris, 1926) p. 2; and William Oualid, *L'Immigration ouvrière en France* (Paris, 1927) pp. 5–6. According to Mesnaud de Saint-Paul, p. 31, in 1902 one out of every seventeen Frenchmen was a foreigner.
13. Anti-foreign sentiment was often expressed in biological terms. Mesnaud de Saint-Paul cites a "M. Laumonier" who compared non-assimilable foreigners in French society to the presence of foreign elements in the human stomach. "To introduce such individuals into society . . . elements who differ in origin, in custom, and in attitude," he concludes, "is to create social unrest

similar to the physiological damage caused by poisoning." (Mesnaud de Saint-Paul, pp. 131–32)

14. For an insightful discussion of the impact of political centralization upon French cultural perceptions, see Dominique Schnapper, *Juifs et israélites* (Paris, 1980), pp. 55–56.

15. The most serious incident of the period concerning homeless Jewish immigrants in Paris occurred in August 1892. It was general practice for representatives of the Jewish Colonization Association to meet Jews arriving from Eastern Europe at the Gare de Lyon and to transport them to the Gare de l'Ouest where they would board trains for Le Havre and ships to North and South America. A group of about one hundred Romanian Jews arrived at the Gare de Lyon in late August 1892 only to find that there was no one to meet them. After camping out at the train station for three days, they were ejected and then proceeded to set up tents on the nearby rue de Lyon. Embarrassed by the sight of immigrant Jews roaming the streets of Paris, French Jewish relief groups put them up at adjoining hotels and arranged for their transportation to Le Havre. *Le Figaro,* in an article entitled "A Jewish Encampment" published on 24 August 1892, assured its readers that the Gare de Lyon was washed down and disinfected after the immigrants were thrown out.

For other discussions of immigrant "nomads" on Paris streets, see *Dass Jüdische Blatt,* (23 February 1912 and 8 March 1912).

16. *Pariser Journal,* September 23, 1910 and October 28, 1910. Even sympathetic Jews in Paris were concerned that unsanitary conditions in immigrant quarters would arouse fears of epidemic among the French populace. Max Nordau, in an article in the *Pariser Journal* (4 November 1910) urged "rich French Jews" to provide doctors and erect public bathhouses in Jewish quarters in the French capital to "avoid any action that could serve as a pretext for anti-Semitic attacks."

17. Edouard Drumont, *Les Juifs contre la France, une nouvelle Pologne* (Paris, 1899) p. 68.

18. Edmond Silberner, *Hasozializm hama'aravi ushe-elat hayehudim* (Jerusalem, 1955) pp. 13–105; Robert Wistrich, *Revolutionary Jews from Marx to Trotsky* (New York, 1976) *passim.*

19. See for example, the article in the 11 January 1911 issue of *Pariser Journal* on a meeting of the brushmakers union. At the meeting, there were cries of "dirty Jew" and demands that the twenty-five Jewish members be expelled. See also the letter from a worker in the women's clothing trade reproduced in *Dass Jüdische Blatt* (9 February 1912). On opposition to separate language sections in trade unions, see Blanc, p. 148.

20. Paula Hyman, *From Dreyfus to Vichy* (New York, 1979) p. 133.

21. Michael Marrus, *The Politics of Assimilation* (Oxford, 1971) pp. 86–87.

22. Weinberg, p. 215. See also the discussion of the attitudes of Joseph Reinach in Marrus, p. 113.

23. In Pierre Abraham's novel, *Les Trois frères,* a French Jew describes his attitudes toward pre-war East European immigrants in the following manner:

> It is with a vaguely piteous repugnance that one considers these unfortunate immigrant Jews from eastern Europe who, with a grand display of *tfiln* on their arms and head and a *tales* on their shoulders, prove to you in a provocative fashion that you are less observant than they. One can flatter oneself in being many generations in advance of these people who are not yet assimilated. (*Les Trois frères* [Paris, 1971] pp. 42–43.)

24. Alliance israélite universelle, *Bulletin*, 2nd series, no. 3 (1881) pp. 53–55.

25. Letters from Emmanuel Veneziani from Brody in YIVO Archives, *Y. Borenstein and M. Eisenberg Collection on Migration*, Folder 13/350–368.

26. Patrick Girard, *Les juifs de France de 1789 à 1860* (Paris, 1976) p. 219.

27. Other members included Jules Gambetta, Pierre Waldeck-Rousseau, Jules Simon, and the Archbishop of Paris. For further information on the committee, see Michel Rudnianski, *Les Relations entre israélites français et juifs russes, 1860–1890*, mémoire de maîtrise présenté . . . dans le cadre de l'U.E.R. d'Histoire de Paris I (1971–72), p. 60.

28. Relations between American and French Jewish relief organizations were often stormy. A joke popular among East European Jews in Paris dealt with a conversation between an American Jewish philanthropist and Rothschild:
The American philanthropist: "Tell me, dear Baron, what have you done for the Jewish poor in the last five years?" Rothschild: "I have donated five million francs so that Russian Jews can be sent from Paris to America. Now tell me what you have done during the same time?" The American philanthropist: "I've collected money from the immigrants so that we can send them back to Paris!" (Quoted in *Ha-Emet*, no. 30 [1895] p. 3.)

29. See, for example, the letter from M.A. Kurscheedt of The Russian Emigrant Relief Fund in New York to S.H. Goldschmidt of the Alliance dated 31 October 1881, and found in the *Borenstein/Eisenberg Collection*, Folder 20/569–584. See also the Alliance circular addressed to immigrants and dated 24 March 1882 which describes the United States as an "immense, rich, and free country where everyone who wants to and is able to work will quickly find employment." (*Borenstein/Eisenberg Collection*, Folder 5/55. Problems were compounded by the existence of competing relief organizations. Paris was also the home of the Jewish Colonization Association.)

30. For a complete list of relief programs for immigrants, see the *Calendrier* [*Calendrier-annuaire*] *à l'usage des communautés israélites pour l'année 1897/98; 1899/1900; 1901/1902;* and *1905/1906* (Paris) *passim*.

31. Cited in Girard, p. 218.

32. See, for example, the letters from the Lyon Consistoire to the Alliance, dated 13 January 1892, and from the *Comité de Bienfaisance* to its Marseilles branch, dated 4 December 1905, contained in *Borenstein/Eisenberg Collection*, Folder 96/4387–4388.

33. See, for example, the *compte-rendu* of a meeting of Jewish relief agencies organized by the Alliance in June 1901 found in the *Borenstein/Eisenberg Collection*, Folder 85/3752–3753.

34. Maxime DuCamp, *Paris bienfaisant* (Paris, 1888) p. 454.

35. An interesting example of how the Consistoire maintained control over immigrants after 1905 concerned marriage and divorce among Russian Jews. After the separation of church and state, the Russian government refused to accept marriages and divorces of immigrants officiated by French rabbis because they were no longer state officials. In 1912, after long and hard deliberation, all consistorial rabbis were recognized as having the same authority as rabbis of the Russian Empire, thus effectively co-opting the power of immigrant religious leaders. (Hyman, p. 125)

36. *Ibid.*, p. 141.

37. *Die moderne Zeit* (13 December 1908). See also the discussion of immigrant attacks upon the rue Rodier facility at the annual meeting of the *Comité*

de Bienfaisance in May 1906, found in the Comité de Bienfaisance, *Assemblée générale du 21 mai 1906*, p. 11.

38. For an example of such attitudes, see André Spire, *Quelques juifs et demijuifs*, (Paris, 1928) I, viii.

39. For a description of the various revolutionary groups, see S. Fridman, *Di profesyonele bavegung tsvishn di yidishe arbeter in frankraykh biz 1914* (Paris, 1937) pp. 57–63, and police reports on Russian militants in the *Archives Nationales*, F⁷, 12519–12520.

40. J. Tchernoff, *Dans le creuset des civilisations* (Paris, 1936–38) II, 82–86.

41. For further information on Lavrov and his impact upon Russian Jewish students, see *ibid.*, pp. 28–37.

42. See, for example, the police report of 9 October 1913 on union activity in the clothing trades in the *Archives Nationales*, F⁷, 13740.

43. Not all newly arrived East European Jews avoided Paris synagogues. *Die Wahrheit* (3 February 1905) recorded an incident at the rue de Lions Saint-Paul synagogue in the Marais where the police had to be called upon to eject a Russian immigrant who had come to a Friday night service to beg for a meal.

44. *Archives israélites* (11 October 1900).

45. Lubetski was not the first important religious figure from Eastern Europe who attempted to organize the Paris immigrant community. Rabbi Israel Salanter, founder of the Musar movement, worked with immigrants during his stay in the French capital from 1880 to 1882. There was also a representative of the Volozhin *yeshiva* who for a brief period in the 1880's vied with Lubetski for leadership of the immigrant community. There were even some efforts by Christian missionaries to convert Eastern European Jews. A "Paris Mission to the Jews" was established at the turn of the century which published a newspaper, *Ha-Emet,* gave lectures in Yiddish, and offered free meals. Though it attempted to play upon the isolation that many immigrants felt in Paris, it had little success.

46. For further information, on the Zionist Federation, see *Der Yid in Pariz* (20 April 1913) and the *YIVO Archives,* RG # 116: France I: *Frankraykh: protokoln,* etc.

47. Arthur Ruppin cited in Nancy Green, "Eléments pour une étude du mouvement ouvrier juif à Paris au début du siècle," *Le Mouvement sociale,* # 110 (January–March 1980), p. 55.

48. See, for example, the article in *Die moderne Zeit* (23 October 1908).

49. See the police report of 10 December 1908 in the *Archives Nationales,* F⁷, 12894.

50. See, for example, the article by A. Karnin in *Die moderne Zeit* (13 December 1908).

51. *Die moderne Zeit* (3 January 1909). For a general discussion of poverty in the Jewish quarters of Paris, see Paul Pottier, "Essai sur le proletariat juif en France," *Revue des revues* (1 March 1899), 482–90. On criminality among immigrant children left alone during the day, see *Die Wahrheit* (17 February 1905).

52. *Der Yid in Pariz* (20 May 1912). According to the article, an immigrant Jewish worker earned approximately 2500 francs a year but was forced to spend over 3200 francs annually to support his family.

53. Weinberg, pp. 16–17.

54. Doris Ben-Simon Donath, *Socio-Démographie des juifs de France et d'Algérie* (Paris, 1976) p. 199.

55. Cited in Green, p. 55.

56. Charlotte Rolland, *Du Ghetto à l'occident: Deux générations yiddiches en France* (Paris, 1962).

57. See, for example, the police reports on Russian revolutionary groups in Paris in the *Archives Nationales*, F^7, 12519–12520.

58. *L'Univers israélite* (11 May 1900).

59. See, for example, the report on the demonstration after the Kishinev pogrom in *L'Echo sioniste* (15 June 1903).

60. On October 18, 1913, for example, Jewish clothing workers held a protest meeting in support of Beilis that drew 800 people (*L'Humanité*, 20 October 1913). On Bundist participation in the meeting sponsored by the French socialists and the League of Human Rights, see *Der Nayer Zhurnal* (31 October 1913).

61. *Le Proletariat juif, Lettre des ouvriers juifs de Paris au Parti socialiste français* (Paris, 1898).

62. See, for example, the essays by Paul Pottier, previously cited, and by Henri Dagan, "Le proletariat juif mondial," *Revue blanche* (15 October 1901), pp. 241–70.

63. Fridman, *Di profesyonele*, p. 36.

64. E. Tcher-ski, "Di Dreyfus-affayr, di arbeter-imigrantn, un di frantsoy-zishe-yidishe firers," in E. Tcherikower, *Yidn in frankraykh*, (New York, 1942) II, 165; and Nelly Wilson, *Bernard Lazare* (Cambridge, 1978), p. 299, n. 19.

65. For information on Nordau's influence upon Russian Jewish immigrants in Paris, see Tchernoff, III, 66. Nordau was attacked by a Zionist militant in December 1903 while attending a meeting of Mebasseret Zion.

66. For information on the activities of the university, see Université populaire juive, *Compte-rendu annuel et Statuts* (Paris, 1904).

67. *Ibid.*, pp. 6–8. A similar ambivalence was evident in the lead article of *L'Echo sioniste* (10 February 1912), which contradicted Zionist teaching by proudly proclaiming the fact that immigrants were assimilating quickly and thus belying anti-Semitic accusations of Jewish separateness.

68. *Dass Jüdische Blatt* (22 March 1912).

69. For further information on Zionist activity among immigrants, see Tchernoff, Volume III, pp. 65–75; and Baruch Hagani, "Les débuts du sionisme à Paris; souvenirs d'enfance," *La Terre retrouvée* (20 March 1929), pp. 2–4.

70. *L'Echo sioniste* (15 August 1904).

71. *Pariser Jüdische Blatt* (June 1912), p. 1.

72. Of course, not all immigrants were optimistic about the possibility of reviving Jewish life in Paris. A writer in *Die moderne Zeit* (27 November 1908) for example, cynically suggested that if Russia was "goles" (exile), then France must be a "golesdikn goles."

73. For information on Sholem Aleichem's visits to Paris, see Yechezkel Kornhendler, *Yidn in pariz* (Paris, 1970), pp. 238–44.

74. An article in a special enclosure in *Die Wahrheit* (6 January 1905) noted that in many immigrant areas in Paris, Yiddish newspapers published in the French capital were often outsold by London papers which were cheaper and of better quality. One French journalist who frequently visited the "Pletzl" observed in 1915 that immigrants flocked to read Russian and Yiddish papers published in Odessa, Warsaw, Lodz, and London. One must remember, however, that at the beginning of the war, the French government banned Yiddish newspapers because the language sounded similar to German and there were no government censors who could read Yiddish.

75. Irving Howe, *World of our Fathers* (New York, 1976), p. 522. For a

discussion of the problem as perceived by East European journalists in Paris, see *Die moderne Zeit* (13 November 1908). Similar attempts by mutual-aid and political organizations to combine entertainment and education met with only partial success. See, for example, the report on the *Agudat Zion* ball in *Dass Jüdische Blatt* (9 February 1912).

76. The famous impresario and Yiddish playwright, Avraham Goldfaden, organized no less than three separate theater groups in Paris before World War I but all failed.

77. "Di vilde Khane" an immensely popular production of the period was a typical example of what Paris immigrant audiences saw in the Yiddish theater. Khane, the daughter of a pious rabbi, falls in love with a rich Christian count. Both leave their parents and live in poverty for nineteen years. Khane's father will only take her back if she leaves her non-Jewish family. Khane loves her father but cannot desert her husband and children. Her daughter is seduced and runs away with her lover. In turn, the seducer convinces Khane's husband to leave with a promise of wealth and his father's title. Khane is alone and goes blind. She stabs the daughter's seducer; the count kills himself. (*Die moderne Zeit* [31 January 1909]).

78. *La Tribune juive* (9 November 1922). For a general overview of the development of Yiddish theater in France, see Zosa Szajkowski, "Yidisher teater in frankraykh," in *Yidisher teater in eyrope* (New York, 1971), pp. 289–321.

79. For an interesting discussion of name changes among immigrants to France, see A. Juret, "La francisation des noms de personnes," in *Population* III (July–September 1947), pp. 451–64.

80. In her work on Jewish assimilation in France in the early nineteenth century, Christine Piette-Samson suggests that there were three discernible steps in the development of daily language patterns among Jewish immigrants. At first, immigrants spoke Judeo-German and shunned French. Within a decade or two, they had begun to blend their native jargon with French, creating strange and colorful hybrid phrases and terms. By 1840, French had "triumphed," a clear indication of successful acculturation. (Christine Piette-Samson, *Les Juifs de Paris [1800–1840]: Problèmes d'acculturation;* thèse de doctorat de troisième cycle présentée à la Faculté des Lettres et Sciences humaines de l'Université de Paris [Paris, 1971], p. 249.) My own research reveals a similar pattern beginning to develop among East European Jews in Paris before World War I. The process was far less rapid than that indicated by Piette-Samson, in part because of the strength of anti-Semitic sentiment among Frenchmen, in part because of the successive waves of immigrants from Eastern Europe which reinforced Yiddish speaking within the community. As the examples in the body of the essay demonstrate, many East European Jews in the French capital had achieved the second stage of language development before World War I intervened.

East European Jews in the *Weltanschauung* of German Zionists, 1882–1914

Jehuda Reinharz
(BRANDEIS UNIVERSITY)

The pogroms of the 1880's and 1890's shattered forever any hope of real emancipation in Eastern Europe.[1] The largest emigration and population transfer in Jewish history followed, whereby most of the emigrés went to the United States. This large-scale movement also affected Germany and German Jewry. From the turn of the century until World War I, Germany shared a border with Russia. Owing to its geographical proximity and access to the sea, Germany became a natural transit country for East European Jews travelling to the United States. Not all those who passed through Germany[2] reached their overseas destination; under some circumstances, or for a variety of personal reasons, many chose to settle in Germany.[3] During these years, therefore, the number of Eastern Jews in Germany increased dramatically. The philanthropic organizations of Western Jewry, and foremost among them, the German Jewish organizations, undertook to help these East European Jews, but above all to organize and direct the emigration to America and other countries.[4]

In general, the pogroms had great impact on some segments of German Jewry and helped shape their attitudes toward settlement in Palestine. Throughout the nineteenth century efforts to rebuild and settle Palestine or to help its Jewish inhabitants came from Orthodox circles whose motivations were religious and philanthropic. Following the pogroms, and the reawakening national feelings among East European Jewry, an increasing number of German Jews began to talk about the settlement of Palestine within a Jewish national context.[5] Plans for rebuilding Palestine became more concrete now and those who joined associations which promoted such ideas were no longer solely of an

Orthodox background. The main problem of these new associations was to find financial support for the execution of their ideas.[6]

The first such association to be founded in Germany in May 1882 was the "Bnei Brith" of Kattowitz founded by Selig Freuthal and Moritz Moses.[7] The association, which had some fifty members, was also in touch with similar associations in Russia, Romania and Austria. It published an information bulletin *(Monatsbericht)* and, toward the end of 1882, it began the publication of *Der Colonist,* which became a weekly in 1883. This was the first organ of German Jewry wholly devoted to matters concerning Palestine.[8] At the initiative of the "Bnei Brith" association, a conference was convened in Kattowitz in November 1884 of all Hovevei Zion associations throughout Europe concerned with the settlement of Palestine.[9] These associations elected a central committee headed by Leo Pinsker.[10] Pinsker had a staunch supporter in Germany in the person of Rabbi Isaak Rülf of Memel who for some twenty years already had been a member of the "Israelitischer Verein zur Kolonisation von Palästina." Under the impact of Pinsker's *Autoemancipation,* Rülf published his *Aruchas Bas-Ammi,* which demanded a return to Palestine.[11]

The first consciously nationalist group in Germany was the "Russischer Jüdischer Wissenschaftlicher Verein"—the Russian Jewish Scientific Society.[12] The "Verein," as it was popularly known, was founded in December 1888 by twelve East European Jewish students some two years before the term "Zionism" had become current.[13] When the "Verein" was founded, there was no other national Jewish student organization in Germany. It was not until March 1892 that Heinrich Löwe, the only German member of the "Verein,"[14] founded a German counterpart called "Jung Israel" which sought to attract German Jews into its ranks.[15] However, by 1894 the "Jung Israel" could boast of only twenty-two members.[16] Thus, the "Russischer Jüdischer Wissenschaftlicher Verein" was the first student organization in Germany to advocate Jewish nationalism, though only gradually.[17] The "Verein" often served as a public catalyst in the 1890's to arouse interest in Jewish national questions among the German Jewish academics. Its fifty members also played a role in helping East European refugees find room and board in Berlin.

The founder and undisputed leader of the "Verein" was Leo Motzkin who had been born in the Ukraine, but had been living in Berlin since the age of fifteen. He led the "Verein" by virtue of his knowledge of German culture and German Jewry and his organizational abilities, but the membership itself consisted of a number of forceful personalities who were to play an important role in Zionist affairs in later years, such as Shmarya Levin, Nachman Syrkin, Victor Jacobson and

Chaim Weizmann.[18] They were all non-conformists, chafing to free themselves from anything smacking of spiritual and cultural bondage. They did not accept authority easily and loved nothing more than to engage in heated ideological debates for hours on end.[19] Yet the "Verein" remained a self-contained group. Its members were marginal men in Berlin society, isolated from both the Russian students as well as the German Jewish community. For all their concern with the fate of their brethren in Eastern Europe, German Jews for the most part, did not interact socially with those refugees and students who lived in their proximity.[20]

Early in 1891 a young lawyer from Cologne, Max Bodenheimer, published a pamphlet called *Wohin mit den russischen Juden? Syrien ein Zufluchtsort der russischen Juden* in which he advocated the settlement of the East European Jews in Syria and Palestine, both to protect them and to rehabilitate them socially in occupations such as farming and crafts.[21] Bodenheimer's brochure enjoyed wide circulation. It proved useful in making contact with other Hovevei Zion groups in Germany and abroad. Soon after Herzl issued the call for the First Zionist Congress, Bodenheimer and his colleagues mobilized and organized those sympathetic to the Zionist idea and in the fall of 1897 their efforts were crystallized in the founding of the "Zionistische Vereinigung für Deutschland" (ZVfD).

Bodenheimer belonged to the first generation of German Zionists, a generation which, unlike Herzl, did not reject Jewish life in the Diaspora.[22] This group continued to live in Germany and considered themselves worthy Germans by virtue of their socio-cultural values and their unquestioned loyalty to the German fatherland. Despite their official adherence to Zionist ideology, they possessed a *Weltanschauung* similar to that of the majority of German Jews. Most German Zionists of this generation were completely estranged from Jewish religion. Their children received the same education as that of other middle class liberal Jews, an education that in no way emphasized Jewish or Hebrew culture. Their concern for things Jewish, such as Jewish folklore, Hasidism, Hebrew and Yiddish, and the Jewish colonies in Palestine, often remained an individual matter or the subject of interesting articles in the official organ of the Zionistische Vereinigung für Deutschland (ZVfD)—the *Jüdische Rundschau*. They did not devise even a limited cultural program in the Diaspora and did not attempt any personal or practical application of their theory of Jewish nationalism. Their Zionist ideology provided them with a systematic worldview that anchored them in Germany and enabled them to see their Jewish identity as compatible with German culture.[23]

The position of these early Zionists was defined by Isaak Zwirn:

"We German Zionists came to Zionism out of different motives from those of the *Ostjuden*. Zionism, as we understand it, is the solution of the moral and economic *Judennot*."[24] Franz Oppenheimer was probably the most articulate representative of the first generation's point of view. While considering himself a "good Zionist" who espoused the Basle Program of 1897, Oppenheimer never intended to emigrate to Palestine. He was appalled at the thought of uprooting himself from his beloved fatherland. The demand by some Zionists that he do so was, in Oppenheimer's opinion, an act of "intolerance" unacceptable to even the most ardent German Zionist.[25] He denounced extreme forms of Jewish nationalism as the "photographic negative of anti-Semitism."[26]

As the "Bnei Brith" statement, Bodenheimer's brochure and Oppenheimer's essay clearly demonstrate, the program of the first generation of German Zionists was directed almost solely to the suffering Jews of the East. It was not designed to change the lives of its adherents in Germany. It was a philanthropic-political brand of Zionism. Critics of the early Zionists called their philosophy "Zionism out of pity" *(Zionismus aus Mitleid)*, mere philanthropy on behalf of East European Jews. These early Zionists had little interest in meeting or learning about East European culture from those East European Jews they met, or had the opportunity to meet, such as members of the "Russischer Jüdischer Wissenschaftlicher Verein."[27]

This point of view persisted until 1910–1912. Shortly thereafter radical revisions in the ideology of German Zionists were made in response to changes in the World Zionist Organization and to the new experiences encountered by the second generation of young German Zionists. On the one hand, these younger men, led by Kurt Blumenfeld, were influenced by the general trend within the World Zionist Organization toward practical and cultural work in Palestine and the Diaspora and by the ideas of Ahad Ha'Am and Martin Buber.[28] Their ideological orientation became a composite whose main features were influenced by Herzl's negation of the Diaspora and Buber's admonition to search for their roots in Judaism. On the other hand, the Zionist youth of pre-World War I Germany was influenced by the ideas that permeated West European middle class youth.[29]

The young Zionists understood the "Jewish Question" in a manner completely different from that of the "confession-oriented" Jews of the older generation. They felt that assimilation into the German *Volk* was undesirable and unattainable. Unlike the members of the older generation, these young Zionists intended to act on their theories. Although they had borrowed some of their ideas and ideals from the same intellectual sources which shaped the German "Wandervogel," they stressed their dissimilarity from the rest of the German population in custom, habit and innermost being. These men and women were no longer satisfied with clichés and conventional ideas. Like many members of the European youth of the period, they too searched for roots and a new, wholesome identity. In turn, this search led to endless discussions about *Deutschtum-Judentum-Zionismus;* debates with anti-Zionists and others forced new definitions and redefinitions of concepts and ideas and a constantly evolving reevaluation of themselves and their Zionist ideology.[30] Under the leadership of Kurt Blumenfeld, the second generation challenged the political-philanthropic orientation of their elders.[31] They could not accept the compromises made by the first generation and tried to achieve a modicum of consistency by seeking to put their theories into practice. An important catalyst in this process and in heightened Jewish nationalism was the Posen Resolution of May 1912, which adopted the concept of Palestine-orientation *(Palästino-zentrismus)* as a cornerstone of the ideology of the ZVfD. With this resolution the second generation declared that Palestine was part of their personal goal.[32] They implicitly affirmed that emigration to Palestine was not solely a vehicle for saving *Ostjuden,* but their responsibility as well.

Both the first and second generations of German Zionists considered the East European Jews to be "better Jews" than they, in closer touch with their tradition and culture. Those of the older generation such as Oppenheimer recognized the differences between German Jews and their East European brethren, but did not draw any implications from this for their own lives. The younger generation, however, looked to the *Ostjuden* as Jews worthy of emulation.[33] This was largely a romantic idealization, however, since very few German Jews had actually come into close contact with the *Ostjuden* prior to World War I. Many young Zionists assumed that the assimilated West European Jew had personality flaws which accounted for the moral and national decline of Western Jewry. Identification with the *Ostjuden* was one vehicle for checking this decline. Idealization of the *Ostjuden* and their East European culture became the answer to the young Zionists' basic and deep personal needs. Blumenfeld exhorted the German Zionists to dedicate themselves more fervently than ever to Jewish nationalist ideology if they were to be as true to the Zionist idea as were their brethren in Eastern Europe. Special efforts would be required for this task because German Zionists lacked the East European Jews' concentrated masses and their traditional ties to their own past. Blumenfeld was the first to urge German Zionists actually to "return to Palestine" even before the mass emigration of the East Europeans would take place. It was only to be expected that someone like Berthold Feiwel, a member of the younger generation, would rise to the "defense" of the *Ostjuden* in light of Oppenheimer's article in *Die Welt*.[34]

One may state that World War I constitutes a turning point in the attitude of German Zionists toward the *Ostjuden*. They were henceforth viewed not merely as objects of philanthropy, but as valuable political and ideological partners in the cause of Zionism and as active participants in alleviating their own miserable condition. Moreover, many German Zionists perceived in the *Ostjuden* a needed source for their own Jewish strength and vitality. An increasing number of German Zionists sought out the East European Jews who lived in their own midst.[35] The *Volksheim* in Berlin served as a meeting place in which Western (mostly Zionist) and East European Jews learned from one another. Those German Zionists—as well as non-Zionists (Franz Rosenzweig is a good example[36])—who met the East European Jews in their own milieu were stamped with an indelible impression. Those Zionists who remained at home during the war often found themselves defending the cause of the *Ostjuden* against those German Jews who feared that an influx of their Eastern brethren into Germany could result in an increased level of anti-Semitism and a diminution of their own rights in Germany.[37] The Zionists were similarly disturbed by the suggestions made by the "Deutsche Volkspartei," the "Wirtschaftsverein" and others that the German border be closed to East European Jews and by the less than forceful defense of the *Ostjuden* by Germany's leading liberal Jewish organizations.[38] In general, the encounter with the *Ostjuden* served as a catalyst for evaluation and reevaluation of German Zionist thought in the period during World War I and in the inter-war period.

Notes

1. See Michael Aronson, "The Prospects for the Emancipation of Russian Jewry During the 1880's," *The Slavonic and East European Review* LV, no. 3 (July 1977) pp. 348–69.

2. By 1891 some 130,000 Jews a year were entering Germany from the East. See Wladimir W. Kaplun-Kogan, *Die Jüdische Wanderbewegungen in der neuesten Zeit* (Bonn, 1919) p. 20.

3. By 1914 there were 90,000 foreign-born Jews in Germany, mostly from territories under Russian control, and from Galicia. See. S. Adler-Rudel, *Ostjuden in Deutschland 1880–1940* (Tübingen, 1959) p. 21. The word "many" is not in relation to the total emigration from Eastern Europe but in relation to the total number of German Jews. The 70,000 foreign Jews in Germany in 1910 comprised 14 percent of the total Jewish population.

4. See Zosa Szajkowski, "The European Attitude to East European Jewish Immigration (1881–1893)," *Publications of the American Jewish Historical Society* XLI, no. 2 (December 1951) pp. 127–60. See also H. Weichmann, *Die Auswanderung aus Österreich und Russland über die Deutschen Häfen* (Berlin, 1913); Michael Aronson, "The Attitude of Russian Officials in the 1880's toward Jewish Assimilation and Emigration," *Slavic Review* XXXIV, no. 1 (March 1975) pp. 1–18.

5. In dealing with the attitude of German Zionists toward the *Ostjuden*, it must be made clear at the outset that the top leadership of the ZVfD was composed throughout its history of Jews born in Germany. There are only very few exceptions to this statement. Though there are many indications that the majority of the rank and file of the ZVfD was composed of East European Jews, it seems that there was a tacit agreement—no doubt due to attacks by anti-Zionists—that German Jews should lead the movement lest it be attacked as a movement of foreigners, not sufficiently loyal to the German fatherland. This statement is based on my interview with Pinhas Rosen (Rosenblüth) on 22 September 1970. Rosenblüth occupied a leadership position within the ZVfD since prior to World War I. See also Kurt Blumenfeld, *Erlebte Judenfrage* (Stuttgart, 1962) pp. 52, 59.

6. Mordechai Eliav, *Ahavat ẓiyyon ve-anshei hod* (Tel Aviv, 1970) pp. 355–56.

7. See letter from Moritz Moses to Alfred Klee, 17 January 1900. Central Zionist Archives (CZA) A142/55/6.

8. See the first public proclamation of the "Bnei Brith" in Central Archives for the History of the Jewish People (CAHJP) GA Beuthen S97/20 (Doc. 1).

9. Prior to the Kattowitz Conference, in early 1884, two more associations were founded in Germany; one in Heidelberg called "Zion" was established by Hermann Schapira whose main aims were "The spread of knowledge of Hebrew history, language and literature among Jews . . . The colonization of Palestine by Jews." Response to this association was meager and it did not accomplish much. See Alter Druyanov, *Ktavim Letoldot ḥibat ẓiyyon veyishuv ereẓ yisrael* (Tel Aviv, 1925) vol. I, 206–11; and CZA, A13/18. In January 1884 a group of young men founded the "Verein Esra Sammelbüchse für Palästina" in Berlin for the purpose of encouraging settlement in Palestine. The national element in this effort was not overt, yet it must be counted as one of the first manifestations of Jewish nationalism in Germany. See *Festschrift zum fünfundzwanzigjährigen Jubiläum des Esra* (Berlin, 1909); *Die Jüdische Presse* (9 April 1884) p. 160; and Jehuda Reinharz, "The Esra Verein and Jewish Colonization in Palestine," *Leo Baeck Institute Year Book (LBIYB)* XIV (1979) 261–89.

10. In Hamburg, the founding of "Ahavass Zijon" in May 1885 was a direct result of this conference. See the first proclamation of "Ahavass Zijon" (May 1885) in CZA, A147/23/2.

11. See Mordechai Eliav, "Zur Vorgeschichte der Jüdischen Nationalbewegung in Deutschland," *Bulletin des Leo Baeck Instituts* XLVIII (1969) p. 289. See also Julius H. Schoeps, "Autoemanzipation und Selbsthilfe: Die Anfänge der nationaljüdischen Bewegung in Deutschland, 1882–1897," *Zeitschrift für Religions und Geistesgeschichte* XXX, no. 4 (1979) 345–65.

12. The association had nothing "scientific" about it; it was a political group which adopted its name in order to hide its true identity. This was necessary because of police restrictions on political activity by foreigners. In fact the police seem to have planted a secret agent in the "Verein." See *Selbst-*

Emancipation no. 3 (1 February 1892) pp. 34–35. On some of the association's activities see: *Jüdische Rundschau* no. 92 (17 September 1933), p. 817: *Selbst-Emancipation* no. 22 (16 November 1891) pp. 6ff: Berl Katznelson, "Ha-eḥad bamaarakha: reshito shel Naḥman Syrkin," *Kitvei Naḥman Syrkin* I (Tel Aviv, 1939). See also Moshe Mishkinski, *Reshit tnuat hapoalim hayehudit berusyah* (Tel Aviv, 1981) pp. 172–73.

13. See *Selbst-Emancipation,* no. 3 (2 February 1891) and Getzel Kressel, "Selbst-Emancipation," in *Shivat ẓiyyon* IV, (eds.) B. Dinur and I. Heilprin (Jerusalem, 1956) p. 81. Alex Bein gives the date of founding as autumn 1889. Alex Bein (ed.), *Sefer Motzkin* (Jerusalem, 1939) p. 40. This is also the date given by another historian, N. M. Gelber, "Agudat hastudentim hayehudim ha rusim harishonah be-Berlin," *Heavar* IV, no. 4 (1956) p. 47. Others who have written on the "Verein" quote Bein or Gelber on this.

14. According to the rules of the "Verein" he had only a "passive membership," i.e., was not entitled to vote.

15. See Heinrich Löwe, "Rede, gehalten in der ersten Sitzung des Jüdischnationalen Vereins 'Jung Israel' in Berlin am 30. Mai 1892." *Selbst-Emancipation* no. 14 (18 July 1892) pp. 142–44 and following issues. See also Eljakim Heinrich Löwe, "Jung Israel," in *Meilensteine, Vom Wege des Kartells Jüdischer Verbindungen in der Zionistischen Bewegung* (ed.) Eli Rothschild (Tel Aviv, 1972) pp 1–3.

16. See letter of Willy Bambus to David Wolffsohn, 20 December 1894, CZA W52I.

17. The statutes of the "Verein," dated January 1890, declared that its aim was to "afford the young Russian Jews in Berlin the opportunity to acquaint themselves with the interests and needs of the Jewish nation." See CZA, A126/12/1 (Doc. 2).

It was only in 1898 that the "Verein," which now changed its name to "Russischer Jüdischer Wissenschaftlicher Verein—Kadimah," stated: "The purpose of the Verein is to cultivate among the Russian Jewish academic youth a Zionist conviction, Jewish knowledge and Jewish life." See CZA, 126/14/1. See also "Unzere hofenung," (Yiddish), CZA, A126/14/1.

18. Other members of the "Verein," during different time periods included: Eliyahu Davidson, Lazare Kunin, David Makhlin, Isidore Eliashev, Joseph Lurie, Israel Motzkin, Selig Soskin, Judah Vilensky, Yehoshua Thon, Mordechai Ehrenpreis, David Farbstein, Fabius Schach and Leo Estermann.

19. See N. M. Gelber, "Agudat hastudentim," pp. 48–50; and Shmarya Levin, *Forward From Exile* (Philadelphia, 1967) pp. 276–77 in which he describes a debate with Parvus.

20. See Chaim Weizmann, *Trial and Error* (New York, 1966) p. 40. See also Steven E. Aschheim, *Brothers and Strangers* (Madison, 1982) pp. 93–4.

21. In the same year the less well known brochure by Paul Demidow—pseudonym of Isaak Turoff—*Wohinaus? Mahnruf an die Westeuropäischen Juden,* also appeared.

22. On the differences among the generations of German Zionists, see Jehuda Reinharz, "Three Generations of German Zionism," *The Jerusalem Quarterly* no. 9 (Fall 1978) pp. 95–110.

23. For a comprehensive analysis of the *Weltanschauung* of the first and second generations of German Zionists see Jehuda Reinharz, *Fatherland or Promised Land: The Dilemma of the German Jew 1893–1914* (Ann Arbor, 1975) chapters III and IV.

24. *Jüdische Rundschau* no. 22 (31 May 1912) p. 206.
25. Franz Oppenheimer, *Erlebtes, Erstrebtes, Errechtes* 6 Köln, 1964) p. 212.
26. Quoted by Adolph Löwe, "In Memoriam Franz Oppenheimer," *LBIYB* X (1965) 139.
27. East European Jews who came in contact with German or other Western forms of Zionism were well aware of this attitude toward them. See, e.g., Yehiel Tschlenow's speech at the Helsingfors Conference of 1906 in *Yehiel Tschlenow, pirkei hayav ufeulato. Zikhronot, ktavim, neumim, mikhtavim* (Tel Aviv, 1937) p. 343.
28. See Jehuda Reinharz, "Achad Haam und der deutsche Zionismus," *Bulletin des Leo Baeck Instituts* LXI (1982) pp. 3–27; and Jehuda Reinharz, "Martin Buber's Impact on German Zionism before World War I," *Studies in Zionism* no. 6 (Autumn 1982) pp. 171–83.
29. See, e.g., Kurt Blumenfeld, "Deutscher Zionismus," *Jüdische Rundschau* no. 35 (2 September 1910) pp. 414–15; and "Der XII. Delegiertentag," *Jüdische Rundschau* no. 38 (23 September 1910). See also Walter Z. Laqueur, *Young Germany. A History of the German Youth Movement* (New York, 1962), and George L. Mosse, "The Influence of the *Völkisch* Idea on German Jewry," in Max Kreutzberger (ed.), *Studies of the Leo Baeck Institute* (New York, 1967) pp. 83–114.
30. See, e.g., "Zur Apologetik des Zionismus," CZA, Z2/409 and Moses Calvary, "Die Erzieherische Aufgabe des Zionismus," *Die Welt* no. 1 (6 January 1911) pp. 5–8.
31. See *Jüdische Rundschau* (12 August 1910) p. 377.
32. See "Persönliches Interesse in Palästina," *Jüdische Rundschau* no. 24 (14 June 1912) p. 222. On the process that led to the resolution and on the conflict that evolved between the younger generation and the first—and the majority of German Jewry—see Jehuda Reinharz, *Fatherland or Promised Land*, chapters IV and V. See also Jehuda Reinharz (ed.), *Dokumente zur Geschichte des deutschen Zionismus* (Tübingen, 1981) pp. 106–43.
33. See, e.g., *Jüdische Rundschau* (16 September 1910), p. 444. This statement is true of a great number of the younger generation; there are countless expressions in various publications which exemplify this attitude. By the same token one can also cite articles and discussions warning against a simplistic view of the role of the *Ostjuden* which dispenses with any critical evaluation of East European Jewish culture and its value for German Zionism.
34. Although born in Moravia, Feiwel belonged to what one might call the *deutscher Kulturbereich*, which refers to the regions of Europe in which the German language and culture predominated. The term thus has primarily sociological and cultural connotations. One need only mention such urban centers as Budapest, Prague and Vienna—all of which are included in the *deutscher Kulturbereich*. Feiwel, in any case, had spent a great many years of his adult life in Germany. For a brief period he was editor of *Die Welt*. He was also one of the few West European Jews who became intimately familiar with East European culture. He edited the Yiddish poems of Morris Rosenfeld— *Lieder des Ghetto*—in 1902 and in 1914 published *Junge Harfen*, a collection of modern Yiddish poetry. See interview with his son, T. R. Fyvel, no date given, Weizmann Archives (W.A.).
35. During World War I, the German government admitted another 15,000–30,000 East European Jewish workers. See Adler-Rudel, *Ostjuden in Deutsch-*

land, p. 39, and Egmont Zechlin *Die deutsche Politik und die Juden im Ersten Weltkrieg* (Göttingen, 1969), p. 201.

36. See Franz Rosenzweig, *Briefe* (Berlin, 1935) pp. 95, 239, 324–25.

37. See for example *Im Deutschen Reich* nos. 1/2 (January/February 1916) p. 23 and *Jüdische Rundschau* no. 10 (10 March 1916) p. 82. See also Stephen Magill, "Defense and Introspection: the First World War as a Pivotal Crisis in the German Jewish Experience," unpublished PhD dissertation, University of California/ Los Angeles, 1977, pp. 176–255.

38. See David Joshua Engel, "Organized Jewish Responses to German Anti-Semitism During the First World War," unpublished PhD dissertation, University of California / Los Angeles, 1979, pp. 174–87. Recently there has been an attempt to provide another view of the attitudes of native German Jews toward the *Ostjuden* before 1914 and to place the blame primarily on government policies. See Jack Wertheimer, "The Unwanted Element: East European Jews in Imperial Germany," *LBIYB* XXVI (1981) 23–46. While it is true that the social and political realities as created by the government must be underscored, it is clear that the attitudes of German Jews toward their East European brethren—regardless of the actual legal status of the *Ostjuden*—were just as important. For this see Steven E. Aschheim, *Brothers and Strangers*.

DOCUMENTS

1. The Bnei Brith Society[1]

May 1882
CAHJP, GA/Beuthen S97/20.

BROTHERS:

The great misfortune which the present time has once again brought upon millions of our co-religionists, the persecutions which would have seemed inconceivable only a few years ago and which are being carried out with a brutality that even the darkest Middle Ages hardly witnessed, can, according to human calculations, no longer be stopped. It is as though an evil spirit makes its way through the great nations, inciting them to murder or at least to oppress the Jews. Those who have succumbed to this spirit have become pitiless towards our brothers—pitiless, as only human beings are capable of.

To whom are these persecuted people looking for help? Who is to save them? Who will espouse their cause?

Brothers! This is not just a question of aid, it is sacrifices that are needed, sacrifices as demanded by great times. Do not merely rely on the work of the Central Committee of the Alliance,[2] thinking that with that you have done your duty; instead, every one of you should put up his own high-altar of aid in his house, in every community, because that is what the times demand. The number of those requiring assistance is so large, the paths of their flight so different, that at present one is hardly able to gain an over-all view of the whole dreadful disaster.

Two directions are especially noticeable, but unfortunately general attention is only focused on one of these, namely on the emigrants who go or are being sent to America. There might well be some justification in preparing a sanctuary for the unfortunates in that free country, but it has already transpired that the plan, even in its beginnings, is inoperable. Already, the Central Committee in Berlin announces that only a limited number, the strongest and most industrious, can be despatched. Where then, should the weak, the aged and the women remain? Is it enough to save the best? Should the weak ones be abandoned to annihilation? It is a misfortune when at a time of emergency the rescuer does not have a clear view of the remedies.

This, dear co-religionists, is one direction which points to Israel's salvation and it is this alone (oddly enough) which enjoyed the attention of the Central Committee in Berlin. In the confusion of the calamity one grasped at a straw disregarding a strong rope.

A large—in fact the largest—part of the Russian Jews and all the Romanians turn towards a different goal, one which is so natural, which shines so brightly before us all that it almost dazzles our beclouded eyes: *the Holy Land*. Who can blame those unfortunates who in view of their expulsion by the various nations, resolve to act on their daily prayers and direct their fleeing feet to the place for which their heart has long been yearning, the place of which it is promised that one day peace and freedom shall blossom for Jacob's descendants?

Is the goal really so far-fetched, is the way there so long, are the obstacles that insurmountable, are the prospects there so poor that those unfortunates would prefer to be killed by the Russian hordes rather than move there? Or is one ashamed to admit that when one is in trouble one turns to Zion, is one ashamed to express the hope of a future for Judah, a future that is to guarantee it an unenvied and secure homeland? The person who does not want to state this, is no longer worthy of the name of Israel and had better renounce it!

Incidentally, these refugees do not indulge in fantastic plans for the future, but reckon with the actual present. The following proves that this is indeed the case.

1. The government of the Sublime Porte agrees to the immigration. Because Palestine is only sparsely populated, it even grants special privileges to the colonists.

2. The land is not barren as biased travellers wrote; on the contrary, it is blessed by the Lord and merely lacks cultivation. It is actually more fertile than the best countries of America.

3. The colonists are not exposed to a dangerous climate, nor to Indian robbers.

4. The cost of immigration to Palestine is so low that for the expense entailed in the journey of a family to America, a family can be set up, provided with a house, a field, tools and cattle.

5. The colonists there would not be scattered over a territory measuring thousands of miles, but would live close together, easily able to defend themselves against any possible attacks.

6. They are not as far removed there from civilization as they would be in Florida, Texas or Colorado and the stream of immigrants which follows them would from year to year strengthen the viability of the colonies.

7. During the last few months several hundred families from Romania and Russia immigrated to Palestine and Syria and have settled quite satisfactorily.[3]

A great deal more evidence to this effect could be furnished, but the above ought to suffice.

Why should these unhappy people, who, following the dictates of their heart, direct their flight in a loftier, holier direction, whose actions are in fact more practical than the decisions of the Central Committee in Berlin, why should they, who form the majority, fail to engage our sympathy and our support and why should they be sent to America against their will?

It was for these reasons that societies and committees were formed in Romania, Russia, Vienna and in the Holy Land itself which work for the colonization of Palestine and, thank God, find thousands of hearts in sympathy with theirs. Such a society is the Bnei Brith founded in Kattowitz U.[pper] S.[ilesia]. It maintains very close contact with all the societies which devote themselves to this holy task. It does not want to work against the Alliance because, in any case, not all the refugees can immigrate to the Holy Land but it sets itself the task to further the exalted holy, *national* idea.

Its desire is to be a high-altar of our nations's *future!*

The following statutes, accounts and business arrangements make it possible to begin immediately with setting up such an altar in every locality.

Everyone of you whose heart still beats for Judaism and Israel's future, lend us a hand. God grant that at least among Jews no disruptive element will seek to hinder its construction.

Every Israelite do his duty.

For the moment, registration and transmission of money for the Society are to be addressed to the Committee att. of the President *Moritz Moses* in Kattowitz, Upper Silesia.

Kattowitz, May 1882.

The Executive Committee

| M. Moses | S. Freuthal | Albert Goldstein |
| President. | Secretary. | Accountant. |

Josef Schmidt   *Phil. Kaminer*
Assessor.   Assessor.

Notes

Romania's gain of independence in 1880 and the murder of Tsar Alexander II in March 1881 unleashed in both lands a series of pogroms and persecutions which prompted a large and unprecedented emigration of Jews from Eastern Europe. The major destination of these emigrés was America, but on their way—because of lack of funds—they also often sojourned for many weeks and months in Western Europe. During this largest population transfer in Jewish history, some 1,750,000 departed mainly on German ships from Bremen, Hamburg and other ports. The Jewish philanthropic organizations of Western Europe, led by the German Jewish organizations, undertook to organize this emigration and to direct it to America, the British Commonwealth, South America, and other lands.

In Upper Silesia, however, there were some Jews who were dissatisfied with the methods and goals of the Jewish philanthropic organizations. They strove for a permanent solution for the emigrés through the establishment of a Jewish national home in Palestine. This society, which soon established branches in other parts of Silesia, began publication toward the end of 1882 of a newspaper called *Der Colonist*.This was the first newspaper in Germany to concern itself solely with questions of settlement in Palestine. The founders of the society were a teacher named Selig Freuthal and Moritz Moses, a businessman.

See letter from Alfred Klee of 17 January 1900. CZA, A142/55/6. For the history of the society and its newspaper see Israel Klausner, "Ha-agudah Bnei Brith be-Kattowitz," in *Sefer hayovel mugash likhvod Dr. N. M. Gelber* edited by Israel Klausner, Raphael Mahler and Dov Sadan (Tel Aviv 1963) and Jacob Toury, "Hagilayon harishon shel halutz kitvei haet shel hovevei zion balashon hagermanit," in *Haẓionut,* edited by Daniel Carpi, III (Tel Aviv 1973). See also the statutes of the Society Bnei Brith of 8 May 1882. CAHJP, GA/Beuthen S97/20 and letter from Moritz Moses to Samuel Pineles of 6 March 1882. CZA, A144/4/7.

1. This is most likely the first public proclamation of the Society Bnei Brith.

2. Alliance Israélite Universelle. A Jewish philanthropic, educational and

defense organization with headquarters in Paris, active in many parts of Europe, the Middle East and Africa. Founded by French Jews in 1860; branches of the Alliance were also established in Germany and in 1906 united under the umbrella of the "Konferenzgemeinschaft der Alliance Israélite Universelle." Following the pogroms of 1881, when thousands of Jews fled to Galicia, the representatives of the Alliance in Brody organized the emigration of these refugees to America with the aid of the "Israelitische Allianz" of Vienna and the German "Zentralkomitee der Alliance Israélite Universelle" which had its headquarters in Berlin. This document refers specifically to a conference of representatives of the Alliance from throughout Western Europe who convened in Berlin on 23–24 April 1882. At this conference the Alliance reiterated its resolve that the emigration of East European refugees be directed to the United States, not to Palestine. For details on the conference, see Shmuel Yavneeli (ed.) *Safer hazionut; tkufat hibbat zion*. Volume I, second edition, Jerusalem 1961.

3. A reference to the Russian, Polish and Romanian Jews who founded Rishon le-Zion and Zikhron Yaacov.

2. Statutes of The Russian Jewish Scientific Association

[January 1890]
CZA, A126/12/1

I. Name and Aim of the Association

1. The name of the Association is: Russian Jewish Scientific Association.

2. The aim of the Association is to enable the Russian Jewish youth who are in Berlin to become acquainted with the interests and requirements of the Jewish people.

3. The above aims are to be attained by the following means:
   a. Lectures on the history, literature and contemporary life of the Jewish people.

   Note: Political matters are not to be discussed.

   b. A reading-room where specialized publications in Hebrew, German and Russian as well as general Russian newspapers, journals and books are available.

II. The Members

4. Members are divided into active, passive and honorary members.

5.
   a. Every Russian Jew can become an active member by a [vote of] two-thirds majority of all active members present, upon having made a declaration that he is in agreement with the aims and intentions of the Association.
   b. Obligations of active members:

1. Every active member has to pay at least 1 Mark at the time of being accepted and later at least 0.05 Mark.

2. Every active member must, regularly and at the specified time attend the meetings of the Association.

c. The rights of active members:

1. To elect the executive committee;

2. To decide business transactions and other matters of the Association;

3. To have free use of the reading-room;

4. To be considered owners of the assets of the Association and to have the use of the reading-room;

5. They can be elected as members of the executive committee.

6.
   a. Anyone can become a passive member of the Association by a majority vote of two thirds of all members present and upon having tendered a written declaration stating his wish to become a member of the Association;
   b. Every passive member is obliged to pay the Association no less than 1 Mark upon being accepted and henceforth a monthly dues of at least 1 Mark;
   c. The Rights of passive members:

1. To have a voice in business transaction, but no voting right;

2. To be entitled to use the Association's reading-room without additional payment.

7. Anyone who has rendered the Association an extraordinary service in the financial or any other sphere can become an honorary member. The decision for such membership is to be made by more than two-thirds of all active members. An honorary member has all the rights of an active member and pays as much as he wishes.

Notes

The *numerus clausus* (enacted in Russia in 1887) prompted many young East European Jews to seek a university education in the West. One popular choice was the University of Berlin which had a liberal admissions policy. After 1887 there were in Berlin many young students from Eastern Europe who had not been admitted to universities in Russia. The Russian Jewish students were isolated from both the Russian Christian students as well as from the native German Jewish students and formed their own associations. Most of the

Russian Jewish students were socialists and belonged to the Russian *Studentenverein* which, despite its overwhelming Jewish membership, refused to be recognized as a Jewish association.

In December 1888 twelve Russian Jewish students founded the "Russischer Jüdischer Wissenschaftlicher Verein." Central to the activity of this association were ideological debates and cultural events during which the Jewish national question was discussed. See *Selbst-Emancipation,* no. 3, 2 February 1891.

The "Verein" had an important and lasting impact on the history of German Zionism, primarily because of the role it played in shaping the ideology of some German Jewish students. See *Selbst-Emancipation,* no. 22, 16 November 1891 and *Jüdische Rundschau,* no. 92, 17 November 1933. In 1898 the "Verein" changed its name to "Russischer Jüdischer Wissenschaftlicher Verein-Kadimah."

3. Whither the Russian Jews? Syria: A Place of Refuge for the Russian Jews

Max I. Bodenheimer[1]

[June 1891]

In placing this outline of a settlement plan before the public, I am guided by the thought that the present circumstances do not warrant presenting a plan worked out with a scientific thoroughness which supplies financial and technical details. Its realization depends, after all, on a number of pre-conditions which cannot be taken into account in advance and which influence the execution of the plan in various ways. I therefore gave up the intention of working out all aspects of the idea of settlement in Syria—for which I have been collecting material for several months—and intend at this stage to provide only a general picture of how the idea of settlement in Syria might be implemented.

However, all those interested ought to be given the opportunity to participate in this plan because its implementation is vital not only for our co-religionists in Russia, but for the whole world. Therefore, all those who are interested in this idea and have experience in and knowledge of economics, geography and technology are invited to advance their suggestions for the implementation of the plan presented here and urgently requested to forward them to the publishing house, marked "Syrian Colonization Project."

The means for implementing the plan, enormous as the sum required might appear, will certainly not be lacking. Why should it be a problem to obtain the collaboration of our financial giants for the construction of a Syrian railway, when for other, far more utopian projects, such as the Panama project, many hundreds of millions were sacrificed for nothing?

Quick action is essential where the fate of six million people depends on the whims of an absolute autocrat who has expressed the definite intention to expel this sector of his subjects from his country because they profess a different faith. One can afford to deliberate and examine when the calm currents of events leave it to our discretion to select a suitable time for the implementation of our intentions, but here, postponement is out of the question. As in a case of a natural disaster, we are being pushed towards a decision. The future of our co-religionists is shrouded in darkness. From ocean to ocean the call for salvation goes out, addressed to all compassionate people. In view of such misery, no petty considerations must restrain us from proffering our aid. The way in which the mass of Russian emigrants appear to us: dejected and unable to make decisions, is the result of centuries of oppression in barbaric bondage. Our faith in the noble spirit of the nations has not as yet been shaken by the hate-filled apparition of anti-Semitism to the extent that we do not confidently expect the nations of the world to condemn this barbarity in the strongest terms. We are equally convinced, and we have already seen this in England, that every feeling human being, irrespective of differences in religion and descent, is happy to contribute his bit in order to help ease this suffering. However, in the first instance, the call for immediate help is addressed to us, who belong to the same religion and are members of the same tribe. Any fragmentation of the forces would hinder the rescue operation and it is therefore necessary to found an organization in order to work according to a definite plan. If there is even the slightest hope for success in the plan outlined here, why should we hold back from energetically setting about its implementation? Everyone with an inclination for social activity is given the opportunity here to utilize it for a purpose which could not be more noble and humane. The gratitude of hundreds of thousands will be a longer lasting memorial to these men than statues of bronze and stone.

First and foremost, it is up to our co-religionists who are blessed with this world's material goods to initiate the implementation of this project with the means necessary to guarantee its success. We must not permit ourselves to be put off by plans which visualize the development of colonies in some distant future. Only an enterprise which immediately supplies the mass of emigrants with the possibility of making a living from the work of their hands should be tackled in the present situation. It is hoped that the committees which are in the process of being formed everywhere take the essential features of this plan into consideration and immediately proceed with its implementation.

When a poor people that is continuously being hounded from one country to another will have found a resting-place in Syria, when within the next decades, trade and industry will impart fresh incentive to its cities, when once large areas that have lain desolate for centuries will become fertile once again, when schools will educate the rising generation and Hebrew literature will approach a new golden age, then, perhaps, also the words of the poet will turn into reality:

> Who hath heard such a thing?
> Who hath seen such a thing?
> Is a land born in one day?
> Is a nation brought forth at once?
> For as soon as Zion travailed,
> She brought forth her children.
>
> Isaiah, Ch. 66, 6ff.

Notes

In 1891 a young lawyer from Cologne, Max Bodenheimer, proposed a new solution to the problem of the East European Jews. Bodenheimer grew up in a completely assimilated milieu. He paid little heed to the Jewish problem in Germany and Eastern Europe until these problems were forced upon his consciousness while coming across some anti-Semitic literature. He became convinced that Palestine must once again become the national center of the Jewish people and a haven for all oppressed Jews.

Bodenheimer's public efforts to settle Jews in Palestine began with his pamphlet *Whither the Russian Jews?* which was published in 1891. The pamphlet enjoyed wide circulation. In it Bodenheimer developed the idea that Jews be settled in Palestine in tandem with the building of a railroad line and ports in Syria and Palestine. Along the railroad he envisaged the founding of Jewish agricultural settlements. See Max Bodenheimer, *So Wurde Israel* (Frankfurt am Main, 1958) and *Selbst-Emancipation,* no. 16, August 18, 1891. See also Henriette Hannah Bodenheimer, *Der Durchbruch des politischen Zionismus in Köln 1890–1900* (Köln, 1978).

1. Max Bodenheimer (1865–1940). Lawyer in Cologne 1890–1933. Member of the GAC 1897–1921. First president of the "Zionistische Vereinigung für Deutschland" (ZVfD) 1897–1910. Director of the "Jewish National Fund" 1907–1921 and chairman of its board 1907–1914.

4. Ethnic Consciousness and National Consciousness

Dr. Franz Oppenheimer[1]

18 February 1910
Die Welt, no. 7, 18 February 1910, pp. 139–143.

I would like to utter a word of truth, not for the sake of truth alone—which is its own reward—but for the sake of peace within our Movement. This is a matter of profound differences in attitude, which could lead to contention and even worse, if they are not stated as clearly as possible. I would like to open the safety valve, to let the excessive pressure in the boiler escape harmlessly.

We Western Europeans regard the Zionist ideal differently from the Eastern Europeans. At least on the average. Of course there are all possible transitions and shadings on both sides, so that many an Eastern European Jew might be a Zionist in the same way as the majority of Western Jews and vice versa. But in general terms there is this basic difference: We Western Jews have ethnic consciousness, Eastern European Jews have national consciousness.

What this actually means can be demonstrated much more easily by means of an example than through long theoretical discussions. The fully naturalized American German, who is proud of his origin, has German ethnic and American national consciousness. The high-ranking official or army officer, who is a member of the French Colony in Berlin and who takes pride in his descent from the "Refugiée," has French ethnic consciousness but German national consciousness. In the same way fully naturalized Jews in America, Holland or England—or at least the ones who were born in those countries—have American, Dutch or English national consciousness, but at the same time Jewish ethnic consciousness, provided they are proud of their origins.

Ethnic consciousness is motivated by past events. It exists, wherever an individual has the feeling that he stems from a people which is at least the equal in glory and nobility of the nation of which he is, at present, a citizen. Where this consciousness does not exist there can be no ethnic consciousness and it opens the road to an anxious striving towards assimilation. In this way all half-castes of colored races, such as the Mulattos and Quadroons of America and the "Eurasians" of India are pretending to be pure-blooded whites, and in times of political strife emigré Germans denied their origins, which they considered shameful and turned as completely as possible into Englishmen or Americans in language, name and custom. In the same way such people of Jewish origin are acting all over the world as "Aryans" and in many cases even as anti-Semites, since they have no pride in their noble origin. But where such pride still exists, there is ethnic consciousness, a consciousness of joint sources, common blood, or at least of a former common nationality, common history with its memories of suffering and joy, heroism and great deeds. We Western Jews, for instance, are proud of our descent from the famous race that presented the world with its three greatest religions, and which, despite its dispersion all over the globe, has proved and is still proving everywhere to be one of the mightiest of cultural factors.

National consciousness, on the other hand, is motivated by the present: the common language, customs, economic and legal relations, etc., and spiritual culture. It is the mental reflection of the society in which and through which we live. This, moreover, is graduated according to the intensity, the joy and advantages which the individual derives from this very integration in that nation. This should be understood most thoroughly, since it constitutes the source of a great deal of self-deception and especially the great many disagreements in the Zionist camp. The above-mentioned joy and advantages depend on two factors: First, on the standing of the nation as a whole amongst all other nations and secondly, on the social position of the individual within his nation. Thereafter the national consciousness can be divided again into consciousness of nationality and cultural consciousness. . . .

Here lies the first enormous gap between East European Jews and those among us Western Jews who grew up in the culture of their native countries. In fact, we are all culturally German, French, English, American, etc., since we were lucky enough to belong to cultural communities who lead all other nations and since it is an honor for us to identify with our world-famous thinkers, scientists, artists and inventors. We cannot be cultural Jews, since what has been saved of Jewish culture from the Middle Ages in the ghettos of the East, is infinitely below the level of modern culture, as represented by our nations. We can't and won't go back. If we well-educated Western Europeans analyze ourselves, for instance, we find that we are composed of 95 percent of Western European cultural elements. But East European Jews cannot possibly be culturally Russian, Romanian or Galician—no more than King Carol or Carmen Silva. They must be culturally Jewish, unless they have already become culturally European, through a rare special advantage of education. This is so, because medieval Jewish culture is at a level which is just as high above East European barbarity as it is below Western European High Culture.

Our ethnic brothers in the East should first of all realize that and try to forgive us, even though this may prove quite difficult for them. After all, for many of them Jewish culture is ordained by God and sacred and our ways may easily appear like blasphemy to them.

Let us now discuss the second part of national consciousness—the consciousness of nationality. Its intensity, the level of "patriotism," depends on the extent to which the individual enjoys the advantages of community life in the state.

That doesn't merely apply to the Jews. It holds equally true for non-Jews. All over the world members of the ruling classes are greater "patriots" than members of the lower class. Industrial workers on the Continent pride themselves on their internationalism and claim not to care a bit for patriotism, which they call chauvinism and "jingoism". Of course, environment often proves stronger than theoretical convictions, or else Polish and Czech socialists would not defend their nationality so stubbornly. But even though no social class can remove itself completely from consciousness of nationality, there can be no doubt that it is classified according to the social position of the individual, the economic class to which he belongs and his status in Society. An acute observer once determined the party affiliation of German lawyers and physicians as follows: "Up to an income of 3,000 Marks they are Social Democrats, up to 6,000 Marks they are unaffiliated, up to 20,000 Marks they are National Liberals and above that Conservatives." This cynical judgement generally holds true, even though some individual cases are of course able to escape the influence of their economic class. On the average, social position determines the degree of the positive attitude towards the State, and the amount of patriotism vis-à-vis state authority.

But we Jews are in the unique situation that our social position is not determined merely by property or education but also by our religion. At this time there is no civilized country which does not have some degree of anti-Semitism. While any non-Jew is accepted automatically by the class to which he belongs according to education and economic level, the Jew always had to face major or minor obstacles. His consciousness of nationality is therefore scaled to that. English and American Jews are necessarily better "citizens" in similar social positions, than German—or even Prussian—Jews, who are suffering much more from anti-Semitism. It is almost an impertinence to demand of us Prussian Jews, who are socially boycotted everywhere and illegally discriminated against by the Authorities—the same degree of "state supporting spirit" as of a country Junker from east of the Elbe, for whom this State constitutes a milk cow, which his class governs and conducts in his own interests and for his own honor.

That is why the American Jew has a much stronger sense of nationality than the French Jew and the latter a much stronger one than the Prussian or Austrian Jew, who, in his turn has a stronger sense of nationality than the Russian or Romanian Jew. For them, the consciousness of nationality must be *negative,* with the exception of some cases of very wealthy and therefore half-way accepted and safeguarded individuals. Such a person has no fatherland, like the American or Englishman, or even a step-fatherland, like the Prussian—but no fatherland, no home at all. He lives in enemy country, a stranger who is threatened in respect of his property and frequently enough his very life—an outlawed pariah. It is hard to see how a Russian or Romanian proletarian Jew could achieve "patriotism", apart from some nostalgia.

This is the second great difference between ourselves and East European Jews. In accordance with our respective individual class and economic conditions and according to our respective citizenships, we are, more or less, national Germans, Englishmen, etc.—but they are only rarely and in the slightest degree national Russians, Poles or Romanians. They are national Jews, just as they are cultural Jews. They are, and therefore feel, as members of a foreign people, living among strangers and having no home of their own, with their own language, religion, tradition, and culture and existing under degrading laws. I am aware of the fact that many of us in the West take pride in calling ourselves "national Jews." In some cases this may actually be true. Some people of the property-owning classes who have an especially highly developed sense of honor and who consider social discrimination an unbearable disgrace. Some others who belong to the "disenfranchised" to whom the state gives nothing and denies everything. Some young firebrands, who overreact and would like to throw out the baby with the bath. Perhaps some who are, so to say, already sitting on packed trunks for their trip to Palestine. It is mainly the latter who deserve our special attention. They are taking the national consciousness for granted, which they will feel as soon as they begin living in a Jewish community. One thing is of course abundantly clear: If a Jew of whatever origin is to be able to live in such a community, he must have Jewish consciousness of nationality, at least to the extent— and in view of the complete social equality—even more than if he had become a citizen of the United States or Canada. "Ubi bene, ibi patria" (Wherever things are good, there is my fatherland). One mocks Jewish emigrants, who are feeling and behaving like American citizens while they are still in the steerage of the boat taking them across. There is nothing to mock them for. What is alright for Germans, who became kings of Romania, Bulgaria, Belgium and Tsars of Russia should be fair enough for poor persecuted Jews. King Alexander of Bulgaria also felt a glowing national Bulgarian sentiment, even before he entered the land of his "pleasant memories." Betrothed princesses have the solemn duty of accepting their new homeland's language, religion and customs even before their wedding. Such great noblemen as the Duke of Arenberg, even manage to have several "fatherlands" and "national consciousnesses". So, if one of us who believes in the phrase "Next year in Jerusalem" has already acquired national Jewish consciousness, he finds himself in excellent company.

In fact, this company is so good, that I am not ashamed to admit it under certain conditions for myself. Assuming that the large Jewish community which Herzl envisioned actually exists—a nation with a culture that is not inferior to any other; assuming, further, that this community entrusted me with tasks that would be satisfactory to me, I have no doubt, that from the moment of taking the decision of immigrating, I would feel to a significant degree as a national and cultural Jew—just as George of Denmark felt as a national Greek. But it may be assumed, that to the day of my death I would have German ethnic sentiments, i.e., I would still feel closer ties to a German than to a Frenchman or an Englishman—in the same way as I suppose George of Denmark prefers to talk to a former compatriot in his old mother tongue rather than to someone else in a foreign language.

But among us only very few believe in the phrase "Next year in Jerusalem" for themselves, and therefore only very few of us get this feeling of nationality in advance, if that is the right expression. There are only very few of those and they are becoming even rarer since the enthusiastic beginnings of the "Charter" have proved ephemeral—just like the hopes of the Christian Primitives for a thousand years' realm and those of the Social Democrats for the Great Upheaval. Most of us, the large majority, call ourselves "national Jews" as a result of a misunderstanding. Since the etymological source of the word "nation" means "origin" they are calling their ethnic consciousness "national consciousness" or "consciousness of nationality".

But while it may be possible to conceal internal conflicts through plays on words for a time, after a while they burst through the cosmetic plasters in dangerous eruptions. The recent [Zionist] Congresses make this abundantly clear. Let us admit clearly that West European national consciousness is an entirely different thing from the East European variety. In the one place we have ethnic consciousness and in the other national consciousness in its double range of cultural Judaism and national Judaism.

Since joining the Zionist movement I have expressed this thought often enough from the lectern, in personal conversations and on the printed page. Almost regularly the people from the East have faced me with the accusation: " . . . in that case you are no Zionist."

That, of course, is untrue. I desire "a publicly and legally guaranteed homeland for the Jewish people in Palestine and its neighboring countries"—therefore I am a Zionist. But as a matter of fact, I and the people who share my convictions have an attitude towards Zionism, which is quite different from that of the Eastern Jews. Sociologically, we have different orientations.

There is a socio-psychological law, which holds true also as a universal physical law in respect of gases and fluids and even for animals and plants: they all flow from locations of higher pressure to those of lower pressure to the point of the least resistance. But since conditions of pressure are different for us than for Eastern European Jews, there is a different direction of the flow.

Russia and Romania are the highest possible locations of pressure for Jews that could be imposed on any mass of humanity anywhere. Those are the countries of complete lawlessness and abuse of human rights, of suppression and exploitation, of the pogroms. Therefore Eastern Jews have the strongest tendency of "flowing away." They wish to and have to get out. They are searching for a country that will not only afford them security for their property and life, but where they can be human beings in the full sense of the word: complete citizens. That is also why they have the actual consciousness of nationality. They want to be "Next year in Jerusalem" and they have already packed their trunks. They have this national sentiment not merely because they are a nation of aliens without a homeland but because spiritually they are already on their journey to the new fatherland.

For them, therefore, Zionism is a cause, which is practical in the highest degree, an aim of the healthiest, well advised self-interest. But for most of us it is an ideological movement, pure and simple, an objective of disinterested altruism.

We are not living at a location of the absolutely highest pressure, from which any flow must be in a downward direction, but at locations of much lower pressure. We enjoy security of possessions and life, and, if we are not assimilation-prone, we have our bearable social position, despite many insults and discriminations. Therefore our currents exist, but we only "flow" to locations having even lower pressure. This means, that many of us would probably move to Palestine, if, everything considered, our total economic and social position would be improved thereby. A few would probably also go if it remained unaltered, i.e., they would make certain material sacrifices for complete political equality. But very few of us would move there if such a move involved heavy material sacrifices: perhaps some very religious people, whose soul yearns for the homeland of the Patriarchs, and some enthusiasts, who want to participate in the creation of a great cultural enterprise.

But since only a very few of us believe that Palestine would become a land of such high culture and prosperity in our times, only a small minority think of their own future when they work for Zionism. If at all, they think of their children or grandchildren but in most cases only of ethnic brothers who must be saved. They think of the good name of the old tribe, that is raped and despised today and which must be reestablished in its old glory through the creation of a people that would prove conclusively the high cultural values of the blood for all the envious and haters to see. They think of liberty and justice, of humanism and self-determination, which they want to lead to their objective in the face of the opposition of unjust barbarity.

Many say that Zionist idealism can only be found in Eastern Europe. The very opposite is true. It is we westerners who are the idealists. The Eastern Jews want things for themselves and no one could blame them for that. We want nothing for ourselves. They serve themselves, and are obliged to do so. We, who are luckier (and that is why there can be no point in bragging about it) are serving an idea. For the sake of this idea we patiently bear the mockery of our countrymen and as often as not of our own co-religionists and continue doing our job. We are not motivated by any dire need, not even by religious drives any more—but merely by our pride in our noble ancestry and our ethnic consciousness.

This our brothers from the East must at long last learn to understand and forgive. Not merely because we are honest co-workers, but because they are making our work much more difficult when they advertise their special attitude to the Zionist problem as the only possible and justified one.

We need, and they need, Western Jewish intelligence and capital very urgently for the sake of their liberation and their humanization. They are pushing back both efforts with their type of propaganda. If you demand of American, Canadian, South African, English, French, Belgian, Dutch, or even Prussian Jews to develop consciousness of nationality in the East European Jewish sense, i.e., to consider themselves only Jews, nationally and culturally—they would in most cases angrily show you the door! And they would be right! Their native countries had afforded asylum to them or their fathers. They gave them language, customs, wealth and education, political, and as often as not, full or partial civic equality. It would be a wicked and unnatural man who could forget that! Anything truly alive takes root where it is living. Anyone who is able to live in a state based on law, as a citizen, would deserve all possible hatred if he doesn't respond with love, and gratitude. When even Russian emigrés over there become patriots as soon as they are able to recuperate from the pressures of the East End— should we feel like aliens, as mere guests in the countries, in which the tombstones of our ancestors have been standing for forty generations? Those unlucky Jews from Eastern Europe, who are suffering spiritually most profoundly, should not feel that their abnormal situation is the rule and they shouldn't rebuke us for our assimilation, when we admit to our patriotism. If we were assimilated, we certainly wouldn't be Zionists and there is every chance that we would have become estranged from Judaism a long time ago.

This one cannot demand of the large majority of Western Jews. But that which *I* call Zionism, they will accept with pleasure. Some sceptics will remain on the outside, for practical reasons. They will refuse to believe that Jews can be turned into farmers or that a dense Jewish population can be settled in Palestine for one reason or another. But in principle, every Western Jew who still considers himself Jewish, is a Zionist in my sense and in that of the people who share my convictions.

So far Zionists have been content in their public appearances to call themselves "loyal citizens of the State." This they are obliged to say, even in Russia and in Romania. But we westerners are more than just "loyal citizens of the State," which is something negative. We are something extremely positive: we are patriots. Not jingoists, but patriots. We love our fatherland and its people, its culture and scenery. We serve wholeheartedly its present and its future, which should also be our own. We are determined to do everything to make the future assume a shape that we can accept wholeheartedly, without conditions or restrictions in its entire complex of social and political composition. We are not guests who will feel like moving on tomorrow, but permanent citizens. Perhaps one or another of us will seek his fortune in Palestine or elsewhere. After all, even pan-German officers have been known to emigrate to America. But we are not thinking of emigration en masse, unless our lives are made so unbearable that we cannot remain here honorably. We have the national consciousness of the nation into which we were born.

All the same we are Zionists and can allow ourselves to be Zionists, since our national consciousness is quite compatible with our Jewish ethnic consciousness.

If this conception of Zionism is no longer merely tolerated as heretofore, but accepted as fully and equally justified, our propaganda work in the West will become much easier. Then we can tell our ethnic brothers who are still on the outside: "No understanding and ethical person could expect patriotism from Russian and Romanian Jews. They want to, have to and shall get out and they should go to the country which for ideological and practical reasons constitutes the point of the lowest pressure, the only country which opens its portals to them, the land of their yearning for thousands of years. We will settle them there in such a dense mass and in a social constellation which will ensure that hatred of Judaism will never again interfere with their social position.

"Any of you Western Jews who would like to take part in this great humanitarian enterprise now or in the future, is welcome. After all the gates of the Jewish country will be open to non-Jews as well. But no one demands or even expects you to be one of the pioneers yourself. Anyone who feels himself a citizen of his country and is rooted in its language, culture, customs and laws should remain. He shall not be rebuked or criticized. He shall continue to strive for civic success within his nation for the good of that nation but also to add honor to the Jewish origins from which he has sprung.

"In addition he should collaborate in that other enterprise which will do honor to the Jewish tribe. Place your intelligence and ability as well as your material means to work for the recreation of a Jewish nation in the land of our forefathers. If you do so you will be inscribed in the scrolls of honor of this new nation, even if you remain loyal citizens of your own nation.

"In this way you will serve a great ideal—but at the same time yourselves as well. After all, you can only steer well for any length of time if you do so by the stars of an ideal. For, the higher the level of the Jewish masses in Eastern Europe, the more anti-Semitism in your own country loses ground. Also, the fewer will immigrate into your own native country, a fact which now imposes such an enormous burden to supply aid and education on yourselves and which brings in anti-Semitism with the immigrants."

If that is what we say, if we can speak without fear of East European Jews denying our words and calling us names such as "assimilationists," "chauvinists," "philo-Zionists," etc., if we are permitted to talk in this way with the approval and understanding of Eastern Jews, our propaganda will become child's play and its success is guaranteed.

But as long as they only recognize as a Zionist, or even as a Jew, he who has the psychology of a Russian outcast, . . . we won't only have to suffer personally (which isn't all that important) because we are between the rock and a hard place—but we won't be able to advance our propaganda work. And that is very important indeed.

At this point we will be challenged triumphantly: "What after all is the difference between this so-called Western Jewish Zionism and Jewish charity works? Weren't Hirsch, Rothschild, the Alliance Israélite Universelle and Hovevei Zion in favor of exactly the same things?"

Not in the least. They were trying to aid individuals, in the best case many individuals. This is far from our mind. We want to organize a community! They wanted to promote thriving Jews, or, at best, thriving Jewish villages. We want to create a Jewish nation.

Not a Jewish State. Since Turkey adopted a constitution, this thought has lost almost all adherents amongst us. The Turkish constitution satisfies us as a "public-legal guarantee" and affords us all we require: namely the autonomous administration of the community and provincial parliaments, provided we achieve what we desire: the creation of a dense Jewish population comprising all trades and professions (but based mainly on farming and agriculture) which would form a majority all over the country. In that case it would be the ruling faction in everything concerning autonomous administration and would also participate in Government at the central parliament. This, of course, is also the intention and the desire of all Ottomans of non-Jewish origin, who are faithful to their constitution.

When this objective is attained, the Jewish people in Palestine will have Jewish national consciousness in addition to Jewish ethnic consciousness and Ottoman imperial consciousness—just as the Bavarians or Provencales have, in addition to their imperial consciousness a large measure of particular national consciousness. And that's a good thing. After all, an orchestra sounds better, the more instruments it contains—but naturally, they must keep in time with one another. The culture of Germany and France depends largely on the competition between the various tribes and areas in the country. Where liberty is the conductor, as for example in Switzerland, even a chorus of different language sources produces a pure sound.

It is in this sense and this sense alone that we want to create a Jewish nation in Palestine. We are not thinking of a Jewish king with ministers, a court and harem and are not worrying about whether a Jewish admiral can be found, who doesn't get seasick. We don't care about any political sovereignty and don't even want to form a vassal state—merely a part of the country with a preponderant Jewish population and Jewish autonomous administration to an extent existing in all civilized countries without damage to the cohesion of the State.

But this we do want—and that is the great difference between us and the philanthropists. We are not motivated by charity, but by Jewish ethnic consciousness. We want the seedling of the old noble tribe, that has been saved throughout the millennia, to strike roots in its mother soil again. We want it to grow into the giant tree of a rejuvenated people, that will carry the blossoms and fruits of a new and exalted Jewish national culture, honoring its tribe as well as brethren the world over.[2]

Notes

1. Franz Oppenheimer (1864–1943). Economist and sociologist. From 1909 Privatdozent at the University of Berlin. From 1919 to 1929 professor of sociology and economic theory at the University of Frankfurt. Strong advocate for cooperative settlement in Palestine. Lectured on forms of settlement in Palestine at the Sixth Zionist Congress (1903) and at the Ninth Zionist Congress (1909). Later he became inactive in Zionist affairs. Left Germany in 1938 and died in 1943 in Los Angeles. See his autobiography, *Erlebtes, Erstrebtes, Erreichtes,* (Düsseldorf, 1964).

2. Oppenheimer's essay unleashed a heated controversy among German Zionists. See the following essay by Feiwel. See also Adolf Friedemann, "Westlicher Zionismus," in *Die Welt,* no. 14, (8 April 1910) pp. 304–5.

5. Two Kinds of Zionism
Berthold Feiwel

March 1910
Jüdische Rundschau, no. 9 (4 March 1910) pp. 97–98; no. 10 (11 March 1910) pp. 109–111; no. 12 (25 March 1910) pp. 133–134.

I

On 18 February Dr. Franz Oppenheimer published an article in the "Welt" entitled "Ethnic Consciousness and National Consciousness." The publishers foresaw (as noted in a footnote) "that it would give rise to a lively exchange of views." Already a few days later the publishers of the paper, in a propaganda circular, were able to call the article "sensational."

"A lively exchange of views," "sensational"—it seems to me that the editorial board and even the publishers of the "Welt" did not do full justice to the work of Franz Oppenheimer. There was too little reserve on the one hand, too little description on the other, in the reactions to a political statement which revolutionizes the prevailing basic concepts, namely splitting Zionism into two Zionisms (please excuse the harsh plural, but the reality is, possibly, even harsher). A sharp incision cuts a supposed unit into two, with West European Zionism on one side and East European Zionists on the other. In the name of the majority of West European Zionists (on the basis of scientific authority, you understand) it is explained: That's how it should be. For the sake of truth and of peace, listen you East European Zionists and learn to understand that *"we West Europeans have a different attitude to Zionism from that of the East Europeans. We Western Jews have a Jewish ethnic consciousness, the Eastern European Jews a national consciousness."*

They represent two different basic Jewish feelings, two kinds of

Zionism with quite different motivations and objectives. There is a reevaluation of Zionist values whose recognition is bound to result in ideological and pragmatic consequences which would basically alter our Zionist microcosm.

And the "Welt" goes and prints such a revolutionary declaration without reservations, merely inviting a discussion. Was it naive to expect that the first to want to participate in a discussion on such an extremely important matter would be the editorial board of the "Welt," the official spokesman, the journalistic representative of the organization? . . . Yet, it is not generally so reticent as regards Zionist views which it does not share. *Qui tacet, consentire videtur*. However, if one not merely appears to be, but actually is in agreement, why is that not stated with the same kind of frankness which distinguishes the author of "Ethnic Consciousness and National Consciousness"?

God knows, I do not dwell on this apparent formality in order to accuse those at the top. But I consider it symptomatic—and I shall still come back to this—how weak the will for honesty really is (obviously only in the philosophical sense) for an uncompromising honest Zionist understanding when the editorial board of the central publication and those deeply involved, do not feel the need for an immediate pronouncement on the implications inherent in Oppenheimer's stand. According to the experience and conjectures of this writer, those most closely concerned are the West European Zionists with the exception of the "disinherited," "several young firebrands" and "a few who are, one might say, sitting on their suitcases, ready for the journey to Palestine."

The likes of us who necessarily belong to the category of exceptions could, of course, keep silent if all that is involved is to know one's theoretical foundation of Zionism remains inviolate. According to Oppenheimer this category is permitted to call itself and to be "national Jewish" with all that this entails. Yet, this category cannot feel indifferent to the "strange bedfellows"—to misquote Shakespeare—with which "Jewish misery has acquainted them." The possible bifurcation of Zionism is too serious a matter for the individual members and the factions as parts of one organism, to agree to forego examination whether it is really justified and necessary. In the event that this is indeed the case, its extent and possible results for pragmatic Zionism need to be examined.

Calling Franz Oppenheimer's announcement revolutionary and cataclysmic is not meant to imply that the views and considerations which form the basis of his article have never been voiced before. Right from the beginning and until the present day the development of Zionism, its actions and its omissions, have been profoundly influenced by a sometimes loud and eruptive and sometimes quiet and tenacious internal struggle between, let us say, a unified and a fractured Jewish nationalism. Whoever has not seen this cannot write Zionist history and whoever does not see it cannot make Zionist history. Though removed from party life, Dr. Oppenheimer has an eye for this. However, two points need to be made: What I called fractured Jewish nationalism did not appear as a uniform system, but rather as a wealth of insistent or reluctant forces whose effectiveness was impaired because they were frequently not consciously and therefore planlessly directed by their supporters. "Philanthropic Zionism," "Opposition or indifference to Jewish culture," "Merely political Zionism," "Opposition to practical work in Palestine"—in order not to waste more words and to be understood more quickly I merely picked out the leading so-called party slogans. Different spheres, different aims. And yet, in the final analysis it is the differentiations and the many variants of the national driving force of the factions which create and feed the contrasts. This was often strenuously denied. The "problem of superior or inferior Zionists" was heatedly dismissed, occasionally it was glossed over and more often than not these things were not seen with any clarity because the original reasons were already hidden behind the facts they had brought into being.

To this one must still add that unbalanced as it might have appeared on the surface and below, in the course of the years it became a kind of basic law that a self-contained Jewish nationalism, encompassing the contemporary and future life of the Zionist individuals and masses must be a prerequisite which motivates and regulates Zionism. (I shall later discuss what was meant by this self-contained Jewish nationalism.) This uniformly basic law was contravened (if you will, sinned against) here, there and everywhere. But it was never attacked theoretically as being applicable to just one category of Jews, but as an inappropriate principle for another category and therefore also not obligatory for it.

It remained for Franz Oppenheimer to do both: to drag the "broken" nationalism—or as he calls it, the "Jewish ethnic consciousness" (in contrast to the self-contained nationalism, the "national consciousness") from its mock-modest subterranean passages into the light of day and to make it the vehicle of a system—precisely what the others could or would not do.

Secondly, to destroy the basic Zionist tenet of a unified Jewish nationalism. He did this by declaring the ethnic consciousness to be the only possible basis of the Zionist confession of the majority of West European Jews. This Zionism, strictly segregated from "national" Zionism, he declared to be a second form with equal justification.

This is what is new and revolutionary in Dr. Oppenheimer's declarations.

He possesses considerable honesty to make no secret of the necessity, to make a virtue of necessity and to raise this virtue into a law.

His conclusion will be energetically opposed, though his courage will be respected, especially when one considers that he revealed it at a moment when he needs the confidence of all Zionists for an important undertaking. Whatever one's attitude to his views, one cannot be sufficiently grateful to him for his frankness and considerable sincerity. Here we have the basis for a future debate which is going to take place in practice and not only in discussion. Even if this discussion will be extremely serious, it would be incomparably more dangerous to remain silent and passive.

Those who are well acquainted with Dr. Oppenheimer's literary-scientific achievements will have another opportunity here to enjoy the author's scintillating and elegant style—the Zionists will regret all the more that precisely on this occasion Dr. Oppenheimer abstained from "theoretical debates," a penetrating analysis of terminology and from a definition of concepts. Notwithstanding the clear construction and thought processes, and however beautiful the correlation between the individual paragraphs of his article, already at a first perusal the serious reader—in addition to subjective differences of opinion—will come up against inner inconsistencies, actual contradictions and above all he will come across instances relating to the author's theory which the author ought not to have passed over in silence. Above all, one misses an unambiguous definition—the lack of which is even more disturbing when one comes to assimilate the material; the author ought here to have come to the aid of the less well-trained reader.

Permit me to give a few brief examples of this before we deal with the heart of the matter.

As we know, the author makes a sharp distinction between ethnic and national consciousness, the latter being sub-divided into consciousness of nationality and consciousness of culture. Ethnic consciousness "concerns itself with the past," it exists where the consciousness of a "common origin, common blood or at least past shared national traditions, a common history" is accompanied by pride in these common possessions. It is "pride in aristocratic descent" which the Jewish assimilationist lacks. The author assumes that a large Jewish community, a nation with a culture, already exists which assigns him to an appropriate task. Having until that moment felt himself to be an ethnic Jew, he thinks that from the moment of his assignment he would "to quite a considerable extent feel himself to be a national and cultural Jew," "but," he continues, "I should presumably retain German ethnic feeling to my dying day," because he "would still feel more closely related to a German than, say, to an Englishman." But what is this ethnic feeling? At one time it is considered to be historic and unalterable and therefore hardly a variable feeling which in the case of the Jew is based on pride in his descent, in his historical nationhood and his blood (Oppenheimer also believes in blood whose "cultural value" he discusses elsewhere). Yet, another time that same Jew is able to acquire a different ethnic feeling, a German ethnic feeling, which is not based on pride in descent, blood, etc., but is a feeling of relationship, apparently of a spiritual and cultural nature.

As a national consciousness, it concerns current issues, such as a common language and customs, economic and legal terms, etc. (there's the surprising absence of the "land." The author does not say "we love our landscape" without emphasizing elsewhere the "national-German" Jews)—and once again it refers to a common spiritual culture. It is the "psychic reflection of the milieu," but the product of a reality in which an individual must stand—and yet, elsewhere, against all physical laws, the author grants even a "passenger" a national consciousness and a magnate, even more than one.

As to cultural consciousness, this is a part or an element of national consciousness, hence something circumscribed in the spatial and spiritual sphere. The German Jew with Jewish ethnic consciousness possesses German cultural consciousness. Yet, suddenly, without further explanation the concept of culture crosses its boundaries and King Carol, in addition to his German ethnic consciousness, is awarded "West European" cultural consciousness.

These were just a few examples—I do not wish to enlarge on how difficult the learned author makes it for us to follow him along straight paths. But enough of this. Let us get on to the main thesis which, somewhat hidden, is to be found in the second half of Oppenheimer's expositions. It states: "We Western Jews are sociologically differently determined from the Eastern Jews." This thesis has to be accepted because it happens to be a fact. To want to deny it for the sake of Zionist unity is as impossible as it is stupid. The "difference" need not look quite the same as Oppenheimer presents it to us and the conclusions too might well differ.

II

There is no need to dwell at any length on the fact that the Eastern Jews are differently determined from the Western Jews. The characteristic differences in Jewish life on either side of the eastern border are sufficiently well known not to require spending time on their enumeration and comparison.

It is all the more strange, therefore, that in several instances Franz Oppenheimer should have erred just here in his diagnoses and deductions. In two places which are decisive for the presentation of his case these errors are crucial.

As we know, Oppenheimer maintains that the West European Jews cannot possibly be "cultural Jews," "because Jewish culture as it survives from the medieval ghettos is much inferior to the contemporary culture of the European nations. The East European Jews are bound to be cultural Jews, because medieval Jewish culture stands as high above East European barbarism as it falls below the advanced West European culture." This reasoning is incorrect and in addition to a mistake in the matter itself, there is an error also in the object of the comparison. Thus, the author places West European Jews vis-a-vis German, English, etc., *culture,* but the East European Jews vis-a-vis East European *barbarism.* The term "barbarism" with its associations of pogroms, the scourge of tyranny and Siberia, confusingly and factually unwarranted—moves from the cultural sphere to that of humanity and civilization. However low one rates Russian culture, one cannot deny Dostoyevsky's and Tolstoy's European cultural status even without consideration of how much European influence this culture has absorbed. To identify Polish culture with barbarism is even more out of place because of the absence of "associations." It just does not apply. The reason why the East European Jews must be cultural Jews is certainly not because the culture surrounding them is inferior to their own. Is the author unaware that hundreds of thousands of Russian and Polish Jews have to work through these "barbarian" cultural groups on their quest for education? Could there be more striking evidence with which to refute Oppenheimer's deduction than the fact that no greater chauvinists, enthusiasts and "patriots" are to be found than the "Jewish Poles"? The second serious error, namely that East European Jewish culture is merely a medieval legacy, identical with the "sacred will of God," that is to say, with religious culture, I shall not even discuss because an additional refutation of Oppenheimer's formula of cultural Judaism "out of necessity" is superfluous.

To mention a related matter—the deduction of Zionism from "necessity," resulting from the social and economic situation of East European Jewry stands on equally shaky ground. As proletarians without rights they have the "natural tendency to run away." True. And where else than "to the place of least pressure along the line of least resistance." If this is true—and it is true—can one go along with Oppenheimer and deduce from this social-psychological tendency a clearly defined national characteristic of East European Jewry which is absent in Western European Jewry? The answer is in the negative, because when the Jews follow this tendency of least resistance, its path actually leads to the industrial centres and the agriculturally and commercially developed areas of America. It is there that the "practical, enlightened self-interest" finds its relatively quickest satisfaction. Here too life supplies the evidence: In the past decade a million Jews went to America, only thousands to Palestine.

Hence, neither with the East European Jews as distinct from the West European Jews is there a "necessity" for a cultural Judaism, forced into being by the inferiority of other cultures, nor is there a national Judaism and Zionism "from necessity" dictated by a law of the least social and economic resistance.

Both are designed to didactically support the other theory which tries to make out a case that the Zionism of West European Jewry is based only on ethnic consciousness—and the existence of a superior culture and the lack of any flight from the soil or tendency to migrate is intended to establish German cultural and national consciousness.

Placing these constructions and the above-mentioned ambiguity of the terminology side by side, one tends to suspect that this tripartite division into ethnic-national-cultural consciousness is a *post hoc, ergo propter hoc,* hardly suitable to clarify the national phenomena of other nations, is meant to explain the Jewish national problem by the following beautiful, but for scientific argumentation dangerous premise: How do I bring about peace between East and West? There is, moreover, the political utilitarian consideration as regards the extent to which the West European Zionists are able to become personally involved, and what is the easiest way to recruit Zionists in Western Europe.

It is possible that this pragmatic tendency led Franz Oppenheimer in the wrong direction right from the beginning, in which case he would not have started out from the divisive elements within the Jewish nation, but would rather have tried to uncover the common ground. This is not the place to go into the entire theory of Jewish nationalism. So much as been said on this subject since Moses Hess, Ahad Ha'Am, Theodor Herzl, Max Nordau, in fact since the beginnings of the Jewish National Movement—though by far not exhaustively and not in sufficient detail—that merely to explain further would mean presenting the commonplace. How schematically simple Oppenheimer finds it to have the Jewish psyche divided into three basic feelings. How enviably healthy is the psyche of the German Jews. Self-satisfied and with a feeling of contentment they condense (or should I say evaporate) their

Judaism to pride in the past and to an altruistic idealism for the "other" Jews; apart from this they tightly embrace Germanness, undisturbed by either doubt or disharmony. Is the "spiritual Jewish suffering" really nothing more than a sentimental delusion, did they only live in the imagination of the poets, those prophetic beings, tormented, inwardly torn and thirsting for redemption who search "for the way to freedom"?

Was it only the altruism of someone happily walking along on European soil who presented the *Judenstaat* to the Zionists with the fiery words: "We are a people. *One* people"?

No, Franz Oppenheimer's formula—though it may appeal to many for its pragmatic-reconciling construction—is not the formula of West European Judaism, as he presumes it to be. Oppenheimer's ethnic consciousness is directed to what has been, recalling a glorious but dead past. It is an abstraction of Judaism and therein lies its basic error, for the past is alive. Jewishness is active in the present. Every Jewish individual brings with him a specific physiological, psychological disposition. Despite the many differences of opinion among the racial theoreticians this can be claimed as a fact, as true. This instinctive Jewishness must come to terms with the environment which it influences and by which it is in return influenced. Wherever there is a Jewish community, imperfect or rudimentary as it might be, as it is in Eastern Europe, there, within the limits of the given possibilities of development, this instinct is able to obtain natural stimulation or at least protection against the alien environment.

Where no such community exists, this instinctive Jewishness either submits to the environment, modifies itself to the milieu or permits itself to be modified by it, or it puts up a fight against the absorbing or modifying power of the environment and tries to hold out against it. True, it is a minor battle, but being repeated a hundred thousand times, it has its grandeur and from an elevated observation point it portrays a real battle with its deserters and cowards, those who surrender on certain conditions, there are the defenseless, the fighters and the wounded. Also "sacrifices are brought here, not lamb and not bull, but—incredibly—human sacrifices." In its general outlines this battle develops along obvious and controlled lines, with groups forming within the battle line: one of the two flanks, the one in retreat, consists of the baptized or about to be baptized and the other, the advancing flank, of the Zionists. We can clearly follow the different stratifications and groupings: The assimilationists pure and simple, cosmopolitans, individualists, the indifferent, the denominationals, the liberals, ethnic Jews (in Oppenheimer's sense), the religious, Diaspora-nationalists, cultural-nationalists, cultural-Zionists, territorialists, political Zionists—these, more or less, represent the different slogans and trends picked out at random. Where, then, does Jewish nationalism begin? Obviously not where the blunting of the instinctive Jewish motivation forms the basis of memory, but rather where this motivation is constantly at work, counteracting the environment in order to preserve what is peculiarly Jewish. Obviously, the psychological and intellectual foundation of Jewish nationalism obtains only where this resistance is not limited to making one's own specific personality dominant but connects up one's personal aims with those of a Jewish community of similar aspirations. It is at this point, where they consciously discuss their own specific characteristics, that Western and Eastern Judaism will meet. Where this tendency is not fixed in time, where the individual and the community by retaining their individuality serve not only their own personal and national needs, but are aware of serving the development of humankind—that is where Zionism comes into being. Hence, on neither side is it "necessity," but rather the will which is the precondition for a national Judaism and for Zionism. Something which in the case of normal nations occurs unconsciously, namely that a person provides meaning to his life just by living, striving and acting within his national entity, effortlessly preserving and handing down the characteristics of his nation merely because he lives and acts, in our case, at least to begin with, has to be a conscious tendency. The inability to tolerate compromise is inherent in its nature. This Jewish nationalism has nothing to do with altruism. The individual can give nothing which it does not first receive, it is a link in the chain. Nor should his personal purpose differ from that of the national entity, his future is inextricably tied to that of the nation as a whole.

Oppenheimer's Zionism which is founded on Jewish ethnic consciousness and at the same time encompasses German national and cultural consciousness, altruistically oriented to help, whose existence therefore terminates with the end or the superfluity of this help, which determines a future which differs for the individual and for the nation as a whole—that is not Zionism. Such a combination of ideas and feelings might further Zionism, it might here and there and without contradiction accompany Zionism in its practical implementation—but it is not Zionism. Only a simple example is needed to prove this: Imagine Oppenheimer's ethnic consciousness to be effective in a mass of individuals and assume that there was as yet no Zionist Movement— what would this ethnic consciousness be whose representatives link their personal future to that of a non-Jewish national entity? Something which needs Zionism as a pre-condition for it to be effective, cannot itself be Zionism. Let us consider for a moment where this ethnic consciousness is likely to lead us. According to Oppenheimer, it is pride in ancestry which insists on the restoration of the good name to the ancient tribe which, in combination with a feeling for freedom, justice and humanitarianism is to lead the Jews to victory against barbarism.

There was once a Jew called Disraeli and later when he was already an Anglican, he was called Lord Beaconsfield. If it can be said of anyone it must be said of him that he carried pride in his ancestry not only in his heart but also manifested it outwardly. Not only did his coat-of-arms bear Jewish symbols, he also altruistically fought in speeches, in his writings and actions for the freedom of the Jews. He travelled to Palestine and immortalized his feelings for the ancestral land in his book *Tancred*. He utilized his political influence in favor of the Jews which earned him considerable opposition, he supported the Sublime Port, etc. A multitude of such Disraelis would leave us with the grotesque phenomenon of a Jewish ethnic-conscious, English-Anglican aristocracy.

Whoever wishes to do so, can no doubt supply further examples of all the possibilities inherent in the abstraction of Jewish ethnic consciousness. Its nature being rooted in the past and lacking the urge to develop in the present environment, it is most likely to lead to inaction.

The fact is that in association with Zionism it can all too easily lead from an idealistic and altruistic striving to a devilishly convenient assimilation: namely, whatever is Jewish in us we classify as belonging to the past. The Judaism of others which "now puts a tremendous burden on our shoulders to provide aid and education"—we shove off to Palestine. No one can deny this possibility, this probability.

However, let us now turn to Oppenheimer's important observations, namely the crucial facts which have been represented in a completely different way only through his dictum "as I see it."

III

We said that it was the will to preserve and to activate the heritage that has come down to us through blood and soul, the inborn quality of Jewishness which forms the basis for Jewish nationalism. Hence, the origin and aim of Jewish nationalism are completely identical for East and West, for North and South. The considerable gradations come about only in the process of the development of nationalism. It is therefore correct—though not in Oppenheimer's sense, for he does not start out from the living and active quality of the Jew—that in West European countries (always excepting Austria) it will generally be the past which will most of all further the will of Jews of national orientation. It must, of course, be a past whose living fusion enables the Jewish individual to create a deeply-felt continuity between the then and the now, between the line of his ancestors and himself. "The blood of our ancestors pulses full of restlessness and pride, the blood of what has been and what will be" as the poet said. The present-day milieu, on the other hand, has little to offer to Jewish nationalism. Religion can (but does not necessarily have to) give it momentum. Apart from this, considering the lack of a Jewish community of economic, social, cultural or political interests in the West European countries one can at most speak of the support given to nationalism by the negative effects of the milieu, namely anti-Semitism in all its manifestations. As against this, Eastern Europe with its active Jewish cultural life (the value of which we do not here assess), its passive Jewish economy and the spatial compactness of the Jewish masses, offers the national tendency an incomparably larger field of activity and scope for development. This does not lead to Oppenheimer's conclusion that: "The West European Zionist has only ethnic consciousness, the East European Zionist national consciousness." (Rather, this applies only if one excepts a not inconsiderable section of East European Jewry which is removed—or has removed itself—from the above-mentioned nationalism-providing factors). The West European Zionist has to make a more concerted effort and face greater difficulties in order to safeguard his nationalism, the possibility to exist and to be creative. An intimate link with the past, a tight rein on his ego in face of the surroundings, social contact with a society sharing similar aims, these form the initial steps towards the attainment of this endeavor. The next step is the emotional and intellectual connection with the Jewish cultural life of the Diaspora which, even if its value and strength as such might not be all that great, nevertheless supplies nationalism with a live element. On such foundations nationalism will be able for a while to defend itself against and stand up to the environment. But in the final analysis these foundations will prove too weak for the individual and of course also for a group merely to maintain a national tendency, not to speak of its reorganization into a creative force. Hence, in place of Oppenheimer's proposition to give in, even to merge completely into the hostile surroundings, a different proposition should be put forward. In order to assure productive facilities for his Jewish nationalism, the West European Zionist needs the connection with the national soil, with Palestine. He needs it more quickly, more urgently than the average East European. This is, of course, only relatively speaking for both need Palestine quickly and urgently.

These are the two conclusions at which one arrives when proceeding from the simplest formulation of Jewish nationalism.

Realistically, organized Zionism, must try to cope with these two conclusions, both of which are also postulates of pure nationalism.

So far, success in this has not been exactly impressive. The majority of West European Zionists have remained stationary on the first few steps, some still on the "threshold" of nationalism as it was phrased above. The majority constitutes a retarding element that occasionally engenders a great deal of pessimism; even so, an as yet small minority has fought its way to a higher step—actually to the highest step—of nationalism and is trying slowly but surely to advance the nonaligned majority.

And then you have Franz Oppenheimer addressing the non-aligned majority: "Stop!" he shouts, "don't bother to exert yourselves. There is no need for you to preserve your own individuality because you haven't any. All you have is pride, and you do not need Palestine because your future lies in the country in which you live."

I find it incomprehensible why serious Zionists, for tactical or other reasons, should try so hard to consider this tendency to be Zionism in spite of everything or because of it, even though it is opposed to nationalism and to Zionism.

An opinion such as Oppenheimer's within Zionism, that is to say, a deliberate renunciation of the strongest integrating elements of Zionism, is impossible in theory and is practically nothing but an invitation to slow but certain suicide. Apart from everything else, with every day which makes the past recede further and advances the political and social position of the Jews, Oppenheimer's brand of West European Zionism cannot but lose its inner vitality. Such Zionism will slowly but surely die of debilitation because such is its nature.

That is why one must put up a strong fight—out of the most primitive Zionist realization—lest Oppenheimer's teaching become tolerated and accepted as Zionism in Western Europe. One might tolerate the rudimentary approach to Jewish nationalism from an historical and tactical understanding if it includes the desire for development and perfection, though, here too, an over-abundance of tolerance has already caused serious disadvantages to Zionism. Even if Germans entertain doubts as to whether Oppenheimer's nationalism paired with Jewish ethnic consciousness constitutes valid German nationalism—we Zionists have no doubt that his German national consciousness paired with Jewish ethnic consciousness neither is, wants to be, nor can ever be Jewish nationalism.

Above all, the younger generation, which can in any case easily be led astray by the picture of an undeveloped nationalism as it is being offered in Western Europe, must be protected from the new heresy which so conveniently and easily unlocks the gate to the Eden of the Diaspora. Precisely with a writer who explains everything on the basis of its utilitarian purpose, it is essential to remind the younger generation that Zionism is the child or rather the development of messianism. It is, of course, a modern movement, employing modern methods. However, by following a rationalistic path one can never hope to plumb the depth, to reach the essence of Zionism, namely the mysterious driving force of a nation's thousand-year-old longing for itself. Zionism originates in the time of antiquity and is accompanied by the heroic quality—almost unknown in our days—which knows not utilitarian purpose but only greatness. It has need of complete human beings, of undivided souls, it must demand them because its nature, its way and its aim demand them.

Oppenheimer's teaching kills off the messianic aspect in Zionism. Thus, judgment has been passed on it.

However, Oppenheimer's way of thinking—and it is this which makes it so valuable—provides the basis for a more generous kind of Jewish Philo-Zionism. Though inside Zionism a dangerous foe, side-by-side with Zionism it could be a valuable ally. For a person unable to identify, for inner or extraneous reasons, with the inherently essential national-Jewish Zionism, but who wishes to extend his help in one sphere or another, to further its cause as an organizing movement, it is preferable if he were a sincere friend of Zion or a friend of Zionists rather than that he call himself a Zionist, without nationalism, without Zionism.

Note

Berthold Feiwel (1875–1937). Poet, journalist and businessman. Co-editor of *Die Welt* 1900–1901, 1906–1907. Member of the Grosses Aktions-Comité of the World Zionist Organization, 1898–1899, 1900–1901, 1905–1921, 1927–1929, 1931–1933. Executive director of the Keren Hayessod in London 1920–1926. Executive director of the Jewish Colonial Trust in London 1928–1932.

Fin-de-Siècle Orientalism, the *Ostjuden* and the Aesthetics of Jewish Self-Affirmation

Paul Mendes-Flohr
(HEBREW UNIVERSITY)

MYSTICISM AND THE CULT OF THE ORIENT

*Wenn Skepsis und Sehnsucht sich
begatten, entsteht die Mystik*
—NIETZSCHE

In the convivial *bohème* of *fin-de-siècle* Munich, surely one of the most flamboyant figures was cut by the person of Omar al Raschid Bey. Dressed in Bedouin robes, a bright yellow and green cummerbund, a red fez, and high leather boots, this grey-bearded patriarch was regarded by his votaries (who included the young Ludwig Klages and Theodor Lessing) as a charismatic, otherworldly sage.[1] A Jew by birth, who had converted to Islam in Istanbul in 1886, al Raschid Bey (né Friedrich Arndt-Kürnberg, d. 1910)[2] taught them the "wisdom of the Orient," a highly syncretistic skein of Indian, Buddhist and Islamic mystical teachings.[3]

This demonstrative Orientalism was indicative of the burgeoning interest in mysticism—and concomitantly in the world of the occult, myth and folklore[4]—that was said to be preserved by the non-Western religions, particularly of the Orient.[4a] The religious traditions of the East were reputedly untouched by the "soulless" rationalism and materialism of the bourgeois West.[5] The Orient—which had hitherto been regarded by Europeans as a distant, debased civilization[6]—had suddenly acquired an alluring prestige as the polar opposite of what was increasingly perceived to be a decadent West. Many European intellectuals at the turn of the century shared Nietzsche's Cassandran premonitions when he exclaimed: "For some time now, our European culture has been moving as toward a catastrophe, with tortured tension that is growing from decade to decade."⁷ In ever widening circles it was fashionable to ascribe this seemingly inexorable decline of Europe to the ruthless hegemony of Reason, and its superficial, mechanistic view of reality, that began with the Enlightenment and the triumph of bourgeois civilization—a civilization centered in the impersonal, spiritually desiccated urban monstrosities that blighted the landscape of Europe.⁸

For the more philosophically inclined, this appreciation of the insidious role of Reason was deepened by the teachings of Arthur Schopenhauer (1788–1860)—the philosophical iconoclast ignored by his own generation whom Nietzsche (together with Richard Wagner) introduced anew to Europe.⁹ In a period still enthralled by the moral and material promise of a world governed by Reason, this lonely sage, dismissed by his contemporaries as a hysterical misanthrope, had decried this promise as inspiring a spiritually jejune optimism. He was particularly enraged by the repeated attempts of his fellow philosophers to enjoin Reason to devise metaphysical and quasi-metaphysical systems to support this optimism. He reminded his colleagues that the revered Kant had decisively demonstrated that Reason is intrinsically incapable of providing such metaphysical knowledge.

True, in contradistinction to the empiricists, Schopenhauer pointed out, Kant had taught that our knowledge of the phenomenal world is not merely a function of sense data but also determined by the very structure of the perceiving mind. The discernment of an individuated world of discrete objects (phenomena) is only made possible by Reason's *a priori* principles of time and space, the *principium individuationis*.¹⁰ Joined by the *a priori* category of causality, the *principium individuationis* presents us with the world of the scientist—the rational, calculable world of phenomena. What particularly distressed Schopenhauer, however, were the ontological and spiritual implications of Kant's principle of individuation, for it posited that all facets of being are locked in eternal separation from—and perforce are in opposition—to one another. Hence, an impenetrable barrier of separateness lies between all phenomenal facts of existence, between man and the world, and between man and man. Such a *Weltbild,* such a picture of reality, Schopenhauer suggested, could only have but the most disastrous affects on our aesthetic, moral and spiritual sensibilities.

Yet, Schopenhauer tirelessly protested, we need not be satisfied with this Kantian *Weltbild*. The individuated world, he underscores, is after all a function of the perceiving mind; and the mind, upon self-reflection, has access to a different order of knowledge. Self-reflection readily indicates that stirring behind our every action is will—and will reveals itself as the noumenal dimension of our phenomenal self.[11] Each of us, in other words, is experientially aware that he or she is eminently more than just a phenomenon—an object among objects, possessing space and time, and passive responsiveness to the laws of causality; each of us has intimate knowledge of ourself as will. And since solipsism is patently absurd, everyone is obliged to assume that his *noumenal* consciousness of the self is true for all human beings.[12] Schopenhauer was so certain of the validity of this extrapolation that he felt no hesitation in extending it beyond the sphere of the human to all phenomena—animate and inanimate: All facts of the world are different only at the phenomenal level, "but they are same according to their inner [noumenal] nature."[13]

This common noumenal ground of all being permits Schopenhauer to posit a unitary, all-pervasive will which is conceived as the world-in-itself, and as such is logically free of the defining properties of the phenomenal world, that is, of space and time.[14] From the perspective of the noumenal will, Schopenhauer now declared the phenomenal, individuated world a "veil of Maya"—a terrible illusion fraught with pain[15]—pain because individuation means endless conflict engendered by the insatiable, rapacious will.[16] In consonance with Hindu Vedänta, from which he borrowed the image of the veil of Maya, Schopenhauer counseled that individuation be overcome by a negation of individual will—that we withdraw into volitional passivity and silence.

While not necessarily accepting Schopenhauer's recommendation to mystical quietism, his critique of the regnant epistemological assumptions of bourgeois civilization—and his dramatic appeal to an Oriental tradition—captured the imagination of the *fin-de-siècle* intellectual. Schopenhauer's interest in Hindu mysticism is a product of the eighteenth-century fascination with esoteric wisdom discussed in note 4, above. He was introduced to the Hindu tradition through a Latin translation of the Upanishads (Vendata) published in 1801 and 1802. This first Western rendition of that ancient body of literature, curiously based on a sixteenth-century Persian translation, became Schopenhauer's "daily prayer book," in which he recognized a pure distillation of his own teachings (Gunter Landczkowski, *Sacred Writings. A Guide to the Literature of Religions,* trans. S. Godman [New York, 1961] p. 98). Indeed, along with Nietzsche's *Thus Spake Zarathustra,* Schopenhauer's *The World as Will and Idea* became *de rigueur* for the generations between 1890 and World War I. His conviction that bourgeois civilization could be overcome only through an alternative *Weltbild* to that offered by Reason inspired many, and his mystical quest resonated the spiritual mood of the period. For disenchantment with modernity had led to profound yearnings for what was often vaguely called "salvation" *(Erlösung)*[17]—this despite the then nigh-obsessive hostility to formal religion and its doctrines. Literature, art and theater now became the most popular vehicles for religious quest.[18] Such inveterate despisers of Christian faith as Stefan George and Rainer Maria Rilke often spoke in their poetry of the yearning for "salvation." In *The Notebook of Malte Laurdis-Brigge* (1910), Rilke, who abhorred the concepts of sin and atonement as an affront to the dignity of the individual, sought "salvation" from the alienation of life in the modern city through a mystical "emptying of the self." Rilke's longing, as Roy Pascal notes, "is typical [of his generation] in that it is associated neither with any particular transgression nor with belief in God; it is the only positive element left over from Christian belief."[19] Further, this longing for salvation was typically mystical, for as Nietzsche pithily observed, "When scepticism mates with longing, mysticism is born" [*Wenn Skepsis und Sehnsucht sich begatten, entsteht die Mystik*].[19]

This sudden fascination with mysticism, especially as embodied in Oriental religious traditions, as already intimated, generated an enormous and wide-ranging literary and artistic activity, touching virtually every area of intellectual and aesthetic endeavor.[20] In music for instance, Gustav Mahler, an avid reader of Nietzsche and Schopenhauer,[21] derived his inspiration for his symphony *Das Lied von der Erde* from Hans Bethge's German anthology of Chinese mystical poetry, *Die Chinesischen Flöte* (1907).[22] His fellow Viennese, the painter Gustav Klimt, used a commission to design a ceiling painting on Philosophy for the ceremonial hall of the University of Vienna in order to present his vision of the human condition. The mural, completed in 1900, was manifestly inspired by Schopenhauer's mysticism, and his vision of the universe, as Carl E. Schorske notes, was "the World as Will, as blind energy in an endless round of meaningless parturience, love and death."[23] A decade later in Munich, Wassily Kandinsky published an essay, "Über das Geistige in der Kunst," which was to become the programmatic statement of modern abstract painting. In it, he called upon his fellow painters to follow the example of contemporary writers and composers and adopt a mystical view of the world's "inner reality."[24] The philosophers and writers of the *fin-de-siècle* to whom Kandinsky referred are legion: we may mention, at random, in philosophy, Fritz Mauthner, Karl Jöel and Georg Simmel; and in *belles-lettres*, Stefan George, Hesse, Hoffmannsthal, Kafka, Robert Musil and Rilke.

To cater to this vigorous interest in mysticism—and the cognate subjects of the occult, myth and folklore—numerous journals and reviews were founded as well as several publishing houses, among the most prominent being the Eugen Diederichs Verlag of Jena established in 1898, and the Kurt Wolff Verlag of Leipzig founded in 1913.[25] Even the more veteran publishing houses of Central Europe established special series to sponsor the new interest (Rütten & Leoning, and Insel Verlag, both of Frankfurt am Main, for example). Eugen Diederichs, who coined the term "New Romanticism" to characterize the "movement," declared that in his publishing activities he was encouraging "a return to a higher transcendent reality;"[26] hence, "the Germans must now pass into mysticism in order again to sense the world as a whole."[27]

THE JEW AS ORIENTAL

> *For the Jew has remained an Oriental.*
> MARTIN BUBER

Despite their eager adoption of modern Western culture, the Jews' Oriental provenance was never quite forgotten, or forgiven. In the nineteenth century, anti-Semites revelled in reminding the Jews of their non-European origins. The Berlin lawyer Karl W. F. Grattenauer exclaimed in his widely read pamphlet, *Wider die Juden* (1803), that the cultured Jews "may talk about Goethe, Schiller, and Schlegel all they please; they nonetheless remain an alien Asiatic people [*orientalisches Fremdlingsvolk*]."[28] The historian Heinrich von Treitschke was only a bit more magnanimous in his *Ein Wort über unser Judenthum* (1879–80), when he noted that despite the "patriotic" efforts of such acculturated Jews as Felix Mendelssohn, Gabriel Riesser, and Moritz Veit, many of their fellow Jews, alas, remained "incorrigibly Oriental" (*unverfälschte Orientalen*).[29] "There will always be Jews," he wrote, "who are nothing else but German-speaking Orientals."[30] It was in the same year, 1879, that Wilhelm Marr ceremoniously introduced the fateful term "anti-Semitism"[31]—the reference to Jews as Semites also sought to underscore their Oriental origin.

In his recent study of various Western conceptions of the Orient, Edward Said has cogently demonstrated that the distinction between Occident and Orient has been axiomatic in much of Western thought since Europe emerged as a self-conscious cultural and political entity in the seventeenth century.[32] The Occident and Orient were, accordingly, seen as contrasting, indeed diametrically opposite, images. Typologically, they denote contrasting epistemological and ontological realities; they demarcate diametrically opposed ideas, personalities and experiences. In general, Said notes, the tendency was to attribute to the Orient—which until the end of the early nineteenth century meant only India and the Bible lands[33]—"feelings of emptiness, loss, disaster."[34] He bases his observations largely on literary sources (primarily, French and English *belles-lettres* of the nineteenth century) with some, albeit cursory, reference to the presuppositions of the Western academic discipline of Oriental studies. One may strengthen his argument with citations from the philosophers, especially Hegel and his disciples. From their historiosophical perspective "the Orient" was invariably treated as an eclipsed, retrograde civilization long deserted by *Geist* in its world-historical march. For Hegel, "Europe is 'plainly' the goal of history. [. . .] The Orientals were the childhood of the world, the Greeks and Romans its youth and manhood, the Christian peoples are its maturity."[35]

The general contempt for the Orient exacerbated and immeasurably complicated the prevailing antipathy toward the Jew in Western Europe. For acculturated Jews who identified with the West, the negative image of the Orient sponsored by European culture understandably caused profound perplexity and self-consciousness. No wonder the Reform movement so hastily sought to purge Jewish religious rite and ritual of its Oriental quality, by eliminating, for example, the Oriental trills and melodies of the *ḥazan,* and, in general, by rendering the prayer service compatible with the aesthetic standards of the West. Eduard Gans, one of Hegel's most distinguished students, presented *Wissenschaft des Judentums* as inculcating an informed awareness of Israel's past and its vital historical contribution to the development of civilization—thus making it possible for the Jews, honorably, to discard their Oriental identity and "merge" with Europe.[36] The often obsessive effort of the Western Jew to free himself of the stigma of his Oriental origin at times took on invidious forms, as in Walter Rathenau's impassioned appeal of 1897, *"Höre, Israel,"* to his fellow German Jews to hasten their assimilation and to cast off all vestiges of their Asiatic manners and appearance:

> [. . .] Look at yourselves in the mirror! This is the first step toward self-criticism. Nothing unfortunately, can be done about the fact that all of you look frighteningly alike [. . .] Neither will it console you that in the first place your east Mediterranean appearance is not very well appreciated by the northern tribes. [. . .] As soon as you recognize [these faults] you will resolve to dedicate a few generations to the renewal of your outer appearance.[37]

Here the self-consciousness of the Western Jew took on the pitiful hues of self-hatred.

To further exacerbate the burden of their public image, the acculturated Jews of the West were recurrently reminded of the manifestly "alien," indeed Oriental reality of their East European brethren, still denizens, as they were, of the "Ghetto" and a pre-modern civilization. Treitschke, for instance, bemoaning the fact that Germany "is invaded year after year by multitudes of assiduous pants-selling [Jewish] youth" from Poland, stressed that "the Jews of the Polish branch"—as opposed perhaps, and only perhaps, to the urbane Sephardim of France—were patently "alien to the European, and especially to the German national character."[38] Not surprisingly the negative image of the so-called *Ostjude* was internalized by the acculturated Jew. Thus when the Viennese Jewish novelist Karl Emil Franzos took the German reader across the frontier from modern Austria to Galicia, where he Franzos, was born and raised, he referred to the remote, backward province and home of close to a million "Polish Jews" as *Halb-Asien:* an exotic world characterized by squalor, ignorance and superstition, and ruled by a fanatic mystical sect known as Hasidim.[39] Through his enormously popular works (translated into virtually every major European language and sold in the millions) Franzos bequeathed the sobriquet of *Halb-Asien* to the vocabulary of the West, indelibly marking the East European Jews as non-European, semi-Oriental people—and to many this undoubtedly meant the genuine Jews, undisguised by Western culture.[40]

The new, positive image of the Orient nurtured by *fin-de-siècle* aestheticism provided an auspicious opportunity to reevaluate the image of the Jew as Oriental. No less importantly it also allowed the Western Jew to develop a new perception of himself, his Oriental origins and his East European brethren. As Hans Kohn observed in 1913 in his preface to *Vom Judentum* (a collection of essays sponsored by the Bar Kochba Jewish Student Association of Prague) the "renaissance" of Jewish culture and identity then characteristic of Jewish youth of the West was grounded in the general struggle against a civilization hostage to "a mechanical dehumanizing, desacralizing order of instrumental, rational aims." "The Occident," he wrote, "has turned to the Orient" in order to renew European cultural and spiritual sensibility.[41] This effort, Kohn added, was of paramount significance for Jewry and humankind alike. Hence both Jew and gentile had much at stake in reevaluating and reaffirming Judaism as representative of the Oriental spirit.

As an example of a gentile who heeded, as it were, Kohn's call we may mention the Austrian novelist Gustav Meyrink, who in his mystery thriller *Der Golem* (Verlag Kurt Wolf, 1915) romanticized the

Prague ghetto and Jewish occultism. Incidentally, in the years that Meyrink lived in Prague writing his powerfully anti-bourgeois novel he had converted from Lutheranism to Buddhism. Another contemporary resident of Prague, Franz Kafka, developed an interest in the occult and even sought the counsel of Rudolf Steiner[42]—the charismatic secretary of the German branch of Madame Blavatsky's Theosophical Society (which was heavily indebted in its teachings to "the wisdom of India")—at the very same time he was drawn to the Yiddish theater and language.[43]

The occult and Yiddish culture were undoubtedly related in Kafka's mind to his struggle to "liberate" himself from the bourgeois world in which he felt himself imprisoned. And this struggle for him, as for many of his contemporaries, also meant the rejection of Judaism, at least as practiced and mediated by their bourgeois parents. For those who were not prepared, or permitted by force of social circumstances, to discard their Judaism totally, there were few genuine alternatives other than to seek an anti-bourgeois (or post-bourgeois) Jewish identity. The Bar Kochba Student Association of Prague, of which Kafka was a member (albeit with his typical tentativeness) sought to forge a Jewish cultural identity which was more "vibrant" and "rooted" than the attenuated Judaism to be found in their largely assimilated homes. The worldview of their parents—primed by a dull rationalism and a naive belief in material progress[44]—was to be transcended by an affirmation of the non-rational realm of the Spirit, a realm best illuminated by the mysticism and myth of the Orient.

In a broad sense, cultural Zionism was the ideological framework of the Bar Kochba Association, but as witnessed by the aforementioned volume *Vom Judentum* (1913), which represented the high point of its productivity, the Jewish "renaissance" it sponsored was not confined to Zionists. Two of the contributors to the volume, for instance, Karl Wolfskehl (of Munich) and Erich Kahler (Vienna) were notable disciples of Stefan George who were remote from Zionism, as were Jakob Wassermann (from Vienna), Gustav Landauer (Berlin) and Margarete Susman (Rüschlikon). What characterized all the essays in the volume by the non-Zionists and Zionists alike was a resurgent Jewish pride and a sustained interest in Oriental spirituality and mysticism. Thus, Karl Wolfskehl inaugurated the volume with a poetic meditation on "Das Geheimnis der Juden" (The Secret of the Jews); Jakob Wassermann followed with a piece entitled "Der Jude als Orientale" (The Jew as Oriental); and Hans Kohn then offered a scholarly disquisition on "Der Geist der Orient" (The Spirit of the East). These three essays, which were grouped together under the rubric "Jüdisches Wesen" (Jewish

Being), set the tone for the following twenty-two articles. The volume appropriately concluded with a collection of passages from the Zohar translated by Hugo Bergmann and Ernst Müller.

Throughout the volume the towering presence of Martin Buber is palpable. The writings and teachings of the then thirty-five year old Buber informed the formulations, vocabulary and illustrative material of many, even most, of the twenty-five essays. Indeed, Buber may be viewed as the patron saint of the Bar Kochba Association. As early as 1901 its members had come under the influence of his writings and unique vision of Jewish renewal.[45] It was only in 1908, however, that he was formally assigned a role as "the spiritual guide" of the society. In November of that year, he received a long letter from Leo Hermann, chairman of the Association,[46] inviting him to participate in a colloquium which would seek to address "the large assimilated public of Prague." Hermann noted that thus far Felix Salten—one of Vienna's most highly regarded feuilletonists—had agreed to speak on "the banality and rootlessness of Jewish society in the big cities." But the organizers of the colloquium were eager to complement Salten's reflections on the negative aspects of assimilation with a discussion of the imperatives of Jewish existence, of "how the *Westjude* can convert what remains of Jewish existence into his own, how it is just these very imperatives that gives the Jewish poet his cultural worth." Buber's correspondent further observed that "for the *Ostjude* this [ability] exists naturally to a significantly higher degree. But for once it is perhaps precisely for the *Westjude* to demonstrate [such an ability as well]." Hermann's letter concluded with a plea to help stem the tide of assimilation among the Jews of Prague: who precisely because of their fervent attachment to high German culture required someone as sophisticated as Buber to inform them about Judaism. "We have nobody today in the West, or anywhere else for that matter, who can interpret Jewish being as sensitively as you." Buber accepted the invitation with alacrity, and came to Prague in January 1909 to deliver a lecture entitled "Der Sinn des Judentums" (The Meaning of Judaism).[47] As Max Brod, who had hitherto been indifferent to Judaism, reports, the lecture deeply touched him and converted him to a passionate Zionism;[48] others were similarly moved.[49] Under the auspices of the Bar Kochba Association, Buber would return to Prague often. Emerging from his first three visits was his *Drei Reden über das Judenthum* (1911), which became the *vade mecum* of Jewish youth for more than a decade.[50]

In *Drei Reden* (and in other lectures he delivered to the Association) he elaborated in a systematic fashion on themes which he had adumbrated in his earlier volumes on Hasidism. In these works—*Die*

Geschichten des Rabbi Nachman (1906) and *Die Legende des Baal Schem* (1908)—he had evoked the mystical strain and spiritual nobility of the hitherto despised denizens of *Halb-Asien*. In Buber's gracefully written and elegantly presented books (he insisted that the lettering and jacket design be executed by the leading *Jugendstil* artists of the day)[51] the Hasid, for so long the emblem of the backward, uncouth *Ostjuden*, was no longer a source of embarrassment. Behind the strange exterior of Hasidism, Buber disclosed a remarkable spiritual universe of mystical profundity. He rendered Hasidism respectable, as it were, by integrating this most distinctive manifestation of East European Jewish spirituality into the general discourse and idiom of the New Romanticism (and later, of Expressionism). By virtue of Buber's inspired presentation, Hasidism—and the millenial Jewish mystical tradition from whence it emerged[52]—was deemed relevant to the concerns of the educated individual involved in the spiritual quest of the *fin-de-siècle*.

What made this transformation possible was, firstly, the favorable comparisons made between Hasidic sensibility and other mystical traditions honored by the New Romanticism. More significantly, Buber presented Hasidism in terms of its legends and myths—pre-Enlightenment "folk" wisdom which Eugen Diederichs, for instance, celebrated as capturing an intuitive and therefore genuine metaphysical experience of the world's primal unity.[53] On a more subtle level, Buber related Hasidism to the overarching problem of the New Romanticism, namely, that defined by Schopenhauer as the problem of individuation. Thus in *Die Legende des Baal Schem* he noted that Hasidic spirituality was dialectically upheld by two poles: *hitlahavut* (ecstasy) and *'avodah* (divine service)—"*Hitlahavut* embraces God beyond time and space, [whereas] *'avodah* is the service of God in time and space".[54] This dialectic of Hasidic spirituality, as Buber explained in the second of his speeches before the Bar Kochba Association, reflected the most fundamental experience of the Jew: his "striving for unity" *(Einheit)*.[55] It was this striving for unity—within the personal, the political and ontological spheres—Buber told his enthralled audience in Prague, "that makes Judaism a phenomenon of mankind, that transforms the Jewish question into a human question."[56]

In a later speech for the Association, entitled "The Spirit of the Orient and Judaism" (1912), he argued that this striving for unity was what distinguished the Jew—as all Orientals—from the European. The latter was fundamentally a sensory man *(ein sensorischer Mensch)*—his senses separated from the "undifferentiated base of organic life."[57] With the aid of Reason's *a priori* principles of time and space he assimilated "static," individuated, sense impressions *(Eindrücke);* as a consequence, sight, the most detached and objective of the senses, tended to predominate in the European's perception of the world. To the sensory man the world, perforce, appeared "as a multiplicity of things, which is spread before his eyes and to which he and his body belong".[58] In contrast (and here Buber developed a theme hitherto only adumbrated in his writings),[59] the Jew *qua* Oriental was *"ein motorischer Mensch"*: his senses—coequal and interrelated and all integrally connected "to the dark side of the organism"[60]—comprehended the world dynamically. Hence to the Jew, as the Oriental in general,

> [. . .] the world appears as a limitless motion, flowing. Though he perceives individual things, he does not perceive them as separate entities, each reposing and complete in itself, but only as an aggregate of nodal points for an infinite motion, which flows through him as well [. . .] He views the world, naturally and primarily, as something happening to him; he senses [*spürt*] rather than perceives [*wahrnimmt*] the world.[61]

The Jew's *Weltbild*, accordingly, was grounded in the totality of his being; all sense impressions gathered from the world diffused throughout his being and thereby linked up with "the undifferentiated base" of his organic life: he thus experienced the dynamic "inwardness" of the world in his own inwardness. Accordingly, the world

> [. . .] lies in repose within [the Jew] [. . .], primevally exempt from all multiplicity and all contrast, perceiving the womb giving birth to and devouring all multiplicity and contrast, the nameless essence and meaning. And just as he comprehends the motion through sensations [*Empfindung*], so are the essence and meaning of the world disclosed to him through his comprehension of the essence and meaning of his own life; the one is revealed through the other, and ultimately the two are one.[62]

In the spirit of Schopenhauer, Buber observed that this experience of the inner unity of the world was the source of the Oriental's incorrigible dissatisfaction with its external reality. The Oriental, and the Jew in particular, profoundly felt "that the full manifestation and disclosure of the world's inner substance is thwarted, that the primarily intended unity of the world is split and distorted."[63] This same experience of the world's inner unity also engendered the passionate, unyielding quest of the Oriental for unity.

In his speeches before the Zionist students of Prague he frequently compared the Chinese, Persian, Indian and Jewish conceptions of redemptive unity. The Indian idea of redemption, for instance, sought to "liberate" the soul from its entanglement in the world; the Indian thus spoke of the need for the "awakening." The Jew, on the other hand, celebrated his involvement in the world, and, accordingly, demanded not the soul's awakening, but its "transformation." For the Indian, redemption, Buber underscored, meant the negation of the world; for the Jew, redemption constituted the affirmation of the world. For the Jew, "the unified world—yet to be built—exists within man himself."[64] For in essence, "the world is not divided. Nor is man divided, he is rather separated; he has fallen, he has become inadequate and unlike God [*gottungleich*] . . . Subjective being is split [*gespalten*], but the external world is split only insofar as it is the symbol of subjective being."[65] Hence, Buber averred, the Jew understood the experience of unity as a demand for the redemption of the world, as a demand to create unity within the divisive world of multiplicity. This dialectic between the subjective experience of unity and a commitment to extend that experience to the objective realm—between what Hasidism referred to as *hitlahavut* and *'avodah*—characterized, according to Buber, the most fundamental sensibility of the Jew, and as such it constituted the abiding significance of Judaism for mankind.

> This, then, is the primal process within the Jew—the process manifested in their personal lives with all the forcefulness of their Asiatic genius by those great Jews in whom the most profound Judaism came alive: the unification of the soul. In those Jews the great idea of Asia became exemplary for the Occident—the Asia of boundlessness and of holy unity, the Asia of Lao-tse and of Buddha, which is the Asia of Moses and of the Isaiahs, of Jesus and of Paul.[66]

The deracinated Jew of the West might be estranged from the Law and Rabbinic learning, but he had not thereby necessarily vitiated his Judaism, for Judaism (and undoubtedly this must have been Buber's most intriguing message to his Prague audience) was ultimately not a matter of formal articles of faith and prescribed ritual practice, but rather of a specific spiritual sensibility. Indeed, Buber contraposed this sensibility, articulated in Israel's mystical tradition, to the "official" Judaism of the rabbis. The former, the truly "creative element" of Judaism, was forever persecuted by the rabbis, and as a result it had been forced to lead a largely "subterranean" existence. At critical moments of history, however, this authentic but submerged spirit of the Jew asserted itself publicly to renew Judaism, as with "the rise of the great religious movement of Hasidism, which gripped Polish Jewry in the eighteenth century and *revealed anew the limitless power of Oriental man.*"[67] To be sure, the creative spirit that animated Hasidism had been checked and eventually stultified by the custodians of "official Judaism," but the possibility for the renewal of the spirit continued to exist, hidden within the very depths of the Jew. Yes, Buber assuringly told the assimilated youth of Prague, the foundation for the renewal of Judaism, "is the Jew's own soul. For the Jew has remained an Oriental [*Denn der Jude ist Orientale geblieben*]."[68]

HASIDISM AS ORIENTAL MYTH: THE APOLOGETIC MOTIVE OF BUBER'S EARLY WRITINGS ON HASIDISM

ex Oriente lux

Buber's novel interpretation of Jewish spirituality enjoyed unique authority among Central European intellectuals, especially those attuned to the mystical inflections of the New Romanticism. Although only thirty when he addressed the Bar Kochba circle for the first time in 1909, Buber was already a renowned author and a central figure in the literary efforts of the New Romanticism. Significantly, his huge output—which at the time of his first Prague address numbered close to one hundred articles and several books—exhibited his distinctive weave of specific Jewish themes within the general purview of the New Romanticism. Thus, in addition to his volumes on Hasidism, by the eve of the First World War he had published editions of Chinese, Finnish, Celtic and Flemish mystical and mythical writings.[69] Each of these volumes was highly acclaimed.

The most successful of his writings from this period, however, was *Ekstatische Konfessionen,* published by Eugen Diederichs in 1909.[70] This exquisitely produced volume presented voices of mystical rapture from various Oriental and Occidental traditions: Indian, Persian, Chinese, Jewish, Gnostic, Eastern Christian, Medieval Catholic and Seventeenth-Century Protestant "ecstatic confessions."[71] These voices, as Buber related in his introduction, each give witness to the most vexing dilemma of the mystic: how to communicate an essentially ineffable experience. In ecstasy the mystic, propelled beyond the bounds of time and space, attains the blissful vision of the world's ultimate unity, but language, alas, is intrinsically wedded to the *principium individuationis,* and is thus an instrument of the world of multiplicity. Yet the mystic has an irresistable urge to proclaim his experience to the world; he feels compelled "to create for the traceless ecstasy a remembrance, he wishes to pull the timeless over into time. He wishes to render the unity without plurality into a unity of all plurality."[72] This is the dilemma of every great mystic, and seeking to give utterance to that which is beyond language, he perforce chooses myth. For, as Buber rhetorically put it, "is not the myth of the Vedas and the Upanishad or the myth proclaimed by the Midrash and the Kabbalah, by Plato and Jesus but a symbol [*Sinnbild*] of that which the ecstatic experiences?"[73]

Ekstatische Konfessionen, which sought to illuminate the inadequacy of ordinary, "rational" language to express "genuine" knowledge, became a central document of the New Romanticism.[74] The volume's impact on its contemporaries is witnessed by Robert Musil, whose epic novel, *Der Mann ohne Eigenschaften,* published in 1930 after a long gestation, contains more than three hundred citations from Buber's collection of mystical testimonies.[75]

Hence, as an honored member of the pantheon of New Romantic authors, Buber's writings on Hasidism were assured of a respectful consideration, and indeed they clearly served, inter alia, an apologetic motive. Upon publishing his first volume of Hasidic tales, Buber sent a copy to his friend Eugen Diederichs, and in the accompanying letter he recalled a conversation several years earlier when the publisher had doubted whether Judaism could provide the soil for mysticism.[76] Fully cognizant that Diederichs' doubts expressed a prevailing prejudice, Buber was exceedingly sensitive to the implied charge of Israel's spiritual impoverishment (a charge, of course, which had its roots in the classical Christian perception of Judaism as an anachronistic religion of law). Among his notes for the Prague lectures (preserved in his archive in Jerusalem) there are several folio sheets with citations in three parallel columns from Werner Sombart, Otto Weininger and Houston Stuart Chamberlain, each asserting that Judaism was utterly bereft of any competence for mysticism and religious mystery (and, by extension, to all "profound" emotions and sentiments).[77]

From the economic historian and sociologist, Sombart, Buber jotted down, for example, the following statement: "The Jewish religion knows no mystery." And: "The Jewish religion does not know the condition of ecstasy in which the believer is united with the Godhead."[78] Among the excerpts Buber made from the writings of Otto Weininger, a Viennese Jewish author whose contempt for Judaism surpassed that of most gentile anti-Semites, we read: "Among the Jews there is no genuine mysticism." And: "To be sure, there are no Jewish murderers, but surely there are also no Jewish saints [*Heiligen*]."[79] The political philosopher and unabashed racist, Chamberlain, who tended to lump the Jew and Arab together, is noted by Buber as observing that "for no human being is mysticism so inaccessible [as it is for the Arab]." And: "The Semite bans from religion all wonder and creative phantasy."[80]

Buber undoubtedly had such views in mind when declaring in the first paragraph of his inaugural work on Hasidism that Rabbi Nachman of Bratslav—"perhaps the last Jewish mystic"—"stands at the end of an unbroken tradition whose beginning we do not know. For a long time men sought to deny this tradition; today it can no longer be doubted."[81] Furthermore, Buber observed, this tradition "is one of the great manifestations of ecstatic wisdom." To be sure, Jewish mysticism, Kabbalah, bears the influence of other mystical traditions, but "the tendency toward mysticism is native to the Jews from antiquity. [Indeed], the strength of Jewish mysticism was drawn from an original characteristic of the people that produced it."[82] In his next work, *Die Legende des Baal Schem,* Buber sought to make a similar point when he asserted apodictically that "the Jews are perhaps the only people that has never ceased to produce myth [. . .], and [Hasidism] is the latest form of Jewish myth that we know."[83]

A similar apologetic motive is likewise discernible in Buber's attitude to the *Ostjuden* as the Jews who had produced Hasidism. After comparing the Hasidic conception of ecstasy to that of medieval German mysticism, he noted in his introduction to *Die Geschichten des Rabbi Nachman,* that it was Polish Jewry "that proved itself creative." Here "the Jew was [. . .] mostly a villager, limited in his knowledge, but original in faith and strong in his dream of God."[84] Polish Jewry may have been primitive and unsophisticated, but spiritually it was a most passionate and creative community. In *Die Legende des Baal Schem,* he again emphasized the East European origins of Hasidism: "[. . .] And suddenly, among the village Jews of Poland and Little Russia, there arose a movement in which myth purified and elevated itself—Hasidism. [. . .] And in the dark, despised East, among simple, unlearned villagers, the throne was prepared for the child of a thousand years," the Kabbalah.[85]

His early pronouncements on Hasidism constituted a veritable revolution in the consciousness of the Western Jew. The emancipated, acculturated Jews of the West, as Gershom Scholem observed, deliberately "excluded and repudiated" mysticism and myth from their understanding of Judaism.[86] And no one, Scholem noted, deserved "more credit for first causing these features of Judaism to come to view again than Buber, who did not approach them with the methods of science and historical research, sociology and psychology, but with all the passion of a heart overwhelmed by a new discovery."[87] A piquant but poignant insight into the resistance of the Western Jew to Buber's efforts to rehabilitate the image of Hasidism and to rescue from oblivion expressions of Jewish mystical piety is provided by a letter, dated 6 February 1908, to Buber from his father, Carl, a successful Austrian businessman:

Dear Martin,
    Please receive my most heartfelt wishes for your birthday: May your work bring you the success you desire and may your life be free of care and worry.

> I would be happy were you to give up this Hasidic and Zohar stuff, for they could only have a mentally debasing and pernicious effect. It is a pity to devote your talents to such a fruitless subject, and to waste so much time and effort [on something] so utterly useless for yourself and the world.[88]

The attitude of his grandfather, Solomon Buber, on the other hand, was more encouraging. This distinguished scholar of Midrash, who actually raised Buber in his home in Lemberg (Lvov), in Austrian Galicia, took an active interest in his grandson's work, and provided him with Hasidic writings unavailable in Berlin.[89] Just before his death, in December 1906, Solomon Buber received a copy of *Die Geschichten des Rabbi Nachman;* the dedication undoubtedly pleased him exceedingly: "To my grandfather, Solomon Buber, the last of the great scholars in the old-style Haskalah, I dedicate this work on Hasidism with respect and love." (*"Meinem Grossvater Salomon Buber dem letzten Meister der alten Haskala bringe ich dies Werk der Chassidut dar in Ehrfrucht und Liebe."*)[90]

In preparing his first studies on Hasidism, Buber also enjoyed the support of several East European scholars, particularly Michah Yosef Berdichevsky, Simon Dubnov and Shmuel Horodetzky,[91] who had already written treatises—in Hebrew, Yiddish and Russian—on various aspects of Hasidism and Kabbalah. In contrast to their interest in Hasidism, however, Buber's was neither historical nor philological. "My aim is not at all to collect new facts," he explained to Horodetzky in a letter dated July 1906, "but simply to provide a new understanding [*Auffassung*] of Jewish mysticism and its interconnections, to give a new synthetic presentation of [this tradition] and its creations, and to make these creations known to a European public in as artistically pure a form as possible."[92] He therefore decided not to translate these creations—the legends and symbolic fairy tales related by the Hasidic masters—but to "retell" them. Selecting various motifs from Hasidic stories, which in his judgment, captured the distinctive message of Hasidism, Buber would "relive" these motifs and the message they conveyed, retelling them as he experienced them. After having tried several times to render the Hasidic story directly into German, Buber related in his essay of 1918, "My Way to Hasidism,"

> I note that the purity [of the original Hasidic story] did not allow itself to be preserved in translation, much less enhanced—I had to tell the stories that I had taken into myself, as a true painter takes into himself the lines of the models and achieves the genuine images out of the memory formed of them. [. . .] And, therefore, although by far the largest part of [my early work on Hasidism] is autonomous fiction composed from the traditional motifs, I might honestly report of my experi-

ence of the legend: I bore in me the blood and the spirit of those who created it, and out of my blood and spirit it has become new.[93]

Buber was later to repudiate his early method of rendering Hasidic tales into German as too undisciplined and free. In an essay of 1957 he admitted that his youthful presentation of Hasidism was too beholden to the contemporary mood and thus tendentious:

> [. . .] I was still at that time, to be sure, an immature man; the so-called *Zeitgeist* still had power over me. To my readiness to make an adequate testimony to the great faith disclosed to me through books and men was joined something of the widespread tendency of that time to display the contents of foreign religions to readers who wavered between desire for information and sheer curiosity. Besides, I did not yet know how to hold in check my inner inclination to transform poetically the narrative material. I did not, to be sure, bring in any alien motifs; still I did not listen attentively enough to the crude and ungainly but living folk-tone which could be heard from this material. At work in me here, too, was a natural reaction against the attitude of most Jewish historians of the nineteenth century toward Hasidism, which they found nothing but wild superstition. The need, in the face of this misunderstanding, to point out the purity and loftiness of Hasidism led me to pay all too little attention to its popular vitality [. . . .] The representation of the Hasidic teaching that I gave in [my earliest works] was essentially faithful; but where I retold the legendary tradition, I still did so just as the Western author that I was.[94]

Buber's free re-working of "the legendary motifs" of Hasidism allowed him—as we now know from an examination of the notes and drafts of his earliest writings on Hasidism[95]—to employ as a "ghost-writer" his wife, Paula (an accomplished author who published highly acclaimed novels under the pseudonym of Georg Munk). Apparently pressed by a publisher's deadline,[96] he supplied his wife with "motifs" upon which she elaborated. Many of *Die Legende des Baal Schem* seem to be the work of her hand, perhaps also parts of *Die Geschichten des Rabbi Nachman*.[97] Paula, who remained Buber's closest intellectual partner until her death in 1958, undoubtedly played a decisive role in shaping the spiritual and ideational direction of his early thought. He met Paula, a Bavarian Catholic who was later to convert to Judaism, during the summer semester of 1899 at the University of Zurich, where Buber came to study German literature. At the time Paula had been a passionate disciple of Omar al Raschid Bey. Indeed, it was al Raschid Bey who sent Paula to Zurich in order to study Sanskrit and Indian religions.[98] Interestingly, until he met his wife, Buber displayed no inclination to mysticism or related subjects,[99] and it is thus reasonable to surmise that it was Paula who introduced him to the world of Oriental wisdom, mysticism and Schopenhauer (upon whose teachings al Raschid Bey based his worldview).[100] During the semester following his meeting and betrothal to Paula, he immersed himself in intense study of mysticism, soon publishing his first article on this subject with a meditation on the sixteenth century German mystic, Jakob Böhme.[101] In 1904 he was awarded a doctorate by the University of Vienna for a dissertation entitled, "Zur Geschichte des Individuationsproblems: Nicolaus von Cues und Jakob Boehme."[102]

It would be mistaken, however, to view Buber's early involvement in Hasidism and Jewish mysticism as purely aesthetic. His interest in these hitherto neglected aspects of Jewish spirituality was ultimately animated by a profound commitment to the Jewish people. The depth and nature of this commitment is mirrored in his wife's "philo-Zionism." When she first met Buber he was engaged in preparations for the Third Zionist Congress which was to take place in Basle in August 1899. Buber, who had joined the Zionist movement shortly after its founding congress, introduced Paula to Zionism and its aspirations. In an essay, "Confessions of a Philo-Zionist," which she published in September 1901 in *Die Welt,* the weekly of the World Zionist Organization, she recalled her response to Buber's speech before the Third Zionist Congress:

> A human mouth spoke to me with wonderful force. [. . .] And my heart stood still [. . .] And then it was again as if he spoke with iron tongues, and all the bells in the world rang out over me. It was no longer an individual man [. . .] the uncanny longing, wish, and will of a whole people came pouring forth. [. . .] It came over me like everything great in life and like life itself—came and carried me with it.[103]

A month following the publication of her "confessions," Paula wrote to Buber that she wanted to take an active role in the Zionist movement: "I have the feeling that I can, I must do something for it [. . .] I grow in your cause. It will be mine and that of our children."[104]

This cause was to secure the dignity of the Jewish people ravished by persecution, assimilation and self-doubt. Although the focus of his Zionist activity would be exclusively cultural, Buber was acutely aware of the suffering and degradation of East European Jewry. In a letter to his wife dated May 1900 he described how he, together with two Zionist colleagues, had gone to a Berlin train station to greet a group of Russian Jewish refugees en route to America. He poignantly described the "forlornness" *(Verlorenheit)* of these hapless, leaderless Jews who "were treated like animals by [the immigration] officials."[105] Appalled, he manifestly identified with their desperation and humiliation. Paula would echo her husband's affection and hopes for his people when she proclaimed:

> How I love you, people of affliction! How strong your heart is and how young it has remained! No, you shall not become another, you shall not go under in the confusion of alien peoples. [. . .] In being different lies all your beauty, all happiness and joy of earth. Remain your own! [. . .] How I love you, you people of all peoples, how I bless you![106]

The pride and identity of the Jew, Buber was convinced, would only be secured through cultural renewal, by which he meant the renewal of Judaism as a framework for a meaningful, creative life. The radical nature of this proposition, which Buber developed together with other "cultural Zionists," above all Ahad Ha'am,[107] lay in the emphasis on culture, as opposed to formal religious observance. With respect to West European Jewry, this renewal required, in the first instance, the re-education of the Jews: they had to be re-acquainted with the literary sources and wisdom of the Jewish heritage. Cultural renewal, Buber averred, also required a restructuring of the Jew's self-perception, especially as it was refracted through the image of the much maligned *Ostjude*. Although still in his early twenties, Buber quickly assumed a leading position among the German-speaking cultural Zionists. In 1902 he founded in Berlin, together with Berthold Feiwel and others, the *Jüdischer Verlag,* the publishing house of the "Jewish renaissance."

The first publication of the *Jüdischer Verlag,* which proved to be an immensely successful and dynamic venture, was the *Jüdische Almanach 5663,* issued in the autumn of 1902. This handsomely produced hardbound volume of some two hundred folio pages contained, inter alia, translations of Yiddish and Hebrew poems by M. Rosenfeld, H. N. Bialik, Sholem Aleichem, Y. L. Peretz, S. Frug, S. Asch and Avrom Reysen; this selection was preceded by an urbane essay on Yiddish literature ("Über Jargon und Jargonliteratur"). Of the sixty illustrations, two-thirds had East European themes, the most famous being a reproduction of Hermann Struck's "Polnischer Jude." This volume was soon followed by a collection of essays, edited by Buber, on Jewish artists. In his introduction to this work, *Jüdischer Kunstler* (1903), he spoke for the first time of Hasidism as a source of the spiritual vitality necessary for the Jewish renaissance; he also wrote in praise of the native Jewish music which "has been preserved in the synagogues of the Ghetto."[108]

In the following year (1904), he published (again with the *Jüdischer Verlag*) a German translation from the Yiddish[109] of *Eisik Scheftel,* "a

Jewish workers' drama in three acts," by Dovid Pinski.[110] He himself translated the hitherto unpublished play from a manuscript supplied by Pinski; and also wrote a foreword in which he hailed the Russian dramatist as an authentic voice of the "Jewish proletariat." In his plays and stories, Buber observed, Pinski sought "to convey nothing but the grim reality [of the Jewish working masses] as he sees and hears it. But in conveying this reality—unadulterated and in all its harshness—he discloses the meaning of this oppressed, enslaved existence. He reveals the prevalence of the most terrible misery." Buber also emphasized that Pinski's language was Yiddish—"the popular idiom *(Volkssprache)* of the Jewish masses." Yiddish, he pointed out, had been falsely regarded as a "jargon"—a crude patois—while in reality it has developed from a dialect into a sophisticated, highly nuanced language, albeit a language *sui generis*. To be sure, it was "not as rich" as Hebrew, but it was "suppler;" it "is not as abstract but is warmer than Hebrew;" it might lack the spiritual pathos of Hebrew, but "it is full of incomparably gentle and rough, tender and graded accents." In Yiddish "the Jewish people [*Volkstümliche*] itself becomes language."[111]

It was this resolute commitment to rehabilitating the image of the *Ostjude*—and concomitantly to securing the dignity of the Jew in general—which clearly provided the primary inspiration for Buber's earliest writings on Hasidism. In a letter of December 1906, he explicitly admitted that these writings had an apologetic motive. In this letter, written while he was still working on *Die Legende des Baal Shem,* he expressed the anguish aroused in him by the recent pogrom in Bialystok, and declared:

> I am now writing a story which is my answer to Bialystok. It is called: *Adonai* [God, i.e., the spiritual reality of the Jew]. [. . .] I am now in the midst of the first real work period of my life. You are my friend and will understand me: I have *a new answer* to give everything. Only now have I found the form for my answer[. . .] I cannot now say more about it, and certainly not about other matters. I have grown slowly into my heaven—my life begins. I experience ineffable suffering and ineffable grace.[112]

Buber viewed his discovery and presentation of Hasidism as a "call" *(Beruf)* to proclaim its spiritual message to the world.[113] In Hasidism, as he explained in his autobiographical essay of 1918, "My Way to Hasidism," he discovered "primal Jewish reality": man's being created in the image of God is to be grasped as a task, as a summons to hallow existence through every action and deed in the world. This reality, which obtained its depth because it was also "the primal human reality," Buber exuberantly affirmed, still lived in Hasidism. For despite its medieval exterior and the inevitable degeneration that had overtaken the movement, Hasidism continued to embody "the inner truth" of Judaism.[114] This spiritual reality "still embraces a large part of Eastern Jewry,"[115] and as he exclaimed in the introduction to *Die Legende des Baal Schem,* "no renewal of Judaism is possible that does not bear in itself the elements of Hasidism."[116]

BUBER'S HASIDIC WRITINGS: A *REZEPTIONSGESCHICHTE*

Buber's early Hasidic writings were accorded wide attention, and by 1914 perhaps some one hundred reviews of *Die Geschichten des Rabbi Nachman* (1906) and *Die Legende des Baal Schem* (1908) had appeared in the popular press and in learned journals.[117] An analysis of these reviews afford us a ready insight into the social and cultural significance of Buber's presentation of Hasidism and Jewish mystical piety. They indicate how Buber was read by his contemporaries, both Jewish and non-Jewish; they apprise us of what ideational and emotional associations he evoked in his readers, thereby resonating for us the contextual and historical connotations of Buber's writings.

Undoubtedly to his profound satisfaction, his Hasidic writings were often reviewed in conjunction with other works on mysticism and Oriental spirituality. In a review in the prestigious Berlin journal, *Das Literarische Echo* (15 February 1907), Ilse Frapan-Akonian discussed *Rabbi Nachman* together with another volume issued by Rütten & Leoning, *Der Pilger Kamanita, Ein Legendenroman* by Karl Gjellerup (the Danish novelist and future recipient of the Nobel prize for literature) who under the influence of Schopenhauer had turned to Buddhism. The reviewer enthusiastically entitled her piece "Ex oriente lux." *Das Literarischen Zentralblatt für Deutschland* (July 1907) included Buber's *Rabbi Nachman* in a long review of eight titles on mystical and Oriental themes which appeared in 1907.[118] Many other reviewers, even when considering Buber's volumes separately, treated them in the context of the current interest in mysticism. *Theosophisches Leben,* a popular journal among votaries of theosophy and the occult, in a review of July 1907 greeted Buber's *Rabbi Nachman* with unbounded excitement. Because it enriched our understanding of the ecstatic experience, the review exulted, "we theosophers especially should be delighted [with the book]."

In a review in the *Preussische Jahrbücher* (September 1907), Marie Fuhrmann found significant similarities between Rabbi Nachman's mystical piety and that of the medieval German mystics such as Johannes Tauler and Heinrich Suso. Another reviewer writing in *Der Kunstwart* of Munich (February 1907) insisted that Rabbi Nachman, although a denizen of eighteenth-century Europe, must be viewed as representing "ancient Oriental" wisdom: "His stories are clearly under the influence of the Oriental genre of fairy tales, such as exemplified in 'A Thousand and One Nights.' " The Jewish literary critic Friedrich Gundelfinger (later, Gundolf), in a review in the *Preussische Jahrbücher* of July 1908, noted the affinities between the teachings of the founder of Hasidism and the doctrines of the Persian Sufis and medieval German mystics. With a hint of Jewish pride, Gundelfinger, however, also recorded his disappointment that in rewriting the Baal Shem's legends Buber so "poeticized" them that the reader was deprived of the joy of "breathing [the unique] spiritual atmosphere of the *shtibl*," the simple prayer room so characteristic of East European Jewish religious life. Buber's legends are not specifically Hasidic, indeed they are hardly Jewish.[119]

Buber would not have denied that he had eliminated the specific Jewish diction and "atmosphere" of the East European *shtibl,* but he would have insisted that he did so in order to illumine the essence and universally significant aspect of Hasidism. Ethnographic fidelity might have indeed provided the Hasidic legends with a more authentic flavor, but such specificity no matter how charming would have entailed the danger of obfuscating the Hasidic message with a veil of parochiality, thus rendering it inaccessible to the educated West European public, Jewish and non-Jewish alike. This public read his Hasidic tales as testimonies of "a primal human reality," yet, much as Buber intended, they also recognized them as expressions of "a primally Jewish reality" preserved by East European Jewry.[120] Thus, many reviewers, Jewish and non-Jewish, saw Buber's writings as serving to correct the negative image of the Jew. An Austrian critic, apparently a non-Jew, reviewing *Rabbi Nachman* in the *Oesterreichische Rundschau* (Vienna, 1 June 1907), observed that "even for Schopenhauer, the most bitter opponent of Jewish-Protestant rationalism," Buber's book would have been a veritable "revelation" *(Enthüllung).* "He would have ceased to generalize so thoroughly his deep antipathy for [certain] Jews. [. . .] I too have never before come across a book that could convince the enemies of modern, half-enlightened, semi-assimilated Jewry of the deep [spiritual] forces that had stirred so powerfully in this people."

The Jewish press also did not fail to appreciate the apologetic value of Buber's Hasidica. Writing a review of *Rabbi Nachman* for the Berlin Weekly *General-Anzeiger für die gesamten Interessen des Judentums* (30 December 1906), Joseph Meisels—a devoted official of the

Jewish community of Berlin who in the twenties was to publish a three volume history of the Jews in Poland and Russia[121]—indignantly observed that due to

> its endlessly complex present and the intricate nuances of its traditional Jewish psyche, East European Jewry is for the European, and no less for the greater part of Western Jewry, an enigma. In the eyes of the educated European, Judaism has hitherto been the very incarnation of materialism, and at best the "Ghetto novels" have provided him with something of the poetry of Jewish family life.

In this respect, Meisels continued, Buber's book "with its aesthetic appreciation of the Jewish spirit [is] revolutionary." Until Buber's *Rabbi Nachman,* Meisels rhetorically asked, "What did Europe know about Hasidism? Nothing, almost nothing whatsoever, and hence the vilest prejudices have sought to reduce the entire movement to an exclusive religious fanaticism." But Buber had demonstrated that "mysticism was the life source of Judaism."

While noting the immense value of Buber's Hasidic writings in correcting the educated European's misconceptions of Judaism, the Jewish press tended to stress the significance of Buber's volumes for Jewry itself, particularly for Western Jews estranged from Judaism and their East European brethren. Writing in the Spring 1907 edition of the semi-annual bulletin of the *Gesellschaft für Jüdische Volkskunde,* the anthropologist and folklorist Samuel Weissenberg averred that "these tales lay bare for uninitiated [Jews] the otherwise misunderstood and misconceived soul of the Jewish people [*die jüdische Volksseele*]." The anonymous writer of a review in the *Populär-Wissenschaftliche Monatsblätter* (April 1907), sponsored by the Mendelssohn-Verein of Frankfurt am Main, described Buber's volume as "a wonderful document of a deep mystical piety from the very womb of our people [. . .] and this [phenomenon] happens to be manifest in the 'dark' East, among the so-called Hasidim who seem to represent for us all that is unlovely, fanatic and superstitious."

To be sure, not all of the Jewish reviewers were inspired by Buber's Hasidic tales. The historian Ludwig Geiger, on 15 February 1907, writing in the *Allgemeine Zeitung des Judentums,* the organ of extreme assimilation which he edited, condemned *Rabbi Nachman* for "leading us into a cultural realm which appears to us not as light but as a deep darkness." In a review of *Die Legendes des Baal Schem* which appeared in the *Literarisches Centralblatt für Deutschland* in March 1910, a critic, S. Kraus, took pains to distance himself as a Jew from the world presented by "M. Buber, a Galician [Jew]": "Most Europeans—and not only Christians but also those of the Jewish faith—will upon reading this book feel themselves thrust into an alien world. Indeed, what is portrayed here is something so extremely peculiar that one might say it is non-European [aussereuropäisches]."

Again, whereas most of the Jewish reviewers, especially those writing in the Jewish press eagerly extended the positive image of Hasidism presented by Buber to all of East European Jewry, there were those who emphasized Buber's distinction between the Hasidism of the founding masters and the movement's contemporary decadence—a decadence, which they intimated, was characteristic of all of East European Jewry.[122] There were, of course, also non-Jewish reviewers who begrudged the Jewish people the mystical sensibilities Buber ascribed to the early Hasidic masters. The highly regarded literary critic—and one of Buber's first mentors in mysticism[123]—Julius Hart did not hesitate to voice the opinion that Rabbi Nachman was an atypical, exceptional spiritual personality among the Jews. Reviewing *Die Geschichten des Rabbi Nachman* in the Berlin daily *Der Tag* (27 January 1907), Hart referred warmly to Rabbi Nachman as "a good-natured character" who evoked "a storm of sympathy," and warmly praised his mystical appreciation of nature "which otherwise is not too strongly developed in the Jewish race."

Another critic, the novelist Frieda Freiin von Bülow, insisted that while Buber may have demonstrated the existence of Jewish fairy tales, these tales are, despite Buber's admirable efforts to spruce them up, clearly inferior examples of the genre. In her review, which appeared in the *Tägliche Rundschau* of Berlin (3 August 1907) and which was devoted to both Lofcadio Hearn, *Izumo. Blicke in das unbekannte Japan* (Rütten & Leoning, 1907) and Buber's *Rabbi Nachman,* she noted that whereas both these works offered a unique insight into "the spiritual world of those remarkable Asian peoples," the latter volume had the added value that its editor, Buber, was "speaking about his own people." Yet, despite Buber's subtle evocation of the authentic atmosphere and despite his superior German style, she found Rabbi Nachman's tales to be spiritually unedifying and aesthetically unpleasant. "Hence, one must conclude that although he was the one and only Jewish story teller [*Märchenerzähler*], Rabbi Nachman did not possess poetic, creative power." A more invidious argument was voiced by an anonymous reviewer in the *Neue Metaphysische Rundschau* (1908, no. 2/3), who suggested that the Jewish reception of the Baal Shem Tov was yet another example of how the Jews had rejected a noble teacher: "If I am not very much mistaken, this new volume of Hasidica will find more Christian adherents [*Freunde*] than it will among the Jews themselves. Speaking through the Baal Shem is a great, holy wisdom, an ancient theosophical teaching whose protective vessel was to be Judaism . . . [But] the wisdom of this teaching has been adopted by other peoples, and the Jewish people continues to err as it has since the time of the patriarchs."

Such scornful reviews, which were clearly inspired by an anti-Semitic animus, were few. Most reviews were to one degree or another sympathetic, although, it should be emphasized, such favorable responses to Buber's Hasidic tales did not necessarily entail a reevaluation of the reviewer's attitude toward Judaism and Jews. The response was often confined to the aesthetic and philosophical value of the tales. Their impact, of course, went far beyond the reviews and made itself felt, for example, in the literary activity of Buber's generation. The poet Rainer Marie Rilke was so inspired by *Die Legende des Baal Schem* that he drew upon its very stylistic and thematic elements in giving shape to his "Ninth Duino Elegy."[124] However, neither in this poetic meditation nor in Rilke's personal life is there to be found any trace of the specific Jewish content of *Die Legende*. Another instructive example of the purely aesthetic impact of Buber's Hasidic tale was Kafka who patterned at least one of his stories—"A Country Doctor"— on a tale he read in *Die Legendes des Baal Schem*.[125] Again, the influence here was strictly literary, and the specifically Jewish elements in Buber's tale were eliminated.[126] On the other hand, Kafka seems to have been drawn to Buber's Hasidic writings as a Jew. In a letter to Max Brod, he noted that "Hasidic stories—I cannot think why—are the only Jewish genre in which I invariably and immediately feel at home, irrespective of my mood: my reaction to other Jewish works is almost entirely fortuitous."[127]

Buber's Hasidica seems to have held a specific attraction for Jews estranged from Judaism. They tended to view the Baal Shem and Rabbi Nachman, as portrayed by Buber, as adumbrating an alternative Jewish identity. They found Buber's image of Judaism as essentially a spiritual sensibility compelling—no doubt, because this sensibility had little to do not only with bourgeois rationalism and materialism, but also with traditional Jewish law and religious practice. Buber's Hasidica allowed them an *aesthetic* affirmation of Judaism. The nature and limitations of such an affirmation of Judaism as sensibility may be illustrated by four avid readers of Buber's early Hasidic writings: Walther Rathenau, Georg Lukács, Ernst Bloch and Gustav Landauer.

Rathenau was so inspired by Buber's Hasidic writings—in which he undoubtedly found affinities to his own mystical conceptions[128]—that he resolved to study Hebrew:[129] a dramatic decision, to be sure, for one who had earlier written the essay, "Höre, Israel," with its remorseless vilification of Jewry. Through his study of Hebrew, Rathenau hoped to gain a more informed understanding of classical, and if one may interpolate, pre-bourgeois Judaism. He pursued his study of Judaism and traditional Jewish sources rather seriously for a number of years, but gradually ceased.[130] Apparently, his interest in Jewish literature, which was not accompanied by any involvement in Jewish communal life, was overwhelmed by his unabated interest in other literary matters and spiritual traditions, especially the teachings of the Oriental sages Lao-tse and Buddha, and the writings of the medieval German mystics, Meister Eckhart and Jakob Boehme. His engagement in Jewish spiritual tradition, particularly as represented by Hasidism, proved episodic; and although it did affect his own Jewish identity, he did not permit this interest to lead him beyond the bounds of the purely aesthetic and intellectual—certainly it did not lead to an expression of Jewish solidarity.[131] Indeed, Rathenau consistently preferred to think of himself, paradoxically, as a German and cosmopolitan.

Georg Lukács, who was later to become one of the central figures in the post-World War One intellectual revival of Marxism, also discovered Jewishness through Buber's Hasidic tales. His close friend the poet Béla Balázs recorded in his diary in 1914: "Gyuri [Georg] has discovered the Jew in himself. The Hasidic sect. The Baal Shem."[132] At the time of his discovery of Buber's Hasidic writings, namely the summer of 1911, Lukács was a political radical, highly disdainful of bourgeois civilization, but he had yet to embrace Marxism. Intellectually, his interests were those of the New Romanticism and the emerging school of Expressionism. His first book, *Die Seele und die Formen* (1911) testified to his intimate knowledge of mysticism, especially Oriental, and also indicated his sympathy for the religious anguish of Kierkegaard. Upon reading *Rabbi Nachman* and *Die Legende des Baal-Schem,* he exuberantly wrote to Buber, with whom he had already corresponded, expressing his "sincere thanks" for these books which "due to various accidents I have not read until this summer."

> [. . .] The *Baal Schem* was for me, particularly unforgettable! It is only a pity that it is so small; it is hardly possible, after all, that this is all that remains. Is there any sort of (German, French or English) edition [which is more complete]? Or will you yourself, my dear Sir, decide all the same to prepare a larger edition? I imagine that here as with the Indian texts there is no possibility of making a complete edition? There is so much—for example, the ethical orientation of the transmigration of the soul—that one would be glad to learn about within the whole extent of the tradition.[133]

In his reply Buber explained that the original sources of the Hasidic tale, being as they were fragmented and often confused, did not permit the type of comprehensive edition that Lukács had in mind. The modern reader, Buber continued, perforce would have to suffice with a "retelling" of the characteristic "motifs" of the Hasidic tale.[134] Nonetheless, Lukács retained his enthusiasm:

> Essentially my [only] wish is a wish for—more. If, as appears to be the case, it is impossible to make a [comprehensive] edition of Hasidic mysticism, similar for example to Deussen's Indian texts,[135] then we for whom these books [*Die Geschichten des Rabbi Nachman* and *Die Legende des Baal Schem*] have been a great experience, wish at least to possess everything obtainable and editable.[136]

In the same letter Lukács indicated that he wrote a review of Buber's two Hasidic books for the Hungarian philosophical journal *A Szellem;*[137] he also indicated that he will hold Buber to his promise to read with him original Hasidic texts.

But Hasidic mystical piety captured Lukács' imagination at a time when he was equally, perhaps even more strongly drawn to the writings and art of medieval Catholicism and Russian Orthodox Christianity. And as evidenced by his correspondence with Buber, he still had an abiding interest in Indian mysticism. Clearly Lukács' interest in Hasidism, which lasted several years, merged easily into the eclectic spiritual universe that he together with so many intellectuals of his generation were so earnestly and studiously exploring. If his affirmation of Judaism à la Buber's *Baal Schem* had any enduring significance for him, it was perhaps revealed by the same diary entry in which Balázs noted his friend's newly discovered interest in Hasidism and "the Jew in himself." This interest, Balázs associated with Gyuri's great new philosophy: "Messianism [or] a homogeneous world as the goal of redemption."[139] Like many radical Jews, one may surmise, Lukács found in the liberal conception of Judaism as essentially a universal messianism a sort of spiritual imprimatur for his social idealism.[140] Buber, incidentally, while eloquently celebrating the universal significance of Israel's messianic vision, as a Zionist insisted—for instance, in his *Drei Reden* (1911) and his famous debate with Hermann Cohn of 1916, writings undoubtedly known to Lukács—that this vision need not entail the self-abnegation of the Jewish people.[141] For all his intense reading of Buber, Lukács seems to have studiously ignored this dimension of Buber's writings. He remained firmly committed to a cosmopolitan messianism, a commitment which eventually found expression in his conviction that communism provides the optimal political strategy for the realization of the *eschaton*.[142]

His friend Ernst Bloch, who was to develop a dialectical ontology of hope and place messianism at the center of the Marxist imagination,[143] also for a time identified with Buber's Baal Shem. In a letter to Lukács, dated May 1915, he notes having been struck once again by Jakobe Solomon, the Jewish heroine in *Hans in Glück*,[144] a novel by the Danish author Henrik Pontoppidan: "[...] I believe I must write [an essay about Jakobe] such that while she is speaking about Hans [her non-Jewish fiancé, whose intense religious urgings she utterly failed to appreciate] with someone of our generation—one who knows the Baal Shem, you and me—she suddenly understands him." Perhaps then, Bloch wistfully suggests, the Jew will no longer be a symbol of religious indifference, of one who has not aptitude for "dreams and transcendence."[145]

Bloch had earlier in 1912/13, written a draft of this contemplated essay: "Symbol: Die Juden."[146] He dedicated this version of nineteen printed pages, published only in 1964,[147] to Else von Stritzky, his first wife. She was a Baltic countess who was raised with a profound admiration and affection for the Jewish people, especially the traditional Jews of her native Latvia.[148] This essay depicted—as a converse symbol to that represented by the Jewess Jakobe—the Jew who knows the spontaniety of religious emotion, especially as exemplified by Hasidism. Resisting the legal formalism of the synagogue, this Jew is "open to the call of the Messiah and the sanctification of God's Name through motoric [i.e., political and social] moral and metaphysical [deeds]."[149] This very conception of Judaism as essentially a spiritual sensibility distinct from the rigid religious formalism of official, "ecclesiastical" Judaism, clearly reflected Buber's influence. Indeed, although Bloch made no explicit reference to Buber, the language and substance of his essay were manifestly indebted to both Buber's Hasidic writings and his *Drei Reden*.

For Bloch, too, the authentic Jewish spirit, which in his letter to Lukács he identified with the Baal Shem, was an emphatically anti-bourgeois principle, and as such it evoked the pride of all those Jews disaffected with the bourgeois ethos. Thus Bloch opened his essay with the exhilirating pronouncement: "The pride of being Jewish has been reawakened [*Neu erwacht der Stolz, jüdisch zu sein*]"[150] Bloch related this dramatic reversal of what seemed to be the ineluctable cadences of assimilation and the flight from Judaism to the anti-bourgeois revolt of the younger generation. "At least it appears that the marked commercial and at the same time formalistic tendency [of Jewry] no longer finds any grounds among the younger Jews."[151] Accordingly, Jewish youth are casting off the attitudes and values accrued through the emancipation and the attendant embourgeoisement of Jewry—a process which had resulted in Jewry's "loss of humility and faith."[152] Indeed, "Shulamit and David with his harp are far from [the emancipated, bourgeois Jews]; in their more or less successful assimilation, these bumptious, energetic Jews evidence no trace of *pride* in belonging to this mysterious race [*der geheimnissvollen Rasse*] and in the *obligation* resulting therefrom."[153] Western Jews, Bloch further observed, were, of course, more severely afflicted by the "free-thinking poison" (*freisinniger Gift*) than the Jews of Poland and Russia.[154]

Bloch, however, refused to glorify the *Ostjuden*—for one had to admit, he insisted, that assimilation had also eliminated "much that is false and typical of the Ghetto, and which still clings to the *Ostjuden* and which is completely un-Jewish and [in essence] also modern."[155] Bloch was apparently referring to what he later in the essay called the "fossilized," "ugly" religious practices, and importunate "haggling spirit" (*Schachergeist*)[156]—"lamentable" features of traditional Jewish life which had disfigured the primal Jewish spirit. Despite this negative evaluation of the Diaspora, Bloch roundly rejected Zionism and its aspiration for a nation-state, an "ephemeral" nineteenth-century ideal—for it amounted to a denial of Israel's election.[157] This election, as Bloch explained in somewhat arcane language, resulted from the primal "Jewish feeling about the world" (*jüdisches Weltgefühl*) which charged the Jews with a "motoric-messianic" responsibility for the destiny of the world.

The term "motoric-messianic" was adapted from Buber who had coined the first word of this compound term to designate Judaism's constitutive intuition and experience of the world's metaphysical unity. This intuition, in contrast to the mystic's typically contemplative posture, produced the intense ("motoric") striving to realize unity at the personal level and in history, preparing the ground for the messianic or "absolute" future.[158] Buber had introduced the term "motoric" in his very first statement on Hasidism,[159] but only elaborated it in his Prague lecture of 1911, "The Spirit of the Orient and Judaism," in which "motoric" spirituality is the focal theme:

> The Oriental begins with the inwardness of the world, which he experiences as his own inwardness. [. . .] He perceives [this inwardness] as lying in repose within himself, invulnerable and invariable, primevally exempt from all multiplicity and all contrast, the nameless essence and meaning. [. . .] But—and this is where all great Asiatic religions and ideologies meet—the unified world must not only be conceived, it must be realized. It is not merely given to man, it is given to him as a task; he is charged with making the true world an actual world. Here the motor character of the Oriental is evidenced in its highest sublimation: as the pathos of command. . . . [And] the supreme sublimation of the Oriental's motor character, the pathos of a divine command, attained its greatest intensity in Judaism.[160]

In the same essay Buber spoke of Hasidism as

> revealing anew the limitless power of Oriental man. [. . .] We need only look at the decadent yet still wondrous Hasid of our own days; to watch him as he prays to his God, shaken by his fervor [. . .]; to observe him at the close of the Sabbath as he partakes with kingly gestures and in concentrated dedication, of the sacred meal to which cling the mysteries of the world's redemption, and we will feel; here, stunted and distorted yet unmistakable, in Asiatic strength and Asiatic inwardness.[161]

These thoughts manifestly intrigued and inspired Bloch, as witnessed by his essay "Symbol: Die Juden."

However, this essay, written when he was twenty-eight, would be the only statement in Bloch's long and prolific literary career in which he expressly spoke as a Jew and in which he addressed Judaism *per se*.[162] Nonetheless, unlike Lukács, he retained even after his adoption of Marxism an interest in Judaism, or rather in those selected strands of Judaism which became for him a key to understanding the eschatological dimension he deemed inherent in all religious faiths and ultimately in all expressions—myth, legend, song—that register the hopeful fantasies of mankind. For him the Jewish eschatological imagination illuminated the essential nature of human hope, namely, that hope—grounded not in the idle desires of an individual but in the genuine social and historical anguish of humankind—which points not only to a better tomorrow but also to the era of "absolute time."[163] As such, Judaism became for Bloch a universal principle, a principle bereft of a specific community. His youthful expression of Jewish pride, inspired by Buber's Baal Shem, did not involve solidarity with his fellow Jews; indeed, when he spoke of "obligation" in "Symbol: Die Juden," it was only to "the primal Jewish sensibility" *(Weltgefühl)*, not to the community of Israel.

In contradistinction to Bloch, the left-wing anarchist Gustav Landauer—who was similarly inspired by Buber's Hasidic tales proudly to affirm Judaism as universally significant—had a refined appreciation of Jewish solidarity. Indeed, in striking contrast to many Jewish socialists of his day, Landauer "found room in his heart for Jewish suffering."[164] In November 1913, he devoted an entire issue of *Der Sozialist,* a bimonthly anarchist newspaper which he founded and edited, to the problem of anti-Semitism. Landauer himself contributed an article "On the Beilis Trial." In this impassioned defense of the aggrieved Mendel Beilis—who "like so many [Jews] before him is tormented without cause"[165]—he chided his fellow socialists as well as bourgeois liberals for permitting ignorance, and hence bigotry to reign with regard to the Jews and Judaism. This ignorance, he complains, is malicious "for one does not know and does not want to know anything about the real life of the Jews, and their customs and practices."[166] Why, for instance, he asked, should Yiddish—"which just like Swiss German has preserved the full splendor of middle high German"—be so derisively dismissed as "Jargon or Kike-talk [*Mauscheln*]?"

> There are dictionaries and scholarly essays about the language of the gypsies, shoppers, criminals—all of which have been written [. . .], not by [them] [. . .] but by scholars. Had not the Jews themselves begun to study their own language and to assemble their folksongs, this area of scholarship would still today be as unknown as the spaces left white on maps.[168]

In a similar vein, Landauer indicted educated Western opinion for having consciously ignored the religious life of the Jew—and he explicitly meant the life of the "authentic" Jewish communities of Eastern Europe: "I am talking specifically about those Jewish communities which are accused [. . .] of baking the blood of murdered Christian children with Passover bread and then eating it!"[169] In conclusion, Landauer told his comrades it was their duty to acknowledge Judaism as part of the universal human culture and "to study the Jews' inner world, and to know their reality."[170] A commitment to attaining such knowledge, Landauer insisted, must be the presupposition of progressive humanity's condemnation of the odious canard of "ritual murder."

Landauer was equally severe in his criticism of assimilated Western Jews who assumed a superior, contemptuous attitude towards East European Jewry. In an article, "Ostjuden und Deutsches Reich," which he contributed to a symposium organized by Buber in 1916 on the increasingly urgent problems produced by the influx of Polish Jews into Germany, Landauer lamented what he perceived as a tendency of German Jews to shun the hapless refugees from the East.[171] What particularly distressed him was the call of some German Jews to close the borders of the Reich to the refugees on the grounds that the unprecedented presence of "unenlightened" *Ostjuden* was aggravating anti-Semitism in Germany. Besides being arrant nonsense, he suggested, this charge betrayed a profound lack of compassion and solidarity. Moreover, he added, the assimilated Jews of Germany had much to learn from their East European brethren—the reality and vitality of life as a *Volk*. And only as a *Volk* (and the Jews as Buber and others had shown were undeniably a *Volk* with their own distinctive "poetry, music and dance")[172] could the Jews *qua* Jews make a genuine contribution to humanity.

Accordingly, Landauer had genuine sympathy for Zionism. As he told a Berlin group of Socialist-Zionists in February 1913, he understood and respected their vision of a national and cultural "renaissance" of the Jewish people in their ancestral homeland.[173] He himself, however, felt that Jewish socialists could best serve Israel's "mission" by resisting the urge to participate in the reconstitution of the Jews as a separate nation, and by remaining in *Galut* (Exile)—bearing with dignity the scourge of dispersion, loneliness and rejection while incessantly prodding the rest of humanity to realize the prophetic vision of justice and brotherhood.[174] Landauer's solidarity with Jewish suffering, then, was confined to the realm of humanitarian, moral concern; he consciously chose not to draw any ideological or personal conclusions from his expressed identification with Jewish anguish. Furthermore, he also chose not to relate his commiseration with his more unfortunate Jewish brethren to his affirmation of Judaism as "a community of sensibility" *(eine Gleichheit des Seelensituation).*[175]

Landauer's primary *political* and *moral* community would remain the workers, whose most passionate advocate he was ever since his student days in the late 1880's. Until the publication of Buber's tales he had remained utterly indifferent to Judaism, which seems to have been associated for him with the despised bourgeois order. The significance of these tales of Landauer's Jewish identity is revealed in a handwritten fragment, possibly a draft of the review of *Die Legende des Baal Schem* that he published in 1910.[176] In this recently discovered handwritten note Landauer is much more personal than in his published statement:

> Several words of appreciation to Martin Buber, who has followed his *Die Legende des Baal-Schem* with *Die Geschichten des Rabbi Nachman*.—When I was a young student I underwent a profound experience in which I—detached and rootless, that is, what one usually calls a radical—found in the spiritual hunger of the proletariat a new cultural milieu [*Kulturelement*]. A cultural milieu which to me had hitherto been totally unknown, indeed something alien—but something that bore the germ of a new people [*Volkstum*] with whom my longings at least, if not my nature craved to merge. At the time, as I fled from the artificial, cold and heartless world of the bourgeois to that of the workers as if they were my people, I had no inkling that in my mature years I would be about to find something like a homeland [*Heimat*] and a primordial people [*uraltes Volk*].

Landauer then added the following passage which he later deleted:

> If I now say that this has come to pass and that it is precisely through the mediation of Martin Buber that I have found Judaism, I must caution all who do not know the world of Jewish spirit to which Buber brings us, not to conjure up a formal religion [*Konfession*] and ritual practices.[177]

In Buber's Hasidic tales, as he wrote in his published review of *Die Legende des Baal-Schem,* Landauer discovered Judaism to be an "inalienable" spiritual sensibility which he shared with his fellow Jews and which was independent of formal belief and affiliation.[178] He also learned from Buber that often those Jews who were most faithful to this sensibility were aligned with an unofficial, indeed heretical tradition—a tradition Landauer associated with such figures as Jesus and Spinoza.

But his newly discovered Jewish identification, prompted by Buber's Hasidic tales, Landauer insisted, was but one of the multiplicity of identities and sensibilities that constituted his mental and spiritual universe. "I have never felt the need," he wrote in a volume sponsored by the Bar Kochba Association of Prague, "to simplify myself or to create an artificial unity by way of denial; I accept my complexity and hope to become an even more multifarious unity than I am now aware of."[179] Accordingly he deeply resented the Zionist demand that the Jew deliberately estrange himself from Europe. In a stinging letter to Siegfried Lehmann (a Zionist educator who during the World War founded a *Volksheim* in Berlin for immigrant Jewish youth from Eastern Europe) he bitterly deplored the cultural seclusion promoted by Zionism. In this letter, dated 30 November 1915, Landauer—who actually participated in the establishment of the *Volksheim* and eventually spoke at its dedication in 1916—sharply criticized both what he perceived as Lehmann's "Western" paternalism towards the East European youth and his Zionist bias that Jewish authenticity and renewal required that the Jew give primacy and even exclusive attention to his Jewish identity: "An inner estrangement from Germany is not in my program; and the *West-East Divan* of the German and European Goethe is incomparably closer to me than any falsifying 'either/or' which a Zionist calls upon me to make between being a German and a Jew, a European and an Oriental."[180]

With Landauer we apparently reach the limits of an aesthetic affirmation of Judaism. Through Buber's writings, especially his Hasidic tales, he recognized himself as an Oriental, as a Jew and bearer of a unique and "inalienable" spiritual sensibility. But as a sensibility—which he limited largely to the realm of an inner, subjective perception—Landauer's "Judaism" blended with the multiple modes of reflection and appreciation that constituted his rich inner world. Culturally, Judaism had for Landauer few objective or material expressions; the cultural renaissance—"the rebirth of the Hebrew language and poetry"—envisioned by the Zionists certainly did not inspire him.[181] Landauer seems to have conceived of Judaism as an almost purely aesthetic category, apparently mediated by the contingency of birth and enshrined in the private sphere of sensibility, through which the Jew *qua* individual obtained a unique "inner experience" of the world.[182] For him, Judaism was thus neither a mode of symbolic discourse shared by Jews nor a specific mode of behavior, certainly not obligatory behavior as would be required by an ideological or religious conception of Judaism. Hence, his public expression of Judaism (apart from the few essays and addresses in which he set forth his conception of Judaism),[183] was confined to humanitarian support for his more unfortunate brethren.

Yet the limited nature of this expression of solidarity with his fellow Jews should not prompt us to minimize the significance of what we have referred to as an aesthetic affirmation of Judaism. The very same knowledge of the vitality of the Jewish *Volksseele* to which Buber introduced Landauer and which inspired him to affirm Judaism as a sensibility, also permitted him to behold the differentiated reality of Jewish life and to realize that not all Jews are votaries of the bourgeois ethos with its crass materialism and narrow rationalism. This realization enabled him to take compassionate cognizance of the precarious existence of the Jewish masses, especially in Eastern Europe and to include them within the purview of his moral concern.[184] Although disappointed by Landauer's ultimate rejection of Zionism, this was undoubtedly the dialectic—from aesthetic affirmation to solidarity—that Zionist apologists such as Buber had in mind when they sought to rehabilitate the image of the Jew as an Oriental.

Notes

1. See Theodor Lessing, *Einmal und nie Wieder. Lebenserrinerungen* (Prague, 1935) pp. 291–96. In the late 1890's al Raschid established a "colony" in the village of Kalusen in south Tirol.

2. The available information on al Raschid Bey is most exiguous. According to Lessing he was born in Germany, but raised in Russia. *Ibid.*, p. 291. In his study of al Raschid Bey's wife, the novelist Helene Böhlau, Friedrich Zillmann is only able to add that she married her husband in Constantinople in 1886. *Helen Böhlau. Ein Beitrag zu ihrer Würdignung* (Leipzig, 1918) p. 18. On my behalf Dr. Ulrich Linse of Munich examined the police registration and nationalization records at the *Stadtarchiv München*. Unfortunately the registration file of Friedrich Arndt (Omar al Raschid Bey) is missing; we only know that he was registered as a Turkish citizen, and, despite his conversion to Islam, a member of the *"mosaische Religion."* His and Helene's son, Omar Hermann Ottokar al Raschid Bey, who was born in Munich in 1895, was interestingly also registered as a Turkish citizen of *"mosaische Religion."* I wish to thank Dr. Linse for his generous assistance.

3. See Omar al Raschid Bey, *Das hohe Ziel der Erkenntnis. Âranâda Upanishad*, ed. Helene Böhlau al Raschid Bey (Munich, 1912).

4. See George L. Mosse, *The Crisis of German Ideology. Intellectual Origins of the Third Reich* (New York, 1964) pp. 54–61; also see Roy Pascal, *From Naturalism to Expressionism. German Literature and Society. 1880–1918* (London, 1973) pp. 161–97; Hans Dieter Zimmerman, introduction, *Rationalität und Mystik* (Frankfurt a/M, 1981) pp. 1–33. Although an interest in mysticism and the occult became intellectually fashionable in *fin-de-siècle* Germany, a "discreet" fascination with these subjects was evidenced already since the late 1700's, and indeed captured the imagination of such *Aufklärer* as Herder, Goethe, Schiller and even Kant. See Antoine Faivre, *Eckartshausen et la Théosophie Chrétienne* (Paris, 1969). I wish to thank my colleague Dr. Moshe Idel for bringing to my attention this monumental study of the theosophical writings of Karl von Eckartshaus (1752–1803) and the enormous influence they exercised on intellectuals from Russia to France.

This interest in the occult and mysticism was not exclusively focused on the Orient, however. *Fin-de-siècle* intellectuals also "rediscovered" the medieval Christian experience—that is, a mystical tradition unadulterated by the "rationalism" of the moderns—as well as pre-Christian myths and legends of Europe, Cf. my introduction to *Ekstatische Konfessionen, gesammelt von Martin Buber* (Heidelberg, 1984) pp. i–xxii; and George Mosse, op.cit., pp. 31–87.

5. There were, of course, those who argued the very opposite, and insisted that the "arid" bourgeois civilization was the product of the Orient, namely of the Jews and their "desert" mentality. See, for instance, Werner Sombart, *The Jews and Modern Capitalism* (1911), trans. M. Epstein (New York, 1962) pp. 299–323; also see Adolf Wahrmund, *Das Gesetz des Nomadenthums und die heutige Judenschaft* (Berlin, 1887).

6. See Edward Said, *Orientalism* (New York, 1978) pp. 57–75. In European discourse the term Orient was used to designate the Asiatic East as a whole including the Near East; indeed, as Said points out, "until the early nineteenth century it meant only India and the Bible lands." *Ibid.*, p. 4.

7. Nietzsche, *The Will to Power*, trans. W. Kaufmann (New York, 1967) p. 3.

8. The pervasiveness of this Cassandran mood in German culture is fully documented in Georg Steinhausen's encyclopaedic study, *Deutsche Geistes und Kulturgeschichte von 1870 bis zur Gegenwart* (Halle, 1931).

9. Cf. Nietzsche, *Schopenhauer als Erzieher* (Leipzig, 1874). On Nietzsche's role in promoting the popularity of Schopenhauer, see R.J. Hollingdale, *Nietzsche. The Man and His Philosophy* (London, 1965) p. 87f.

10. Schopenhauer, *The World as Will and Representation*, trans. E. F. J. Payne (New York, 1958) par. 23, p. 113.

11. *Ibid.*, par. 18, pp. 99–103.

12. *Ibid.*, par. 19, pp. 104ff.

13. *Ibid.*, par. 22, pp. 109–10.

14. *Ibid.*, par. 23, p. 113.

15. *Ibid.*, par. 66, p. 370.

16. *Ibid.*, par. 51, p. 253.

17. Pascal, *From Naturalism*, p. 194.

18. *Ibid.* p. 195.

19. Nietzsche, *Gesammelte Werke*, edition Musarion (Munich, 1928), XIV, 22.

20. Cf. "Almost all the writers of [*fin-de-siècle* Germany] show at least sporadically a lively interest in occultism." Pascal, *From Naturalism*, p. 175. Also see, Peter Wust, *Die Aufstehung der Metaphysik* (Leipzig, 1920), and Zimmermann, *Rationalität und Mystik*, pp. 1–33. The cult of the Orient also had an impact on Jewish circles beyond Germany. In Warsaw of 1910's the Yiddish writer Y.L. Peretz, for instance, belonged to a circle around the person of the artist Krako, a fervent Zionist who dressed in Oriental attire, kept a live goat painted in gold, and bedecked his garret with Oriental carpets and draperies. Y. Trinek, *Poyln, zikhroynes un bilder* (New York, 1949) vol. 5, chapter on Peretz. On the influence of Orientalism on early Hebrew literature and later Hebrew theater, see the forthcoming paper by Freddie Rokem, "The Habima Theatre and the Biblical Play."

21. See Bruno Walter, *Gustav Mahler*, trans. James Galtston, with a biographical essay by Ernst Krenek (New York, 1941) pp. 128ff; also Allan Janik and Stephen Toulmin, *Wittgenstein's Vienna* (New York, 1973) p. 109f.

22. This volume was published by Insel Verlag in 1907.

23. Carl E. Schorske, *Fin de Siècle Vienna. Politics and Culture* (New York, 1981) p. 228.

24. First published in Munich in 1911. Part A of the essay is reprinted in Zimmermann, *Rationalität und Mystik*, pp. 96–113.

25. See Gary D. Stark, *Entrepreneurs of Ideology. Neo-Conservative Publishers in Germany, 1890–1933* (Chapel Hill, 1981). On the significance of the Kurt Wolff Verlag for the Expressionist movement, see the succinct but insightful discussion in John Willett, *Expressionism* (London, 1970) pp. 95–96.

26. Cited in George Mosse, *The Crisis of German Ideology*, p. 54. Many of the interests cultivated by the New Romanticism, especially appertaining to mysticism and myth, "spill over" into the Expressionist movement which began to crystalize in the years immediately preceding the outbreak of the First World War. Thus in this paper when we speak of New Romanticism we are also referring to early Expressionism. On mysticism and the Expressionist movement, see Willett, *Expressionism*, p. 13f.

27. Cited in Stark, *Entrepreneurs of Ideology*, p. 75.

28. *Wider die Juden* (Berlin, 1803) p. 36.

29. Separatabdruck aus 44. und 45. Bande der *Preussiche Jahrbücher* (15 December 1879) p. 18.

30. *Ibid.*, p. 9.

31. See Wilhelm Marr, *Der Sieg des Judenthums über das Germanenthum vom nicht confessionellen Standpunkt ausbetrachtet* (Bern, 1879). For a discussion of this pamphlet and translation of some key passages, see P. Mendes-Flohr and J. Reinharz, *The Jew in the Modern World* (New York, 1980) pp. 271–73.

32. Said, *Orientalism*, pp. 1–3.

33. *Ibid.*, p. 4.

34. *Ibid.*, p. 56. Despite his wide and sensitive reading of the pertinent literature, Said tends to overlook the tendency to regard the Jew as an Oriental. He also ignores the positive image of the Orient that emerged from the *fin-de-siècle* fascination with the Orient.

35. Karl Löwith, *Meaning in History* (Chicago, 1949) p. 56.

36. E. Gans, "Halbjähriger Bericht im Verein für Cultur und Wissenschaft der Juden (28 April 1822)," in S. Rubaschoff, "Erstlinge der Entjudung. Drei Reden von Eduard Gans im 'Kulturverein,'" *Der jüdische Wille* II (1919) pp. 109–15.

37. Walter Hartenau [pseud.], "Höre Israel!" *Zukunft* 18 (16 March 1897), p. 460. Translated in Mendes-Flohr and Reinharz, *Jew in the Modern World*, p. 232.

38. Treitschke, *Ein Wort*, p. 9.

39. Franzos first used the term in his collection of tales of East European life, in which sketches of the Jewish "ghetto" figure most prominently, *Aus Halb-Asien. Kulturbilder aus Galizien, der Bukowina, Südrussland und Rumänien* (Stuggart/Berlin, 1876), 2 vols. He used the term "Halb-Asien" often in his writings, applying it rather indiscriminately to all those lands which lie "nicht bloss geographisch, sondern auch in ihrem Kulturleben zwischen dem gebildeten Europa und dem barbarischen Asien." Franzos, *Von Don zur Donau* (Stuttgart/Berlin, 1878) 2 Band, p. 193.

40. The term "Halb-Asien" was "to become a familiar word throughout Europe, connoting that area of Eastern Europe which was a bit Oriental and barbaric, as to be considered partially Asiatic by Western Europeans." Mary L. Martin, *Karl Emil Franzos. His Views on Jewry as Reflected in His Writings on the Ghetto*. Ph.D. thesis, The University of Wisconsin (1968) p. 114. On the significance of Franzos' writings in shaping the popular image of the *Ostjuden*, see Martin, *ibid;* Marian Wynxynski-Roshwald, *The Stetl in the Works of Karl Emil Franzos, Shalom Aleichem and Shmuel Yosef Agnon*. Ph.D. thesis, University of Minnesota (1972); also see Sander Gilman's brief but provocative discussion, "The Rediscovery of Eastern Jews: German Jews in the East, 1890–1918," in D. Bronsen (ed.), *Jews and Germans from 1860–1933: The Problematic Symbiosis* (Heidelberg, 1979) pp. 338–42.

41. H. Kohn, "Geleitwort," *Vom Judentum. Ein Sammelbuch*. Herausgegeben vom Verein Jüdischer Hochschuler Bar Kochba in Prag. (Leipzig, 1913) p. VI. It is of interest to note that this volume was published by Kurt Wolff, who was one of the leading patrons of the Expressionist movement. In fact, many of the participants—e.g., Max Brod, Margerete Susman—in the volume were associated with Expressionism, and indeed were published by Kurt Wolff.

42. Kafka met with Steiner, then visiting Prague, in March 1911. See Ronald Hayman, *Kafka. A Biography* (New York, 1982), p. 93.

43. This "romance" began when a Yiddish theater troupe visited Prague in October 1911. See Hayman, *Kafka*, pp. 108–20.

44. See Kafka's famous criticism of his father's "respectable" but spiritually desiccated Judaism. "Letter to His Father" (November 1919), in Kafka, *Dearest Father: Stories and Other Writings*, trans. E. Kaiser and E. Wilkins (New York, 1954), pp. 171–76.

45. See Hans Tramer, "Die Dreivölkerstadt Prag," in *Robert Weltsch zum 70. Geburtstag von seinen Freunden* (ed.), H. Tramer and K. Loewenstein (Tel Aviv, 1961), p. 159f. Buber first spoke before the Bar Kochba Association in 1903, when he delivered a lecture on "Jewish Renaissance."

46. L. Hermann to Buber, letter dated 14 November 1908, in Buber, *Briefwechsel aus sieben Jahrzehnten*, Grete Schaeder (ed.), (Heidelberg, 1972), I, 268–69. On the circumstances of this correspondence, see Leo Hermann, "Erinnerungen an Bubers 'Drei Reden' in Prag." *Mitteilungsblatt der Hitachduth Olej Germania* (Tel Aviv) No. 48 (26 November 1971), pp. 4–5.

47. The lecture was revised and published in *Drei Reden* under the title "Das Judentum und die Juden." Cf. Buber's note to this lecture in the *Martin Buber Archive*, The Jewish National and University Library, Ms. varia 350, Mappe 22.

48. Tramer, "Dreivölkerstadt," p. 168.
49. See Hermann, "Erinnerungen"; also see Hans Kohn, *Martin Buber. Sein Werk und seine Zeit. ein Beitrag zur Geistesgeschichte Mitteleuropas 1880–1930*, 2. ed. (Cologne: Joseph Melzer Verlag, 1961) pp. 89ff, 314f; and Maurice Friedman, *Martin Buber's Life and Work*, pp. 125–147. "The Prague Bar Kochba became Buber's community, and from it emerged some of Buber's most influential disciples and lasting friends, men such as Hugo Bergmann, Max Brod, Robert and Felix Weltsch, and Hans Kohn." *Ibid.*, p. 125.
50. "[Buber's *Drei Reden*] exuded a considerable magic in their time. I would be unable to mention any other book about Judaism in these years, which even came close to having such an effect—not among the men of learning, who scarcely read these speeches, but among a youth that here heard the summons to a new departure[. . .]" G. Scholem, "Martin Buber's Conception of Judaism," in Scholem, *On Jews and Judaism in Crisis. Selected Essays*. trans. W. J. Dannhauser (New York, 1976) p. 138.
51. On the importance Buber attached to the aesthetics of publishing, and in particular his relationship to *Jugendstil*, see my *Von der Mystik zum Dialog. Martin Bubers geistige Entwicklung bis hin zu 'Ich und du'* (Königstein/Ts., 1978) pp. 111–12.
52. "Buber was," as Scholem observes, "the first Jewish thinker [in modern times] who saw in mysticism a basic feature and continuously operating tendency of Judaism." Scholem, "Buber's Conception of Judaism," p. 145.
53. See Mosse, *Crisis of German Ideology*, pp. 52 ff.
54. Buber, *The Legend of the Baal-Shem*, trans. M. Friedman (London, 1978) p. 23.
55. "Judaism and Mankind," In Buber, *On Judaism* (ed.), N. N. Glatzer (New York, 1967) p. 25.
56. *Ibid.*
57. "The Spirit of the Orient and Judaism," in *On Judaism*, p. 58; "Der Geist des Orients und das Judentum," in Buber, *Vom Geist des Judentums. Reden und Geleitworte* (Leipzig, Verlag Kurt Wolff, 1916) p. 59.
58. "The Spirit of the Orient and Judaism," p. 59.
59. See, e.g., Buber's introduction to *Jüdischer Kunstler* (Berlin, 1903). Therein he observes that "der Jude des Altertums [ist] mehr Ohrenmensch als Augenmensch und mehr Zeitmensch als Raummensch [. . .]" p. 1. In this very same essay he also makes his first published reference to Hasidism: "Der Chassidismus ist Geburt des neuen Judentums," p. 5.
60. "The Spirit of the Orient and Judaism," p. 58.
61. *Ibid.;* "Der Geist des Orients und das Judentum," p. 15.
62. "The Spirit of the Orient and Judaism," p. 60; "Der Geist des Orients und das Judentum," p. 16.
63. "The Spirit of the Orient and Judaism," p. 64.
65. "Judaism and Mankind," p. 26.
66. *Ibid;* p. 29.
67. "The Spirit of the Orient and Judaism," p. 75.
68. *Ibid.;* "Der Geist des Orients und das Judentum," p. 18.
69. *Reden und Gleichnisse des Tschauung-Tse* (Insel Verlag, 1910); *Chinesische Geister - und Lebensgeschichte* (Insel Verlag, 1911); *Kalewala. Das nationalepos der Finnen* (Verlag G. Müller, 1914); *Die vier Zweige des Mabinogi. Ein keltisches Sagenbuch* (Insel Verlag, 1914).
70. On the popularity of this volume, see Zimmermann, *Rationalität und Mystik*, pp. 25 ff.; also see my introduction to the recent edition of *Ekstatische*

Konfessionen (Heidelberg, 1983). Buber was also the editor of the immensely successful forty volume series of "social-psychological" monographs *Die Gesellschaft* which appeared between 1906 and 1912.

71. Buber originally conceived of the volume as focusing exclusively on European mysticism with separate sections devoted to German, Slavic and Jewish mysticism respectively. Cf. Buber to Gustav Landauer, letter dated 10 February 1903, in Buber, *Briefwechsel,* I, 186. In the published version, the Jewish mystical tradition is represented by several short pieces from Buber's *Rabbi Nachman.*

72. "Ekstase und Bekenntnis" (Geleitwort), *Ekstatische Konfessionen,* p. XXV.

73. *Ibid.*

74. See Zimmermann, *Rationalität und Mystik,* pp. 25 ff. Incidentally, this presumed ontological limitation of speech remained one of Buber's central convictions. "[. . .] the language of things touches only the lips of real life." *I and Thou,* trans. W. Kaufmann (New York, 1970) p. 69.

75. See Dietmar Goltschnigg, *Mystische Tradition im Roman Robert Musils. Martin Bubers 'Ekstatische Konfessionen' im 'Mann ohne Eigenschaften.'* (Heidelberg, 1974).

76. "Sie werden sich vielleicht erinnern, dass wir einmal—vor mehreren Jahren—über die Frage der Exsitenz einer jüdischen Mystik miteinander gesprochen haben. Sie wollten nicht recht daran glauben. Mit dem Nachman-Buche habe ich eine Serie von Dokumenten dieser Existenz eröffnt? [. . .]" Buber to Diederichs, letter dated 21 January 1907, Buber, *Briefwechsel,* I, 253 f. Diederichs' attitude toward Judaism is discussed in Mosse, *Crisis of German Ideology,* p. 57 f.

77. *Martin Buber Archive,* varia 350, Mappe heh 22.

78. Buber lists these citations without giving their source, but he does note the pagination, thus enabling us to trace the source. Hence the Sombert quote is from *Die Juden und das Wirtschaftsleben* (Munich/Leipzig, 1911) p. 237.

79. *Geschlecht und Charakter* (Vienna, 1903) pp. 467 f, 421.

80. For this citation Buber provides neither the source nor the pagination. We may surmise, however, that it is from Chamberlain's *magnum opus, Die Grundlagen des neunzehnten Jahrhunderts* (Munich, 1901).

81. Buber, *The Tales of Rabbi Nachman,* trans. M. Friedman (Bloomington, 1956) p. 3.

82. *Ibid.,* p. 4.

83. *The Legend of the Baal-Shem,* trans. M. Friedman (London, 1978), pp. xi, xiii.

84. *The Tales of Rabbi Nachman,* p. 11.

85. *The Legend of the Baal-Shem,* p. xxi.

86. Scholem, "Martin Buber's Conception of Judaism," p. 142.

87. *Ibid.*

88. Buber, *Briefwechsel,* I, 260 f.

89. See, e.g., Salomon Buber to Martin Buber, letter dated 26 November 1906, Buber, *Briefwechsel,* I, 248.

90. After his grandfather's death, Buber changed the dedication to read: "Dem Gedächtnis meines Grossvaters Salomon Buber des letzten Meisters der alten Haskala bringe ich in treuen dies Werk der Chassidut dar."

91. Buber consulted with each of these scholars, whose assistance he acknowledged in the preface of the first edition of *Die Geschichten des Rabbi*

Nachman. See also the relevant correspondence in Buber, *Briefwechsel,* Vol. 1.
  92. Buber, *Briefwechsel,* I, 244.
  93. "My Way to Hasidism," Buber, *Hasidism and Modern Man,* ed. and trans. by M. Friedman (New York, 1958) pp. 61–63. Hans Kohn suggests that the principles governing Buber's rendition of Hasidic tales may have been inspired by his friend, Gustav Landauer's first modern German translation of Meister Eckhart's mystical writings, *Meister Eckharts Mystische Schriften* (Berlin, 1903). See Kohn, *Martin Buber,* p. 30. Cf. Landauer's explanation of his Eckhart translation, cited in *ibid.,* p. 293. Both Landauer's and Buber's concept of translation as an act of empathic retelling seems to be influenced by the doctrines of Wilhelm Dilthey. See Mendes-Flohr, *Von der Mystik zum Dialog,* Ch. 1.
  94. *Hasidism and Modern Man,* p. 22.
  95. See G. Schaeder, "Einleitung," Buber, *Briefwechsel,* I, 34 f.
  96. See M. Buber to Paul Buber-Winkler, letter dated 1 December 1906, *Briefwechsel,* I, 249 f; also cf. *ibid.,* pp. 250–252.
  97. See C. Schaeder, "Einleitung," p. 34 f.
  98. Lessing, *Einmal und nie Wieder,* pp. 293–295.
  99. In Buber's first years of study through the end of the summer semester 1899 in Zurich, "er hat [. . .] Philosophie, Kunstgeschichte, Literaturgeschichte, Psychiatrie, Germanistik, klassische Philologie und Nationalökonomie gehört. In diesem reichen Programm fehlen alle religösen oder auf den Orient bezüglichen Kollegia." Kohn, *Martin Buber,* p. 23.
  100. Lessing, *Einmal und nie Wieder,* p. 291.
  101. "Über Jakob Boehme," *Wiener Rundschau,* v/12 (15 June 1901) 251–53. "Wir stehen heute Boehme näher als der Lehre Feuerbachs, dem Gefühle des heiligen Franciscus von Assisi, der Bäume, Vögel und Sterne seine Geschwister nannte und noch nähr dem Vedanta." *Ibid.,* p. 252.
  102. *Martin Buber Archive,* Ms. varia 350, Mappe 2/a.
  103. Paula Winkler, "Betrachtungen einer Philozionistin," *Die Welt,* Nr. 36 (6 September 1901); reprinted in *München ehrt Martin Buber,* (ed.) Hans Lamm (Munich, 1961) p. 16.
  104. Paula Buber-Winkler to Buber, letter dated 19 October 1901, *Briefwechsel,* I, 169.
  105. M. Buber to Paula Buber-Winkler, letter dated 14 May 1900, *Briefwechsel,* I, 155 f.
  106. Paula Winkler, "Betrachtungen einer Philozionistin," p. 19.
  107. Buber was instrumental in the founding of the Democractic Fraction, an organized group which appeared in the 5th Zionist Congress (1901). Consisting of about 37 delegates the Fraction sought to promote a greater measure of democracy in the movement and greater attention to cultural activity.
  108. *Jüdischer Kunstler,* p. 5.
  109. Buber was raised by his paternal grandparents in Lvov (Lemberg), then capital of Austrian Galicia. Although he spoke Polish and German at home, he presumably learned Yiddish from his daily contacts with the Yiddish speaking Jews of Lvov. Buber's son, Rafael, informs me that his father would avail himself of every opportunity to speak Yiddish. "He would especially like to meet with Agnon, to converse in Yiddish and tell one another *mayselech* [stories]."
  110. *Eisik Schafter. Ein jüdisches Arbeiterdrama in Drei Akten von David*

Pinski, Autorisierte Übertragung aus dem jüdischen Manuskript von Martin Buber (Berlin, 1903). Buber himself apparently initiated this project and solicited the manuscript from Pinski. Cf. his correspondence with Pinski, *Martin Buber Archive*, Ms. varia 350, Mappe 585, chet 1. Earlier he had translated a short story by Pinski: "Das Erwachen. Eine Skizze," *Jüdischer Almanach*, 5633 (Berlin, 1902) pp. 209–215.

111. *Ibid.*, pp. 1–2. In contradistinction to his later rendering of Hasidic tales, Buber sought to be as true as possible to Pinski's original text. "[Ich habe] mich bemüht, die Redewendungen und Stazordnungen des Originals getreu widerzugeben und so wenig als möglich das Jüdische zu 'verdeutschen' [. . .] Hier redet das Volk selbst; und seine Worte in hochdeutsche Syntaxis transponieren, hiesse dem Wesen dessen, was es sagt, Gewalt antun [. . .]" *Ibid.*, p. 2 f. Parenthetically, at the time Buber was engaged in the *Jüdische Verlag*, he was also one of the principal sponsors of *Ost und West,* a non-party monthly founded in Berlin in 1901 to promote "Jewish solidarity" and reconciliation between East and West European Jewries. Cf. editorial, *Ost und West. Illustrierte Monatsschrift für Modernes Judentum*, No. 1 (January, 1901) p. 3.

112. Cited in Kohn, *Martin Buber*, p. 310. Kohn fails to give the addressee of this letter. It is not included in Buber's published *Briefwechsel*. Given his use of the familiar form of second person singular *((Du)*, which he rarely used at the time, the recipient of the letter may have been Hans Lindau, his closest friend in those years. I have been unable, however, to trace the letter in the Buber archive.

113. "Mein Weg zum Chassidismus," Buber, *Schriften zum Chassidismus* (Heidelberg, 1963), *Werke*, Vol. 3., p. 968.

114. "My Way to Hasidism," *Hasidism and Modern Man*, p. 59.

115. *Ibid.*, p. 48.

116. *The Legend of the Baal-Shem*, p. xii f.

117. Most of the reviews considered here are based on clippings that Buber himself collected and which were later arranged by Ms. Margot Cohen, director of the Martin Buber Archive. I wish to express my gratitude to Ms. Cohen for assistance. From a somewhat different perspective than that assumed in this essay, many of these reviews are discussed by Steven E. Aschheim, *Brothers and Strangers. The East European Jew in German and German Jewish Consciousness. 1800–1923* (Madison, 1982) pp. 128–34.

118. Buber's *Rabbi Nachman* was reviewed by Ernst Hlandy together with the following titles all published in 1907; Hans Nehls, *Der Weg zur Sonne. Geschichte und Märchen;* Karl Schulz, *Der Prophet;* Karl Gjellerup, *Der Pilger Kamanita. Ein Legendenroman;* Arthur Schnitzler, *Dämmerseelen;* Th. Lindemann, *Holunder. Ein romantishce Erzahlung;* Bruno Koch, *Klaus Ohm und andere Erzählungen;* Hans Lons, *Mein braunes Buch.*

119. *Preussiche Jahrbücher,* Nr. 1 (July 1908) pp. 149–51.

120. "My Way to Hasidism," p. 59.

121. *Geschichte der Juden in Polen und Russland* (Berlin, 1921–25), 3 vols.

122. Cf. "Hätte Israel ben Eliezer würdigere Apostel gefunden, so wäre des Chassidismus nicht zu einer entarteten Sekte samtischer Dunkelmänner herabgesunken, sonder wäre bis heute der Träger der schöpferischen Glut der jüdischen Volksseele geblieben." Alfred Nossig, "Messianismus und Kabbalistik," *Berlin Lokal-Anzeiger*, 28 June 1908 p. 151. Although more guarded, Buber also expressed such ambivalence toward contemporary Hasidism: "Im Chassidismus siegt für eine Weile das unterirdische Judentum über das

offizielle. [. . .] Für eine Weile nur. Es gibt in unseren Tagen noch Hunderttausende von Chassidim; der Chassidismus ist verdorben. Aber die chassidische Schriften haben uns seine Lehre und seine Legende übergehen." *Die Legende des Baal-Schem*, pp. v–vi. The English translation deletes all but the last two sentences of this passage. On Buber's ambivalence to contemporary *Ostjuden*, see the insightful observations in Gilman, "The Rediscovery of Eastern Jews," pp. 345–49.

123. Buber's relation to Julius Hart and his brother Heinrich is discussed at length in my *Von der Mystik zum Dialog*, pp. 42–54; also see Paul Mendes-Flohr and Bernard Susser, "Alte und Neue Gemeinschaft. An Unpublished Buber Manuscript." *Association for Jewish Studies Review* (1976), I, 41–49.

124. Benjamin Joseph Morse, "Rainer Maria Rilke and Martin Buber," in Irmgard Bück and Georg Kurt Schauer (eds.), *Alles Legenige meinet den Menschen. Gedenkbuch für Max Niehans* (Bern, 1972), pp. 102–128.

125. Hayman, *Kafka*, p. 216f. Kafka, however, was even more impressed by Buber's edition of *Chinesische Geister-und Lebensgeschichte* (1911). See Kafka, *I Am a Memory Come Alive*, (ed.) N.N. Glatzer (New York, 1974), p. 73.

126. With respect to "A Country Doctor," Kafka drew upon several of Buber's Hasidic tales, eliminating not only the specific Jewish reference but also reversing the spiritual message of the tales. See Hayman, *Kakfa*, p. 216f.

127. Cited in Kafka, *I Am a Memory Come Alive*, p. 160.

128. Rathenau's biographer, Harry Graf Kessler, reports that he read Buber's *Rabbi Nachman* in 1906 and that "er fand dort die Antwort auf die Frage nach dem 'Wozu' des Lebens, genau die, die er als Ergebnis jener inneren Einkehr aus Greichland mitbrachte: dass zweckfreie Eingehen der Seele in Gott, das seine volkommenste Erfüllung in der Ekstase erreicht." Kessler, *Walter Rathenau. Sein Leben und sein Werk* (Berlin, 1928) p. 89f. Cf. Buber's letter to Kessler, dated 16 January 1928, in which he recalled his friendship with Rathenau and their many discussions about Hasidism. Buber, *Briefwechsel*, II, 300.

129. *Ibid.*

130. Kessler, *Walther Rathenau*, p. 90.

131. See Robert A. Pois, "Walther Rathenau's Jewish Quandary," *Leo Baeck Institute Year Book* XIII (1968), pp. 120–31.

132. Bela Balàzs, "Notes from a Diary (1911–21)," *The New Hungarian Quarterly* XIII, no. 47 (Autumn 1972) p. 124. Cited in Palema Vermes, "The Buber-Lukàcs Correspondence." *Leo Baeck Institute Year Book* XXVII (1982) p. 371.

133. Lukács to Buber, letter dated November 1911, in Georg Lukács, *Briefwechsel. 1902–1917*, E. Karadi and E. Fekete (eds.) (Budapest, 1982), p. 258.

134. Buber to Lukács, letter dated 3 December 1911, in *ibid.*, p. 260.

135. Paul Jakob Deussen, *Die Sutras und die Vedanta* (1887), *Sechzig Upanishads der Veda* (1897), *Die Geheimlehre der Veda* (1907).

136. Lukács to Buber, letter dated 20 December 1911, in Lukács, *Briefwechsel*, 264f.

137. This short review in Hungarian appeared under the title "Jewish Mysticism" in the inaugural issue of *A Szellem* (1911).

138. See Andrew Araton and Paul Brines, *The Young Lukács* (London, 1979) pp. 3–13.

139. Balázs, "Notes from a Diary," p. 124.

140. This argument was made famous by Eduard Bernstein in his pamphlet, *Die Aufgabe der Juden im Weltkrieg* (Berlin, 1917).

141. Extensive excerpts of the Buber-Cohen debate are presented in Mendes-Flohr and Reinharz, *The Jew in the Modern World,* pp. 448–53.

142. See his seminal discussion of Marxism as "a practical epistemology of the future," "Moses Hess and the Problem of Idealist Dialectics," in Lukács, *Political Writings. 1919–1929* (London, 1972), pp. 181–223.

143. Cf. my " 'To Brush History Against the Grain.' The Eschatology of the Frankfurt School and Ernst Bloch," *Journal of the American Academy of Religion* (forthcoming).

144. This eight volume novel, *Lykke-Per* in the original Danish, was published in Copenhagen from 1898 to 1904. A German translation appeared in 1906.

145. Bloch to Lukàcs, letter dated May 1915, in Lukács, *Briefwechsel,* p. 346.

146. In his aforementioned letter to Lukács, Bloch makes elliptical reference to an earlier, in his judgment, unsatisfactory attempt to confront Jakobe with religiously sensitive Jews. Because of its discussion of Jakobe, we surmise that the essay "Symbol: Die Juden" is the earlier version Bloch was referring to. He apparently never managed to write the essay he outlined to Lukács.

147. In E. Bloch, *Durch die Wuste. Frühe kritische Aufsätze* (Frankfurt a/M., 1964) pp. 122–140.

148. Geertruda M. van Asperen, *Hope and History. A Critical Inquiry into the Philosophy of Ernst Bloch* (unpublished doctoral dissertation, University of Utrecht, 1973), p. 18. Also see Karola Bloch, *Aus meinem Leben* (Pfullingan, 1981), p. 51.

149. "Symbol: Die Juden," p. 138.

150. *Ibid.,* p. 122.

151. *Ibid.*

152. *Ibid.,* p. 122 f.

153. *Ibid.,* p. 123.

154. *Ibid.*

155. *Ibid.*

156. *Ibid.,* pp. 123, 137.

157. *Ibid.,* p. 123 f.

158. Buber, "Renewal of Judaism" (third lecture of *Drei Reden*), in Buber, *On Judaism,* p. 51.

159. *Jüdische Kunstler,* p. 1.

160. "The Spirit of the Orient and Judaism," in Buber, *On Judaism,* pp. 60f, 66.

161. *Ibid.,* pp. 75–76.

162. Disregarding or unaware of Bloch's early but episodic essay on Judaism, the historian and life-long colleague of Bloch, Hans Mayer observed, "the Jew Ernst Bloch never finds Jewishness of significance or cause for reflection." H. Mayer, *Outsiders. A Study in Life and Letters,* trans. Denis M. Sweet (Cambridge, Mass., 1982), p. 2. On Bloch's attitude toward Judaism, also see G. Scholem, "Wohnt Gott im Herzen eines Atheisten? Zu Ernst Bloch 90. Geburtstag." *Der Spiegel* (7 Juli 1975), pp. 110–14.

163. "Symbol: Die Juden," p. 140. Cf. note 158 above, where Buber speaks of "the absolute future."

164. Cf. Rosa Luxemburg, "No Room in My Heart for Jewish Suffering," in Mendes-Flohr and Reinharz, *The Jew in the Modern World*, p. 225.
165. "Zum Belis-Prozess," in G. Landauer, *Zwang und Befreiung. Eine Auswahl aus seinem Werk*, introd. and ed. by Heinz-Joachim Heydorn (Cologne, 1968), p. 207.
166. *Ibid.*, p. 202 f.
167. *Ibid.*, p. 202.
168. *Ibid.*
169. *Ibid.*, p. 204 f.
170. *Ibid.*, p. 207.
171. "Ostjuden und Deutsches Reich," *Der Jude*, I/6 (September 1916), 433–39. Due to technical reasons, the article was actually published separately from the other contributions to the symposium included in *Der Jude*, I/1 (April 1916).
172. "Zur Poesie der Juden," *Die Freistatt: Alljüdische Revue*, I (1913–14), pp. 321–24. Cited in Eugene Lunn, *Prophet of Community. The Romantic Socialism of Gustav Landauer* (Berkeley, 1973), p. 269.
173. "Judentum und Sozialismus" (lecture to the *Zionistische Ortsgruppe West Berlin*, 12 February 1912), *Die Arbeit*. Organ der Zionistischen Volkssozialistischen Partei (June 1920). Cited in Ruth Link-Salinger (Hyman), *Gustav Landauer. Philosopher of Utopia* (Indianapolis, 1977), p. 74 f.
174. *Ibid.*
175. G. Landauer, Review of Buber, *Die Legende des Baal-Schem*, in *Das Literarische Echo* (1 October 1910), p. 148.
176. *Ibid.*
177. I found this handwritten fragment among Buber's collection of reviews of his *Die Legende des Baal-Schem*. Martin Buber Archive. Ms. Varia 350, Mappe yud-gimmel 49. I wish to thank Ms. Margot Cohen for her assistance in deciphering Landauer's script.
178. Landauer, Review of *Die Legende des Baal-Schem*, pp. 148–49.
179. Landauer, "Sind das Ketzergedanken?" in *Vom Judentum*, pp. 250–57; excerpts trans. in Mendes-Flohr and Reinharz, *The Jew in the Modern World*, p. 241.
180. "Brief an Dr. Siegfried Lehmann" (30 November 1915), *Der junge Jude*, II (November 1929), pp. 114–115. On the Volksheim, see S. Lehmann, "Idee der jüdischen Siedlung und des Volksheims" (lecture given in September 1916), in Jehuda Reinharz (ed.) *Dokumente zur Geschichte des Deutschen Zionismus. 1882–1933* (Tübingen, 1981), pp. 183–85. Also see the excellent discussion in Aschheim, *Brothers and Strangers*, pp. 194–97.
181. "Judentum und Sozialismus," cited in Link-Salinger (Hyman), *Gustav Landauer*, p. 74.
182. Cf. "Sind das Ketzergedanken?"
183. For a thorough inventory of Landauer's essays on Jewish themes, see Link-Salinger (Hyman), *Gustav Landauer*, pp. 73–82, esp. n. 113, p. 74.
184. For a somewhat different understanding of Landauer's relationship to Judaism, see Norbert Altenhofer, "Tradition als Revolution: Gustav Landauers 'gewordenes-werdendes' Judentum," in David Bronsen (ed.) *Jews and Germans from 1860 to 1933: The Problematic Symbiosis* (Heidelberg, 1979), pp. 173–208. Our interpretation also differs fundamentally from that offered by Heinz-Joachim Heydron, foreword to Landauer, *Aufruf zum Sozialismus* (Frankfurt a/M., 1967), p. 24; also cf. Lunn, *Prophet of Community*, pp. 267–74; and Link-Salinger (Hyman), *Gustav Landauer*, pp. 73–82.

Jewish Lobbyists and the German Citizenship Law of 1914: A Documentary Account

Jack Wertheimer
(JEWISH THEOLOGICAL SEMINARY OF AMERICA)

The acquisition or loss of citizenship in Imperial Germany was regulated by a highly decentralized and arbitrary procedure. According to the "Law Concerning the Acquisition and Forfeiture of Federal and State Citizenship" of 1 June 1870, each German state exercised jurisdiction in matters of citizenship. Germans, in fact, possessed citizenship *in* a German state, rather than *of* Germany; they were Germans by virtue of their citizenship in states such as Baden, Bavaria, or Prussia. While the law of 1870 outlined minimal criteria for acquiring or forfeiting citizenship, it granted states wide latitude to reject or accept applicants for naturalization. In practice questions of citizenship were resolved by local officials who were not obligated to explain their decisions.[1]

The leaders of German Jewry frequently expressed concern over the equity of these procedures because they were convinced that state officials routinely discriminated against Jews seeking to acquire citizenship. It was, however, exceedingly difficult to prove such allegations. On occasion, ministers and bureaucrats inadvertently conceded that policies were anti-Semitic, but generally governments denied that they discriminated and successfully kept bureaucratic directives clandestine. In the latter years of the Second Reich, the two largest defense agencies of German Jewry were sufficiently disturbed by the state of affairs that they pooled their resources to challenge discriminatory governments. A joint commission founded in 1909 by the Federation of German Jews *(Verband der deutschen Juden)* and the Central Union of German Citizens of the Jewish Faith *(Central Verein deutscher Staatsbürger jüdischen Glaubens)* gathered statistical evidence in order to substantiate charges of anti-Semitic discrimination. In light of this long-standing concern with German naturalization policies, it is not surprising that when in 1913 the Reichstag deliberated over a new Reich and State Citizenship Law, German Jewry lobbied actively on behalf of Jewish interests.[2]

Jewish lobbyists strove above all else to convince legislators of the need to include in the new law a specific prohibition against religious discrimination. Such an injunction was necessary because foreigners were not entitled to the same legal protection as citizens, and, as a result, foreign Jews did not enjoy protection from discrimination in the manner of their emancipated German coreligionists. Furthermore, foreigners possessed no legal recourse to challenge the policies of state officials. When, for example, a Jewish woman from Russia petitioned the Prussia Minister of Interior after she had been imprisoned without trial, the Minister ruled that she even had no right to appeal her detention.[3] Rather, foreigners enjoyed legal protection only insofar as their native countries represented their interests, a condition that left the Jewish subjects of anti-Semitic regimes in Eastern Europe at a severe disadvantage.[4]

A second goal of Jewish lobbyists was to ameliorate the condition of German women who had married foreigners. Under the law of 1870, a married woman bore the citizenship of her husband. If a non-citizen married a German, she automatically acquired his citizenship. But if a German woman married an alien, she immediately forfeited her citizenship—regardless of whether she acquired citizenship in her husband's native land (Doc. 1). This latter regulation was particularly burdensome to Jews. To begin with, in most marriages between German and foreign Jews, native women married foreign men—and, accordingly, lost their citizenship.[5] Furthermore, anti-Semitic regimes in Eastern Europe usually did not naturalize these women. Deprived of their German citizenship, native-born Jewish women often suffered expulsion along with their husbands and even forfeited the right to return to Germany after divorce or the death of their husbands (Doc. 2).

The third issue on the agenda of Jewish lobbyists concerned the status of foreigners employed by synagogues. Under the prevailing law (article 9), all foreigners seeking employment as religious functionaries were required to obtain state authorization. Once granted, this authorization guaranteed naturalization to the religious official. Some states, therefore, directed bureaucrats to avoid authorizing foreigners to work for synagogues. Prussia, the most important offender, since the mid-1880's had repeatedly forbidden local officials to approve the hiring of foreign Jews as religious teachers, cantors, and ritual slaughterers (Doc. 3). This policy created a severe crisis for German synagogues which relied upon Polish Jews to serve their ritual needs. While some congregations successfully convinced their provincial governors to grant temporary permits to their foreign employees (Doc. 4), others simply broke the law by surreptitiously employing unauthorized foreigners.[6]

The draft version of the new citizenship law (article 10) threatened to make matters even worse. Whereas the existing law had guaranteed naturalization to all foreigners performing in "the service of a church" (ecclesiastical service—*Kirchendienst*), the new law offered such a guarantee only to those employed by a "church" *(Kirche)*. If allowed to stand, this wording would be understood to exclude foreigners employed by synagogues from the right to citizenship enjoyed by Christian religious functionaries from abroad.

The new citizenship law contained one additional provision that concerned Jewish leaders. Unlike the law of 1870 which insured complete decentralization in matters of citizenship, the new law granted each state the right to veto naturalization applications filed in neighboring states. This revision was designed to plug a loophole that had for decades frustrated state bureaucrats and benefited aliens, including Jews. For precisely because naturalization proceedings were not centralized in the hands of federal bureaucrats, it was possible for foreigners to go from one German state to the next in search of a bureaucrat who might approve their naturalization. Once they obtained citizenship in one state, these individuals were then entitled by law to acquire citizenship in any state where they had established legal domiciles. Bureaucrats in more xenophobic and anti-Semitic states repeatedly vented their rage at their counterparts in more liberal states for naturalizing unwanted foreigners.[7] To prevent such occurrences in the future, they wrote a provision into the new law that required Germany's chancellor to inquire of each state whether it objected to the naturalization of a foreigner who had applied to a member state of the German federation. This stipulation raised fears among Jewish leaders that an anti-Semitic regime in one state might veto every Jew who applied for naturalization in Germany.

As the Citizenship Law successfully proceeded through each of the required three readings in the Reichstag, a variety of Jewish lobbyists tried to sway German legislators on behalf of Jewish interests. Representatives of Jewish groups drafted petitions, met privately with legislators, and testified before the commission that was empowered to shepherd the bill through the Reichstag. The *Central Verein* and *Verband der deutschen Juden* were particularly active; and their efforts were augmented by a variety of synagogue organizations, professional associations and Jewish factions, ranging from the Zionist *Volkspartei* to the Association for the Interests of Orthodox Judaism (Docs. 5 and 6).[8]

The most concerted efforts were directed at reversing the exclusion of foreign synagogue employees from equal treatment along with all foreign employees of religious institutions. If the wording of article 10 were permitted to stand uncorrected, it would not only cause serious harm to synagogues, but would also legitimize the unequal treatment of one category of Jews—foreign religious functionaries. For native Jews it was unthinkable to permit such a breach in the principle of Jewish legal equality, lest other breaches follow.

Jewish groups, therefore, sought to recruit a Reichstag deputy who would work to alter the wording of article 10. During the third and final reading of the law, Deputy Gröber of the Catholic Center Party took responsibility for this campaign.[9] Due to Gröber's strong defense of Jewish religious equality and his forthright confrontation of the Interior Minister, the Reichstag voted to approve an amendment that permitted foreigners authorized for service in "a recognized religious association" (and not only in a "church") to acquire automatic naturalization (Doc. 7).

Jewish lobbyists proved only partially successful in achieving their other goals. They failed to alter the law in a manner that would protect native women from losing their citizenship upon marrying a foreigner (Doc. 7). Such women were assured, however, of more lenient treatment if they returned to Germany as widows or divorcees. The Reichstag also refused to include a prohibition in the law against religious discrimination in matters pertaining to citizenship. This rejection was partially mitigated by the repeated promises of government ministers and spokesmen that they would respect Jewish legal equality when evaluating naturalization requests. Jewish groups were pacified by these assurances (Doc. 8). In truth, however, discrimination against Jewish aliens continued unabated. Moreover, with their newly acquired power to veto applicants for naturalization, anti-Semitic officials in a few states repeatedly rejected Jewish applicants in other German states. Thus, the new citizenship law failed to eliminate the arbitrariness and subjectivity that had characterized German naturalization policies since 1870.[10]

Despite their limited success, the lobbying efforts of German Jewry are worth noting because they add to our understanding of German Jewish responses to East European immigrants. Contrary to oft-repeated generalizations about the hostility and condescension of German Jews toward *Ostjuden,* the leadership of native Jewry consistently strove to improve conditions for foreign Jews in matters of citizenship. Individual German Jews, to be sure, felt threatened by the influx of newcomers and worked against their interests (Doc. 9). But the leadership of German Jewry rejected this narrow perspective (Doc. 10). It acted upon the conviction that discrimination against any Jews in Germany—whether citizens or foreigners—insulted and harmed all Jews.[11]

Notes

I acknowledge with appreciation the translating assistance provided by Mrs. Charlotte Schoeman. Financial aid from the Leo Baeck Institute and the German Academic Exchange Service (DAAD) helped to defray research expenses for this essay.

1. For the text of the law, see Ernst Rudolph Huber, *Dokumente zur Deutschen Verfassungsgeschichte* II (Stuttgart, 1964) 249–53.

2. For examples of protest resolutions issued by the *Central Verein*, see *Im deutschen Reich* XI (April 1906) 241 and (June 1906) 358–60. On protests by the *Verband der deutschen Juden*, see *Allgemeine Zeitung des Judentums (AZJ)* 18 October 1907, p.495. For reports of concessions by government officials that discrimination occurred, see *Geschäftsberichte des Verbandes der deutschen Juden* VIII, 17–18, 36. Activities of the joint commission are reported in *Geschäftsberichte* V, 20 and VI, 27–28. The commission gathered information by sending questionnaires to Jewish leaders throughout Germany. It also prepared legal opinions on naturalization issues, but refrained from challenging the government with test cases (presumably because German law provided little protection to aliens).

3. There are press clippings about the case of Jannina Berson in the Preussisches Geheimes Staatsarchiv, Berlin, Dahlem. Rep. 84a, Nr. 14, Justizministerium, *"Die Ausweisungen von Ausländern"* (press clippings from January 1905).

4. For a discussion of the indifference displayed by the Russian and Austro-Hungarian governments to the fate of their Jewish subjects residing in Germany, see my doctoral dissertation "German Policy and Jewish Politics: The Absorption of East European Jews in Germany, 1868–1914" (Columbia University, 1978), pp.80–83.

5. Jewish contemporaries asserted that more Jewish women than men married foreigners (see Doc. 6). See, also, "German Policy . . ." (chapter V), where I concur with this assessment.

6. At the orders of Interior Minister Puttkamer, Prussian governors were required after 1884 to apply directly to the Interior Ministry for permission to authorize a foreign Jew to work as a religious functionary. See Alfred Michaelis, *Die Rechtsverhältnisse der Juden in Preussen* (Berlin, 1910), pp. 215–16. (This policy was justified on the basis of an article in Prussia's Jewry Law of 23 July 1847.) For reports about synagogues fined for employing foreigners illegally, see Michaelis, p. 559ff and *AZJ*. 28 August 1908, p.410; 19 March 1909, p.134; and other references cited in "German Policy . . ." chapter I, note 35.

7. See, for example, Document III appended to my essay, "The 'Unwanted

Element': East European Jews in Imperial Germany," *Yearbook of the Leo Baeck Institute* XXVI (1981) 45–46.

8. On the activities of various Jewish organizations, see *Israelitisches Familienblatt,* Hamburg 4 July 1913, *Beilage,* pp. 1–2 and *Jüdische Rundschau,* 4 July 1913, p.274, as well as *Geschäftsberichte* VIII, 16–18, 31–39, 40–43.

9. During the bill's second reading in the Reichstag, deputies of the Progressive parties unsuccessfully campaigned for a similar revision.

10. During the Weimar era, the Bavarian government repeatedly exercised its veto against Jews who applied for naturalization in other states. For some cases, see Preussisches Geheimes Staatsarchiv, Berlin, Dahlem, Rep. 90/151, II 1747/27B, 10 March 1927. The text of the new citizenship law passed on July 22, 1913, appears in Huber II, 382–89.

11. For a broader discussion of German Jewry's response to discrimination against immigrant Jews, see my essay, "The 'Unwanted Element'," pp. 33–39.

DOCUMENTS

I. THE STATUS OF GERMAN WOMEN MARRIED TO FOREIGNERS

1. The Betrothal of a German-Jewish Woman

Bayerisches Hauptstaatsarchiv, Munich, MINN #74140, Ministry of Interior, *"Einwanderung und Aufenthalt von Ausländern, Generalia 1871–1919."*

Berlin 12 February 1913.

To the Royal Bavarian Ministry of Interior, Munich:

I am respectfully submitting the following case to the Royal Ministry of Interior for its gracious consideration:

A well-respected physician in Berlin, a close acquaintance of mine, hesitates to betroth his only child to a young merchant of a well-to-do Jewish family because the latter, even though born in Germany and never having crossed its borders, is a Russian due to the nationality of his father (who has also lived for many years in Germany). There exists the legal possibility of his expulsion and the deportation of the physician's daughter since she would become a Russian through her planned marriage.

I respectfully beg the High Royal Ministry for its gracious response: Under what conditions would Bavaria naturalize this Russian of unblemished reputation after he has established a domicile here? I do not want to omit to mention that the physician would like to express his joy over the finalized naturalization and the ensuing happiness of his only child through a contribution to any charitable or scientific project you may suggest.

> Most respectfully,
> Thiel, Attorney

> Munich, 15 February 1913.

Attorney Thiel
Berlin NW 87
Concerning naturalization

The question whether a foreigner may be naturalized in Bavaria can be decided only after a residence *of many years* in Bavaria and a consideration of all personal circumstances.

> Signed for the Minister of the Interior

[Marginal Note.] It would be advisable not to state officially that Russian Jews are normally not naturalized.

2. A Newspaper Appeal

Allgemeine Zeitung des Judentums, 12 March 1909, supplement p. 4. [Hebrew terms in this document appear in Hebrew characters in the original.]

K'rahem av al banim ken t'rahem [As a father shows compassion toward his children, thus shall you show compassion]

Compassionate Co-religionists!

Open your hearts and hands to perform a great *mizvah* [pious deed]. A religious official who aged in the service of the community, as a *yerei shamayim* [pious man] and an *ish nikhbad* [respected man], a man whose reputation extends far beyond the borders of his district, has sacrificed greatly to marry his daughter, a native-born German, to a Russian living in Germany but not naturalized; the latter, together with his family, was subsequently expelled from Germany. Now, a short time later, the wife has returned with a child born in Russia (another child died in the meantime) in a very sad condition, denuded and robbed of everything, to her aged and weak parents. The woman bent with sorrow is half blind; the child had to be taken to a hospital as soon as it reached German soil. This is not yet all that fills their cup of suffering. When the mother reported her arrival, she was informed by the German police that she and her child would be expelled from Germany . . . *Raḥmanim bnei raḥmanim* [Jews, renowned for your compassion]! Have sympathy for this suffering and help, *raḥmanut av al banim* [with the compassion of a father] help, so that this unhappy family can regain the courage to live and find some means of support. We also most sincerely entreat officials of the congregations to take an interest in this charitable case and to provide some help by collecting contributions. God will reward each contribution with a twofold blessing. Dr. S. Freund, Rabbi in Hanover, as well as Rabbi Dr. Wiesen in Stadtlengsfeld are ready to provide any requested information and to forward contributions to the proper address.

Biz'khut zeh hakadosh barukh hu yazilekha min oniut umidalut ush'felut [In return, may the Holy One, Blessed Be He, preserve you from poverty, want and humiliation].

II. THE STATUS OF JEWISH RELIGIOUS FUNCTIONARIES FROM ABROAD

3. A Statement of Prussian Policy

Staatsarchiv Wiesbaden, Abt. 407. Polizeipräsidium Frankfurt am Main. Nr. 83. *"Isr. Kultusangelegenheiten 1867–1905."*

Copy
Interior Ministry   Berlin, 6 November 1980
Pursuant to regulation Ict. 9454 of 19 December 1887, I am herewith informing your Excellency very respectfully, as I consider it proper, that the Provincial Governors may in the future agree to the employment of foreign Jews as rabbis or synagogue officials—insofar as this is made necessary by the relevant regulations—only after obtaining my consent. Since the acceptance of foreign Jews as religious officials can in general be described as undesirable, the special reasons why such an application should be granted must be described in detail in the required reports.

Your Excellency will guide himself accordingly.

The Minister of the Interior
Signed: Herrfurth

4. A Russian *Shoḥet* in Dirschau

Preussischer Geheimes Staatsarchiv, Berlin, Dahlem, XIV Hauptabt. Rep. 180, Regierung Danzig #13550, *"Aufenthalt von Ausländern 1899–1901."*

Dirschau, 4 October 1907

Congregation Dirschau
Concerning: Authorization for the employment of the Russian citizen Israel Zaklikowski as ritual slaughterer

[Seen
The statements by the presiding officers of the congregation are correct. I support the application for Zaklikowski's authorization for 1 year.

Dirschau, 8 Oct. 1907
signed
... The Landrat]

To the Royal Provincial Governor in Danzig]

Because of the unavailability of German citizens, it has become impossible in recent years to fill the post of assistant cantor, a job which also includes the responsibility for ritually slaughtering animals. An advertisement published in several newspapers proved unsuccessful. In order not to deny the enjoyment of meat to the faithful members of our congregation, we were therefore forced to hire a Russian citizen, Israel Zaklikowski, to serve as ritual slaughterer in the municipal slaughterhouse and in the poultry-slaughtering pen belonging to the congregation. However, his pay is relatively small. In the last fiscal year, the fee for slaughtering in the slaughter-house amounted to 435 Mark; the fee for the slaughtering of poultry is collected directly by Zaklikowski and it is estimated to amount to 200 to 250 Mark for the year. Since the slaughterer could not defray even a most modest living from these receipts, he is paid a supplement out of the communal budget for the ritual slaughterer and assistant cantor. Zaklikowski is not, however, occupied with religious services. He is neither a rabbi nor synagogue official in the sense of the law of 23 July 1847. The rabbi of the Danzig congregation will be able to confirm this fact. (The post of assistant cantor is filled by the teacher and cantor, Mr. Jaffe.) The authorization for residence which had previously been given to Zaklikowski has expired and the District Governor of Danzig, through the regulation of 15 August 1907, Nr. O.P.I. 3013, has made a further authorization subject to our requesting the permission for Zaklikowski's employment according to Paragraph 71 of the law of 23 July 1847.

Our efforts to fill the position with a German citizen so far remain unsuccessful. According to the religious commandments, the office of ritual slaughterer cannot be assumed by just any person of the Jewish faith. It is simply untrue as stated in a recent petition submitted by a man from Krotoschin, that a sufficient number of German ritual slaughterers are available. The author of that petition served a jail sentence and therefore cannot be entrusted with a position that requires a person with high moral qualifications. (These facts will be confirmed upon request by the police department and by presiding officers of the Jewish community in Krotoschin.) Our efforts to train members of the congregation as ritual slaughterers failed; the only local Jewish butcher is completely occupied with his trade; other members of the congregation do not want to give up their secure income to take over the poorly remunerated position of ritual slaughterer.

Under these circumstances we beg Your Honor most respectfully to authorize provisionally the employment of Zaklikowski as ritual slaughterer of our congregation for the duration of one year. By the end of that period we hope to be able to fill the position with a German citizen.

                          The Board of the Synagogue
                          Congregation of Dirschau

Minister of the Interior   Berlin, 30 October 1907

To the Provincial Governor of Danzig

Regarding the report of the 19th of this month—communication No. A.I. 4987—I grant permission herewith—subject to recall at any time—for the Russian citizen Israel Zaklikowski to function as ritual slaughterer of the Jewish community in Dirschau. This permit will remain in force for the duration of one year at the most.

According to the report, Zaklikowski has apparently assumed these functions for several years already without authorization. Therefore I request your honor most respectfully to kindly see to it that the regulations of 30 September 1885 will be strictly observed in the future.

                          By order of the Minister of
                          Interior

III. JEWISH LOBBYING

5. A Petition From Berlin Synagogues

Geschäftsberichte des Verbandes der deutschen Juden VIII (Berlin, 1913) 40–43.

To the Reichstag   Berlin, 7 June 1913

Berlin
To the Esteemed Chamber,
Regarding article 10 of the Citizenship Law, we most respectfully sub-

mit a petition by the Union of Synagogues in Berlin and Its Environs (to which belong about twenty societies) that we also support.

Verband der deutschen Juden.
(The Federation of German Jews)
Dr. Horwitz, Chairman.

Petition Concerning the Draft of a Reich and State Citizenship Law.

To the Reichstag.

To the Esteemed Chamber of the Reichstag,
The Undersigned union submits the following proposal regarding the draft of a citizenship law presently under discussion: in Article 10 instead of the words . . . "Church service" it should say "service in a religious association officially recognized by the state [. . .]"

The rationale for the draft proposal was presented by Representative Dr. Blunck (session 153 [. . .] and session 155[. . .]). He pointed out that this proposal aims in no way to widen the circle of persons currently authorized by the law for naturalization, but aims merely to clarify the intention of article 9 of the law governing citizenship of 1 June 1870 which is presently in force. The preamble to the draft of said law states: "In most states, employment confirmed by the government in the service of a religious congregation is the equivalent of official naturalization." Hence there can be no doubt that already in the law of 1 June 1870 the term "church" is used to refer to all religious congregations recognized by the state. This is defined explicitly in a later federal law, the national law governing inheritance taxes, where article 12, paragraph 2, reads: "church is understood to mean all officially authorized religious communities in the country which have the rights of judicial persons[. . .]"

If in the new law, the word "church" were indeed to be understood in the sense in which it is used in the laws of various states, this would signify a worsening of the current legal situation. Yet, according to the government's statements, a change in legal principles is precisely what the commission does not intend [. . .]

Deputy Dr. Beltzer has stated during the first session that "the meaning of 'employment by a church' is decided by the relevant laws of the states. We want to maintain the right of state legislators to interpret the law." Deputy Beck declared (153. session) that "up to now the regulations concerning official recognition of religious congregations had been up to the individual states. We have heretofore been reluctant on principle to permit the federal government to interfere, and, indeed, state laws have varied to date."

These latter statements especially demonstrate that our proposal is attacked on the basis of unwarranted assumptions. The right of each state to "regulate the official recognition of religious associations," that is to decide which religious associations should be "officially recognized," will not be affected by a federal law stating that official authorization—without reservations—for "employment in a recognized religious congregation" implies naturalization.

If there remained any possible doubt in spite of Deputy Blunck's explanations of the draft proposal, then these concerns would surely be eliminated through the acceptance of the version proposed at the beginning of this petition. According to it, the religious association must be one which is officially recognized in the state whose government or central or higher authority executes the confirmation. This has also been the legal situation until now.

On the other hand, if the version of article 10 accepted in the second reading were to be retained, the consequence would be the dilution of presently guaranteed rights [. . .]

A number of Jewish congregations share our urgent interest that this should be avoided. The medium-sized and smaller Jewish congregations have found themselves for some time in ever increasing need. The emigration by numerous members of those congregations to the large cities and the decline in the income of many members of those congregations have weakened the financial solvency of those congregations. Therefore, they are generally not in a position to increase the salaries of their cantors, teachers, etc. to keep up with the general increase in the cost of living.

The result is that the supply of well trained cantors capable of leading the prayers and possessing a solid knowledge of religious laws, who serve the needs for smaller congregations in the provinces as well as those of the growing religious congregations of the cities, continues to shrink. Therefore, the small and medium-sized congregations are often forced to engage foreigners as cantors. These individuals, born generally in Austria or Russia, were able to acquire the necessary special knowledge in their native lands during their youth. Their mother tongue is most often German. In most cases they are able to further their general education in Germany in such a manner that they can successfully fill positions. Many congregations have therefore appointed foreigners as cantors and they are satisfied in every way. Such is also the case with a number of synagogues in Greater Berlin.

It must be pointed out particularly that irreproachable conduct is a prerequisite for a person's appointment as a cantor or teacher of religion. This condition is made not only for general ethical reasons, but it is a specific prescription of Jewish religious law which sees in the man who leads the prayers the representative and guardian of the congregation. In order to be worthy of his position, he must be absolutely above reproach in his moral, as well as in his religious, conduct. The same is true for the religious school teacher since, in the Jewish view, the religious instruction of the young is equivalent to the performance of a religious activity.

However, lately the government has objected in many cases to the employment of foreigners as cantors or religious school teachers, even though there were no objections to the applicants concerned except the very fact that they are foreigners. In other cases, foreigners were hired only temporarily. But this continued uncertainty has created very unsatisfactory conditions for the congregation, as well as for the employee. It should be unnecessary to list in this connection the numerous individual cases which have come to our attention.

A positive decision on behalf of the above proposal cannot hurt or threaten the interests of the state. On the other hand, the vital interests of many congregations, in particular also those of our congregations, depend on their ability to continue their religious service in a dignified manner. On this point the interests of the Jewish religious community coincide with those of the state.

> The Union of Synagogues in Berlin
> and Its Environs
> A. Lewinski
> Chairman

6. The Lobbying Activities of the *Verband der deutschen Juden*.

Geschäftsberichte des Verbandes des deutschen Juden VIII
(Berlin, 1913) 17–18.

The petition addressed to the Reichstag by the *Verband der deutschen Juden* pertained to two of the law's stipulations.

1. Regarding the article setting forth conditions for naturalization (#7), the addition of the following paragraph was proposed: "In the evaluation of a naturalization application, it is inadmissible to discriminate on the basis of the applicant's professed faith or his membership in a specific religious community."

The desire to include such a prohibition was prompted by concern over the prevailing practice when Jews apply for naturalization. As anticipated, this proposal was not accepted due to resistance by the government and the majority of parties to any infringement on the power of state authorities to reject petitions for naturalization. (Some exceptions have in fact been made in regard to state prerogatives in the case of applications submitted by former Germans and their descendants. One of these exceptions, that in favor of a German-born woman who had married a foreigner, particularly interests the *Verband* because among German women who marry foreigners, the percentage of Jewish women is relatively greater than that of other confessions. Consequently, the *Verband* has attended to this issue since the commission began its deliberations.) Much has been achieved by keeping the deputies—particularly commission members—constantly apprised of statistics, relevant cases, and decisions concerning Jewish foreigners. As a result of these efforts, representatives of nearly all political parties emphatically reproached the government for its practices to date. The representative of the Prussian government was forced to issue a statement—which was included in the commission's report—confirming that: for the Prussian government and its officials, the applicant's professed religion is in itself not a major factor in naturalization decisions. Furthermore, the government representative issued the following statement [. . .]:"A state may never base its objections to a foreign applicant on the applicant's confession if he belongs to a religious community which is officially sanctioned by that state."

According to the commission's report, the government representative added the following remarks to his statement, remarks that deserve to be reported verbatim:

> To the assertion that Jewish foreigners have been told that 'as long as they are Jews they would not be naturalized, but if they were to adopt the Christian faith, the matter could be discussed,' we must declare that, on the contrary, the Prussian Minister of Interior considers it undignified when an individual changes his professed faith for the sake of material advantage. The government can even cite cases where the Minister of Interior rejected an application for naturalization precisely because the applicant had expressed his intention to give up the Jewish confession for the sake of naturalization or because the applicant had already converted in order to acquire citizenship.

It would be a welcome development in the ceaseless struggle for legal equality were these principles acted upon not only where the Prussian Minister of Interior exercises jurisdiction but by all branches of the administration.

2. According to the second petition of the *Verband der deutschen Juden,* the new law should state clearly that when a government approves of a foreigner's employment in the service of a church, and this also applies to the religious functionaries of a Jewish community, naturalization will ensue. This was already implied in the present law but it

had not been made sufficiently explicit. During the second reading of the new law, when the Progressive Party introduced proposals along these lines, the *Verband* submitted a petition supporting this position; but the proposal was rejected. Nevertheless, as a result of a new petition drafted with the cooperation of the Union of Synagogues in Berlin and Its Environs and thanks to the repeated written and oral communications with deputies of virtually all political parties, it became possible to persuade the Center Party to introduce a slightly reworded proposal during the third reading. This was accepted. . . .

IV. THE CITIZENSHIP LAW OF 1914

7. The Reichstag Debates Two Amendments

Stenographische Berichte über die Verhandlungen des Reichstags. 13 Legisl. P., I Session 1912/13. 169 Sitzung, 25th June, 1913, pp. 5773–5775.

DEPUTY GRÖBER: Gentlemen, according to article 10, naturalization may also ensue from government approved employment in the service of a church within a federated German state (as long as the letter of appointment and authorization does not specifically rule out naturalization). This regulation is not new; it is already incorporated into the Law of 1870 currently still in force. The preamble to that regulation in the present law declares: "In most of the federated states, government authorized appointment in the service of a government approved religious association confers explicit naturalization upon the appointee." According to the current laws of individual states, the various religious associations recognized by the state are given the same rights as Christian churches. This applies in all the states of southern Germany, in a large part of Prussia, namely in the new Prussian provinces, especially in Hessen-Nassau, Hannover, Schleswig-Holstein, also in Hohenzollern, and furthermore in Mecklenburg-Schwerin, Sachsen-Weimar, Oldenburg, Braunschweig, Anhalt and in the German territories of Alsace-Lorraine. You see then: what was contained in the preamble to the draft of the 1870 law has become lawful in most of Germany; but not everywhere, particularly not in the areas where Prussian law obtains.

Such inconsistencies in the law have had a particularly deleterious effect on the German Jews. The cause of this unfortunate state of affairs can be traced to the fact that the German Jews recruit ever fewer German citizens to serve as religious functionaries. This is true not only for small and medium-sized German Jewish congregations, where one could perhaps assume that the necessary emoluments are unavailable for religious officials; but it is also the case for quite well financed larger congregations, for instance the congregations in Berlin, where one surely cannot speak of a lack of financial resources to pay salaries. The cause is deeper; it is not the lack of adequate remuneration but, most of all, that Jewish teachers are not particularly inclined to perform ritual functions. This is not surprising in light of the development of the teaching profession. Thus, the most profound reason for the pressing need of the German synagogues has to do with the peculiar circumstances of the Jews. I surely do not need to discuss this point in detail. The circumstances are known and undisputed. The more the synagogues have been forced to meet their religious needs by employing foreigners, particularly those from Russia and Austria, the more the situation has worsened. And in this respect, the proposed new law creates even greater hardship with its harsh stipulation that appointment in an officially recognized religious association is not the equivalent of employment in the service of a church. It is this bad state of affairs that our petition seeks to remedy.

Our motion is based on the same principles which shaped the federal law of 1869 governing the equal legal rights of religious denominations. Gentlemen, we do not ignore [the fact] that the federal law of 1869 on the equalization of religious denominations concerns German citizens. But we are of the opinion that the same principle must also apply to the appointment of foreigners to serve in an officially recognized religious congregation and to the eligibility of such individuals for naturalization. Our petition in no way trespasses on the independence of states to decide such matters. We do not want to dictate to the individual states which religious societies they must recognize; we do not want to dictate in any way to the states which specific individuals they must appoint to the service of a recognized religious society, or whether they should authorize and confirm an appointment. In other words, as long as there exist any reservations concerning the appointment of a foreigner, for instance because the foreigner is not yet well enough known to the authorities, we certainly want governments of individual states to exercise the option, as in the past, either to refuse an appointment if they do not consider the persons concerned suitable, or to authorize his appointment only with reservations (to declare, for instance, that they wish to hold a decision in abeyance until the individual concerned demonstrates his suitability for appointment and thereby for obtaining German citizenship).

Gentlemen, in submitting this proposal for your approval, we act upon religious impulses. Our concern is the religious need of a confession in Germany. The Jewish religious community, in fact, is unable to recruit religious officials in sufficient number in Germany proper and therefore finds itself in straitened circumstances when it tries to organize religious services in a traditional and dignified form. We deem it appropriate and even incumbent upon ourselves to help the Israelites in this religious matter. And we base this on the conviction that religious communities which are officially recognized in Germany should be treated as equal under the law.

Therefore we beg the esteemed Chamber to approve our proposal. (Applause from the Center)

Vice-President Dove: The Minister of Interior, Dr. Delbrück, has the floor.

Dr. Delbrück, Minister of State, Minister of Interior, Plenipotentiary of the Bundesrat: Gentlemen, proposals with the same tendencies as the one which has just been defended by Deputy Gröber have already been submitted and argued in earlier stages of the debates, and the federal government has repeatedly pointed out the risks inherent in these proposals. In consideration of the Chamber's busy schedule, I refer only in general to the objections raised against these proposals in earlier debates and want to repeat that the federal government continues to harbor the most serious concerns over the acceptance of this proposal [. . .]

Concerning the recognized religious communities, legal conditions vary. This is an area which up to now has been the province of individual states and I can only urgently recommend that, in this respect, present conditions not be changed. This should not be an occasion for intervention in such a privileged area.

Furthermore, it is my opinion that the aim pursued by Deputy Gröber would not be achieved, because the individual states retain the right to formulate reservations, and it must even be feared—that too has been expressed specifically in an earlier case—that a regulation such as Deputy Gröber wants to introduce now would not make the procedures concerning Jewish religious officials in the East easier, but would make matters for those concerned more uncomfortable than before.

I beg therefore that the regulations of the draft proposal be left as they were after the second reading.

Vice-President Dove: Deputy Gröber has the floor.

Deputy Gröber: Gentlemen, the Minister of Interior's contention that acceptance of our motion would make matters more difficult for Israelites does not augur well for the treatment of the question in the eastern regions of our Empire. Here is the critical point we are debating.

Gentlemen, we are concerned here most of all with resolving the principles of the question. That the principle of the federal law of 1869 should apply also in this case was something that I had hoped would encounter no contradiction. If that principle is respected and applied to the present matter, its practical application will improve over the years. That is a hope we do not want to abandon in spite of the Minister's explanation.

PRESIDENT: The debate is closed; we shall now vote. Before us is the proposal by Deputy Gröber to replace in article 10 the words "in the service of a church" with the words: "in the service of a religious association recognized by the state." I beg the gentlemen who wish to accept this proposal to rise. (Done) That is the majority. The proposal is accepted . . . Concerning paragraph 13, Deputy [Eduard] Bernstein has the floor.

DEPUTY BERNSTEIN: Gentlemen, I must put it to your conscience to at least consider our proposal. This paragraph concerns the conditions under which citizenship is lost. Paragraph 13, no. 6 reads: "for a German woman through marriage to a citizen of another German state or to a foreigner." Now we have been shown cases where, in spite of such a marriage, a German woman does not obtain citizenship in another state. Why, then, should this German woman lose her German citizenship? It is, after all, the most elementary demand of justice and the result of the here established *jus sanguinis,* the right of descent, that German women under such circumstances at least not lose their citizenship. Gentlemen, I beg you, accept this proposal. (Bravo! from the Social Democrats)

PRESIDENT: The debate is closed. We arrive at the vote on article 13 . . . [to change the wording] as follows: "for a German woman through marriage to a citizen of another state of the federation or to a foreigner, provided she acquires thereby citizenship in another state." Will the gentlemen who wish to accept this proposal please rise. (Done) This is the minority. The proposal is rejected.

8. A Threat Posed by the New Law is Minimized
Israelitisches Familienblatt, Hamburg, 28 August, 1913, p. 9.

The New Citizenship Law

The *National Legal Notices* has just published the text of the new *Reich* and State Citizenship Law of 22 July, 1913, that takes effect on

January 1, 1914. According to the legal authority Freudenthaler of Berlin, it will be more difficult for foreigners to acquire citizenship in the future. As under the presently applicable law, naturalization will still be linked to the applicant's financial resources, unblemished record, ownership of a domicile, and ability to support himself and his dependents. The increased difficulty, however, stems from a new paragraph (number 9) that conditions naturalization in one state upon the Chancellor's verification that no other state harbors any misgivings about the applicant's naturalization. The law thereby intends to safeguard the interests of all states—and not only the state where the application is submitted—since once an applicant is naturalized by one state he may request citizenship in any state where he has established a residence. This new regulation has been actively fought in the Reichstag. In particular, some concern has been voiced that the administration will allow itself to be influenced by the applicant's religion. The commission in fact discussed a case, for which there is documentary proof, in which Prussia's Minister of Interior rejected on religious grounds an application for naturalization submitted by an Israelite. A representative of the Prussian government denied this allegation during his testimony before the commission investigating the proposed new law. He offered assurances based on official figures that in Prussia neither religious, nor plutocratic, nor political considerations holds sway. And in any event, he claimed, applications for naturalization are rejected only in exceptional cases. At the same time, he stated categorically in the name of the Prussian government that religion as such carries no appreciable weight in the eyes of authorities who act upon requests for naturalization. Rather, the deciding factor is whether the state views the applicant as a desirable addition to its population . . .

But in addition to these assurances, the danger to foreigners inherent in the government's draft was reduced considerably when the Reichstag's commission . . . added a sentence to the present article 9: "Reservations raised by a state can only be based on facts which justify concern that the applicant's naturalization would endanger the well-being of the country or a state." According to a speech by a Reichstag Deputy, the Minister of Interior has expressed the urgent desire and hope that article 9 will create a certain uniformity in the naturalization practices of all states.

9. A German Cantor Responds to the Gröber Proposal.

Israelitisches Familienblatt, Hamburg. 7th April, 1913, p. 11.

Article 10 of the New Citizenship Law

During the third reading of the Citizenship Law, article 10 was changed in order to make it easier for Jewish congregations to employ foreigners as religious officials (insofar as official approval of an appointment is tantamount to naturalization). This proposal was presented by the Center Party's Deputy Gröber over the objections of Interior Minister Delbrück and at the behest of the Union of Synagogues in Berlin and Its Environs and the Free Associations for the Interests of Orthodox Judaism. Though it may be perceived as a great victory for equal rights, this article contains such great dangers that it would be an injustice not to point out, before it is too late, the law's consequences and the reasons why communities can do without the rather dubious benefits of article 10.

According to Deputy Gröber's explanations, the term "religious officials" is to be understood as ritual slaughterers. But what prevents congregations from employing naturalized religious slaughterers as cantors or teachers of religion? (Should the authorities require a certificate attesting to the appointees' qualifications, this can be obtained easily, judging by the practices of certain parties!) Therefore, article 10 may lead to a development in the German synagogue which seemingly had been overcome, thank God, through the enlightened efforts of the professional associations. We certainly harbor no animosity toward foreigners and do not demand the expulsion of colleagues presently employed; we also do not demand out of fear of competition that they be kept out of official religious positions. Nonetheless, their appointment must be considered a danger for German Jewry so long as the foreigners have not proven their qualifications by taking examinations administered by an official authority who will test not only their knowledge of religion but their education. Moreover, the religious slaughterer should not be permitted to avoid such an examination without suffering demotion to the rank of an ordinary butcher.

And how often has it been shown in the last decade among professionals how greatly the congregations sin against the religious spirit? How they dishonor our religious services in the eyes of every educated person when they employ as cantors men who bring to this job almost nothing other than a "voice"! When will they recognize that an inferior social status, which usually results from a lack of a general education, is not only regrettable for the employee but even more so for the employer? It may well be that for some officials of the community the appointment of a foreigner is more desirable than that of a well educated native. For such a man does their bidding more easily because he is glad to make a living: he had been so much worse off in his own country, is used to "pressure," and always bends under it. Little fuss is made about a *"Pollack"* (that is the *terminus technicus* popular among the powers that be in the congregations). He is fired if he complains in the least! They believe they have no obligations whatever toward such a man! And how pitiful is such a religious employee! However hard he tries to acquire a German education and German manners, he remains a *Pollack* in the eyes of the communal leaders, men who bear him little good-will. And what effect this has on his work! It undermines children's religiosity when such a foreigner becomes a teacher of religion (not to mention that he lacks the proper qualifications!). If therefore the Gröber proposal should result in the more benevolent treatment of foreigners serving as authorized religious functionaries, two things must be requested from the authorities:

1) No religious functionary, whether a native or a foreigner, may be employed unless he has proven his qualifications to a board of examiners appointed by the state.

2) No religious civil servant may be dismissed without the authorization of the state government.

If this latter regulation is also applied to foreigners, many congregations will probably desist from appointing foreigners as religious officials.

Those who supported Gröber's proposal prepared a statement for him contending that . . . "The problem does not stem from a lack of adequate remuneration, but primarily from the fact that Jewish teachers show no particular inclination to perform ritual functions." No, dear Mr. Gröber, there is an even deeper reason than that which you indicated! Even if it is difficult for small, poorly financed congregations, particularly in the East, to obtain native religious functionaries, we doubt that this is also the case for larger, well financed congregations. Here is the heart of the matter. These religious appointments offer so little attraction both from the material and the social point of view that one cannot hold it against any German teacher if he shows "no particular inclination to perform ritual functions." And can congregations even expect elementary school teachers to find satisfaction when they are supposed to serve only as religious slaughterers?

It therefore should be made a condition that religious employees who perform only manual functions receive a sufficient and honorable livelihood . . . If religious institutions provide for the above, they will entice German youths to this profession.

However, such a development requires the existence of institutions which prepare religious officials thoroughly; the private preparatory institutions currently available are not satisfactory. Contrary to recent proposals, it is not necessary to establish new professional schools; instead, existing Jewish teachers' seminaries should be reformed so that they could also become preparatory institutions for religious functionaries, such as teachers of religion, cantors, and ritual slaughterers. This would also aid the seminaries, which presently suffer from a dearth of students and may soon close due to the shrinking demand for elementary school teachers.

If we have demonstrated above ways in which to prevent or at least limit the threatened flooding of religious positions with foreigners, we were not motivated by prejudice against foreign colleagues who, after all, have contributed numerous capable officials. But rather, this matter is closely connected with the preservation of German Jewry. In view of the absolutely overriding importance of this question, personal sympathies or antipathies are secondary to the question, "What is to become of German Jewish communities?" If the Union of German Cantors opposes the threatened flooding of German congregations by foreign religious functionaries, it does so not for selfish reasons, such as the fear that the German functionaries might then not find jobs. No, such petty arguments are remote from the concerns of German cantors and religious officials. First, because we do not suffer from an oversupply; and second, because our sacred task leads us to strive not for our personal well-being, but for the good of Israel, for the flowering and growth of Judaism. Our hearts bleed when we observe that one of our officials is held in low esteem. We recognize in this a withering of the religious spirit, a lack of respect for our holiest possession—our religion.

Therefore we admonish the Jewish communities in Germany to take care that:

1) All religious positions provide material and social support so that officials will be assured a sufficient and honorable livelihood.

2) Existing teachers' seminaries must provide for the preparation of religious functionaries, such as cantors, teachers of religion, and ritual slaughterers.

Then German congregations will not need to fill their requirements with religious officials from abroad and the proposal of Mr. Gröber and his backers will not—we hope—enjoy a very frequent application. . . .

10. In Defense of Foreign Religious Functionaries.

Der Israelit, 4 September 1913, p. 12.

. . . We say: "An open track to all applicants, provided they are properly qualified for the job!" He who wants to function as a teacher of religion must possess the knowledge required by the state of its teachers in addition to *Wissenschaft des Judentums* [Jewish scholarship]; he who wants to function as a cantor must show evidence of a thorough education in religion, as well as in music; and he who wants to function as a ritual slaughterer must demonstrate his qualifications to a rabbinical authority as prescribed by the religious laws. Whether the applicant is a citizen or an alien, the requirements must always remain the same.

From this point of view we can only regret it deeply when, in the most recent issue of the "Monthly Bulletin of the General Association of German Cantors," my colleague Fabisch (Göttingen) goes so far as to assert that Gröber's proposal contains great dangers [. . .] It is kind of him that he does not demand the explusion of colleagues presently employed, but we can undestand when the latter express their displeasure with his statements in rather excited letters to us [. . .]. Cantors, especially, count among their ranks a great number of excellent representatives of their profession whose cradle stood neither on the banks of the Rhine or the Main, but on those of the Weichsel [Vistula], the Memel [Nieman] or the Duna [Dvina]. These ornaments of their profession until now did not have to demonstrate to any authority their level of religious knowledge and general education, as is requested in Fabisch's article.

. . . The success of article 10 will at best be moderate. But only those who are intent on predicting disaster because it suits their purposes can speak of a "threatening flood." The narrow-mindedness expressed in the above mentioned article does us no honor.

Judah L. Magnes' Trip to Przedborz

A. Goren
(HEBREW UNIVERSITY)

On October 24, 1900, Judah Magnes, who would make his mark as a Zionist orator, American Jewish communal leader, and first chancellor of the Hebrew University, arrived in Berlin to pursue his postgraduate studies. For the twenty-three year old, San Francisco-born rabbi—he was ordained at Cincinnati's Hebrew Union College three months earlier—earning a doctoral degree at a German university promised to enhance his prospects for a successful career in the American rabbinate. His teachers at the college and his mentor and sponsor, Jacob Voorsanger, rabbi of Temple Emanu-El of San Francisco, had encouraged the gifted young graduate to continue his studies in Germany. Magnes did not disappoint them. In December 1902, he returned to the United States with a Heidelberg doctorate in Semitics.[1]

His two years in Germany, most of which he spent in Berlin studying at the university and at the Lehranstalt für die Wissenschaft des Judenthums (the liberal rabbinical seminary), did more than broaden his intellectual horizons and enrich his Judaic background. They proved to be the most formative period of his life. The handsome and affable Californian, who grew up in a middle class Reform Jewish milieu, underwent a metamorphosis, a time he later called "those days of a great Jewish awakening." In Berlin, Magnes embraced Zionism with the ardor of a convert. It became, as he declared in a letter to his parents in October 1901, "my *Lebensprogramm*." His view of life had changed, he explained, and how best to serve the Zionist cause would now determine his calling and his future. "My hopes, my prayers have changed. The questions concerning the Jewish people—and the Jewish religion is but one of these questions—are the questions that are consuming my days and my nights." No longer could he be content in the role of liberal preacher ministering to a congregation of wealthy Jews.

Zionism had also changed his mode of life. "I seek to live more like a Jew, i.e., you would call it more like an Orthodox Jew."[2] In what was, in a sense, a symbolic act of rebirth, Magnes informed his family that he intended to change his given name from Julian Leon to Judah Laban. On the eve of his return to the United States, he signed a letter to his parents with the name Yehudah Leibush Magnes: the Hebrew-Yiddish name of his paternal grandfather which he used the rest of his life.[3]

For Magnes, Zionism meant more than subscribing to a political program. It entailed an affirmation of Jewish life in all its forms. Because of his Zionism, he explained to his parents (who feared his espousal of Zionism would ruin his career), his studies at the Lehranstalt were now more important to him than his university courses. He had enlisted in a movement, he declared, which would not only provide a homeland for the persecuted Jews but would bring about the "cultural renaissance of the Jewish people."[4]

Like the circle of young German Zionists to which he belonged, he saw the Jews of Eastern Europe, the *Ostjuden,* as the bearers of the authentic traditions of the Jewish people. Firmly rooted in their ethnic heritage, they were the antithesis of the assimilated Jewry of the West. On one occasion, deeply moved by a meeting with his father's relatives, immigrants from Lodz who were passing through Berlin, he wrote:

> How they cling to life and to hope—what a fine intellectuality they all have, and what a tremendous spiritual power is in them. It is our Talmud Judaism that has kept them alive until this day. God help them if ever in their present condition our cracked-up ideas of "progress" ever reach them. My fervent prayer is that they be given the opportunity to develop themselves in the land of our fathers, in Palestine. There their great dormant powers will come to life and the world's finest civilization will result.[5]

Magnes encountered Jewish students from Eastern Europe at Zionist meetings, in efforts to form a society of Jewish nationalists at the Lehranstalt, and at Hebrew study circles. During the months he lived in Heidelberg he joined a "Hebrew Conversation Verein" organized by Saul Tchernichowsky, the Hebrew poet, then a medical student at the university. When a Lemberg (Lvov) Yiddish theater company performed in Berlin he attended the performance. He planned a summer trip to Galicia. "I shall make a *Judenreise,* i.e. I shall visit Galicia, and by touring on foot for about two months I think I shall become acquainted with my brethren."[6]

Magnes also met East European Jews in their synagogues. Following *seliḥot* services in a Hasidic synagogue he described the "wild and tragic scene": "They want to tear God from heaven. They pour out the pain of ages in their wild cries."[7] But as another visit to an immigrant congregation indicated, he identified with the worshippers. "There was the repetition of prayers learned years ago and mumbled as fast as possible. There was the interest in the reading of the Scroll; the love of literature as manifested in the reading of the lesson from the Prophets; the vanity of the Reader and his trills and the roulades; the delight of singing out of tune and making your voice last longest in the congregational singing. There was the social converse, the passing of the snuffbox, the 'shhh' of the Beadle to people who were talking." He had seen Orthodox services before, he noted, "but never one in which I took so much interest and felt so much pride. It was as noisy as any Orthodox service. The worshippers were of the same stripe that compose other Orthodox congregations. It was I who was different, who saw it all with different eyes."[8]

During his years of active leadership in the American Jewish community, Magnes' empathy for the East European Jews enabled him to play a notable role as mediator between the immigrant and the established German Jews. This was possible because, on the one hand, German Jewish society accepted him as one of theirs: As rabbi of New York's Temple Emanu-El he formed close ties with the leading patrician families, ties which were further cemented by marriage. On the other hand, his Zionism, which he conceived broadly as a commitment to the preservation of Jewish group life in all of its manifestations, led him to support a whole range of cultural, social and ideological interests which were indigenous to the life of the Jewish immigrants. As head of the Jewish Defense Association, organized in 1905 to raise funds for Jewish self-defense in Russia, he established ties with radical elements within the immigrant community. He aided the Socialist-Zionists raise funds for their journal, the *Yidisher kemfer*. Dissatisfied with the rabid partisanship of the Yiddish press, he was instrumental in the founding of *Der tog* in 1914. Magnes supported the literary endeavors of David Pinski, Sholem Asch, and Chayim Zhitlovsky. A group of young Orthodox Jews on New York's Lower East Side, the nucleus of the Young Israel movement, turned to him for counsel and aid. When European and Palestinian Zionists visited the United States to raise funds for a variety of Hebrew cultural and educational undertakings, they depended upon Magnes to intercede with the men of wealth. His visits to Palestine in 1907 and 1912, and his missions on behalf of the Joint Distribution Committee to Poland in 1916 and 1922, raised his esteem in the eyes of American Jews of both German and East European origin.[9]

There is a peculiarly American dimension to the interplay of East and West in Magnes' family history. His father, David, was born in Przedborz, southeast of Lodz, in the Kielce province of Poland. His mother's family, the Abrahamsons, came from Filehne, a small town in western Posen. Both arrived in America old enough to have acquired a thorough grounding in the traditions and culture of their respective regions. David, aged 15, was brought to San Francisco by his older brother in 1863. Sophie arrived in the city with her parents and six brothers and sisters in 1868, an older brother having preceded them. She was 16.

David retained warm sentiments towards the Hasidic Judaism of his youth. His letters to his son were laced with Hebrew phrases, and Judah recalled fondly the Hasidic melodies his father sang. Sophie Abrahamson's parents spoke German and proudly passed on the language and culture to their children. In the marriage, the German side dominated. There were more Abrahamsons and they were wealthier. By the time Sophie married, her brothers had established a flourishing department store in Oakland across the bay from San Francisco. David Magnes' dry goods store—the young couple moved to Oakland in 1882—remained a modest affair. In the Jewish social order of the late nineteenth and early twentieth centuries, the German stratum, more Americanized and affluent, occupied the pre-eminent place. As an infant, Judah had a German-speaking nurse, and the presence of grandmother Abrahamson exposed the Magnes children to the German language during their youth.[10]

The marriage of a Polish Jew to a German Jewess would have been unlikely in the older, more socially stratified cities of the East Coast or Middle West. But San Francisco and Oakland were less than a generation removed from their frontier beginnings. The open, fluid, egalitarian society (for whites) combined with a Jewish community in its first stage of organization to blur social differences. Moreover, David and Sophie arrived in America young enough to learn English quickly and well and enter the cultural life of the city and the Jewish community. Their letters to their son during his years in Cincinnati reflect the typical domestic interests of a middle class American family. Thus Judah, although aware of the two Jewish traditions represented by his parents, grew up in a home where both blended with the American component to form an authentic American Jewish style of life. In Berlin, Magnes—this new American Jew—became profoundly aware of his European roots.

Yet for all his admiration for the *Ostjude,* his closest friends remained Westerners. In Berlin, he forged a lifelong friendship with Max Schloessinger, son of a Heidelberg family and a fellow student at the

Lehranstalt. Schloessinger later became his principal aide at the Hebrew University. Other friends included Arthur Biram, Gotthold Weil and Emil Cohn, all of whom were German-born. Like Magnes, they were drawn to Jewish studies as an expression of their group pride, and they turned to a career in Jewish public life or Jewish scholarship as a way of serving their people. During this period, Magnes also established especially warm ties with his mother's cousins, formerly from Filehne and now typical middle class Berliners. In New York, his most intimate friend was Solomon Lowenstein, who graduated from Hebrew Union College a year after Magnes and entered Jewish social service. Magnes' intimate social circle included the Marshall, Herzog and Wertheimer families, who were related to his wife by marriage. After he settled in Jerusalem, he felt more at ease with the small colony of English, American and German academics and officials. Zionist leaders like Chaim Weizmann considered him the important link between the Zionist Organization and America's German Jewish elite.

Magnes wrote the following account of his visit to his father's birthplace on 5 August 1922. He and his wife and three children left the United States the previous May to spend a year in Jerusalem, a visit that led to permanent settlement. On the way to Palestine, Magnes carried out an assignment for the Joint Distribution Committee to survey Jewish cultural life in Eastern Europe. While on this mission he made the trip to Przedborz. The text as published below is taken from a typed manuscript in the Judah Leib Magnes Papers located in the Central Archives for the History of the Jewish People in Jerusalem. The orthography and transliterations of the original have been retained. I was unable to locate the handwritten text from which the typed copy was transcribed. I wish to acknowledge with thanks the permission granted by the Central Archives to publish the document.

Journal Entry, August 5, 1922

It is now two weeks since I made the trip to Przedborg, but the impression of it all is still strong upon me.

When I was in Poland in 1916 a trip to Przedborg was out of the question. It would have been difficult to get military permission for it. But I was determined that this time I should make the journey under all circumstances. On thinking of another trip to Poland, one of the attractions was the visit to Przedborg, and the account about it for Daddy.*
With him gone, much of the zest of the adventure is gone.

Almost since I can remember looking at maps, I have looked for Przedborg on the Pilica. One of the first trips I took in the Russian

---

*Magnes's father died in April, 1922.

Baedeker I got in 1916 was the trip by train to the station near Przedborg, and then the wagon the few miles from the railroad. That wagon ride I always wanted to take at night, because when Daddy left home it was in a wagon at night in order the better to get smuggled across the border. Jews travelling in wagons—that is one of the familiar sights as you ride over the countryside. Narrow wagons, drawn by one or two tired-looking horses, and piled high with household goods or crates of ducks or hay, and on top Yidden and Yiddenes, some asleep, some back to back, some sprawling over others. Over the Polish roads and through the tall pine woods, and over grassy paths, you see Jews riding, walking, going to market, visiting relatives and friends. There is a saying: "Yidden gehen zu fohren" [go traveling]. They may be city and town and village dwellers, but they certainly move about from place to place.

What interesting people they are, too, in the landscape. The long black coats of the men, the white collars, the beards, the small black cloth cap with peak, and the black boots, and, most of the time, the Zizis* hanging over the belt. There are those who despise or object to these distinguishing outward gabardine marks; but, as for me, I vote for and not against, particularly when, as sometimes happens, you find a clean Jew with clean raiment, and clean collar and clean peat. Some of the young men look quite Byronesque or Schillerlike, and the boots of some make them look like Oriental cavalry men. Some of the young merchants are quite elegant with Kapottes (long coats) not quite of black (?) and golden pince-nez, and well-combed reddish beards, and canes, and well-shined shoes.

The way from Warsaw is about 150 kilometers, and we were supposed to do it in the J.D.C. car in about five hours. But owing to a defective wheel, we had to stop several times, and although we left Warsaw at 6:30 a.m., we did not get to Przedborg until about 2:30 p.m. Mr. Emerson, the J.D.C. Administrator in Warsaw, and another member of the staff whose name I never shall remember, and the 10-year old boy of the Polish chauffeur—the boy dressed in red blouse and blue military cap—made up our party.

Not much has changed on this countryside since Daddy was a boy. The automobile road is better, there is electric light, and here and there you see an American farming machine. But for the most part the mowing of the splendid rye fields is done by hand, and groups of women pass in the wake of the mower, and tie up bundles of grain, which are later gathered and stacked. The peasants live together with their pigs

---

*"Fringes," sewn to the four corners of the undergarment in knotted tassels worn by Orthodox males.

and chickens and goats and cows—side by side—and at intervals you see the well-wooded parks and fine houses and farming-out houses of the Poritz, the land-owner and political lord of the neighborhood. Every once in a while you pass through a town where you look for a Jew in vain; then through others where the Jews occupy one end or other of the place, and then through other towns almost entirely Jewish. It is such Jewish towns, with their old synagogues and crowded quarters, and Jews of all descriptions filling the market-place and standing at the doors and looking through the windows, that give you an idea of how deeply rooted the Jewish community is in the Polish soil, and what primitive forces must be at work to be uprooting so old and native a tree.

As we approached Przedborg, the ground grew more hilly, and it was clear from the map that after we crossed the dark range in the distance we should be in sight of Przedborg and the Pilica Valley. Did Daddy as a boy walk these roads? Surely his people had something to do with the ancestors of those Polish peasant men and girls in their colored Sunday clothes, now resting under trees or walking the roads into the nearest town with a Catholic Church. This beautiful place, with its noble trees lining a driveway to a white door—was that the Poritiz's place of Daddy's town? Did he make my family's life miserable? Did they dance with Yofis* for him? These fields—were they part of the lands granted Jews a hundred years ago by the first Nicholas if they would return to the soil—and was it here that some of Daddy's early recollections of the family "farm" had their origin? It is taking long to get to Przedborg, and that bare-legged Jewish boy has already jumped on the running board of the car to take us to the Rov's house. Yes, past a few more old, well-cultivated gardens, and there is the lazy, narrow stream, and here we are in the market-place of another Jewish town—this time Przedborg.

It is a broad market-place paved with cobble stones as all such are. It is lined with shops on all four sides, and there are little alley ways leading away—some down towards the stream, others up towards the castle-fortress on the hill. A little boy with imagination could find considerable material here. The color of the day, the pink color of the paint on some of the houses, the shops closed at Midday (it was Sunday and no business is opened on the holy day in Poland) gave their market-place the appearance of an Oriental gathering place.

But the people soon arouse you from any dreaming you may want to do. I suppose automobiles do not get to Przedborg every day with

---

*Corruption of "mayofis"—"how beautiful"—a song sung Friday evening which figuratively came to mean servile. Jews were forced to dance to the melody by their persecutors.

people asking for the Rov [rabbi]. By the time you get out to follow the little boy, he is lost in the crowd, and there are fifty others, old and young, who want the job of being guide. He lives down one of the alleys toward the stream. The old wooden synagogue is right there in front. But you think most of the filthy street, with the shallow gutter as sewer, and the bad smells (Oriental also?)—and the people! I am for the Jewish garb, and the Jews, and they are my people and the chosen people, and the greatest of all peoples. But how offensive they get when they mob you in Przedborg and ask for money. How dirty, and sick, and ragged and unfortunate.

The Rov lives across the alley from the Schul [synagogue], and right back of the Beth Hamedrash [study house] and School. A Melamed is perched on a bench pounding the old lesson into the heads of about twenty little David Magneses. We are showed into the Rov's room unceremoniously, and the door is bolted to keep the crowd out. The noise outside indicates that a considerable percentage of Przedborg's 7,000 Jews are gathering.

The Rov is writing at the table in the middle of the room. A Jew is standing alongside, and it is evidently a document for this Jew that the Rov is preparing. He looks up annoyed, and stands up to greet us, dignified, distant as though we were Polish military breaking into his sanctum to search his premises. He is young, has a high forehead, his cap thrust back, no collar, his long coat open in front showing his shirt, and his trousers mussed in slippers. He is red-bearded and golden-spectacled and cross-eyed, and it was difficult to begin before this silent, rather indignant Rabbi. After a Sholem Aleichem [peace unto you], and a rather awkward pause, I plunged right in and said we were from America, that my father had been born in Przedborg, and that I had come to visit Kever Ovos (graves of ancestors). He unbent a little and gave us his hand. What is the name? Magnes. Magnes? Magnes? He thought long. He had never heard the name before. My Seide [grandfather] was Jehuda Leibush Magnes, I said, and his wife's name was Chava, and Chava was a well-known woman in these parts. Chava, Chava, Reb Jehuda Leibush's wife, well-known, ... The Rov shook his head, and I was somewhat crestfallen. But then a woman dared to speak up and said, "I know whom he means. The Chava whom I knew when I was a girl. She with the white cap about her head and across her forehead." And then an old man said that Itzek Becker in Widoma would know because Reb Leibush Magnes really lived in Widoma. This was an authentic voice. Daddy often had told of Widoma being on the other side of the stream. And then I remembered to say that in some of the books that my father and his brother had brought from Home my grandfather had written his name, and after that, "Verleger von Widoma." Then the old man said quickly, "Yes, when my father was Rov in Widoma, your grandfather was Dosser (Head of the Community) there." This was also an authentic voice, because Tante Fromme had told how her father was the most prominent gentleman of the Community, and its representative whenever there was anything (friendly or unfriendly) to do with the Goyim. That is a Dosser. I felt sure enough of my ground to show the Rov the Yichus Brief (genealogical records) which I had received a couple of years back from "a man named Seligfeld, in Czenstochan," who claimed to be a relative, and who traced the family history back to illustrious beginnings. The Rov read it through carefully without a word. It is a lengthy document. When finished, he began at the beginning and read through to the end again, and handed it back to me, saying, "Es stimt" [it appears to be correct].

While he was reading, I had glimpses through some of the many windows of the large room. Directly in the shadow opposite me was the door of the old Schul. Then through another window to the north lay the stream, 100 feet away; across the stream the little houses of Widoma, and beyond Widoma across the stream the trees, and the dark, bent, crowded gravestones of the cemetery.

What the old man and woman said about my grandparents, the Rabbi's reading of the Yichus Brief, the glimpses of the Synagogue, the stream, the bridges, Widoma, the graveyard—this was the heart of the visit—and whereas all the rest was interesting, those moments in the Rabbi's room had a grace of their own, and I should have been satisfied to be lifted away from this old world of my ancestors to my own world far away.

Several attempts were made to storm the Rabbi's door from without, and a few people succeeded in slipping through and bolting the door after them. Soon the real trial was to begin. We were first to visit the Synagogue. The tradition makes its age 600 years old—the same as the beautiful wooden Synagogue at Koniez. "Scholars" say it is not so old. Some woman also said that the Peroches (pulpit cloth) is a piece of the coronation robes of Napoleon. "Legendarisch, legendarisch," declared the Rov, thereby showing his own superior modernity.

We found our way through the crowd into the Synagogue. The Shammes [sexton] opened the carved doors with a good-sized key. I have a feeling that I did not give the Shammes enough, many a beggar getting more. He looked at what I gave him, and was the only man who gave no sign of satisfaction or dissatisfaction. But I left a considerable amount with the Rov, and I hope the Shammes gets his proper share.

Mr. Emerson took some pictures of the Schul, inside and out, and the Rov promised to have others taken, and also to send me a transcript of the various inscriptions on the walls. They are eulogies of some of the wise and pious and great men who prayed in that Synagogue in the course of its long history. A certain Reb Schlemele was among the greatest of these, and for a moment it appeared that I was one of his descendants. That was before the Rov came into the Schul. He killed the genealogical excitement by declaring authoritatively that my Yichus Brief mentions a very excellent Reb Schlemele, but hardly *the* Schlemele.

There arrived a Jew in the sixties—a dark, reddish beard, flattish nose, rather squat himself—a clean Jew—who soon took possession of the situation. Your grandfather? Of course, I knew him well. Leibush, Jehudah Leibush, of course. He was the son of Yankef. "No," said I, "a son of Abraham." "Of course, Abraham," said he. "I knew his wife well, Rachel." "No," said I, "his wife's name was Chava." "Why, of course," said he. "The Chava Jovente, the well-known Chava. And you say your father was her youngest son. I knew him well. Ephraim was his name." "No," said I, "his name was David." "David, David, that's it. He and I used to play together. We were of an age." "How old are you?" "I am in my sixties." "But my father was 75 when he died." "Yes, yes, that is probably so, but I knew the whole family well. I remember them perfectly. I shall show you where they lie buried."

"No, no," said a ragged creature, with a black beard and a rag tied over one eye and about his head. "I am the only one who knows."

The Rabbi pointed out the ark which he said had an inscription showing it to be at least 276 years old. (Date given here.)

I had expected to go over to Widoma to see Itzek Becker. But the way from the Schul to the car was a procession of miserables. Miserables stretching forth their hands for money, myself miserable in that I was tempted to empty my whole purse upon the ground, so ashamed was I of the money in my pocket. But I kept my head, and acted the scientific charity expert giving only here and there in small amounts. Before we got into the car, one woman shrieked that there was a relation of mine in town—the widower of a daughter of one of my father's brothers. He himself appeared. Nebich [pitiful]. I gave both him and her something on the chance she might be right.

She followed the car across the bridge to Widoma, and us along the path into the cemetery. But she was not the only one. A whole line of people stood on the Przedborg side of the bridge and ever so many crowded into the cemetery after us. It is an old place. Members of the Cemetery Committee were on the spot. They pointed out the mole holes. The moles dig their way from the river through the graves. Many a stone had fallen on account of it. There they lay, the fence of the cemetery had been broken down, and any kind of animal was at liberty to come in and graze and dirty up the place. Would I not help? Twenty-five thousand Polish marks would help. I promised this provided a properly authenticated letter came from the Committee.

But the graves of my grandparents, where were they? A number of people knew absolutely, but each time the stone was that of another. But soon the ragged, black-bearded man with the rag about his one eye came limping hurriedly from Przedborg. He found his way among and over the stones like a goat in its native mountain crags. This way and that, through tortuous rows of stones, and here lies the body of that Chava who was our grandmother. I see her picture hanging in our home—the enlargement from a small photograph she sent Daddy. The white ruching about her forehead, the grey shawl about her head and neck and shoulders, the firm, kind mouth, the straight nose, the shrewd eyes. Tante [Aunt] Fromme talks of this Ashes Chayil the "virtuous woman" of Proverbs as though the fame of her would always be alive and fresh among the Jews of that world. Were not her potatoes, her crops, always the best? Was she not the only one during the rebellion of 1863 to have supplies for the whole neighborhood? Was she not the Bobe par excellence? Well, here she lies, and only a few of the old know her name. The stone is taller than most of its neighbors. It is colored and has a flowery inscription, which they have promised to copy for me. It is not an old grave. I remember our mother saying that she had had a letter from the Bobe.

But not even the ragged one could find the grave of Jehudah Leibush Magnes. He died before our father was Bar Mitzvah. While we were searching, the Rov of Przedborg came. He was dressed now in official black, and made a handsome appearance. He carried with him the Pinkas—the official register of the Przedborg community. He had consulted it at home, and had the book open at the place recording Jehudah Leibush's burial. It read (Hebrew text which translates as follows): The man learned in Torah, the authorized Rabbi, R. Leibush Mag*de*s, and he is buried next to R. Benish, 5506, 29 Marcheshvan erev Rosh Chodesh Kislev.*

You will note two things. The one is that the name does not in the Pinkas spell Magnes, but Magdes. I looked twice to make sure of this. Further, that the year as I have it is 5506; that is 76 years ago. Either I have the figure wrong (the Rabbi promised me an exact copy), or Daddy was older than he thought. I think I copied the date wrong. They looked for the grave "next to R. Benish" but it could not be found. There stood the Rov with finger on the opened page, and there others ran about bending over, trying to locate the Torah scholar,

---

*The 29th of the Hebrew month of Mar'heshvan, the eve of the new month of Kislev.

R. Leibush, or the grave next to him, R. Benish. Meanwhile, the alleged relative of a daughter of a brother appeared, and declared that she would show us the grave of Daddy's brother Shaye (Isaiah). There it is between those two trees. No, there on that mound. What, have you not found it? Fine Shamosim (Sextons) of a community not to know where important people are buried. Soon the hunters wearied of the hunt. Only the ragged one stood by wisely saying, "Someone told him once to remember where Chava was buried, because someday someone was going to come and ask about it." The beggars were crowding the mourners hard by now. I gave one of the Committee men 2,000M. and deflected the stream somewhat to him. It was time to go. As we passed beyond the gate towards the Widoma street where the car was, others were still coming towards us from Przedborg way. A blind woman led by a little boy came running and stumbling in the wrong direction. They were soon turned back towards us. She fell on a pile of sand. She was satisfied when I gave her something. A little boy was crying about his sick mother. The grave-digger needed funds for himself. A lame man who was a mighty strong walker promised to share what I gave him with anyone I designated. . . .

Should I stop in to see the Widoma Rov, to see Itzek Becker? I should have liked to. But I was weary at heart. I had had a glimpse into that old world far away, long ago, through the Rov's windows. This world about me, feverish, chattering, miserable, had its claws in my flesh. I had seen the graves. No living member of the family was here. Perhaps Itzek Becker, too, would be of this world, and not of that of long ago. We jumped into the car, and were off for Lodz.

I comforted myself by saying that I should come back again to see Itzek Becker—some night perhaps, when not so many would see me come and go, and when some of the squalor might be softened by the darkness.

The soul of R. Leibush I knew before I came to Przedborg. Having been there, R. Leibush has taken on flesh for me.

It was good to touch the soil out of which our Daddy came. I think I know his soul better, and my own.

Notes

1. Norman Bentwich, *For Zion's Sake: A Biography of Judah L. Magnes* (Philadelphia, 1954) pp. 23–26, 31.

2. Arthur A. Goren, *Dissenter in Zion: From the Writings of Judah L. Magnes* (Cambridge, MA, 1982) p. 65.

3. Magnes to parents, 13 September 1901; 12 October 1902. Magnes Papers, Jerusalem. All archival sources cited are from the Magnes Papers.

4. Goren, pp. 64–66.

5. Magnes to family, 7 November 1901, quoted in Yohai Goell, "*Aliya* in the Zionism of an American *Oleh:* Judah L. Magnes," *American Jewish Historical Quarterly* LXV (December, 1975) 103.

6. Magnes to family, 11 November 1902; 16 May 1901; 7 July 1901; Bentwich, pp. 29–30.

7. Magnes to family, 8 September 1901.

8. Bentwich, pp. 27–28.

9. Goren, pp. 14–19, 131–134.

10. Bentwich, pp. 10–14; David Magnes, Autobiographical notes, 8 March 1909; 5 October 1911; 18 July 1915.

The East European Jew in the Weimar Press: Stereotype and Attempted Rebuttal

Trude Maurer
(UNIVERSITY OF TÜBINGEN)

The mass migration to the West that started with the catastrophic famine and epidemics of 1868/9 sent some two million Jews from Eastern Europe through Germany in the years up till the outbreak of the First World War. It also created a resident East European Jewish community, which comprised some seventy thousand persons in 1910, or 11.4 percent of the German Jewish population.[1] The Jews in Western and Eastern Europe had developed separately from each other for at least two centuries, and with the passage of time the Western image of the *Ostjude* took on a negative coloring: the Jew from the East was the "Ghetto Jew," a cultural and physical type contrasted with the emancipated German Jews.[2]

The First World War brought with it the recruitment of East European Jews for labor in Germany and their number was swelled by mass flight from economic distress and pogroms. About one hundred thousand East European Jews entered Germany between 1914 and 1921, of whom some 40 percent moved further on or else returned to their homes by the end of this period.[3]

With the war there also came an increase and a radicalization of anti-Semitism, now implanted in a larger system of values and all-embracing goals directed toward Germany's recovery.[4] The German occupation of Poland and fear of mass immigration from that region gave fresh impetus to agitation against the East European Jews, climaxing in the demand to close the frontiers. The war, however, also brought a great number of German and German Jewish soldiers into direct contact with East European Jews for the first time, and while this often tended to strengthen the stereotype of the "Ghetto Jew," it sometimes led to the "discovery" and even to the "cult" of the *Ostjude*—at least on the part of a small group.[5]

In the discussion which follows, we will examine the *Ostjude* image as it was presented in the German press in the aftermath of the war and in the context of the socio-economic crisis that burdened the new German republic. What should be made clear at the outset is that opinions expressed publicly may have differed considerably from views privately expressed in Jewish and non-Jewish circles. The analysis here will be based on periodicals, mainly weeklies, representing various political parties and extra-parliamentary groups as well as the Christian denominations and the main trends of opinion within German Jewry.[6] It also draws on the minutes of the Reichstag and the Prussian Diet (Landtag) to complement the picture.[7] We shall compile an inventory of the stereotypes, and in so doing we shall see who disparaged—even attacked—the East European Jews and who defended them. To what extent did attitudes differ on the part of Jews and non-Jews? What weapons were used in attack and defense? What was the relation between what non-Jews wrote about East European Jews and what they thought about German Jews?

ECONOMIC PARASITISM, PHYSICAL AND MORAL HYGIENE, AND CRIMINALITY

The itinerant Jew from the East who begged his way from one community to another was a well-known phenomenon in German Jewish life long before the First World War. The *Ostjude* concept was in fact linked from the outset with the figure of the wandering beggar.[8] Immediately after the war Jewish sources spoke mainly of the recrudescence of *Schnorrertum* (begging) and only later of its resurgence.[9] On the other hand, in non-Jewish and even in anti-Semitic pronouncements, hardly anything was said about it.[10] The most important characteristic of the beggar—that he does not work—was, however, brought up over and over again,[11] and the same idea was intended in the use of the term "parasite."[12] When Jewish newspapers agreed that "work-shy" elements did exist among the East European Jews, they countered with the argument that the disinclination to work had become so general a phenomenon in European society, and in Germany in particular since the war, that the East European Jews would have had to be angels to escape this malady entirely.[13] German soldiers and German employers were cited as witnesses to the East European Jews' remarkable diligence.[14]

But the East European Jews were relatively seldom reproached with beggary and idleness largely because the constant tendency in Germany was to assume that they were all traders. A Reichstag representative of the Deutsche Demokratische Partei (DDP) referred to their well-known "passion for trade."[15] With their "pedlar mentality,"[16] they were seen as a threat to honest merchants. Church periodicals likewise resorted to this one-dimensional portrayal, long enshrined in the popular mind.[17] More specifically, the *Ostjuden* were criticized on two counts: one, that they "traded in everything" (thus, for example, the Socialist *Neue Zeit*);[18] the *Alldeutsche Blätter* put it more concretely—the *Ostjude* even sold information about other people like shares on the stock-exchange thereby rating even their passions and failings.[19] The main point of the criticism, however, was that buying and selling was not a productive activity.[20]

Jews who tried to counter the charge that their only function was trading seldom argued that trade was economically essential, that distribution was, for example, of vital benefit to the German army of occupation in wartime.[21] It was exceptional for the economic activity of the East European Jews in Germany to be described as useful. Only rarely was the point made that they were active in branches neglected by the indigenous economy; that they thus created jobs and stepped up production; that they had started trade going with the East early on and kept it going.[22]

Sixty percent of the Jews in Prussia in 1925 were in the "trade and commerce" classification. That German Jews not only refrained from defending trade, but at the same time promoted occupational deconcentration *(Berufsumschichtung)* among themselves as well as among Eastern Jews seems to show that they agreed at least in part with the judgment that trade was unproductive.[23] Rather, the attempt was made in general to explain the concentration of East European Jews in this line of work by referring to the adverse economic and legal conditions prevailing in their countries of origin. It was typically argued that they had been cut off from the soil and had had acquisitiveness forcibly stamped upon them; trading was their only way of earning a living, not freely chosen.[24]

The regulations governing demobilization in Germany, it was argued, had only exacerbated the problem. Albert Einstein wrote in the *Berliner Tageblatt:*

> The mistaken policy of discharging thousands of East European Jewish workers who were forcibly brought to Germany during the war, leaving them unemployed and denied opportunities of working, must in actual fact force people who do not want their families to starve into illicit trading.[25]

Only the *Verband nationaldeutscher Juden* (The League of National German Jews), which always spoke out sharply against the East European Jews in terms hardly to be distinguished from those of the anti-Semites, spoke of the propensity of the *Ostjuden* for trade (with its accompanying "instinctive" skills) without going into the issue of causes.[26]

Jewish spokesmen sometimes referred to the willingness of the East Europeans to work as artisans or in agriculture and to the fact that these were actually the occupations of most of the immigrants.[27] Non-Jews were eagerly quoted in support of this theme—as, for example, the President of the Reichstag, Paul Loebe, who had studied these issues as an editor in Breslau and later on journeys in Poland, and who found the pioneering activities in Palestine "moving," as he told a Poalei Zion meeting in 1925.[28]

From travels in Eastern Europe, it was generally known at this time that there was little question in those parts of German cleanliness. It is not surprising, therefore, to find a German Jew who described the Galician Jews in the Austrian army as "caftan soldiers," whose conduct was "dirty and untidy."[29] The OSE, transferred to Berlin in 1922 as the "International League for Jewish Health Protection," opened a Migration Health Museum. That the explanations were in Yiddish and that the exhibition would later be taken to the larger urban centers of Poland, Lithuania and Latvia showed where hygienic education was thought to be necessary.[30]

And, of course, the anti-Semites could not help dwelling on the dirt of the *Ostjude*. "The complete lack of any sort of sense of cleanliness, bodily care and hygiene is the signature of the *Ostjude*." "In all Germany there wasn't a single dog as verminous as the richest Jew here or as the Rabbi."[31] The absence of hygiene and the presence of vermin were often adduced as the cause of illnesses allegedly or actually widespread among the *Ostjuden*—scabies, trachoma, tuberculosis, cholera and other infectious or contagious diseases.[32] In the low anti-Semitic paper *Hammer,* a reader wrote about a Romanian Jew with a chronic veneral disease who boasted of having seduced and infected many German women.[33] The alleged danger from the *Ostjuden* could not have been more clearly demonstrated. Most of the accusations of immorality were tied up with reports on sexual debauchery. The *Hammer* always gave details (place, name, date) and referred to reports in local newspapers so as to convey the impression that the report was a matter of actual fact.[34] From these examples the reader was, of course, expected to draw general conclusions.

Alongside personal, private debauchery, business exploitation of sex also played an important role in the anti-Semitic portrayal of the

Ostjude. The Führer-to-be wrote in 1925 that in his Vienna days he already recognized the "relation of Jewry to prostitution and still more to the white slave trade" even though this tie was still hidden from "the majority of the German people."[35] Jewish sources were often quoted by the anti-Semites to prove that the trade in girls was in the hands of Jews.[36] Names and figures would be given—for example, in reports of arrests—when treating this theme, again in order to stress the credibility of the anti-Semitic agitation. "Facts" of this kind would be urgently needed by the *Hammer,* for example, when it had allowed the subject to simmer down for a long time for lack of new cases and was reduced to repeating a quotation from the London *Jewish Chronicle* of 1910, or of a report (dating from 1911) on the pre-war period, or even an article on the tenth century envoy Ibrahim ibn Jaqub.[37]

The subject of the "white slave trade" attracted great interest in the Jewish press when two international conferences on the matter took place in London—one actually sponsored by Jewish organizations. At the non-sectarian conference, Regierungsrat (government councillor) Kundt, chairman of the German *Nationalkommittee gegen Mädchenhandel,* presented a report. This Committee was in fact a private organization, but Kundt had managed to attach himself to the director of the police branch dealing with the matter on an official tour. Kundt linked the trade with activities in smuggling people across the frontier between Poland and Germany, and named only East European Jews as guilty parties.[38] Various Jewish organizations successfully took steps to counter these insinuations, although many German Jews were hesitant to admit the reality of the traffic and many denied it outright—primarily, of course, from fear of anti-Semitic reactions. When Jewish writers attributed the alleged traffic to economic necessity, this did not only correspond with the general structure of their argument against anti-Semitic charges, but also with the analysis of non-Jews who fought the "white slave trade."[39]

The whole field of sexual offenses was widely used to demonstrate how immorality was organically linked to criminality. The *Ostjude* was thus numbered among the "typical Berlin crooks." Over and over again, the *Hammer* gave reports about pickpockets, street bag-snatchers, gangs of thieves and receivers of stolen goods.[40] The anti-Semitic press regularly directed suspicion against the *Ostjude* in cases of murder. The disappearance of children and young people was reported, with veiled references to ritual murder.[41]

> The number of young people who have disappeared has increased in direct proportion to the numbers of *Ostjuden* sneaking in! In the last two years several hundred children and young people of both sexes have

disappeared without a trace. We express the suspicion that the two phenomena are causally connected, for there is no other explanation and anything can be believed of this bestialized rabble.[42]

That there were criminals among both Eastern and Western Jews was in no way contested in German Jewish circles: In the Jewish press Jewish institutions frequently warned each other of swindlers and imposters. But Jews permitted themselves to suggest that "criminal elements" existed in other circles of the population as well.[43] The roundups in the Berlin "Scheunenviertel" where many *Ostjuden* lived were cited to discount the alleged criminality of the East European Jews, because the police soon released almost all those they arrested.[44]

CONSUMERS OF SCARCE RESOURCES, PROFITEERS AND REVOLUTIONARIES

The East European Jews were reproached not only for their supposedly timeless character traits but also for specific post-war problems, for which they were held responsible: the food supply difficulties and the housing shortage. The frequent repetition of these accusations made them into part of the stereotype. "Mass immigration" of East European Jews was being tolerated, so the angry charges went, in spite of the shortage of consumer goods and it increased this shortage intolerably.[45] For example, a Stadtverordneter (City Councillor) in Elberfeld saw the German patrons of a middle class eating house as being displaced, because the number of East European habitués had risen from two to twenty and these conducted themselves insolently. In response, the Oberbürgermeister pointed out that there were only some seven hundred East European Jewish immigrants residing in Elberfeld, and this, according to the *Jüdische Rundschau,* was less than 0.5 percent of the total population.[46]

Similarly, the Social-Democratic deputy Heilmann was of the opinion that in a country of sixty million Germans, forty thousand East Europeans Jews could hardly make much difference to the food situation;[47] while his party colleague, Limbertz, quoted the trade unions of Essen that no particular food shortages had resulted from Eastern Jewish immigration.[48] The assertion by Paul Nathan that many of the immigrant Jews had been brought in during the war specifically to help solve the food problem in the occupied territories could also be understood as an argument against the allegation that they were creating a food shortage.[49]

Still more frequent were the complaints over the housing shortage.

The causes of the problem and its possible solutions had been discussed repeatedly in the general press in the last years of the war. As late as mid-1918, however, a *völkisch* paper could express surprise at the "constant outcry over the frightful housing shortage" and ask whether this might not be "a fantasy picture painted by land and building speculators."[50] The director of the Statistisches Landesamt (State Bureau of Statistics) could explain the causes of the housing shortage in the same paper,[51] but this did not prevent the East European Jews from being made the scapegoats over and over again.[52] Even if the *Alldeutscher Verband* (Pan-German League) did once or twice mention German refugees from the former Prussian provinces in the East, this paper, too, later called the housing shortage in the big towns simply "a consequence of the immigration of East European Jews."[53]

But the association of the shortage with the Jews from the East had deeply penetrated the general consciousness as well. The German nationalist *Eiserne Blätter* saw Jewish money and Jewish influence as the answer to the riddle of how two hundred thousand foreigners could be living in Berlin while three hundred thousand Germans were looking for dwellings fit for human habitation.[54] In the *Deutsche Stimmen,* published by Stresemann (DVP), in the middle of lengthy reflections on separatist tendencies ('Los von Berlin'), the East European Jews suddenly turned up, "taking away flats from the residents."[55] A deputy belonging to the Deutschhannoversche (Hanover-German) Party called the situation in Germany "scandalous" and spoke of the feeling that must be experienced by the simple German when he found a caftaned immigrant given precedence in the choice of living quarters. A representative of the Zentrum (Catholic Center), Loenartz, cited the example of the Housing Bureau, which had offered the minister for welfare and his family the prospect of one room and a kitchen after a wait of several months, and he insisted that under these circumstances it would be "inappropriate if Jews, especially foreigners, were in some way to claim housing in Berlin, as is actually the case."[56] Even some Jews joined in the chorus.[57] Proposed countermeasures—from stopping immigration[58] to expulsions[59]—were always said to aim at making housing available for German refugees, whether they had been expelled from the Volga region or from the Ruhr.[60]

German Jews publicly recognized that the appearance of "numerous fellow-consumers from the great human reservoir of the East [. . .] is naturally found disagreeable." At the same time, however, they warned against exaggerating the number of immigrants.[61] The accusations were met by accounts of the real housing situation, of the crowded quarters in over-expensive lodgings in which the *Ostjuden* were living.[62] East European Jews were satisfied with housing that

German lodgers would not take, or they stayed with relatives and acquaintances.⁶³ Occasionally, the standard attacks on the *Ostjude* were thrown back against the rich foreigners in the "fashionable quarters"—Baltic barons, Russian ex-generals and nobility, who rented ten- to twelve-room apartments by underhanded means.⁶⁴

Food and housing shortages were often cited or at the same time as arguments against permitting Jews to immigrate from the East, not only by the *Hammer* but also by the Deutschnationalen in the Prussian Diet and by a DDP representative at a meeting of the *Centralverein deutscher Staatsbürger jüdischen Glaubens* (Central Union of German Citizens of the Jewish Faith). To be sure, the DDP-member called for equal treatment and equal respect for German Jewish citizens; but this equality did not apply to the immigrant Jews.⁶⁵ The fact that other (not formally anti-Semitic) parties took up the argument from time to time shows that it was broadly popular, at least until 1924. After that, references to shortages in connection with East European immigrants were far less frequent.

The East European Jews were attacked not only as consumers but still more as profiteers destroying the economy. It was not out of necessity that they stole food-stocks; traded in bread ration cards; corrupted city officials; sent up the price of furniture with installment payments so that a German couple could no longer afford to get married. This anti-Semitic agitation found powerful supporters among the National German Jews:

> Whole stretches of Berlin's streets pass into their hands, without any of the residents ever getting to see his landlord. They don't give a hoot for the rent receipts, for the authorities, who demand taxes and upkeep, and above all for the wishes of the lessee residents [. . .] They are not keen solely on houses, by no means. For them whatever is to be had for money is an object that can be bought and sold. Old clothes and the latest art, jewels and furs, metals, and hard currency, they sell everything and then buy it up again. In the meantime they buy our food, our linen, our textiles, clothes and footwear.⁶⁶

There were frequent complaints that city properties were passing into more and more foreign hands.⁶⁷

The German Jews naturally put a distance between themselves and profiteers and demanded that the latter receive well-deserved punishment.⁶⁸ They did attempt all the same to assess both the general situation in which profiteering occurred and the particular circumstances of the East European Jews:

> How far trade in itself is to be thought of today as profiteering we shall not go into here. We have only to affirm that even for German mer-

chants it has publicly been called practically impossible to observe all the innumerable wartime and post-war regulations, and it can be tacitly confessed that every merchant has at some time been guilty of a breach of these regulations.[69]

It was further argued that profiteering resulted invariably from the far-reaching ban on the employment of foreigners following demobilization, and picking out the immigrant Jews from profiteers in general distracted attention from other, large-scale speculators.[70] Finally, the tactics of defense included counter-attacking the reactionary circles that made billions in profiteering deals with the West across the unguarded post-armistice frontiers.[71] All these arguments demonstrating the limited and conditional nature of Jewish profiteering made not the slightest impression on opponents. The *Nationaldeutsche Jude* contemptuously dismissed "the uncritical defense and hushing-up tactics of some Jewish organizations."[72]

The Jews were also said to inflict damage on the finances of the state by trading in gold and other precious metals. Already during the war, a Polish newspaper report was semi-officially distributed about some Polish Jews arrested in Hamburg, who had tried to smuggle a large quantity of gold into Poland. The *Centralverein* sought to explain this case away in its journal, *Im deutschen Reich:*

> Jews in the occupied territories could pay the fees for passports, certificates and the like and buy *matzos* only with gold. That the scene of events was a port seemed to show that it was a matter of bringing gold in from the enemy and neutral foreign countries. And even if it was not done specifically for this purpose, these Polish Jews were still deserving well of Germany [. . .] since they were getting good German gold away from foreigners. And even if this gold did not go directly to the German State Bank where it belonged, it went all the same to a country under German control and from there in the way indicated above to the coffers of the *Reichsbank*.[73]

East European Jews were attacked by the anti-Semites simultaneously as both capitalists and revolutionaries. Either these contradictory roles were made to appear directly complementary—proletarians and capitalists together pursuing similar, and in fact Jewish, aims;[74] or alternatively, they went a good part of the way together towards their different final goals:

> In order to achieve power, Jews without possessions need the complete inner and external ruination of the people among whom they dwell. Jewry with possessions needs only inner national attrition and the national inability to resist [. . .] In the last resort, however, anarchist Jews

unintentionally supported the possessing Jews, because in anarchy they themselves become the possessors; anarchy does not last long, while Jewish capital then still finds a broadened economic sphere in the rubble of the state.[75]

Many saw the Russian revolution as an example, as they believed, of the decisive influence of the Jews.[76] In Germany as well, Russian Jews were seen to be producing plans, propaganda and money for the revolution.[77] It was even argued that the attempted revolutions in Germany had been the work of a small clique of Jews, mostly of Russian origin.[78] The leaders of the revolt in Munich, above all Toller and Eisner, were repeatedly stigmatized as *Ostjuden*.[79] In March 1919 the *Alldeutsche Blätter* could state that "under Eisner the leadership was Galician-Jewish; and now it is Russian-Jewish."[80] Alongside the prominent leaders, minor figures were everywhere seen at work: the director of a ministry who had just been naturalized, artists, students.[81] There also seems to have been a widespread belief that the Spartacus rising in the Ruhr had resulted for the most part from the subversive activities of *Ostjuden*. The *Kölnische Volkszeitung* said it was remarkable "how these people, easily recognizable by their long caftans and the rest of their outlandish appearance, have the main say at popular meetings."[82] Anti-Semitic periodicals produced lists of "ringleaders."

For its part, the *Centralverein* tried to counter with detailed information about the persons mentioned.[83] The Jewish Workers' Welfare Bureau affirmed that the participation of Jewish workers in the German Communist forces was "absolutely minimal and completely normal, reflecting the situation in a time like the Kapp days."[84]* The Prussian Minister of the Interior was quoted by the journal of the *Centralverein* affirming that there could be no question of East European Jews being prominent in the uprising.[85] Nevertheless, the endless repetition of the idea that Jews equalled Bolsheviks also played a role for many parliamentary parties: for example, the DVP and DNVP.[86] It enjoyed some credence even among Jews,[87] making the refutation of such generalizations all the harder. True, there were also calls not to react to such charges, as being undeserving of serious discussion; but attempts were made all the same to contest, or explain away, the entire notion.[88]

Sometimes the moral commitment of the revolutionaries was stressed,[89] but more often oppression and social distress were cited as the factors responsible for Jewish participation in the revolutionary movement. It was declared surprising that more or even all Russian

---

*Kapp was a conservative politician who for a few days became chancellor in a *Putsch* against the republican government, led by General Lüttwitz and himself in March 1920.

Jews had not turned into revolutionaries. This argument did not prevent thoroughgoing criticism of the revolutionary position. A major thesis put forward in this area was that the revolutionaries inwardly no longer belonged to Jewry at all, or else that they had forfeited this attachment because their life contradicted the Jewish *Weltanschauung*.[90] Further, it was stressed that the very hardships brought down on most of the Jews by the social upheavals were enough to turn them against Bolshevism.[91]

DEHUMANIZATION

The catchword "The *Ostjude* Peril" was always driven home by comparisons with animals. Designating all East European Jews without distinction as "vermin," for example, was very widespread in anti-Jewish circles.[92] However, they were also called "beasts" and "hyenas" as well.[93] "A horrible sight," declared the *Hammer*, "this look of predatory animals—no trace of human emotions—spotting the prey, stealing up on it, springing on it and strangling it."[94] Insects, too, were pressed into service as when they appear in swarms like locusts.[95] Regardless of the absurdity of the thing, the image of the nation eaten away and "writhing in its death-throes" was to be found even in such ecclesiastical journals as the *Evangelische Kirchenboten für die Pfalz*. This extraordinary magnification of something so minute into something so powerful, corresponds entirely to the language of mythification generally to be found in *völkisch* and Nazi publications.[96]

The image of the hyena, of the "march of the vultures from Vienna to Berlin"[97] spoken of by a National-German deputy, graphically evoked death and putrefaction. The aim was similar when East European Jews were characterized in the Reichstag as a cancerous affliction and in a Liberal paper as pests.[98] Animal comparisons directed mostly against political opponents were not so rare then and were in no way used exclusively by the extreme Right,[99] but on the whole this was a sporadic phenomenon except when it came to anti-Semitic rhetoric. There the *Ostjude* was not *compared* to animals, but *identified* with them.[100]

PRIMITIVE ASIATICS

It was a basic anti-Semitic assumption that the East European Jews were "a racially foreign, inferior and therefore highly undesirable section of the population."[101] There were nevertheless difficulties in defining their racial affiliation. The *Ostjuden* were said to be "a product of the most unnatural mixture of races." "The Slav-Jewish-German mongrel is the most abominable human being that has ever been propagated on the Earth."[102] Since racial mixture was seen as highly dangerous, the Eastern Jew had *a priori* to be rated an inferior being.[103] The Socialist *Neue Zeit* quoted with tacit approval a mayor in Switzerland, who said that the East European Jews "were strictly speaking not Europeans at all." The Evangelical paper, *Türmer,* called their immigration a "Tatar invasion," and to others they appeared as "Asiatics from the lowest levels." Such ideas were even publicized by the National-German Jews in their column for the comment of non-Jews, "Voices From the Other Shore."[104]

In rebutting these anti-Semitic attacks on the Jews as primitive Asiatics, a distinction was drawn between merely external civilization, on the basis of which modern culture was stated to be judged, and spiritual and ethical values. The latter were the criterion applied in evaluating ancient culture and should be applied to *Ostjuden* as well.[105] Another line of defense emphasized what can be called "the Germanness of the East European Jew." According to this approach, the East European Jews were in fact former German Jews who had migrated eastwards in the Middle Ages or had fled thither to escape persecution. There they had waged "a hard struggle for German language and culture."[106]

Yiddish, which had been discarded by German Jews since the emancipation, was discovered in this context to be a German dialect that could be presented as "paving the way for the Germans" (or the German language) in Eastern Europe.[107] The Catholic chaplain Roedel affirmed in the *Israelitischen Familienblatt* that the Jews had preserved the German language better than the Christians who had migrated to the East and who in the course of the centuries had "gradually shed everything German."[108] They would appear to have surpassed even the Germans themselves in their love and knowledge of German culture and especially literature.[109] It was rare for Jews to criticize this line, as Jacob Klatzkin once did referring to Jewish policies during the First World War: "People looked for and found all sorts of relations between Jews and German-ness. In Zionist circles, too, people were not ashamed to claim Yiddish as a German dialect in order to proffer it to victorious Imperialism as a tie between East European Jewry and Germany's Eastern policy."[110]

On this basis new immigrants after the war, it was suggested, should actually be considered returnees.[111] But this idea received short shrift from the authorities, as was noted by Hermann Badt (a high official in a Prussian ministry and a Zionist): "The centuries-long residence of their forefathers on German soil was not as a rule of any avail to those East European Jews who wanted to re-immigrate as Germans, laying claim to rights of precedence over the Germans living to the east of the Elbe, who had been hostile to everything German for centuries."[112]

In internal Jewish discussion, German Jews sometimes made the reverse point—that the German Jews as such were originally descended from East European Jewish immigrants.[113] And, of course, anti-Semites used the same contention in order to attack the German Jews. The danger from the East European Jews was that they would eventually become German Jews, since the "Grenadierstrasse becomes the breeding place for would-be German citizens of the Jewish faith."[114]

The Jews from the East were sometimes stated to be the main cause of anti-Semitism. This argument was often put forward in an attempt to pressure the German Jews themselves to work against immigration. The implication was that if they failed to do so, anti-Semitism would increase. In general, anti-Semites advocated the curtailment of Jewish equal rights by "legal means." The low press, however, compounded this with threats of pogroms.[115] For the extreme anti-Semite, behind the German Jewish businessman there lurked an *Ostjude:* a swindler or thief; behind the theatrical agent the white slave trader; behind the doctor the Jew who perverted German women. The two communities were joined by common behavior, racial affiliation and origin. German Jews for the most part recognized that the anti-Semites made no distinction between Western and Eastern Jews. The East European Jews were "the main target only tactically" and in fact it was the German Jews or the Jews as such that were meant.[116]

This may be one explanation of the discrepancy between the often-cited widespread antipathy felt by German Jewry for the *Ostjuden* and the picture given here of the German Jews over a broad spectrum doggedly defending their fellow Jews from the East. Individual pronouncements apart, the one Jewish group that agitated consistently against the East European Jews was the *Verband nationaldeutscher Juden*. With that one exception, the assault was conducted by non-Jews.

IN DEFENSE OF THE *OSTJUDE*

At this point, in order to see the full picture, it is necessary to recall that Germans—primarily Jews but also, on occasion non-Jews—were ready in this period (more so than before the war) to note favorable traits in the *Ostjude*. The positive approach found expression not only in direct response to anti-Semitism, but also in other and varied contexts.

Contemporaries thus could emphasize the propensity of the East European Jews for charity and for frugality in personal life. These were praised by the orthodox journalist of the *Israelit* and by German-Jewish soldiers and confirmed by noble landowners who employed Eastern Jews on their manors.[117] Christian soldiers were quoted describing their hospitality and readiness to help.[118]

A feature story in the *Israelit* was devoted to a poor, illiterate East European Jew who had risen to riches in Berlin but still remained simple and modest in his way of life and showed his concern for synagogue and welfare institutions by making large contributions. Here frugality and generosity went together in ideal conjunction.[119] The marked sense of family among the East European Jews was depicted in different ways in the Jewish journals[120] and also, at times, by non-Jews on various occasions.[121] Their love of their home country expressed in their yearning from afar for Russia, where they had languished in the obscurity of the "ghetto" was likewise the subject of admiration.[122] Their religious devotion was highly praised by the most varied Jewish currents, and Jewish officers in the German army waxed emotional over the piety they had come to know in the East.[123]

As a result of their religiosity, which made for constant "learning," the East European Jews were seen as peculiarly apt for spiritual activity in general. The attributes accorded them were thus intelligence, appetite for knowledge and a strong drive for education.[124] Since he considered study as an aim in itself, it would be quite natural for the East European Jew "to earn his bread in some hard and often humble way without any connection with his studies."[125] Some commentators, alarmed by this romanticizing trend, complained that even poverty and dirt were found picturesque by some enthusiasts, and that the East European Jews were being idealized inordinately. But there were few real grounds for such fears. In general, Jewish observers from Germany noted above all the economic distress and backward civilization of the Jews of Eastern Europe, and sought ways to have them raised to a "higher level."[126]

Among non-Jewish groups, only part of the Social-Democrats and the Communists were found ready to defend the East European Jews. However, Communists especially defended them not as Jews or as a national or religious community, but as proletarians suspected of being revolutionaries and agitators. Communist protest against the discriminatory treatment of East European Jews was part of their fight against the political system, whose treatment of foreign workers seemed to them to be perpetuating the policies of Imperial Germany. If foreigners were held responsible for depressed conditions, this, rebutted the Left, was in order to divert the workers' attention from the really guilty parties.[127]

In the SPD organ *Neue Zeit,* there was only one article (in several installments) about East European Jews—and it was copied for the most part word for word from a Pan-German pamphlet of 1915. The author distinguished himself from both the Jews and the anti-Semites writing on the *Ostjuden;* included a few sentences on the Jews as a cultural force and on the significance of the Jewish Bund for Russian socialism; and closed with a modest demand for the regulation of immigration in accordance with the state of the labor market. Nonetheless, his article can only be called anti-Semitic.[128] In the *Sozialistische Monatschefte,* on the other hand, Jews active in welfare work for East European Jews wrote some well-informed and sympathetic articles, which corresponded to some extent with the views of the Workers' Welfare Bureau of the Jewish organizations.

An analysis of the debates and motions presented in the Prussian Diet and the German Reichstag confirms that the Independent Social-Democrats (USPD) and the Communists tended to defend the East European Jews. In contrast, not only did the *Völkische* and National-Germans (DNVP) introduce motions to limit the immigration of Jews and restrict their rights; the Liberals (Deutsche Volkspartei and the Deutsche Demokratische Partei) also attacked immigrant Jews, despite the fact that both these parties stood in principle for the equal rights of Jews in Germany and that both were critical of the *völkisch* groups. For the DVP equal rights for Jews—within the party at least—was considered to be conditional on their aligning themselves with the way of life and thought of the German people. At the same time, that party was worried that anti-Semitism would push the Jews to the Left.[129] Moreover, a clear affinity existed between DVP and the *Verband nationaldeutscher Juden.*[130] The attitude towards Eastern Jews was totally negative.

Das demokratische Deutschland always argued against anti-Semitism, urging that people must be judged according to their individual integrity and achievements,[131] but within the party anti-Semitism existed in moderate form and Jews were discriminated against—in the choice of candidates for example—for tactical political reasons, ostensibly.[132] Eastern Jews were at times defended against open discrimination—the expulsion of Jewish students in Bavaria, for instance. The party supported measures against "mass immigration," however, with the proviso that the measures as implemented by the states be narrowly interpreted: immigrants were not automatically to be classed as "burdensome foreigners" just because there was unemployment in Germany or because they were suspected of holding radical views. On the other hand, speeches about aggravation of the housing shortage; the food shortage; the threats to the national health; all as possible consequences of immigration, together with explanations of just how the East European Jews contributed to these problems, were clearly reminiscent of those made by the self-declared anti-Semites.[133] Precisely through complaints over post-war problems, the concretization of stereotypes in a defined situation, anti-Semitic modes of thought were spread further and further in the democratic camp.

CONCLUSIONS

What conclusions can be drawn from this extensive reading of the journals of the Weimar period? Clearly, the relatively large population of *Ostjuden* left in Germany in the wake of the war proved an ideal target for every form of anti-Semitic agitation. The idea of any significant Jewish immigration from the East was highly unpopular with the mass of the German people. As a result, the center and conservative parties tended to join in the hounding of the *Ostjude,* although with a less obsessive perspective than that shown by the overtly anti-Semitic, *völkisch* camp. Only on the Left were there movements ready to raise their voice—by no means unanimously or loudly—in defense of the immigrants and of a measure of immigration.

Faced by the broad spectrum of hostility to the immigrants, the German Jews were thrown very much on to the defensive. The marginal group of Jews who defined themselves as national German *(Verband nationaldeutscher Juden)* chose (in loose alliance with the Deutsche Volkspartei) to mark themselves off totally from the *Ostjuden,* calling for a complete halt to immigration. At the other extreme, there were Jews—individuals and even groups (primarily Zionist)—who idealized the *Ostjude,* seeing in him the true embodiment of authentic Jewish values. The mainstream spokesmen for German Jewry chose to defend the *Ostjude*—at least publicly—with a high degree of persistence. In general, it was realized that in attacking the *Ostjude,* the anti-Semites were simply selecting the weakest flank of Jewry as a whole. But the Jewish spokesmen were clearly unsure of how best to present their case. While apologetic overtones in a number of statements might have weakened the power of their argument, their method of *Aufklärung* (enlightening), i.e. of explaining circumstances and drawing on statistics to prove that the *Ostjuden* were a productive, non-criminal element rested on faith in reason and the reasonableness of their fellow men. Given their high degree of isolation on the *Ostjuden* issue and the totally unrestrained emotionalism of the anti-Semitic camp, their efforts were to be without any major result.

List of Periodicals

I. Jewish
Allgemeine Zeitung des Judentums (AZJ). Liberal
Im deutschen Reich (IdR) and *CV-Zeitung* (CVZ), organs of the Centralverein deutscher Staatsbürger jüdischen Glaubens.
Jüdisch-liberale Zeitung (JLZ), of the Vereinigung für das liberale Judentum.
Israelitisches Familienblatt (IF). Inclined toward the views of the CV.
Der Israelit (I), of the "Austrittsorthodoxie" (Agudas Israel).
Jüdische Presse (JP). Orthodox, central organ of the Mizrachi from 1920 on.
Jüdische Rundschau (JR), organ of the Zionistische Vereinigung für Deutschland.
Der national-deutsche Jude (NdJ). Until 1924: *Mitteilungsblatt des Verbandes nationaldeutscher Juden*.
Ost und West (OuW) founded 1901 to promote communication between German and East European Jews.

II. Non-Jewish
Völkisch periodicals:
Deutschlands Erneuerung (DE). Circulation ca. 6500.
Alldeutsche Blätter (AdB) of the Alldeutsche Verband. (In 1922, ca. 40,000 members)
Hammer (H) (ca. 6–8,000 subscribers).
Party organs:
Eiserne Blätter (EB) of the Deutschnationale Volkspartei (DNVP)
Deutsche Stimmen (DS) of the Deutsche Volkspartei (DVP).
Das demokratische Deutschland (DD). After 1923, *Deutsche Einheit;* of the Deutsche Demokratische Partei (DDP).
Neue Zeit (NZ) and *Sozialistische Monatshefte* (SM), Social-Democrats.
Das Zentrum (appeared only 1921 to 1923) and *Historisch-politische Blätter für das katholische Deutschland* which represented the Catholic Center Party (with reservations to be made in the case of the latter after 1918) did not include any articles on the problem of *Ostjuden*.

Notes

1. J. Wertheimer, "German Policy and Jewish Politics. The Absorption of East European Jews in Germany." (Unpublished doctoral thesis, Columbia University, 1979) pp. 13, 193, 199 note 9 and p. 568.
2. Cf. S. Aschheim, *Brothers and Strangers. The East European Jew in German and German Jewish Consciousness, 1800–1923* (Madison, 1982), esp. Ch. 1.

3. This was the estimate of the *Arbeiterfürsorgeamt* of the Jewish organizations in Germany, an estimate which was also used by the Reich Minister of the Interior in a memorandum. JR (12 August 1921) p. 460; cf. IF (18 August 1921), p. 3 and IdR (July–August, 1921), p. 226; *Verhandlungen des Reichstags. Anlage zu den Stenographischen Berichten,* Vol. 372, no. 4084, pp. 4382–4404, esp. p. 4385 (30 March, 1922). In the population census of 1925, 107,747 Jews out of a total of 564,400 were listed as foreigners. Among these, 14.2 percent were East European Jews (i.e., some eighty thousand), citizens of Poland, Hungary, Romania, Russia, Lithuania and Latvia, as well as stateless persons. Cf. S. Adler-Rudel, *Ostjuden in Deutschland 1880–1940* (Tübingen, 1959), p. 165ff. On the recruitment of labor, J. Berger, *Ostjüdische Arbeiter im Kriege. Ein Beitrag zur Arbeitervermittlung unter Juden* (Berlin, 1919); Central Zionist Archives (CZA), Jerusalem, Z3/167, 168, 169 (on Berger's activity in the German Arbeiterzentrale in Warsaw).

4. Cf. W. Jochmann, "Die Ausbreitung des Antisemitismus," in W. Mosse and A. Paucker (eds.), *Deutsches Judentum in Krieg und Revolution, 1916–1923* (Tübingen, 1971), pp. 409–45.

5. For the image of the East European Jew during the war, see Aschheim, *Brothers and Strangers,* Ch. 7 and 8; T. Maurer, "Die Ostjuden in deutschsprachigen Publikationen der Ersten Weltkriegs" (unpublished, Tübingen, 1980).

6. Aschheim makes use of only a few Jewish and non-Jewish periodicals in his chapter on the Weimar period (although most of the publications referred to here appear in his bibliography).

7. The Minutes of the Prussian Diet (Sitzungs berichte) and of the German Reichstag (RT, Stenographische Berichte) are cited with the numbers of the volume and page or column and the date of the session, but without the date of publication or the place (always Berlin).

8. For itinerant beggars in the nineteenth century see e.g. R. Straus, *Wir lebten in Deutschland. Erinnerungen einer deutschen Jüden 1880–1933* (Stuttgart, 1961), p. 20. There was even a certain amount of "professionalization" in the way this trade was plied. A book circulated in Eastern Europe concerning German towns with a guide to how to act in the matter. See M. Daniel, in M. Richarz (ed), *Jüdisches Leben in Deutschland,* vol. 2 (Stuttgart, 1979), p. 218.

9. See *Ostjuden in Deutschland* (Berlin, 1931), p. 23. On the recrudescence of professional begging in general: *Zedakah* no. 1 (December, 1925), p. 19. The increase in begging in the second half of the 1920's was explained by the worsening economic condition. IF (24 June 1926) p. 14; *Jüdische Arbeits- und Wanderfürsorge* I (July–August 1927) p. 9.

10. An exception was the Protestant *Kirchliches Jahrbuch* (1924) p. 126, cited in W. Altmann, "Die Judenfrage in evangelischen und katholischen Zeitschriften zwischen 1918 und 1933," (unpublished doctoral thesis, Munich, 1971), p. 197.

11. DE (June 1922), p. 358.

12. *Kasseler Sonntagsblatt* (21 March 1920) and *Hessisches Evangelisches Sonntagsblatt* (21 January 1923), cited in I. Arndt, "Die Judenfrage im Licht der evangelischen Sonntagsblätter von 1918–1933," (unpublished doctoral thesis, Tübingen, 1960) pp. 35, 37.

13. OuW (March–April 1920), column 59.

14. IF (7 August 1919), p. 2; IdR (July–August 1921) p. 216; AZJ (26 March 1920), p. 135.

15. General tendency: *Ostjuden in Deutschland,* p. 34: DDP-Deputy: DD

(22 August 1920), p. 528.

16. Quoted in JR (12 October 1920), p. 544. "Peddling" (Schacher) originally meant ambulatory trading, as contrasted with a firmly established business, but in Germany by the 1920's it had already received the connotation of haggling and unfair dealing.

17. Altmann, "Die Judenfrage in evangelischen und katholischen Zeitschriften," p. 192.

18. NZ (24 June 1921), p. 295.

19. AdB (18 October 1919) p. 353.

20. See, for example, the estimate of Deputy von Eynern (DVP) in: Prussian Diet, *Sitzungsberichte* I, Election period, Vol. 10, Columns 13577–79 (29 November 1922). The "unproductivity" of the East European Jew was also the reason given for the heavy sentence given to a peasant convicted of "favoring the unauthorized border crossing of two East European Jews." He had given them hospitality and shown them the way. JLZ (5 November 1926).

21. *Ibid.;* SM (15 October 1918) pp. 942, 944.

22. IF (5 March 1925), p. 2.

23. H. Silbergleit, *Bevölkerungs- und Berufsverhältnisse der Juden im Deutschen Reich. Auf Grund von amtlichen Materialen bearbeitet* (Berlin, 1930), vol. I, p. 109, Table 37a. That the Jews, as the weaker, permanently threatened group, assumed the stereotyped role of the foreigner is also the view of T. Bermann, *Produktivierungsmythen und Antisemitismus* (Vienna, 1973) p. 60.

24. AZJ (12 September 1919), p. 414. (Article from the *Mitteilungsblatt des Jüdischen Volksrats*-Posen, May/June 1919).

25. *Berliner Tageblatt* (30 December 1919); cf. IdR (December 1920), p. 366 and JR (15 October 1920), p. 547.

26. NdJ (May 1925), p. 2.

27. JR (6 January 1920), p. 3; cf. *Die Einwanderung der Ostjuden, Eine Gefahr oder ein sozialpolitisches Problem* (Berlin, 1920), p. 14; I (26 August 1920) p. 2, from an article by the secretary-general of the "Verband der Ostjuden" in the Berlin *Nationalzeitung.*

28. IF (26 March 1925), p. 10.

29. AZJ (4 January 1918), p. 10.

30. JLZ (10 April, 1925); JR (21 April 1925), p. 288; IF (21 May 1925), p. 3.

31. H (1 February 1918), p. 51, quoting E. Starkenstein, *Miesbacher Anzeiger* (7 April 1921), reprinted in *Das Duftigste aus dem Miesbacher Anzeiger* (Miesbach, 1921), p. 9; on uncleanliness, see also NZ (24 June 1921), p. 296.

32. AdB (18 October 1919), p. 352; H (1 May 1920), p. 174 and (15 January 1920) p. 31; *Miesbacher Anzeiger,* (7 April 1921) quoted in *Das Duftigste,* p. 10. In 1925, the OSE reported on the relatively high number of tuberculosis sufferers in the Berlin East European Jewish population and in this connection pointed to the unhygienic conditions in many homes. See IF (14 May 1925), p. 2.

33. H (January 1923), p. 29. Despite the relatively small number of subscribers this periodical can be considered as representative not only of the low type of anti-Semitic journals, but of a larger *völkisch* audience, since the argument of the *Hammer* is very similar and often identical with that of the publications of the Deutschvölkischer Schutz-und Trutzbund which had about 200,000 members. The leadership as well as the membership of the *Bund* and the *Hammer* circles overlapped.

34. H (1 July 1925), p. 258; (15 June 1923), p. 224; (15 September 1922), p. 369.

35. A. Hitler, *Mein Kampf* (Munich 1925) vol. I, p. 60.
36. This question has recently been treated by M. Kaplan, *The Jewish Feminist Movement in Germany* (Westport, CT and London, 1979) and by Edward Bristow, *Prostitution and Prejudice* (Oxford, 1982).
37. H (15 August 1929), p. 431; (1 May 1927), pp. 247 f; (1 January 1929), p. 23; (15 August 1928), p. 415.
38. IF (30 June 1927), p. 2; JLZ (1 July 1927); JR (28 June 1927), p. 367.
39. For examples, see: *Jüdische Arbeits- und Wanderfursorge* I, (Sept/Oct., 1927), pp. 66–71; (November 1927), p. 100; (December 1927), pp. 116 ff; JR (23 August 1927), pp. 479 ff; IF (24 November 1927), p. 8b; Kaplan, *The Jewish Feminist Movement*, pp. 107 ff.
40. H (15 May 1922), p. 204. Cf, for example, H (1 February 1923), p. 56; (15 February 1923), p. 75; (15 October 1923), p. 408.
41. IF (24 June 1926), p. 2; H (15 October 1929), p. 534; IF (18 April 1922), p. 2.
42. H (1 March 1923), p. 94.
43. CVZ (14 November 1924), p. 701.
44. JR (12 March 1920), p. 137. Similar contentions were put forward later about internment.
45. H (1 November 1919), p. 429 and (1 May 1920), p. 174.
46. JR (26 October 1920), p. 631. At the 1925 census, Elberfeld had 387 foreign Jews (0.23 percent) in a total population of 167,577 inhabitants. Silbergleit, *Bevölkerungs- und Berufsverhältnisse,* p. 24, Table 11.
47. Prussian Constitutional Assembly, *Sitzungsberichte* Vol. IX, col. 11704 (7 July 1920).
48. Prussian Diet, *Sitzungsberichte* I, Election period vol. VIII, col. 10764, (17 June 1922).
49. AZJ (15 April 1921), p. 89.
50. H (1 July 1918), p. 280.
51. H (1 October 1918), p. 411.
52. See, e.g., H (1 November 1919) p. 425; (1 May 1920), p. 168.
53. AdB (22 November 1919), p. 396; (10 January 1920), p. 11.
54. EB (22 October 1922), p. 251.
55. DS (18 April 1920), p. 260. This was presumably written by the publisher Stresemann himself who was to become chancellor and minister of foreign affairs in 1923.
56. Prussian Diet *Sitzungsberichte* I, Election period Vol. 10, col. 13612 and 13621 (29 November 1922).
57. JR (19 June 1923), p. 300 (about a member of the Committee of Directors of the Reichsbund jüdischer Frontsoldaten); *Das Grundeigentum* (1922) no. 39, p. 690.
58. I (27 March 1924), p. 2 (Motion in Diet of Saxony), and JR (5 December 1919), p. 675 (Schoeneberg City Council).
59. JR (12 December 1924), p. 689 (Director of Berlin Housing Bureau).
60. Two motions of the DVNP: RT annexures Vol. 370, no. 3302, p. 3243 (2 February 1922); RT annexures vol. 376, no. 5568, p. 6281 (22 February 1923). Cf. *Das Grundeigentum* (1922) no. 39, p. 690.
61. This quotation is representative of many from I (18 December 1919), p. 4.
62. JR (12 March 1920), p. 137 ff; AZJ (29 October 1920), p. 400; I (28 October 1920), p. 3.
63. I (15 January 1920), p. 3; Prussian Diet *Sitzungsberichte* I, Election period vol. 8, col. 10764 (17 June 1922).

64. *Einwanderung der Ostjuden,* p. 40; IF (12 February 1920), p. 3.

65. H (15 July 1922), p. 276; Prussian Constitutional Assembly, annexures Vol. IV, no. 769, p. 1138 (18 September 1919); IF (10 February 1920), p. 2. Cf. DD (22 August 1920), p. 526.

66. H (15 December 1919), p. 486; (15 February 1920), p. 78); (1 September 1918), p. 366. Quotation: *Kölnische Zeitung* (18 December 1922—Evening edition; also in NdJ (September–November 1922).

67. EB (1 January 1923), p. 347. Cf. W. Treue, "Zur Frage der wirtschaftlichen Motive im deutschen Antisemitismus," in Mosse and Paucker (eds.), *Deutsches Judentum,* pp. 400 ff. According to this source, in Prussia in 1930, 16,891 out of 492,000 pieces of real estate acquired since 1 July 1918 belonged to foreigners. In total, 21,284 out of 1.442 million plots of land belonged to foreigners (physical, not legal persons). Treue considers that foreign ownership would not necessarily be identical with East European Jewish ownership; but he assumes that most of the 14,692 buyers (out of a total of 21,284) from Holland and Central and Eastern Europe would have been Jews. This statistic is misleading, since Czech and Dutch citizens were also among the fourteen thousand, some of them Jews, but mostly not of East European origin.

68. OuW (March–April 1920) col. 58; I (11 March 1920), pp. 2ff.

69. *Ostjuden in Deutschland,* p. 27. The German term "schieben" means trading not complying with the law and refers particularly to times of need.

70. JR (3 October 1920), p. 543; AZJ (18 February 1921), p. 38 and (26 March 1920), p. 135; JP (20 February 1920), p. 60.

71. JR (3 October 1919), p. 543; cf. I (24 December 1922), p. 3.

72. NdJ (October 1924), p. 3.

73. Summarized from IdR (January 1918), pp. 12–15. On the trial of gold profiteers, see JP (14 June 1918), p. 223. On speculation in foreign currency and the ruin of finances see e.g. H (1 December 1921), p. 459 and the Protestant *Kirchliches Jahrbuch* 1924, p. 125f as quoted in Altmann, "Die Judenfrage," p. 216.

74. DE (June 1922), p. 368.

75. DE (January 1919), p. 31 (quotation and, following the brackets, summary).

76. DE (July 1920), p. 432. Cf. H (15 January 1921), p. 38.

77. DE (August 1919), p. 578; AdB (7 June 1919), p. 186; H (15 July 1922), p. 236.

78. H (15 February 1920), p. 80.

79. For example: AdB (22 March 1919), p. 91 and (3 June 1922), p. 89; H (15 May 1919), p. 210.

80. AdB (22 March 1919), p. 91.

81. H (1 February 1919, 15 June 1926, 15 March 1919); JR (23 October 1923), p. 536; etc.

82. Quoted in H (1 May 1920), p. 168.

83. IdR (June 1920) pp. 210ff.

84. AZJ (25 June 1920), Supplement p. 2.

85. IdR (July–August 1921), p. 217.

86. DS (18 September 1921), p. 624; Prussian Diet *Sitzungsberichte* I, Election period vol. 10, col. 13554 (29 November 1922).

87. NdJ (September–November 1922). Reports on other cases in: JR (17 January 1919), p. 38 and (9 July 1920), p. 359.

88. IF (25 December 1919), p. 1.

89. IF (26 September 1918), pp. 1ff; I (20 March 1919), p. 6.

90. JR (13 April 1923), p. 180; OuW (January–February 1920), col. 38; I (24

April 1919), p. 1; AZJ (9 January 1920), p. 16 and (28 February 1919), p. 86; IF (25 January 1919), p. 1; JP (22 February 1918), p. 70.
91. I (6 November 1919), p. 3; IdR (January 1920), p. 25; I (30 December 1919), p. 2.
92. Statement: CVZ (14 November 1924), p. 701. See, e.g., H (15 August 1922), p. 331. IF (12 February 1925), p. 9 quoted the *Deutsche Zeitung:* "Germans and East European Jews are to each other as men to bedbugs." This paper represented the *völkisch* wing within the DNVP.
93. H (15 January 1923), p. 3; IF (12 February 1925), p. 9 (quoting from *Deutsche Zeitung*).
94. H (15 December 1919), p. 486.
95. Statement concerning the *völkisch* press: IF (20 May 1920), p. 2. NdJ (September–November 1922) used the picture as well.
96. *Evangelischer Kirchenboten für die Pfalz* no. 26, 1926; quoted in IF (5 August 1926), p. 5. Cf. H (1 January 1930), p. 20. A. Bein, "Der jüdische Parasit, Bemerkungen zur Semantik der Judenfrage," in *Vierteljahrshefte für Zeitgeschichte* XIII (1965) pp. 121–48. See esp. p. 133.
97. Prussian Diet *Sitzungsberichte* I, election period vol. 10, co. 13614 (29 November 1922).
98. RT, *Stenographische Berichte*, vol. 358, p. 9861 (23 February 1923); *Berliner Tageblatt*, quoted from JR (24 February 1920), p. 2.
99. E.g., DS (21 September 1919), p. 654; DD (17 November 1923), p. 1075.
100. Cf. Bein, *"Der jüdische Parasit,"* p. 123 and 130 on the development from comparison into identification with animals in *völkisch* language.
101. AdB (10 January 1920), p. 11.
102. DE (July 1922), p. 426, 424. The well known "race-researcher," Hans Günther, defined the Jews not as a race, but as a people and *Ostjuden* as "vorderasiatisch-mongolisch-ostisch-nordisch-orientalisch-hamitsch-negroide Mischung." H. Günther, *Rassenkunde des deutschen Volkes* (Munich, 1922), p. 370, 406.
103. H (1 August 1928), p. 266 and (15 November 1919), p. 433; low cultural level: DE (June 1922), p. 351; DS (14 October 1919), p. 717 and (18 September 1921), p. 624.
104. NZ (24 June 1921), p. 296; *Türmer* (1923), p. 350, quoted by Altmann "Die Judenfrage," p. 189; cf. NdJ (January–March 1924), p. 6.
105. *Hickl's illustrierter jüdischer Volkskalender (26) für das Jahr 5687-1926/27*, p. 84. A similar judgment is implied in CVZ (25 January 1923), p. 27.
106. IdR (January 1921), p. 23 and (February 1921), p. 54.
107. IF (27 January 1921), p. 2. Cf IF (28 May 1925), p. 9 and (18 June 1925), p. 10ff; CVZ (19 September 1930), p. 506 ff.
108. IF (10 December 1925), p. 10.
109. AZJ (14 June 1918), p. 285 and (1 October 1920), p. 380; IF (8 August 1918), p. 4; JR (27 February 1920), p. 111.
110. *Freie Zionistische Blätter* 1921, no. 1, p. 6.
111. IF (8 July 1920) (Marum, Jewish Deputy in the Baden Diet).
112. Summarized from IF (30 June 1927), p. 1.
113. AZJ (29 October 1920), p. 401; JR (26 October 1926), p. 601; I (14 October 1926), p. 5.
114. H (1 March 1927), p. 136.
115. DE (March 1922), p. 155, H (15 August 1919), p. 317. Pogrom e.g. H (15 January 1922), p. 46.
116. IF (6 January 1921), p. 1; CVZ (12 May 1923), p. 150; I (25 November 1926) p. 1.

117. I (25 November 1926), p. 1; AZJ (4 January 1918), p. 10; IdR (July–August 1921), p. 216.
118. AZJ (26 March 1920), p. 135; JP (31 May 1918), p. 211.
119. I (3 April 1924), p. 9.
120. I (16 June 1921), pp. 4ff; IF (8 September 1926), p. 3; *Einwanderung der Ostjuden,* p. 6.
121. IF (22 October 1925), p. 12; (11 May 1922), p. 2; SM (18 September 1923), p. 574.
122. I (14 February 1918), p. 5ff (from a Berlin daily); *KC-Blätter* 17 (1927) no. 3, p. 109.
123. NdJ (January–February 1926), p. 11. Report of a German Jewish soldier, AZJ (4 January 1918), p. 10.
124. IF (22 November 1918), p. 2; AZJ (4 January 1918), p. 10; JR (27 February 1920), p. 11 *(Vossische Zeitung).*
125. IF (2 September 1926), p. 1.
126. IdR (January 1921), p. 25; "Uplift," IdR (January–February 1916), pp. 15ff; IF (28 February 1918), p. 1; JR (23 August 1927), p. 484.
127. Till the mid-1920's, the Communist Party's theoretical organ, *Die Internationale,* did not have a single article on the Jewish question and anti-Semitism. We have therefore drawn on *Die rote Fahne* for the period 1919–1923; it appeared seven days a week, on five of them twice daily. In each case the issues have been scrutinized for the week after the discussion on East European Jews in the Prussian Diet or in the German Reichstag. Examples of details adduced for this general interpretation: *Rote Fahne* (7 August 1920), (8 November 1921—morning edition), (30 November 1922—morning edition).
128. Passages are quoted from: G. Fritz, *Die Ostjudenfrage. Zionismus und Grenzschluss* (Munich 1915), pp. 23, 29–32, 39–43. There was no "distancing" commentary of the editorial board of the *Neue Zeit.* Moreover, in an article about the *völkisch* movement, it was said that anti-Semitism had imperceptibly received fresh nourishment from the "influx" of "masses of East European Jews . . . from whom we should protect ourselves." (NZ, 10 March 1923), p. 439. The paper stopped appearing during the inflation of 1923. Its successor, *Die Gesellschaft,* had no more articles on anti-Semitism and the Jewish question.
129. DS (23 January 1921), p. 64 and (18 September 1921), p. 627.
130. DS (23 January 1921), pp. 63ff and (6 February) pp. 95 ff. Some articles of the NdJ first appeared in the *Kölnische Zeitung,* which belonged to the DVP and Naumann, the leader of the union, was a party member.
131. DD (19 September 1920), p. 600.
132. BB Frye, "The German Democratic Party and the 'Jewish Problem' in the Weimar Republic," in *LBIYB* XXI (1976), pp. 143–172, esp. p. 165, 167, 170ff.
133. DD (13 June 1920), p. 377 and (22 August 1920), p. 526ff. Anti-Semitic attitudes: "But the immigrants manage by deals with all sorts of 'pull' that they know how to use to get apartments that Germans would try to rent in vain." (p. 526).

Essays

The Place of the Holocaust in Contemporary History[1]

Yehuda Bauer
(HEBREW UNIVERSITY)

In recent discussions on the place of the Holocaust in the history of our century, there has been a clear tendency to find a way to reconcile the concept of its uniqueness with the idea of its universal importance. Most observers feel that both concepts are valid and indeed can hardly exist without each other. However, such attempts rarely link definitions with historical analyses of what the Holocaust actually was. It is therefore essential to devote attention first of all to questions of definition.

The Holocaust is the name now customarily used in English for the planned total annihilation of the Jewish people, and the actual murder of six million of them at the hands of the Nazis and their auxiliaries.[2] What sets the Holocaust apart from other crimes committed by Nazis, or by others, against many millions of other people, was neither the number of victims nor the way of their murder, nor the proportion of the murdered compared to the total number of the targeted victims. Many more Russians were murdered by the Nazis than Jews. In past history there have been cases in which a much higher proportion of a given community was annihilated than the thirty-five percent of the Jewish people that died in the Holocaust. And, while most of the victims of the gas chambers were Jews, some were not—Gypsies, Soviet POWs and others.

What made the Holocaust different from other cases of what is loosely termed "genocide" was the motivation behind it. It is perfectly clear that Nazi ideology saw in the Jew the non-human antithesis of what it considered to be the human ideal: the German Aryan. In the controversy regarding the problem of whether there was a Nazi ideology or not, it seems obvious that there were some tenets that were generally held by the Nazi elite, whether or not they constitute an ideology. Above all, there was the Manichean approach that saw in the world victory of the Germanic Aryans not only a geopolitical necessity for the survival of the Germanic race and its peoples, but a precondition for the continued existence of humankind. At the other pole stood the Jew, a Satanic element and a parasitic one, both weak and contemptible, and yet also immensely powerful and absolutely evil.

The Jew, though he looked human, was not. He controlled most of the world through his control of both capitalism and Russian Bolshevism; only Germany and, to an extent, England were still outside his grasp. His victory was imminent, and with it the destruction not only of Germany, but of all humanity. Germany's war against its enemies was therefore waged for two complementary reasons: the "positive" one of ensuring the victory of the Germanic peoples in Europe, and then in the entire world; and the "negative" one, of defeating the Jewish Satan and his world government. The former was unattainable except through the latter.[3]

An analysis of the events leading up to World War II and of the war itself shows that the expansionist policies of Nazi Germany were motivated primarily not by concrete German interests—political or strategic or economic—but rather by ideological considerations. These were expressed often enough in no unmistakable terms, but some historians tend to ignore documents that do not fit into their preconceived picture. Nazi Germany sought "Lebensraum" for the Germanic peoples (primarily, but by no means solely, for the Germans) so that they might control Europe and the world; in order to do so, war had to be waged against enemies, who were united by the arch-enemy that lurked behind all of them: the Jew. The anti-Jewish struggle was one of the two inextricably connected motivations which underlay the Nazi decision to wage World War II. The struggle against the Jews was a crucial part of the Nazi eschatology, an absolutely central pillar of their world-view, and not just one part of their program. The future of humanity depended on their "victory" over the Jew. This pseudo-religious motivation made their anti-Jewish actions unprecedented. There could be no exceptions to the murder of Jews, once that was decided upon, because Satan had to be extirpated completely, or else he would arise again. Anyone with three Jewish grandparents was sentenced to death, and the principle was that anyone with two Jewish grandparents should either be killed or sterilized. What was unique in the Holocaust was the totality of its ideology and of its translation of abstract thought into planned, logically implemented total murder. More than that—it became a central part of the rationale for a total war that caused some 35 million casualties[4] in the six-year long struggle. That is the uniqueness of the Holocaust.

What is the universality of that experience?

Mass murder of noncombatants in times of war or of quasi-peace has been with us since time immemorial. Massacres of civilian populations by conquering or marauding armies or police can be documented for most of human history. The very concept of mass murder, however, is highly problematical. When does murder become mass murder? With ten victims? Or a hundred? Or a thousand? When somebody causes mass starvation and epidemics—is that mass murder? When masses of prisoners are killed, is that on the same level as the murder of civilians? When, in the course of World War I, masses of soldiers were killed by gas, was that mass murder, or an acceptable taking of life in the course of armed action?

A detailed comparative analysis of such occurrences in past centuries is a task for the future. But, it may be argued, is not this all too scholastic? If a person was murdered at Verdun by German gas, at Dresden by British bombers, at Auschwitz by gassing, at Hiroshima by atomic fallout or at My Lai by an American bullet—or in the thirteenth century at Isfahan by a Mongol knife—it is all the same. Or is it? We do, after all, differentiate between different types of good. We know that there is a difference, however hard it may be to define, between helping an old lady across the street, and rescuing that same old lady from a burning building. We try to differentiate between different types of—in this case—socially commendable action which we call morally good, because we accept the Kantian approach which would see in such action an example to be, ideally, universally followed. In order that that may be so, we grade and differentiate. In effect, we usually do the same with actions that most of us would consider to be evil. In human history, judicial norms have clearly differentiated between crimes according to socially accepted criteria of what was seen as more serious or less so. The argument presented here is that the same consideration applies to different types of arbitrary life-taking. True, it makes, perhaps, no difference to the victim of My Lai or Auschwitz or Verdun, but it does make a great difference to the survivor.

Let us then try to differentiate. After a relatively civilized nineteenth century, in the course of which "only" tens of thousands of soldiers died in the many wars that took place between 1815 and the American Civil War, methods of more efficient mass killing brought about an increase in what one might call the level of brutalization. This process reached its apogee in World War I, with its hecatombs of soldier-victims. But, one might argue, they died in the course of war, when ordinary social norms do not apply to the armies which butcher armed men. The murder of civilians in large numbers was the exception rather than the rule in 1914–1918. The most obvious such case was of course the destruction of the Armenian people in Anatolia, and we will return to this case later.

Whether one considers the murder of millions of soldiers, by more and more sophisticated means, mass murder or an unfortunate act of war—and it is suggested here that the former seems to be the more appropriate—it is clear that George Mosse's analysis of the First World War as a catalyst of aggressions manifesting themselves in a general brutalization of modern civilization is very convincing.[5] Surely the major point is that while mass murder was not the norm in a society which prided itself on its 'progress,' the First World War constituted a watershed event after which mass murder first becomes acceptable, or perhaps acceptable once again. One can point to the events of the Russian Civil War, including the murder of perhaps a hundred thousand Jews, as an example; or to the frightful wars that rocked China in the twenties, even prior to the Japanese invasion of 1931. The Holocaust, surely, is unimaginable without this shift in attitudes to mass destruction of human life.

What, then, is the relation of mass murder to what we know as 'genocide'? Much has been written on the origin of the term and its meaning. The legal mind has, of course, no difficulty in defining a term that has received the sanction of the proposed United Nations Convention on Genocide. As approved on 9 December 1948, it reads as follows: "In the present Convention, genocide means any of the following acts committed with intent to destroy, in *whole* or in *part* (our emphasis added), a national, ethnical or religious group, as such:

(a) Killing members of the group; (b) Causing serious bodily or mental harm to members of the group; (c) Deliberately inflicting on the group conditions of life calculated to bring about its physical destruction in whole or in part; (d) Imposing measures intended to prevent births within the group; (e) Forcibly transferring children of the group to another group". The wording seems to indicate that genocide is meant, in the extreme case, to be an act designed to destroy a group totally. However, a group can be totally destroyed without killing all of its members, so that the planned total physical annihilation of a group would appear not to be necessarily included in this definition.

These definitions followed those offered by the inventor of the term, Raphael Lemkin. Lemkin, in early 1943, under the influence of the information received from Europe on the Holocaust as well as on the persecution of other nationalities, formulated a contradictory definition. On the one hand, he defined genocide as the total "extermination" of a people; on the other hand, he defined it as extreme deprivation, destruction of educational institutions, interference in religious life, general denationalization and even moral poisoning by the introduction (for example) of pornography. In effect, we have here two definitions, which are obviously mutually exclusive: one cannot interfere in the religious life or destroy the educational institutions of a people who has been exterminated. Nor does it make sense to see in these actions steps necessarily leading to extermination, because in the case of many of the peoples under Nazi rule this did not happen. The first definition fits the case of the Jews during the war, while the other is suited to the fate of the Slav nations, for instance, under the Nazis.[6] It is here suggested that Lemkin's second definition be called 'genocide'—whatever the United Nations have to say about the matter; while the first be called, for want of a better term, Holocaust, or more accurately *Shoah* (Catastrophe), using the Hebrew term, which is more appropriate.

Lemkin's secondary definition of his term does indeed fit the fate of the Czechs, the Poles, the Serbs and others. Their institutions of self-government were destroyed; the social cohesion of these nations was disrupted; their intelligentsia largely killed; their churches harassed; the masses reduced to near-starvation. But only one people was sentenced to total and absolute annihilation: the Jews.

Some historians reject this description and maintain that the Nazi intention was to destroy all the members of certain Slav nations, such as the Czech and the Polish. This was simply not so. Because of the importance of this issue of differentiating between evil and evil, it is important to examine this problem more closely.

As far as the Slavic nations were concerned, documentary evidence makes it clear that the intention of the Nazis was to kill the leadership, to deport a part of these peoples, and to enslave the rest. There never was a plan for the physical mass annihilation of any one of these nations. To argue that Nazi policies would logically have led to such total annihilation policies has no basis in fact, and is a hypothesis at best. It is illogical, too, because the Third Reich needed millions of slave laborers, and a policy seems to have been evolving to turn the Slav peoples into a permanent population of Helots to serve their German masters.

Basic to the way the Nazis saw these things was the need to reconcile the racial, the economic and the political-strategic aims of a future Germanic world empire. In the writings of Nazi officials and ideologists alike, however, the racial-ideological element clearly dominates.

The Nazis viewed the Slavic peoples as Aryans, albeit of a lower racial order.[7] The Czechs, Poles, Ukrainians, Byelorussians and the Russians fell into this category. In addition, the Nazis had to contend with the three non-Slavic peoples in the Baltic states: the Lithuanians, the Latvians and the Estonians.[8]

"Nordic" elements among these populations were to be identified—a racial survey, based largely on external characteristics, was to be conducted—and those found racially akin to Germans would be germanized, voluntarily or by force. This meant, among other things, the kidnaping of racially "valuable" children, to be raised in Germany. Nordic leadership elements among the Poles, the Czechs and the Russians would be eliminated, because they might provide rallying points for anti-German resistance movements. The rest of the population was to be divided, part to be exiled to the East and part to form the slave labor force needed to make life bearable for the master race.

In the period before the Barbarossa Plan took shape (the plan to invade the USSR), Nazi planning for the future had to contend with the fact that one could not evict the existing Slav populations—the Czechs and the Poles—who were now living in territories controlled by the Germans. In a discussion that took place on 17 October 1939, Hitler declared that in the General-gouvernement the Nazi officials were to ensure "a low standard of living. We want only to get labor from there."[9] He repeated this view on 2 October 1940, when he said that he wanted to establish the General-gouvernement as "a Polish reservation, a big Polish labor camp."[10]

Prior to the German invasion of the USSR, therefore, we find the main lines of Nazi policy towards the Slav peoples clearly defined. It was indeed a program of genocide—slavery, removal of leadership groups by murder and intimidation, germanization and deportation—a program intended to destroy these nations as nations; it was not a program of holocaust: a planned, total physical annihilation.

After the decision to invade the USSR was taken, a new situation arose. In the time span between early 1941 and the end of 1942, we find the development of plans dealing with the future treatment of East European populations after a German victory. These plans revolved around the so-called Generalplan Ost, a first draft of which was submitted to Himmler at the end of 1941.[11] Meyer-Hetling dealt mainly with the problem of resettling the eastern areas that Himmler wanted cleared of the Slavic populations. Of the forty-five million "foreigners" (*Fremdvölkische*) who were in these areas, which included the Baltic states, Poland and most of the western part of European Russia, all of White Russia and the Ukraine, thirty-one million were to be deported and the rest germanized. It did not, however, go into the details, as its attention was focused on the resettlement of Germans and other "Teutonics" in the areas to be cleared. If we want to follow Nazi plans regarding the indigenous populations, we have to turn to two main sources: the comments on the "Generalplan" submitted to Himmler by

Dr. Erhard Wetzel, and Heydrich's speeches on the "Czech question."[12]

Wetzel saw considerable difficulties in the plans for germanization *(Eindeutschung)*, mainly because of the lack of German manpower to settle areas from which other populations would be removed. He also foresaw grave political difficulties in separating the populations, giving favorable treatment to one part and deporting the other.

Regarding the Baltic peoples, Wetzel opposed deportation by force, lest those whom the Germans hoped to germanize realize "that such a forcible evacuation would probably bring with it the demise *(Untergang)* of their brothers and sisters." Wetzel therefore proposed a program of more or less voluntary removal of the "Ungermanizables," the motivation to be the opportunity for the evacuees to become the middle class in eastern areas ruled, but not settled, by Germans. If, says Wetzel, we can use these racially unsuitable people to save German manpower in the East, we would have gained a great advantage from both the 'racial-political' and also the political viewpoint."[13] In contrast to the plans for the Poles and the Czechs, this strategy envisaged the elimination of the Baltic nations as such and the use of their members for German power strategies.[14]

As for the Poles, he thought that most of them were not fit for germanization, and would have to be deported to western Siberia. Dispersed among the local population there, they would form an anti-Russian element. The transport of seven or eight hundred thousand people each year for the next thirty years would ensure the realization of this plan.

"It is obvious that the Polish question cannot be solved in such a way that one would liquidate the Poles in the same manner as the Jews. Such a solution of the Polish question would be a standing accusation against the German people into the far distant future and would deprive us of all sympathy, especially as the other neighboring nations would have to assume that they would be treated similarly when the time came."[15]

The Ukrainians would be concentrated in the northern and eastern parts of the Ukraine, and there be used for the Ukrainization of the considerable Russian minority. Wetzel opposed the deportation of the 'ungermanizable' *(nicht eindeutschungsfähige)* Ukrainians to Siberia. Those who were 'germanizable' would be treated in the same way as similar groups among the other peoples. As far as the Byelorussians were concerned, Wetzel believed they should mostly be left where they were, to be used as laborers. Many of the groups which were sound socially could be used as permanent slaves in Germany, and replace the South and Southeast Europeans who were then, in 1942, streaming to Germany and who were racially farther removed than the Slavs from the master race.

The main problem as he saw it was the Russian question. A leading German intellectual, Prof. Dr.phil. Wolfgang Abel, of the Kaiser Wilhelm Institute for Anthropology at Berlin-Dahlem, had suggested that either the Russians be exterminated *in toto* (the term used was '*Ausrottung*'), or that the Nordic part of the Russian people be selected for germanization (I could not find out what the professor intended to do with the non-germanized Russians, but it is not very difficult to guess what he thought). Wetzel rejected Abel's proposal: "The policy proposed by Abel, to liquidate the Russian people, is impossible, not only because it is hardly possible to implement it, but also for political and economic reasons." In other words, it would be technically difficult, and then of course Germany needed the Russians for labor. The political difficulties would be the same as with the Poles. Instead, Wetzel proposed the subdivision of the Russian area into administrative units independent of each other in order to foster separatism. He also suggested giving Finnic and Turkic groups autonomy within these areas, and he joined a number of others in the Nazi hierarchy who advocated a policy of discouragement of population growth by various quasi-medical and political-hygienic measures. He mentioned that the racial experts of Nazi Germany had discovered among the Russians a so-called 'primitive europide' race, which had not been taken into account by Hans Günther. There were also many Nordics among the Russians. These should be germanizable and/or should be used in the Reich for labor.

Himmler's response to these ideas was generally positive.[16] They fitted well into the conception which he shared with Hitler of a future Pax Germanica in Eastern Europe—apart of course from the general injunction that anyone in the least opposed to the Germans should be immediately shot.[17]

For our purpose the above considerations seem to be sufficient. They show that there was an explicit rejection of ideas of total mass annihilation—not, of course for moral reasons—and instead the older ideas of a destruction of nations as such, their enslavement, forced germanization and deportation, in different proportions for the different nations, was to be adopted.

As far as the Czechs are concerned, we have Heydrich's speeches to tell us what the Nazi plans were. We must use the Czechs as Helots, Heydrich said on 2 October 1941.[18] On 2 February 1942, Heydrich further suggested that the removal of non-germanizable elements should be camouflaged as labor outside the country, with those sent for labor being granted the right to bring their families.[19]

What emerges quite clearly from Heydrich's speeches is the same line of policy as that favored by Wetzel towards the Poles and others: genocide, not holocaust. There was not only no plan for the physical annihilation of all or some of these nations, but there was an explicit rejection of such ideas by those who had the decision-making power.

However, the case of the Gypsies was different again. Nobody really knows the precise number of Romany people living in Europe in 1939. Some estimates put the number of Romanies murdered by the Nazis at 810,000[20] and their number today at 6 million in Europe, and 10 million in the entire world.[21] The first figure can hardly be proved, and both are probably considerably higher than the facts would indicate. However, in sheer demonic, cold-blooded brutality, the tragedy of the Romanies is one of the most terrible indictments of the Nazis. The fact that their fate is hardly ever mentioned, and that the mutilated Romany nation continues to be vilified and persecuted to this day should put all their European host nations to shame.

Branded and persecuted as thieves, sorcerers and child-kidnapers, the Romanies (Gypsies) in Germany largely belonged to the Sinti and to the Lalleri in Austria. Their numbers were given in Himmler's *Runderlass* of 7 August 1941, as 28,607 in Germany, and 11,000 in Austria.[22] Of those in Germany, 2,652 were "persons wandering about in Gypsy manner."[23] The figures for those murdered are unclear, but we know that 13,080 were deported to Auschwitz (this does not include non-German Romanies), and 5,007 Austrian Lalleri were deported to Lodz, and murdered at Chelmno. Three thousand more Austrian Romanies were put into concentration camps, and two and a half thousand deported to Poland, mostly into Jewish ghettoes. Most of these probably perished. When we add up all these victims, we arrive at 23,587, of the 39,607 total indicated above, most of whom died. We shall see that 14,017 Sinti and Lalleri were exempted by Himmler. The figures seem to tally.

What was the principle according to which the Gypsies were treated? Romanies (Gypsies) were considered *"artfremd"* (radically alien). The 1935 Nuremberg Laws really applied to them as well, as the two Nazi experts, Wilhelm Stuckart and Hans Globke made clear.[24] As they were considered to be asocial, their fate was affected by Himmler's order of 14 December 1937, to arrest 'asocials', defined as persons "who, without being criminals, endanger the community by their asocial behavior."[25] Further explications of that decree (4 April 1938) mentioned "e.g., beggars, vagabonds (Gypsies), prostitutes, etc." As this seemed to be a bit too extreme, Himmler issued a clarification on 1 June 1938, which included among the "asocials" "Gypsies and persons wandering about in Gypsy manner, when they do not show any desire for regular work or when they are the subject of criminal proceedings."[26]

Himmler's own attitude to the Romanies was ambivalent. In his *Runderlass* of 8 December 1938, he stated that in accordance with experience gathered in fighting the "Gypsy scourge" *(Zigeunerplage)* and with the results of racial-biological research, the Gypsy problem would be solved in the light of the "inner characteristic of that race" *("aus dem Wesen dieser Rasse heraus")*. "For the final solution *(endgültige Lösung der Zigeunerfrage)* of the Gypsy problem it is therefore evidently essential to treat the racially pure Gypsies and the mixed breeds [*Mischlinge*] separately." In his explanation of the correct attitude to the Gypsy question, Himmler stated quite clearly the obvious dilemma of the racialist struggling between theoretical racialism, which would accord an equal status to all pure human races, and the variety adopted by the Nazis, which, of course, established a hierarchy led by the Nordic Aryans: "It must be established as a basic thesis in the fight against the Gypsy scourge that the German *Volk* also respects every race that is alien to its *völkish* essence . . . [and advocates] the racial separation of Gypsydom from the German *Volk,* and thus the prevention of race mixing and finally the ordering of the lives of racially pure and mixed-breed Gypsies [becomes necessary]."[27] Himmler did indeed try to solve the Gypsy problem in this way. His "Regelung" of 13 October 1942, separated the "racially pure" Sinti from the rest, and assimilated to them "good *Mischlinge* in the Gypsy sense" *(im zigeunerischen Sinne gute Mischlinge)* who should be again led towards Gypsydom *(sollen einzelnen reinrassigen Sinte-Zigeunersippen wieder zugefürt werden)*. In line with Nazi policies, nine Romanies were appointed, who would be responsible for the organization of the segregated "pure" and "assimilated" Sinti and Lalleri and lead them in a Nazi-approved non-sedentary Gypsy life. This indeed appears to have happened, and 14,017 Romanies were exempted.

The fate of the others was eventually sealed, in close connection with the other racial policies of the Nazis. On 6 December 1942, an SS order established that the non-protected Gypsies should be sent to Auschwitz, except for ex-Wehrmacht soldiers, socially adapted Gypsies, and armament workers. For these, sterilization was to be provided. Prior to that, Gypsy soldiers were to have been dismissed from the army.

The execution of the December order was harsher than the order itself. In a "Schnellbrief" of 29 January 1943, the SS provided for the sending of Gypsy *Mischlinge*, Gypsies of the Rom tribes (presumably those in the Reich area) and "members of Gypsy clans of Balkan origin who are not of German blood" into concentration camps.[28]

In effect, we have limited knowledge as yet of what exactly happened, beyond the fact that two-thirds of the German Romanies were murdered, many of them (2,897) gassed in Auschwitz, on 2 August 1944. We do know that many of the survivors were put into German uniforms in the last period of the war and deployed in punitive battalions, on dangerous missions and the like. Others were sent to be slaves in armament factories. We have even less knowledge of what happened to the large Gypsy populations in the Balkans and in Eastern Europe. But it is known that Einsatzgruppe D under Otto Ohlendorf murdered all the Romanies it could find in its area of operations. Many Polish Gypsies were killed where they were—in forests, on the roads, etc. At least fifty (and possibly ninety) thousand Romanies were killed in Yugoslavia. But despite pioneer efforts by some writers, we are still in quest of a detailed description of the fate of the Romany people in Europe as a whole.[29]

And yet, what stands out very clearly are both the parallels and the differences in the Nazi treatment of the Gypsies and the Jews. These two peoples shared certain characteristics in the Nazi period: they both lacked a national territory and basic cultural differences separated them (each people in its own way) from their European host nations. The Nazi technique of dealing with both was similar, not only bureaucratically (they were handled by the same SS organizations) but also ideologically (Himmler applied the same racialist theories to them). The difference is indeed of great significance—Gypsies who were racially "pure" in Nazi eyes, or could be re-assimilated to "gypsydom" were spared. This could be done because the Nazis could live with another, albeit inferior, race, provided there was no 'mixed breeding'. Therefore the *'Mischlinge'*, but not the "pure" Gypsies, had to die. The murder even included 2,652 Germans who lived as Gypsies.

With the Jews, only quarter-Jews were relatively safe, because, contrary to the Gypsy case, Jews were not just another race, but the anti-race, Satan, bacteria, contaminators of culture, and mortal enemies of the Aryan peoples. Gypsies were just another inferior race, to be dealt with according to the rules of Nazi racial hygiene. The murder of innocent humans was the same; we are here interested in the motivation, and its implications, and these differed.

Let us now return to the discussion of genocide. The contradiction inherent in Lemkin's original definition became even clearer in the resolution passed by the U.N. General Assembly in December 1946. There, as we have seen, genocide is defined as "a denial of the right of existence of entire groups." There is an obvious difference between the denial of the right to exist and actual total murder.

In any case, the U.N. Convention is a purely arbitrary document, arrived at as a result of heated discussions between delegates of member states at the U.N.[30] There is actually no clear definition of genocide, because such a definition would have to emerge inductively, and not, as has in fact been the case, deductively—i.e., as a result of politically and ideologically motivated pressures. Lemkin did indeed try to define inductively: he was, naturally, affected and influenced by what he knew—in late 1942 and early 1943—of Nazi policies. He defined, as we have seen, what happened to Czechs, Poles and Serbs. When he came to discuss Jews, he seems to have been unable to comprehend fully what was happening to them. It seems that cognitively, he "knew" that they were being totally annihilated. But this was not something that could be accepted, or grasped. He therefore left his "first" definition—that of total "extermination"—in, and then went on to describe something else.

An argument evolved as to the correctness of including the destruction of political groups in the definition of genocide. One point to be remembered is, it seems, that political associations are voluntary, and the destruction of political groups is conditioned by the decision of the intended victims to stick to their convictions—with the exception, perhaps, of the leadership elites. Social Democrats and Communists were not killed in Germany, by and large. Millions of them recanted, or kept their views to themselves. Even leaders were—in the thirties—often arrested, and after a while, released from concentration camps. Many survived in the camps, having become part of the *Prominenz* in them. The other point is that in the destruction of political groups, the annihilation of their families is the exception rather than the rule. The destruction of political groups, whether by Nazis, Soviets, Chilean dictators, or Chinese Communists, while utterly to be condemned, is not genocide, though it is true that in their motivation, political and racial issues are at times intermingled. In some cases, such as that of the Communists in Indonesia—for the most part, ethnically Chinese—total mass murder, usually including the families, was aimed at.

Genocide should really be left where the etymology places it—the destruction of racial, tribal, national or ethnic groups. Even the destruction of religious groups poses problems, because there again, religious affiliation is a voluntary act. Admittedly, there are obvious cases where the element of choice is hardly there: the Druse are a religious community, but although they define themselves as ethnically Arab, persecution of the Druse has had a clearly religio-ethnic tinge about it. Persecution of the Jews in pre-modern times had that same quality about it. The mass murder of heretics in France in the Middle Ages was intended to be total, and included the total annihilation of whole towns (Beziers), without providing much choice to the hapless inhabitants whether or not to recant. But then, the concepts of ethnic, national or racial groups were much less clear in pre-modern times than they are today. Christians saw themselves as in some sense a "nation", as did the Muslims. In the industrial era, with the rise of nationalism, religion has become increasingly more voluntary, and the persecution of religious groups more and more parallels that of political ones. It would seem, therefore, that genocide ought to be defined so as to exclude religious persecution.

We thus arrive at a much narrower definition, and it seems that one ought to concentrate on the modern era, or the last one hundred years, because pre-modern genocide cannot really be subsumed under the same category as the modern variety. Bloody massacres there undoubtedly were. Entire cities were razed to the ground (Carthage by the Romans). But this was done for political power reasons. Those who ran away were not pursued, and there seems to have been little desire to eradicate ethnic groups or cultures as such, unless there were weighty power-political reasons to do so. Modern genocide, by contrast, has two decisive characteristics: it is ideological, and it is relentless, in that it desires the disappearance of a racial, national or ethnic group as such.

A limited, and therefore, it seems, more realistic definition of genocide would therefore run somewhat as follows: the planned destruction, since the mid-nineteenth century, of a racial, national, or ethnic group as such, by the following means: (a) selective mass murder of elites or parts of the population; (b) elimination of national (racial, ethnic) culture and religious life with the intent of "denationalization"; (c) enslavement, with the same intent; (d) destruction of national (racial, ethnic) economic life, with the same intent; (e) biological decimation through the kidnaping of children, or the prevention of normal family life, with the same intent.

Genocide, as thus defined, would include the Nazi policies towards Czechs, Poles, or Gypsies, for example, and Soviet policies towards the Chechens, Volga Germans, or Tatars. It would include the policies of American settlers towards many native American tribes (Seminoles, Blackfoot, Arapaho, Apache and others), though there are cases where policies went beyond what is here defined as genocide (Nez Percé, Lakotas). It would probably also include the cases of the Hutus, the Biharis and the Ibos.

Two cases are obviously outside the definition as offered here: one is that of so-called auto-genocide, when both the perpetrators and the victims of mass murder belong to the same national group—as in the case of Cambodia, or, earlier, Stalin's anti-kulak campaign. In all such cases, the mass murder is the result of tremendous internal upheavals, and should be seen as constituting a category of its own. Understanding such tragedies will not be made easier by lumping them together with cases of genocide as here defined. The other case is that of the use of nuclear weapons. Here warfare is escalated to the mass destruction of enemy populations, but there is no intention to "denationalize". In a sense, of course, the use of nuclear weapons indicates the danger of what might be called *urbicide,* i.e., the destruction of civilized life as such, going beyond both genocide and holocaust.

We are then left with a re-statement of Lemkin's "first" definition, namely, the planned physical annihilation, for ideological or pseudo-religious reasons, of all the members of a national, ethnic or racial group. That, indeed, seems to be the true meaning of holocaust. So defined, it becomes a general term, not limited to the Jewish experience in World War II, though that experience is the most thorough-going to date, the only case where "holocaust" (or *"Shoah",* as previously suggested) would appear fully applicable.

We then arrive at a kind of continuum of evil that would lead from 'mass murder' in recent times through 'genocide' to 'holocaust' *('shoah').* Such a continuum does not imply a value judgment as to the degree of moral condemnation, so that one could argue that 'mass murder' is in some way less reprehensible than 'genocide' or 'holocaust'. Whatever it is called in the context of our definition, any particular event of the sort we are describing will have to be put somewhere on the continuum, and may not fit precisely the three orientation points.

We would suggest that some of the most tragic events that have occurred in this century have to be placed between the terms 'genocide' and 'holocaust'. The two outstanding examples are those of the Romanies and the Armenians. The fate of the Romanies has been discussed above. Outside of Germany, there was wanton and near-total, but not very precisely organized, murder. The motivation was social rather than political; in Germany, racism operated almost the other way: it tended to save a remnant (one-third) of the Romany people. Escape from the general fate was made possible either by settled status, or by disappearance into the crowd of non-Romanies. We do not know of any special hunts for individual Romanies—it was the wandering groups that were the hardest hit. The massive destruction went beyond selective mass murder and therefore beyond our definition of genocide, but paradoxically, in Germany itself no attempt was made to destroy the life-style of the protected 'racially pure' remnant. This, at least, was the case in theory; in practice, things were different. We would therefore argue that what befell the European Romanies under Nazi rule has to be placed on our continuum between genocide and holocaust.

The case of the Armenians is grimmer still. There had been massacres of Armenians in 1894–1896, including the murder of three thousand Armenians burnt in the Armenian cathedral at Urfa on 28/29 December 1895. The total number of victims at that time has been estimated at three hundred thousand. Although the Armenian nationalists were welcomed among the Young Turks who gained control over Turkey in 1908, the triumvirate of Talaat, Enver and Djamal which gained control in 1913, finally broke with the Armenians. Massacres took place in 1909 (Adana) and 1912.

The Armenians in Turkey numbered, according to some sources, 1,850,000 in 1914. They were a Christian nationality, mostly peasants, but with a strong middle class and a significant stratum of intellectuals who played an important role in Ottoman society. Ostensibly, the Young Turks wanted to eliminate the Armenians in order to create a Pan-Turkic empire extending into Central Asia. The Armenians were an important element in the population of eastern Anatolia, which was regarded by the Turks as part of the Ottoman heartland. Frustration over the loss of the Ottoman Empire in Europe, and a resulting extreme nationalism played their part. The instigators and organizers of the murder were intellectuals who had seized the government. They utilized a war situation, and used primitive tribesmen and criminals, driven by sadistic instincts, greed and lust, to aid in mass murder. Religious factors may have been part of the general background, and appear from testimonies to have partially motivated the execution of government policy. However, the Young Turks themselves were not only secularist, but anti-religious. Post factum, Turkish apologists argued that the massacres were the result of an Armenian rebellion, or a threat of a rebellion. This is clearly incorrect.

Starting on 24/25 April 1915, with the arrest of two hundred and thirty five top Armenian intellectuals and leaders, the massacres spread in Anatolia, and lasted until early 1916. Armenian soldiers in the Turkish army were first disarmed, then used for slave labor, and then murdered. Women, children and the aged were "evacuated" from their villages and towns. En route, a high proportion were murdered, in part by Kurdish and Circassian tribesmen. The rest were brought to the Syrian desert, and there most of them died.[31]

It is very difficult to arrive at an agreed figure of the number of victims. The German expert on the Armenian question, Johannes Lepsius, says that 1.4 million Armenians were deported. Others put the number of the victims at between eight hundred thousand and over a million. The massacres were committed by central planning and the use of modern technology (the telegraph, the rail transportation of troops, modern propaganda and disinformation techniques, modern bureaucratic procedures). No contradiction appears to exist between that and the use of the most primitive methods—killing with clubs and knives, mass rapes, the denial of water and food.

The decisive document appears to be a cable of the ruling Turkish group to the provincial governors of 28 February 1915: "Jemiyet has decided to free the fatherland from the covetousness of this accursed race and to bear upon their shoulder the stigma that might malign the Ottoman history. Unable to forget the disgrace and bitterness of the past, filled with vengeful episodes, Jemiyet, hopeful about its future, has decided to exterminate all Armenians living in Turkey, without allowing a single one to remain alive."[32] At the trial of the killer of Talaat in Berlin in 1921, another cable by Talaat to the prefect of Aleppo, of 9 September 1915, was quoted: "The right of the Armenians to live and work on Turkish territory is totally abrogated. The government, which assumes all responsibility in this respect, has ordered not to leave even children in their cribs. In several provinces the execution has been evidenced. Out of reasons unknown to us, exceptions were made with (sic) persons who were allowed to stay in Aleppo, instead of being sent to the place of exile, thus causing new difficulties for the government. Make women and children, whoever they may be, leave, without giving any reason, even those who cannot walk, and do not give the population any grounds for defending them . . . Wipe out every Armenian from the eastern province whom you can find on your territory" (text quoted as in the original).[33]

The parallels with the Holocaust are too obvious to require elucidation. Due to the corrupt and disorderly nature of the Young Turkish regime, some Armenians survived: women were taken to Turkish harems or carried off by tribesmen; children were kidnaped and brought up as Turks; some people were left in villages, and there were small numbers who survived the death marches to the Syrian desert. In Istanbul and Izmir relatively large numbers of Armenians were spared, largely because of the proximity of foreign representatives. But, clearly, the intention was the planned, total annihilation of the Armenian nation in Turkey. This is the closest parallel to the Holocaust.

However, there are differences. They become evident in the above quote from Talaat Bey of 28 February 1915. The perpetrators announced that they had decided "to bear upon their shoulders the stigma that might malign Ottoman history." In other words, they were part of a moral world that rejected their deed, but for political-ideological reasons they decided to persist in it nevertheless. They saw themselves, no doubt, as Turkish patriots, and saw the murder of the Armenians as in line with the interests of the Turkish people; but they also knew that the murder could not be justified by appealing to national interest, and they took the responsibility on themselves for something they had difficulty in justifying. Compare this to Himmler's well-known speech at Posen on 4 October 1943: speaking of the "extermination of the Jewish people," he called it "an unwritten and never-to-be-written page of glory in our history." Himmler accepted petit-bourgeois morality (in the same speech he insisted that SS murderers must not take any Jewish property); he prided himself on the SS having "stayed decent" and "suffered no harm to our inner being, our soul, our character."[34] At the same time, he literally turned accepted morality upside-down: instead of 'thou shalt not kill', he decreed—'thou shalt kill'. Killing the Jewish enemy was a moral command, not as in the Armenian case, a practical "necessity" known to be in contrast to standards accepted even by the initiators of the murder.

This consideration is linked to another, perhaps more obvious one: the Nazis saw the Jews as *the* central problem of world history. Upon its solution depended the future of mankind. Unless International Jewry was defeated, human civilization would not survive. The attitude towards the Jews had in it important elements of pseudo-religion. There was no such motivation present in the Armenian case; Armenians were to be annihilated for power-political reasons, and in Turkey only. No anti-Armenian ideology developed in the writings of the Turkish leadership, and the Armenians were not seen as a universal threat. The motivation, in other words, was different in the two cases.

The differences between the holocaust and the Armenian massacres are less important than the similarities—and even if the Armenian case is not seen as a holocaust in the extreme form which it took towards the Jews, it is certainly the nearest thing to it. On the continuum, the two events stand next to each other.

The two definitions of holocaust indicate the dialectical tension between the universal and the particularistic aspects of that watershed event: holocaust has to be seen as a general category, as the outermost pole on a continuum of evil; yet at the same time, as an event which has (so far) overtaken Jews alone—for reasons which have to be explained in part by reference to the specific nature of Jewish history and to the inter-relationship of Jew and gentile throughout the ages. Being general, as well as specific, the term holocaust carries with it the implication that, because it happened once, it may happen again—to any group if the conditions are right.

Unless both parts of this duality are borne in mind, one runs the risk of making misleading and false comparisons between the Holocaust and other events. Any serious attempt to determine the contemporary significance of the Holocaust must start from the awareness that historical analogies usually distort and that history does not repeat itself.

Indeed, because political leaders, in particular, have recently indulged so frequently in the kind of nonsense that equates every act of war, every isolated terror attack, with Auschwitz, Belsen and Dachau,[35] it is not out of place here to point out that there has not been a holocaust since World War II. Such equations are certainly misleading, and often dangerous.

Moreover, Jews are no less vulnerable to the trap of false analogy. Two different kinds of historical error frequently recur in Jewish thought on the Holocaust.

A number of Jewish religious authorities have said that the Holocaust is not essentially new, and represents a continuation of the persecution which has plagued the Jews for two thousand years. The need to integrate the Holocaust into the tradition of Jewish martyrology is understandable from a religious point of view, but it is historically erroneous. For one thing, never before was there a plan to annihilate the Jewish people everywhere. Persecutions were limited in area—Jews usually had the possibility of escaping elsewhere. The attacks and expulsions were the result of local social, religious, economic or political tensions. And the Jews had, as a rule, the option of abjuring their faith—sometimes only temporarily—and if they chose to do so, their lives were usually spared. There was never a persecution that saw in the total annihilation of the Jewish people a panacea for the ills of humanity. In that sense, Nazi anti-Semitism represented a new departure, because while the elements on which it built were familiar, their combination was qualitatively unprecedented, total and murderous. From a Jewish historical perspective, therefore, the Holocaust, while containing many elements familiar from the long history of Jewish martyrdom, is unique.

The second type of false analogy increasingly common among Jews involves references to the Holocaust in the attempt to draw "lessons" for application to topical political situations. For example, it is absurd to compare (as some have done) the plea of a democratic French government that acts of anti-Semitic terror be regarded as an internal French problem which it will confront resolutely, with the Nazi claim in the thirties that the "Jewish problem" was an internal German one.[36] The context is entirely different—French society in the eighties is not Germany of the thirties.

When Israeli politicians thus invoke the Holocaust, accuse foreign statesmen of anti-Semitism reminiscent of the Nazi period, or engage in similar analogies, they often do so because they are under the influence of a collective (sometimes personal) trauma, with which they do not know how to deal. The Holocaust remains an unhealed psychic wound.

Collective traumatization has also produced a type of Jewish backlash. Jewish people and Jewish leadership, especially in Israel, seem to be developing a stance which assumes that anyone who is critical of actions by Jews anywhere, especially in Israel, is anti-Jewish and that therefore the only possible reaction of Jews must be to regard all non-Jews as potential or actual enemies, and to respond to any incipient danger with the threat of force. This attitude seems to be based on two misinterpretations of the events of the Holocaust.

On the one hand there is the assumption that all gentiles as individuals, and all nations (save for the Danes and sometimes the Bulgarians) somehow joined forces with the Nazis. And on the other, it is assumed that the Jewish reaction to the Nazi threat was almost wholly passive, and that therefore the lesson to be learned is that Jews must never again be caught in passivity.

Both these arguments are wrong. I have discussed them elsewhere[37] and will not repeat myself at length here. Belgians, Italians, Serbs and other nations, as well as individuals and groups elsewhere, proved ready by and large to help Jews. True, the picture is dark indeed, especially in Eastern Europe; but were it not for those who helped, not even the small remnant would have survived.

The charge of passivity is uniquely Jewish—no other people has similarly accused itself (though some of them would have had good reason to do so). Czechs and Hungarians glorify almost non-existent undergrounds, and no Soviet writer has yet asked the question why there were no major rebellions among the millions of Soviet POWs who were starved to death or were tortured and murdered by the Nazis. In reality, unarmed active resistance to Nazi policies permeated Jewish life under the Nazis. In Europe in general, armed resistance was marginal, except in Yugoslavia and, debatably, in the USSR (especially in Byelorussia); nevertheless, Jewish armed resistance was relatively widespread.

Peculiarly, the very uniqueness of the Holocaust on which so many Jewish leaders insist—rightly so—contradicts facile analogies. Nonetheless, because the Holocaust was certainly unique but also has its place on a continuum, room has to be found for carefully controlled historical comparisons. The fact that there are no facile "lessons" to be learned does not mean that nothing can be learned, or that this event should be beheld simply in mute horror.

First of all, and probably most important of all, there is the sense of the continuity of Jewish history, in which the Holocaust was a watershed event. The sense of continuity obliges us to know the 'why' and 'how' of the Holocaust, both because we are the heirs to the civilization of the victims and because we or our parents were intended to be the victims no less than those who actually were.

Behavior of the victims ranged from one extreme to the other. In part, this behavior was conditioned by the Jewish environment, by Jewish education, Jewish religion, culture and civilization, or specifically Jewish family and social structures. We can learn what these influences were, and whether they resulted in patterns of behavior that were different from those of non-Jews persecuted by the Nazis. We may be able to understand better who we are, as a Jewish society, by analyzing the history of those who were like us and whose heritage we share. We may be able to empathize with them through our learning, and empathy may lead to a deeper feeling of identification with them and their lives. All this need not be limited to an understanding of Jews only—though there is no possible way to understand universal problems unless we also approach them through the discrete, particular instances of particular people at a particular time.

Beyond these basic issues, more immediate historical and political problems emerge, because the context of the Holocaust is that of our century and our era, and we cannot escape from it. One problem is that of retaining a sense of moral values opposite to that espoused by Himmler, in an increasingly violent, increasingly cynical world.

An analysis of Jewish policies, Jewish leadership reactions in Europe and in the free countries during the Holocaust is called for: not in order to accuse and "draw lessons," but in order to see what the dynamics are that operate on the leadership of a largely dispersed people in times of stress; whether certain historic patterns of Jewish behavior tend to repeat themselves; and whether, in the extreme case of the Holocaust, there were not beginnings of behavior patterns that were different from the traditional ones and that might indicate new developments. By 'old' patterns, we mean attempts by Jewish philanthropic groups (JDC, HIAS, ICA) to come to the aid of victims of persecution within the legal framework of, and in complete loyalty to, the host societies; squabbles between individuals and groups as to primacy in leadership; attempts to influence governments by 'quiet diplomacy,' etc. The abandonment of strictly legalistic attitudes, even by JDC leaders (in Europe); the growing awareness of the need for publicity and of the efficacy of grass-roots organization and democratic procedure; the relatively quick adjustment to the new conditions by some Jewish groups both inside and outside Nazi-occupied Europe—

all these appear to be new departures, or at least new emphases, influencing the post-Holocaust Jewish world.

Jewish contemporary consciousness of the Holocaust is troubled by the dialectical tension between the Holocaust as a traumatic caesura in Jewish history and the Holocaust as a part, albeit a tragic part, of the continuity of Jewish history. As such, the current argument about whether the Holocaust is over-emphasized, as some would have it, becomes rather irrelevant. It is a crucial, central event in general and Jewish history. It is set in this history. It has exerted and still exerts a vast impact on our objective situation and on our subjective reaction to events. It therefore has to be dealt with within the context of Jewish life in our era as the central event it is. Its interpretation is bound to have a vital influence, for good or for bad.

Notes

1. This article is based on a very fruitful discussion that took place on 4 August 1977, at the Hebrew University in Jerusalem. The participants should not be surprised if some of their input is being used here, though of course, the sole responsibility for the views expressed lies with the author. Those who participated, and to whom I wish to extend my thanks, are: Moshe Davis, Emil Fackenheim, Israel Gutman, Dov Otto Kulka, Seymour M. Lipset, Deborah Lipstadt, Malcolm Lowe, Avraham Margaliot, Michael Meyer, George Mosse, Leni Yahil. The symposium, and the research on which this article is based was made possible by the Philip M. Klutznick Fund in Contemporary Jewry. I am grateful to Mr.Philip M. Klutznick for his constant encouragement and great personal interest in these topics.
2. Cf. Uriel Tal, "On the Study of the Holocaust and Genocide," *Yad Vashem Studies* XIII (1973) pp. 7–52.
3. Cf. *Hitler's Secret Book* (New York, 1961); Joshua Trachtenberg, *The Devil and the Jews* (New Haven, 1944); Norman Cohn, *Warrant for Genocide* (New York, 1967); Andreas Hillgruber, "Die Endlösung und das deutsche Ostimperium," *Vierteljahreshefte für Zeitgeschichte* 1972, no. 2, pp. 133–53; Jacob Talmon, in: *The European Jewish Catastrophe* (Jerusalem, 1974); Uriel Tal, "Anti-Christian Anti-Semitism," *ibid.* Alice L. and A. Roy Eckardt, "The Holocaust and the Enigma of Uniqueness," in: *Reflections on the Holocaust, The Annals of the American Academy of Political and Social Science* (July 1980) pp. 165–78; Yehuda Bauer, "Genocide: Was It the Nazis' Original Plan?," *ibid.*, pp. 35–45.
4. Cf. Lucy S. Dawidowicz, *The Holocaust and the Historians* (Cambridge, Mass., 1981) pp. 5–11.
5. E.g., George L. Mosse, *Nazism: A Historical and Comparative Analysis of National Socialism* (New Brunswick, 1978) p. 55.
6. Raphael Lemkin, *Axis Rule in Occupied Europe* (New York, 1943) pp. xi–xii.

7. The Slavs were supposed to be a mixture of what the racial anthropologist Hans Günther had defined as "eastern" and "east Baltic" racial sub-groups, with additions from the Mongol and Finnic peoples, some Nordic influences, and even some Jewish influence.

8. In all the discussions on this matter there were two centers of power that had the most impact on policy-making: Alfred Rosenberg's *Ostministerium,* set up before the German invasion of the USSR to deal with the civilian administration of the territories to be conquered from the Soviets; and the various power structures controlled by Heinrich Himmler. Of these two, it was not the "Chaosministerium" (as it was known among Nazis in the know) but Himmler's empire that had the decisive voice. Himmler's general ideas on the subject were articulated in May 1940 in his memorandum on the treatment of foreign peoples, which he submitted to Hitler and which was approved by the Führer. (Printed in the original German in the *Vierteljahreshefte für Zeitgeschichte (VfZG)* 1957, no. 2, pp. 196–98; at Nüremberg this was Prosecutor's Exhibit 1314, NO-1880. For a partial English translation see my *A History of the Holocaust* [New York, 1982] p. 22).

9. PS-864; quoted in: Martin Broszat, *Nationalsozialistische Polenpolitik, 1939–1945* (Stuttgart, 1961) p. 22.

10. *Ibid.*, p. 24; USSR-172. It is hardly surprising to find the same basic attitude prevailing in the case of the Czechs. In a report on a speech of the state secretary to the German viceroy ('Protector') of Bohemia-Moravia, Karl H. Frank, of 9 October 1940, we read that Frank opposed "the most total solution, namely the deportation *(Aussiedlung)* of all the Czechs *(des Tschechentums).* He proposed the dissolution *(Aufsaugen)* of about one half of the Czech people in the German Folkdom, insofar as they are of any value from the point of view of their blood and anything else. This will occur through increased labor by Czechs in the Reich area (not in the Sudeten border areas), that is, through the dispersion of the concentrated Czech people. The other half of the Czech people must be made powerless, must be removed *(ausgeschaltet)* and deported . . . Elements opposed to the germanizing tendency must be dealt with harshly and must be removed . . . The Führer has approved the assimilation solution." (PS-867. Report of 15 October 1940 by Friderici, Wehrmacht plenipotentiary with the Reichsprotektor, on Frank's speech of 9 October.)

11. See Helmut Heiber, "Der Generalplan Ost," VfZG 1958, no. 2, pp. 281–325; also Josef Ackerman, *Himmler als Ideologe* (Göttingen, 1970) pp. 222–31.

The author of the plan's final version, Dr. Konrad Meyer-Hetling was not just another Nazi official. He was responsible for population matters in another of Himmler's offices, the *"Reichskommissariat zur Festigung des deutschen Volkstums"* (Reich Office for Strengthening the German Volkdom), in charge of the planning of racial and population policies. Closely allied with Heydrich's *"Reichssicherheitshauptamt"* (Reich Main Security Office), the RKF proposed its policies—and that included Meyer-Hetling's plan—with Heydrich's approval.

12. Dr. Erhard Wetzel (he survived the war) was not an old Nazi, but a latecomer: he joined the Party on 1 May 1933. A servile and intelligent bureaucrat, he became a leading light in the office of Racial Policy of the Nazi Party *(Rassenpolitisches Amt der Reichsleitung)* in 1939. He then became involved with the RSHA, especially with its section III B dealing with racial problems, and in 1941 received a post in Rosenberg's Ostministerium.

13. *VfZG* 1958, no. 2, pp. 302–03.

14. Before Wetzel dealt with the problem of the Slav nations, he had some

interesting things to say about the Jews. Wetzel was not only informed of the mass murder by the Einzatsgruppen in the East, but actively supported it from his office. It was therefore very significant when he said this about the Jews: "A deportation *(Aussiedlung)* of the Jews as envisaged in the plan (i.e., Meyer-Hetling's plan—Y.B.) becomes redundant with the solution of the Jewish question. A possible removal *(Überführung)* after the end of this war of the still remaining Jews into forced labor camps in the area of northern Russia or Siberia is no 'removal.' " We have here a clear indication that the term *'Aussiedlung'* (removal, resettlement) as used towards the Jews has a different meaning in the language of German bureaucracy from the same term when used towards others. The context makes it clear that as far as the Jews are concerned, *'Aussiedlung'* means murder, rather than forcible deportation. (*VfZG* 1958, no. 2, p. 305)

15. *Ibid.*, p. 308.
16. *Ibid.*, p. 325.
17. *Ibid.*, p. 221–26.
18. Vaclav Kral, *Die Vergangenheit Warnt* (Praha, 1961) Doc. 19, pp. 122–23. "We have the following people: some are racially good and well disposed; this is very simple, we can germanize them. Then we have the others, that is, the other extreme: racially bad and ill-intentioned. These people I have to get out. There is plenty of room in the East. We then remain with the middle group, which I have to check out precisely. There are those who are racially bad but well-intentioned, and racially good but ill-intentioned. The racially bad and well-intentioned ones we will probably have to use for labor somewhere in the Reich and see to it that they do not have any more children . . . But we should not antagonize them . . . Then we are left with the racially good but ill-intentioned. Those are the most dangerous ones, because they are the racially good leadership group . . . only one thing will be left to do, namely . . . to settle them in the Reich, in a purely German environment, and educate them ideologically and germanize them, and if this does not work, to stand them up against the wall; because I cannot deport them, since they would form a leadership group over there in the East and would turn against us."
19. *Ibid.*, Doc. 22, pp. 145–48. For some of these people Heydrich foresaw the possibility of using them as labor stewards *(Vorarbeiter)* in the arctic area "where the concentration camps will, in the future, be the ideal homeland of the eleven million European Jews." Waxing enthusiastic about the possibilities of developing the arctic areas for utilization of their raw materials, Heydrich added that he did not want the non-germanizable Czechs to go there as enemies of the Reich, but to give them certain material advantages, so that they could serve as guardians of European culture. (*Ibid.*, Doc. 22, p.. 145–48.) Heydrich's speech took place about two weeks after the Wannsee conference (20 Jan. '42) the figure of eleven million Jews is that used by Heydrich at that conference. At Wannsee, the arctic concentration camps were not mentioned; but Wetzel alluded to them (see note 14).
20. Tilman Zülch (ed.), *In Auschwitz vergast, bis heute verfolgt* (Hamburg 1979) p. 382; Annegret Ehmann, "Gerechtigkeit für Zigeuner," *Zeichen* no. 4 (Dec. 1970) p. 25; Ulrich Völklein, "Lästig ist das Zigeunerleben," *Die Zeit,* (7 March 1980) pp. 9ff.
21. *Ibid.*
22. *In Auschwitz vergast, bis heute verfolgt,* p. 315.
23. "Nach Zigeunerart umherziehende Personen."
24. *Kommentar zur Deutschen Rassengesetzgebung,* I (Munich, 1936).

25. *In Auschwitz vergast, bis heute verfolgt,* p. 76.
26. *Ibid.* In 1936, Dr. Robert Ritter was nominated to head a special research department for genetic science dealing specifically with Romanies *("Erbwissenschaftliche Forschungsstelle").* This became, in 1937, a research department on race hygiene and population biology *("Rassenhygienische und bevölkerungsbiologische Forschungsstelle").* Their researches into the racial purity of Gypsies resulted in a well-ordered card index, which was deposited with the health authorities. Just as those who decided on the murder of children and women in Auschwitz were medical doctors, so the fate of Gypsies was determined by pseudo-scientists attached to the Nazi health authorities. Does one have to mention that none of these Nazi women and men were ever punished?
27. Rd.Erl. des RFSS u ChdDtPol, 12/8/38, S-Kr. I., No. 557 VIII 38-2026-6; *In Auschwitz vergast, bis heute verfolgt,* p. 78.
28. The wording of the order is contradictory. Obviously, Gypsies were not of "German blood" so that what appears to have been meant is non-Sintis and non-Lalleri Romanies of Balkan origin. RSHA VA2 Nr. 59/43g; *In Auschwitz vergast, bis heute verfolgt,* pp. 327–28.
29. Cf. Donald Kenrich and Grattan Puxon, *The Destiny of Europe's Gypsies* (London, 1972); Siegfried Wölffling, "Zur Verfolgung und Vernichtung der Mitteldeutschen Zigeuner," *Wissensch. Zeitsch. der Martin-Luther Universität* 1965, H. 7.
30. Cf. Leo Kuper, *Genocide, Its Political Uses in the Twentieth Century* (New Haven, 1981) pp. 24–39.
31. The above has been culled from a number of sources: Richard G. Hovanissian, *Armenia on the Road to Independence* (Berkeley, 1967); Stanford J. Shaw and Ezel K. Shaw, *History of the Ottoman Empire and Modern Turkey* (Cambridge, Mass., 1976/77); Robert Melson, "A Theoretical Enquiry into the Armenian Massacres of 1894–1896," *Comparative Studies in Society and History* XXIV, no. 3 (1982) pp. 481–509; Johannes Lepsius, *Deutschland und Armenien, 1914–1918* (Potsdam, 1919); Tessa Hofmann, *Der Prozess Talaat Pascha* (Berlin, 1921/Göttingen, 1980); St. Stephanian, "Deutsche Armenien Politik," *Pogrom* X (1964) pp. 22–28.
32. Quoted from Helen Fein, *Accounting for Genocide* (New York, 1979) p. 15. Original document to be found in: *The Memoirs of Naim Bey* (Neuton Sq., Pa., 1966).
33. Stephanian, "Deutsche Armenien Politik;" cf. Hofmann, *Der Prozess . . . ,* p. 133ff.
34. *Documents on the Holocaust* (Jerusalem, 1981) pp. 344–45.
35. In an Israel TV interview on 8/20/82, Lebanese Christian leader Dany Chamoun referred to Bashir Jemayel's responsibility for the murder of men, women and children as tantamount to being responsible for Belsen and Dachau.
36. Prime Minister Menachem Begin made that comparison in a Knesset speech on 12 August 1982.
37. Yehuda Bauer, *The Holocaust in Historical Perspective* (Seattle, 1978) and *idem, The Jewish Emergence From Powerlessness* (Toronto, 1979).

Jewish Enrollment Patterns in Classical Secondary Education in Old Regime and Inter-war Hungary

Victor Karady

(ÉCOLE DES HAUTES ÉTUDES EN SCIENCES SOCIALES)

This essay is based on preliminary findings of a work in progress on the social uses of education in modern Hungary, and addresses only some strictly defined aspects of this subject. Though mainly of a sociological nature, this study of Jewish involvement in schooling will also touch upon many essential features of the historical fate of what was once the third largest Jewish community in the world.[1]

During the pre-1914 period, Hungarian Jews provided a sizeable portion of the country's professional and creative elites. This was due to their heavy investment in education, especially higher education. Schooling in general was an essential part of Jewish social strategies aimed at both class and status mobility and cultural assimilation.[2]

At the outset of the post-Liberal, inter-war period, Jewish educational overrepresentation became a major anti-Semitic argument of the radical Right. The *numerus clausus* law on university enrollment (1920) was enacted explicitly to curb further "Jewish expansion" in the educated classes.[3] This was the first instance since the civic emancipation of the Jews of a legal restriction on their access to higher education in any country of Catholic and Protestant Europe.[4] The ensuing emigration of Jewish students and members of the intellectual and professional elites created a conspicuous diaspora whose representatives appeared in lists of Nobel Prize nominees, conducted some of the best orchestras of Europe and the Americas, and taught physics, medicine or economics in the most prominent centers of higher learning in the Western world. All these, regardless of their particular destinies, were products of Hungarian classical secondary schools.

Classical secondary schools include here *Gymnasia* and *Real* schools granting academic diplomas *(matura)* entitling graduates to

Table 1. Denominational Distribution of Hungarian Adults by Sex, Denomination, Illiteracy and Levels of Education in 1910 and 1930

Denominations	Dates	Men			Women		
		% of Illiterates among 6 Years Old and Over	% of Those Having Completed 4 or More Secondary Classes among 15 Years Old and Over	% of Graduates from Secondary school among 20 Years Old and Over	% of Illiterates among 6 Years Old and Over	% of Those Having Completed 4 or More Secondary Classes among 15 Years Old and Over	% of Graduates from Secondary School among 20 Years Old and Over
Jews	1910	9.9	33.3	18.2	16.6	22.2	2.7
	1930	1.4	45.0	22.1	3.3	46.4	6.0
Others*	1910	18.2	6.9	4.3	26.1	4.1	0.8
	1930	7.4	9.8	4.1	11.4	9.6	1.7

*Only Catholics, Lutherans and Calvinists have been taken into account as other Christian denominations were overwhelmingly drawn from non-Hungarian ethnic minorities.

Sources: Computation according to data in *Magyar statisztikai közlemények* [Hungarian statistical reports] 61, 1910, pp. 392–431 and *ibid.* 114, 1930, p. 46 (for the size of the population by sex, age and denomination) and *ibid.* 61, Népszámlálás [Census] V, 1910, pp. 526–541 and *ibid.* 96, 1930, pp. 314–325 (for data on schooling and illiteracy).

enter universities—a key rung up the ladder of socialization which prepared young people for the assumption of elite positions under the old regime.[5] Most of the evidence derives from official statistics, the excellence of which is widely attested, and which usually allow comparisons between Jewish and non-Jewish educational patterns. Thus, we can point to the specificity of Jewish uses of education in terms of the needs and objectives of this particular group, given the changing socio-political situation as well as the changing institutional structure of the educational system. Four main areas will be touched on: a global measure of Jewish educational attainment and its regional variations; the historical trends of Jewish secondary schooling (by age group, sex and residence); the cultural or social, class-determined nature of Jewish "over-production" of educated men; school excellence and variable segregation as related to discrimination and the compensations for it.

EDUCATIONAL ATTAINMENTS

Table 1 offers an overall measure of the general educational superiority of the Hungarian Jewish population at two dates, one during the Dual Monarchy (referring to historical "Great Hungary" without Croatia) and one in the inter-war years (referring to the Rump State of "Little Hungary"). "Little Hungary" was carved out of those parts of the former Hungarian Empire that were in many respects more developed,[6] so that these data do not allow a direct comparison, relating as they do to two different territorial and societal formations. Jewish educational attainment is nonetheless well documented in both.

The pre-World War I situation can be summarized by two observations. In 1910, the rate of illiteracy was still substantial among Jews (one-tenth of the male but one-sixth of the female population), though it was considerably lower than among Hungarian gentiles. On the other hand, a significant proportion of Jewish adults (one-third of the men, one-fifth of the women) had by that time received (or participated in) secondary schooling, while this was true of only a small proportion of the other denominational groups. Hence, although it is true that the pre-war Jewish community was by far the best educated among the denominations—so much so that it provided the country with one-fifth to one-quarter of its formally educated men (which compares very favorably with the Jews' 6 percent share in the national population)—the group still included a large number of people who had received little or no schooling.

The regional breakdown of Jewish educational achievement in 1910 (Table 2) shows that the community was at that time composed of at

Table 2. Distribution of Jewish Men in the Hungarian Empire by Region of Residence and Levels of Education in 1910

Geographical Region	Residence	% of those Jewish men in 1910 who				Total Number	% of Regional Distribution of Jews
		Had Completed 8 Secondary School Classes	4 Secondary School Classes	Were Illiterates	Were Illiterates among Those Over 6 Years of Age		
Transdanubia (West)	Cities	12.2	29.2	13.9	2.3	8,740	1.9
	Counties	8.1	19.4	16.6	4.1	35,171	7.6
Western Slovakia (North-West), Left of Danube	Cities	11.0	28.7	13.5	2.3	4,725	1.0
	Counties	8.6	22.4	17.6	4.3	38,649	8.3
Eastern Slovakia (North-East), Right of Tisza	Cities	10.6	25.9	17.6	4.2	8,742	1.9
	Counties	3.7	9.2	30.9	12.6	60,952	13.2
Central Plain Between Danube and Tisza (exc. Pest County)	Cities	16.7	38.9	13.1	2.9	9,567	2.1
	Counties	10.2	21.9	17.3	3.6	15,388	3.3

Eastern, South-Eastern Plain, Left of Tisza (exc. Máramaros County)	Cities	12.3	27.7	16.4	3.9	22,684	4.9
	Counties	5.3	13.1	25.1	8.6	58,348	12.6
Transylvania	Cities	12.6	26.7	19.7	5.6	4,921	1.1
(South-East)	Counties	5.0	13.9	29.6	12.2	26,812	5.8
Croatia	Cities	20.5	40.1	12.0	2.1	3,951	0.9
(South-West)	Counties	10.2	22.6	16.4	3.9	6,641	1.4
Pest County (exc. Budapest)		8.6	20.8	19.3	4.1	19,516	4.2
Máramaros County		1.6	3.6	64.8	42.9	31,637	6.8
Budapest		20.3	38.0	11.6	2.1	105,022	22.7
Hungarian Empire		10.2	21.9	22.5	8.4	462,442	100.0

Source: *Magyar statisztikai közlemények* [Hungarian statistical reports] 61, *Népszámlálás* [Census] V., 1910, pp. 540–541.

least two sub-groups of distinct geographical location. The less educated were placed well below the national educational average, often below the level observed among non-Jews. A breakdown by age groups of the same data yields similar results. For example, in the 20–29 age group, one-quarter had completed eight secondary classes by 1910 (as compared with 5 percent of this age group in the gentile population); but only 6 percent of those in the 70 years and over age bracket (3 percent among gentiles) had reached this educational level.[7] Jewish educational advance must have progressed over time. More significantly, in Budapest, literacy data for the early years of the century show a considerable advantage of Jews over non-Jews in the younger age brackets but also an equally noticeable disadvantage among the elderly (60 years and over).[8]

Such contrasting evidence of the regional and age-group breakdowns makes it necessary to bear in mind, when interpreting the global findings on educational attainments, that Jewish supremacy in this sphere was the outcome of historically recent efforts. The differences between age-groups closely correlate with the historical localization and migration patterns of Jewish sub-groups endowed with quite different educational potential. These often enormous disparities bar any attempt to understand Jewish educational attainments in terms of some sort of general ethnic or cultural propensity for learning.

While the problem of group-specific uses of learning cannot be dealt with here in all its complexity, it must be stated that the attraction that secondary education exerted on Jewish Hungarians tightly overlapped with their willingness, and perceived chances, for social assimilation. Historically, such chances and such willingness grew in the post-1867 Liberal era,[9] and tended to be better secured (together with other assets for socio-economic mobility) in the central and western parts of the country which experienced in this period an unprecedented measure of economic growth and social modernization.[10]

This changing socio-historical setting helps us to understand later developments. By 1930 almost half of the adult Jews in "Little Hungary" (both men and women) had attended secondary school, although the increase in the proportion of graduates proved to be more limited, probably because of the heavy war losses among male graduates.[11] Geographic and residential factors are a major clue in explaining the disparities in Jewish educational attainments (illustrated in Table 2).

Without underestimating the intricacies of the socio-historical reality that underlies this data, the gist of the findings from Table 2 can be put rather simply: urban groups had everywhere better educational scores than rural groups (in the counties); the west and the center were much better off than the eastern regions. The contrast between urban and rural areas was itself less conspicuous in the west and the center than in the east. Some eastern sections of the Jewish community belonged manifestly among the educationally most backward social sectors, as attested most prominently in Máramaros County, with over two-thirds of Jewish adults illiterate.

These disparities largely if not completely overlap with historical patterns of Jewish migration. The northeastern regions were necessarily the passage way and the first stopping places for the Yiddish-speaking Polish and later Russian and Balkan Jews who provided the bulk of immigrants in the nineteenth century and, for that matter, the overwhelming majority of Hungarian Jewry proper. The west Hungarian Jews were either of long-established local stock or immigrants from German-speaking Austrian, Bohemian or Imperial German communities. The social distance between the two groups can be expressed in terms not only of mother tongue, cultural identity or class—to which must be added the marked opposition between Orthodox and Reform Judaism—but also in terms of their attitudes to gentile society (i.e., to issues related to emancipation and assimilation)[12] and to the agencies, like secondary schools, that promoted social mobility and integration. The typical movement of social ascent for most Jewish families was regularly associated with a residential transfer to the cities, and often to the capital city—the only really important conurbation in the country—which entailed, for most of them, a move from east to west.[13] Urban residence, especially in Budapest, represented in its turn a supplementary incentive for educational investment, not only because of the availability of better educational facilities, but also because the cities were the actual market place where skills, linguistic competences, entitlements to higher studies, and social manners, all gained through secondary education, could be turned to best account.

In the form of a statistical shorthand, these data offer an overall picture of Jewish social mobility and cultural assimilation patterns in Old Regime Hungary. Differences between east and west indeed correlate with all the indicators of collective behavior, values and social class position which together fix the distance from or proximity to the secular, urban, educated middle class ideal. It should be noted that this ideal was developed in Hungary above all by sections of the new bourgeoisie and intelligentsia that were alien in ethnic origin (Jews, Germans and Slavs) and by social extraction (commoners) from the Magyar gentry, who formed the bulk of the ruling elite.

Secondary schooling proved to be the paramount expression and criterion of a meritocratic principle that could partly compensate for the social handicaps of birth, and was structurally adopted in society as a major test of a "gentleman." A Jew with a secondary school *matura*

Table 3. Secondary School Attendance in Hungary by Denominations from 1869/70 to 1946/47 (Yearly Averages)

Dates	All Pupils in Gymnasia and "Real" Schools	All Graduates (Matura)	% of Jews among All Pupils	% of Jews among Graduates	% of Jews among Pupils in Budapest	% of Jews among Pupils in The Provinces
1869–1879/80*	—	—	10.9	—	32.0	—
1881–1885/86	38,059	—	20.3	—	36.8	—
1886–1890/91	39,557	—	19.8	—	35.8	—
1891–1895/96	47,774	2,499	21.1	—	38.8	18.4
1895–1900/01	56,316	3,230	22.4	—	35.3	20.2
1901–1905/06	62,082	4,228	22.8	—	41.4	19.2
1906–1910/11	72,674	4,935	20.8	23.0**	40.0	17.2
1911–1914/15	75,682	5,533	21.7	25.5	39.8	18.6
1915–1917/18	—	6,576	—	24.1	38.0	—
1918–1920/21	58,667	4,200	27.6	26.9	38.5	23.9
1921–1925/26	58,628	4,630	20.7	24.2	29.4	16.6
1926–1930/31	61,381	5,464	16.6	19.6	28.4	12.1
1931–1935/36	66,970	5,644	16.1	15.3	27.5	11.4
1936–1940/41	83,585	7,185	12.8	14.3	22.8	9.1
1942–43	104,448	8,953	9.2	11.3	17.2†	7.1†
1946–47	51,217	—	4.0	—	5.1††	—

* 1869/70 for nation wide data and 1872/73–1880/81 for data relative to Budapest.
**1908/09–1910/11 only for the denominational distribution of graduates.
† The only available evidence for 1941/42 is for Budapest. Regional proportions are thus only a rough estimate for 1942–43.
††Data relative only to 16 secondary schools in Budapest, computed individually for lack of aggregate statistical information.

Sources: *Magyar statisztikai évkönyv* [Hungarian statistical yearbook] annually (for nation wide data) and *Budapest Székesfőváros statisztikai évkönyve* [Statistical yearbook of the residential capital Budapest], annually. Data on the provinces derive from extrapolations from the above sources. Data relative to Jewish pupils in 16 secondary schools of Budapest in 1946/47 have been gathered from published yearly reports of these schools and for all Budapest schools of the nineteenth century from *Budapest Székesfőváros Statisztikai Közleményei* [Statistical reports of the residential capital Budapest].

was no longer a social outcast but an enfranchised citizen (a distinct privilege in a country where only 6 percent were voters), entitled to curtailed "voluntary" military service, and eligible to become an officer. The completion of even four secondary classes was recognized as a valid passport into the lower echelons of the established middle classes. Secondary education thus became part and parcel of any strategy of integration into the ruling classes and a major incentive to upwardly mobile Jewish Hungarians.

EVOLUTION IN SECONDARY SCHOOL ATTENDANCE

The main regional variations and historical developments in this respect can be directly traced in Tables 3 and 4, which are closely interrelated. The overrepresentation of Jewish youth is obviously more pronounced in schools of the capital city than in the provinces throughout the long period surveyed. It is striking from the very earliest decades of liberal rule.[14] In fact, the progressively higher proportion of Jewish secondary pupils from the 1880's onward, until well past World War I, suggests that, of all denominational groups in the country, Jews were the foremost users of the newly developed educational system. National and regional schooling frequencies even underestimate localized Jewish predominance in some privileged sectors of the educational hierarchy (with, for example, Jews accounting for two-fifths of pupils in the capital around the turn of the century).

Jewish pupils indeed often filled the majority of benches in some of the best Protestant and state *Gymnasia* before the First World War.[15] In addition, given the channeling effect towards the more traditional (especially clerical) middle class positions exerted by many denominational *Gymnasia*—especially the Catholic schools—from which Jewish students remained exempt, they were much freer than their gentile counterparts to maximize the profitability of their educational assets in the fast developing new professional markets of free-lance intelligentsia, business executives and the service professions.[16]

A reversal in this trend took place in the inter-war years, as is apparent from the figures showing a falling proportion of Jews among secondary school pupils after 1920 (Table 3). This decline can be traced to purely demographic factors: the dramatic decrease in the number of those eligible, given the ever-declining Jewish birthrate since the beginning of the century. In reality, the statistical chances of completing a secondary education increased considerably for the Jewish youth of the Rump State not only in the provinces—which was to some extent a consequence of the loss of many educationally backward areas—but also in the capital (Table 4).

Table 4. Age-Specific Rates of Secondary Schooling in Budapest Denominations, 1900–1947 (Selected Dates)

Dates	Denominations	Estimated % of Secondary School Pupils among 10–18 Years Old		Estimated % of Secondary Graduates among 18 years Old
		In Budapest	In the Provinces	
1880–	Jewish	11.9	—	—
1881	Other	6.5*	—	—
1890–	Jewish	10.1	—	—
1891	Other	6.0*	—	—
1900–	Jewish	13.1	8.3	4.5
1901	Other	6.0	1.6	0.85
1910–	Jewish	13.9	8.5	6.2
1911	Other	6.2	1.9	1.1
1920–	Jewish	24.2	18.1	10.8
1921	Other	12.1	2.35	1.9
1930–	Jewish	25.6**	21.6**	15.5
1931	Other	15.0	4.1	2.9
1940–	Jewish	25.9†	23.8†	16.3†
1941	Other	17.2†	5.0†	4.4†
1946–	Jewish	19.1††		—
1947	Other	6.1§		—

* Only for Catholics, Calvinists and Lutherans.
**Based on an estimation of the size of relevant age groups according to the distribution of the literate population. (Cf. *Magyar statisztikai közlemények* [Hungarian statistical report] 96, p. 358).
† Based on estimations of the size of relevant age groups according to combined data of the *World Jewish Congress* (cited below) and the 1941 Census.
††Based on an estimation of the relevant age group according to data of the *World Jewish Congress, Hungarian Section,* n°10, 1948, p. 8 (in Hungarian).
§ Based on an estimation of the relevant age group according to data of the 1949 census. (Cf. *Az 1949 évi népszámlálás. 9. Demográfiai eredmények* [The census of 1949, demographical results], Budapest, Központi Statisztikai Hivatal, 1950, p. 4 and p. 36.)

Other sources: *Magyar statisztikai közlemények* [Hungarian statistical reports] 5, pp. 470–517; *ibid.* 61, pp. 392–423; *ibid.,* 73, pp. 154–169; *ibid.,* 114, p. 46 (for the size of age groups nation wide) and *Budapest Székesfőváros Statisztikai közleményei* [Statistical yearbook of the residential capital Budapest] 1933, p. 66 (for the size of age groups in Budapest). Data for 1940 are estimated according to the census of 1941. (Cf. *Az 1941. évi népszámlálás* [The census of 1941] Budapest, Központi Statisztikai Hivatal, 1979, pp. 20–21 and 39.) Data on the number of pupils was gathered as in Table 3.

The educational boom of the inter-war years that affected Jews and gentiles alike (in fact, the latter even more, given their lower initial educational level) can be interpreted, paradoxical as it may appear, as a collective response to the worsening position of the established and upwardly mobile middle classes in their respective socio-economic markets. As unemployment increased, the offspring of those groups that already possessed a propensity to seek educational assets were increasingly spurred to an even greater accumulation of these assets. This search for better bargaining positions, competition for middle class jobs becoming all the more desperate as a sizeable proportion of the traditional ruling elite of Great Hungary lost its livelihood, was also expressed in the upsurge of university enrollments. In a way, the *numerus clausus* law of 1920 was aimed at the artificial limitation of Jewish competition in the professional markets. Academic anti-Semitism buttressed the legal restrictions. But neither of these succeeded in modifying the demand of Jews for secondary schooling.

This demand in fact rose to a historically unprecedented level between the wars. By 1930 over one in four in Budapest and over one in five among provincial Jewish youth received some secondary education; almost one-sixth of them actually graduated. Residential disparities in educational opportunity became relatively insignificant (if one considers that about one-fifth of the enrollments in the *Gymnasia* of the capital were accounted for by pupils living in the provinces). The general progress of women's education, for which demand grew drastically during and after the war, was partly responsible for these developments. But once again, it is easy to observe that this new extension in the provision of education (women's *Gymnasia*)[17] and other educational innovations (the science-based *Realgymnasia,* for example, created in 1924)[18] were preferentially made use of by Jewish Hungarians. Undoubtedly, relative over-schooling went hand in hand with an attitude of openness to possible new educational strategies and with a measure of eagerness to benefit fully from the new forms being offered.

Jewish educational demand was broken indeed only by the Holocaust. Absolute enrollment proportions among Jewish youth fell to less than one-third of the pre-war level and to less than half of the early war years that were already marked by anti-Jewish legislation. It is true that registered Jewish enrollments fail to take account of many more or less forcibly converted youth whose relative numbers were probably much higher among *Gymnasium* students than among others. It is even probable that the Holocaust itself, however enormous were the losses it caused in the younger age brackets, decimated less the better educated, especially those from Budapest (who did not systematically suffer deportation) than those from the provinces (who were all subject to deportation). This is why it is possible to estimate that age-specific enrollment ratios of surviving Jewish youth after the Holocaust remained approximately as high as before (that is, somewhat higher than indicated for 1946–47 in Table 4).

Our findings in Table 4 suggest that well after the first anti-Jewish

Table 5. Sex Ratio among Secondary School Pupils in Budapest by Denominations between the Wars (Selected Dates)

A. *Proportions of Girls*

	Jewish	Non-Jewish
1924/25	34.9	26.8
1929/30	27.8	17.4
1934/35	38.6	28.0
1937/38	42.7	29.4
1938/39	43.0	34.7

B. *Age Specific Proportions of Jewish Pupils by Sex*

	1930/31	1937/38*	1937/38**	1940/41†
% of Male Pupils among 10–18 Year Old Boys	39.0	45.1	40.1	29.1
% of Female Pupils among 10–18 Year Old Girls	12.2	35.6	30.4	23.1

* High hypothesis: number of pupils compared with 10–18 years old in 1941.
**Low hypothesis: number of pupils compared with 10–18 years old in 1930.
† Sex ratio of pupils, by hypothesis, as in 1938/39, the last year for which data is available separately for boys and girls.

Source: As in Table 4 (for the size of age groups) and *Budapest Székesfőváros Statisztikai Évkönyve* [Statistical Yearbook of the residential capital Budapest], annually (for the number of pupils).

law in 1938 the educational propensity of Jewish Hungarians did not cease growing; while Table 3, by contrast, hints at a constant fall in the proportion of Jewish pupils and graduates in the same period. Apparently this fall was due only to demographic factors. Globally, in its first years, the anti-Semitic legislation does not seem to have affected directly the secondary educational chances of those concerned. This development would indeed be consistent with the fact that the new legislation did not explicitly restrict the right of Jews to attend *Gymnasia* in the same way as it limited (practically to a *numerus nullus*) their access to higher education.

The key to the data presented in Tables 3 and 4 is to be found in Table 5. Briefly, it appears that age-specific enrollments could well increase in the beginning of the era of persecutions if losses among some potential students were counter-balanced by an additional propensity to enroll among others. This happened most conspicuously in the considerable growth of secondary education among Jewish girls. To be sure, Table 5 shows that till 1937–38—the last academic year not affected by the Anti-Jewish Laws—the educational propensity of both Jewish boys and girls advanced to an unprecedented level. Decline was brutal in the following years, but it was more limited for girls than for boys. The educational chances of the latter group lay by 1940-41 much below those of 1930, while those of the former were still much above.

The high marks of the global indicator in Table 4 express these contradictory developments. Obviously it provides no indication of significant regional disparities. More importantly, it hides disparities in educational propensity linked with socio-economic status, as it is well known that the social class recruitment of female pupils was high above the male average.[19] We can conclude that the first stage of the anti-Jewish legislation brought about a significant transfer of educational opportunity within the Jewish community at the expense, most probably, of the lower middle classes whose use of secondary education had been up to then mostly reserved for boys. The relative over-schooling of the Jewish bourgeoisie continued for a while.

Indeed, as indicated above and contrary to expectations, institutionalized anti-Semitism at first did not affect the global chances of admission. Jewish pupils were, to be sure, often denied entry to individual establishments.[20] But the school market was large enough, especially in Budapest, to secure admission elsewhere. The Jewish propensity for schooling was nevertheless at risk from the outset of the anti-Jewish legislation since it threatened with economic ruin those middle class groups which supplied the majority of candidates for the *Gymnasia*. These very strata were also among the culturally most assimilated and socially most readily accepted in the gentile environment. Many of their numbers, especially in Budapest and in the other cities, had only a loose connection, if any, with Judaism and were liable to seek conversion in order to escape at least partly the consequences of the legal restrictions.[21] Even though conversion at that time was far from providing real protection from further persecution, converted pupils nonetheless disappeared from the Jewish rubrics in the educational statistics. Similarly, the educated middle classes, which possessed skills and competences representing an eminently mobile social capital, were among those most inclined to emigrate. Their selective departure must have contributed to a decline in the global educational propensity of the remaining Jewish Hungarian population.

When, in spite of all these detrimental circumstances, observed Jewish secondary enrollments remained, till the first years of the war, at as high a level as ever, one must ask whether education did not become *an essential form of compensatory long term investment,* one of the very few still within reach. When all other prospects, both economic and social, appeared to be suddenly blocked, secondary education remained open, providing, if anything, the last field of symbolic competition on equal terms between Jews and gentiles. Such compensatory over-investment in education is by no means an exceptional phenomenon in the history of the middle classes. It actually occurred in the not entirely dissimilar post-World War I predicament when suddenly all avenues of middle class success were saturated; professional unemployment rose sharply; and, to Jewish youth, even the gates of the universities were half closed. Yet (as is shown in Table 4) age-specific indicators of secondary schooling jumped ahead significantly, even in Budapest where these data are comparable from one period to another.

The trend is apparent if we take into account age-specific provincial enrollment figures (as in Table 4) which were the highest ever for Jews and non-Jews alike in 1940–41, though the share of the former in global enrollment figures continued to decline until 1942–43, the last year observed (as in Table 3). The apparent contradiction between the two sets of data can be explained in part by the numerical decline of Jewish youth as a consequence of the long term fall of birth rates. Moreover, the Vienna Awards (1938, 1940) reunited with Hungary some of the formerly detached southern and northeastern territories of the Empire where the Jewish minorities belonged, as we have seen (Table 2), to the least educated sections of the Hungarian community. If global indicators of Jewish secondary schooling in the provinces remained high, a measure of compensatory relative over-schooling must have been achieved there too. Indeed it is significant in this context that by 1940–41, inequalities in age-specific Jewish enrollment frequencies all but disappeared between Budapest and the provinces.[22]

Let us also remark that this relative and temporary over-schooling—linked paradoxically to a desperate historical juncture—rested also on several necessary if not sufficient demo-economic conditions, among them the constant decrease of the cost of education per family, due to the dramatic diminution of the number of children in Jewish families (generalization of the one-child family).[23] This could not be offset by the common practice in denominational schools—which were attended by Jews, if at all, only from the most affluent sectors—to charge extra fees for all non-coreligionist pupils.[24]

Further research is needed to clarify all the factors that determined these trends. But it seems reasonable that pre-Holocaust relative Jewish over-schooling can be explained as a last-minute effort at *basically assimilatory* self-assertion by a status group with middle class aspirations—and well advanced on its way to being absorbed on specific margins of the middle classes[25]—which had now been declared a pariah.

A concluding remark is imperative about the almost consistent superiority of the frequency of Jewish graduates as compared with general Jewish secondary school attendance (see Table 3). In some instances, especially in the early years of the century, this can be interpreted as a degree of relative over-schooling implying a higher probability for Jewish pupils to achieve graduation than for non-Jews. However, in the inter-war years, when—as a consequence of regularly falling birthrates—the cohorts of Jewish candidates for schooling declined from year to year, the differences are largely due to the diminishing size of the classes admitted in the first forms of secondary education.[26]

DIFFERENTIAL SCHOOLING FREQUENCIES: A JEWISH OR A SOCIAL CLASS PRIVILEGE

With this we get to the most controversial sociological aspect of the problem of Jewish schooling in Old Regime Hungary. It is indeed tempting to argue that the above-documented quite remarkable propensity of Jewish Hungarians to attend secondary schools derives from some group-specific intellectual superiority, when it is not attributable to inborn, individual qualities. As against this thesis one might argue that, given the largely middle class nature of the Hungarian Jewish community, especially in "Little Hungary," trends of Jewish overschooling might well reflect nothing but class-bound social privileges. In Table 6 an attempt has been made to construe a battery of chronological indicators of schooling which explicitly neutralizes the effects of social class. The measure of denominational group-specific differential schooling is the gap between the indiciary number and 100. A positive difference (more than 100) is a sign of group-specific school attendance above the average; a negative difference signals attendance below the average.

The efficiency of the indicator is subject to two conditions: the equal relative size of age-groups liable to attend school for Jews and non-Jews belonging to the same socio-economic category (that is, broadly speaking, the equality of birthrates); and the equal allocation for Jews and non-Jews of social class assets (income, housing conditions, wealth, educational stock of the family)—which can influence propensity for schooling *within* each social class category. Indeed, if we suppose that within each social group where the Jewish component was sizeable (mostly in the urban middle and lower middle strata) the proportion of the young among Jews was less than among gentiles of the same strata, the *expected* number of Jewish pupils must also be less that what is presumed here. This hypothesis is unverifiable for all practical purposes, since age-group or fertility data are never broken

Table 6. Relative Secondary Schooling Propensity of Jewish Hungarians Independently of Social Class (1900–1935)

Real Number of Jewish Pupils per *100 Expected* Pupils**

	In Budapest	In Hungary
1900/1901*	143	—
1910/1911	143	125
1920/1921	—	127
1930/1931	98	118
1935/1936	97	—

* Number of pupils only for 1902/1903.
**Expected numbers correspond to the number of Jewish pupils *if* proportions of children of secondary school age and, among them, proportions of those attending secondary school had been the same *in each social class category* among Jews as in the whole Hungarian population (Jews included). Here is an example of calculation for Budapest in 1900/1901:

Social Class (occupational categories)	1 Male Active Population in Budapest	2 Pupils by Father's Categories	3 = 2:1 Number of Pupils for Each Active Male	4 Active Jewish Males	5 = 3 × 4 Expected Number of Jewish Pupils
Farmers	5,496	453	0.082	363	29
Independents (in industry)	31,219	1,241	0.04	9,087	363
Industrial Employees	122,623	355	0.0028	18,047	51
Traders, Shopkeepers	15,328	1,563	0.102	10,092	1,029
Shop Assistants	43,160	441	0.013	9,422	122
Civil Servants	31,240	3,020	0.097	5,626	546
Professionals, Executives, Clerks, etc.	25,654	1,078	0.042	13,224	555
Officers, Soldiers	15,846	104	0.0066	1,011	7
Servants	19,195	549	0.0286	1,361	39
'Rentiers', etc.	26,323	854	0.0324	4,221	136

N = I. *Expected* number of Jewish pupils = 2,877
II. *Observed* number of Jewish pupils = 4,104
II:I = 1.43 (or 143 for 100)

Sources: *Magyar Statisztikai Évkönyv* [Hungarian statistical yearbook] and *Budapest Székesföváros Statisztikai Évkönyve* [Statistical yearbook of the residential capital Budapest] for relevant years (for the number of pupils); census data for relevant years (on active population) in *Magyar Statisztikai Közlemények* [Hungarian statistical reports] and the above cited Statistical yearbook for Budapest.

down both by social class and denomination, and the regularly falling Jewish birthrates in this century may well be part and parcel of decreasing fertility trends characteristic for all middle or lower middle class denominational status groups. As for the differential availability of social advantages within class categories, some indicators suggest that, in Budapest at least, the Jewish sections of the major middle class groups succeeded in securing by the end of the Liberal era a substantial bonus, compared with their gentile counterparts, in terms for example of housing conditions and wealth.[27] This in its turn means that at least part of Jewish superiority in schooling, when observable in the figures of Table 6 (where the social class variable is formally controlled) must nevertheless be attributed to differentials in social condition. This happens to be the case more and more in later periods as embourgeoisement and relative enrichment of the Jewish middle classes progressed.

Let us remark, to start with the interpretation of Table 6, that a significant part of the heretofore registered Jewish educational hegemony appears to be indeed a "class property," owing mostly to the virtual absence of the poor peasantry and to the small urban proletariat—the two strata most deprived of educational opportunity—within the social stratification of the Hungarian Jewish community. Global indicators of schooling (as in Table 4) show a Jewish overrepresentation, compared with the gentiles, of over two to one in Budapest but above five to one in the provinces at the beginning of the century. This advantage proves to be much more limited—less than three to two—once the influence of differentials in social structure is eliminated. In reality, the Jewish advantage can probably be even further reduced, particularly in the capital where the wealthiest sections of the Jewish middle class were concentrated. But this limitation does not essentially weaken the implications of the data which establish that *Jewish Hungarians, whatever their social class, invested more heavily in secondary education* than their non-Jewish counterparts during the Liberal era.

This is certainly not to say that one should look for any sort of cultural or anthropological explanation here. There are enough purely sociological reasons for relative Jewish overschooling which can be substantiated, without resorting to others which lie beyond proof. Even if a truly sociological discussion of the findings cannot be improvised here, reference should be made both to the state of intense social mobility in which most sections of the Jewish community found themselves during most of the period considered and, concomitantly, to its relative social deprivation, resulting from ethnic prejudice; the weakness of its "social capital" (links with the ruling elite); and its effective exclusion from traditional ruling class positions (e.g., the civil service).

All aspects of the observed Jewish mobility pattern, including transfer to the cities and to the west and center, ascent on the occupational ladder and linguistic-cultural assimilation, were liable to promote schooling. The frequency of urban residence was a necessary, if not sufficient, advantage in this regard. More important, the skills and entitlements obtainable through secondary education appeared to be a most profitable capital investment as it procured assets easy to transfer and to mobilize at will. It was an eminently mobile capital (contrary to landed property) which, as such, was preferentially sought by and proved to be accessible to even some of the lower middle class Jewish families. To boot, its social profitability was immediate, as secondary education automatically conferred middle class status (if not necessarily income) on its graduates, while other economic investments promised comparable returns—if any—only in the long run. Finally, secondary schooling was the golden gate to complete cultural assimilation including above all the learning of the dominant language and the internalization of the cultural values and assets of the ruling elite.[28]

All this said, once again the compensatory function of preferential recourse to instruction should not be overlooked in the case of Jewish Hungarians who suffered discrimination in many avenues of social promotion (even in the service professions like health care and teaching, insofar as they fell within the public sector). Learning was not only itself a form of open market (even if a transitory one) where Jews could compete with gentiles on equal terms; it also led to the fast-expanding market of the emergent modern professions (engineering, business executives, trading staff, the bar, free-lance intelligentsia, the press, publishing, etc.) where discrimination was either ignored or inefficient and where, indeed, Jewish Hungarians had long-consolidated vested interests.

Still, specific Jewish secondary overschooling seems to have been a historically circumscribed phenomenon. It ceased to be of any significance between the wars when, most probably, the non-Jewish middle classes and lower social strata adopted with growing intensity the educational model already represented by the assimilated Jewish bourgeoisie.[29] Our data reflects by no means the weakening of Jewish educational efforts but simply the effect of "catching up" achieved by gentiles.

ACADEMIC QUALIFICATIONS AND SEGREGATION

After having discussed in some detail the entry ratios that define the general use of schooling by Jewish Hungarians, we can briefly deal with their behavior and the position they occupied within the school system. The available indicators in these respects include a measure of Jewish academic "overperformance" (which might be connected with a social mechanism of compensation) and a measure of selectivity in the use of, or access to, the different kinds of secondary schools. In Hungary, perhaps more than elsewhere, these institutions were stratified and graded in terms not only of academic level and social class recruit-

Table 7. Results at Graduation from Secondary Schools ('Matura') by Sex and Denominations (1908–1935, Selected Dates)

Date		% of the Best Marks Among			
		Jewish* Graduates	Other* Graduates	Jewish** Graduates	Other** Graduates
1908/9	Boys' Gymnasiums	21.9	18.1		
	Boys' 'Real' Schools	21.5	16.3		
1914/15	Girls' Schools	36.7	36.3		
1927/8	Boys' Schools	19.1	14.8		
1930/1	Girls' Schools	30.2	26.5		
1931/2	Boys	14.4	9.4	6.0	5.6
1932/3	Girls	23.4	16.7	8.4	10.5
1936/7	Boys	12.5	9.2	6.3	7.9
	Girls	17.4	15.5	17.0	16.1

* Mark 'Honors' (4)
**Mark 'Special Honors' (5) introduced in 1931.

Sources: For 1908/09–1914/15, *Magyar Statisztikai Évkönyv* [Hungarian statistical yearbook], annually: for 1927/28–1933/34; J. Asztalos, *A magyar középiskolák statisztikája az 1932/33-as évig* [Statistics of the secondary schools in Hungary till the year 1932/33], Budapest, 1934, p. 114; for 1936–37 *Statisztikai Szemle* [Statistical review], 1937, 1, p. 9.

ment, but also in terms of anti-Semitic potential. In both cases one should be warned from the outset that these indicators are heavily overladen with historically changing significations.

According to Table 7, Jewish secondary school graduates received as a rule more often than others the best marks at graduation. Apparently a persistent Jewish academic overperformance can be considered as proven. A more detailed study would show, however, that Lutheran graduates were usually as well qualified as the Jews—sometimes even better.[30] As the Lutherans, of all denominational groups, included the largest German-speaking components of Hungary's rising middle class, it seems possible to suggest that educational overperformance among them and among Jews was linked to a compensatory mechanism typical of those in a process of cultural assimilation. Beside this, the school success by Jews and Lutherans alike can be interpreted in more than one way, in particular as an achievement connected with a school population coming, in this century, more often from an urban middle class background endowed with a relatively high level of formal education[31] than pupils belonging to other denominations.[32] Moreover, Lutherans and Jews both belong to denominations in which a degree of

Table 8. Percent Distribution of Classical Secondary School ('Gymnasium') Graduates by Denominations and the Authorities in Charge of the Schools (1893/94–1946/47, Selected Dates)

Dates	Graduates or Pupils	Jewish	State	Muni-cipal	Lutheran	Unitarian Other Protestant	Calvinist	Private	Catholic Congre-tional	Other Catholic	Other Christian	Total (%)	Total Number
1893/4*	Jewish	—	14.1	7.5	12.8	1.1	15.0	0.7	28.2	20.1	0.6	100	6,895*
	All	—	9.5	1.9	13.6	1.8	17.8	0.4	28.5	18.3	4.5	100	39,268*
1908/9–1914/5	Jewish	—	42.8	6.6	10.4	1.6	10.7	1.7	15.2	10.9	0.1	100	6,816
	All	—	26.2	4.4	11.1	1.8	15.3	1.7	21.9	13.0	4.5	100	32,478
1925/6–1930/1	Jewish	8.8	59.3	2.1	7.9	—	8.4	0.5	9.6	3.3	—	100	3,776
	All	1.5	42.1	1.9	7.0	—	14.9	0.8	26.1	5.7	—	100	22,855
1931/2–1936/7	Jewish	16.0	54.5	1.4	7.8	—	8.4	0.9	8.7	2.3	—	100	3,013
	All	2.1	38.0	1.6	6.9	—	15.7	1.3	28.5	5.8	—	100	28,321
1938/9–1941/2	Jewish	14.8	59.1	3.9	4.9	—	6.2	0.9	7.0	3.2	—	100	3,329
	All	1.8	44.9	3.3	5.5	—	13.7	1.1	25.0	4.7	—	100	28,227
1946–1947*	Jewish	36.0	48.0	4.1	3.7	—	5.6	0.4	2.3	—	—	100	1,239*
	All	1.1	44.6	5.4	5.7	—	15.8	1.5	25.8	—	—	100	38,962*
% of Jewish Graduates or Pupils within the Schools
1893/4*		—	26.0	24.0	16.5	11.0	14.7	29.6	17.3	19.2	2.1	—	—
1908/9–1914/15		—	34.2	31.2	19.7	19.3	14.7	20.9	14.6	17.5	0.6	—	—
1925/6–1930/1		99.4	23.3	17.8	18.7	—	9.3	10.1	6.1	9.6	—	—	—
1931/2–1936/7		97.8	18.5	11.3	14.6	—	7.0	9.4	3.9	5.1	—	—	—
1938/9–1941/2		99.2	15.5	13.8	10.5	—	5.4	9.3	3.3	7.9	—	—	—
1946–1947*		100.0	3.4	2.4	2.1	—	1.1	0.9	2.7	—	—	—	—

*Pupils of all classes. No data available separately on graduates.

Source: *Magyar Statisztikai Évkönyv* [Hungarian statistical yearbook], annually.

religious literacy (if only the individual reading and interpretation of the Bible) is an indispensable condition of religious practice. Once again, instead of falling back on anthropological presumptions to explain school success, it seems more conclusive to regard overperformance as the outcome of sociologically determined skills and habits which are not only Jewish but characteristic for other groups of similar social condition.

Paradoxical as it may appear, even school segregation, which at its face value one should be inclined to assign exclusively to the differential anti-Semitic disposition of the various school authorities and clienteles, has much to do with the state of the school system—notably with the local availability of educational choices in terms of the number, the quality and the social qualification of accessible schools. The progressive narrowing of Jewish educational options, as demonstrated in Table 8, was thus the outcome of at least two major historical trends. The first of them—and the more general one—was linked directly to the growth of the school system proper. The rapid expansion of the denominationally neutral public sector (which educated only one-tenth of the secondary school clientele at the end of the nineteenth century but almost one-half in the inter-war period) guaranteed the extended availability of non-denominational schooling for all those who had reasons to prefer it. But this very structural change allowed some private school authorities—the Catholic above all—to practice a progressively isolationist policy of enrollment leading to the development of general denominational segregation in secondary schooling.[33]

The more specific trend concerns of course institutionalized anti-Semitism as expressed in the restriction of admission of Jewish pupils and, as a defensive reaction, in isolationist Jewish schooling strategies (the transfer to the public sector; the foundation of Jewish secondary schools: two in Budapest—in 1919, and one in Debrecen—in 1921). The evidence displayed in Table 8 presents the combined effect of the two trends. As it is observed here, school segregation is simultaneously the result of the scope and the structure of the school system and the expression of social distance between denominational groups.

Historical changes in this respect appear to be very sharp though some historical continuities are also apparent. To start with the latter, Jewish over-representation in the public sector proved to be constant. After World War I the majority of Jewish pupils attended state schools. It is easy to observe, even if on a smaller scale, a frequent Jewish preferential option for Lutheran *Gymnasia*. In the years preceding the first anti-Jewish law (1938), these schools educated *relatively* more Jewish than other pupils and there remained hardly any imbalance between them even during the period of anti-Jewish legislation. Calvinist schools came third among Jewish choices, increasingly at some distance from options for the Catholic sector. In the inter-war years, Calvinist *Gymnasia,* whose share of this educational market was half that of the Catholic schools, educated practically as many Jewish pupils as the latter. The major change observable in the long run has to do also with the access of Jewish pupils to Catholic schools: this declined dramatically over time, especially after World War I. In the late nineteenth century Jewish pupils sought admission indifferently and sometimes even preferentially[34] to Catholic *Gymnasia,* while half a century later, either they were excluded outright or they themselves opted out. No such evolution can be traced as regards Lutheran schools, and the post-war decrease was much less conspicuous in the Calvinist sector. Data on growing but differential educational segregation clearly indicates that the social distance that separated Jews from Catholics after the First World War was much larger than the one that divided them from their Protestant social partners, especially from the Lutherans.

Such measurable social distance observed in school segregation cannot however be equated directly with the anti-Semitic valence of various Christian groups in inter-war Hungary. It may well be that further scrutiny would demonstrate in many walks of life less alienation or even a degree of community between Jews and Protestants[35]—a subject far too complex to tackle here in any significant manner. School segregation may be more directly related to the clientele policies pursued by individual school authorities and by local heads of schools, as well as to the different enrollment strategies of potential student populations. Some topical remarks should be made in this respect. Catholic segregationist policies, probably never insignificant in some schools, seem to have been directed, traditionally, more against Protestants—rivals in Christianity—than against Jews, who were considered as more open to possible conversion.[36] Catholic proselytism intensified after the political crisis of 1893–95 that led to the enactment of several "lay" laws, regarded as equivalent to the separation of Church and State (civil marriage; Judaism granted the status of a "received faith"). This was expressed in further Catholic efforts at school segregation: Some Catholic schools encouraged the enrollment of converts (including converted Jews) while discouraging or even denying admission to all non-Catholics. However, various Catholic teaching congregations and other school authorities diverged in their policies, the Piarist Fathers advocating the most open policies.[37] The maintenance of a sizeable Jewish clientele in Protestant schools was consistent with the absence or weakness of proselytizing pressures in the Lutheran and Calvinist environment. It was also due to the fact that a good part of the Jewish clientele remained true to its assimilationist educational preferences and was eager to stay in denominational schools while it could. It is worth noting in this respect that the newly established Jewish community schools, after a rapid initial growth in the 1920's, attracted relatively *less* pupils in the late thirties than in the early years of the decade. Moreover, the Jewish *Gymnasia* appear to have drawn their pupils from the more traditionalist sections of the bourgeoisie rather than from the modern-educated middle classes.[38] Subject to the existing institutional and societal constraints, schooling preferences in the Jewish community, as elsewhere, were dependent on the class-specific social strategies of status maintenance and mobility.

Notes

1. After Russia proper and the territories that would later form the Polish state, the Hungarian Jewish community (over 900,000) ranked third in strength before World War I. They represented 4.5% of the population of the Hungarian Empire (Croatia included) as a whole and almost one-quarter of that in the capital. Budapest, with over 200,000 Jewish inhabitants, had one of the biggest Jewish concentrations of any city in the world in the early years of the century.

2. A detailed sociological analysis of the place of Jews in the social stratification of pre-1914 Hungary was attempted in Victor Karady and István Kemény, "Les juifs dans la structure des classes en Hongrie: essai sur les antécédents historiques des crises d'antisemitisme du XX. siècle," *Actes de la Recherche en sciences sociales* XXII (juin 1978) pp. 25–59.

3. See Victor Karady and István Kemény, "Antisemitisme universitaire et concurrence de classe. La loi de *numerus clausus* en Hongrie entre les deux guerres" in *Actes de la Recherche en sciences sociales* XXXIV (sept. 1980) pp. 67–96.

4. For all practical purposes anti-Semitism in those countries of Eastern Europe where Orthodox Christianity predominated should be dealt with as a separate problem—even from a comparative view. The social setting of the Jewish problem was radically different there, and so, for example, civic emancipation in Russia and in Romania remained incomplete well beyond the turn of the twentieth century.

5. Practically this excludes two types of secondary education which, in some ways, had similar social functions to the classical one but did not, as a rule, lead to university studies. These were the Lower Grammar School, comprising six forms for boys and four for girls (equivalent to the German *Bürgerschule*) and the Commercial Secondary School which provided an additional three forms above the Lower Grammar School. The latter could lead to a formal graduation (commercial *matura, érettségi*). None of these schools taught Latin which remained the privilege of the classical track including the *Gymnasia* and the *Real* schools. The latter gradually lost ground and, between the wars, vanished from the educational scene, after the creation in 1924 of the

Realgymnasia which took over the preparatory training for the scientific professions, to emphasize the difference between the social destination of pupils. In the years preceding World War I some 84% of all *Gymnasium* and *Real* school graduates intended to pursue higher studies as against less than 3% of graduates of commercial secondary schools. (Annual data from *Magyar Statisztikai Évkönyv*/[Hungarian statistical yearbook].) Girls' secondary schools (*lycées* and later *Gymnasia*) were progressively established and integrated into the classical secondary school network during and after World War I.

6. The Treaty of Trianon (Versailles) left the Hungarian Rump State with only 42% of the population of the former Empire (7,615,000 out of 20,880,000) including a majority (471,000) of the Jewish population. Most of the northern, eastern and southern territories were lost for Hungary which henceforth consisted only of the Central Plain and Transdanubia (the West).

7. Cf. *Publications statistiques hongroises* no. 64, Budapest, 1924, p. 181, table 50. (In French.)

8. Cf. Jozsef Körösi and Lajos Thirring, *Budapest főváros az 1901-ik évben* (The Capital City of Budapest in the Year 1901), Budapest, 1905, p. 102. For example, 37% of Jewish women of 60–65 years of age were illiterate in 1901 in Budapest, as against only 27% of the Calvinists, 22% of the Lutherans and 34% of the Catholics. In the same age group the rate of illiteracy for men was 11% for Jews, as against only 4% for Calvinists, 8% for Lutherans, but as much as 15% for Catholics.

9. The 1867 Compromise Treaty with Austria granted complete independence to Hungary in every respect except foreign and military affairs, the so-called "common affairs" of the dual monarchy. Jewish emancipation (1867) was the object of one of the first acts of the new nationalist legislation, a mere confirmation of a former law adopted in 1849 by the revolutionary National Assembly. In 1895 the Jewish religion became one of the "received faiths" of the country, legally equal to the other four (Catholic, Calvinist, Lutheran, and Greek Catholic or Uniate) and as such entitled to State subsidies and to official representation in the Upper Chamber, etc. The social reception of the emerging Jewish intelligentsia and bourgeoisie was conspicuously marked by public honours conferred on their members, knighthood, aristocratic titles, honorary court functions. Cf. William O. McCagg, Jr., *Jewish Nobles and Geniuses in Modern Hungary* (New York, 1972).

10. This fact can be illustrated by the high proportion of professional groups which, after the dismembering of the Empire, found themselves inside the frontiers of the Rump State; that is, 84% of the medical staff, 68% of the lawyers and 64% of the engineers (as against only 42% of the total pre-war population).

11. This is the only way to interpret the progression of the proportions of graduates—both Jewish and non-Jewish—among women and the relative stagnation of the proportion of graduates among Jewish—and their regression among gentile—males.

12. This fact is well demonstrated in the ever growing rate of mixed marriages or—in limited cases—conversions in the capital and the west. Some sections of Jewish Orthodoxy, especially in the east, went so far in rejecting any form of assimilation that they refused to comply with some of the essential lay legal dispositions. This is, for instance, why the proportion of allegedly illegitimate births remained overwhelming among the Máramaros Jews well after the enactment of the long awaited law on civil marriage (1895), while

illegitimate births were exceptional among Jewish Hungarians at large. A good part of the Máramaros community apparently neglected the civil contract that gave legal status to religious marriages.

13. The growth of the Jewish population of the capital—from 48,000 in 1873 to 204,000 in 1910 and to 216,000 in 1920—is a case in point: more than half of this growth (118,000) derived from immigration. Cf. *Budapest Székesföváros Statisztikai Évkönyve*/[Statistical Yearbook of the Residential Capital], Budapest/1921–24, pp. 48 and 49.

14. Table 4 shows that since 1880–81 age-specific Jewish enrollment rates in secondary schools were almost twice as high as among gentiles in Budapest. The long term stagnation of these rates till World War I (a decrease till 1900–1901 among Jews and a slow increase thereafter) bears probably the complicated and perhaps partly contradictory effects of Jewish migration trends into the capital. Thus, the turn of the century possibly witnessed the growth of the poor Orthodox Jewish population in Budapest with a low immediate educational potential, hence the low global enrollment rates.

15. For example, in the Lutheran *Gymnasium* of Budapest the proportion of Jewish pupils reached 43% in 1897–98 but grew by 1913–14 to 56%. Similarly, in the state *Gymnasium* of District V. in Budapest (an area of large Jewish upper middle class population) the comparable proportions rose from 56% to 70% in the same period. Data gathered from the published yearly *Reports* of the schools.

16. Indeed it is impossible to account for the overwhelmingly Jewish recruitment in the new professions at the turn of the century (with 49% of physicians, 45% of lawyers, 40% of veterinarians, 42% of journalists, 38% of engineers, etc.) if we disregard the concomitant diversion of the best Catholic pupils—belonging to by far the largest denomination in the country and trained mostly in Catholic *Gymnasia*—towards the clerical occupations (priests, members of teaching congregations) or towards those sections of the civil service (the military or county administration) where members of the dominant faith retained historically established privileges. Thus, the academically often first-rate Catholic *Gymnasia* channelled, on their own initiative, some of the brightest graduates away from the new professions and indirectly opened the road to what the anti-Semitic propaganda would call later "Jewish expansion" or the "conquest" of the "economic" middle class positions.

17. See the relevant data for Budapest in Table 5.

18. Soon after their creation, the *Real Gymnasia* were attended by approximately three-fourths of all the Jewish male secondary pupils as against two-thirds of the non-Jewish pupils. It is to be recalled in this context that Jewish over-representation had been constant in *real* schools leading to scientific and technical professions as compared with the *Gymnasia*.

19. In 1937–38 among all the female secondary pupils only 5.5% belonged to lower class (blue-collar) families as against 14.5% among male pupils. 67.2% of pupils in girls' *Gymnasia* came from the educated middle classes (professions, business executives, civil servants) and 24% from various groups of the propertied classes ("independents") as against 51% and 30.1% respectively in the boys' *Gymnasia*. Unfortunately there are no similar social background data for Jewish pupils. (Cf. *Magyar Statisztikai Évkönyv*, 1938, p. 290.)

20. In point of fact in the school year 1942–43 there were hardly any Jewish pupils left in Catholic *Gymnasia* (except for those of the Piarists).

21. The year 1938 saw a peak in Jewish conversion frequencies, second only to 1919 in the pre-Holocaust years. The index of conversions stood at

2,088 in 1938 and at 1,473 in 1939 compared with 100 for 1925. In the two years of the first anti-Jewish law over 14,600 conversions took place, more than during the two inter-war decades. The frequency of family conversions rose particularly sharply.

22. Unfortunately there is no direct statistical way to prove this for the period after 1940 because of the changing territorial and demographic base of the relevant quantitative information. The paramount trend towards the equalization of educational chances till 1940 is described in Table 4.

23. Jewish demographic decline was progressive since the beginning of the century but accelerated between the wars. Since 1925, approximately, the Jewish population had a negative natural growth rate (-0.6 per 1,000 in 1926–30 but -3.1 per 1,000 by 1934). Jewish birth rates fell from 15.4 per 1,000 in 1921–25 to 11.0 by 1934. Cf. *Statisztikai Szemle* [Statistical Review] IX (1936) p. 765.

24. The usual practice in Christian schools was to charge *other* Christians double and Jews triple or quadruple the normal fees paid by pupils belonging to the faith of the school authority.

25. This absorption process can be best attested by the constant growth in the proportion of marriages between Jews and gentiles in the very inter-war period of increasing anti-Semitism. In 1906–1910, 10% of Jewish men married gentile women, 15.7% in 1921–25 and as much as 20% in 1936 in Budapest. The last year before the enactment of the First Anti-Jewish Law (1937) also saw the absolute peak (nationwide) of mixed marriage frequencies. Even in 1940, a year before the third anti-Jewish law actually outlawed mixed marriages, some 15% of Jewish bridegrooms chose gentile brides in Budapest. (Data from the Statistical yearbooks of Budapest in relevant years.)

26. Indeed between the wars the rate of maintenance of Jewish pupils in the schools (and, consequently, the probability of graduation) was approximately the same as for the non-Jews. Comparing pupils in form 3 in 1928–29 with those in form 8 in 1932–33, this rate was 66.5% for Jews, 68.9% for Calvinists, 67.0% for Catholics and 66.3% for Lutherans. (Calculated according to data in Jozsef Asztalos, *A magyar közepiskolák statisztikája az 1932/33-as évig* [Statistics of the Hungarian secondary schools till 1932/33] Budapest, 1934, p. 72.)

27. Housing statistics—a particularly sensitive indicator of economic welfare—show that within each section of the middle strata in Budapest (businessmen, civil servants, shopkeepers, executives, members of the professions), Jews were far better housed on the average than their gentile partners since 1906 (the first year when these data are available). See particularly Illefalvy Lajos, *A föváros polgári népességének szociális es gazdasági viszonyai* [The Social and Economic Condition of the Middle Classes in the Capital] (Budapest, 1935) pp. 241–42.

28. This is probably the reason why relative overschooling can also be traced among the Lutherans, a good part of whom—especially in Budapest and the cities—consisted of members of ancestral German stock.

29. Such "imitation of the Jewish model," though mostly unavowed, can be observed elsewhere in the educational field, especially in the post-World War I transfer of gentile students from law schools and theology—where they had been over-represented before the war—to the polytechnic and to medical schools which they had rarely attended earlier. The Jewish ethos of learning, which large sections of the Christian secondary school clientele (mostly the Catholics and the Calvinists) tended to reject before the war, is also expressed in academic overperformance as shown in Table 7, and discussed below.

30. See data in the sources of Table 7. Both Jewish and Lutheran excel-

lence as against a markedly lower average school performance at graduation among pupils of other denominations is the permanent feature of graduation statistics throughout the thirty-odd years during which such aggregate data was gathered.

31. Though no data is available to bear out this statement directly, it can be brought together with what is known for students in higher education. In 1929–30, for example, Jewish and Lutheran students had the smallest proportions of farmers among their parents and the largest proportion of those having received a university degree. Cf. Laky Dezső, *A magyar főiskolai hallgatók statisztikája az 1929–30 évben* [Student Statistics in Hungary for 1929–30] (Budapest, 1934) p. 33.

32. This is negatively confirmed by the poor academic performance of Greek Catholic and Greek Orthodox pupils. It is well known that the proportion of the educated elite groups (except the clerical) and of the bourgeoisie was extremely low among members of these denominations.

33. A detailed study of the historical trend of growing denominational segregation in Hungarian schooling under the old regime will be attempted in another article. Let us observe simply that while in 1893–94, for example, approximately one-fourth of pupils attending Catholic *Gymnasia* were non-Catholics (31% in Piarist schools) and some 15% Jewish, by 1937–38, the comparable proportion fell to less than 10%, and of them only 3.2% Jewish. (Data computed from *Magyar Statisztikai Évkönyv* [Hungarian statistical yearbook] 1895, pp. 376–77 and *ibid.*, 1938, p. 291.) Conversely, it is worth noting that Protestant *Gymnasia* (with some 15% Catholics in 1893–94 and 18% in 1937–38) remained more open to pupils of other faith throughout the long period considered, in particular to Jews.

34. Jews were indeed significantly overrepresented in Piarist *Gymnasia* in 1893–94 (with an indicator of 109 if 100 is taken for their overall representation in *Gymnasia*) and only slightly under-represented (83 to 100) in Premontree schools. Their relative frequency in the so-called "Royal Catholic *Gymnasia*" was at that time 147 to 100, only a little less than in schools run by the State (157 to 100). (See note 33 above for the data source.)

35. This could probably be traced even in fields as diverse as basic theology (respect for the Bible); political ideals (since the assimilationist policies of the Liberal Period—1867–1918—were mostly implemented by Protestant politicians); or economic modernization (whereby German-Lutheran capitalists fulfilled functions and pursued investment strategies often hand in hand with the Jewish bourgeoisie).

36. Lutheran and Calvinist attendance at Catholic schools was decisively *rarer* than Jewish in the late nineteenth century. In 1893–94 Jewish pupils made up a not insubstantial fraction of Catholic school clienteles, their proportions ranging from 9% in episcopal *Gymnasia* to 19% in schools of the Piarist Congregation and as much as 25% in "Royal Catholic" establishments. At the same time, the share of Protestants, almost as numerous in secondary education as Jews (16.1% as against 17.1% of all pupils), nowhere exceeded 9% in Catholic *Gymnasia* (with 7.4% under the Piarists but only 1.9% in episcopal schools). (Same sources as in note 33.)

37. In 1942–43, under the full weight of the anti-Jewish legislation, when Jewish pupils were practically excluded from Catholic schools, the Budapest *Gymnasium* of the Piarist fathers still had four Jewish graduates, a significant if only token reminder of the very relative liberalism of the largest teaching congregation in Hungary whose principal, at that time, was himself a Jewish

convert. It must be noted, though, that in the same academic year, 1942–43, two years preceding the Holocaust in Hungary, twenty-four Jewish pupils still attended the Calvinist *Gymnasium* and sixty-five the Lutheran *Gymnasium* (9% of all pupils) in Budapest. (Data gathered from individual published school reports.)

38. Jewish community *Gymnasia* educated 12.6% of all Jewish secondary pupils in 1925–26, 16.9% in 1930–31, 15.6% in 1934–35 and only 14.6% in 1937–38, the academic year immediately preceding the enactment of the first anti-Jewish law. These community schools attracted the offspring of a distinctively non-educated and non-professional social bracket with, for example, almost half of them (48.8%) belonging to the families of traders, shopkeepers and shop assistants (as against 22% of pupils in state *Gymnasia* and 21% in Lutheran *Gymnasia*) while the proportion of children of the educated middle classes, teachers, professionals, civil servants, was among the lowest: 14% (as against 29% in state and Lutheran *Gymnasia*). (Data for 1934–35 computed from *Magyar Statisztikai Évkönyv* [Hungarian statistical yearbook], 1935, p. 312.)

The Jewish Anti-Fascist Committee in the USSR in Light of New Documentation

Mordecai Altshuler

(HEBREW UNIVERSITY)

The Jewish Anti-Fascist Committee in the USSR has been assigned a prominent place in memoirs published in the West during the 1960's and 1970's.[1] Many articles and books on Soviet Jewish history have been devoted, in whole or in part, to the study of this organization.[2] An important monograph was recently published on the subject.[3] All historical analysis has been based on Soviet publications, memoirs and fragmentary information culled from correspondence between members of the Committee and its supporters and friends abroad.

The Committee was disbanded in 1948 and the majority of its members were executed in 1952. Over thirty years have passed since these events, and in most countries such a time span would have been sufficient to warrant the opening of archives. In the USSR, however, all documentation on this subject, as on so many others, remains sealed, so that the appearance in the West of fresh scraps of primary data on the Committee can contribute significantly to our knowledge of Soviet Jewry during the war and in the immediate post-war years.

Through unconventional channels, the Central Archives for the History of the Jewish People (in Jerusalem) has recently acquired a number of documents (in copy form) which apparently belong to the archive of Solomon Mikhoels.[4] Shortly after Mikhoels was murdered (14 January 1948), his daughter Natalia was appointed director of the Solomon Mikhoels Museum, located in his study and in the office of the GOSET (the Moscow State Yiddish Theater). Mikhoels' papers (including theater reviews, stenographic copies of his speeches and other material related to his activities) had been transferred some time in 1948 to the Bakhrushin Museum, according to the testimony of his daughter, where most of it was destroyed in a subsequent fire. According to the same witness, any remaining material of an archival nature that was left in Mikhoels' apartment was confiscated during a search that took place in early 1953.[5] But a certain amount of archival material concerning Mikhoels' activities as an actor, director and as head of the Jewish Anti-Fascist Committee, was preserved in a collection at the Central State Archive for Art and Literature in Moscow (TsGALI).

The collection is divided into two sections. The first (no. 2308) consists of 209 items containing material on the Moscow Jewish School of Theater. This includes instructions and directives received by the School from 1933 to 1939, as well as annual reports on its activities between 1936 and 1938. There are, in addition, notes for Mikhoels' lectures (1936–37) and material related to personal matters for the years 1933–1948.[6] The other section (no. 2307) consists of 108 items of papers from the Moscow State Yiddish Theater (GOSET). Among them were directives received by the theater from 1938–1949; work schedules and reports from 1940–49; agreements with writers, composers and directors; lists of theater employees; and minutes of the "liquidation committee" that oversaw the dismantling of the theater. (This constitutes the only direct evidence, to the best of our knowledge, for the existence of a special "liquidation committee" for the GOSET).[7]

The documents acquired in Jerusalem most probably come from this material, and include personal papers and letters, as well as material relating to Mikhoels' work as director, teacher and manager at the State Yiddish Theater. Mikhoels' role as a public figure, identified with the Jewish Anti-Fascist Committee, also finds reflection in a number of the letters in the collection. Some of the latter appear below, in translation from the Russian original.

The late 1930's saw the restriction and decline of legitimate Jewish activity in the Soviet Union. In mid-1938, the OZET (Society for the Agricultural Settlement of Jewish Workers) was forced to disband as was the KOMZET (State Committee for Agricultural Settlement of Jewish Workers).[8] Thus, the Soviet Jews were left without any public or state body to deal with their specific problems on a nationwide level.

In January 1938, the Russian-language organ of the OZET, *Tribuna,* which had disseminated a certain amount of information about Jewish life in the Soviet Union, was closed down.[9] On 14 September of that year, publication of the main Communist Yiddish newspaper, *Der emes,* ceased.[10] There was a steep decline in Yiddish publishing in general, both from a qualitative and quantitative point of view. While 437 pamphlets and books in Yiddish were published in 1935, the number in 1938 was down to 348.[11]

Soviet Jewish research institutions ceased activity almost completely, though they continued to exist officially on a reduced scale.[12]

The number of Yiddish schools dwindled considerably,[13] and in those few that remained, Russian became the language of instruction, while Yiddish was taught only as one of the subjects in the curriculum—a reversal of the situation in the 1920's.

A considerable number of those involved in communist Yiddish culture were arrested and exiled or executed in the great purges of 1936–37. Among them were several Jewish writers[14] but in the main, Jewish writers continued to publish in whatever literary forums remained, and Jewish dramatists continued to stage plays at the four professional Jewish theaters (in Moscow, Kiev, Minsk and Birobidzhan). Willingly or not, literary and theatrical figures became the only visible representatives of the Soviet Jewish community, and the regime used them in this capacity whenever it was considered expedient. Thus, people whose main activity had previously been in artistic fields now found themselves becoming public figures. Of these, one of the most prominent was director of the GOSET, Mikhoels.[15] When the Soviet authorities organized a series of rallies (in November 1938) to protest against the Nazi attacks on German Jews on "Kristallnacht," among the participants were the Yiddish author, Itzik Feffer, and Mikhoels.[16] The authorities decided once again to use Jewish literary and theater figures as propagandists when the Soviet annexation of parts of eastern Poland (following the Molotov-Ribbentrop Treaty and the subsequent invasions of September 1939) brought with it the resident Jewish population of 1.3 million—ten percent of the total in the area. In addition, the new regions contained some three hundred thousand refugees fleeing, or expelled, from the German-occupied areas. Delegations of writers and artists were sent to the annexed territories and appeared at meetings and rallies, where they sang the praises of Jewish life in the Soviet Union.[17]

Thus, for example, in February 1940, a delegation of Soviet Yiddish writers arrived in the newly annexed western part of the Belorussian SSR, on the eve of the elections to the Supreme Soviet. The delegation included Yiddish novelists and poets Peretz Markish, Leyb Kvitko, Shmuel Halkin, Aron Kushnirov, Shmuel Godiner, Shmuel Rosin, Ber Orshansky, Buzi Olievsky and Elye Gordon. Among its members were also the literary and stage critics, Yehezkel Dobrushin and Yitskhok Nusinov; the director of the Moscow Yiddish publishing house, Leyb Strongin; and the secretary of the Jewish section of the Writers' Union in Belorussia, Hirsh Kamenetsky. This, like the other such delegations, met with employees in factories where a high proportion of the work-force was Jewish, appeared at literary evenings in public halls, and spoke about the achievements of Soviet Yiddish literature.[18] While they thus fulfilled their assigned task, they were able to get an in-depth view of the difficult economic situation and low morale of the Jews in the area—especially among the refugees. Upon their return, members of the delegation felt obliged to approach the highest government echelons with suggestions of ways to ease this situation. They drew up memoranda to this effect, and drafted a letter to Stalin.[19] In their letter, they noted, inter alia, that

> Jewish workers and the entire unfortunate mass of the Jewish poor, and the Jewish intelligentsia, are animated by the thirst to build life on new Soviet principles. This requires the implementation of systematic and organized economic and cultural-educational measures; at the present time it is not being carried out or is done poorly.

Along with criticism of the lack of practical action appropriate to the specific needs of the Jews in the annexed territories, the letter noted that

> Young patriots of our homeland [the reference is to Jews of the annexed territories] are experiencing a tragedy whose equal has not been seen in the history of the Jewish people. Jews of the liberated areas and even more so the hundreds of thousands of refugees are the blood relatives of the three million Jews who remain in the zone of German interests. This by itself suggests the need for a series of immediate measures.

In drafting this appeal, to say nothing of sending it (if indeed it was sent), these literary personalities deviated from the role to which they had been assigned. Such behavior might well have aroused the suspicion in government circles that those involved were trying to assume leadership of the Jewish population. Indeed, Mikhoels' wife testified that in the late 1930's he claimed that "Sometimes it seems to me that I alone am responsible for my whole people."[20]

Jewish literary and stage figures thus found themselves in an extremely difficult position at this time. Part of the Jewish community considered them a sort of unofficial leadership, turning to them with complaints about the decline of officially-sanctioned Jewish culture in the Soviet Union, and in fact demanding that they take appropriate action to change the situation (Doc. 1). The writers knew very well, however, that not only in the large urban centers but even in the Jewish Autonomous Region (upon which some of them had placed so much hope), Jewish cultural life had been all but destroyed in the purges of the late 1930's (Doc. 2).[21] The authorities had clearly indicated that there would not only be no expansion of Jewish cultural activity, but that it intended to cancel the publication of Yiddish literary works in the original, and publish Russian translations instead.[22]

Furthermore, the writers and others active in the cultural sphere sensed that a growing segment of the Jewish population was losing interest in Soviet Yiddish culture—whether as a consequence of government pressure or of assimilatory processes. All this promoted among them a sense of helplessness, isolation and even depression, feelings expressed by Mikhoels in a letter (a copy of which is now in Jerusalem) to his wife.

In May 1941, the Moscow State Yiddish Theater staged a series of performances in Leningrad—the second-largest Jewish population center in the Soviet Union, with an estimated 200,000 to 250,000 Jews. After a number of these performances, Mikhoels wrote to his wife:[23]

> I do not know what is the matter with me. I have the feeling that something has burst inside: apparently, an unprecedented tiredness [. . .] I think that it is not simply tiredness, but a special tiredness from everything that accompanied my latest work; both the difficulty of the work and the resistance of the ever slower and slower older actors led me to the end of my tether.

In addition to the difficulties that the authorities placed in the path of any new production, to which Mikhoels alludes in his letter, the theater, he implies, also encountered indifference among the Jewish public:

> Here in the meantime things are joyless. At "Tevye"[24] on the opening day of the tour the hall was only fifty percent filled. At "Maimon,"[25] "Ispantsii [The Spaniards]"[26] and "Kunelemel"[27] there were even fewer. It was performed heavily and unwillingly. Tomorrow is a premiere. [. . .] Solitude here is just as thick as the noisy surroundings of businesslike Moscow [. . .]

The sense of loneliness and the nagging question, "For whom do I toil?" was almost certainly uppermost in the minds of many Soviet Jewish artists in the Soviet Union on the eve of the German invasion.

The sudden German invasion of the Soviet Union on 22 June 1941 once again encouraged the Soviet regime to use the Jewish intelligentsia in a propagandist role—this time with the Jews of the free world, particularly of the USA, in mind. Assigned a positive function, many Jewish artists found their spirits revived. On 24 August 1941 a gathering of "representatives of the Jewish people" was called in Moscow. Mikhoels spoke at the assembly, as did the Yiddish writers, Peretz Markish and Dovid Bergelson; the Russian authors of Jewish origin, Samuil Marshak and Ilya Ehrenberg; the journalist, Shakhna Epstein; and others. Addressing the Jews of the world, they emphasized that "we are one people," and that "the ocean between us has not divided us, even for a moment."[29] The speakers stressed that "the very existence of the Jewish people is now at stake, more than ever before in the history of this tormented people,"[30] and called upon "the members of this ancient people [. . .] this people which has been persecuted for generations,"[31] "Jews throughout the world, wherever they may live, regardless of differences in ideology and world view, to join without delay in the sacred battle against Fascism."[32] This appeal greatly impressed many Soviet Jews, soldiers at the front as well as civilians, who were now more confident about addressing various requests to Jewish literary figures (Doc. 3).

Now, in contrast to the late 1930's, these intellectuals appeared publicly as representatives of the Jewish people in the Soviet Union, which seemed to legitimize their leadership position. This situation was institutionalized with the establishment of the Jewish Anti-Fascist Committee in the first quarter of 1942. The regime created the Committee for the specific purpose of collecting material and disseminating it, primarily abroad, among the Jewish communities in the West. The work of the Committee was conducted, at least in the first stage, according to specific instructions from Kuibyshev, where the government offices were located after their evacuation from Moscow. The Secretary of the Committee, Shakhna Epstein, lived in Kuibyshev at the time, while Mikhoels, the Chairman, was in Tashkent, to which the GOSET had been evacuated from Moscow in October 1941. The operating procedure of the Committee can be inferred from the following telegram, which Epstein sent, apparently in May 1942, to Mikhoels:

> *They proposed* [emphasis added] convoking a meeting of the Jewish intelligentsia in Moscow. At the same time, of the plenum of the committee, also a continuation of the collections for the tank column.[33]

At the gathering that took place in response to this telegram, the speeches were similar in tone to those of August 1941, but at the first plenary meeting of the Committee the question of its role inside of the Soviet Union was brought up. Several of the participants stressed the view that the Committee should not limit itself to propaganda activity aimed at those outside the Soviet Union, but should also deal with the problems of Soviet Jews. Proposals for expanding its sphere of activity came clearly to the fore in its second plenary meeting, which took place 18–20 February 1943, following the Soviet victory at Stalingrad.

A number of the participants urged the Committee to take upon itself the task of resettling the hundreds of thousands of refugees, and not to remain merely an office for the transmission of propaganda abroad. They proposed that the Committee establish branches wherever there was a concentration of Jews.[34] In this way, many of the participants sought to break out of the existing framework and expand the scope of the tasks originally assigned to the Committee. Such demands most probably were not to the liking of those in authority, but given the policy of relative tolerance toward "nationalist deviations" during the war, and the Committee's utility as a propaganda tool, the authorities permitted the discussion of these ideas to continue.

Following this meeting of the Committee, Mikhoels and Itzik Feffer were summoned to Kuibyshev and asked to undertake a mission to the United States. Mikhoels thought the idea through very carefully, and was ambivalent about it up to the moment of departure, as he revealed in a letter to his wife of 15 March 1943:

> I have thought over an awful lot during these days. Apparently, it has to be this way. You prepare for something your whole life and when finally the need arises to accomplish this thing, you turn out to be unprepared, everything seems unexpected and even unnecessary [. . .] The prospect of that situation in which, factually, I would find myself alone, appears to be awfully difficult and complicated. For my second colleague who is travelling with me can hardly offer me any support. And the complications then will increase with every passing day. I will just have to plunge right in. But in truth this is not like playing a role. A flop here is unthinkable—that means to ruin oneself, to behead oneself.

In these obscure lines, Mikhoels hinted at his awareness that the mission could prove fateful and that any slip could cost him his life, and made a point of stressing that Itzik Feffer might not be the best possible companion for such a difficult task. This may explain the cautious manner with which Mikhoels responded in the United States to those Jews who tried to raise the problems of Jewish life in the Soviet Union.

Preparations for the departure of the delegation took longer than initially expected. Feffer and Mikhoels had been scheduled to leave during the last part of March and to return to the Soviet Union at the end of June,[36] but they left the Soviet Union only at the beginning of May 1943 and arrived in the United States in mid-June. The delegation was received with great enthusiasm in the United States, Canada, Mexico and England and its mission was carried out to great advantage. In meetings which the delegation held with representatives of the Joint Distribution Committee and the World Jewish Congress, the American hosts expressed their willingness to help in resettling the hundreds of thousands of Jewish refugees in the Soviet Union, and even to renew the discussion of possible support for Jewish resettlement in the Crimean Peninsula.

In November 1943, the delegation returned to the Soviet Union, filled with impressions from their trip. During the spring of 1944, the Crimean Peninsula was liberated from Nazi occupation. Most of the local Tatar population was exiled for alleged collaboration with the enemy. The ethnic Germans from the Volga region had suffered a similar fate. These two areas seemed most suitable for a concentrated settlement of the Jewish population. Accordingly, the Jewish Anti-Fascist Committee requested that the Soviet authorities allot one of these areas for such settlement, and for the establishment of a Jewish republic (Doc. 4). The fact that this request was apparently rejected by Stalin personally did not have an immediate impact on the status of the Jewish Anti-Fascist Committee. It was only in the late 1940's and early 1950's that the idea was denounced as a Jewish-Zionist plot to detach the Crimea from the USSR and hand it over to American imperialism.

Once most of the Nazi-occupied territory had been liberated, the Committee received an increasing number of appeals from the Jews who were encountering official difficulties in their attempts to return to their old homes (Doc. 5). There was also an increasing number of complaints against the lenience of the authorities towards those who had collaborated with the Nazis and had taken part in the murder of Jews (Doc. 6). After the final victory over Nazi Germany, the number of appeals to the Committee connected with manifestations of blatant anti-Semitism likewise increased (Docs. 7 and 10). For their part, Jews who had been exiled to the interior at the beginning of the war similarly appealed to the Committee to help them reunite with their families (Doc. 9). When the survivors returned to their former homes—in the Soviet Union as elsewhere—they devoted an intense effort to memorializing those who died at Nazi hands. The Jewish Anti-Fascist Committee, and particularly its head, Solomon Mikhoels, became the main source of aid and counsel in this sphere, too (Doc. 11). The Committee also received complaints concerning discrimination against Jews in acceptance and promotion at Soviet academic and research institutions. The first signs of such discrimination were already becoming apparent by 1947 (Doc. 13).

It was to the Anti-Fascist Committee, then, that Soviet Jews directed most of their complaints. Some even considered it the proper address for venting their criticism of Soviet policy toward the Yishuv (Doc. 12). However, in reality the Committee had its hands tied. It was never recognized by the Soviet authorities as the representative of Soviet Jews, with the official right to speak in their name and voice their demands and requests. Those actively involved in its work, beginning with Mikhoels himself (who had excellent connections) made concerted efforts to deal as best they could with the matters brought before them, and took advantage of personal contacts in government and among the intelligentsia. One of the former actors of the GOSET has given the following description of Mikhoels' activities at the end of 1947:

> In the corridor next to the entrance [. . .] sat a number of aging women, a young man, an actor in the Russian theater and a soldier. They, as many others, had come to Solomon Mikhailovich Mikhoels to ask for advice and help [. . .] When my friend and I entered his room, Mikhoels was busy talking on the phone. "His name is Alexander Davidovich Milner . . . That's how it's listed on the passport . . . Does that affect his acceptance into the university?" Mikhoels said in an excited tone. "You understand" [he said, turning to the writer of this account, and to his friend] "this is not an isolated case, but is becoming part of a pattern. They don't allow an old woman to enter her own apartment because she comes from Tashkent, where she had been 'hiding' from the war. 'Your people stayed in Tashkent while we fought,' they claim, 'so why don't you stay there?' . . . Another man is rejected wherever he seeks employment, without any explanations. A third man has been rejected from every university. Where are we heading?[37]

This question indeed seemed to preoccupy Mikhoels during his last trip to Minsk, where he was cruelly murdered on 14 January 1948.

It is fair to assume that one of the several factors that led to the murder of Solomon Mikhoels and to the arrest and execution of many Committee activists was the fact that so many Soviet Jews saw them as leaders.

Notes

1. The following memoirs devote some attention to the Jewish Anti-Fascist Committee and to the fate of its members: Yosef Kerler, *12 Oygust 1952* (Jerusalem, 1978); Israel Emiot, *Der birobidzhaner inien* (New York, 1960); Hersh Smoliar, *Vu bistu, ḥaver Sidorov?* (Tel Aviv, 1975); Yitzhak Yanasovitch, *Mit yidishe shrayber in rusland* (Buenos Aires, 1959); Esther Markish, *Laḥzor miderekh arukah* (Tel Aviv, 1977); Hersh Smoliar, *Oyf der letster pozitsie, mit der letster hofenung* (Tel Aviv, 1982).

2. S. M. Schwarz, *The Jews in the Soviet Union* (New York, 1951) pp. 202–05; S. W. Baron, *The Russian Jew Under Tsars and Soviets* (New York, 1976) pp. 261–64; Benjamin West (ed.), *Beḥevlei klayah* (Tel Aviv, 1963) pp. 225–53; L. Schapiro, "The Jewish Antifascist Committee and Phases of Soviet Anti-Semitic Policy During and After World War II," in Vago and Mosse (eds.), *Jews and Non-Jews in Eastern Europe, 1918–1945* (New York, 1974) pp. 283–300; Yehoshua Gilboa, *Hashanim hash'ḥorot—yahadut brit hamo'aẓot, 1939–1953* (Tel Aviv, 1972) pp. 37–59.

3. Shimon Redlich, *Propaganda and Nationalism in Wartime Russia; the Jewish Anti-Fascist Committee in the USSR, 1941–1948* (New York, 1982).
4. The collection in the Mikhoels archive at the Central Archives for the History of the Jewish People is numbered P166.
5. Natalia Vofsi-Mikhoels, *Avi Shlomo Mikhoels* (1982) pp. 38–40.
6. *Tsentral'nyi gosudarstvennyi arkhiv literatury i iskusstva SSSR, putevoditel'—iskusstvo* (Moscow, 1959) p. 300.
7. *Ibid.*, p. 309.
8. See Yaakov Levavi (Babitzky), "OZET-GEZERD (Ḥevrah lesidur ḥaklai shel yehudim amelim bivrit hamo'aẓot)," *He'avar* XVI (1969) 118–30.
9. See Yehuda Slutsky, "Tribuna—ktav-et yehudi-rusi-sovieti (1927–1937)," *Beḥinot* VIII-IX (1977–78) 68–88.
10. *Gazety SSSR, 1917–1960; bibliograficheskii spravochnik* (Moscow, 1970) p. 48.
11. Khone Shmeruk, "Hapirsumim be-yidish bivrit hamo'aẓot bashanim 1917–1960," in Kh. Shmeruk (ed.), *Pirsumim yehudiim bivrit hamo'aẓot, 1917–1960* (Jerusalem, 1961) p. lxvi.
12. Alfred A. Greenbaum, *Jewish Scholarship and Scholarly Institutions in the Soviet Union, 1918–1953* (Jerusalem, 1978) pp. 72–76.
13. The Polish Jewish writer Melekh Tshemny was told the following about the closing of Yiddish schools, by a librarian in the Jewish library of the small town of New Zlatopol, in March–April 1941: "The Jewish school is closed. [The authorities] in Kremenchug wanted to find out how many Jews were interested in the Yiddish school . . . They took a vote and afterwards turned the school into a Ukrainian school. It has been several years since we had a Jewish school." (Interview by Dov Ben-Yaakov, 15 May 1971, p. 19 of transcript).
14. Among the prominent writers liquidated during this time were Izzy Kharik and Moshe Kulbak, as well as literary critics Yoisef Liberberg and Max Erik.
15. Mikhoels' role as a public figure, other than in the theatrical realm, became evident at a conference of Yiddish writers held in Moscow in April 1941. For reports of this conference, see *Ufboy* 1941, no. 9, pp. 12–13.
16. For a report on these gatherings see: *Der shtern* (28–29 November 1938); *Pravda* (28 November 1938).
17. For an account of the impact of the annexations on the expansion of Yiddish publishing, see Shmeruk, "Hapirsumim be-yidish bivrit hamo'aẓot (misof shnot hashloshim ad 1948)," in *Sifrut yehudei brit hamo'aẓot biyemot hashoah veaḥareḥah,* Yad Vashem special publication.
18. On this visit, see the letter of Y. Dobrushin in *Yidishe kultur* (1940) no. 4, p. 54; Hersh Smoliar, "Haḥayim ha-yehudiim bema'arav byelorusiah hasovietit 1939–1941: priḥah ushki'aḥ," *Shvut* IV (1976) 133–34.
19. Among the items from Mikhoels' archive which have reached Jerusalem is the first page only of the letter to Stalin, which mentions the memorandum. The memorandum itself is not in our hands. Citations are from the text of the letter.
20. A. Pototskaya-Mikhoels, "O Mikhoelse bogatom i starshem," in *Mikhoels* (Moscow, 1965) p. 508.
21. On the purges in the Jewish Autonomous Region, see: Yaakov Levavi (Babitzky), *Hahityashvut hayehudit bebirobidzhan* (Jerusalem, 1965) pp. 64–66, 362–70.
22. Such views were expressed to Itzik Feffer by a prominent cultural figure in the Ukraine in the summer of 1939, according to Soviet writer

H. Bloshtein: "This figure was of the opinion that it would be more practical to translate works by Jewish writers into Russian and Ukrainian, directly from the manuscript. He justified this by saying that the rising generation of Jews is not being educated in Jewish schools and no longer speaks Yiddish, while at the same time the older generation understands either Russian or Ukrainian fairly well. This approach would also permit the non-Jewish reader to become better acquainted with Yiddish literature." (H. Bloshtein, "Er volt itster alt gevorn 75 yor (a bintl zikhroynes vegn Dem Nister)," *Yiddishe kultur* (1959) no. 8, p. 22.

23. The letter, in Mikhoels' handwriting, is not dated, but from the context it is clear that he refers to the tour made by GOSET in Leningrad just prior to the outbreak of the Soviet-German war.

24. "Tevye der milkhiker," adapted for the stage by Y. Dobrushin and N. Oyslender, based on the story by Sholem Aleichem. Solomon Mikhoels staged the play and played the role of Tevye. Music was written by L. Pulver, and the set was designed by Y. Rabinowitz. The premiere performance was held at the Moscow State Yiddish Theater on 27 November 1938. Writing about the play after the signing of the Molotov-Ribbentrop Pact, Peretz Markish alluded to its contemporary resonance. In describing the scene in which Tevye and his daughters are expelled from the village, he emphasized:

> This is how Jewish and non-Jewish anti-fascists are being persecuted in Germany, Austria and Fascist Italy. In this one little scene, presented in all its simplicity, we can feel history—the tragic history of a people that has not been broken by tragedy; of a people standing against the worst possible conditions and resisting them . . ."

(Peretz Markish, *Mikhoels* [Moscow, 1939] pp. 48–49. The book was approved by the censor for publication on 3 October 1939.)

25. The play "Solomon Maimon" was written by the Soviet Yiddish writer M. Daniel, and the music was by L. Pulver. The set was designed by R. Falk; Solomon Mikhoels directed. The premiere performance took place on 22 October 1940 in Moscow and in 1941 the play was performed for the first time in Leningrad.

26. Lermontov's play "The Spaniards" was first staged at the GOSET in 1940 or 1941. Referring to this play in 1941, Mikhoels wrote:

> Though there were many differences between Fernando and Emilia, there was one further factor that divided him from Naomi. It was not just the gap of social inequality, as the one which stood between Fernando and Emilia, but the difference in nationality as well. And these days, when ideas about biological distinctions among peoples are rampant in the capitalist countries—distinctions that can be made to separate lovers—we can appreciate the tragedy of "The Spaniards" as a truly contemporary one

(Mikhoels, "Ispantsii," in *Mikhoels* [Moscow, 1965] p. 235).

27. A comedy by Avrohom Goldfadn, the father of the Yiddish theater (1840–1908).

28. During a visit to Leningrad, the theater staged "Wandering Stars" for the first time. The play was written by Y. Dobrushin, adapted from the work by Sholem Aleichem. The musical score was arranged by L. Pulver and the set was designed by A. Tishler. Solomon Mikhoels directed.

29. The words of Peretz Markish in *Brider yidn fun der gantser velt!* (Moscow, 1941) p. 14.

30. David Bergelson, *ibid.*, p. 18.
31. Solomon Mikhoels, *ibid.*, p. 8.
32. David Bergelson, *ibid.*, p. 20.
33. Cited from the documents in the Mikhoels archive, now at the Central Archives for the History of the Jewish People in Jerusalem.
34. "Tsveyter plenum fun yidishn antifashistishn komitet fun FSSR," *Einikayt* (15 March 1943).
35. Cited from a letter written by Mikhoels, undated, which dealt mainly with final arrangements prior to his departure. The letter mentions the date 16 March as "tomorrow" and further on stated that "The trip will take from a week to ten days . . . and I will be there by the end of March." From this one can infer that the letter was written on 15 March 1943.
36. In the letter cited in note 35, Mikhoels wrote: " 'How long will I be away? I have tried to clarify this matter here. Lozovsky told me that it would not be more than two months, apart from travel time . . . He said that had been the decision."
37. Yosef Sheyn, *Arum moskver yidishn teater*. (Paris, 1964) pp. 192–94.

DOCUMENTS[1]

1.

Leningrad, 25.4.39

To the People's Artist of the USSR
Comrade Mikhoels

We greatly regret that Leningrad has no Jewish theater, no Jewish club, no society and no one with whom to talk.

Sholem Aleichem's jubilee is passing here almost unnoticed.[2]

The public library has an exhibition, but the Jewish population is completely unaware of it; the newspapers don't mention it and there are no posters. At the entrance to the library hangs a poster—"Sholem Aleichem Exhibit." Whoever notices the sign will drop in to have a look.

A concert was held in the Academic Capella [hall] in connection with the jubilee, but this concert was most unsuitable for the jubilee.[3] The little theater was full, there were no tickets, a large crowd stood by the doors and on the street, asking for tickets, and the public went away embittered, because they couldn't go to the concert.

In the exhibition hall of the public library a meeting was scheduled for 5:00 PM (as if on purpose so that the public wouldn't be there). About two dozen people attended, no more. No one knew about this meeting. Someone from the group who arranged the jubilee spoke and someone from the public. And that was all. When many Jews learned about this, they were indignant and offended by such inattention, such lack of activity and organization and inability to conduct a jubilee.

It is very annoying and very sad that Jews pay so little attention to their outstanding writers, poets, etc. They discredit themselves, place themselves beneath all others. This jubilee should be respected according to its worth, as an event of worldwide magnitude, which should be the pride of the people.

They comforted us that the artist Mikhoels will come to Leningrad which would enhance the jubilee.

We should be most happy and grateful.

(Signed for all) Soloveichik
[signature]

2.

Birobidzhan, 15.6.39

Asyonok,[4] my dear, you see how I remember you and write frequently. The day before yesterday the theater received a telegram from Solomon Mikhailovich [Mikhoels] from which I understood that he is in Dnepropetrovsk. How is the People's [Artist][5] there and how are you in Moscow? Write to me, please; at the address which I already indicated in the previous letter (Khabarovsk. Regional Board for the Arts. Comrade Smolianov. For I.A. Belikov).

I have begun to feel a little more cheerful since the theater began to perform, had the premiere of "Wandering Stars"[6] (not a bad show). Today is a jubilee evening and on the 20th I shall travel to Khabarovsk. In addition, the weather has become pleasant and sunny. And although clouds of dust are drifting about Birobidzhan, this is better than impassable mud and autumn rains. To top it all, Zhemchuzhina[7] spent a day here on her way from Vladivostok to Moscow and I was with her for several hours. She asked about the health of the People's [Artist] and of Zuskin[8] who, it turns out, visited her two days before her departure to the Far East, complained of insomnia, etc. I assured her that the insomnia had ended. (I don't know whether V. L. [Veniamin L'vovich Zuskin] will thank me for that.) Polina Semenova [Zhemchuzhina] watched two acts of the dress rehearsal of "Wandering Stars," was very pleased and found that the female troupe here is stronger than in Moscow GOSET. ("They act well, but in Moscow the women don't know even what to do with their hands. I pointed that out to Mikhoels when I watched 'Tevye.' ")[9]

I tried, of course, to uphold Moscow's honor, but except for

Romm,[10] she doesn't like any of the women in "Tevye." Particularly Rotbaum[11] and Karchmer. Here there is a truly capable gang (not only the women) and one can only be amazed how in these unbelievable conditions in which they live and work the performances turn out quite well. (I mean specifically "Wandering Stars" since I have not yet seen their other standard works. Despite a few deficiencies, this is a performance of good theater). They relate to Mikhoels with some kind of reverence, incessantly emphasizing that he is their teacher (this does not hinder them, it is true, from admiring Goldblatt).[12] And truly, People's [Artist], you can be proud of many of them, your students. Despite everything, they have some kind of creative daring, they set important tasks for themselves and accomplish them simply, with self-sacrifice.

Keep in mind that to work in their circumstances is quite a feat. They have disgusting facilities, no leadership and no audience. The living conditions are very bad. And it is no wonder that their enthusiasm flags somewhat, their creative flame begins to dim.

There is no nourishment for the fire, the flame cannot blaze up. And I am very sorry for this capable, young, self-sacrificing group, who in the name of hollow fireworks (the creation of a Jewish republic) are to a certain degree sacrificing themselves. For a Jewish Autonomous Region (as specifically Jewish)—this is a bluff.

Factually, everything comes down to signs in Yiddish, two or three Jewish villages and several kolkhozes. Altogether in the region, the Jewish population numbers about twenty thousand people (the others are much more numerous) and resettlement in the past two years has almost ceased (somewhere around 150 families). In addition, assimilation is occurring. The circulation of the two regional newspapers is characteristic. Twelve thousand copies of the *Birobidzhanskaia zvezda* [Birobidzhan Star] (in Russian) are distributed, but the *Birobidzhaner shtern* [Birobidzhan Star] (in Yiddish) barely reaches 1,500, although by the order of the regional Party committee the press run of both newspapers was set at 5,000 each. The literary Jewish journal printed here appears in a few hundred copies altogether.[13] Its quality is not worth talking about. From conversations with the regional committee secretary[14] and the editor of *Birobidzhanskaia zvezda,* I have the impression that not only will the creation of a Jewish republic not succeed (there can be no talk of that, I think), but that even the region is unlikely to be maintained as Jewish. For what, then, the sacrifices; for what all the enthusiasm? And it is no wonder that people fade; they have drunk all the eau de cologne, shampoo, even valerian drops (this is serious!), they rot while still on the stalk.

Well, today my letter did not come out very cheerful; for that reason it's better to end quickly! Again I ask you to write me about everything. When you meet him, kiss the People's [Artist] for me (please send him the letter. How good it would be if he would scribble even a little something to me). With greetings to all. With a hug and kiss,

Osia[15]

3.

[1941]

Dear Comrade Professor!

I am now in the field with the army. I read the report on the Jewish meeting in Moscow with bated breath, with great joy. I am particularly pleased with the appeal to stop the tears, sobbing, sitting *shive* over the dead and mourning *golus*. Now is the time to act. It's so right—"Now or never!"

In the name of my Jewish comrades, I assure you that each of us, at his post, will kill the enemy and destroy him no worse than our Slavic brothers in the struggle. The enemy will be beaten!

In addition, dear professor, I have a request. At the meeting of 24. VII.41.,[16] a journalist, a correspondent of the Jewish press in the USA—Shakhna Epstein—spoke. From the photograph I recognized him as a Jewish activist in the leftist organizations in Paris. (I myself am from Riga, but in 1938–39 I lived in Paris in order to improve my skills—I am a pianist). If Shakhna Epstein is only his pseudonym and I am not mistaken that he is *Leo Glezer*[17] (at whose place I lived in Paris), then I ask you to help me make contact with him. If I am mistaken, please let me know. Excuse me for the trouble to which I am putting you.

We waited and waited for your visit to Riga as a guest of our Jewish theater,[18] but unfortunately, it didn't come about. But I am sure that in the new Soviet Riga we shall have the honor to greet you as our dear guest.

My address: Field post station No. 557
              Post station No. 4, Orchestra
              G. I. Braun

I await your reply and remain yours,

G Braun [signature]

4. [Memorandum on Jewish Resettlement][19]

[1944]

[. . .] In the course of the Patriotic War [Soviet-German War 1941–1945] there arose again a series of urgent questions connected with the life and organization of the Jewish masses of the Soviet Union.

According to approximate data, before the war there were about five million Jews in the USSR. Of them more than a million were killed by the Fascists in the Soviet areas which were temporarily conquered.[20]

Among the Jews living in the USSR, a significant portion reside in the western regions of the Ukraine and Belorussia, former eastern Poland, the Baltic republics, Bessarabia and Bukovina. With the exception of those capable of bearing arms who are in the ranks of the Red Army, the entire Jewish population is scattered in groups throughout the Central Asian republics, Siberia, the banks of the Volga and in certain central regions of Soviet Russia.

The question of returning a significant part of the Jewish population to their native locations loses its real meaning in that some—for example, the Polish Jews—having become Soviet citizens, cannot return to Poland. And a part of the indigenous Jewish population of the USSR again faces the question of shelter, for the areas which they had inhabited for so long have been thoroughly destroyed and none of their relatives remain alive. On the other hand, those hurriedly evacuated to new places cannot regard their situation as stable and in good order.

As for political and cultural educational work in their native language, in that respect the matter is even worse since the overwhelming majority know no language other than Yiddish sufficiently well, and almost no work is done in Yiddish. This fact makes it easier for harmful elements to increase their influence in this milieu. Further economic recovery and the building up of Soviet Jewish culture, which has attained important achievements, is made extraordinarily complicated by the above-mentioned circumstances.

At the same time, whether under the influence of Fascist propaganda or as a consequence—during the war—of the intensification of certain capitalist vestiges in the psyche of certain strata of the population, including part of the intelligentsia, new outbursts of anti-Semitism have become noticeable. These unhealthy phenomena are extremely painful to literally all strata of the Soviet Jewish population, which is natural, given the fact that the entire Jewish people is experiencing the greatest tragedy in its history, having lost about four million of its number at the hands of the Fascist barbarians, i.e., more than a quarter of its total population. This development evokes on the other hand the growth of nationalistic and chauvinistic feelings [among the Jews].

In its time the Jewish Autonomous Region was created in Birobidzhan, with the prospect of transforming it into a Jewish Soviet Republic, thus [resolving the anomaly of a non-territorial nationality group by] granting the Jewish people normative state and legal status. Such a development would have equalized its position in the family of fraternal peoples of the Soviet Union in this respect also. It must be acknowledged that the Birobidzhan experiment, for a variety of reasons, including its extreme distance from the primary locations of the Jewish working masses, did not produce the desired effect. The national Jewish districts in the Crimea and in the Kherson area were reputedly more successful in this sense, both economically and culturally.

In view of the above, we consider it timely and expedient to place for discussion on the agenda of post-war problems the question of creating a Jewish Soviet Republic in one of the regions where, subject to political considerations, this is possible. We would consider that such a region could be either the territory of the former republic of Volga Germans or in the Crimea.

The creation of such a republic would solve once and for all the problem of the Jewish people, its life and development in a Bolshevik manner. Such a solution, which was impossible for so many centuries, is still impossible in all states other than our Great Socialist Motherland.

In the construction of such a republic the Jewish masses of all countries, in particular of the USA, would offer us essential help.

Among the Jewish working masses of the USSR—who were not behind hand among those fighting against the German invaders, both at the front and in the rear during the Great Patriotic War—such an idea enjoys unusual popularity [. . .]

5.

20.8.44

Anti-Fascist Committee
To Comrade Mikhoels

From a captain's wife, L. V. Berdakina, temporarily living in Simferopol, Lenin 19, Apt. 18

Petition

I am appealing for your intercession in obtaining permission for me and my family, consisting of two children: a son Veniamin Yakovlevich Berdakin, b. 1927, a student of automechanics; and a daughter, Sofia Yakovlevna, b. 1940; and myself, Liubov Veniaminova Berdakina, b. 1900 to return home to Kalinindorf,[21] Kherson Region. I was evacuated from there and was located for the duration in Siberia, in the Altai Region. A month ago I succeeded in traveling to Simferopol, but I want to go home. But it is impossible to get there without an official permit; I have received no answer to my repeated requests. I wrote to friends and they advised me to turn to you. My husband, a military doctor with the rank of captain, was conscripted and has been at the front the whole time, and he also received no answer to his requests, that we be permitted to return home. In addition, we are in difficult material circumstances, and it is very difficult for us to live in a strange city. In Kalinindorf I worked in the hospital. Now I would perform any kind of work, I am ready to work in a kolkhoz, if only I can live at home.

I ask for your intercession in obtaining authorization to go to Kalinindorf. My husband is a member of the Kalinindorf district Soviet and RIK [district executive committee], a deputy of the village Soviet, and chief doctor of the district hospital.

L. V. Berdakina

6.

26.8.44

Dear Comrade Chairman of the Anti-Fascist Committee!

Recently I succeeded in visiting the motherland, and shtetl of Minkovtsy,[22] Kamenets-Podolsk Region of the USSR, where I learned of the tragic death, at the hands of the German Fascist invaders of my family—my wife and my son as well as my wife's parents and all her relatives among the 2000 Jews of the shtetl who were murdered.

The slaughter was carried out on 31.8.41, i.e., at the beginning of the war; it was the first such action in all the regions of the Kamenets-Podolsk Region and almost the entire Ukraine. According to the testimony of the few surviving inhabitants of the shtetl, I was convinced that it was the action of a particular band of local inhabitants from the surrounding villages (Antonovka, Kuzhelovka etc.), who conducted secret meetings and submitted their decisions about the annihilation of all Jews and Communists of the entire region to the Gestapo, which quickly—31.8.41 dispatched a detachment there and with the help of local police [*politsai*] drove all the Jews and Communists to a hill beyond the shtetl, shot them all and threw them into three ditches.

At present these police go about freely and work in the region. An especially savage member of the police now works as a cinema technician, and the local organs of authority tolerate this.

It is difficult to describe everything that I experienced and heard from the remaining inhabitants. For a more vivid familiarity with the situation which occurred in Minkovtsy during the occupation by the German bandits, if you find it necessary, you can summon an inhabitant of this shtetl, Haim Ikhilevich Ingberman, who lived underground the whole time and knows more than a little about those evil deeds which were committed there.

> With a greeting from the front
> Captain [signature]

7.

12 July 194[5]

Anti-Fascist Jewish Committee—Moscow

To Comrade Mikhoels

An incredible moral depression, oppressing us to the utmost, forces us to turn to you with a request to dispel our doubts, calm us all, and to undertake appropriate measures.

Recently, cases of anti-Semitic attacks have become more frequent: Jews have been beaten and insulted at the market, in stores, schools and even in institutions and enterprises; simply on the street; some of the public witnessing such incidents join in the hooting and egg on the hooligans.

Here are some concrete facts from reality in Rubtsovsk:[23]

1. In the middle of May at the market one woman, with the clear connivance and even participation of the market supervisor, took away a chicken—purportedly stolen—which had been bought by the mother of Comrade Belekhov, director of the tool shop of the factory; meanwhile all this was accompanied by insults in an anti-Semitic spirit!

2. Gazizov, a worker of the TsES [central electric station] of the factory committed a series of hooligan attacks, accompanying his excesses with anti-Semitic declarations. On 3 July of this year in the

bread store of the factory Gazizov insulted in word and deed the factory worker I. G. Lvovskaya, wife of a front officer of the Red Army several times decorated; he hit one old lady who was felled by the blow, but upon discovering that she was Russian, he helped her get up and apologized, adding, "but I thought you were a Jewess," after which he beat the OTK [technical control division] worker, Patukhova, wife of a senior worker with more than thirty years experience at this factory; and finally he beat until he bled a Polish Jew, D. Lazarovsky, who interceded on behalf of Patukhova.

3. On the night of 4 July in the same store a band of five people, under the leadership of Nikolai Podprugin, a worker in shop No. 2, and of Bondarenko, a worker in shop No. 1, beat the Polish Jew Zilbershtein, and rained insults and threats upon I. N. Tkachenko, a senior worker of factory shop No. 1 because he interceded.

4. The daughter of senior factory worker Lerner, Comrade Rusobrova, ORS [workers' supplies section] worker, turned to the *Gorzdravotdel* [municipal division of public health] for a certificate in connection with the notice she had received via the *Raivoenkomat* [regional military commissariat] about her husband's death on one of the war fronts; instead of help, she was asked the question—"what nation are you from?" Astonished at this question, she asked, "What does nation have to do with anything here," and not attaining anything other than poisoned grins, Rusobrova left the *Gorzdravotdel* with nothing.

5. On 8 July the hooligans completely lost all control of themselves and caused something like a pogrom at the stadium during a football match. The director of subsidiary agriculture at the *Gorpishchepromkombinat* [city food processing combine], a certain Markov, with a chest decorated with medals (since the organizers of these excesses generally do not appear themselves, but put up invalids or decorated participants of the patriotic war) beat the factory engineer Eistrakh, decorated with a medal for the defense of Odessa; tried to beat another engineer and defender of Odessa, also decorated with a medal, Comrade Gimpelman; but was hindered in this by engineer Mirsky. Then Mirsky was approached by a citizen who called himself an NKVD worker; he led Mirsky to a room where Mirsky was beaten by this same Markov and others. When engineer Eistrakh, pale, with a torn shirt, burst away from the crowd surrounding him and hooting at him, it seemed to us like we were witnessing a scene from the movie *Professor Mamlok*.[24]

The anti-Semitic excesses, which also occurred earlier, but have intensified recently and acquired terrible dimensions, undoubtedly are the result of the actions of a special group of ill-meaning people who conduct secret anti-Semitic propaganda and sow national enmity because here in Rubtsovsk both in 1941 and early 1942 there was no notion of anti-Semitism.

We are disturbed by the fact that the local prosecutor's office, the militia and party organizations often play down the political side of these excesses, considering them simple hooliganism and rather frequently leaving these crimes completely unpunished.

Among us are direct participants and family members of participants in three wars: World War I, the Civil War and the Great Patriotic War. In these wars many of our dear ones gave their life for the Soviet Motherland and many were decorated. After this should we hear threats—"Wait until our own people return from the front, we'll slaughter all the Jews"? And this is taking place in a country which was the first in the world and in history to give the much suffering Jewish people the opportunity to live freely and develop after two thousand years of persecution. And this is the country which has crushed and annihilated the most savage enemy of the Jewish people—Fascism.

We can not be silent any longer!

The atmosphere now is inflamed: the excesses increase with every day, we are demoralized and in no condition to work.

We beg you to send a commission as soon as possible to investigate the facts presented here, to check the reaction of the local Party and Soviet organization to our complaints.

>A group of workers of the "Altaiselmash" [Altai agricultural machinery] factory in Rubtsovsk, Altai region:

[original signatures]: Shop director Sigal, OKS [capital construction division] [two signatures blurred], foreman Goldin, construction engineer Medvedovsky, engineer Bogudnov, foreman Shnaider, shop director [signature smudged], director of the financial dept. Korotin, dept. directors of the OTZ [labor and wages division] Boim, Kaufman, Shraiman, foreman Grinberg, Vainer, [signature blurred], foreman Pesmel, technical director of the shop Shnaider, director of the ODK [quality control section] M. Bernshtein, engineer Limeniuk, accountant Grinshtein, deputy chief accountant Talmapolsky, deputy director Geibtman, sr. designer Khmelnitsky, sr. designer Levit, dispatcher-engineer Komriz, director of the OTZ [labour and wages division] Lifshits, shop director Fridman, assistant shop director Krushan, director of the kindergarten [signature illegible], store director [signature illegible], electrician Lepkin [not very legible], director Yablonsky, electrical engineer Maze, deputy director [signature blurred], shop mechanic Mirsky, [two signatures blurred].

8.

[1945]

Dear Solomon Mikhailovich!

Today is the premiere of *Freylechs* [cheerful tune].[25] Unfortunately I am unable to attend the theater as a spectator.

And so: *Freylechs*. One only has to think briefly about this one word.

After the greatest tragedy in the history of the existence of the Jewish people, their theater in the USSR is sold out for every performance with the slogan *Freylechs*.

You know, my friend, this is very significant and promising. This means that our people is alive, we are living and we shall live—we, its sons and daughters.

Sholom Aleichem said: *"Gute fraynd veln zikh freyen—shlekhte veln tsepuket vern kukndik."* [Good friends will rejoice—and ill-wishers will bust watching.] Retribution awaits the latter *(shlekhte)* sooner or later—they will be no more.

The Jewish people has occupied a worthy place in the general concord of all our peoples. It—our people—will work and rejoice.

And so, the application of the post-war five year plan in the field of art, the Jewish State Theater opens with the premiere *Freylechs*.

Good luck, dear one!

I am confident of the success of the premiere, with which I and Khena Naumovna congratulate you!

Greetings, congratulations and best wishes to the entire theater collective.

Boris Shimelovich[26]

9.

30.11.45

Moscow Jewish Theater

To the Honored People's Artist of the USSR
Comrade Mikhoels

Our very dear friend!

We are sending to you our collective petition to the Chairman of the Presidium of the Supreme Soviet, M. I. Kalinin on the issues:

1. About removing from us and the members of our family the appellation *"spetspereselentsy."*[27]

2. On the granting of permits to the members of our families to go from Tomsk Oblast to the city of Prokopevsk, Kemerov Region—to our place of work—the construction of the third level of the Stalin coal mine since August 1943.

The same declaration, along with our individual petitions was sent directly to M. I. Kalinin.

Why did we decide to turn to you. We know about your interesting and important social activity. As a deputy of the Supreme Soviet,[28] as a great, widely recognized talent, you are ready and willing to offer various kinds of help to individuals and groups from our much suffering Jewish people. With your sensitivity you will know what forms of help you can give to expedite the approval of our petition.

We are confident that your expeditious, authoritative, active participation in this matter will help in a positive and more speedy outcome.

Be assured of our deep respect for you. The success of this matter will earn you our collective gratitude. From our hearts we wish you health and success in all your undertakings.

[Signatures]: 1. Smolian, I. M.; 2. Levin; 3. Ess, B.; 4. Sadovnik; 5. Khanzhi; 6. Rubinshtein; 7. Rotshtein; 8. Feldman; 9. Kolitsman; 10. Fenster; 11. Nussenbaum, S. I.; 12. Steikovsky; 13. Shlafer; 14. Shvartsman; 15. Yagolnitser; 16. Traiber; 17. Goldman; 18. Kupershtein, Sh.; 19. Dorfman; 20. Vishmit.

To the Chairman of the Presidium of the Supreme Soviet of Workers' Deputies of the USSR, Kalinin, Mikhail Ivanovich

Moscow

Declaration

We, the following signatories, turn to you, our deeply respected president of the USSR, Mikhail Ivanovich, with a petition to issue governmental instructions:

1. To remove from us and the members of our families the appellation *spetspereselentsy*.

2. To have the Tomsk Oblast NKVD permit the departure of mem-

bers of our families from Tomsk Region to the city of Prokopevsk, Kemerovsk Region.

Our petition is dictated by our difficult situation which would be significantly eased if you could solve this problem.

The circumstances are as follows: From various places in Lithuania, Northern Bukovina, Moldavia and Bessarabia we were resettled in June 1941 together with our families in the Tomsk Region.[29] We are deeply convinced that such a massive resettlement of Jewish families from these localities was not intended as a class repression.

Yes, many of us—under the capitalist order (before the advent of Soviet power) were forced to live specifically in these localities (the zone of the Jewish ghetto and eternal border wars) and to engage in commerce. It is not difficult to become convinced that this was not our fault but our great misfortune. In these localities there was no developed manufacturing, industry, many were unable to obtain office positions. Unemployment and competition thrived among the congested population. Dry goods, hardware and grocery shops saved the situation and afforded a middling existence. We are convinced that in this case the repressions imposed upon us were not because our parents belonged in the past to the petty-trade stratum under capitalist conditions.

The repressive measures with regard to our parents, and all the more so to the majority of our younger generation were entirely uncalled for according to all considerations:

a. We ourselves all willingly transferred under Soviet power to employment in administration or labor since it is these positions which now and in the future promise a better existence, stable qualifications, a more favorable moral and material way of life.

b. We always felt, and the four years of war showed ever more graphically, that the Soviet Union alone is the sole true defender of national minorities. The nationality policy of the Soviet state seeks the revival and development of the physical and cultural strength of all the formerly oppressed nations and of the Jewish people, in particular.

c. As against this healthy Soviet nationality policy, the German Fascists during the entire period of Hitler's rule, especially during the war years, gave a lesson in multi-millioned annihilation of all Jews without exception, not distinguishing between poor and rich, young and old. These victims cry out for vengeance.

d. This means that the Jewish people naturally seeks to live and work in any corner of the Soviet Union sincerely and loyally, for only the Soviet state offers the right to life, labor, rest, and cultural development.

e. A rational use of our labor was achieved in the construction of the third level of the Stalin coal mine.

Many of us also participate actively in social activity, improve our qualifications. We have all begun to live an active life. In comparison with the past, this new life is more interesting and full. We consider that our resettlement was dictated only by military circumstances, for we have been living in a zone where the battle front was drawing near. Now, thanks to the great victories of the Heroic RKKA [Workers and Peasants Red Army] and of the entire Soviet people, naturally the time has come to consider easing, abolishing the consequences of resettlement.

The July decision of the GKO [State Defence Committee] recommended the unification of the coal miners' families in order to offer us the conditions and opportunities for still better work. The Construction Board of the third level of the Stalin coal mine (city of Prokopevsk) and the National Coal Commissariat have also lent their support to this request.

Aside from family ties, the question of uniting the coal miners' families is also of material and practical importance. Under the existing conditions in the Tomsk Region and in the Bogcharsk District, the family members left there cannot apply their knowledge, strength, and labor. Bringing them from Tomsk Oblast to the city of Prokopevsk, Kemerov Region, where entry is permitted, will end the dependent condition of family members, attract new young forces to the work of construction, and increase the workers' energy.

Along with a positive solution to the question of resettling our families and uniting them with us, we also sincerely hope, dear Mikhail Ivanovich, our father and teacher, that you will also justly solve the basic issue of eliminating our appellation—accidentally and temporarily ascribed to us—of *spetspereselentsy*.

In doing so you will give us the opportunity to live better, to work and study better, and to devote all our strength, energy and knowledge more calmly and fully to the aid of socialist construction.

One can write with regard to all the attached declarations to one address:

Kemerov Oblast, City of Prokopevsk, Construction Board of the third level of the Stalin coal mine—Nussenbaum, S.I.

[All the signatures are as given in the former document]

10.

Kuibyshev, 4.1.46

Dear Comrades Mikhoels and Zaslavsky[30]

I decided to inform you of my thoughts, which have long been upsetting me and, as far as I know, have been upsetting many citizens of our city and of other cities in the Soviet Union.

Perhaps it is no secret to you that the anti-Semites are trying to raise their heads and are becoming more and more brazen. At least in the city of Kuibyshev this is very noticeable. In street-cars, on queues, in railroad cars and in other places one can hear all sorts of attacks against Jews, along with attacks and ironic comments against other national minorities.

People frequently slander and inform on the Jews to various organs completely without any serious basis (by the way, such incidents occurred even before the war). There have been cases where Jews have been rejected for work. There have also been instances where various organs such as social welfare have adopted a bureaucratic attitude toward members of Jewish families—even toward old people whose children were killed and toward women left alone with their children when their husbands were killed.

In Kuibyshev during 1945 there were several instances of the murder of Jewish families. After these murders generally rumors are spread that they were committed with the intent to rob. No one knows the results of the investigations. Some time ago, the family of a Jewish dentist was murdered. The murderer was arrested. The results of the investigation and trial remain unknown.

In addition to such deplorable instances, it should be noted that the Jews' internal social life is more and more going to ruin. Ever more frequently one can encounter Jews who live alone, far from other Jews and consequently deprived of the opportunity to socialize with people of their own nationality. People forget their own native language and culture. Many of them change their first names and family names for various reasons and often because of the unfavorable circumstances in which they find themselves.

Jewish girls often become the wives of men of another nationality who afterwards reveal their anti-Semitism. I'm not even mentioning that we know very little about the international situation of the Jews, and little about how the Jews live in other cities in the Soviet Union. The circumstances [in which we live] demand that Jews have the opportunity to socialize with each other, to turn to a leading comrade for advice, help or support. Although Jewish societies exist here and there, they are usually religious in spirit. The Soviets and trade unions are often insufficiently sensitive when it comes to inquiries from Jews, to settling their complaints, appeals, etc.

Furthermore, the Jewish people is now experiencing (as a result of the war) various kinds of difficulties more than any other people. Difficulties connected with the fact that many Jews lack living quarters. Material difficulties. Many Jews, men and women (particularly old people and widows deprived of their breadwinners) live half-starving, don't have enough to eat. The mortality rate among them is very high. No one organizes a collection for them.

Presumably, many Jews abroad (especially in the USA) would respond and offer material support to Jews who have suffered from German and other Fascism. Indeed, there are philanthropists in that same USA who concern themselves with raising the material standard of living of the Germans, scrupulously calculating how many calories each one of them gets.

We don't know whether the Jews who are still in German concentration camps receive material support from their brethren in the USA. Many Jews are becoming ill as a result of the insults and the humiliations which they suffer at the hands of the anti-Semites.

In the initial years of the Soviet regime, Jewish sections of the party organs were in existence.[31] Then they justified themselves since Jews had barely arisen from former oppression and humiliation. Now, clearly, there is an urgent need to create such organs at least in the trade unions or at the very least in those unions where there is a significant number of Jews.

In some of the trade union regional committees there should be workers specially designated to work among the Jews and the other national minorities. These organs must be established, even if it means having to reduce the staff in other areas of work (physical culture, chess etc.). It is also necessary to establish All-Union and republic aid funds for Jewish families who have suffered loss at the hands of German Fascism (aged parents who have lost their children, widows, orphans). This fund should be created from payments made by Jews, both those living in the USSR and those abroad. Each Jew can make a contribution, without an upper limit to this fund. Any monetary sum or property could be willed to it.

In general, an insufficient amount of anti-racist agitation and propaganda is conducted among the urban and rural populations. No anti-racist journals or newspapers are published. No anti-racist films, explaining the question scientifically are produced. Up until now no anti-racist socio-scientific society has been organized, although this question could interest many in the most diverse circles and is in itself a very interesting problem. The international unification of peoples of different nations and races, after all, serves the growth and progress of mankind in all respects, including anthropologically.

What I have presented is a statement, on the one hand of several facts of life and, on the other, proposals derived from the need to eradicate anti-Semitism and racism, which have revived and increased as the result of:

1. The Hitlerite agitation and propaganda, which put down roots among the vacillating and insufficiently conscious elements.

2. The amnesty of many imprisoned criminals.

3. The return from Germany of many war prisoners and other prisoners (who were captured by the Germans even before the war)—many of them were undoubtedly subjected to a Gestapo work-over.

4. The contamination of many Soviet institutions and trade unions (and frequently party bodies, it must be confessed) with blatantly anti-Semitic elements, who are also disposed against other national minorities, who camouflage themselves and do their dark, dirty work secretly, "on the sly," by conversations amongst "their own," by intrigues, slander, etc.

5. The weak agitation and propaganda activity directed against anti-Semitism, racism and various types and forms of chauvinism.

6. The lack of any kind of organizational socio-political activity among the Jews.

I beg you, comrades Mikhoels and Zaslavsky, to examine my letter and to send me an answer. I thank you in advance for your answer.

Engineer G. Sher [signature]

To the Jewish Anti-Fascist Committee

Please send this letter (copy) to Comrade Zaslavsky, D. of the editorial board of the newspaper *Pravda*.

G. Sher [signature]

11.

14.9.46

Dear Solomon Mikhailovich!

I am sending you a photo of the first slab to be placed on the grave of the victims of Fascism in the city of Chervin,[32] Minsk Region. Altogether forty slabs will be cast.

I am asking you to solicit the Soviet of Ministers of the Belorussian SSR to authorize 30,000 rubles for the establishment of a memorial at the grave of the victims of Fascism in Chervin as an addition to the 15,000 r. which we have collected to manufacture the above mentioned slabs in Moscow. Some have suggested that we assemble the slabs in the side wall of one of the stone houses in the city of Chervin itself, and place a single slab with a common inscription on the grave of the victims of Fascism.

Please give us your opinion.

Greetings, Vi . . .

12. On the Struggle to Eradicate Fascism and on the Fate of the Jewish People

[1946][33]

The ashes of the crematoria of Auschwitz, Treblinka and other German death factories have not yet cooled. The specter of the gas ovens where the Germans suffocated millions of people has barely vanished, the massive annihilation of millions of Jews by German and other Fascists has barely ended. Over Kiev's Babi Yar there still hovers, clearly, distinctly, the vision of the horrible shooting of 114,000 Jews. Tens of thousands of homes in numerous shtetls in the Ukraine, Belorussia and Poland stand empty for their age-old inhabitants—Jews—were murdered by the Fascists. In the fertile villages of the Jewish areas of the Ukraine and Crimea one can no longer hear the talk of industrious Jewish farmers, who lived there for centuries.

There is no measuring rod which can measure the magnitude or suffering and loss borne by the Jewish people from bloody, misanthropic Fascism; from its protectors; from the "diplomatic" attempts to strengthen Fascism under various masks—attempts which were conducted openly during the Fascists' brief time in power. There is no measuring rod which can measure the baseness and loathsomeness of the friends (both open and secret) of Fascism, of the enemies (both open and secret) of the ancient but young, powerful but weak Jewish people, which has brought much benefit to mankind, but remains so defenseless!

The very history of the people was defamed, the foundations of human knowledge were falsified, and the genius of the Jewish people was held down—all in preparation for the annihilation of the Jews by the Fascists.

It was the cursed, infinitely despised German Fascist killers and their various henchmen who did the actual murdering, but it was their hidden associates and friends who were chuckling and rubbing their hands with pleasure. Now, cowed by the magnificent struggle of all freedom-loving mankind against Fascism, these people have crept into every loophole in literature, art, science (it was the most difficult to creep into the latter field since science itself is completely incompatible with unnatural Fascist obscurantism). They crept in here by stealth and there under the heaviest disguise tried to incite hatred against Jews, to defame the people as a whole, particularly certain of its most outstanding sons, who consistently fought for the fate of their people.

But Fascism, as a state organization, has been destroyed in all the countries where it temporarily was in power and where it raged most savagely. The peoples of the world turn away with contempt from Francoist Spain in which a blatant Fascist dictatorship has so far been preserved and they demand the destruction of this stronghold of Fascism and the liquidation of Fascist elements everywhere once and for all.

It is against this background that various pseudo-scientific, *ex cathedra* pronouncements have been appearing in the press, supposedly in defence of a national liberation movement but in essence almost openly fomenting anti-Semitism. They appeal in reality for the further annihilation and suppression, both spiritual and physical, of the Jewish people in Palestine. These articles, lectures and all kinds of pan-Arab appeals constitute a particularly brazen juggling of Fascist anti-Jewish propaganda. This entire screech, all these "howls" have as their cause the decision to allow one hundred thousand Jews into Palestine. The whole world knows the terrible deprivation of rights under which the Jews have to live in Greece, where monarchical-Fascist terror is in full swing and is forcing the Jews to emigrate. It is well known that there are tens of thousands of Jews who have been made homeless by Fascism—they cannot return to Germany where Fascist elements are still far from eradicated, or to other places destroyed by Fascism. They cannot continue to live in the refugee camps; they cannot immigrate to America. Why is it impossible for these people, saved by a miracle from death, to immigrate to Palestine, where there is a compact group of Jews who wish to help them? What danger can these hundred thousand unfortunate Jews, saved from death in the death camps, constitute for the development of the sixty million Arabs?

Clearly, they do not present any danger to the Arab national liberation movement. It is obvious that the fierce hue and cry which this issue has unleashed is a patently Fascist anti-Jewish campaign. Clearly, this campaign is part of the struggle for the revival of Fascism;

clearly, it is inspired by certain pro-Fascist elements who wish to disrupt the peaceful postwar development, who desire war with the Soviet Union. In their subversive work they are willing to use any provocations and in their activity in the Middle East they resort to the tried method of inciting hatred between peoples and, before all else, hatred toward the Jewish people. But if the anti-Semites, the cannibals calling for the destruction of Jewry, the various Purishkeviches,[34] Petliuras,[35] Makhnos,[36] Hitlers, did achieve temporary successes in the anti-Jewish activity, their end was all the more ignominious and terrible for that. This time, these anti-Semitic gentlemen, enemies of the Jewish people—even if they have the impudence to array themselves in the guise of would-be Marxists heralding a "national liberation" (read a pan-Arab) movement—will not attain even a transient success.

Irrevocably gone are the times when the interests of the Jewish people were grist for the mill of political scoundrels. The times will never return when for every plausible and implausible reason it was permissible to destroy what had been built up by the Jewish people and to agitate for their destruction.

Indeed, one need only approach the question impartially to become convinced that the Jews have justice on their side. A people oppressed for millenia, annihilated, has found for a million of its sons and daughters some semblance of autonomy in their historical homeland—in Palestine. The Arabs are a people who share the same origin as the Jews, and moreover, of course, they are not going to lose the right to any of their numerous states. The only ones who lose rights in Palestine are the pro-Fascist political foxes. The presence of the Jews there makes it more difficult for them to rush about from Hitler to Churchill, from the League of Arab Nations to those "decent" forces who lend their protection to all kinds of anti-Jewish outbursts. No matter how strange it might seem, such elements have found a place for themselves even on the platform of Soviet lecture halls (the lectures of Milogradov, Lutsky[37] and others).

From 1936 to 1939 anti-Jewish pogroms occurred in Palestine—this is presented as the Arab liberation movement. During the war, many Arab figures migrated to Hitler in Berlin (the Mufti of Jerusalem and others). These Arab politicians did not take any active part in the war against the Fascist Axis of Germany, Italy and their allies, the true enemies of the Arabs and of all mankind. On the contrary, some came out in support of Fascist Germany. Consequently, they—these figures of pan-Arabism, this league of united nations—do not deserve any credit from the United Nations.

These political foxes and scoundrels are trying to wipe the Jewish people from the face of the earth even though this people, which had to endure the savage hatred of Fascism against freedom-loving mankind, fought consistently and actively against German and other Fascism. They are trying to crown the physical annihilation of the Jews with the spiritual destruction of those left alive. Their plot to deny the right of the Jewish people to a governmental system is utterly repulsive and disgusting. This denial is patently unscientific, anti-Marxist. It is a patent pro-Fascist affirmation. Luxemburg, with a population of 300,000 has the right to be, and should be, an independent state! Various small nations have the right to preserve their governmental system! This is completely true as long as class society exists.

But why must a great nation, the Jews, with many millenia of history, with a powerful culture, which has given so much to mankind, be deprived of this right?

Clearly, depriving the Jews of the right to settle in a compact mass is a manifestly pro-Fascist action, an attempt to revive the times when the Jews were being annihilated. But this attempt must be and will be brought to nought. Progressive humanity will put an end to the incitement of hatred against the Jews and against their achievements in Palestine and in other countries. All the Fascist ravings, all the Fascist pogroms and actions have cost all the peoples too much blood, sufferings and horror!

It is time to end this! It is time to understand that this is inadmissible!

The Jewish people has lived, lives, and shall live!

It will disappear only when classes, states and nations disappear, only when communism triumphs *throughout the world!* The path toward this aspiration of all mankind is long. On the road toward it, the existence of the Jewish people—like that of other peoples—is a natural law of social development.

Roizen, M. A. [signature]

13.

[1947][38]

For Reference

The Commission of the Presidium of the AN SSSR [Academy of Sciences, USSR] has rejected the confirmation of all the Jews (eleven people) [who had applied]. Five of them did not have a low grade ("satisfactory") on any of their exams.

Gurevich

The only one of all the candidates who passed *all* the exams with a "five,"[39]—a member of VKP(b) [All-union Communist Party (Bolsheviks)]. The reason for the rejection—he is an orientalist, and since the country needs orientalists, it is inexpedient to accept him for another speciality. The Institute of Philosophy is interested in Comrade Gurevich since he knows oriental languages and can work in the field of Eastern philosophy. Comrade Gurevich presented a certificate obtained from the Oriental Institute, that the Institute does not need him and permits him to use his own discretion and recommends him for graduate studies at the Institute of Philosophy.

Vorsovskaia

A member of the VKP(b); she has sixteen years of pedagogical experience in propaganda work, and her speciality is suitable—she graduated from the Faculty of Russian Language. The reason for the rejection is not indicated since there aren't any reasons. Korotaev refers to the Institute; the Institute had accepted her and refers to Korotaev.

Kantorovich

A partisan; a candidate for membership of the VKP (b); decorated; her speciality is suitable (she graduated from the Faculty of Russian Language and Literature). As there is no reason for rejection the case has been put off and drawn out for the second month already, they refer to technical reasons, do not confirm and reject.

Zibel-Vaisman

Decorated; a front-line soldier; a candidate for the VKP (b). Third year working in school. His speciality is suitable—a historian who has gone into the area of historical materialism. The reason for rejection— he finished the Institute this year and has not yet shown his capability for scholarly work (although his academic supervisor, Prof. Konstantinov, in evaluating his research paper, noted his aptitude for scholarly work).

Pritsker

Decorated; a front-line soldier; a member of the VKP(b). The reason—he studied in graduate school before he joined the army and did not distinguish himself.

The remaining candidates (Levit, Finkelshtein, Rukhovich, Nemirovskaia, Shafran, Kabalnitskaia) do have one poor ("satisfactory") grade either in language or in one question in philosophy. But among the Russians who have been confirmed, there are only five or six who do not have a "satisfactory" mark. The Presidium did not reject one of the Russians who passed before the examination and admissions committee. There is a big shortage in the sector of psychology. They announced an additional selection, but are not taking Jews (Pritsker, Levit). Five months ago, all the Jews passed the credentials committee, after which they were accepted by the examination and admissions committee and by the bureau of the division of graduate studies and the historico-philosophical sciences.

The rejection is signed by the member of the Presidium of the AN SSSR, Academician Nikitin and by the director of the division of graduate studies, Korotaev.

Notes to the Documents

1. All documents have been translated from the original Russian manuscripts by Stefanie Hoffman. They are arranged in chronological order. My own interpolated comments appear in square brackets [].

2. 1939 marked the eightieth anniversary of the birth of the great Jewish writer Sholem Aleichem (Sholem Rabinowitch). The event was marked publicly throughout the Soviet Union during 1939–40. Seventeen of his works in Russian translation were published, in addition to new editions of books in the Yiddish original. A special committee was formed to mark the jubilee by the Writers' Union in Leningrad. The Russian writer Mikhail Zoshchenko (1895–1958) headed the committee, which also included actor Boris Gurin-Guryanov (1883–1944) and the composer Ermler. (*Oktyabr,* 6 March 1939).

3. According to press reports, a recitation (in Russian), of passages from Sholem Aleichem's works, dedicated to the writer's memory, took place in the Leningrad Conservatory. The readings were performed by Emanuel Kamenka. (*Oktyabr,* 6 March 1939)

4. The letter was written to Anastasia Pavlovna Pototskaia-Mikhoels, whom friends called Asyka, Asyonok, etc. Anastasia, the daughter of Varvara Vaikov-Pototskaia, founder of the "Progressive *Gymnasium,*" was born in 1907 and was trained as a biologist. In 1936 she married Solomon Mikhoels.

5. On 31 March 1939, Mikhoels received the title "People's Artist of the Soviet Union," along with the Order of Lenin medal.

6. The play was staged in Birobidzhan by Samuil Margulin, and the premiere performance took place on 12 June 1939, in honor of the fifth anniversary of the founding of the Jewish Autonomous Region and of the establishment of the theater there. F. Arones, "Five years of the Birobidzhan Jewish State Theater," *Nay-lebn* (New York) August/September, 1939; *Oktyabr* (Minsk) 3 May, 1939.

7. Polina Semyonovna Zhemchuzhina (?–1970), the Jewish wife of Vyacheslav Molotov, was born in Odessa, and was active in the revolutionary movement until 1917. After the Bolshevik takeover, she fulfilled a variety of functions in the Soviet *apparat*. During 1939–40 she served as Minister of Fisheries, and in the second half of the 1940's was a member of the Central Committee of the CPSU. Despite her involvement in general Soviet affairs, she displayed great interest in Jewish matters and made a point of sprinkling her conversation with Yiddishisms—as is reported by Mordecai Namir, at the time, first secretary of the Israeli embassy in Moscow. Zhemchuzhina was apparently connected indirectly with the proposal to establish a Jewish republic in the Crimea. She was arrested in 1949 and exiled to Kazakhstan. She was permitted to return only after Stalin's death. (See Mordecai Namir, *Shlihut bemoskvah* [Tel Aviv, 1971] pp. 83–84; *Khrushchev ma'aleh zikhronot* [Tel Aviv, 1971] pp. 186–87.)

8. Veniamin Zuskin (1899–1952) became associated with the Yiddish Theater in Moscow in 1921, and played a number of outstanding roles. From 1935 on, he served as an instructor in the drama school attached to the theater. In 1939 he was awarded the title of "People's Artist" of the RSFSR. After the murder of Mikhoels (14 January 1948), Zuskin became the director of the GOSET. He was arrested at the end of the 1940's and was murdered in prison in 1952.

9. See note 24 in my introduction.

10. Leah Romm (1894–1959) joined the Yiddish theater in Petrograd in 1919, where she continued to perform until its demise in 1949. During the last years of her life, she avoided all public activity.

11. Sarah Rotbaum (1899–1970) studied in drama schools in Warsaw (1916–1918) and Berlin (1918–1921). In 1921 she joined the Yiddish Theater in Moscow, where she performed until its closure in 1949. During the 1950's she returned to Poland.

12. Moyshe Goldblatt (1896–1974) started his career as an actor in a travelling troupe in 1918. In 1924 he graduated from the Yiddish Theater studio in Moscow and continued to perform there for a number of years. From 1931 to 1936, he was the theatrical director of the Gypsy Theater in that city. In 1935 he was awarded the title of "Outstanding Artist" of the RSFSR. He was appointed as the theatrical director of the Lazar Kaganovich Yiddish Theater in Birobidzhan, in 1937. He contributed significantly to the artistic level of the theater, but left the area in 1939 for "health reasons." In 1940–41 he was a director at the Yiddish theater in Kiev. From 1941 to 1944 he served as theatrical director at the Kazakh Drama Theater in Alma-Ata. From 1944 to 1951 he worked as a director at the Russian theater in Kharkov and while there (1945) received the title of "Outstanding Cultural Figure" of the Ukraine SSR. The rising wave of anti-Semitism led him to return to Alma-Ata, where he continued to work in the Kazakh theater until 1959. He emigrated to Israel in 1972. (For his activity in the Gypsy theater, see *Shvut* IV, pp. 119–22.)

13. From 1936 to 1940, a "journal for the arts, politics and society" appeared in the Jewish Autonomous Region, called *Forpost*. From 1936 to 1938 it was printed in Moscow, and afterwards it was transferred to Birobidzhan. The journal printed work by Jewish writers living in the Region, as well as by those living elsewhere in the Soviet Union.

14. During this time, Grigori (Hirsh) Sukharev was the Party secretary of the Region; he was also a delegate to the Council of Nationalities (of the Supreme Soviet).

15. Isai Belikov, a theater critic, wrote reviews for Russian theatrical journals. For a few years in the early 1930's, he served as the administrative director of the GOSET, and was an intimate of the Mikhoels household.

16. On this meeting, see my introduction.

17. Shakhna Epstein (1883–1945) received a traditional Jewish education. In 1903 he joined the Bund, and published a number of articles in that party's press. He was arrested for revolutionary activities, but escaped and in 1909 reached the United States. After the February Revolution of 1917 he returned to Russia, was active in Bund affairs, and wrote for Bund journals in Yiddish and Russian. In 1919 he joined the Communist Party and was active in its Jewish Section (Evsektsiia). In 1921 he was sent to the United States to help organize a split in the socialist parties and facilitate the entry of their leftist factions into the Communist Party. He returned to the Soviet Union at the end of the twenties and continued his work as editor of various journals and newspapers. It appears that during the 1930's he was assigned rather important work by the Soviet espionage service, and was sent to Germany, France, Switzerland and the United States. It is quite possible, then, that Epstein indeed lived in Paris towards the end of the 1930's under an assumed name. During the Soviet-German war, he served as the secretary of the Jewish Anti-Fascist Committee and as the chief editor of its newspaper, *Einikayt*.

18. The Red Army entered Latvia on 16 June 1940. From this moment on, sovietization of Jewish life there proceeded apace. It was in this context that a state Yiddish theater was established in Riga, directed by Y. Lanin. In its first year, the theater staged ten plays by Soviet playwrights, both Jewish and non-Jewish. (See Dov Levin, *Im hagav el hakir* [Tel Aviv, 1978] p. 37.)

19. This document, consisting of two typewritten pages, has reached us in this form, with neither its beginning nor its conclusion. It is, most likely, part of the memorandum presented to the authorities by the Jewish Anti-Fascist Committee on the question of allocating territory in the Crimea or in the former Volga German area for Jewish resettlement. The document is undated, but it can be assumed with a good deal of certainty that it was drafted sometime between April/May and September of 1944. It was in April and May 1944 that the Red Army liberated the Crimea. In September 1944, the pro-Soviet Polish government signed a repatriation agreement with the Ukrainian and the Belorussian SSR's, according to which Polish Jewish refugees in the Soviet Union were recognized as Polish citizens and granted the right to return to Poland.

20. The estimate here of the number of Soviet Jews murdered by the Nazis is much smaller than that usually accepted. The low figure may be attributed to the fact that the memorandum was drafted in the second quarter of 1944, before the authors of the document had received accurate figures on the full extent of the Holocaust.

21. The Kalinindorf settlement was the direct heir of Seidemenukha, the Jewish agricultural colony founded in the steppes of Kherson province during the reign of Alexander I. In 1897 the colony's Jewish population stood at 1,284;

one year later, it was 1,146. Many Jews fled during the Civil War, out of fear of pogroms, but returned to the village when the situation stabilized. In the second half of the 1920's, the village served as a center for Jewish agricultural settlement, and a number of new villages were established in its environs. In 1927 a Jewish District Center was built, and was given the name Kalinindorf. It contained 902 Jews in 1931. The village boasted a large cultural center, a hospital and a school which served the surrounding villages, most of them Jewish.

22. The settlement was founded in the seventeenth century by Adam Stanislawski. In 1765 the Jewish community there consisted of 378 taxpayers. The local registry listed 1,151 Jews there in 1847. At the end of the nineteenth century the town was incorporated in the Podolsk province, Ashitsk district. According to the census of 1897, the Jewish population at that time was 2,196, representing 67 percent of the total population. During the twentieth century there was a general trend toward emigration from the town, and the number of Jews living there in 1926 was 1,796, constituting 94.7 percent of the population. It may be assumed that during the Second World War, Jews from the surrounding area fled or were driven to Minkovtsy.

23. Rubtsovsk is a district center in the Altai province. It experienced particular growth during the Second World War, when many refugees from the German-occupied areas were evacuated there. Plants for the manufacture of tractors, agricultural machinery and spare parts for electrical equipment were built there. Among the refugees, apparently, were quite a few Jews.

24. The script for the film "Professor Mamlok" was written by Frederich Wolf, a German writer who settled in the Soviet Union. It was staged by two German Jewish immigrants, Adolf Minkin and Herbert Rappaport. The film focuses on anti-Jewish and anti-communist persecution in Germany of the 1930's. The hero of the film, Mamlok, a Jewish doctor, is the victim of Nazi persecution and dies from a bullet fired by a German soldier. The film was completed in the Soviet Union in 1938 and was shown in cinemas until the Soviet-German pact was signed, and again after the German invasion in 1941.

25. The official debut of the play, under Mikhoel's direction, took place on 23 July 1945, but an earlier version had been staged in 1943. Prior to his departure for the United States, Mikhoels proposed to writer and poet Zalman Shneyer (Okun), then in Tashkent, that he write the script for a revue about Jewish life. The play was staged during Mikhoels' stay in the US, as is apparent from the following (cited from a letter dated 11 August 1943 from Fishman, the administrative director of the GOSET, now in the Mikhoels archive): "We are now showing the play 'Freylechs.' It is a joyful and very successful show." A description of the play as staged in 1945 noted that its content was quite simple really, and centered around a wedding—which, in Mikhoels' words, represented the "table of life." What made the play was not the plot but Mikhoels' staging (with music by L. Pulver and set design by A. Tishler). As the curtain rose on a darkened stage, burning candles—representing the victims of the Holocaust—were slowly extinguished, and were replaced by the wedding scene, which was accompanied by Jewish dances and folksongs.

26. The writer of the letter was the son of an assistant sexton in a Riga synagogue. He studied medicine at the university in Voronezh and was well known as an outstanding doctor. He served as the director of the Botkin Hospital in Moscow. He was a member of the presidium of the Jewish Anti-Fascist Committee and in this capacity was made a member of the editorial committee for the publication of the *Black Book* in the United States. In 1946

he received the Stalin Prize for his achievements in medicine. During the "Doctors' Plot" affair, he was arrested and accused of having been, together with Solomon Mikhoels, a link in the connection between the "Joint" in the United States and Jewish doctors who were alleged to have carried out activities in an attempt to murder Soviet leaders. Shimelovich apparently died in prison.

27. *Spetspereselentsy:* The name given to the special class of "migrants," people who were taken from their homes and forced to live and work in kolkhozes and villages, particularly in Siberia and Central Asia. Those thus exiled were forbidden to leave their new residence, and were obliged to present themselves regularly at the NKVD office, which was the authority responsible for them. The exiles were free to move about in their place of residence, and lived in private homes.

28. The writers of this letter were in error: Mikhoels was not a member of the Supreme Soviet of the USSR.

29. In the course of the sovietization of the territories annexed to the USSR during the Second World War, hundreds of thousands of families of those labelled as "anti-Soviet" elements, in a political or social sense, were sent into exile. The deportations continued literally until the Nazi invasion. As agricultural and industrial areas were liberated from Nazi occupation, some of the exiles—young people in particular—were transferred to work on the rebuilding of the destroyed areas. This petition apparently came from among those young people, asking to be reunited with their families and to be recognized as free Soviet citizens.

30. David Zaslavsky (1879–1965) received both a traditional and a secular education. He completed his secondary education and attended university in Kiev, where he attached himself to revolutionary circles. From 1903 on he was active in the Bund, and published political articles in party journals in Russian and Yiddish. He also published articles in the Russian progressive press. After the Bolshevik takeover, Zaslavsky attacked the new rulers vehemently. When the Bund was dissolved in the early twenties, he did not join the Communist Party, and avoided political activity. In 1925 he published an "Open Letter" in *Pravda* in which he criticized his own political past. Beginning in 1928, he became a regular contributor to *Pravda*. He was a member of the Jewish Anti-Fascist Committee and published articles in its newspaper, *Einikayt*. He was among the few members of the Committee who were not arrested when it was liquidated at the end of the 1940's. After the death of Stalin, he became involved in anti-religious propaganda, and on this subject published a number of articles and pamphlets.

31. From 1918–1930 there existed within the CPSU Jewish sections, set up to deal with special Jewish matters.

32. In the town of Chervin (until 1923, Igumen), there lived, according to the 1897 census, a total of 2,817 Jews, who represented 62 percent of the inhabitants. In 1899 almost the entire town was wiped out in a fire, but Jewish life was reestablished there soon afterwards. In 1926 the Jewish population stood at 2,027 (about 41 percent of the total) and in 1931 at only 968 (about 34 percent of the total population). On the eve of the Second World War the town had tanneries, a flour mill, artisans' workshops and a total population of some 6,400 people. The copy of the list appended to this letter shows the names of twenty-five of those murdered during the war. If the writers intended to prepare forty such lists, then what was being proposed was the memorialization of some 1,000 Jews. The copy of the list appended to the letter includes five

families, comprised of five men over age 45; five women aged 40 and over; a young woman of 19; and fourteen children up to age 15. The Soviet Belorussian Encyclopedia notes that a monument was erected over the mass grave near the town to commemorate those killed there on 2 February 1942. It can be inferred from this that the plan outlined in the letter was not implemented.

33. The document is undated, but it is very likely that it was written at the end of 1946, based on the fact that it mentions the permission given to 100,000 Jews to immigrate to Palestine, but does not mention the referral of the Palestine problem to the UN (2 April 1947). In addition, it mentions the pamphlet by Lutsky (see note 37 below).

34. Vladimir Purishkevich (1870–1920) was one of the founders of the Union of the Russian People *(Soiuz russkogo narod)* and later of the Union of Archangel Michael *(Soiuz mikhaila arkhangela)*, right-wing anti-Semitic organizations that participated in the anti-Jewish pogroms of Tsarist Russia.

35. Semyon Petliura (1879–1926), a member of the Ukrainian Social-Democratic Party, was active in the underground as a revolutionary and journalist. In 1917 he was one of the organizers of Ukrainian fighting units and a member of the Ukrainian parliament (Rada). In November 1918 he became a member of the Directorate that established the independent Ukrainian People's Republic, the commander of its army, and afterwards its supreme commander. After the conquest of the Ukraine by the Red Army, he fled abroad. His forces carried out cruel pogroms against the Jewish population, and his name became a symbol for pogromists. He was assassinated in Paris on 26 May 1926 by Sholem Schwarzbard in an act of vengeance for the pogroms.

36. Nestor Makhno (1884–1934) was an anarchist who fought during the Civil War in the Ukraine at the head of a peasant army against—in turn—the Bolshevik and the White forces. After the stabilization of Soviet rule he fled abroad and died in Paris.

37. V. B. Lutsky, "Palestinskaia problema: Stenogramma publichnoi lektsii, prochitannoi 9 avgusta 1946 goda v tsentral'nom parke kultury i otdykaia im. Gorkogo v Moskve" (Moscow, 1946).

38. The document is undated, but since it appears in the Mikhoels archive, it cannot date from after the end of 1947. (Mikhoels was murdered on 14 January 1948.)

39. "Five" is the highest grade given in the Soviet Union.

40. Vasily Petrovich Nikitin (1893–1956) was a scientist in the field of electro-chemistry and a member of the Soviet Academy of Sciences since 1939. Between 1933 and 1950 he served as a professor at the N.E. Bauman Higher Technical School in Moscow. In 1950 he became the director of that institute. During 1947–1953 he was a member of the presidium of the Academy of Sciences of the USSR.

On the Differential Frequency of Western Migration to Israel

Sergio DellaPergola
(HEBREW UNIVERSITY)

A common typological distinction in the study of migration contrasts "mass" migration movements with smaller and more selective "free" migrations.[1] The former are assumed to involve social groups in their entirety, or large numbers of migrants reacting similarly to unfavorable conditions at their places of origin. The latter, by contrast, involve relatively small, homogeneous and specialized groups, whose range of options and whose ability to adjust to factors affecting migration would appear to be somewhat greater. Although both types of migration may occur quite close to each other in time, from the same places of origin to the same places of destination—thus making difficult a clear-cut distinction between them—they seem nevertheless to involve different conceptual frameworks and to have different demographic, socio-economic and policy implications in the long run.

This paper focuses on some aspects of one of these relatively small and selective migration flows: the movement from free-emigration Western countries to Israel—a country which is not only open to free migration (aliyah) but actually strives to encourage it. Although this type of migration constitutes one of the major potential sources of Jewish population growth in Israel, comparatively little attention has been devoted in the past to clarifying its characteristics, determinants and implications. Thorough investigation of these matters is of central importance, especially in view of the recently renewed interest in estimates and projections concerning the size of the Jewish population in Israel and in the Diaspora. Furthermore, in view of the assumption that socio-demographic policies might be initiated—including policies affecting migration—with the aim of influencing the future size, composition and dynamics of Israel's population, it appears that a detailed understanding of the factors that generated past Jewish migration trends is essential if one wishes to gain informed insights on possible future developments. Although the relationship between the world Jewish population and Israel is essentially unique, some of the problems discussed and the hypotheses suggested here, are also applicable to other small, selective migration movements.

Israel's (and formerly Palestine's) past experience with immigration has typically been one of wave-like fluctuations. Such aliyah waves, originating in a variety of countries, were influenced not only by political and ideological determinants, but also by the varying accessibility of alternative destinations.[2] Taking into consideration the social structure of the Jewish Diaspora populations and the material conditions under which migration to Israel took place, it is possible to identify most migrating groups as belonging predominantly either to the "mass" migration or "free" migration category—though shifts from one to the other have occurred over time for some groups. Although the volume and geographical composition of aliyah waves have undergone periodic changes, the rate of Jewish immigration has been consistently higher from certain regions—especially the Asian Middle East, North Africa and the Balkans—than from others. Jewish communities in Western and Northern Europe, North and Latin America, South Africa and Oceania have exhibited comparatively low emigration propensities.[3]

In these regions—referred to hereafter as the Western countries— the Jews have enjoyed during the last century more favorable political and economic conditions, have been more integrated within the framework of the local society, and have had fewer feelings of immediate danger. In various periods, Western countries have drawn Jewish immigration from other countries, including Israel. Consequently, a sharp geographical polarization has developed within world Jewry: in 1975, 77 percent of diaspora Jews lived in Western countries, but only 9 percent of Israeli residents were of Western origin.

Immigrants from Western countries (as defined in Table 1)—in all, about 250,000—accounted for only 15 percent of all aliyah between 1948 and the end of 1980, though they have constituted a higher share of the total since the late 1960's. Examining recent aliyah trends one finds that soon after the war of June 1967 and its aftermath, a new immigration wave—the fourth since 1948—started, achieving momentum in 1969. For the purpose of our discussion, we shall focus here on two comparable eight-year periods (1961–68 and 1969–76), each including a migration peak (1963 and 1972) and a low (1967 and 1976, respectively). Western aliyah accounted for 13 percent of the total immigration for the first period, and 39 percent during the second. The yearly rate of migration for the total aggregate of Western countries increased from about 7 per 10,000 Jewish population in the countries of origin in 1961–68, to 18 per 10,000 in 1969–76. These rates contrast with a worldwide total aliyah rate of 36–37 per 10,000 Jews in the Diaspora during both periods. These figures also indicate that immigration from non-Western countries could not respond as freely to the new political and economic situation in Israel: aliyah rates from non-Western countries actually declined from 115 per 10,000 in 1961–68 to 95 per 10,000 in 1969–76, and were essentially affected by whether and when governments allowed Jews to emigrate.

Within the context of the lower-than-average frequency of migration from the countries considered in Table 1 as a group, a remarkable range of variation can be observed. Aliyah was—with no exception—more frequent in 1969–76 than in 1961–68, ranging between less than 2 immigrants per 10,000 Jews (United States) and 59 per 10,000 (Uruguay) in the former period, and between 8 (United States) and 176 (Chile) in the latter. Comparing the changes in the rates of migration over the two periods, we find a pattern of considerable similarity (as indicated by a correlation coefficient of .72).

Apparently, the dynamics of Western migration to Israel was influenced over time by a highly consistent set of determinants, which dominated internal variation and overall levels of aliyah rates. These intensity differentials are of greatest importance in determining the overall volume of aliyah. Thus, for example, the combined aliyah rate of all non-European, English-speaking areas (North America, Southern Africa, Oceania) was 2 per 10,000 Jews in 1961–68, and 10 per 10,000 in 1969–76, while the combined rates of all Western European countries were 17 and 43, respectively, and those of Latin America were 37 and 63 per 10,000. Should the 1969–76 aliyah rate of English-speaking countries have been similar to that of Western Europe, immigration would have been larger by 170,000 persons, and should it have equalled that of Latin America, there would have been 270,000 more immigrants. On the other hand, should the 1969–76 aliyah rate of all Western countries have been as low as that of the United States, there would have been 65,000 fewer immigrants to Israel. What, then, stood behind these substantial differentials?

THE CAUSAL STRUCTURE OF WESTERN ALIYAH

The study of aliyah must confront a number of central questions related to the changing volume of migration over time, its sociodemographic composition, and its absorption patterns in Israel. These questions cannot be answered without due consideration of the societal and personal determinants of migration to Israel, and of the selectivity of immigrants as compared to members of the same Jewish communities who did not migrate, or preferred to emigrate to alternative destinations.[4] The examination of these topics should not only focus on the specific conditions of the Jews in the Diaspora and in Israel, but should also make reference to certain broader concepts, which emerge from the general study of human migrations.

Analytic understanding of emigration from countries which neither raise obstacles to the free emigration of their citizens, nor are particularly active in encouraging it, requires that research be focused on the monetary and non-monetary costs and benefits presumably associated with the decision to migrate.[5] Thus, the existing degree of relative satisfaction among potential migrants must be defined, together with a set of relationships between positive and negative factors—whether correctly or incorrectly perceived—in the places of origin and destination. The following chart summarizes the various possible effects of such factors on an individual's migration status.[6]

Type of factor affecting individual	Expected effect on individual's migration status following perception of factor operating:	
	At place of origin	At place of destination
Positive	Hold	Pull
Negative	Push	Repel

In other words, a distinction is suggested between factors encouraging, and factors acting as a disincentive to, migration. Such a distinction, though certainly relevant in the analysis of relatively infrequent migration (such as in the case of Western aliyah), is not always taken into account in the literature: while standard reference is made to the pull-push factors, the hold-repel forces have been less often investigated. Furthermore, as in other voluntary processes involving social and demographic change, decision-making connected to potential migration also depends on a number of intervening factors affecting the desirability and the feasibility of migration.[7] It can be expected that migration will actually occur only after given thresholds of migration desirability and feasibility will have been attained.[8] Such thresholds may shift over time. With regard to Western aliyah, changes probably occurred in connection with events such as the June 1967 war, which opened a new chapter in the relationship between the Jewish people and Israel, and as a consequence of which the salience of Israel as an ideal place of domicile considerably increased in the perception of Diaspora Jewries. It can be assumed that among persons who already possessed some latent migration propensity, events of this sort can have a decisive effect on the actual decision to migrate.

In the specific case of Israel, conventional wisdom holds that immigration, particularly from Western countries, has responded essentially to ideological factors.[9] Aliyah thus seems to constitute a particular case of a more general situation in which geographical mobility, *prima facie*, is not exclusively or even essentially determined by economic factors, but rather results from the existence of certain religious, political or cultural values and norms. Such migrations at times seem to contradict the rules of conventional rational economic behavior, especially when they involve the move from a more to a less developed country, thus bringing about for the migrants the loss of some material benefits.

Other scholars have focused on a broader range of determinants, namely the periodic changes in the economic absorption potential of Israeli society, and changes in the migration policies of Israeli governments, over time.[10] Indeed, the volume of aliyah has been found to correlate strongly and positively with the main economic indicators in the receiving country. However, the relationship between migration and economic cycles is rather complex, and may not coincide with a one-way causation. In fact, it can be reasonably assumed that economic conditions in Israel not only stimulated but often responded to the changing volume of aliyah. It seems that after the 1967 Six Day War, changes in Israel, such as a rapidly expanding economy, growing differentiation for the labor market, and an improving technical infrastructure for immigrant absorption combined in attracting a larger volume of immigration.[11] Potential Jewish immigrants from Western countries may have been especially affected by such changes. There were, however, other factors at work that should not be ignored, such as an increasing salience of Jewish identity among Jews in the Diaspora. Moreover, the early 1970's witnessed serious political crises in various Western countries, including the violent overthrow of a number of regimes. Economic difficulties were partly due to the consequences for the West of the sharp increase in the price of energy sources that was connected, at least indirectly, with the Arab-Israeli war of October 1973.

Beyond these impressionistic notions, we shall not be able to assess the actual presence and relative weight of the various above mentioned factors in determining the peculiar characteristics of Western aliyah unless an attempt is made to organize them into a more systematic framework. A more complete explanation of aliyah trends and differentials should consider three main sets of factors which generate a range of challenges and opportunities for Jews considering aliyah: (a) the different general political and socio-economic contexts of the countries from which migration originates; (b) the different demographic, socio-economic and ideological characteristics of the Jewish communities in each country; (c) the socio-economic and ideological characteristics of Israeli society.

One of the basic characteristics of the type of migration considered here is that it can be expected to be associated with a very peculiar and narrow "space awareness."[12] The choice of destination clearly implies a well-defined set of goals among migrants. At least some of these goals, and the benefits expected to be associated with their attainment, cannot be achieved in indifferent destinations, and can only be pursued in relation to a certain "ideal place." Migration to Israel, in fact, does not usually constitute one of many alternatives being equally considered by potential migrants; the typical alternative to aliyah for Jews in Western countries is non-migration. A sample survey of the Jewish population of South Africa (1974) shows that 22 percent of heads of households were considering emigration (though only 1.3 percent had definitely decided to leave). Israel was indicated as the preferred country of destination by 80 percent of all those who considered emigration, and by 74 percent of those more committed.[13] Similarly, in a sample study of Italian Jews in Israel (1975) it was found that only 16 percent of migrants had considered alternative destinations when leaving Italy.[14] Israel's dominant position in the migration-related space awareness of Western Jews is confirmed by the predominance of ideological determinants for migration. For example, the most frequent reason given by Italians in Israel for migration (to a multiple-answer question) was "the desire to live in a Jewish state" (76 percent). The least frequent was "economic reasons" (11 percent). Quite similar findings appear in studies of North American migrants to Israel[15] and of Israelis abroad, either considering a return to Israel or actually returning.[16]

The data available on Western immigrants from the longitudinal survey of immigrant absorption currently being carried out in Israel, and the analyses (based on the same source) of selected Western origin groups (such as North Americans or Latin Americans) point to a higher percentage of "religious" or "Zionist" immigrants than that currently existing among the Jewish populations of the respective countries of origin.[17] The desirability of migration to Israel, and perhaps also the feasibility of such a move, are perceived quite selectively in diaspora Jewish populations depending on demographic, socio-economic and ideological factors. Jews migrating to Israel do not constitute a representative cross-section of the population in their communities of origin; and as a group they are structured differently from groups of Jews migrating to alternative destinations.[18]

When considering the Western Jewish diaspora cross-nationally, however, it should also be ascertained whether the same rules that govern migration selectivity within countries also operate between countries. Investigating individual as against aggregate social behavior requires somewhat different approaches and assumptions, although both analytic levels are ultimately interrelated. We mainly focus, here, on aggregative generalizations, assuming that exposure to similar environments tends to introduce a common basis into the possible range of individual responses.

Even within the general situation of freedom and affluence that characterizes Western Jewish communities, variations in economic development and political freedom may be expected to be significantly related to the degree of complexity in the occupational structure and in the socio-political institutions of the countries considered. These general aspects of a country's social structure, in turn, may affect the likelihood that occupational and social opportunities exist that are more or less congenial to the particular structural characteristics of Jewish populations, with their diffuse and higher-than-average educational attainment, their nearly total urbanization, and their concentration in a number of occupational branches in industry, trade and services.[19] Some very preliminary research actually suggests that Jewish populations in the Diaspora may be strongly attracted by places offering a combination of high average income, occupational diversification, modern technology and well-developed cultural services.[20] Where such greater opportunities are available, it can be expected that stronger societal hold will be experienced among members of the group: feelings of satisfaction with the present situation are likely to reduce the desire to migrate.

On a shorter term perspective, rapid changes in existing economic and political conditions—such as high rates of inflation or frequent manifestations of political violence, including violence against the group in question—may disrupt the framework on which previous evaluations of place satisfaction were based. Such society push may clearly be expected to increase the perceived need to migrate.

From the internal perspective of the Diaspora Jewish communities, a situation of relative societal openness—which we assume as more characteristic of Western than of other countries—may engender two contrasting processes. On the one hand, freedom and equality may be positively associated with the intensity of interaction between Jews and members of other groups, leading to an increasing degree of cultural and structural similarity, and in the longer run to increasing frequencies of marital and identificational assimilation.[21] Assimilation, in turn, is presumedly associated with a decrease in the salience of particularistic values and norms, including those concerning ideal places of residence. On the other hand, freedom may stimulate socio-cultural groups, including Jewish minorities, to organize themselves voluntarily to achieve their preferred collective goals. It may be expected that the more a community is able to strengthen its self-supportive institutions—such as, for example, an independent educational network—the higher the likelihood that its members will internalize the group's norms and values, including, in the case of the Jews, those related to emigration to Israel.

The absolute size of a community, or its percentage relative to the general population of the community, may provide a further important indication of the influence and visibility of local Jewry, of the share of general power that it holds, and of its ability to offer opportunities for local community life as an alternative to the ideological forces that would lead to aliyah. The weight of Diaspora Jewish populations reflects a complex interplay of political, socio-economic and demographic forces.[22] Keeping in mind gravity theories of migration,[23] one may assume that the greater or denser a Jewish community, the stronger is its potential for holding the existing population, and also for attracting new Jewish migrants.

Turning now to the pull and repel factors related to the country of destination, the availability of levels of socio-economic reward compatible with the potential migrants' expectations can significantly affect the overall migration volume.[24] In the case of Israel, physical security as well as occupational absorption may be important components in this pull-repel complex. However, in the case of ideologically oriented migration, further attention should be devoted to factors affecting the level of place idealization among residents of the place itself. Changes in the cultural-ideological environment of the absorbing society may affect migration fluctuations over time.

When the focus is—as in our case—on migration differentials, two different groups of pull-repel factors should be discussed. At a greater generalization level stands the degree of appeal of the country of destination. An intriguing question is whether Israel's society projects only one image towards various other outside societies. It seems likely that local differences exist in the media presentation of Israel's image—in terms of its security problems, political regime, economic situation—which tend to affect the attitude of different Jewish communities in the Diaspora.

The differential impact of the receiving country on migration is probably easier to measure in terms of the absorption feedback of former immigrants from each country of origin. The experience of earlier immigrants can substantially affect the decision-making processes of those contemplating migration from the same country.[25] Perception from the outside of the degree of satisfaction prevailing among members of an origin group currently living in the country of destination seems likely to influence others in the country of origin. It can be assumed that differences will emerge in the degree of adaptation of various immigrant groups, due to their different occupational and cultural backgrounds. Absorption is a time-related process,[26] and consequently, the length of stay in the country appears to be a reasonable indicator of the degree of satisfaction among members of an immigrant group. Important components of the absorption process are the degree of efficiency and goodwill displayed by the absorptive system. Although the latter is supposed to treat all new immigrants equally, regardless of origin, some groups may be more favored than others. In the case of Israel, a high degree of communication exists with Western countries through family and other links, including rapidly expanding streams of tourism in both directions. Return migration, which is part of a larger stream of emigration from Israel, and which indicates that persons of the same origin group—presumably with similar backgrounds and characteristics—had to face difficulties that prevented their permanent settlement, seems most likely to deter further migration.

Finally, one should consider a set of factors related to financial or other costs of migration. Distance can (other things being equal) be considered a broad attrition factor in the propensity to migrate, because of transportation costs, and possibly also because of cultural, climatic and other environmental differences involved. In the context of migrations which, like aliyah, are subsidized by the governments of the countries of destination, however, migration costs should not be expected to play a very significant role in reducing the perceived feasibility of migration.

DEFINITIONS, DATA AND METHOD

Having outlined the essential components of a conceptual framework for the analysis of variation in the rates of aliyah from Western countries, we should try to check its validity empirically. To do so we should translate each of the general concepts now defined into an appropriate quantitative variable. Comparing the values of each variable for each of the countries investigated here should provide an

Table 1. Yearly Rates of Migration to Israel from Western Countries per 10,000 Jewish Population, 1961–68 and 1969–76

Country	1961–1968	1969–1976
World, total	37	36
Western countries, total	7	18
Other countries, total	115	95
United Kingdom, Ireland	10	27
Scandinavia	23	68
Netherlands	31	61
Belgium, Luxembourg	23	48
France	24	50
Switzerland	31	62
Germany	38	55
Austria	33	59
Italy	31	58
Yugoslavia	14	23
Greece	41	92
United States	1	8
Canada	4	17
Mexico	14	43
Argentina	42	64
Brazil	25	39
Uruguay	59	97
Chile	41	176
Rest of Latin America	31	47
South Africa, Rhodesia	22	49
Australia, New Zealand	11	43

Sources: Immigrants, potential immigrants, and tourists settling in Israel: Israel Central Bureau of Statistics.
Jewish population size in the countries of origin: censuses, surveys, and population estimates, Division of Jewish Demography and Statistics, Institute of Contemporary Jewry, The Hebrew University, Jerusalem. See also Table 2.

indication of the ability of our model to explain the observed differentials in aliyah rates, and to assess the relative weight of each variable in such an explanation.

Unfortunately, the quality and quantity of the relevant data available are uneven. Relatively copious and accurate data exist as to the general demographic and economic characteristics of Western societies. Fewer comparable indicators are available to throw light on their internal socio-political and cultural dynamics. Data on Jewish minorities the world over are far less numerous and standardized, notwithstanding the recent expansion of Jewish population studies.[27] Only in the case of a few variables is there complete coverage for the entire Western world—that is, for each of the twenty-one geographical units listed in Table 1. Data on characteristics of particular Western immigrant groups in Israel are available from a special processing of the

1961 Israeli census. Fewer data are available so far with the desired detail from the more recent—and for our purposes more interesting—1972 census. In certain cases, therefore, data operationalization will correspond only partially, or indirectly, to the needs of our model.

Such data constraints suggest that a first exploratory analysis of differential rates of Western migration to Israel (the dependent variable) be confined to a rather simplified version of the conceptual framework discussed above. The model tested consists of ten independent variables, divided into five categories of up to three variables each: (a) *general societal hold:* energy consumption per capita (an indicator of industrial and technological development); press freedom (an indicator of a country's political emancipation); (b) *general societal push:* consumer price increase; domestic violence (measured by indicators such as the number of deaths in internal political events); (c) *Jewish community structure:* the weight of the Jewish in the total population; the degree of Jewish assimilation; frequency of Jewish education; (d) *immigrant feedback:* the length of stay in Israel; return migration; (e) *migration costs:* the distance of each country from Israel. A synopsis of the variables used in the statistical analysis of migration rates from Western countries to Israel is given in Table 2.[28]

The multiple regression analysis discussed in the next section aims to test the strength and direction of relationships between Western migration rates to Israel and each independent variable, or category of variables. Since it may be argued that the quality of the data and their correspondence to the theoretical specifications of the model are better suited for measuring societal hold and push than other factors, an additional line of investigation will consider how much of the observed migration differentials can be explained solely by these factors. Consequently, in this analytic perspective the interest of other variables, including those related to Israel, is somewhat secondary.

In order to test our hypotheses empirically, we present in the next section a brief description of the characteristics of the independent variables, followed by a separate examination of the relationship of the dependent variable to each independent variable, and by an overall assessment of validity of the model and of its components.

RESULTS

Means and standard deviations of each of the variables studied are reported in Table 3. The main changes over time refer to increases in the aliyah rate, energy consumption, assimilation and prices. Jewish population weight and the length of stay in Israel were relatively stable. (Other variables could not be compared over time.)

Interrelationships among independent variables are reported in Table 4. The data points to a pattern of overall consistency over time in the correlations between factors relating to general societal hold and push, and Jewish community structure in the countries of origin. Energy consumption and press freedom, both of which represent societal hold factors, are strongly and positively correlated. High correlation coefficients also appear within the societal push category between price increase and domestic violence in the countries of origin. The relationship between general hold and push factors is generally negative. With regard to the variables related to the structure of Jewish communities in the Diaspora, a clear negative link exists between the frequency of assimilation, on the one hand, and the weight of Jewish population and the frequency of Jewish education on the other. Jewish population weight, in turn, is directly correlated with the general societal hold factors.

Turning now to the variables related to the country of destination, a strongly negative relationship appears between the length of stay in Israel and the frequency of return migration. The attractive power of a given diaspora on Jewish migrants is indicated by the fact that Jewish population weight is negatively correlated with the length of stay in Israel among former immigrants from that country, and is positively correlated with the frequency of return migration among the same origin group. All these relationships confirm previously discussed hypotheses and the results of previous research.

These findings do not indicate the direction of causal relationships between variables; but only the sign (positive or negative) and the robustness of such relations. The very high correlation coefficients emerging in Table 4 suggest that some of the variables we defined above as independent are in fact dependent on further variables. This calls for additional caution in assessing the role of single variables in determining differential rates of Western migration to Israel, as in general, the interpretation of findings from multivariate analysis is on safer ground when it focuses on the larger categories of variables, rather than on single variables.

Analytic relationships between independent variables and the dependent variable are shown in Table 5. Looking first at the consistency over time of the sign of relationships, six correlation coefficients and eight standardized regression coefficients, out of ten, pointed in the same direction in both periods examined. The two measures, however, were in disagreement for four variables in the former period, and for six in the latter. The relationship of the dependent variable to several independent variables therefore may be intrinsically different from what it appears to be. (Correlation coefficients describe the relationship between a given independent variable and (in our case) aliyah

Table 2. Variables Used in Multiple Regression Analysis of Migration Rates from Western Countries to Israel, 1961–68 and 1969–76

		Years Considered		
Variable name	Description	First Period	Second Period	Source
Dependent variable				
Migration rate	Yearly rate of migration to Israel (incl. new immigrants, potential immigrants, and tourists settling) per 10,000 Jewish population in the countries of origin	1961–68	1969–76	a,b
Independent variables				
A. *General societal hold*				
Energy consumption	Energy consumption pro capite (equivalent of coal kgs.)	1965	1972	c
Press freedom	Index of press freedom, ratings given by judges-experts (range 0–4)	1965	1965	d
B. *General societal push*				
Price increase	Logarithm of percentage increase in consumer price index	1961–66	1969–74	c
Domestic violence	Logarithm of number of deaths from domestic violence	1963–67		d
	Index (range 0–100) based on detailed chronologies of events such as: deaths from domestic violence, violent overthrows of governments, interventions of armed forces in internal affairs		1969–76	e
C. *Jewish community structure*				
Jewish population weight	Jews per 1,000 population of country	1961	1972	b,c

Assimilation	Percent of non-Jews among immigrants to Israel from country: this indicator displays a correlation coefficient of .8 with percent mixed marriages (for the countries with available data on the latter subject)	1948–68	1969–76	a
Jewish education	Percent Jewish children aged 6–17 receiving any kind of Jewish education	1960	1967	f

D. *Immigrants absorption feedback*

Length of stay	Median length of stay (years) among persons born in given country and living in Israel	1961	1972	g
Return migration	Percent "missing" among persons born in given country when comparing 1961 and 1972 Israeli censuses, after taking into account new immigrants and estimates of mortality	1961–72	1961–72	g

E. *Migration cost*

Distance	Distance of given country from Israel (measured in conventional units of 25 kms.)	—	—	

Sources:

(a) Israel, Central Bureau of Statistics, *Immigration to Israel 1948–1972*, Part I and II, Special Series, Nos. 416 and 489; *Immigration to Israel*, yearly publication; and unpublished data provided through the courtesy of the Central Bureau of Statistics.

(b) Figures of Jewish population size in individual countries according to censuses, surveys, population estimates, Division of Jewish Demography and Statistics, The Institute of Contemporary Jewry, The Hebrew University, Jerusalem.

(c) United Nations, Statistical Office, *Statistical Yearbook*.

(d) Taylor, C. L., and M. C. Hudson, *World Handbook of Political and Social Indicators*, Second Edition. New Haven and London: Yale University Press, 1972.

(e) Stebbins, R. P., and A. Amoia. *The World This Year. Supplement to the Political Handbook and Atlas of the World*. New York: Simon and Schuster for Council on Foreign Relations, 1971, 1972, 1973; Banks, A. S., editor, *Political Handbook of the World*. Sponsored by the Council on Foreign Relations, Center for Social Analysis of the State University of New York at Binghamton. New York: McGraw-Hill, 1975, 1976–7, 1978.

(f) Engelman, U. Z. *Jewish Education in the Diaspora: Preliminary Report*. Jerusalem: World Conference of Jewish Organizations, 1962; Duskin, A. editor, *Jewish Education in the Diaspora*. Jerusalem: The World Zionist Organization, 1971.

(g) Israel, Central Bureau of Statistics, *Population and Housing Census, 1961*, Vol. 22; *Census of Population and Housing, 1972*, Vol. 10; and unpublished data provided through the courtesy of the Central Bureau of Statistics.

Table 3. Means and Standard Deviations of Variables,[a] 1961–68 and 1969–76

	1961–1968		1969–1976	
Variables	Mean	Standard deviation	Mean	Standard deviation
Migration rate	25.98[b]	14.12	56.43[b]	34.88
Energy consumption	3,080.43	2,324.62	4,023.19	3,027.39
Press freedom	2.03	0.81	2.03	0.81
Price increase	3.56	1.29	4.36	1.31
Domestic violence[c]	1.86	2.04	43.10	29.39
Jewish population weight	5.64	6.66	6.07	7.18
Assimilation	0.57	0.79	4.82	4.79
Jewish education	41.91	20.91	40.42	18.33
Length of stay	11.00	5.54	12.96	10.42
Return migration	260.58	213.13	260.58	213.13
Distance	330.00	204.76	330.00	204.76

(a) N = 21. Measurement units for each variable are specified in Table 2.
(b) Unweighted means. Weighted means in Table 1 were 6.8 and 18.1, respectively.
(c) Data are not strictly comparable for the two periods of time. See Table 2 for further explanations.

rates, while incorporating the indirect effects on migration of additional variables. Standardized regression coefficients reflect the "net" effect of a single independent variable on aliyah rates, after controlling for the effects of the other variables.) Two examples of a "hidden" positive relationship between an independent variable and aliyah rates—despite the negative "apparent" relationship indicated by correlation coefficients—are offered by press freedom and Jewish education. Taken by themselves, these two factors (proxies for societal liberalism and Jewish identity, respectively) tend toward a positive impact on aliyah rates.

Economic hold, represented in the model by energy consumption in the countries of origin, shows up as the strongest single explanatory factor of variation in Western aliyah rates in 1961–68, while economic push—as indicated by inflation in the countries of origin—was the strongest factor in 1969–76. An alternative variable partially tested, and then rejected in the course of this study—the ratio of Israeli price increase to price increase in the country of origin—resulted in a substantially weaker correlate of both migration to, and return migration from, Israel than inflation rates in the countries of origin alone.

Standardized regression coefficients for other independent variables mostly behaved according to expectations. After controlling for all other variables, positive effects on migration to Israel were exerted by price increase, Jewish education, domestic violence and press freedom in the countries of origin, and by the length of stay in Israel of

Table 4. Zero-order Correlation between Independent Variables,[a] 1961–68 and 1969–76

Variables	Societal Hold		Societal Push		Jewish Community			Migration Feedback		Cost
	Energy consumption	Press freedom	Price increase	Domestic violence	Jewish population weight	Assimilation	Jewish education	Length of stay	Return migration	Distance
1961–1968										
Energy consumption	1.000									
Press freedom	.593[c]	1.000								
Price increase	−.473[b]	−.328	1.000							
Domestic violence	−.061	−.377[b]	.037	1.000						
Jewish population weight	.591[c]	.236	.160	.282	1.000					
Assimilation	−.110	−.398[b]	−.002	−.231	−.296	1.000				
Jewish education	.245	.229	−.550[c]	.194	−.143	−.268	1.000			
Length of stay	.088	.158	−.458[b]	−.457[b]	−.350	.281	.308	1.000		
Return migration	.381[b]	.036	−.131	.524[c]	.468[b]	−.331	.174	−.574[c]	1.000	
Distance	.055	−.019	.420[b]	.493[b]	.438[b]	−.478[b]	.088	−.691[c]	.421[b]	1.000
1969–1976										
Energy consumption	1.000									
Press freedom	.609[c]	1.000								
Price increase	−.482[b]	−.393[b]	1.000							
Domestic violence	−.444[b]	−.471[b]	.679[c]	1.000						
Jewish population weight	.592[c]	.274	.006	.103	1.000					
Assimilation	.090	.264	−.247	−.446[b]	−.426[b]	1.000				
Jewish education	.094	.304	−.271	−.168	−.037	−.263	1.000			
Length of stay	−.124	−.084	−.302	−.073	−.523[c]	.533[c]	−.055	1.000		
Return migration	.345	.036	.099	.014	.505[c]	−.458[b]	.311	−.652[c]	1.000	
Distance	.005	.019	.451[b]	.316	.418[b]	−.617[c]	.247	−.741[c]	.421[b]	1.000

[a] N = 21
[b] Significant at .05 level
[c] Significant at .01 level

Table 5. Zero-order Correlation Coefficients and Standardized Multiple Regression (Beta) Coefficients between Migration Rates from Western Countries to Israel and Independent Variables[a]

Variables	1961–1968		1969–1976	
	Correlation coefficients	Beta coefficients	Correlation coefficients	Beta coefficients
Energy consumption	−.665[c]	−.804[c]	−.482[b]	.063
Press freedom	−.089	.255	−.148	.340
Price increase	.500[c]	.398	.789[c]	.998[c]
Domestic violence	−.180	.022	.528[c]	.168
Jewish population weight	−.231	.359	−.300	−.314
Assimilation	−.205	−.332[b]	.041	−.042
Jewish education	−.201	.138	−.124	.131
Length of stay	.141	.164	.047	.015
Return migration	−.531[c]	−.264	.340	−.047
Distance	−.093	−.326	.100	−.293

[a] N = 21
[b] Significant at .05 level
[c] Significant at .01 level

former immigrants. Negative effects on aliyah resulted from assimilation, return migration and distance. On the other hand, standardized regression coefficients for energy consumption and Jewish population weight, as they relate to aliyah rates, displayed a certain instability. (Such intriguing findings suggest that the reality of the situation is far more complex than can be encapsulated in this type of schematic model.) With the important exception of assimilation in 1961–68, none of these other variables, however, exerted statistically significant effects on aliyah rates.

Alternative analyses, not presented here, did show that demographic factors such as the age structure of diaspora Jewish populations may assist in explaining variation in Western aliyah rates. Migration rates were weakly positive in correlation with the population's percentage of aged persons, and weakly negative in correlation with the percentage of younger adults. Such variables were excluded from the final analysis in order to retain a number of countries for which such data were not available.

In order to ascertain the relative importance of each main category of variables in determining the variations in Western aliyah rates, three different multiple regression procedures were run (see Table 6): (a) each category was inserted alone to see how much of the variance it could explain on its own; (b) each category was removed, one at a time, while all the others were retained in the model, in order to see how large a change in the variance explained would result from that omission; (c) all five categories were retained in a stepwise regression. The general explanatory power of the model is high: after adjustment for degrees of freedom, about 72 percent of Western aliyah rate variations are statistically explained by the ten independent variables examined here. The same value of determination coefficient (71.5 and 71.6 percent respectively) was obtained for the two periods of time for which the model was tested, although this involved a different internal balance amongst the variables. However, the relatively small number of countries examined and the relatively high number of variables indicate the need for caution in interpreting the high explanatory power of our model.

On the whole, referring back to our earlier discussion, general societal factors of hold and push in the countries of origin seem to produce much stronger effects on aliyah rates than the factors related to Jewish community structure and to immigrant absorption feedback. The last column of Table 6 shows that societal hold alone (two variables: energy consumption and press freedom) accounted for 68 percent of the explained variance in Western aliyah rates in 1961–68; while societal push alone (two variables: price increase and domestic violence) accounted for 52 percent of the explained variance in 1969–76, with societal hold contributing a further 31 percent. However the second column in Table 6 shows that, usually, when one category of variables is omitted, very little of the model's explanatory power is lost, because of the high correlation existing between general societal and Jewish variables. A remarkable exception appears in the 1969–76 data: when omitting societal push variables, the model loses more than half of its capacity to explain variation in Western migration rates to Israel.

DISCUSSION AND CONCLUSIONS

The main thrust of this study is that to understand free Jewish migration one has to assess not only the determinants of individual migrant selectivity—which in the case of aliyah is known to have a strong ideological bias—but also the causes of fluctuation in the migration from different countries. Since Jewish communities in the Diaspora have very different population sizes, the total number of immigrants to Israel depends on the combination of these weights with the variable propensities to emigrate from each country.

During the period studied here, significant changes occurred in the total volume of Western aliyah. On the average, migration rates in 1969–76 were about three times higher than in 1961–68. Such a change

Table 6. Contribution of Each Category of Independent Variables in Explaining Variation in Migration Rates from Western Countries to Israel, 1961–68 and 1969–76

	Change in R^2			
Category of independent variables	Category inserted alone	Category removed, all other categories retained	All-inclusive stepwise regression[a]	Percent of explained variance
1961–1968				
General societal hold	.585	.107	.585	68
Jewish community structure	.258	.112	.081	9
General societal push	.290	.043	.047	6
Immigrants absorption feedback	.322	.067	.121	14
Migration cost	.009	.022	.024	3
Total R^2			.858	100
R^2 adjusted for degrees of freedom			.715	
F			6.035[b]	
Regression standard error			7.53	
1969–1976				
General societal hold	.266	.053	.266	31
Jewish community structure	.129	.042	.103	12
General societal push	.622	.514	.450	52
Immigrants absorption feedback	.169	.001	.018	2
Migration cost	.010	.020	.021	3
Total R^2			.858	100
R^2 adjusted for degrees of freedom			.716	
F			6.057[b]	
Regression standard error			18.57	

[a] Categories were hierarchically inserted in the equation, in the same order in which they are listed in this table.
[b] Significant at .01 level

has generally been explained by the renewed interest for Diaspora Jews of the state of Israel, and by the economic growth in Israel in the wake of the June 1967 war. However, due weight must also be given to the fact that during the early 1970's many countries—including a number of Western countries—were facing serious economic and political problems.

The variation in rates of aliyah from Western, free-emigration countries was studied in this paper through a multiple regression technique. Selected hypotheses were explored over two consecutive periods of time, and a statistical interpretation was found for most of the observed differentials. However, significant statistical relationships emerged for very few of the single correlates of the aliyah rates. General societal hold and push factors in the countries of origin contributed most of the explanation for the observed migration differentials. More frequent migration was highly associated with both long term factors, such as relatively lower levels of economic development, modernization and political emancipation; and short term factors, such as higher levels of economic and political instability. Structural—mainly cultural—factors in the Jewish communities of origin, and factors relating to the process of absorption in Israel of earlier immigrants from the same countries, had a relatively minor impact on the frequency of Western aliyah. Distance from Israel had a very minor effect.

The different balance of explanatory factors in the two periods examined here suggests that elements of economic and political stress may substantially affect Western migration to Israel—which would otherwise be depressed by hold factors in the countries of origin—although Jews in Western countries are less likely to be exposed to such unfavorable societal circumstances than Jews in Eastern Europe or in Moslem countries. In other words, the findings of this study support the popular assumption that full "fleshpots" do deter free aliyah. Moreover, the fact that research focusing essentially on factors operating in the countries of origin succeeds in illuminating important aspects of migration propensities has its own policy implications. Indeed, one possible conclusion is that Western aliyah is so responsive to general societal conditions in the countries of origin that factors operating in Israel do not appear to play a very significant role. Provided that these findings are confirmed by further, more systematic research, they suggest that the geographical composition—and implicitly, the volume—of Western migration to Israel may be largely determined by factors lying beyond the control of the Jewish polity—either in the state of Israel or in the Diaspora Jewish communities.

These facts notwithstanding, there seems to be no justification for rushing to the conclusion that more aliyah from the West will only be induced by a substantial deterioration in the socio-political environment of the Jewish communities there. The intrinsic relationship between the frequency of Jewish education in the Diaspora, or the frequency of assimilation, and aliyah rates suggests that it would be in the best interest of Israel to encourage efforts to strengthen the Jewish content and character of the Diaspora communities. Such efforts, if successful, could lead to a rise in aliyah, provided that additional factors conducive to migration materialize. It also appears, perhaps indirectly, that an environment of societal freedom and openness is advantageous to aliyah, other things being equal.

The question of the general effects on aliyah of changes in Israeli society was examined here only very marginally. It can be legitimately argued that such factors do influence the total volume of aliyah, and perhaps its geographical composition as well. But, as has already been pointed out, an examination of the factors acting chiefly outside Israel provided a self-contained interpretation of Western aliyah rate differentials.

A broader issue for discussion is how to interpret aliyah, and more generally, free ideological migration, in the framework of allegedly homogenizing global modernization processes, which, according to some theories, lead irrevocably from particularistic to universalistic attitudes and behavior.[29] Migration that enhances the particularism of an ethno-religious group may seem anachronistic in the framework of a broad conception of the modernization process. Our exploratory analysis indicates that such a contradiction is more apparent than real. It is true that most migrants to Israel would not move unless ideological factors were at work. Ideology, however, is in most cases a necessary but not sufficient factor for migration. Aliyah is thus quite congruent with the experience of general migration movements in which socio-economic variables act as prominent determinants.

Our findings suggest, more generally, that free migration, though largely inspired by "the relation of man to his higher aspirations,"[30] may more often occur under the influence of factors similar to those which would tend to generate other, quantitatively larger, types of migration. Free migration tends to draw from relatively small, selected and at times even elitist social strata. This upward selectivity with regard to the internal stratification of each country of origin contrasts with a downward selectivity with regard to each country's socio-economic and political status, free migration gaining momentum in those countries which offer less attractive prospects.

In summarizing the results of this research, its preliminary and exploratory nature should be unequivocally stressed. The data upon which we have relied have many limitations, which should ideally be removed in further attempts of this kind; furthermore, time coverage should be considerably extended, and an effort should be made to tie the explanatory variables more directly to periodic changes in the overall frequency of Western aliyah. Repeated verifications of our experiment are necessary before it can be ascertained with some certainty that consistent determinant patterns affect the variation of aliyah rates, and make them partially predictable.

A further warning relates to certain recent trends which have some bearing on the very concept of migration. Nowadays one may observe an increasing spread of bi-local (or higher order) residential patterns among Jews (and non-Jews) in Western countries—and to some extent also among Israelis living in the West. Such circular movements aim at fulfilling complementary economic and non-economic needs that cannot be satisfied in one place only. Quite a few Western immigrants (olim) and especially potential immigrants[31] *(olim bekhoaḥ)* may have intended to reside in Israel only for limited periods of time—for purposes of study, perhaps—before returning to their countries of origin. Again, other people keep a home in Israel, and make great efforts to pay frequent visits to the country but nevertheless never formally immigrate. To the extent that observed migration lacks a lifetime commitment, its analysis too can only lead to provisional conclusions.

On the other hand, the approach presented in this paper seems justifiable when considering that the migration of Jews from Western countries and their absorption into Israeli society are extremely complex social processes, which need to be dealt with on the basis of systematic research. It would appear, by contrast, that the prediction of expected or potential aliyah has relied more often on evaluations based on feelings of hope or fear. Clearly, combined use of comprehensive theoretical frameworks and of more sophisticated instruments of statistical inference may help in attempts to monitor and also to predict the volume of aliyah in current and future years, especially with regard to countries which permit free emigration.

Notes

Research for this paper was partially undertaken during my stay as Visiting Research Associate at the Population Studies and Training Center, Department of Sociology, Brown University in 1978/79; and at the Institute for Advanced Studies, the Hebrew University of Jerusalem, in the framework of the Study Group on Demography of the Jews directed by Prof. Roberto Bachi, in 1980/81. In the course of this research, I greatly benefited from the comments and criticisms of Professors Barbara A. Anderson, Calvin Goldscheider, Sidney Goldstein, Fran Kobrin, Robert M. Marsh, Dietrich Rueschemeyer and Alan S. Zuckerman. Responsibility for contents of the paper is, of course, my own.

1. W. Petersen, "A General Typology of Migration," *American Sociological Review* XXIII (1958) 256–66; W. Zelinsky, "The Hypothesis of the Mobility Transition," *Geographical Review* LXI (1971) 219–49.

2. L. Hersch, "International Migration of the Jews," *International Migration* II (1931) W. F. Willcox (ed.) 471–520; S. N. Eisenstadt, *The Absorption of Immigrants* (London, 1954); M. Sicron, *Immigration to Israel 1948–1953* (Jerusalem, 1957) 2 vols.; Jacob Lestschinsky, "Jewish Migrations 1840–1956," in *The Jews: Their History, Culture and Religion,* Louis Finkelstein (ed.), (New York, 1960) 3rd edition, Vol. II, 1536–96; U. O. Schmelz, "Migrations," *Encyclopedia Judaica* Vol. 16: 1518–29; Roberto Bachi, *The Population of Israel* (Jerusalem, 1977).

3. Bachi, *Population of Israel*.

4. Sergio DellaPergola, "Aliyah and Other Jewish Migrations: Toward an Integrated Perspective," in *Studies in the Population of Israel*, U. O. Schmelz and G. Natan (eds.), *Scripta Hierosolymitana* XXIX (Jerusalem).

5. J. Wolpert, "Behavioral Aspects of the Decision to Migrate," *Papers of the Regional Science Association* XV (1965) 159–69.

6. See also the general discussion of migration theories in: E. Lee, "A Theory of Migration," *Demography* III (1966) 47–57; Calvin Goldscheider, *Population, Modernization and Social Structure* (Boston, 1971).

7. R. Dixon, "Explaining Cross-cultural Variations in Age at Marriage and Proportion Never Marrying," *Population Studies* XXV (1971) 215–33.

8. A. Speare, Jr., S. Goldstein and W. H. Frey, *Residential Mobility, Migration and Metropolitan Change* (Cambridge, Mass., 1975).

9. United Nations, "International Migration Trends, 1950–1970," *The Population Debate*. New York: United Nations, Department of Economic and Political Affairs, 1975. Vol. 1, pp. 237–48.

10. D. Friedlander and Calvin Goldscheider, *The Population of Israel* (New York, 1979).

11. B. Thomas, *Migration and Urban Development* (London, 1972).

12. See Speare, *et al*, *Residential Mobility* . . .

13. S. DellaPergola, *South African Jewish Population Study, Advance Report No. 2: Emigration* (Jerusalem, 1977). It would appear that the proportion of migrants to Israel who actually left South Africa during the late 1970's was substantially lower than the prospective percentages reported here.

14. Sergio DellaPergola and A. Tagloacozzo, *Gli Italiani in Israele* (Roma, 1978).

15. G. Engel, "North American Jewish Settlers in Israel," *American Jewish Year Book* LXXI (1970) 161–87; A. Antonovski and D. Katz, *From the Golden Land to the Promised Land* (Jerusalem, 1979).

16. D. Elizur, "Attitudes and Intentions of Israelis Residing in the U.S. Towards Returning to Israel," *International Migration* XI (1973) 3–14; N. Toren, "Return to Zion: Characteristics and Motivations of Returning Emigrants," *Social Forces* LIV (1976) 546–58.

17. Calvin Goldscheider, "American Aliyah: Sociological and Demographic Perspectives," in *The Jew In American Society*, Marshall Sklare (ed.), (New York, 1974) pp. 335–84; M. Sicron, "Immigration to Israel from Latin America," *Papers in Jewish Demography 1973*, U. O. Schmelz, *et al* (eds.), (Jerusalem: 1977) pp. 347–54.

18. Sergio DellaPergola, "Aliyah and Other Jewish Migrations . . . ;" E. Leshem, Y. Rosenbaum and O. Kahanov, *The "Drop-Out" Phenomenon Among Soviet Jews: Main Findings and Recommendations* (Jerusalem, 1979).

19. Simon Kuznets, "Economic Structure and Life of the Jews," in Finkelstein, *The Jews*, II, pp. 1597–1666.

20. Sergio DellaPergola, "Toward a Typology of Jewish Population Distribution in European Towns," paper presented at the Seminar on Urban Ecology of the Jews, Hebrew University, Institute for Advanced Studies, 1981.

21. Milton M. Gordon, *Assimilation In American Life* (New York, 1964).

22. Roberto Bachi, *Population Trends of World Jewry* (Jerusalem, 1976).

23. G. K. Zipf, "The P_1P_2/D Hypothesis: On Intercity Movement of Persons," *American Sociological Review* XI (1946) 677–86.

24. R. T. Appleyard, "Economic and Non-economic Factors in the Dynamics of International Migration," *International Migration, Proceedings of a*

Seminar on Demographic Research in Relations to International Migration (held in Buenos Aires), G. Tapinos, ed. (Paris, 1974) pp. 95–101.

25. C. Price, "Chain Migration and Immigrant Groups With Special Reference to Australian Jewry," *Jewish Journal of Sociology* VI (1964) 157–71.

26. J. Goldlust and A. H. Richmond, "A Multivariate Model of Immigrant Adaptation," *International Migration Review* VIII (1974) 193–225.

27. U. O. Schmelz, Paul Glikson, and S. J. Gould (eds.), *Studies in Jewish Demography, 1972–1980* (Jerusalem, 1983).

28. Further details on the characteristics and limitations of data employed in this study are reported in the original and extended version of this paper, "Western Migration to Israel: Some Explanatory Hypotheses," Jerusalem, Hebrew University, Institute of Contemporary Jewry.

29. S. P. Huntington, "The Change to Change: Modernization, Development and Politics," *Comparative Politics* III (1971) 283–322.

30. Petersen, "A General Typology of Migration."

31. "Potential immigrants" as used here follows the terminology of Israel government offices and denotes a person who is entitled under the Law of Return to an immigrant visa or an immigrant certificate, and who intends to stay in Israel for more than three months.

Recent Work on the Jews in Inter-war East Central Europe: A Survey

Ezra Mendelsohn
(HEBREW UNIVERSITY)

The history of the Jews in inter-war East Central Europe[1] is of obvious interest and importance. In this region large and mostly unassimilated (although acculturating) Jewish communities, living in an environment of anti-Semitism, economic backwardness, but political and cultural freedom, maintained and developed the rich traditions of Austro-Hungarian and Russian Jewry at a time when Soviet Jewry was becoming increasingly paralyzed by the new Communist regime. Here, too, gentile obsession with the "Jewish question" reached new heights of intensity, as the growth of local fascist movements challenged the conservative and pluralistic regimes which came into being immediately after World War I.

It is only recently, however, that trained historians and other scholars have begun to work on this short but dramatic chapter in the modern history of the Jewish people, and even now the number working in the field is not impressive. There are several reasons for this. The impact of the Holocaust on East European Jewish historiography is obvious. Survivors or those who were fortunate enough to leave the region before the war have contributed much to our understanding of the inter-war years, but a whole generation of Jewish scholars was decimated and invaluable archival materials destroyed. The new Communist regimes set up after World War II have hardly encouraged their historians and social scientists to deal with the immediate Jewish past, and of course there are not too many Jews left to take an interest in their history. With a few notable exceptions, therefore, scholarly work on the Jews of East Central Europe must be carried out beyond the borders of that region—in Israel, Western Europe and America.[2]

Moreover, the overriding emphasis on and attraction of the Holocaust as a subject of inquiry which characterizes Jewish scholarship today has meant that among the relatively small number of researchers competent to deal with Eastern Europe a disproportionate number are working on the 1939–1945 period. The experts on the Holocaust will, of course, sometimes turn their attention to the pre-war period, but only as an introduction to their main subject, much as historians of the French Revolution will attach to their books a chapter devoted to the old regime.[3] Finally, there are perfectly good reasons why the new generation of modern Jewish scholars, educated in Israel or in the West, should avoid a subject which demands the acquisition of esoteric languages and which is rarely taught at the university level. To the extent that this new generation has taken an interest in Eastern Europe it has naturally gravitated to Russian and Soviet Jewry and not to the less well known communities lodged in between Russia and Germany.

Thus scholarly work on Jews of inter-war East Central Europe is being carried on today by a small group whose achievements cannot be compared to those of the much larger group of scholars working on German, French, Russian or American Jewish subjects and which has little in the way of a historiographical tradition to draw upon. The fact is that, with a few exceptions, objective scholarly work of the kind encouraged by Israeli, American, and European universities began to appear only in the 1970's. To be sure, during the 1950's and 1960's much was published on the subject, but it was chiefly of the amateur variety, produced by enthusiastic and nostalgic survivors whose commitment was not usually accompanied by objectivity or by acquaintance with the tools of modern historical research. They published the often valuable but hardly scholarly *yisker-bikher* and other compilations, which are still appearing, though in a steadily diminishing stream. This distinct historical genre, half memoir, half descriptive history, does much to re-create the now lost world of East European Jewry but does not usually qualify as serious historical research.[4]

The heyday of the *yisker-bukh,* however, also witnessed the beginnings of serious post-war research on the inter-war period. This research was mostly produced by survivors who had begun their scholarly careers in the 1930's, often in the pages of the *Yivo bleter* published in Vilna or in the other Jewish scholarly and semi-scholarly journals which appeared in independent Poland and elsewhere in East Central Europe. I am thinking here of the work of the historian Rafael Mahler, of the economist Yankev (Jacob) Leshchinski, and of the sociologist Aryeh Tartakover.[5] In the 1960's and 1970's representatives of the slightly younger generation of scholars born in Eastern Europe but educated in Israel and in the West began to write (and occasionally publish) dissertations on inter-war Jewish Eastern Europe.[6] Finally, in the 1970's a distinct group of young scholars, usually not born in the "old country" (but augmented here and there by scholars who had grown up in the new Communist states and who had left for the West or for Israel) made its appearance. This new generation will, of course, determine the future of East European Jewish historiography.

What has been achieved up to now? General, comparative surveys of the entire region are few and far between. (There is, however, a selective bibliography of secondary sources in English, Hebrew and Yiddish, published in 1978 and now, happily, somewhat out of date.[7]) A worthwhile if uneven collection of survey articles on the Jewish communities of twentieth-century Eastern Europe was published in Hebrew in 1975.[8] Three other collective works, all bearing a scholarly character, are worthy of mention: *Jews and Non-Jews in Eastern Europe*, a compilation based on a conference held at the University of Haifa in 1972;[9] *Jewish Assimilation in Modern Times*, also the result of a conference at Haifa;[10] and *Patterns of Jewish Leadership in Nazi Europe, 1933–1945*, the result of a Yad Vashem symposium held in 1977.[11] Bela Vago's *The Shadow of the Swastika. The Rise of Fascism and Anti-Semitism in the Danube Basin, 1936–1939*, is a valuable collection of documents on Jewish-gentile relations in Hungary, Czechoslovakia, and Romania.[12] Among the mostly older, less academic but still useful studies of specific subjects relating to the Jewish condition in inter-war East Central Europe are the collection on the Jewish press edited by Gothelf, Flinker, Tsanin, and Rosenfeld;[13] the book on minority rights edited by Robinson, Karbach, and Laserson;[14] Mirsky's volume on traditional Jewish learning;[15] the book edited by Sharfstein on Jewish education;[16] and the various works on Jewish economic life by Yankev Leshchinski.[17] My own book on the Jews of East Central Europe recently appeared.[18] There are also a few scholarly journals specifically devoted to modern East Central European Jewish history. Of particular importance is *Gal-ed*, edited by Moshe Mishkinsky at the Tel-Aviv University and concerned exclusively with Jewish history in Poland.[19] *Toladot*, a journal dealing with Jewish history in Romania, has unfortunately ceased publication.[20]

It is only natural that of all the Jewish communities of inter-war East Central Europe, Polish Jewry should attract the most scholarly attention. Poland, with by far the largest Jewish population in Europe outside the USSR, was the great center of autonomous Jewish cultural and political life during the 1920's and 1930's. Here the traditions of pre-war Russian and Galician Jewry were maintained within the context of an anti-Semitic, nationalistic, authoritarian, but far from totalitarian regime which, while very unfavorable to Jews as individuals, constituted an extremely favorable environment for Jewry in the collective sense. The contribution of inter-war Polish Jewry to the preservation of orthodox Judaism, to Yiddish literature, and to the Yishuv in Palestine—to cite only three examples—was immense. Poland also served as a paradigm of the inevitable worsening of relations between Jews and gentiles in the nation-states of East Central Europe, where liberalism and democracy rapidly gave way to chauvinism and where economic backwardness and the growing economic crisis had tragic consequences for the minority nationalities in general and for the Jews in particular.

It was not, however, until the 1960's and 1970's that serious scholarly works on inter-war Polish Jewry began to appear. In the 1960's the studies of Mahler and Bronsztejn, continuing the pioneering work of the inter-war period itself, laid the foundations for the study of the demographic and economic condition of Polish Jewry.[21] General interpretive efforts first appeared in the 1970's. In 1974 YIVO (the Institute for Jewish Research established in Polish Vilna in 1925 and reestablished in New York during the war) published a collection of articles edited by Joshua Fishman and entitled *Studies on Polish Jewry 1919–1939: The Interplay of Social, Economic and Political Factors in the Struggle of a Minority for its Existence*. The articles, published in English and Yiddish, were mostly written by scholars of the older generation, products of the Jewish world destroyed by Nazi Germany, who eventually found refuge in America, Western Europe and Israel. The contributions are certainly respectable, if rather old-fashioned, but they most certainly do not give the reader a comprehensive understanding of the Jewish experience in inter-war Poland. The subject best covered is anti-Semitism (in two lengthy articles by Trunk and Korzec). There is also an interesting (but ideologically slanted) description of Jewish youth movements in Poland by Moyshe Kligsberg and a solid account of the *hakhsharah* activities of the pioneering *(ḥaluẓ)* Zionist movements by Yisrael Oppenheim.

The first major effort to come to grips with Jewish history in inter-war Poland appeared in 1977: Celia S. Heller's *On the Edge of Destruction, Jews of Poland Between the Two World Wars*.[22] It cannot be denied that this book remains the best single-volume introduction to the subject in any language. It is, however, somewhat under-researched and fails to explicate, among other things, the most basic characteristic of the inter-war Polish Jewish community—namely its division into at least three distinct Jewries; Polish, Galician and Lithuanian, each with its own historical traditions and socio-economic and cultural profile. The best part of the book deals with the small but interesting "assimilated" section of the Jewish community, a subject on which Professor Heller has published several enlightening articles. As usual, anti-Semitism is emphasized at the expense of internal Jewish developments, on which material is less readily available. Jewish politics is described in a cursory and over-simplified way.[23]

Somewhat more scholarly, although not quite what its title proclaims it to be, is Pawel Korzec's *Juifs en Pologne* (the subtitle, *La question juive pendent l'entre-deux-guerres,* is a more exact definition of the contents of the book).[24] The author, a member of the small group of historians who began publishing in Communist Poland and later departed for the West, is also mostly concerned with anti-Semitism. His book reveals a good grasp of the Polish context and is valuable on the subject of negotiations between Jews and Poles and on the Jewish question in the Polish parliament. It too is weak on internal Jewish developments, and while a very worthwhile book it clearly does not answer the need for a general, synthetic treatment of the subject.

It may well be that such a synthetic work will not appear until we possess a substantial number of monographic studies on the manifold aspects of Polish Jewish history. In this regard the situation is improving rapidly, although much remains to be accomplished. In the area of economics, demography and sociology, relatively little has been published since the pioneering studies of Mahler, Leshchinski, and Tartakover mentioned above. Another scholar whose roots are in Communist Poland, Lucjan Dobroszycki, has written on Jewish demography, and Bina Garncarska-Kadari has written on the Polish Jewish proletariat.[26] Little general work has been done on the sociology of Polish Jewry, aside from the early studies of Aryeh Tartakover.[27]

Much more satisfying is the situation with regard to the closely linked subjects of the legal situation of Polish Jewry, its efforts to attain national minority rights, and relations between Poles and Jews. In this field the work of three Polish-born but Israeli-educated scholars is particularly important: Shlomo Netser has written on the Jewish struggle to attain equality and national rights during the years 1918–1922;[28] Moshe Landau on a very similar subject;[29] and Emanuel Meltser on the Jewish condition in Poland during the vital period of the late 1930's.[30] Another Israeli of the same pre-war Polish Jewish generation, Yosef Te'eni, has completed a dissertation on the impact of Hitler's rise to power on Polish anti-Semitism.[31] Much valuable work has also been done on the subject of anti-Semitism by non-Israeli scholars. The American expert on modern Polish history, Edward Wynot, has written an excellent study on the 1930's,[32] and very recently a major book, the last section of which pertains to the inter-war years, has been published by a young and very promising German scholar of Polish Jewish origin, Frank Golczewski.[33] These works, along with those of Korzec, Heller, and Trunk, provide a solid foundation for an understanding of inter-war Polish attitudes toward the Jewish question, although we still lack a comparative study which would place this issue firmly in the context of Polish policy toward the nationalities problem as a whole.[34] Scholars have also not really come to grips with the ambiguous attitudes of the various Polish political parties toward the Jews. One and the same party was capable at times of preaching assimilation while at other times demanding severe anti-Semitic measures.

As for internal Jewish developments, politics has attracted the most attention. Poland in the inter-war period constituted an ideal environment for modern Jewish politics of every conceivable ideological persuasion, and this subject has an obvious topicality and appeal for scholars, particularly of the new generation. (The fact that there exists an immense amount of material, printed and archival, also makes the subject attractive.) Nevertheless, it cannot be said that a great deal of satisfactory work has been done. Polish Zionism, for example, the single most powerful political trend within Polish Jewry and of great importance for the world Zionist movement and for the establishment of the state of Israel, has not yet been thoroughly studied. My own book, the first to attempt a synthetic treatment of the whole range of Zionist activities in Poland, covers only the years 1915–1926.[35]

General Zionism, the central trend within the movement, has not yet found its historian, and there are no biographies of its outstanding leaders—Yitshak Grünbaum, Leon Reich, and Ozjasz (Yehoshua) Thon. (Grünbaum, the personification of the new type of Jewish politician in Eastern Europe, and one of the most interesting of all modern Jewish political leaders, would make a brilliant subject.)[36] We possess no scholarly study of Polish Revisionism, the importance of which for Zionism could be easily grasped by a glance at the political leadership today in Israel. Nor have the parties of the Zionist socialist and labor left been studied. Yisrael Oppenheim, a prominent representative of the "middle generation" of Polish Jewish historians, born in Poland and educated in Israel, has written extensively and objectively on the Pioneer,[37] but the vitally important youth movements (with a few exceptions) have been largely ignored.[38] Religious Zionism has likewise been neglected—a recent monograph on the early years of the Polish Mizrachi is little more than a disappointing collection of the protocols of a few conferences.[39]

The anti-Zionist political forces have not fared too well either. The socialist Bund, whose "Polish chapter" is perhaps no less interesting than its incomparably better studied Russian origins, has not inspired much scholarship since the appearance in the 1960's of an unsatisfactory monograph by Bernard Johnpoll.[40] There is a good article by a young American historian on the Folkist party,[41] and a very important dissertation on the Polish Agudas Israel by Gershon Bacon, another American-born (and now Israel-based) representative of the new generation of Jewish historians working on Eastern Europe. His dissertation, when published, will constitute a very significant contribution to Polish Jewish studies.[42]

Apart from the work on the various political parties and movements, a few articles deal with Jewish political strategies in and out of the Polish parliament. Joseph Rothschild (a leading political scientist and professor at Columbia University) has written an interesting study on this subject,[43] and both the establishment of the minorities' bloc in 1922 and the celebrated "Ugoda" affair of 1925 have been particularly well covered.[44] However, a number of subjects have been almost entirely ignored. The question of Jewish voting patterns, for example, has not been analyzed. It would be interesting to know to what extent Jewish voting was affected by regional factors, and whether Jews voted one way in elections to the parliament and another way in elections to municipal institutions or to the *kehillot*. The involvement of Jews, as individuals, in general Polish politics is also a neglected subject, in particular the important and sensitive question of Jewish involvement in the Polish Communist Party.[45] We also know all too little about the processes of political mobilization of Polish Jews and the factors which governed the choice of party and youth movement. (The invaluable collection of autobiographies by Jewish youth available at the YIVO archives in New York contains the raw data on which such studies could be based.)

Jewish cultural and religious life in inter-war Poland also offers a rich and little investigated field for the scholar equipped with the necessary languages (Yiddish, Hebrew, and Polish). There are several rather outdated studies on Jewish education, but this subject is still virtually virgin soil. Such school networks as Tarbut, Tsisho, and Bes Yankev would make extremely interesting research subjects.[46] Orthodox Jewish life in Poland in general—its social institution, yeshivas, Hasidic dynasties—has been sadly neglected. While most historians speak of the decline of Jewish orthodoxy they rarely document their assertions, and we really do not know if this decline was precipitous or gradual, or whether it took place at all. To recall the fact that the majority of interwar Polish Jews grew up in religious homes is to realize what a striking lacuna this is in Polish Jewish historiography. The Jewish Polish press has been more fortunate in finding historians (there is an important contribution in this field by a Polish Jewish scholar working in present-day Poland).[47] The activities of Jewish historians in inter-war Poland have also been studied, and there is even a biography (though not a very satisfactory one) of the famous Jewish historian, Mayer Balaban.[48]

I am not competent to review the scholarship on various aspects of secular Jewish culture in Poland—Yiddish and Hebrew literature and the Jewish theater, for example—but I believe it would not be too risky to say that these subjects have been little studied by contemporary scholars. Nor have scholars investigated the fascinating contribution of Jews to Polish culture.[49] On the other hand, recent years have witnessed the publication of several important regional studies of Polish Jewry between the wars, which to some extent follow in the tradition of the *yisker-bukh,* but are more scholarly and therefore particularly welcome.[50] However, there is still an almost complete lack of studies on the importance of regionalism in the life of inter-war Polish Jewry, above all on the crucial distinctions, already mentioned, between "Litvaks," "Galitsianers," and "Polish" Jews.

This brief review leads us to several conclusions as to the state and the future of historiography on inter-war Polish Jewry. While the situation in 1982 is considerably better than it was in 1972, the fact is that basic work remains to be done in almost every aspect of the Jewish experience in independent Poland. The main question now is whether the inevitable decline and disappearance of the generation which up until today has been responsible for most of the work done on this period—the generation born in Eastern Europe in the 1920's and 1930's—will be offset by the work of a new generation of mostly North American and Israeli scholars, born in the 1940's and 1950's. In the current atmosphere of academic depression it is difficult to be sanguine, although the work of such historians as Gershon Bacon and Frank Golczewski certainly justifies a degree of guarded optimism. One thing is certain; the new generation of historians working on modern Polish Jewish history, having grown to maturity far from the bitter internal political and cultural wars of Polish Jewry, and never having experienced inter-war Polish anti-Semitism, is bound to write a very different kind of history—more academic, and above all less partisan—than that of its predecessors. The ideological commitment and occasional political bias, the general assumption that "all Poles were anti-Semites," and the possibly overdrawn picture of Jewish suffering in the bourgeois Polish republic, typical of much of the work of the two previous generations of scholars, will in all probability be absent from the historiography of the 1980's. This is all to the good, though it may not entirely make up for the lack of first-hand knowledge of this last chapter of Polish Jewish history, so close to us chronologically and yet so distant in every other way.

Prior to World War I there was no such thing as "Czechoslovak Jewry," and in fact no such entity emerged between the wars. As was the case with Polish Jewry, three very different Jewries constituted the Jewish community of the new state—those of Bohemia-Moravia, Slovakia, and Subcarpathian Rus. Despite its relatively small size this was a remarkably heterogeneous and interesting community, but its very heterogeneity complicates matters for would-be historians, who ideally must know German (the "high language" of many Czech and Slovak Jews), Hungarian, Czech, Slovak, Yiddish, and perhaps even Ukrainian. In the event, little has been accomplished, and we possess no scholarly works on the inter-war years to rival the work done on the immediate pre-war period, the golden age of Jewish-German culture in Prague.[51]

The major work on the inter-war Czechoslovak Jewish community is the two volume compilation entitled *The Jews of Czechoslovakia*.[52] It is of mixed quality, part memoir, part scholarship, informative but not really adding up to a sophisticated synthesis. There is also a very useful compilation in Hebrew, *Yahadut chekhoslovakiya*, which deals both with the pre-war and with the inter-war period and which contains a valuable study on the Zionist movement by Haim Yahil.[53] The fascinating story of Jewish demography, with its three distinct patterns (Bohemian-Morovian, Slovakian, and Subcarpathian Rus), has been analyzed by Jan Herman in a publication of the demography section of the Institute of Contemporary Jewry.[54] The no less interesting question of Jewish linguistic acculturation and the various competing national identities of Czechoslovak Jewry (German, Czech, Hungarian, and Jewish) has also been studied, although here too most scholars have emphasized the pre-World War I period at the expense of the inter-war years.[55] There is no serious study of Jewish-gentile relations in Czechoslovakia, despite the fact that the relatively low level of anti-Semitism in this multi-national state presents the historian with an important problem with obvious implications for the general study of anti-Semitism. Only Thomas Masaryk's unique attitude towards the Jews has attracted attention, although not always of an objective nature.[56] It would be particularly interesting to compare attitudes towards the Jews area by area in order to determine just why anti-Semitism was so much stronger in the Slovak and German than in the Czech regions.

No satisfactory scholarly work exists on Jewish politics in Czechoslovakia (again, the pre-war origins of Czech Zionism are better covered in the literature than the inter-war period).[57] The emergence of a national Jewish Party in the state, a rather surprising development given the "Western" character of Czech Jewry, has not been seriously studied, and other Jewish political formations have likewise been virtually ignored.[58]

This rather gloomy picture is to some extent relieved by the existence of several useful regional studies. The remarkable Jewish community of Subcarpathian Rus—Hasidic, proletarian, and even agrarian, the very antithesis of the Jewish communities of Bohemia and Moravia—is the subject of a highly informative if rather old-fashioned volume in the series, *Entsiklopediya shel galuyot*.[59] Jewish Prague has been much studied, though once again the emphasis is on the pre-war period, and there is a reasonably good monograph on the important Jewish community of Pressburg (Bratislava, Pozsony).[60]

As in the case of Polish Jewry, there are encouraging signs that a new generation is beginning to take an interest in the Jews of Czechoslovakia, but this interest has been confined, up to now, to the Czech lands (Bohemia and Moravia) and to the pre-World War I period. A serious, analytical, comparative study of Jewish communities of the inter-war state, which despite their great diversity joined together in an alliance with the enlightened, liberal Czech regime in Prague, is surely one of the crying needs of modern Jewish historiography.

As bad as the situation is with regard to Czechoslovakia, it is even worse with regard to Romanian Jewry. The remarkable neglect of Romanian Jewish history is itself a worthy subject for investigation. During the inter-war period Romanian Jewry, composed of at least four distinct sub-groups (the Jewries of the Regat, of Bukovina, of Bessarabia, and of Transylvania), was second only to Poland in numbers and in cultural and political creativity. In Romania, too, the "Jewish question" played a great role in public life. And yet scholarly work in this field is virtually non-existent. This is both because of the exotic languages which the field requires, and because the historical hegemony of Polish-Russian-Lithuanian Jewry in Eastern Europe has thrust the smaller Romanian Jewry into an obscurity which, at least in its much enlarged inter-war conditions, it clearly does not deserve.

We possess nothing approaching a sophisticated synthetic history of inter-war Romanian Jewry, although Bela Vago, whose main concern is with the Holocaust, is preparing one as the first volume of his study on the Romanian Jewish community during the war years.[61] The Romanian volumes in the series *Pinkas ha-kehillot* are extremely useful, especially for the information provided there about the numerous Jewish communities of the country.[62] The history of inter-war Bessarabian Jewry is the subject of an informative but far from objective study by David Vinitsky,⁶³ and there is an interesting interpretive book on the Jewish community of the Regat by Yitzhak Berkovich.⁶⁴ The important dissertation by Jean Ancel, while devoted to Romanian Jewry during the Second World War, contains some material on the inter-war period.⁶⁵

As for monographic studies, the only subject which has attracted a fair amount of modern scholarly attention is the Jewish struggle for equal rights and the linked subject of anti-Semitism. On the question of Jewish emancipation we have a new and very welcome survey by the young Romanian-born and French-based historian, Carol Iancu, which unfortunately only reaches 1919.⁶⁶ There is an important early article by the late Joshua Starr on the vexed problem of Jewish citizenship,⁶⁷ and several notable studies on anti-Semitism by Bela Vago.⁶⁸ Also of interest in this connection is the work of the well-known Romanian historian Stephen Fisher-Galati.⁶⁹ The short-lived journal, *Toladot,* naturally published a considerable amount of material on Romanian anti-Semitism.⁷⁰

Other major subjects of inquiry have been all but entirely neglected. Fisher-Galati has written on the question of Jewish assimilation,⁷¹ but I am not aware of any recent work on Jewish demography or economics. Jewish politics, a fascinating subject in this so diverse and creative Jewish community, is only marginally better represented by one compilation on a youth movement,⁷² some memoirs on Romanian Zionism and the Jewish national party,⁷³ and a study by Vago on Jewish voting patterns.⁷⁴ The Union of Romanian Jews and its famous leader Wilhelm Fildermann have been ignored, at least so far as the inter-war years are concerned, and Vago's important article on Jewish leadership in Romania concentrates, once again, on the Holocaust period.⁷⁵

It is therefore only a slight exaggeration to claim that the dynamic and influential Jewish community of inter-war Romania still awaits the attention of modern scholarship. We can only hope that the generation born in Romania (preferably in Transylvania, where both Romanian and Hungarian are spoken) and educated in Israel and the West will generate some work on this subject, building on the work of the older generation so ably represented by Bela Vago. There are some signs that this is in fact happening.⁷⁶

It is interesting to remark that Hungarian Jewry, smaller than that of Romania, much more uniform, and much less creative from a Jewish point of view, has succeeded in attracting considerable attention. Indeed, it is probably true that the historiographical record here is more satisfactory even than the study of Polish Jewry, let alone of the Romanian and Czechoslovakian Jewish communities. This may reflect both the high level of education enjoyed by Hungarian Jews in the inter-war period and the fact that a relatively large proportion of Hungarian Jews survived the Holocaust period. Whatever the case may be, during the 1970's and continuing into the 1980's, a number of talented historians have devoted themselves to this subject. Two recently published books in English survey the entire inter-war period—Randolph Braham's *The Politics of Genocide. The Holocaust in Hungary* (in two volumes, the first of which deals with the 1920's and 1930's);[77] and Natanel Katzburg's *Hungary and the Jews. Policy and Legislation, 1920–1943*.[78] Of the two Braham's is the more inclusive, while Katzburg's study focuses more narrowly on the Jewish question.

Apart from these two rewarding volumes, there is also the rather uneven collection edited by Braham and entitled *Hungarian-Jewish Studies*;[79] a newer but also uneven compilation in Hebrew;[80] and a volume in the *Pinkas ha-kehillot* series.[81] We must also mention the short but brilliant interpretive essay by the prominent Hungarian-born Jewish historian Jacob Katz,[82] required reading for anyone interested in the special characteristics of this remarkable Jewish community, the only one in Eastern Europe to embrace, at least in part, both assimilation and Reform Judaism.

As is definitely not the case with regard to other East European Jewish communities, the sociology of Hungarian Jewry has been rather extensively studied. William McCagg, in a few articles and in an unconventional but extremely interesting book, has investigated both the causes of the rapid upward mobility of Hungarian Jewry and its remarkable penetration into the Hungarian economic and intellectual elite.[83] Victor Karady, in collaboration with Istvan Kemeny, has also tackled this subject.[84] The key issue of Jewish acculturation and assimilation—its causes and its limits—has been studied in a long and highly suggestive article by George Barany[85] and in an interesting piece by George Schöpflin.[86] The remarkably conspicuous role of Jews in the Hungarian Left is the subject of an article by McCagg[87] and of a study (in Hebrew) by Shlomo Yitshaki.[88] Articles on Jewish demography and economic structure may be found in *Hungarian-Jewish Studies,* although this is a field which warrants considerably more work.[89]

Hungarian anti-Semitism, rather quiescent before World War I but a powerful force during the interwar period, has also been closely studied. Professor Katzburg has written an impressive number of articles on this subject, as have several others, including the celebrated historian of modern Hungary, C. A. Macartney.[90] A documentary account of Hungarian anti-Semitism is available in German.[91] Particularly well covered is the notorious *numerus clausus* affair which began in

1920.[92] Professor Katz, in his recent book on anti-Semitism, has a chapter on Hungary which is especially useful for the pre-World War I background.[93]

Much less impressive is the treatment of internal Jewish affairs. Studies on Jewish political leadership have concentrated, as usual, on the Holocaust period.[94] Secular Jewish politics were weakly developed in the inter-war years, but it would be nice to know more about the Zionist movement. (Hungary, after all, was the birthplace of both Herzl and Nordau, although admittedly Jewish nationalism failed to flourish on its soil.)[95] Jewish religious life, both the orthodox and neolog varieties, has been largely ignored.[96]

Almost all work on Hungarian Jewish history has been accomplished by Jews native to Hungary. (McCagg is the outstanding exception, being neither Hungarian nor Jewish.) The language barrier here is such that one can hardly expect too many scholars born outside that country to maintain and develop the traditions of Hungarian Jewish historiography. On the other hand, the relatively liberal regime which prevails today in Hungary has allowed scholarly work to proceed on the Jewish community, and this fact may to some extent offset the inevitable problems afflicting this field in Israel and the West. Unfortunately, those who have no command of Hungarian (including the present writer) have no access to the fruits of modern Hungarian historiography on what was once a leading if somewhat idiosyncratic East Central European Jewish community.

The small but interesting Jewish communities of the Baltic States have received little modern scholarly attention, although there are numerous *yisker-bikher* available, at least for the communities of Lithuania. Lithuanian Jewry, famous in the inter-war period for its temporarily successful struggle for national rights, is the subject of several rather good compilations, especially volume two of the series *Yahadut Lita*.[97] The issue of national autonomy has been well covered in an article by Gringauz,[98] and the status of the Jewish *kehillah* has been studied by a representative of the new American-born generation of East European Jewish historians, Mark Friedman.[99]

Still, we very much need a scholarly book on the whole question of Jewish national autonomy in the land where conditions seemed ideal, both externally and internally, for the realization of the schemes of Dubnov and other theorists. Yankev Leshchinski has done some important work on the economic structure of the community,[100] while Jewish politics has on the whole been the subject only of older, traditional studies.[101] Dov Levin, perhaps the greatest living expert on the Jews of the Baltic region, has published some work on inter-war Lithuania, although he is primarily interested, like so many of his colleagues, in the Holocaust period.[102] Anti-Semitism in Lithuania has been studied by Azriel Shochat,[103] but the remarkable upsurge of secular Jewish education in this small state has been ignored by modern scholarship.

The smaller but more heterogeneous community of inter-war Latvia has been even more neglected than that of Lithuania. There are several collected works, of the traditional type.[104] Perhaps the best general introduction to Latvian Jewry is to be found in the first chapter of the book by Itay and Naishtat on the youth movement, Netsah.[105] Yudel Mark has written on Jewish education.[106] There is little else on Latvia, and virtually nothing at all on Estonian Jewry, by far the smallest of the East European Jewish communities but an interesting one, nonetheless, which enjoyed a singular degree of national-cultural autonomy.[107]

We are witnessing today a changing of the guard in Jewish scholarship on modern East Europe. If we broaden, for a moment, the framework of this brief survey and consider the entire nineteenth and twentieth centuries and the Russian Empire, it will become clear to what an extent the new generation is coming to the fore. One only has to think of the works of Frankel, Gitelman, Altshuler, Stanislavski, Zipperstein, Grunbaum, Bartal, Orbach, Etkes, Salmon, Aronson, Stampfer, and a number of others (of those named only Altshuler is a native of Eastern Europe) to appreciate to what extent this generation of Western- and Israeli-trained scholars, equipped with the modern tools of research and often interested in fields of study hitherto neglected, has been changing our traditional notions about East European Jewish history. The impact of the new generation on East Central European Jewish history, as we have seen, is also growing. It is safe to assume that ten years hence we will know a great deal more about Jewish history in the inter-war successor states than we do today, at least in the academic sense, while, at the same time, the living link between the old Jewish East European world and the present becomes ever more tenuous.

Notes

1. The region is notoriously difficult to define. In this paper I include the almost exclusively Ashkenazic communities of Poland, Romania, Czechoslovakia, Hungary, and the three Baltic States (Lithuania, Latvia, and Estonia) and omit the Jews of Bulgaria and Yugoslavia.

2. For examples of work being done now in Communist Eastern Europe see below, notes 21, 40, 47. Mention should also be made of two important journals appearing in this region today—the Polish *Biuletyn Żydowskiego Institutu Historycznego,* and the Czech *Judaica Bohemiae.* Both publish, on occasion, articles on the inter-war period.

3. One thinks, for example, of Yisrael Gutman, author of the standard work on the Warsaw ghetto; of Bela Vago, now engaged in writing a book on the Holocaust in Romania; of Randolph Braham, the historian of the Holocaust in Hungary; and of Dov Levin, the authority on the Baltic region. The number of dissertations written at Israeli universities on the Holocaust in Poland is certainly much greater than the number produced on pre-Holocaust twentieth-century Polish Jewish history.

4. For a bibliography of these works, which deal mostly with Poland and Lithuania, see David Bas, "Reshimat sifrei-zikaron sheyaz'u bashanim 1943–1972," *Yad Vashem: kovez mehkarim beparshiyot hashoah vehagvurah* IX (1973) 231–263.

5. See, for example, Lestchinsky (Leshchinski), "The Industrial and Social Structure of Interbellum Poland," *Yivo Annual Jewish of Social Science,* II (1956–57); the same author's "Hapra'ot befolin (1935–1937)," *Dapim leheker hashoah vehamered* II (February, 1952) 37–92; Mahler, "Antisemitism in Poland" in Koppel Pinson (ed.), *Essays on Antisemitism* (New York, 1946) pp. 146–72; Tartakover, together with B. Dinur and Leshchinski (eds.), *Klal yisrael. prakim basoziologiah shel ha'am hayehudi,* (Jerusalem, 1954); Tartakover, *Shivtei yisrael,* vol. 2 (Tel Aviv, 1966).

6. See below, notes 28, 29, 30, 31, 37.

7. Ezra Mendelsohn, *Yehudei mizrah-merkaz eiropah bein shtei milhamot ha'olam: bibliografiah nivheret,* (Jerusalem, 1978).

8. Yaakov Tsur (ed.), *Hatfuzah: mizrah eiropah* (Jerusalem, 1975). This book also contains chapters on the Soviet Union, Finland, and Greece. There is even an article on Albania, despite the virtually total absence of Jews there.

9. Edited by Bela Vago and George Mosse and published in New York and London, 1974. This volume includes a general introduction by Shmuel Ettinger, "Jews and Non-Jews in Eastern and Central Europe Between the Wars: An Outline," pp. 1–20.

10. Edited by Bela Vago and published in Boulder, Colorado, 1981. This collection includes articles on Hungary, Romania, and Poland along with work on Western Europe, America, and the Soviet Union.

11. Edited by Yisrael Gutman and Cynthia Haft and published in Jerusalem, 1979. The book contains a general introduction by myself entitled "Jewish Leadership Between the Two World Wars," and articles on most of the countries of East Central Europe. It is chiefly concerned with the Holocaust period.

12. London, 1975.

13. *Itonut yehudit shehaytah* (Tel Aviv, 1973).

14. *Were the Minorities Treaties a Failure?* (New York, 1943).

15. Shmuel Mirsky (ed.), *Mosdot torah be-eiropah bevinyanam uvehurbanam* (New York, 1956).

16. Tsvi Sharfstein (ed.), *Hahinukh vehatarbut ha'ivrit be-eiropah bein shtei milhamot ha'olam* (New York, 1957).

17. For example *Mazavam hakalkali shel hayehudim be-eiropah hamizrahit vehamerkazit* (Tel Aviv, 1935).

18. *The Jews of East Central Europe Between the World Wars* (Bloomington, 1983).
19. So far five volumes have appeared. It began publication in 1973.
20. In all six volumes appeared, during the years 1972–1977. Two other Israeli journals, *Beḥinot* (now defunct) and *Shvut,* are mostly concerned with the Soviet Union, as is the London-based *Soviet Jewish Affairs.*
21. Rafael Mahler, *Yehudei polin bein shtei milḥamot ha'olam* (Tel Aviv, 1968). This valuable but misnamed book deals exclusively with demography and economics. Szyja Bronsztejn, *Ludność żydowska w Polsce w okresie międzywojennym* (Warsaw, 1963). See also the latter author's article "The Jewish Population of Poland in 1931," *Jewish Journal of Sociology* VI, no. 1 (July, 1964) pp. 3–29.
22. New York, 1977. See also the earlier and not very impressive book by Harry Rabinowicz, *The Legacy of Polish Jewry* (New York, 1956).
23. For a more detailed discussion see my comments in *Slavic Review* XXXVII, no. 4 (December, 1978) pp. 694–95.
24. Paris, 1980. See the comments by Gershon Bacon, p. 355 below.
26. Dobroszycki, "Jewish Fertility in Modern Poland," in Paul Ritterband (ed.), *Modern Jewish Fertility* pp. 64–77. Garncarska-Kadari, "Shkhavot ha-'ovdim hayehudim befolin bein shtei milḥamot olam (nituaḥ statisti)," *Gal-ed* III (1976) 141–89. See also the thorough survey of Jewish agriculture in Poland by Yaakov Levavi, "Maamadah shel haḥakla-ut hayehudit befolin bashanim 1918–1939," *Gal-ed* II (1975) 179–207.
27. See above, note 5, and Leshchinski, "Al pi hatehom, Lasoẓiologiah shel yahadut polin," *Molad* I, no. 5 (April, 1948) pp. 265–72; no. 6 (September, 1948) pp. 334–39. See also Heller's work on the "assimilationists" mentioned above, p. 514. Also worthy of mention in this context is the remarkable socio-psychological study by Max Weinreich, *Der veg tsu unzer yugnt* (Vilna, 1934).
28. *Maavak yehudei polin al zekhuiyoteihem ha-ezraḥiyot vehaleumiyot, (1918–1922)* (Tel Aviv, 1980). See the comments by Gershon Bacon in this volume, p. 355. There is also a valuable study of the central organ of Jewish autonomy: William Glicksman, *A Kehillah in Poland During the Inter-War Period* (Philadelphia, 1969).
29. *Hayehudim kemiut leumi bashnoteha harishonot shel polin haaẓmait, 1918–1926* (Ph.D. dissertation, Tel Aviv University, 1972). See also Landau's published article on the 1926 crisis and the Jews, "Hafikhat mai 1926—ẓipiyot beyahadut polin letmurah medinit vetahalikh hitbadutan," *Gal-ed* II (1975) 237–86.
30. *Yahadut polin, hamaavak hamedini al kiyumah bishnot 1935–1939* (Ph.D. dissertation, Tel Aviv University, 1975); now available in book form under the title *Maavak medini bemalkodet. Yehudei polin 1935–1939* (Tel Aviv, 1982). Meltser has published several articles incorporated into or based on his excellent dissertation: "Ha-diplomatiah hapolanit uve'ayat hahagirah hayehudit bashanim 1935–1939," *Gal-ed* I (1973) 211–49; "Yaḥsei polin-germaniah bashanim 1935–1939 vehashpa'atam al be'ayat hayehudim befolin," *Yad Vashem: koveẓ meḥkarim befarshiyot hashoah ve-hagvurah* XII (1977) 145–170.
31. *Aliyat Hitler lashilton vehashpa'atah shel haantishemiyut hapolanit al maẓavam shel yehudei polin bashanim 1933–1939* (Ph.D. dissertation, The Hebrew University, 1980). See also his article "Ḥelkah shel ha-ideologiah haantishemit hanaẓit al haantishemiyut hapolanit," *Yalkut moreshet* XX (December 1975) 127–48.

32. "'A Necessary Cruelty': The Emergence of Official Anti-Semitism in Poland, 1936–1939," *American Historical Review* LXXVI, no. 4 (October, 1971) pp. 1035–1058.

33. *Polnisch-Jüdische Beziehungen 1881–1922* (Wiesbaden 1981). This book is the first to be based on an exhaustive study of the Polish sources. See Bacon's review in this volume, p. 355, and my review in *Soviet Jewish Affairs* XIII, no. 1 (1983) pp. 71–74. Another recent German study is by Dietrich Beyrau, "Antisemitismus und Judentum in Polen, 1918–1939," *Geschichte und Gesellschaft* VIII, no. 2 (1982) 205–32.

34. There is a Polish book on this subject by Andrzej Chojnowski, *Koncepcje polityki narodowosciowej rządów polskich w latach 1921–1939*, (Wroclaw, etc., 1979). I should also mention in this context the remarkably interesting comparative study of William Hagen, *Germans, Poles, and Jews. The Nationality Conflict in the Prussian East, 1772–1914* (Chicago and London, 1980). This book, however, does not deal with the inter-war period.

35. *Zionism in Poland. The Formative Years, 1915–1926*, (New Haven and London, 1981).

36. The third volume on Warsaw in the series *Enziklopediah shel galuyot*, edited by Haim Barlas, Aryeh Tartakover, and Dov Sadan (Jerusalem, 1973) is devoted in part to Grünbaum and contains valuable biographical and bibliographical materials. See also Shlomo Netser, "Yizhak Grünbaum ke-ish za'ir—zmihato shel manhig ziyonei polin," *Kivunim* X (February, 1981) 73–92.

37. His Hebrew University Ph.D. dissertation, *Reshito shel he-Haluz befolin, hashanim haformativiyot* (1974), has now been published by Magnes Press (Jerusalem) in a revised and expanded form: *Tnu'at he-Haluz befolin;* see my review in this volume, p. 515. On this subject we also possess two other less impressive studies written by members of Oppenheim's generation—Yisrael Otiker, *Tnu'at he-Haluz befolin, 1932–1935* (Tel Aviv, 1972), and the exhaustive two-volume work of Levi Aryeh Sarid, *He-Haluz utnu'ot hano'ar be-folin, 1917–1939* (Tel Aviv, 1979).

38. Elkana Margalit's excellent book *"Ha-shomer haza'ir me'edat ne'urim lemarksizm mahapkhani* (Tel Aviv, 1971), deals mostly with the movement in Palestine, but an interesting book on the Warsaw branch of this important movement has recently been published: Moshe Zartal, *Ken ne'urim. Hashomer haza'ir bevarsha 1913–1943* (Tel Aviv, 1980). There is a good article by Rivka Perles, "He-Haluz haza'ir befolin bereshito (tnu'at no'ar bezmihato);" *Gal-ed* IV-V (1978) 197–229. See also Leizer Ran, "'Bin (dvorah)'— irgun zofim sozialisti shel no'ar lomed ve' oved bevilna uvesvivatah," *Gal-ed* III (1976) 191–212; Rafael Mahler, "Yugnt: tnu'at no'ar shel Po'alei Ziyon smol," *Haziyonut* III (1973) 247–57. For a general though not very objective survey see Kligsberg's work mentioned above, p. 319. I know of no serious scholarly work on Betar, Gordonia, or the Bund youth movement.

39. This odd book is by Avraham Rubinstein and is entitled *Tnu'ah be'idan shel tmurah. Perek bereshit ha-Mizrahi befolin* (Ramat Gan, 1981). See also the collective work *Sefer Shragai*, edited by Mordecai Eliav and Yitshak Refael (Jerusalem, 1981) which contains several articles on Polish religious Zionism, including a study on relations between the Mizrachi and Agudas Israel by Yosef Elihai.

40. *The Politics of Futility. The General Jewish Workers Bund of Poland 1917–1943*, (Ithaca, 1967). See also the fourth volume of the official history of the Bund, *Di geshikhte fun bund,* edited by S. Dubnov-Erlich, Y.Sh. Herts,

Kh. Sh. Kazdan, and E. Sherer (New York, 1972), and the interesting Polish monograph on the Jewish section of the PPS by Henrik Piasecki, *Żydowska organizacja PPS* (Wroclaw, 1978).

41. Mark Kiel, "The Ideology of the Folks-Partey," *Soviet Jewish Affairs* V (1975) 75–89.

42. *Agudath Israel in Poland, 1916–39: An Orthodox Jewish Response to the Challenge of Modernity* (Columbia University, 1979). See also my article on this subject, "The Politics of Agudas Yisroel in Inter-War Poland," *Soviet Jewish Affairs* II (1972) 47–60.

43. "Ethnic Peripheries Versus Ethnic Cores: Jewish Political Strategies in Interwar Poland," *Political Science Quarterly* XCVI, no. 4 (Winter 1981–82) pp. 591–606. See also my earlier article on the same subject, "The Dilemma of Jewish Politics in Poland: Four Responses," in Vago and Mosse (eds.), *Jews and Non-Jews in Eastern Europe*, pp. 203–20.

44. Ezra Mendelsohn, "Reflections on the 'Ugoda'," in *Sefer Refael Mahler* (Merhaviah, 1974) pp. 87–102; Pawel Korzec, "Heskem memshelet V. Grabski im hanezigut hayehudit," *Gal-ed* I (1973) 175–210; Moshe Landau, "Mekomah shel ha-'ugoda' (mishnat 1925) bamasekhet hayaḥasim hahadadiim hapolaniim-yehudiim," *Ziyon* XXXVII (1972) 66–110. On the minorities bloc see the relevant chapters in Mendelsohn, *Zionism in Poland;* Korzec, *Juifs en Pologne;* and Netser, *Maavak yehudei polin*.

45. This is, of course, a difficult subject to study, given the inaccessibility of archival material; see the article by Ester Rozental-Schneiderman, "Hayehudim batnu'ah hakomunistit befolin," *Molad* III, no. 13 (January–February 1970) pp. 81–96.

46. Miriam Eisenstein, *Jewish Schools in Poland* (New York, 1950); Nathan Eck, "The Educational Institutions of Polish Jewry (1921–1934)," *Jewish Social Studies* IX, no. 1 (1947) pp.3–32; Menahem Gelerter, *Hagimnaziah ha'ivrit 'tarbut' berovna* (Jerusalem, 1973); Haim Ormian, "Beit hasefer hapolani ha'ivri haziburi befolin bein shtei milḥamot ha'olam," *Gal-ed* IV-V(1978) 231–263. Still useful is the old survey (heavily weighted towards the Yiddish secular school system, which the author led) by Kh. Sh. Kazdan, *Di geshikhte fun yidishn shulvezn in umophengikn poyln* (Mexico City, 1947). See also Shmuel Rozenak, "Al ma'arekhet haḥinukh befolin bein shtei milḥamot ha-'olam," in Yisrael Halperin (ed.), *Beit yisrael befolin*, vol. 2 (Jerusalem, 1953) pp. 142–55.

47. Marian Fuks, *Prasa żydowska w Warszawie 1823–1939*, (Warsaw, 1979). (On this book see the comments of Chone Shmeruk, "A Pioneering Study of the Warsaw Jewish Press," *Soviet Jewish Affairs*, XI, no. 3 [November, 1981] pp. 35–54.) See also Haim Finkelstein, *Haynt. A tsaytung bay yidn 1908–1939* (Tel Aviv, 1978).

48. Phillip Friedman, "Polish Jewish Historiography Between the Two Wars (1918–1939), *Jewish Social Studies* IX, no. 4 (1949) pp. 373–408; Yishayahu Trunk, "Letoldot hahistoriografiah hayehudit-polanit (skirah)," *Gal-ed* III (1976) 245–68; Israel Biderman, *Mayer Balaban, Historian of Polish Jewry* (New York, 1976). See also Shlomo Idelberg (ed.), *Yiẓḥak Schipper, ktavim nivḥarim vedivrei ha'arakhah* (Jerusalem, 1967).

49. See the suggestive book by Aleksander Hertz, *Żydzi w kulturze polskiej* (Paris, 1961).

50. I have in mind the Yad Vashem series *Pinkas hakehillot, Polin*. See, for example, the first volume, devoted to Lodz and its environs, published in

Jerusalem, 1976, and edited by Danuta Dabrowska and Avraham Wein, and volume two, on East Galicia, edited by Dabrowska, Wein, and Aaron Weiss (Jerusalem, 1980).

51. See, for example, two very new studies by young American-born historians: Gary Cohen, *The Politics of Ethnic Survival: Germans in Prague, 1861–1914* (Princeton, 1981), which contains very interesting material on Prague Jews (see review by Kieval in this volume, p. 424), and Hillel Kieval, *Nationalism and the Jews of Prague: The Transformation of Jewish Culture in Central Europe, 1880–1918* (Ph.D. dissertation, Harvard University, 1981).

52. New York and Philadelphia, 1968, 1971.

53. This collective work is published as a separate volume in the journal *Gesher* II-III (September, 1969).

54. "The Development of Bohemian and Moravian Jewry, 1918–1938," in U.O. Schmelz, Paul Glikson, and Sergio DellaPergola (eds.), *Papers in Jewish Demography* (Jerusalem, 1969) pp. 191–206.

55. Bruno Blau, "Nationality Among Czechoslovak Jewry," *Historia Judaica* X (1948) 147–154; Wilma Iggers, "The Flexible National Identities of Bohemian Jewry," *East Central Europe/L'europe du centre-est* VII, Part 1 (1980) pp. 39–48. This subject is central to Cohen's book mentioned in note 51.

56. See the very early work of Ernest Rychnovsky, *Thomas Masaryk and the Jews* (New York, 1941). A recent intellectual biography of Masaryk by Roman Szporluk, *The Political Thought of Thomas G. Masaryk* (New York, 1981), contains some very interesting material on his attitude toward the Jews.

57. Thus there is a dissertation on the origins of Czech Zionism by Stuart Borman, *The Prague Student Zionist Movement 1896–1914* (University of Chicago, 1972), but no modern, serious work on the inter-war years. The best work is the essay by Yahil in the above-mentioned collection *Yahadut chekhoslovakia* which has been published separately under the title *Dvarim al haziyonut hachekhoslovakit* (Jerusalem, 1967). See also Oskar Rabinowitz's long essay in Volume Two of *The Jews of Czechoslovakia*.

58. See, however, Aharon Rabinowicz's article "The Jewish Party," *The Jews of Czechoslovakia*, Vol. 2, 253–346.

59. Yehuda Erez (ed.), *Karpatorus, Enziklopediya shel galiyot* (Jerusalem, 1959). See also the articles of Aryeh Sole in *The Jews of Czechoslovakia*, Vol. 1, 125–54, and Vol. 2, 401–39.

60. Hans Tramer, "Prague—City of Three Peoples," *Leo Baeck Institute Yearbook* IX (1964) 305–39; Feliks Weltsch (ed.), *Prag vi-yerushalayim, sefer zikaron lezekher Leon Herman* (Jerusalem, 1954); Shmuel Ha-Cohen Weingarten, *Toldot yehudei bratislava (presburg), 'Arim ve-imahot be-yisrael* VII (Jerusalem, 1960). Hugo Gold's compilations on the Jews of Bohemia, Moravia, and Bratislava, though published in the 1920's and 1930's, are still useful. It is striking that virtually nothing in the way of a synthesis has been written on the important Slovakian Jewish community.

61. The as yet unpublished manuscript is entitled *Jews and Anti-Semitism in Interwar Romania, 1919–1940. Prologue to the Holocaust*.

62. *Pinkas ha-kehillot: romaniah*, Vol. 1 (Jerusalem, 1970), deals with the Regat and southern Transylvania, and includes introductory articles by Theodore Lavi and Bela Vago; Vol. 2 (Jerusalem, 1980) deals with northern Transylvania, Bukovina, and Bessarabia. Also very useful is the volume *Yahadut besarabiah* in the series *Enziklopeda shel galiyot* (Jerusalem and Tel Aviv, 1971).

63. *Besarabiah hayehudit bema'arakhoteha*, 2 vols. (Tel Aviv, 1973).

64. *Pirkei rumaniah zramim tarbutiim ufolitiim bekerev yahadut romaniah bein 1918–1941* (Tel Aviv, 1975).
65. *Yahadut romaniah bein 23.8.1944 levein 30.2.1947* (Hebrew University, 1979).
66. *Les juifs en Roumanie 1866–1919. De l'exclusion a l'emancipation* (Provence, 1978).
67. "Jewish Citizenship in Rumania (1878–1940)", *Jewish Social Studies* III (1941) 57–80.
68. See especially "Hamediniyut hayehudit shel hadiktaturah hamalkhutit beromaniah (1938–1940), *Ziyon* XXIX (1964) 133–51.
69. "Fascism, Communism, and the Jewish Question in Romania," in Vago and Mosse (eds.), *Jews and Non-Jews in Eastern Europe*, 157–75.
70. For example T. Armon, "Antishemiyut halegionerim kegorem beyahseihem im hafashizm ha-italki," II (1972) 5–6; Ana Kolombo, "Yorga vehayehudim," I (1972): II; Artur Aksenfeld, "Gzerot kalkaliyot neged yehudei romaniah," IX (1975) 14–18.
71. "The Radical Left and Assimilation: The Case of Romania," in Vago (ed.), *Jewish Assimilation in Modern Times*, pp. 89–104.
72. Meir Zayit (ed.), *Sipurah shel tnu'ah: Gordoniah-makabi haza'ir beromaniah* (Tel Aviv, 1978).
73. Michael Landau, "Hatnu'ah haleumit hayehudit beromaniah bameah ha-esrim," *Gesher* I (1957) 77–94; II (1957) 78–91; III (1957) 101–13. See also Landau's memoirs *Maavak hayay* (Ramat Gan, 1970), and the collection of articles by Leon Mizrahi, *'Im dori umaavakav* (Tel Aviv, 1970).
74. "The Jewish Vote in Romania Between the Two Wars," *Jewish Journal of Sociology* XIV, no. 2 (1972) pp. 133–56.
75. Bela Vago, "The Ambiguity of Collaborationism: The Center of the Jews in Romania (1942–1944)," in Gutman and Haft (eds.), *Patterns of Jewish Leadership in Nazi Europe*, pp. 287–309.
76. I am thinking of Efraim Ofir, currently writing a dissertation at the Hebrew University on Romanian Zionism, and of Irina Livzeanu who is working on Romanian anti-Semitism at the University of Michigan.
77. Published in New York, 1981.
78. Ramat Gan, 1981.
79. Two volumes, New York, 1966 and 1969.
80. M. E. Gonda, I.I. Cohen, and I. Marron (eds.), *Yehudei hungariah mehkarim historiim* (Tel Aviv, 1980). Most of the articles in this volume deal with the pre-World War I era.
81. *Pinkas ha-kehillot: hungariah* (Jerusalem, 1976).
82. "Yihudah shel yahadut hungariah," in *Hanhagat yehudei hungariah bemivhan hashoah* (Jerusalem, 1976), pp. 13–24. This article is also available in English in *Forum* (1977) pp. 45–53.
83. *Jewish Nobles and Geniuses in Modern Hungary* (Boulder, 1972); "Hungary's 'Feudalized' Bourgeoisie," *Journal of Modern History* XLIV, no. 1 (1972) pp. 65–78. See also below, note 87.
84. "Les juifs dans la structure des classes en Hongrie: essai sur les antécédents historiques des crises d'antisemitisme du XXe siècle," *Actes de la recherche en sciences sociales* XXII (June, 1978) 25–59.
85. "Magyar Jew or Jewish Magyar?," in Vago and Mosse (eds.), *Jews and Non-Jews in Eastern Europe*, pp. 51–98.
86. "Jewish Assimilation in Hungary: A Moot Point," in Vago (ed.), *Jewish Assimilation in Modern Times*, pp. 75–88. See also the article in the same

volume by Asher Cohen, "The Attitude of the Intelligentsia in Hungary Toward Jewish Assimilation Between the Two World Wars," 57–74.

87. "Jews in Revolutions: The Hungarian Experience," *Journal of Social History* (Fall, 1972) pp. 78–105.

88. "Hayehudim bemahapekhat hungariah 1918/1919," *Yalkut moreshet* XI (November, 1969) 113–34; XII (July, 1970) 107–27.

89. See, for example, Istvan Veghazi, "The Role of Jewry in the Economic Life of Hungary," in Braham (ed.), *Hungarian-Jewish Studies* II, 35–84.

90. C.A. Macartney, "Hungarian Foreign Policy During the Interwar Period, with Special Reference to the Jewish Question," in Vago and Mosse (eds.), *Jews and Non-Jews in Eastern Europe*, 125–36; Braham, "The Rightists, Horthy, and the Germans: Factors Underlying the Destruction of Hungarian Jewry," *ibid.*, 137–56; Bernard Klein, "Hungarian Politics and the Jewish Question in the Interwar Period," *Jewish Social Studies* XXVIII (1966) 79–98; Katzburg, "Leredifot hayehudim behungariah, 1919–1922," *Universitat Bar-Ilan: sefer ha-shanah* III (1965) 225–251; Katzburg, "The Jewish Question in Hungary During the Interwar Period—Jewish Attitudes," in Vago and Mosse (eds.), *Jews and Non-Jews in Eastern Europe*, 113–24.

91. Johann Weidlein (ed.), *Der Ungarisch Antisemitismus in Dokumenten* (Schorndorf, 1962).

92. Karady and Kemeny, "Antisemitisme universitaire et concurrence de classe: la loi du numerus clausus en Hongrie entre les deux guerres," *Actes de la recherche en sciences sociales* XXXIV (September, 1980) 67–96; Katzburg, "Hamaavak behever haleumim neged ḥok numerus klauzus behungariah," *Universitat Bar-Ilan: sefer hashanah* III (1965) 270–288; Thomas Spira, "Hungary's Numerus Clausus, the Jewish Minority, and the League of Nations," *Ungarn-Jahrbuch* IV (1972) 115–28.

93. *Sinat yisrael. Misinat hadat leshlilat ha-gez'a*, (Tel Aviv, 1979). This book has also been published in English under the title *From Prejudice to Destruction: Anti-Semitism 1700–1933* (Cambridge, Mass., 1981).

94. See the collective work mentioned above, *Hanhagat yehudei hungariah bemivḥan hashoah*, and Braham, "The Official Jewish Leadership of Wartime Hungary" in Gutman and Haft (eds.), *Patterns of Jewish Leadership in Nazi Europe*, 267–86.

95. See Livia Bitton, "Zionism in Hungary—The First Twenty-Five Years," *Herzl Yearbook* VII (1971) 285–320.

96. But see A.N. Ts. Rot, "Beit midrash lerabanim behungariah" in Mirsky (ed.), *Mosdot Torah* 635–54, and A. Moskovits, *Jewish Education in Hungary, 1848–1948* (Philadelphia, 1964).

97. Tel-Aviv, 1972. Volume 3, (Tel Aviv, 1967), includes articles on Jewish leaders and on Jewish communities.

98. "Jewish National Autonomy in Lithuania (1918–1925)," *Jewish Social Studies* XIV (1952) 225–46. See also the important articles by Leib Garfunkel in *Yahadut lita*, Vol. 2.

99. "The Kehillah in Lithuania 1919–1926: A Study Based on Panevezys and Ukmerge (Vilkomir)," *Soviet Jewish Affairs* VI, no. 2 (1976) pp. 83–103.

100. See his early article "The Economic Struggle of the Jews in Independent Lithuania," *Jewish Social Studies* VII, no. 4 (1946) pp. 267–96, and his article in *Yahdut lita*, Vol. 2, 91–100.

101. See the articles in *Yahadut lita* and in another compilation, *Lite*, Vol. 2 (Tel Aviv, 1965), edited by Mendel Sudarski, Uriah Katznelenboigen and

Y. Kisin. See also L. Shimoni, "Poale Ziyon smol belita," *Asufot* IX (1965) 95–110.

102. See his "The Jews in the Soviet Lithuanian Establishment, 1940–1941," *Soviet Jewish Affairs* X, no. 2 (May, 1980) pp. 21–38, and also "The Jews in the Election Campaigns in Lithuania," *ibid.* X, no. 1 (February, 1980) pp. 39–51. Levin has also published documents pertaining to the internal Jewish political struggle in *Mikhael* VI (1980) 69–109.

103. "The Beginnings of Anti-Semitism in Independent Lithuania," *Yad Vashem Studies on the European Jewish Catastrophe and Resistance* II (1958) 7–48; "Jews, Lithuanians, and Russians, 1939–1941," in Vago and Mosse (eds.), *Jews and Non-Jews in Eastern Europe*, 301–14.

104. B. Eliav, M. Bobe, and A. Kremer (eds.), *The Jews in Latvia* (Tel Aviv, 1971); *Yahadut latviah* (Tel Aviv, 1953). See also Mendel Bobe, *Yidn in letland* (Tel Aviv, 1972).

105. *Koroteha shel tnu'at: nezah be-latviah* (Tel Aviv, 1972).

106. "A kurtser iberblik iber der yidisher shul in letland," *Yivo bleter* LIV (1973) 231–47.

107. See Emanuel Nodel, "Life and Death of Estonian Jewry," in A. Ziedonis, W. Winter, and M. Valgemae (eds.), *Baltic History* (Cleveland, 1973), 227–36. There is also some material on Estonian Jewry in the aforementioned *The Jews of Latvia* and in the general article on the Baltic region by Binyamin Eliav in the volume edited by Yaakov Tsur, *Hatfuzah: mizrah eiropah*, pp. 95–118.

Review Essays

Metropolis and Periphery in American Jewry

Myron Berman, *Richmond's Jewry, 1769–1976: Shabbat in Shockoe*. Charlottesville: The University Press of Virginia for the Jewish Community Federation of Richmond, 1979. xxii + 438 pp. $12.50

Deborah Dash Moore, *At Home in America: Second Generation New York Jews*. New York: Columbia University Press, 1981. xiii + 303 pp. $20.00

Nathan M. Kaganoff and Melvin I. Urofsky (eds.), *"Turn to the South": Essays on Southern Jewry*. Charlottesville: University Press of Virginia for the American Jewish Historical Society. xiii + 205 pp. $7.95

The most characteristic genre of American Jewish historiography is local history, but the quality of local historiography has not made it the finest genre. Its weaknesses are too well known to require elaboration. Swollen with names and places, obsessively laudatory, dull and ponderous while lacking discussion or analysis of significant problems, these studies deliver what the local community leaders who frequently foot the bill usually expect of them. Humor, irony, or a critical sense are at a large discount. Yet with all these and other failings, it is local history that can show American Jewish life as it has been lived. Moreover, the genre has improved in recent years, thanks mostly to the stimulation coming from the new social history, which has focused on local history often with exciting results.

Local communities, not national organizations, hold the real power in American Jewry. Besides financing themselves they also raise the money in unified campaigns for the national and overseas commitments of American Jewry, and they then decide, in virtually sovereign fashion, how to distribute the money raised. Much of the fanfare which issues from New York or Jerusalem aims to impress local communities with the merits of the institutions which are seeking allocations.

More than is often realized, it is local Jewish communities which urge Israel's case before the Senators and Representatives they elect. No one underestimates the significance of the Kansas City Jews who had access to their fellow townsman Senator Truman and did not completely lose it when he went to the White House. Ohio Jewry was close to Robert A. Taft, while Hubert H. Humphrey had important ties with the Jewry of Minneapolis-St. Paul.

Is the history of New York City Jewry local history? Formally the answer must be yes. Yet the question itself arises because its immense scale has made New York City different not only in degree but in kind from every other local diaspora community. One who seeks local Jewish history for New York City ought to examine works dealing with bygone or existing Jewish neighborhoods such as Harlem, Brownsville, Williamsburg, or Borough Park. Face to face acquaintance, which is so much part of communal life and leadership, becomes impossible to sustain when there are two million faces. Moreover, New York City, as the capital of American Jewry since the 1890s and of the Diaspora since 1945, has seen many of its best Jewish talents drawn into national and international Jewish affairs which are based in Manhattan, thus diminishing that available for the Jewish community of the city. For the historian, to be sure, the vastness of the New York City Jewish scene grants comparative freedom from pressures to conform to some Jewish image derived from public relations gospel. But the city as a whole has had few Jewish historians.

Deborah Dash Moore is one of these few intrepid historians, and her *At Home in America* deserves more than perfunctory attention. Its theme is the coming of age between 1920 and 1940 of the children of the mass immigration from Eastern Europe as New Yorkers. Strictly speaking, this is the history of a loosely defined age cohort rather than the history of a city or community. However, the age cohort was so important and its size so great that it reshaped New York City Jewry as a whole. This point is implicit in the book. Its title, *At Home in America*, is inappropriate since Dr. Moore is writing about the aspiration of the second generation, not about its actual status, and to be at home in New York is not the same as being at home in America. New Yorkers who stray west of the Hudson River surely learn this.

Conflicts between Jews and other ethnic groups have been described, especially by Glazer and Moynihan as well as by Bayor, but not the consciousness and sensibility of the Jews themselves. In contrast, *At Home in America* hardly contains gentiles at all. Dr. Moore follows her Jews into their neighborhoods, especially in Brooklyn and the Bronx, and characterizes each. Every neighborhood possessed a distinct socio-economic level—although one far more heterogeneous than that prevailing in the post-World War II suburbs—as well as its palpable cultural and religious quality. Of particular interest is the description of the Jews in the building trades, who were responsible for erecting entire neighborhoods to accommodate the spreading Jewish population. The awareness of neighborhood variety is the strength of Dr. Moore's book.

What is missing, however, is some account of the economic changes among the Jews which underlay these huge neighborhood developments. This in turn leads the reviewer to what seems the weakest point in the book. The immense force of the Great Depression is hardly noticed, despite its shattering effect on every neighborhood and its inhabitants. Nazism and anti-Semitism were truly menacing, and within the Jewish world highly articulate ideologies were everywhere to be heard, but they hardly appear here. Dr. Moore fails to divide the 1930s from the 1920s with sufficient clarity, and her work tilts towards the earlier decade.

The author describes the synagogue-centers of Brooklyn and the Bronx, emphasizing their ideology as derived especially from Mordecai M. Kaplan. These usually Conservative congregations were housed in imposing edifices, and some of their rabbis (for example, Harry Halpern, Israel H. Levinthal, the Orthodox Leo Jung, and Kaplan himself) were distinguished men. The synagogue-centers aimed to be places of prayer and study while also providing sports, a social club, banqueting facilities, and even swimming pools for their members. "A shul with a pool," neighbors jested. "If they come to play they won't stay to pray," Abba Hillel Silver is reported to have responded when he vetoed the installation of a center at his Cleveland congregation.

The synagogue-centers served more prosperous Jews, while numerous local community centers and Young Men's and Women's Hebrew Associations, disregarded by Dr. Moore, drew much larger numbers. The transition of these institutions from the original immigrant districts to the new Jewish neighborhoods, and the professional rationales which they developed, merit attention. The nearly exclusive focus on synagogue-centers, with only the *hevrah** mentioned as a counterfoil, also leads to the omission of the many local Orthodox synagogues. These were modern congregations, some of which had notable rabbis and supported Talmud Torahs and charitable activity. They usually featured virtuoso *hazanim*, who could attract worshippers for the High Holidays to rent the unoccupied seats. This financial expedient was scorned by the better-heeled synagogue-centers.

Public schools, where enrollments were proportionately even more Jewish than that of their neighborhoods (because Catholic children often went to parochial schools), were Jewish in an equivocal sense. Dr. Moore stresses the accomodation between the public schools and the Jews, without disregarding the pressures exerted by the schools against overt Jewish expression. To judge from my experiences and those of my contemporaries in New York City high schools during the 1940s, her appraisal of the Jewishness which could be openly ex-

---

*traditional-style devotional or charitable society

pressed in them is somewhat too generous—nor were most Jewish teachers by any means favorable to such attempts, which included the teaching of Hebrew. Dr. Moore's chapter on politics is a lively tale of local Jewish politicians fighting their way into the Brooklyn Democratic machine, long under Irish control. Unfortunately, that and the description of the American Labor Party hardly do full justice to the subject as a whole.

Dr. Moore's account of the way in which the Federation of Jewish Philanthropies raised funds by means of a plutocratic Business Men's Council makes a valuable contribution to our understanding of the Jewish communal structure in New York City. However, she practically terminates her discussion in 1929, when this body began to lose its leadership role with the onset of the Depression. The way was then opened for more ideological, democratic conceptions of Jewish community organization, as typified by the Jewish Community Council movement and the American Jewish Congress. The popular democracy stimulated by the New Deal offered inspiration, at a time when the Nazi and anti-Semitic peril cast a dark shadow. Nothing about the Business Men's Council prepared it to lead the Jewish community under such circumstances.

In her text, Dr. Moore often quotes the dicta of sociologists as though theirs were the last word, and they also provide some soggy epigraphs for her interesting chapters. She is at her best in depicting the Jewish neighborhoods of New York, especially during the 1920s. Hers is not, and lays no claim to being, a full-scale history of New York City Jewry between 1920 and 1940. It treats sensitively, with attractive illustrations, the intense efforts of the post-immigration generation to find their place in the middle class of the cosmopolitan metropolis.

To "*Turn to the South*" was rarely if ever the aspiration of a Jewish New Yorker during those years. The South was perceived, not without some reason, as an impoverished region held in the vise of fanatical racism and provincial bigotry. Soldiers sent there from the North during World War II generally detested the experience. Merely one to two percent of East European Jewish immigrants had settled in the South, a proportion resembling that among other immigrants during the same period. Throughout the century which began with the outbreak of the Civil War, the South played a minimal role in American Jewish life, and the history of Southern Jewry meant mostly the celebration of its antebellum heritage. The conference on Southern Jewry which the American Jewish Historical Society convened at Richmond in 1976 exemplifies a change that is taking place. Very little in "*Turn to the South*", which is the result of that event, precedes 1860.

All the authors, Jewish and gentile from North and South alike, display keen appreciation of the Jews as a small ethnic and religious minority within a region which in a sense constituted a minority within the social and economic development of the country as a whole. The Southern Jewish minority in many ways represented the values of the American majority. The most culturally northern city in the South, Miami, was geographically the furthest south. Of four articles dealing with rabbis, that by Gladys Rosen skillfully presents the leading rabbi of Miami, Irving Lehrman. Malcolm H. Stern and Jack D. Spiro discuss their rabbinic service in Norfolk and Richmond respectively, while Byron L. Sherwin's subject is Bernard C. Ehrenreich (1876–1955), whose varied career included a term in Montgomery between 1906 and 1920.

Two Jewish politicians are included. Richard S. Tedlow, thinking of all the Jewish statesmen to whom Judah P. Benjamin may be compared, arrives at Benjamin Disraeli. Even if the attempt were convincing, it seems quite pointless. (To Tedlow's list of novels about Benjamin may be added *Judah,* by Allan Appel, published in paperback in 1976.) Charles Jacobson's significant political career in Arkansas between 1891 and 1915 is described in an instructive study by Raymond Arsenault.

The core of *"Turn to the South,"* however, consists of five chapters on the place of the Jews in the South, by Stephen J. Whitfield, Arnold Shankman, Abraham D. Lavender, John Shelton Reed, and Alfred O. Hero, Jr. These come to grips with central issues—Jewish status in Southern culture and society, Jews and Blacks, Jewish ethnicity and acculturation. Perhaps the most stimulating contribution is Whitfield's lively "Jews and Other Southerners: Counterpoint and Paradox," which enumerates incompatibilities between Southern and Jewish traditions before arriving at the paradox—the acceptance of the Jew as individual, the rejection of his people and religion. This volume, with all its unevenness, is a lively introduction to Southern Jewry.

Jack D. Spiro's rabbinic colleague in Richmond, Myron Berman, has written a history of *Richmond's Jewry,* a community which can trace its beginnings back to the late eighteenth century. Dr. Berman's research has been thorough, especially among the extensive papers of the pioneer Mordecai family. With this plenitude of sources, he tells in leisurely fashion a story of family relations, intermarriage, and ultimate departure from Judaism. Unfortunately *Richmond's Jewry* is too slow-paced a work; we stand at page 203 of the 330 pages of text when the Civil War terminates with the capture of the Confederate capital city. Economic data is very sparse, while communal and institutional information is perhaps excessive although welcome in itself. Had maps been included and the book been half its present length, it would have been better for all concerned.

Between 1865 and 1910, during a period of mass immigration, Richmond Jewry increased merely from 1,000 to 1,400. During the following sixty years, their numbers multiplied, from 1,400 to 10,000. It seems obvious that this is largely a new community amid historic remains. Why the Jewish population of Richmond increased in this fashion at a time when the numerical strength of American Jewry stagnated is not clarified. Was this the true turn to the South?

LLOYD P. GARTNER
Tel-Aviv University

The Emerging Colossus of the North: Three Recent Books On Canadian Jewry

Victor Teboul, *Mythe et images du Juif au Québec*. Montreal: Editions de Lagrave, 1977. 234 pp. No price given.

Morton Weinfeld, William Shaffir, and Irwin Cotler (eds), *The Canadian Jewish Mosaic*. Toronto: John Wiley & Sons, 1981. 511 pp. No price given.

Irving Abella and Harold Troper, *None Is Too Many*. Toronto: Lester & Orpen Dennys, 1982. xiii + 336 pp. $ 19.95 Cdn.

On the eve of the Holocaust the Jewish community of Canada was still largely *terra incognita* to scholars and laymen, Jews and gentiles, both in the country and out. This is not surprising, for the community was still young and relatively insignificant. At the turn of the century there were still no more than sixteen thousand Jews in all of Canada; even in the late thirties, eighteen other countries had larger Jewish communities. On the eve of the war Canadian Jewry was still overshadowed by the more populous and much older community in Great Britain, the mother country, and by the vastly larger Jewry of the United States. Canada's Jewish star was further dimmed from the twenties on by an immigration policy in Canada most inhospitable towards Jews.

Today much has changed. In the years after 1948 Canadian immigration laws were relaxed and the Jewish population doubled in size, while sharing North American prosperity. Because many Jewish communities in Europe and the Middle East declined or disappeared during World War II and the immediate post-war years, Canadian Jewry is today the sixth (possibly the fifth) largest in the world. The community has not only grown in size; its internal organization and its relations with other groups in Canada have matured. This coming of age has been much assisted in the last quarter century by the energetic and generously funded multi-cultural policy of the federal government, which has created a conducive atmosphere for strong ethnic loyalties. One expression of that policy has been the subvention of books, such as those under review here, which both reflect and stimulate the growing interest in Canada's ethnic minorities.

Perhaps because the community is now larger, perhaps because contemporary history is happier, it is the most recent experiences of Canadian Jews which have been the focus of much of the scholarly attention, as these three works indicate. Each of them deals with a different aspect of contemporary or almost contemporary Jewish life in Canada. Abella and Troper have written a political history of Canadian policy towards Jewish refugees in the 1930s and 1940s. The Teboul book concentrates on the image of Jews in French-Canadian *belles lettres* in the last 25 years, while *The Canadian Jewish Mosaic* offers a *tour d'horizon* of present-day Jewish life in Canada.

The best of the three is *None Is Too Many,* a meticulous documentation and analysis of governmental activities, or, rather, inactivity. The publication of the book has been something of a media event in Canada: unprecedented efforts by the publishers (including a cocktail party debut of the sort not generally held for Holocaust books) to arouse interest in a scholarly monograph on Jews; public appearances by the authors across the country; and the publication of lengthy excerpts in the prestigious Toronto *Globe and Mail* and elsewhere. As is not often the case, the ballyhoo is proportionate to the merits of the book. It reflects, too, the awareness of Canadians, that however flawed their society may seem at present, they—but especially those belonging to ethnic minorities, like the Jews—"have never had it so good."

None Is Too Many presents a particularly mean, petty, even vicious variation on an all too familiar theme. In Washington during the war years Breckenridge Long, the assistant Secretary of State with responsibility for immigration and an unregenerate anti-Semite, did what he could (and it was quite a lot) to block the entry of Jews into the United States. In Ottawa Frederick Charles Blair, from 1935 to 1943 director of the Immigration Branch of the Department of Mines and Resources, "an anti-Semite," a religious man, and "a narrow-minded bureaucrat," who was also "a dedicated civil servant," devoted himself most enthusiastically to keeping Jews out of Canada.

No matter how villainous Long and Blair may have been, of course, one should not overestimate the power of any one middle-level civil servant. Abella and Troper show, that while Blair may have seized the initiative with regard to Jewish refugees, his behavior reflected the wishes of the majority of cabinet ministers, most certainly those who were French-Canadians, but also his own superior, Thomas Crerar, and even Prime Minister Mackenzie King. Blair was a cog in the wheel, although nonetheless culpable for that. Through his efforts and those of his successor, backed by the government and broad public opinion,

Canada more than any other country kept her doors shut in the face of Jewish refugees from Hitler's Europe.

The authors give the lie to revisionist claims of Jewish complacency during the Holocaust, at least in Canada. They record the indefatigable efforts of *shtadlanim**, especially Saul Hayes, the executive director of the Canadian Jewish Congress from 1940 and the right-hand man of Samuel Bronfman, the country's wealthiest and most powerful Jew. Hayes, Bronfman, the three Jewish MPs, and others made repeated, unwelcome, representations to the government after 1933. At most, they were able to pry open the doors of the country by a crack in individual cases. While pressuring the government, the *shtadlanim* were also attempting to hold back the impatient Jews of recent immigrant origin, most of whom had relatives in Nazi Europe. Occasionally, as on November 20, 1938, in the wake of Kristallnacht, the *shtadlanim* bowed to public pressure and supported demonstrations. They preferred to work in quiet, however, fearing that public activities would reinforce the image, all too prevalent in Canada, of Jews as aggressive and unassimilable barbarians, who were altogether too powerful. They hoped not to provide an additional excuse for excluding the refugees.

As time went on and no change in government policy was forthcoming, Zionists, Communists, the Federation of Polish Jews, and others began to suspect that the leadership was selling out; and they demanded a more activist posture. They naively believed that gentile Canadians could not possibly be so inimical towards Jews, that they would acquiesce in their certain murder. That belief was mistaken. Abella and Troper offer ample evidence to corroborate Yehuda Bauer's thesis, that the political powerlessness of Jews in the era before the establishment of the Jewish state exposed them to murder in Hitler's Europe. It certainly meant that they would not be rescued by inward-looking, sometimes backward-looking, Canadians, many of whom were anti-Semitic, and none of whom had any tangible interest in saving Jews. Had they known, or faced, the truth, Canada's Jews might have despaired. Instead they bickered among themselves, as the Jewish Immigrant Aid Service, the Federation of Polish Jews, and others sparred with the more broadly representative Canadian Jewish Congress. The bickering may have been unseemly, but it did not affect the fate of the refugees. Nothing would have moved the adamant government.

While Jewish powerlessness helps to explain the Canadian response to the refugees as well as that of other countries, it is clearly not a sufficient explanation. The authors of *None Is Too Many* point to

*intercessors

other factors, some of them uniquely Canadian, others operative elsewhere, particularly in the United States. There was the Great Depression, which hit Canada very hard, creating anxiety about the future and reinforcing traditional racist doubts about "indiscriminate" immigration. Hostility towards all foreigners, but especially towards Jews, allegedly the least assimilable group, was much in evidence. (People of color were beyond consideration altogether.) There was the long-standing prejudice against city dwellers in Canada, reflected in an immigration policy heavily weighted in favor of agriculturists and against Jews, considered to be the most urban people of Europe. There were the Canadian fascist movements of the thirties. There was also the need of the federal government to retain the loyalty of French-Canadians, who tended to oppose immigration in general and the Jewish presence in particular. The reigning Liberals were especially sensitive when it came to this issue, since their majority depended upon broad support in Quebec. And finally, there was Frederick Charles Blair.

Even this list, however, does not represent a sufficient explanation of the extraordinary nastiness of Canadian behavior. After all, the Depression took its economic and psychological toll in the United States, and polls there also showed anti-Semitism on the rise in the thirties and forties. Yet that country admitted about three times as many Jewish refugees per capita as Canada, despite Breckenridge Long. The authors claim that while Blair was an anti-Semite, his successor, A. L. Jolliffe, was not. But they do not explain why, then, Jolliffe proved as vigorous as his predecessor in fending off Jewish refugees. Even after the war with the horrors of the Holocaust well publicized, Canada severely restricted the entry of Jews, sometimes giving preference to Germans. And finally, although Jewish immigration was indeed objectionable to French-Canadians, so, too, were other policies, such as conscription, on which the government did not give way.

How, then, is one to account for this dismal record? The explanation undoubtedly lies deep in the social, cultural, and historical makeup of pre-war Canada. The country was then a bi-national, bi-lingual, bi-religious, bi-"racial" country of French and Anglo-Canadians. The two groups had little love for each other, less for others, and almost none for Jews, who were outsiders on every count. This cultural and historical background is missing from *None Is Too Many,* which is not a social history of the times, but a work of political history, and a masterly one at that. Still, full understanding of the period must await examination of the social context within which the government acted.

How far Canada has moved beyond the insular duality of the

Holocaust era is manifested in *The Canadian Jewish Mosaic,* a collection of popular essays on the present-day Jewish condition by some of the country's leading Jewish scholars, all of whom agree in their positive assessment of the present. Arnold Ages reports that "during the last two decades . . . bigotry has declined steadily," and he anticipates the increasing acceptance of Jews in Canadian society. Harold M. Waller and Morton Weinfeld concede that there is considerable unease among Jews in Quebec, justified to a degree, although they claim that "the reality of anti-Semitism in Quebec compares favourably with that in Europe and is no worse than in other Canadian provinces or the American states." Stuart Schonfeld, a sociologist, observes that the power of conservative Christianity, both Protestant and Catholic, has declined greatly in Canada in the last two decades, that religion has become largely "a private matter," rather than a communal enterprise. As a result, he sees more space for Jews and Judaism than formerly.

There are several yardsticks by which to measure the new sense of belonging felt by Jews in Canada. One is the rapidly rising rate of intermarriage, 26.5 per cent of all Canadian Jews marrying gentiles in 1978, according to Weinfeld. Another gauge is Zionism. Once Canadian Zionism was unusually vigorous, enjoying almost universal support, offering Jews an alternative to the French and Anglo-Canadian nationalisms which excluded them. Today, however, in Waller's assessment, Canadian Zionism consists of little more than vague sentiments of support for, and the donation of money to, Israel. It is little different from the American brand of Jewish "nationalism," indicating a similar level of rootedness on the part of Jews in both North American countries.

Although acceptance in pluralistic Canada has led to the attenuation of some aspects of Jewish life in recent years, it has strengthened others. In a report on Jewish education, Yaacov Glickman notes that in the early seventies almost 60 per cent of the children in Toronto and Montreal receiving any Jewish education were enrolled in day schools. (It is unfortunate in a book about the present day, that the figures are not more up to date.) In comparison to communities of similar size in the United States, this is an extraordinary percentage. Although he offers no supporting data, another sociologist, Leo Davids, believes that "a committed and identified Jewish sub-community continues to involve itself with synagogues, organizations, and philanthropy . . ., maintain[ing] Jewish practices vigorously at home," despite the allure of alternative life styles. Howard Stanislawski, a political scientist, finds that "the political awareness" of Canadian Jews and their "involvement . . . at all levels of the political process" has increased in recent years to a degree that augurs well for their future well-being.

Some shadows do creep into this generally sunny book. Eugene Orenstein notes that Yiddish culture and institutions, which only a quarter century ago appeared to be flourishing, have all but withered away. Dwindling too are the Jewish communities in outlying areas, those in the Atlantic provinces and the prairie farm colonies now threatened with extinction. The most ominous decline is that of Montreal, the once proud "capital city of Canadian Jewry." Although Waller and Weinfeld speak in guarded terms about the city's problems, they do hint that the handwriting may be on the wall. And, finally, it may be noted, that the rising number of intermarriages marks not only the integration of Jews into Canadian society, but also the disintegration of the tight-knit Canadian-Jewish community.

These signs of trouble ahead notwithstanding, Canada's Jewry seems in fairly sound health at present, certainly in comparison with the period described in *None Is Too Many*. (That this is also the perspective of the editors of *The Canadian Jewish Mosaic* is evident from their inclusion of a portion of the former book in their own historical introduction.) Still, some of the good cheer is clearly forced: Waller and Weinfeld's suggestion that the decline in fertility and the exodus of young Jews from Montreal "may have happier results" than once foreseen, for example; or Stanislawski's optimism, despite the failure of the federal government to follow the example of Ontario which in 1978 enacted legislation against the Arab boycott, and despite the whirlwind Jews reaped over the Progressive-Conservative Party's 1979 election promise to recognize Jerusalem as the capital of Israel. Perhaps this almost apologetic optimism comes from the "official" character of the book, which seems meant, in part at least, to present contemporary Canadian Jews to their neighbors. More to the point, however, the book celebrates the present, which is, indeed, an improvement over the past.

One serious shortcoming of *The Canadian Jewish Mosaic* is the failure to include a chapter on the impact of the Holocaust. This is surprising, since some forty per cent of the Jews in Canada are survivors or their descendants. The editors' explanation of "limitations of space, time, and energy" is not very satisfying. Another shortcoming is that some of the essays lean heavily on data borrowed from the United States, adding little to our knowledge of Canada. A few of the contributions rehash old data and views published elsewhere, although this may be inevitable in a "state of Confederation" volume such as this. Despite such relatively minor failings, *The Canadian Jewish Mosaic* is a seminal work. Its attempt to survey contemporary Canadian Jewry breaks new ground; the book adds considerably to our knowledge of the Canadian Jewish community, especially from a sociological perspective.

And Canadian Jews deserve attention, since in many ways their community is, at present, a model of both integration and autonomy!

Victor Teboul's *Mythe et images du Juif au Québec* is a flawed book, but it is most definitely not apologetic. In fact, it is a very disturbing work, which casts considerable doubt on the optimism of *The Canadian Jewish Mosaic,* posing the question of whether public opinion regarding Jews has really changed in Quebec since the Holocaust era. Teboul suggests that anti-Semitism remains a concept fundamental to the self-understanding of French-Canadian society, and he provides a voluminous catalogue of recent Quebec films, fiction, and critical and historical writing to illustrate his thesis. Teboul claims, in fact, that the "current attitude in Quebec" towards anti-Semitism is simply to deny its existence in past or present.

According to Teboul, Jews appear in contemporary French-Canadian writing as little more than stock characters, and negative ones at that. They are depicted as newcomers, who unlike the French-Canadians, are not rooted in the land. They are urban, commercial, rapacious and rich, in contrast to the simple, rural *habitants:* they are parasites guilty of exploitation, who embody dark, hostile forces. Jewish women are painted as dangerously erotic.

Novelists whose works Teboul sees as reflecting such an approach are among French Canada's most highly regarded: Yves Thériault, Roch Carrier, and Gabrielle Roy, for example. (He might have noted that one Montreal Jewish writer, Mordecai Richler, has employed the same stereotypes.) According to Teboul, writers in Montreal papers, including *La Presse,* the country's largest French-language daily (founded, ironically, by a Jew) use such stereotypes to attack everything associated with Jews from the policies of Israel to Woody Allen. So, too, does Robert Rumilly, author of the definitive French-language history of Quebec. The list is long and impressive, the more so in light of the role played by intellectuals in present-day Quebec, a point Teboul fails to make. After the manner of their European counterparts, French-Canadian intellectuals are to be found in the vanguard of the current political and social renaissance of the province. This is one reason why Quebec Jews find the new nationalism so threatening.

As a catalogue of present dangers, *Mythe et images* is quite effective. As a work of cultural history and literary criticism, however, it is very weak. Teboul gives the impression that the anti-Semitism of contemporary Quebec was born full-blown from the head of Zeus. Missing is any discussion of the hoary tradition of literary, cultural, political, and religious anti-Semitism in the province, which would make the current manifestations understandable by placing them in context. Teboul's offhand mention of earlier eras is not helpful in this regard.

What he needs to do in order to transcend reportage is to reach back even to the French colonial period, when Jews were barred from settling in New France. Present-day attitudes and stereotypes had their genesis then, and their evolution should be traced historically to the present.

None Is Too Many, The Canadian Jewish Mosaic and *Mythe et images du Juif au Québec* are very different from each other, then, not only in methodology and focus, but also in quality. And yet, together they present an interesting and, in some respects, a coherent view of contemporary Canadian Jewry. Abella and Troper write of the recent past, when anti-Semitism governed immigration policies and Jews were powerless to counteract it. In Teboul's view French-Canadian writing indicates that little has changed in Quebec, and he implies that independence for that province could signal for Jews a return to the bad old days. The present, however, is rather pleasant, in some respects ideal, almost everywhere in Canada, even in the trouble spots, as is evident from *The Canadian Jewish Mosaic*. The future, of course, even the immediate future, is uncertain. But whatever it holds for Canadian Jews themselves, students of the community will enjoy a much improved situation thanks to the books under review here. Scholars cannot but be grateful that at last the Jewish northland, hitherto virtually unknown, is today being confidently explored and assertively charted.

MICHAEL BROWN
York University
Hebrew University

The Jewish Question in Pre-World War II Poland

Frank Golczewski, *Polnische-Jüdische Beziehungen 1881–1922*. Wiesbaden: Franz Steiner Verlag, 1981. 391 pp.

Pawel Korzec, *Juifs en Pologne*. Paris: Presses de la Fondation Nationale des Sciences Politiques, 1980. 326 pp.

Shlomo Netzer, *Maavak yehudei polin 'al zekhuyoteihem haezrahiyot vehaleumiyot (1918–1922)*. (The Struggle of Polish Jewry for Civic and National Rights). Tel Aviv: Tel Aviv University, 1980. 338 pp. + 4-page English summary.

One of the more lamentable aspects of the recent Polish crisis has been the demonstrated durability of the "Jewish Question" in Poland, which has managed to survive the changes of regime, the destruction of ninety percent of Polish Jewry in the Holocaust, and the post-war flight of most of the surviving remnant. Even the 1968 "anti-Zionist" purges, which reduced the size of the Polish Jewish community to a few thousand, have not put an end to the debate over the place or lack thereof of Jews in the Polish state.

The roots of the modern debate on the "Jewish Question" lie in the era of the partitions. As part of a more general effort to reform and strengthen the already truncated Polish state, the position of the Jews and possible reforms in their legal status came under discussion. After the loss of Polish independence, the question of the Jews still remained on the national agenda. Some political thinkers were hesitant to support equal rights for the Jews, while others urged emancipation as the best way to bring about the total assimilation of the Jews. Neither school looked with favor on a nationally identified Jewish community.

In the second half of the nineteenth century, the growth of Polish cities and industry, and the concomitant rise of a strong self-conscious Polish middle class created a fertile ground for anti-Jewish agitation. The development of mass politics in the latter part of the century, as well as the growing nationalist sentiments of the various national minorities raised the minorities question and the Jewish question in an intense form. The powerful Polish Right rejected the old vision of assimilation of the Jews, replacing it with a drive to eliminate Jews from the Polish economy and culture.

The economic boycott of Jews called for by the Polish Right (begun in 1912) was the practical expression of this desire for Polish "independence" from Jewish influence. Polish Jewry thus entered the period of renewed Polish independence feeling the effects of built-up political and economic antipathy. In inter-war Poland, Jews suffered some instances of outright physical attack but, more important, had to contend with far-reaching economic and bureaucratic discrimination. Jewish politicians had to function in a generally hostile atmosphere in the Polish parliament and city councils.

The three works under consideration shed much light on the position of Polish Jewry during the period of the rise of mass politics under the partition regimes and during the inter-war Polish Republic.

The first, Frank Golczewski's *Polnische-Jüdische Beziehungen 1881–1922*, is a pioneering full-length study of anti-Jewish outbreaks on Polish territory in the critical formative period of modern Polish party politics. It opens with the Warsaw pogrom of 1881, and ranges through less well-known episodes such as the worker unrest in Lodz in 1892 and peasant unrest in western Galicia in 1898. It then leads into the 1912 boycott movement, the pogroms and legal harassment at the onset of Polish independence, culminating in the assassination of Narutowicz, the first president of the reborn Polish Republic. The author notes that histories of Poland as well as general histories of anti-Semitism have tended to overlook Polish anti-Semitism, and he has gone far to fill this gap. His rich documentation draws on newspapers, books, and archival materials, using to good advantage the files in German and Israeli archives. Golczewski received access to Polish archives only after the present work was completed, so we must await future works to see the amplification and reconfirmation of his present findings.

The subtitle of the book, a study of the history of anti-Semitism in Eastern Europe, more accurately reflects its nature. It is more a study of the development of Judeophobia than of the Jewish reactions or of the Jewish self-image. Similarly, Golczewski makes relatively minimal use of Hebrew and Yiddish sources, while attempting to compensate through the use of Jewish sources in Polish, German and English. The ideology of Polish anti-Semitism and its development also receive a less than systematic treatment, and Golczewski himself admits that further research needs to be done in this area.

One area where Golczewski covers territory not usually touched by Jewish historians of Eastern Europe is in his attempt to apply the findings of theoretical literature on the nature of anti-Semitism to the specific case of Polish Jewry. Throughout this interesting book we find insights into the many and varied ways in which the Jew was perceived as "other" as well as into their psychological significance. Phenomena as varied as the anti-Jewish boycott, the barring of caftaned Jews from public parks, and accusations of Jewish collaboration with German or Bolshevik invaders take on an added dimension. A rich bibliography, (with the exception of the scanty references to Hebrew and Yiddish sources), rounds out this important volume.

The first part of Pawel Korzec's *Juifs en Pologne* covers much the same territory as does Golczewski, but the bulk of the book focuses on the political situation of the Jews in inter-war Poland. Korzec follows the evolution of the Jewish Question from the period of high hopes in the years of Polish national rebirth through the years of political struggle in the parliament, the "tempered" anti-Semitism after the Pilsudski coup d'etat, and the official anti-Semitism of the colonels' regime immediately preceding World War II. The several abortive attempts at a Polish-Jewish rapprochement receive particular attention, benefiting greatly from Korzec's earlier monographic treatment of those episodes. Korzec also presents an adequate survey of the goals, strategies and activities of the many Jewish political parties.

The reader finds no startlingly new conclusions regarding either Polish or Jewish policies. Korzec's searches of French and German archives have turned up, among other things, internal publications of the respective foreign ministries surveying the Polish and Yiddish press in Poland which are sure to be invaluable to scholars working on the inter-war period. Yet these new sources and others that Korzec refers to serve to confirm what has more or less been the scholarly consensus for decades.

This notwithstanding, *Juifs en Pologne* deservedly should take its place among the standard surveys on inter-war Polish Jewry. This is clearly the work of a seasoned scholar in control of the diverse sources, published and unpublished, in many languages. It is also a labor of love and of great pain by someone whose passionate involvement in the historical issues animates a lively yet informative narrative. Particularly in the notes, Korzec carries on a spirited polemic with current Polish historiography, both in Communist Poland and in the West, on the national minorities question. Though he is occasionally carried away by his own rhetoric, Korzec has produced a major new synthesis. The book lacks a bibliography, and this is doubly unfortunate, since the notes show that Korzec has a knack for finding bibliographic treasures in unexpected places.

The Jewish side of Polish-Jewish relations during the critical years of the Constituent Sejm (1918–1922) is the subject of Shlomo Netzer's *Maavak yehudei polin*. Here we see described in great detail the lonely struggle of Jewish elected representatives to guarantee the civil and national rights of the Polish Jews and of the other national minorities as well. Netzer documents both the attempts made to consolidate Polish Jewry as a functioning national organism, and also the tensions and frictions that this process engendered. He draws on an impressive array of archival and published sources, as evidenced by the notes and the rich bibliography. Though acknowledging the leading role of Zionist politicians in Jewish parliamentary and extra-parliamentary dealings with the Polish regime and though he leans heavily on Zionist archives and publications, Netzer makes a noteworthy attempt to provide a balanced portrayal of the role played by the Bund, the Folkists and Agudas Israel in the Jewish politics of this period. In sum, Netzer's thoroughness and attention to detail can serve as a model for scholars examining this difficult era.

Taken together, these three works lead to several important conclusions about Polish-Jewish relations. First of all, Polish anti-Semitism was not of one piece and varied in intensity. At least at the outset of the period under consideration, significant voices in Polish society denounced anti-Jewish violence as alien to the Polish spirit. Even though anti-Jewish sentiment may have grown beneath the surface, the situation of Polish Jewry remained relatively good until 1900 (or even until 1912), even though it was marred by scattered violent outbursts. On the other hand, from 1912 on we note the virtual disappearance of the liberal segment of Polish public opinion. The Polish Right, whether in power or out, came to mold Polish national thought and called the ideological tune for all of Polish society. On several occasions, the Jewish Question became an issue of crucial importance for Poland, but throughout the period under discussion here it served as a faithful barometer registering the problems of Polish society in its search for unity and political independence.

Within the Jewish community, diaspora politics reached its zenith in the inter-war period. Even without full government recognition and financial support, Jewish political autonomy became a reality. No matter what the strategy adopted, however, Jewish politics had few successes. Though Jewish leaders often complained of the lack of Jewish unity, even when the major parties did unite, the political results were little enhanced as a result. The futility of Jewish politics on the external level did little to dampen and indeed probably intensified the internal Jewish political and ideological struggle. The works considered above document these struggles, and help explain at least in part the background of the ultimate tragedy that befell Polish Jewry.

GERSHON C. BACON
Bar-Ilan University

On Dissidents and Refuseniks

Mark Azbel, *Refusenik: Trapped in the Soviet Union.* Boston: Houghton-Mifflin & Co., 1981. 513 pp. $17.95

Evgenia Guinzbourg, *Sous le ciel de Kolyma.* Paris: Editions du Seuil, 1980. 476 pp.

Lev Kopelev, *The Education of a True Believer.* London: Wildwood House, 1981. 328 pp. [Harper and Row, $15.95]

Eduard Kuznetsov, *Mordovskii mirofan.* Ramat Gan: Moskva-Jerusalem Edition, 1979. 254 pp. (French edition: *Lettres de mordovie,* Paris: Gallimard, 1981)

Writings by dissident Soviet authors, many of whom are of Jewish origin, have been published in the West since the early 1960's. The literature is constantly expanding and has begun to assume considerable importance as a source for research on Soviet history in general and the nationalities problem in particular. It is enough to recall the names of Alexander Solzhenitsyn, Nadezhda Mandelstam, and Vasily Grossman in order to see how great has been the contribution of such works to our understanding of Soviet reality. The four books under review here are unquestionably in the direct line of this literature.

They have much in common, despite some striking differences. All four authors are of Jewish origin (at least in part) and this fact made them both highly vulnerable and especially sensitive to the metamorphoses in Soviet society. Secondly, all were dissidents in the full sense, who were driven to revolt and paid a high price, which in the case of some of them included arrest, long-term imprisonment and limitless suffering of body and soul. Their books belong to the category of committed *(engagé)* literature—it can even be called a literature of combat—that aims to show how a tiny handful fought against a fearful apparatus of almost unparalleled terror. This fight was at the same time a desperate struggle on their part to free themselves from accepted ideas in which they themselves had believed for many years.

There are also significant differences between the books, some purely technical and some more significant, differences of form and structure, content and character. In the first place, the writers belong to different generations, and this fact goes far to explain their markedly contrasting views of the Jewish national question. On the one hand, Ginzburg and Kopelev were born before the Revolution (the former in 1905 and the latter in 1912) and embarked on communist activity in the 1920's; while Azbel and Kuznetsov on the other hand were born in the 1930's (the former in 1932 and the latter in 1939) and grew up under Stalin. The first two remained in the Soviet Union while both the younger men became Zionists and emigrated to Israel. They divide along the same generational lines in their view of the nationalities problem.

It should also be pointed out that the books of Kopelev and Azbel belong to the genre of narrative autobiography while the other two memoirs concentrate on camp life. (It is worth noting, finally, that except for Azbel's book, which has appeared so far only in the edition reviewed here, all of them are editions of works already published in the West in other languages.)

Lev Kopelev became known all over the world as the model for Rubin, the philologist and scholar in Solzhenitsyn's *The First Circle*. Kopelev served as an officer in the Red Army during World War II, and at the time of the Soviet occupation of East Prussia he tried to intervene on behalf of the civilian German population, to put an end to acts of rape and indiscriminate slaughter by Soviet troops. It was on this account that he was accused of treason and sentenced to a long term of imprisonment. These dramatic events in his life are described in his valuable and gripping testimony *Khranit' vechno* (To Keep Forever) which, though published first, in fact constitutes the chronological sequel to the memoirs reviewed here. The English title of the book, *The Education of a True Believer,* is not a translation of the Russian title: *I sotvoril sebe kumira* ("And He Made Himself an Idol").

The ten chapters of the book give a more or less chronological account of the author's childhood, from the age of five (1917) through his adolescence in the 1930's, when he personally took part in the bloody and devastating collectivization of the Ukraine. Interestingly enough, two of the early chapters have titles connected with his attitude to religion: "Without the Tsar but still with God" and "The loss of God." Belief in divine presence—never specifically in Judaism *per se*—gave way to the fuller and stronger faith in the new religion, the communist god. Chapter 5, "Esperanto", is particularly important for its discussion on the nationality question, and Chapter 9 for its description of Soviet life during the collectivization campaign; "The lost grain collections." The emphasis throughout is on the system of indoctrination employed to turn the young people into a cadre of zealots. Thus the author tries to explain—perhaps not only to his readers but to himself, first of all—how it happened that he and his whole generation created for themselves a Moloch idol, which they were ready to serve without qualification or pangs of conscience, though its demands became ever more voracious.

Kopelev's strength is his ability to describe the experience of the individual, the family and a broader public over a wide range of subjects—geographical, social and national. His weakness is his inability or perhaps unwillingness to draw ultimate conclusions from his own criticism of the idol. The reader is perturbed, even astonished. Can the author's ambivalent attitude really stem from an attempt to avoid arrest or exile and to stay in his beloved Russia, or is he perhaps incapable of consistency and unable to draw devastating conclusions? (Be that as it may, in 1977 he was nonetheless expelled both from the Party and from the Union of Soviet Writers.)

Kopelev devotes almost two chapters in his book to the nationalities problem. Even if his approach is not original (and has undoubtedly been influenced by Ilya Ehrenburg, Julian Tuwim and Osip Mandelstam) it is of some importance because even today it is representative of the attitude of a large percentage of Soviet Jewish intellectuals.

Officially—that is, when forced by law to answer the question—he has given his nationality as "Jew" (p. 102). This is his obligatory answer, stemming from his personal pride; but to his comrades and to himself he speaks differently: "I have never found in my conscious mind anything that would link me to the nationalistic ideals or religious traditions of Jewry" (p. 112). He is confirmed in this stand by a letter from a friend of his, a new immigrant in Israel, who had suffered greatly from anti-Semitism in the Soviet Union, had learned Hebrew, and now after a year in Israel wrote to him: "I feel myself a Russian and nothing but a Russian" (p. 113).

The book by Azbel, as we have already said, resembles Kopelev's in form and general character. There is also a certain resemblance between the two men themselves. They both belong to the world of Soviet scholarship, one in the humanities and the other in natural science. They have a similar social origin: Kopelev's father was an agronomist and Azbel's a doctor. They were both educated in the Ukraine and their development followed a similar path. Nonetheless, the positions they reached on the Jewish question are absolutely poles apart.

Refusenik (the title is most apt) divides in two almost equal parts. The first part ends in 1972, when after much hesitation the author submitted his request to emigrate. He gives lively and interesting reminiscences of his childhood and youth before the war, during it (when his family was evacuated to Siberia) and after it (when they lived in the Ukraine and Moscow). There is an impressive description of the Soviet educational system and, most important, of the Soviet scientific world. The second part of the book is largely devoted to the Jewish nationalist revival which burgeoned in the Soviet Union after the trials of Jewish dissidents in Leningrad, Riga and Kishinev (1970–71). The author was a leader in this movement and his very full account of the methods that were used to outwit the KGB constitutes a most important source for the outside observer.

Azbel is generous with reflections, ideas and digressions, and even if they are not very original they lead us to a better understanding of the Soviet scientist, torn between his ambition to make a career for himself and the price he has to pay in order to achieve it. With Azbel, we penetrate into the secret recesses of the soul of *homo sovieticus* as scientist fighting to survive.

There are some inaccuracies in the book (for example, the statement that Chmielnicki [seventeenth century Ukranian hetman and anti-Polish rebel] murdered a million Jews) and certain notes jar (such, to take one example from many, as the affirmation that a given school or institution is the best not only in the Soviet Union but in the whole world). But all these faults do not fundamentally detract from the great value of the book.

Sous le ciel de Kolyma belongs to a completely different genre. The author recorded her *via dolorosa* in her first book of memoirs, *Vertigo* (Into the Whirlwind), which described her life up to her despatch to the Kolyma concentration camp. In the present work she rises to unparalleled artistic and literary heights. The reader cannot remain indifferent. From the first page he is swept away on the flood of terrifying atrocities described and must be moved to pity, sorrow and agony. As we are swallowed up in the successive circles of the hell of Kolyma we ask ourselves whether there can really be any life there at all. The answer is yes—"In spite of the fact that everyone defends his place under the sun of Kolyma in a ceaseless fight against everyone else" (p. 9).

In *Vertigo*, Guinzbourg did not treat the matter of nationality directly at all, and she also completely ignored her family origin and her upbringing. It was not hard to guess, of course, that she came from an assimilated Jewish family, and fitted perfectly into Russian surroundings and culture together with her Russian husband, a senior official in the Communist Party, and her son (by her first husband), Vasily Aksenov, who became a major Russian novelist. In the book under review, the nationality theme—general and Jewish—receives only sporadic treatment, which is nevertheless highly significant as live testimony from the "planet Kolyma."

Although the camp filled up at different periods with large numbers of given nationalities (Lithuanians, Latvians and Estonians in 1940; Soviet Germans in 1941; Jews in 1949), Guinzbourg asserts that relations between the groups were not strained until the camp administration began to exploit the nationality factor to set the inmates against each other. She devotes considerable space to the Soviet-German minority *(Volksdeutsche)* because of her personal ties with her friend in the camp (and future husband) Dr. Walter. He was a doctor from Simferopol, one of the many thousands of ethnic Germans arrested in the second half of the 1930's, collectively and falsely accused of anti-Soviet activity and collaboration with a foreign power.

In 1949, as we have said, the Jews began to arrive. Even the command personnel of Jewish origin were influenced by the anti-Semitic "anti-cosmopolitan" campaign—as, for example, the NKVD colonel who feared he would lose his job because of the nationality clause in his identity certificate. It was only in 1953, however, that the anti-Jewish campaign really began to be felt in Kolyma, after the announcement on 13 January that a group of doctor "poisoners" had been arrested. The author affirms, "This was the first time that this poison penetrated even into our distant planet" (p. 411); Dr. Walter, who had previously suffered because he was German, was victimized now as a "Jewish doctor." As the author reports, Walter commented, "I shall soon have to get documents from Germany to confirm my German race purity."

Eduard Kuznetsov has already given us his unforgettable *Prison Diary,* written and published while he was still in the labor camp. This important new work, *The Mordovian Marathon,* combines a description of the cruel life in the concentration camps in a period of supposed liberalization with an analysis of the Soviet prison world to which he applies an original and penetrating intellect. In the form of letters smuggled out of prison, the author gives a finely worked and stingingly ironical account of his life from the moment when he was sentenced at the notorious Leningrad trial to fifteen years' imprisonment. All in all, he has spent about half of his life in the forced labor camps (including the period 1961–68, for his part in general dissident activity).

The discussion of the nationalities question is somewhat restricted in this book, because it is in some ways a sequel to Kuznetsov's *Prison Diary,* where he explained how he came to Zionism. Nevertheless, *Mordovskii mirofan* throws further light on the relations among nationality groups in Soviet prison camps. The hatred of Jews on the part of the authorities in the Mordovian camps was not very different from that in Kolyma, but times had changed. Fear that Jews in the West would "kick up a row" and the freer flow of information from the camps themselves inhibited the anti-Semitic zeal of the authorities. "If it depended on me," says one of the KGB men, "I would banish them from the Soviet Union" (p. 16). However, the existence of the state of Israel and events such as the rescue at Entebbe shattered stereotypes of the Jew as coward. Friendly relations were struck up with dissident prisoners of other nationalities, especially with Ukrainians.

Finally, there are Kuznetsov's interesting reflections on the difficulty of solving the Palestinian problem. In contrast to the generally extreme views expressed on this painful subject by Soviet immigrants to Israel, Kuznetsov in far-off Mordovia can say of the Arabs: "I recognize their being in the right also. Even if their right is less than that of the Jews, it is impossible not to recognize it. What is the way out, then? How can one compromise between two truths? It is impossible, I'm afraid" (p. 237). The tone is pessimistic but, in view of the course of events since the publication of the book, not unrealistic.

How, then, are we to explain the radically different attitudes of a Guinzbourg or a Kopelev on the one hand and a Kuznetsov or an Azbel on the other to the national Jewish awakening? When and why does an assimilated Jew, bound to Russian culture heart and soul, begin to concern himself with his national origin and future?

Azbel tells us that it was from the "outside" world that he learned at an early age that he was Jewish. The "folk" anti-Semitism that is native to Russian soil rises to the surface during times of crisis and strain as in World War II: insulting nicknames, accusations, blows dealt out and the need to defend oneself against them, all sharpen the child's senses and sow doubts in his mind. As he grows up, he begins to understand that official, state anti-Semitism exists, too, in a country where fraternity between peoples is preached. Against this background, the creation of the state of Israel acted as a catalyst of great potency: "To see Jews for the first time in two thousand years responsible for their own fate, and in a position to defend themselves, was an immense source of gratification to me and to all my friends" (p. 61).

Discrimination in education and career opportunities; plain fear at the time of the anti-"Cosmopolitan" campaign and the "doctors' plot;" the first encounters with the KGB—all contributed their share to the process of national awakening. Then there was the period of liberalization, the "thaw" in the USSR, which made it much easier for people to move about, exchange opinions and even, within limits, to express themselves. Like many other Zionist activists, Azbel first went through the stage of dissidence. His friendship with Yuli Daniel, who was tried in 1966 together with Sinyavsky for anti-Soviet activity, was Azbel's baptism of fire. The June War of 1967 on the one hand and the 1968 invasion of Czechoslovakia on the other completed the process and drove Azbel to take the hard, dangerous road of Zionist activism. "The first time [. . .] it ever crossed my mind that my work in the Soviet Union might come to an end was at the very beginning of 1970," he writes (p. 234); but it was not until the first large Zionist group was granted exit visas on 11 March 1971 that he finally made up his mind and submitted his fateful request.

The conclusion from this book is that his struggle finally succeeded because of a historic conjunction of international and internal pressures—above all, the stubborn fight of Soviet Jews themselves.

BENJAMIN PINKUS
Ben-Gurion University of the Negev

Aharon Appelfeld: The Search for a Language

Aharon Appelfeld, *Tor hapelaot* (Hakibbutz Hameuḥad, 1978).

———, *The Age of Wonders,* trans. Dalya Bilu. New York: Washington Square Press, 1981. $12.95

Aharon Appelfeld, *Mikhvat Haor* [*Searing Light*] (Hakibbutz Hameuḥad, 1980). (Untranslated)

The appearance in English translation of the work of a Hebrew writer hitherto relatively unknown outside Israel signals a significant change in the public status of that writer. Some of the recent fiction of Aharon Appelfeld, who is the 1983 recipient of the Israel Prize for literature, has crossed the boundaries of an intimate community of Hebrew readers and is now available to a much wider public through the English translations of Dalya Bilu.*

Translating Appelfeld is a complex enterprise, though not for the usual reasons; the insularity of the classical allusions which laminate the prose of S.Y. Agnon, for example, does not apply here. Quite the contrary. There is the quality of a primal struggle in Appelfeld's prose, a chiseling and shaping of language by a writer who encounters Hebrew unencumbered by layers of classical association; this struggle with the linguistic medium, which resists transposition into another idiom, is the focus of the present discussion. Some of the chisel-marks which show through the Hebrew text, like Michelangelo's "Captive" sculptures just barely emerging from yet still imprisoned in the unhewn rock, have been polished over in the English version, which is otherwise faithful to the original.

The signs of an acquired language are literary evidence of Appelfeld's personal odyssey. He was born in the German-speaking Jewish

---

*Translations of individual stories have appeared in various journals and anthologies. The first of Appelfeld's full-length books to appear in English translation was *Badenheim, 1939* (trans. Dalya Bilu [New York: Washington Square Press, 1980]). And in 1983, the novella *Tzili* appeared (trans. Dalya Bilu [New York: Dutton]). Most of his fiction, however, remains untranslated.

community of Czernowitz in the Bukovina region of Romania; when he was eight years old the Germans entered his town and he was separated from his family and sent to a work camp in Transnistria. He managed to escape and then spent the war years as a fugitive in the forests of Europe. In 1944 he was picked up by the Red Army and brought to the Ukraine; the end of the war found him in Italy, from whose shores he was transported to Palestine in 1946.

In examining the fiction of Appelfeld and of certain other writers within the confines of what has come to be known as "Holocaust literature," one may tend to overlook dimensions of the experience of upheaval and displacement which these writers share with other writers of the twentieth century and with a long line of exiled artists who can trace their lineage in one direction to Ovid on the shores of the Black Sea and in another to the psalmist by the waters of Babylon. From Ovid banished from Rome through Dante banished from Florence, from the voluntary exile of Nabokov and Beckett through the forced exile of Solzhenitsyn, from the wanderings of Judah Halevi to those of S.Y. Agnon, "the history of civilization itself could be reckoned," as Harry Levin claims, "by an endless sequence of migrations." The personal malaise that such wanderings often induced was diagnosed as early as 1688 as an affliction called "Heimweh" (nostalgia or homesickness).[1]

Our century seems to abound with examples of prominent literary exiles. In some cases they continued writing in their native tongue which, as with Ovid nearly two thousand years ago, compounded their sense of exile and often brought about a loss of linguistic facility ("Lo! I am ashamed to confess it; now from long disuse Latin words with difficulty occur even to me! And I doubt not there are even in this book not a few barbarisms, not the fault of the man but of the place"[2]). Other displaced writers labored to acquire the languages of their adopted countries. George Steiner refers to twentieth-century writers "driven from language to language by social upheaval and war . . . as apt symbols for the age of the refugee."[3] Those who most tragically exemplify this status are the expatriates from Nazi Germany. German writers such as Thomas Mann, Berthold Brecht, Stefan Zweig, Franz Werfel and Erich Maria Remarque, who managed to emigrate to North or South America before the full forces of destruction had been unleashed, have been the subject of a growing critical study of *Exil Literatur*.[4] In an impassioned speech delivered at the memorial service held for Stefan Zweig in Los Angeles after his suicide in 1942, Franz Werfel said that

> like all the rest of us he was banished from his native country not only geographically but spiritually. Later generations will one day plumb the

tragedy of poets and writers separated from their mother tongue, beggars doomed to wander eternally on the borders of a foreign idiom and a foreign mode of thought, with neither the youthful energy nor the desire nor the humility to go across.[5]

Yet their state of exile is still fertile ground when compared to the barren landscape of the transplanted Jewish writers who managed to survive the Holocaust in Europe and who found themselves, at the end of their long ordeal, far from their homeland and deprived of their native tongue. Piotr Rawicz, Anna Langfus and Elie Wiesel writing in French, Jurek Becker in German, Ilona Karmel and Jerzy Kosinski in English—the linguistic displacement is perhaps the most telling characteristic of the total upheaval of those years.[6]

Albert Memmi has argued that language for the Jew has always been a provisional possession which the mandates of history periodically force him to exchange.[7] The condition of exile which was inherent in the Jewish condition and perception for two millennia had found its literary expression in nearly every generation.[8] Yet the upheavals were local; it would take World War II to empty Europe of its Jewish voices. Though it may still be too early to assess the impact of such massive displacement on the cultures from which Jews were expelled or on the survivors' adopted languages, there are a few writers, such as Nelly Sachs or Paul Celan, whose continuing post-war presence in the German language, even while in physical exile in Sweden or France, has already had a profound effect on contemporary German letters. Choosing not to exchange his native tongue together with his citizenship, Celan nevertheless had to reinvent the language in order to find a home in it. John Felstiner has written that Celan's poems "do not enjoy the emotional closure and vocal integrity that lyric verse traditionally embodies. Each line struggles not just with, but against the language itself, against the 'thousand darknesses of death-bringing speech' which Celan says his native German had to pass through during the Holocaust."[9] In a speech in 1958 acknowledging the literary prize awarded him by the city of Bremen, Celan identified his own poetry and that of others of his generation as the " 'efforts of someone . . . shelterless in a sense undreamt-of till now and thus most uncannily out in the open, who goes with his very being to language, stricken by and seeking reality.' "[10]

When Celan came to Jerusalem in 1969, some of his sense of exile seems to have lifted. His posthumously-published Jerusalem poems are entitled "Zeitgehöft" (Homestead of Time).[11] And for several years before this visit he had made frequent, incantatory use of untranslated Hebrew words and phrases. The poem "Du sei wie du," ends with the

Hebrew imperative "kumi/ori" which, as Felstiner elucidates, refers to Isaiah 60:1, promising a renewal of the covenant and a return of the exiles: "I see [Celan] breaking free in [the poem's final words], renewing his bond with them in messianic speech."[12] Hebrew here carries the promise of light beside the "darknesses of death-bringing speech," of a haven for the "shelterless" and an access to ancient, pristine layers of speech and of being.

Celan himself was a sojourner in the land of Israel on his way, it now appears, to an inexorable rendezvous with death which was administered by his own hand in 1970. But the intimations of connectedness in his last poems suffuse the writing of many of the adopted sons of Israel. In the early post-war period, the linguistic exchange undertaken by every European refugee who arrived in Palestine seemed to entail more gains than losses. Palestine had been a land of immigrants and pilgrims since the Babylonian dispersion, and in most recent times had seen an influx of writers who wrote in Hebrew but still dreamed in Russian, Yiddish, German, whose portraits of the Judean desert still invoked the steppes of Russia. Yet by the time the survivors of the Nazi Holocaust began to arrive, there was already a generation of native speakers. And for the writer attuned to its sounds, there were echoes of ancient voices keening the dead of two millennia, providing literary models.

In acquiring the language, the writer moving into Hebrew acquired an apparatus of discourse on Jewish suffering, a set of paradigms of protest and consolation, of piety and even irony. To the extent that, like the poet and ghetto fighter, Abba Kovner, his childhood memories resonated with the language of sacred texts, Hebrew became the avenue of retrieval of the writer's personal as well as the collective past. Kovner illuminates this process in describing his own agonized search for a bridge to the dead; he states that as he was completing the fortieth chapter of his long poem, "Aḥoti Ktanah," (My Little Sister), a chasm suddenly opened up before him and, without a rope to pull him across, he could not proceed:

> The end of the rope was not in my hand. And my hands were over my eyes:
>
> > The shorn head of my sister
> > Breaks out of a wall.
>
> She stands on the other side and does not hear me, does not understand my language. My God! There must be a language which will make a bridge between us. A language of the living which the dead will also hear and understand.

> And then I hear the voice of the syllables like drops of rain which fall on a hot tin roof: ridudi. . . midadi . . . gdudi . . . kitvi . . . metfi . . . dodi . . . litsvi . . . li . . . bemar li . . .
>
> I didn't know how they came to me. And I didn't ask at this time or this hour about their origins. Like a woman beaten by a dry season who comes hesitantly toward the first rain, I collected the drops in a small bowl.
>
> Still I remember the magic sound of the words while they fell. Like the weeping of many violins.[13]

The language of ancient piyyut, erupting like grace from the depths of the collective unconscious, is a bridge to the poet's private as well as public memory; it evokes the sounds of a childhood in Vilna—or elsewhere in Jewish Europe. In another image of access, Kovner claims that the medieval piyyutim came into his poems "like windows . . . cut in a prison wall. Through them comes a small light and through them is reflected, near, yet unattainable, another world, real and imagined."[14]

Hebrew then, is not a neutral instrument, indifferent to Jewish experience, like French or English, in which survivor writers grope for a vocabulary to accommodate biographies that cannot fit the common mold. The Hebrew writer inherits a language infused with forms of Jewish historical memory that both liberate and constrain the poetic imagination.[15] Even when the writer is subverting the tradition from within, through irony or *"Widerruf,"* he is affirming its boundaries as the demarcations of the collective consciousness. A dialectical process of appropriation runs through the lamentation literature from the binding of Isaac on Mt. Moriah through the massacre of Jews in Bialik's Kishinev, to the devastation of Kovner's Vilna.[16]

In this context, Aharon Appelfeld stands out as one survivor writer for whom the Hebrew language seems to provide neither a bridge nor a window onto the past. In the land which was envisioned by prophets, poets and philosophers as a haven for the dislocated soul of Israel, Appelfeld remains, in a fundamental, linguistic sense, an exile. Like his fictional characters, he grew up in an assimilated family ("assimilation was passed on as our inheritance"[17]) which had totally embraced German culture as their own. Their credo was an advanced form of liberal humanism, accompanied by a disdain for the *Ostjuden* for their parochial practices and appearance and anachronistic beliefs. The major theme in his later fiction is not the atrocities of the Nazi years, but the retrieval of childhood: imagination as the only possible vehicle of return to a world that now exists solely in the memory of the survivor and language as the only possible mortar of reconstruction. Yet in Appelfeld's case the inaccessibility of classical layers of symbol and meaning integral to the fabric of childhood render Hebrew a partial or even intractable medium of return.

In two of Appelfeld's recent novels, the return journey takes on variant, even alternative, forms. *The Age of Wonders,* published in Hebrew in 1978, consists of a long novella and a short independent story which also serves as its sequel. Book One is a first-person narrative of the twilight hours of bourgeois German-Jewish culture in Europe on the eve of World War II, related from the perspective of the child but informed by the hindsight of the adult. The story concludes as the Jews of the little Austrian town find themselves crowded into "the cattle train hurtling south."[18] A blank page follows, separating the two stories and signifying what Harold Fisch calls the great "silence"—the unarticulated event that disrupted the normal continuity of biography and subverted the normal literary course of the *bildungsroman*;[19] where the youth should, like Pip or Stephen Dedalus or Wilhelm Meister, have gone out into the world to shape his destiny, he fell instead into the abyss.

The second part, narrated in the third person, takes place over twenty years later, when the protagonist, Bruno, revisits his hometown of Knospen and tries to put together the pieces of the puzzle of his past. Both sections focus essentially on the same period of time but the first part of the novel is an *artistic* reconstruction of the pre-Holocaust world in which the writer exercises his creative prerogative to construct fictions out of the gaps of memory. The story has inner and symbolic logic, a chronology—a beginning, a middle, and an end (in this case an ominous "end" which informs the entire narrative, though it is clearly not perceivable to the actors during the events themselves). The second part, on the other hand, is a *psychological* reconstruction of the past from the limited vantage point of the present. Here, where there is no artistic privilege, memory erupts as fragmentary; psychological barriers to coherent memory, which were overcome through the fiction-making of the writer in the first part, shape the work of retrieval which is necessarily involuntary and incomplete. The same logic prevails in Appelfeld's later novel, *Mikhvat Haor* (Searing Light), which traces a group of liberated refugees in their wanderings along the shores of Italy and in their journey to and arrival in Palestine.

All of Appelfeld's attempts to retrieve "un temps perdu" focus on the struggle between inherited and acquired languages. The first and most fundamental property of which the hapless German-speaking Jews who populate his fiction were dispossessed was their language, their mode of intercourse with the world at large. Appelfeld dramatizes repeatedly how, in the earliest stages of exile, in the crush of deportation to ghettos and train stations, "the words got lost."[20] The language of home was not simply forgotten, having fallen into disuse—it was *denied*. None of the lessons that had been learned were useful in the present struggle. Not algebra or Latin, nor the pride of belonging to the glorious Weimar Republic. German was now the language of National Socialism, of a territory in which the Jew had been disenfranchised. In the first part of *The Age of Wonders*, the father of the protagonist is remembered as having protested in anguish to his detractors in the twilight weeks preceding deportation:

> I am an Austrian writer. German is my native tongue. I have no other language. In German I have composed six novels, six collections of short stories, two books of essays. Haven't I brought honor to Austria? For a moment there was silence. Very nice. So why don't you go to the Jews and write for them? They must need writers. We'll manage with what we've got![21]

There emerges, throughout these two novels, a scarcely-veiled disdain on the part of the adult narrator for the culture of his childhood which had bred such trusting and deluded cosmopolitan Jews; the contempt is focused primarily on the father—a figure that carries over from one novel to another and whose solipsism penetrates every inch of the narrative. Still, although the German Jewish culture prepared the child neither for survival in a hostile world nor for participation in the post-war enterprise of national rebirth in the Jewish homeland, its substance, its beliefs, its prejudices, its language are the child's only inheritance.

The Austrian Jewish writer, Jean Améry, in his book, *At the Mind's Limits,* subtitled "Contemplations by a Survivor on Auschwitz and its Realities," writes that "home is the land of one's childhood and youth. Whoever has lost it remains lost himself. . . ." For those who were exiled from the Third Reich, the loss of home also meant the loss of a "'mother tongue.'"[22] The younger one was at the time of deportation the more far-reaching the ultimate effects of this process seem to have been. The child of eight—Appelfeld himself or nearly any of the characters in his recent fiction—who had barely mastered the rudiments of language, could retain no articulate formulas of experience to protect the integrity of his past. Memories, associations, one's own native tongue, remain trapped forever in that pre-articulate stage of young childhood.

As in *The Age of Wonders*, the war years are obscured in most of Appelfeld's stories by a thick veil of silence, punctuated in the early fiction by oblique tales of persecution and flight that are largely non-referential.[23] This silence regarding the events themselves is not only a form of amnesia as response to trauma,[24] but the muteness of those who have, quite simply, *lost their tongue*.

In the fiction that traces the wanderings of groups of refugees following liberation, the survivors begin to appropriate fragments of speech from one another. And each acquisition, it seems, consigns to oblivion another article from one's own past. "How many years has it been since I saw father's study," muses the narrator of *Mikhvat Haor*; "Even my mother tongue, German, comes out of my mouth corrupted irreparably. I lost it somewhere along those endless roads. Now I speak Yiddish in all the jumbled accents of the refugees."[25] Elsewhere, in an essay, Appelfeld remarks that the "bit of warmth that resided in the few words we had brought from home, evaporated."[26] On the shores of Italy and after the refugees' arrival in Palestine, a few words of Hebrew were learned—as a cover and a camouflage over the negated past.

The new culture facilitated the escape from and denial of one's former identity. Whatever remained of the languages of *Galut* to which the "smell of death"[27] still clung, was baggage to be cast off in order to qualify for the Procrustean bed provided by the Jewish Agency. The image of the helpless, ignominious Jew was exchanged along with one's name and mannerisms, for the proud, swarthy appearance of the self-reliant Israeli. It was fairly easy to pour language into a mind which had been emptied. Rather than providing a vocabulary to rescue private as well as public memory, the language of the Sabra spoken in Appelfeld's house of fiction constitutes an effective shield against any claims the past might still assert. Cliché is the language of enforced consensus that intrudes upon and usurps the remnants of memory which still manage to infiltrate the private domain. Soon after his arrival in Eretz Yisrael, the narrator of *Mikhvat Haor* dozes in the company of a group of refugees who spend their time playing cards and declaring their political and religious allegiances:

> And I close my eyes for a moment and see clearly the small village where my mother and I spent our last vacation. It was a sparse village bisected by a stream. And when it was time to leave, mother packed the suitcases and wept. I, fool that I was, tried to comfort her. But she refused to be comforted and continued to cry. As if her whole world had been destroyed. I can now see her teary face clearly, as if under a magnifying glass.
> "Now we are all in one boat." This sentence penetrated my daydream and awakened me. One of the cardplayers, who was losing, had said it.
> "You are asleep. Who will build the country? We need *halutzim* here and not dreamers."
> "What do you want from the boy?"
> "I want him to be a *ḥalutz*. A fighter."
> There is no meaning to the words. They issue forth by themselves

and do not harm anybody, but they roused me from my sweet daydream. How long has it been since I last saw my mother. Now that she has appeared to me, they have snatched her from me.[28]

It is only later that the narrator learns the pragmatic value of the Hebrew idioms and clichés which he masters slowly. "We spoke a broken babel of tongues, and now to this mix were added a few Hebrew words. He [Dormant (sic), the refugee who has made the quickest adjustment] absorbed the clichés first and made effective use of them. At that time we did not yet realize that they were his fins and that it was with their help that he navigated."[29] In what emerges as a Darwinian process of acculturation, acquired words are like new appendages enabling this transplanted species to adapt to a new environment.

There is, then, a clear dialectical antagonism here between the languages of past and present, between the diminishing store of warm words salvaged from home—like the marks of speech organs from an earlier biological phase—and the foreign clichés grafted on but never fully assimilated, between the privacy of biography and the tyranny of collective existence.[30]

In most of Appelfeld's stories set after the war, the past, the world of childhood, is a fragmented estate which cannot be voluntarily recalled. In S. Y. Agnon's *A Guest for the Night*, which is the great interbellum Hebrew novel of return on which the second part of *The Age of Wonders* is largely patterned, the associational mechanism is primarily sensory: the aroma of "millet boiled in honey"[31] accompanies the narrator in his arrival to and departure from his hometown, and frames the entire narrative. It recalls Proust's "petite madeleine," that cake dipped in tea in the first part of *A la recherche du temps perdu*, which invokes the dormant memories of childhood that the intellect had failed to summon:

> And so it is with our own past. It is a labour in vain to recapture it: all the efforts of our intellect must prove futile. The past is hidden somewhere outside the realm, beyond the reach of intellect, in some material object (in the sensation which that material object will give us) which we do not suspect. And as for that object, it depends on chance whether we come upon it or not before we ourselves must die. . . .
>
> But when from a long-distant past nothing subsists, after the people are dead, after the things are broken and scattered, still, alone, more fragile, but with more vitality, more unsubstantial, more persistent, more faithful, the smell and taste of things remain poised for a long time, like souls, ready to remind us, waiting and hoping for their moment, amid the ruins of all the rest; and bear unfalteringly, in the tiny and almost impalpable drop of their essence, the vast structure of recollection.[32]

For Proust and for Agnon, smell and taste are the essences of the organic material world of the child that can be reaffirmed even at a distance and beyond the normal ravages of time. Yet for Appelfeld to retrieve a past which was lost not in the natural course of time and aging, but wrested brutally from the eight-year-old child, more radical means of recall seem to be needed. The words, as intermediate between body and spirit, remain the primary associative mechanism that can survive the ultimate ruin of the physical world and serve to reconstruct it; it is words that evoke the past, and memory is triggered primarily through verbal rather than non-verbal sensory association.[33] The narrator of *Mikhvat Haor* is confronted by the man who claims to have been his father's literary adversary:

> 'I wrote about 12 long articles and not a few critical essays [reẓenziot] against your father, mostly in German, but some in French' [he tells the boy]. The word 'reẓenziah' evokes in me, like magic, the smells of home. Books, galleys, my father sitting bent over his table, writing. He is engulfed in a screen of cigarette smoke and the aroma of coffee: 'What does the 'reẓenziah' say?' I hear mother's voice.[34]

Sometimes memory is embodied in a name, a name which is no longer legitimate in a world of Yorams and Rinahs. " 'Zossi,' Dormant says (addressing our group), 'wouldn't you like to go to Zossi's and celebrate her birthday?' Strange, this sweet name evoked, like magic, the sweet smells of parquet, of a stove emitting comfortable heat and a window decked with flowers, the enchanted remains of our homes."[35]

The old words, then, are independent entities, they are of the essence of time past; they *are* the past, as palpable as any artifact salvaged from one's childhood—a picture or a scarf—could be. They erupt, unbidden, autonomous, into the business of constructing one's present life out of stone and cliché. Retrieval of childhood will, inevitably, remain partial, incomplete, since the process of remembering is involuntary[36] and since when one succeeds in retrieving one detail, one loses the others. At one point the narrator forgets everything—father, mother, all of the properties and personalities of his childhood home except for Louise (the chambermaid) and her room.

But there *is* another form of narrative in Appelfeld's fiction in which the past becomes more palpably accessible: the stories of actual return—stories such as "Reparations" from Appelfeld's first volume of stories, *Ashan* [Smoke] and "Many Years Later, When Everything Was Over," the second part of *The Age of Wonders*. In these stories, the narrator actually takes the journey back to his hometown and confronts the physical environment and even some of the people with whom he grew up.

In fact, perhaps the most dramatic and tragic epilogue to the story of the struggle for survival in all of Holocaust literature is that moment when the survivor returns to the rubble of his former home; in a representative story of return to post-war Warsaw by Adolf Rudnicki, devastation of place is an objective correlative for the desolation of soul and there is nothing tangible on which to hang a memory.[37] Yet where survivors return to find their homes *intact*—but expropriated by strangers—their cities unscathed by the war but divested of all their Jewish inhabitants, the contrast between the internal state of bereavement and the immutable environment is in a way even more terrible than the vistas of ruin that Warsaw presents.[38]

The sparse realism as a projection of floating selves that characterizes most of Appelfeld's post-Holocaust stories evolved, in the stories of return, and especially in "Many Years Later. . .," into a kind of hyper-realism, a close focus on the physical properties that remained untouched by the earthquake that shook the town and emptied it of its Jews. Its fixation on geometrical patterns and designs, on the positioning of objects in this unchanging world, calls to mind the radical spatial focus of a nouveau roman such as Robbe-Grillet's *La Jalousie*. The riveting of attention on minute detail is a displacement for the emotions which would seem to have been appropriate to such a momentous occasion:

> A week already gone in this familiar exile and nothing done. Most of the day he spends sitting on a bench measuring the shadows of the church spires; realizing again that nothing has changed here, only him—he is already his father's age.
>
> And when he tires of measuring the shadows, he strolls along Hapsburg Avenue, and here too nothing has changed. As if the scenes of his childhood have been embalmed in all their subtlest nuances of light and shade, from the awnings above to the paving stones below. . . . Even the Jewish shops have preserved their outward appearance, like the Lauffers' drapery shop. None of them have survived but their shop is still standing at exactly the same angle as before, perfectly preserved, even the geraniums in their pots.[39]

These operations, which at one level seem to recapitulate the child's-eye view of the world, are in a more basic sense what Frederick Hoffman would call "calculations of existence." Hoffman sees Samuel Beckett's characters as calculating "truths, moral and ontological, in a limited geometrical estimation of their spatial positioning with respect to other objects. Indeed, they are mostly concerned to establish the most elementary facts and lines of existence. . . . they attempt to answer the question, not why do I exist but do I exist at all; that is, is there a recognizable set of spatial and temporal coordinates which, by means of certain calculations, I can use to arrive at the fact of my existing?"[40] In the case of the lone survivor of the Holocaust, the spatial coordinates are not the measure of his present existence, but of all the *absences*. On the platform of the train station, "paving stones lay side by side in the familiar pattern, but they seemed more worn."[41] Worn perhaps by all the shoes of all the Jews deported from the town. Bruno's scrupulous observation, extreme objectivity and concreteness serve to camouflage the unmentioned scenes of violence that divide part I from part II of *The Age of Wonders*.

Between the immutable shadows of the church spires and the shop awnings, Bruno finds no foothold for himself. Except for a mild reception on the part of a group of half-Jewish "mongrels," Bruno has not been welcomed by the few people who still remember his family, and the very awkwardness of his presence confirms how totally the Jews have been eliminated from the vistas of the town. Staring at the "dark green geranium pot, looking as out of place and artificial as ever," Bruno suddenly says, "in any case what difference does it make." Then "words deserted him, as did the fevered excitement. Only weariness remained. It was as if a scaly armor had sprouted on his back."[42] Here we have an image of reversal of the process of natural selection that we saw (in *Mikhvat Haor*) in the acquisition of fins as the survivor species adapted to its new environment. The survivor who dares to return home becomes an anachronism, a prehistoric creature who has outlived his time. Still, this meeting with a lost world has provided at least a physical catalyst to his memory, and his sojourn on native ground—rather than the random associations removed in time and space—has conjured up and sustained images of the past. Here the linguistic environment, rather than being antagonistic, is organic with the memories themselves, and the suppressed words are allowed to surface freely. The speech he hears in the familiar dialect is exhilarating and liberating:

> Words he had not used for years rose to the tip of his tongue and he was glad to have them back again.[Later, Bruno heard two old women speaking and it was] as if the words had filtered toward him through a heavy curtain of water.[43]

Finally, though, it seems that the past which was so unnaturally aborted and which is so discontinuous with his present, cannot be fully recalled or redeemed, and the writer is condemned to begin again and again. At the end of *The Age of Wonders,* Bruno is at the train station waiting to leave Knospen and return to Jerusalem. He recapitulates

Marcel's act of eating the "petite madeleine" in a rather obvious denial of the Proustian model of childhood retrieved through sensory association and infused with meaning through art; ordering a cake and dipping it into his coffee, he realizes that "not a memory remained with him. It was as if they had been devoured and left not a trace behind."[44]

Yet, although the mechanisms of retrieval are different, and art does not seem to constitute a redemptive mode, the parameters of memory in Appelfeld's fiction are ultimately closer to Proust's in being grounded in the private self, rather than in the intertextual codification of collective experience retrieved by the individual that characterizes the language of Agnon or Kovner. The process remains private, personal, a struggle against the currents of the Hebrew language. The writer and his characters remain expatriates, never fully "in-gathered" in the land, never fully at home anywhere again. Bruno will return from Knospen to a Jerusalem without shadows, to a Hebrew without echoes.

SIDRA DEKOVEN EZRAHI
Hebrew University

Notes

1. "Literature and Exile," in Herbert Dieckmann, Harry Levin, Helmut Mutekat, *Essays in Comparative Literature* (St. Louis, 1961) pp. 6, 8.

2. *Tristia,* V. vii, 11.56–60, trans, Arthur Leslie Wheeler (Cambridge, Mass., 1975) p. 239.

3. *Extraterritorial: Papers on Literature and the Language Revolution* (New York, 1971), p. 11.

4. One of the most up-to-date bibliographies of studies of *Exil Literatur* can be found in Egbert Krispyn, *Anti-Nazi Writers in Exile* (Athens, Ga., 1978).

5. "Stefen Zweig's Death," *Stefen Zweig: A Tribute To His Life and Work,* ed. Hanns Arens (London, n.d.), p. 140.

6. It is, still, rather astonishing that after only a few years, most uprooted Jewish writers found their tongue in the language of their adopted home; by contrast, it appears that those Armenians who managed to survive the massacres of 1915 did not for the most part succeed in mastering the languages of the countries in which they settled or in creating a "survivor literature" in languages other than Armenian. See: Leo Hamalian, "The Armenian Genocide and the Literary Imagination," and Vahe Oshagan, "The Impact of the 1915 Turkish Genocide on West-Armenian Letters," papers delivered at the International Conference on the Holocaust and Genocide, Tel Aviv, Summer, 1982.

7. *The Liberation of the Jew,* trans: Judy Hyun (New York, 1966), p. 185.

8. "My heart is in The East and I am at the/edge of the West," wrote Judah Halevi in the 12th century ("Libi bamizraḥ", *The Penguin Book of Hebrew Verse,* trans. & ed. T. Carmi [Harmondsworth, Penguin, 1981], p. 347); "I do

not know the speech/Of this cool land/I cannot keep its pace," wrote Elsa Lasker-Schüler in the early part of this century, long before her own expatriation from Germany. ("Heimweh," Elsa Lasker-Schüler, *Hebrew Ballads and Other Poems*, ed. Audri Durchslag and Jeannette Litman-Demeestere [Philadelphia, 1980], p. 17.)

9. "Translating Celan's Last Poem," *The American Poetry Review (A Special Supplement)*, July/August 1982, p. 22.

10. Quoted in *Ibid.*, p. 23.

11. *Ibid.*, p. 24.

12. "Translating Paul Celan's Du sei wei du," *Prooftexts* III, no. 1 (January 1983) p. 104.

13. *A Canopy in the Desert: Selected Poems by Abba Kovner*, ed. Shirley Kaufman (Pittsburgh, 1973), pp. 214–15.

See also Abraham Sutzkever's poem, "Under the Earth," for a similar affirmation of the power of words over the Yiddish poet (*An Anthology of Modern Poetry*, selected and translated by Ruth Whitman [New York, 1966], p. 127).

14. Kovner, pp. 213–24.

15. When S.Y. Agnon, a native of Galicia who emigrated to Palestine long before the outbreak of World War II, comes, in a short story, "Hasiman" (The Sign—set at the end of the war), to summon the dead of his hometown of Buczacz, he turns in a vision to the master of the medieval *paytanim*, Solomon Ibn Gabirol. The language provides an unmediated discourse between the twentieth-century writer and the eleventh-century poet (in *Ha-esh veha'ezim* [The Fire and the Wood] Jerusalem, 1971). For a discussion of this story, see my "Agnon Before and After," *Prooftexts*, II, no. 1 (January, 1982), pp. 78–94.

16. For a more detailed discussion of the processes of literary adoption and subversion in martyrological literature, see my chapter on "The Legacy of Lamentations," in *By Words Alone: The Holocaust in Literature* (Chicago, 1980); and David G. Roskies, "The Pogrom Poem and the Literature of Destruction," *Notre Dame English Journal*, XI, no. 2 (April, 1979), pp. 89–113.

17. *Masot b'guf rishon* [Essays in the First Person] (Jerusalem, 1979), p. 10. All translations from this book are mine.

18. *The Age of Wonders*, p. 132.

19. "Et lahashot v'et ledabber: al *Tor hapelaot* l'Aharon Appelfeld" [A time to be silent and a time to speak: On Aharon Appelfeld's *The Age of Wonders*], (Hebrew), *Zehut* I (April/May 1981) p. 151.

20. *Masot be'guf rishon*, p. 12.

21. *The Age of Wonders*, p. 8.

22. *At the Mind's Limits: Contemplations by a Survivor on Auschwitz and its Realities* (trans. Sidney Rosenfeld and Stella P. Rosenfeld [Bloomington, Ind., 1980]), pp. 48, 54.

23. These stories appear in such collections as *B'gai haporeh* (Jerusalem, Schocken Books, 1964), and *Adnai hanahar* (Hakibbutz Hameuhad, 1971). Appelfeld's recent, longer, fiction tends to be more realistic and socially engaged than the earlier stories. The latter, as Dan Miron has written, were often shrouded in an impressionistic, metaphoric mist that obscured psychological process and engagement with reality. (See: "Facing the Father: Renewal and Power in the Work of Aharon Appelfeld," [Hebrew], *Yediot Ahronot*, June 2, 1978, Literary Supplement, p. 1.)

24. See, for example, the story "Bertha," in *Hebrew Short Stories*, Vol. II, ed. S.Y. Penueli and A. Ukhmani (Tel Aviv, 1965).

25. *Mikhvat haor*, p. 31. All translations from this novel are mine.
26. *Masot beguf rishon*, p. 36.
27. *Ibid.*, p. 63.
28. *Mikhvat haor*, p. 33.
29. *Ibid.*, p. 98.
30. This was the period of the Yishuv and the young state which, as Gershon Shaked writes, was epitomized in a "code of behavior . . . and a set of values above life and death. This generation [of writers] . . . has no significant affinity . . .to the Jewish past and the Diaspora experience, all these were exchanged for myth . . . The collective novel is a fitting expression for a society whose gaze is directed at the collective and not the individual." ("First Person Plural—Literature of the 1948 Generation," *Jerusalem Quarterly* no. 22 [Winter 1982] pp. 111, 112).
31. *A Guest for the Night*, trans. Misha Louvish (New York, 1968), p. 463. Again, however, it should be stressed that for Agnon, as for Kovner, the realm of memory is not enclosed within the bounds of the self but often extends to encompass collective experience.
32. *Remembrance of Things Past*, trans. C.K. Scott Moncrieff (New York, 1934), Vol. I, pp. 34, 36.
33. There is, of course, a sensory-auditory quality to the verbal mechanism, to memory which is almost invariably triggered by the *spoken* word; nevertheless, the process of recovery and the mode of retrieval focus on the associative content of language as the *primary* medium. The father in both novels is a writer whose identity is embodied in his language, and it is through language that the struggle of the son manifests itself.
34. *Mikhvat haor*, p. 30.
35. *Ibid.*, p. 86.
36. "I am exercising all the powers of memory but I cannot summon up a thing," (*Ibid.*, p. 117).
37. For a discussion of the theme of return in Holocaust literature, see my *By Words Alone*, pp. 89–95.
38. See, for example, the end of Anna Langfus' novel, *The Whole Land Brimstone*, trans. Peter Wiles (New York, 1962).
39. *The Age of Wonders*, p. 166.
40. Frederick Hoffman, *The Mortal No: Death and the Modern Imagination* (Princeton, 1964), pp. 463–64.
41. *The Age of Wonders*, p. 138.
42. *Ibid.*, p. 138. I have altered the English translation somewhat to conform with the original.
43. *Ibid.*, pp. 146, 152.
44. *Ibid.*, p. 204.

The Holocaust in Lithuania and Latvia

Yitzhak Alperovitz (ed.), *Sefer Gorzd* (The Book of Gorzd). Tel Aviv: Gorzd Society in Israel, 1980. 417 pp.

Fruma Gurvitch, *Zikhronot shel rofah: im yehudei lita biyemei shoah* (A Doctor's Memories: With the Jews of Lithuania in the Holocaust). Tel-Aviv: Beit Lohamei Hagettaot and Kibbutz Hameuhad, 1981. 171 pp.

Gertrude Schneider, *Journey into Terror: The Story of the Riga Ghetto.* New York: Ark House, 1979. 229 pp. $12.95

One characteristic of survivors of the East European Holocaust is the drive to perpetuate in book form the memory of those near and dear who were exterminated and of their own communities that were destroyed. This characteristic, very human in itself, is also of very great historiographical importance. These commemorative volumes are often practically the sole source of information on what happened to some of the communities both during, and prior to, the Holocaust.

Books of this type, dealing with individuals (mainly memoirs) or with communities (usually called *yizkor,* memorial books), first came out during World War II itself and have been appearing ever since in a constant stream in different languages and different forms. By now there are thousands of them, and there is as yet no end in sight. Most were published in Israel, many in America and Europe, and some even in Africa and Australia. The peak from the numerical point of view seems to have been reached in the 1950's and sixties, but still more books of this kind are to be expected up to the end of the present century and beyond, as long as here are still Holocaust survivors and their children alive.

Here we shall review three publications that appeared recently which differ in language and form, but all relate to the Baltic Jewish communities, to Lithuania and Latvia.

The first of these publications is a bulky volume on the model of a typical memorial book, devoted to the small Lithuanian village of Gorzd—"its life and its ending." Gorzd—Gargzdai in Lithuanian—was a village in the District of Zamut (Samogitia) near the German frontier. The Jewish community, which had lived there for some four centuries up till the German invasion in June 1941, numbered about eleven hundred souls in its last years. Gorzd is one of only a dozen or so out of the more than two hundred Jewish communities in Lithuania that have been memorialized like this.

The bitter fate of the thousand Jews of Gorzd at the time of the Nazi occupation in mid-1941 is described from the testimony of eyewitnesses and from the official report of the post-war trial of Nazi war criminals in Ulm (Germany). There are details, inter alia, of the desperate resistance of two young Jews at the moment of conquest. Elsewhere, the share of the local non-Jewish inhabitants in the slaughter of the Jews in the village is pointed out. There is a list of twenty-one of the people of Gorzd who were killed in the Kovno Ghetto and in concentration camps, and a list of sixteen other men of the village and their sons who fought in the ranks of the Lithuanian Division of the Red Army and in other units, six of whom were killed in battle.

The rest of the book is the fruit of memories of life in the village and of a number of the principal families there. One way and another, the reader is given a comprehensive and varied picture of the shtetl: the prayerhouses, the educational institutions—secular and religious—the youth movements, the parties and the different political currents, public institutions and leaders, as well as of natives of this place who dispersed to many different countries, some to become persons of importance in the Jewish world, such as Haim Shoys, the poetess Yudika, the rabbi "Reb" Itzele Ponivezher, Dr. Hershel Meyer and others.

Thanks to a few determined enthusiasts with a measure of literary and organizing ability (led by Yehudit Leshem), and thanks to the experienced editor, a valuable addition has been made to the ranks of memorial books.

The next publication in this brief survey is far smaller, more modest and altogether different in its structure. This is the story of a Jewish family in Lithuania from the twenties to the seventies of this century, in the form of the personal memoir of the mother of the family, a pediatrician. She wrote most of the book after she, at the age of seventy, had come to Israel with her three daughters. Her husband was killed in Dachau concentration camp. The stress on personal experience, natural and legitimate in a book of memoirs, does not detract from the work because the author and her three daughters are not untypical of other families that were saved from the Holocaust.

As a schoolgirl the author lived through the Russian Civil War, returning to her native Lithuania in 1921. Her chapter on her medical practice in the village of Mazeikiai (in northwest Lithuania), where she lived until shortly before World War II, is likely to be of interest to readers in the fields of medicine, medical sociology and social welfare. She describes her patients, most of them non-Jewish peasants: their way of life, the treatments usually prescribed, and their attitudes to the doctors. From the Jewish point of view, important details are recorded here about the work of the OZE health association on behalf of the local Jews as well as the refugees from Russia and elsewhere. With the annexation of Lithuania to the USSR in 1940, this association was liquidated by the authorities.

The third chapter, which, together with its appendices, takes up nearly half of the book, is called, "Three years in the (Kovno) Ghetto." She describes the bewilderment and confusion among the Jews of Kovno in the first days of the war and the desperate attempts of many of them to escape eastwards in the wake of the retreating Red Army. In her account of the ensuing pogroms and the orgies of bloodshed inflicted on the helpless Jews, she points to the large part played by the Lithuanian masses, who had a hand in the "spontaneous" deeds of death, as well as in the systematic murder of their Jewish neighbors.

Against this ugly background, she recalls particularly striking, exceptional instances when a handful of Lithuanians summoned up the courage to extend a helping hand to the persecuted Jews. She herself and her three daughters owe their lives to the shelter provided by gentiles.

The fourth and last chapter describes the writer's work as a pediatrician in various institutions in Kovno during the period 1944–69. Like so many memoirs of survivors of the Holocaust in Europe in general and in the Soviet Union in particular, this one too closes with an account of the extraordinary exertions she made to emigrate to Israel and to bring over her three daughters.

Unlike the two works reviewed above, the third publication before us focuses on the Holocaust period alone. Its core is the "German" ghetto in the Latvian city of Riga. The author reached Riga from Vienna together with her parents and her little sister in February 1942, when the Jews from Germany, Austria and Czechoslovakia were deported. Part of the group was liquidated at once in the forests of Rumbuli, at Jungfernhof and other places of slaughter near Riga, while the rest were put into houses left by the original owners: Latvian Jews who had for the most part been killed. This is how the "German" ghetto, which remained in existence for nearly two years, alongside the "Latvian" ghetto of the surviving local Jews, was established. They were all deported later to the Kaiserwald and other camps in Latvia and Germany. However, some eight hundred persons from the "German" ghetto remained alive, among them the author, her mother and sister.

She wrote her book in English many years after the events as a research piece, relying not only on her own memories but also on her historical training, original documentation and other sources. She has also used the testimony of survivors, most of whom, like herself, live in the USA and support a very active association, the Society of Survivors of the Riga Ghetto.

The thirteen chapters of this book briefly and clearly present various aspects of the story of this special ghetto, of which there are perhaps only one or two other examples in the whole of Eastern Europe (Minsk, Lodz). However, apart from the fact that the "German" ghetto in Riga included many families with children, it was not substantially different from the nearby ghetto of Latvian Jews: they were both practically cut off from the outside world; there were similar institutions in both of them, such as internal police and a few services; and the main thing—the population in both was left alive by the Nazi authorities as a practically unpaid labor force serving the war effort.

At the same time the people in the "German" ghetto felt they had a superior status to that of their fellow Jews, the *"Ostjuden"* in the nearby Latvian camp. For their part, the Latvian Jews suspected that if it had not been for the need to house the Jews from Germany, their own wives and children would not have been exterminated at the end of 1941. The Jews from Germany were also accused of being too puffed up, of having boundless trust in the Nazi authorities, of treacherous collaboration.

These and other complaints about the relations between the "German" and "Latvian" ghettos have up to now found their echo mainly in publications drawing their material from the survivors of Latvian Jewry. Now, almost for the first time, we have before us a discussion of these contentions by someone who was herself an inhabitant of the "German" ghetto. Anxious to uncover the truth, she treats the relevant facts cautiously. The relative security felt by the Jews in the "German" ghetto was the result in no small measure, she demonstrates, of systematic indoctrination on the part of the Nazi authorities who assured the inmates that the ghetto had been readied specially for them, because they spoke German and were "different" and far better qualified to contribute to the war effort.

The book confirms what has been published in the past based on Latvian Jewish sources on the aid the local Jews afforded the German Jews when they arrived and on the personal contacts that developed later, mainly between the young men of the Latvian ghetto and young women of the German ghetto. Sabbath Eve *(oneg shabbat)* and other social gatherings permitted almost regular encounters which had a Zionist ideological tone to them. In the ghetto itself the Jews were permitted to lead their lives in accordance with their culture and their tradition and even along lines similar, at least symbolically, to what they had known in their home countries. The streets in the "German" ghetto were officially called Berlinerstrasse and the like. Moreover, in the period of relative calm in early 1942, concerts, plays and other cultural events, given only in German and presenting well-known performers from Vienna or elsewhere in Central Europe, were held almost every Sunday. The Nazi commander of the ghetto and his entourage would visit them accompanied sometimes by their guests.

"Routine" life went on, including parties and flirtations, almost until the liquidation of the ghetto. "Eventually," writes the author in her epilogue to the book,

> after the liquidation of the Riga ghetto, the German Jews were to realize how well the Latvian Jews had understood the diabolical Nazi plan right from the start. In the death camps, they were to see at long last that in the eyes of the non-Jewish world it did not matter whether the Jews had come from the Reich or from some East European country.

The large amount of space devoted to the relationship between the Central Europeans and the local community—with the sword of extermination hanging over the heads of both—endows this book with special significance. It constitutes a real contribution to the historiography of the Holocaust from a hitherto little-known vantage point. The bibliographical and archival apparatus, as well as the rare photographs and the other appendices are of great assistance to the reader.

Dov Levin
Hebrew University

The Nazi Legal System and the Jews in Germany

Joseph Walk (ed.), *Das Sonderrecht für die Juden im NS-Staat, eine Sammlung der gesetzlichen Massnahmen und Richtlinien—Inhalt und Bedeutung.* Unter Mitarbeit von Daniel Cil Brecher, Bracha Freundlich, Yoram Konrad Jacoby, Hans Isaak Weiss. Heidelberg—Karlsruhe: C. F. Muller Juristischer Verlag, 1981, xvii + 452 pp.

In his illuminating analysis of the moral significance of the Eichmann trial (*Yad Vashem* V [1963] pp. 17–29), Nathan Rotenstreich pointed out that F. C. von Savigny, one of the founders of the historical school of jurisprudence at the beginning of the nineteenth century, noted that while the law is to be understood as the product of a people's historical development, that does not exempt the individual from moral and legal responsibility for his acts or way of life; within both historical conditioning and historical causation a person remains morally autonomous.

Indeed the historical school of law contends that historicity does not necessarily lead to relativism of moral values or norms. The comprehension of civilization, including law, as the product of historical conditions does not make the values of that civilization, such as truth, justice and responsibility, devoid of binding authority. Moreover, while morality is conditioned by history, a change of the historical conditions does not necessarily make it obsolete. Hence, the historical school of law stressed that a historical conception is not necessarily a historistic one. According to Savigny, the course of historical development provides the nation with only the material of law *(Stoff des Rechtes)* whereas the criteria for the evaluation of that material are determined by man's cognitive faculties *(Erkenntnis)*. Consequently, the value criteria in the area of morality and law and even on the plane of the state are historical in their origin, juridical in their cognitive nature, and socio-political when in operation. This theory ensures both the binding authority of morality and law, despite their historic character, and their universal validity despite their national origin. It was shared not only by Savigny's teacher and friend, Niebuhr, the editor of *Corpus Scriptorum Historiae Byzantinae,* but also by Eichhorn and by

Wilhelm von Humboldt, one of the eminent humanists who laid the foundations of non-relativist historicity. This spirit also moved some of the founders of the "historical" school of Judaism, especially the brilliant popular philosopher Fabius Mieses and the great scholar and rabbi, Zacharias Frankel.

The historical school of law and the struggle against the relativity of moral values within historicity reached the height of its development during the last quarter of the nineteenth century and first quarter of the twentieth, most notably in the methods of Otto von Gierke, Paul Laband, Georg Jellinek and Ernst Troeltsch. Troeltsch most aptly defined the danger of the relativization of values presented by historical research by emphasizing the dichotomy of history and theology. Thus, historical research uncovers the interests, motivations and functional needs underlying civilization, including justice, law and morality, and thereby may discredit its binding authority. Theology, on the other hand, extricates civilization from the relativity of values by its insistence on the "absolute" (*Die Absolutheit des Christentums und der Religionsgeschichte*, 1902, 1969, 14th edition). Troeltsch hoped in this way to fill the spiritual vacuum in which the generation spanning the turn of the century found itself, and he sought thereby to prevent members of that generation from being drawn to the radical Right, including modern racism and anti-Semitism. And in fact, the course of history, particularly following World War I, reinforced the sway of the concept of *Absolutheit* to which Troeltsch had referred but in a sense opposite to the one he intended.

The National Socialist movement in Germany understood very well the yearning of that generation for *Absolutheit* but, contrary to the cultural Protestantism of the Troeltsch type, it developed an absolute secular political religion. In thus reversing meanings, Nazism also rebelled against the historical school of law and transferred law and justice from the plane of history to that of politics and racism. This process was clearly demonstrated from the viewpoint of both theory and action, including the annihilation of European Jewry, in the work of Hans Frank.

Frank became a member of the Nazi party in the early 1920s, leader of the union of Nazi attorneys in 1926, head of the legal bureau *(Reichsrechtsamt)* of the national headquarters of the Nazi party in 1929; President of the Academy of German Law in 1934; and finally head of the General-gouvernement in Poland. He was thus one of the people chiefly responsible for the Holocaust, its planning, its implementation and its justification. It was his view that the legislation on race and on sterilization represented the most important section of the legal code, and that the purification of the "blood of the people" and the "soil of the people" were the most important duties of the state in maintaining law and order (in his speeches on 20 March 1934 and 29 January 1936). And on 14 January 1936, Frank published in *Deutsches Recht* (vol. 6, p. 10), the guiding principles that expressed the juridical attitude of Nazism from the late 1920s on, and that shaped its legal policy in practice until the end of the Holocaust and the collapse of the Third Reich. Frank's guiding principles (as reprinted in F. A. Six, [ed.], *Dokumente der deutschen Politik.* Berlin, 1942, IV, p. 337) read as follows:

> 1. It is not his [the judge's] . . . task to help apply a legal order that is higher than the racial community, or to enforce some system of universal values. What we must do, rather, is to safeguard the concrete order of the racial community, to exterminate those who undermine it . . .
> 2. . . . The basis for interpreting all legal sources is the National Socialist philosophy, especially as expressed in the party program, and in the utterances of the Führer . . .
> 3. . . . A judge has no right to examine a decision of the Führer which has been issued in the form of a law or decree. . .

Against this background, the book in question has historiographical value of the first rank, in regard both to the history of the Jews in Germany during the Third Reich era and also to the history of German jurisprudence under Nazi rule. Moreover, it involves issues of fundamental significance in the history of law and morality, as noted by Samuel Hugo Bergman in his consideration of the Eichmann Trial (*Yad Vashem* V [1963] p. 9): "In the entire Torah there is no agent for a transgression" (B. T. *Bava Kamma,* p. 79a).*

The volume here reviewed is a rich and illuminating collection of the laws, ordinances, judgments and instructions which determined the legal status of Jews (including non-Jewish "non-Aryans") in the Germany of pre-Nazi borders during the Third Reich. The book covers the subject extremely well, is edited with great expertise, care and precision, and includes laws and orders from the most diverse juridical areas.

Each item is fully identified, and the explanatory information includes the date of issue; the legal authority which issued it (Reichchancellor; Reich Ministry of the Interior, of Justice, of Labor; various provincial agencies such as the Sachsen Ministry of the Interior, or police units at various levels such as *Gestapo Stettin*); and the form of legislation involved (law, command, order, regulation, instruction for

---

*I.e., the individual committing an act of transgression bears full personal responsibility, and cannot plead that he is acting at another's behest.

the implementation of laws and decrees, proclamation, ordinance, circular letter, enactment). The text of the item is given (in part or in full), along with references to its original publication, to other simultaneous or later publications, and to scholarly studies. The editor has also provided helpful additions: he has numbered the items (for easy reference in the index) and supplied each with a caption describing its main point, as well as notes.

The collection is divided according to four main periods: 1) from the Nazi rise to power up to the Nuremberg laws—31 January 1933 to 15 September 1935: 2) from the Nuremberg laws to "Crystal Night"—15 September 1935 to 9 November 1938; 3) from "Crystal Night" to the outbreak of World War II—10 November 1938 to 1 September 1939; 4) from the outbreak of World War II to the annihilation of German Jewry—1 September 1939 to 16 February 1945. The editor has limited the collection of sources to the actual laws and regulations that were publicly announced or secretly passed from authority to authority. He does not provide, nor would the one-volume format allow for, information on the implementation of the laws. And yet, the very evolution of the laws, regulations and decrees in their chronological order reflects successes and failures, planning and improvisation, consistency and internal contradictions, enforcement and non-enforcement. Most of the laws applied to the entire Reich, but much can also be learned from the laws, included in this volume, which were promulgated by the local authorities in various states of Germany, such as Bavaria, Baden, Wurttemberg, Thuringen and Sachsen.

The editor notes that the initiative for a collection of the sort came from the late Dr. Saul Esh, a leading scholar of the Yad Vashem research staff and an early member of the Institute of Contemporary Jewry. And indeed, Dr. Esh's *Studies in Holocaust and Contemporary Jewry* (Jerusalem, 1963) contains material relating to the history of the legal status of the Jews in Nazi Germany, especially in the chapters on "The Background of Nazi Anti-Jewish Legislation, and Its Beginnings" and "Racist Madness—The Background of the Eichmann Trial." The editor notes as well that his collection is a continuation and development of several earlier studies, in particular Bruno Blaw's *Das Ausnahmerecht für die Juden in Deutschland 1933–1945* (Düsseldorf, 1965).

The excellent source collection, *Documents on the Holocaust*, edited by Yitzhak Arad, Yisrael Gutman and Abraham Margaliot (Jerusalem, 1981) was published too late to be referred to by Walk. Another collection of sources unfortunately not referred to is *Documents on Nazism 1919–1945*, introduced and edited by Jeremy Noakes and Geoffrey Pridhaim (New York, 1974). This omission is regrettable since this volume views the Jewish question and its legal aspects against the background of the overall development of Nazism, a perspective which is perhaps a *sine qua non* for an understanding of the special nature of the Jewish question.

The many legal issues cited in the Walk book enhance its great historiographical value, and we shall discuss only a few examples. Particular interest is generated by the legal status of emigration, one of the questions nowadays raised again and again which will certainly require further study. Why was it that more Jews did not leave Germany while it was still possible? Why did some even return in the midthirties? Didn't they know what was happening? Did they know but were unaware of their knowledge? Were they informed and aware, and yet rejected that awareness? Did the Nazi regime purposely obscure its policy of annihilation, or did it actually lack a clear policy and have only the explicit principle that the Jews had no right to exist? Did the Jews not dare to emigrate because they were too attached to their home, their German culture or their property? Did they wish to leave? Was it mainly the well-to-do who were able to leave? What did the Jewish and Zionist leadership do about emigration? Walk's book contributes a great deal to the understanding of the legal framework surrounding these complicated problems, and reinforces Nora Levin's conclusion that the "dilemma of the victim was how to cope with a fitful, inconsistent persecutor who . . . occasionally let his victim slip away . . ." (in her book, *The Holocaust.* [New York, 1975] p. 57).

This collection shows that at various times both the Reich and the individual states issued laws and regulations for the encouragement of emigration, though with gradually increasing strictness. Just a few months after the establishment of the Third Reich, on 8 August 1933, the Reich Ministry for the Economy issued a decree that eased foreign currency restrictions for emigrants to Palestine (p. 48). A later decree, however, of 13 May 1938, placed substantial restrictions on the removal of foreign currency and other kinds of property from the country (p. 225). Then on 25 January 1939 the Ministry of Foreign Affairs issued a declaration favoring the encouragement of Jewish emigration, but not to Palestine, for "under no circumstances is the establishment of a Jewish state to be facilitated" (p. 276). And yet, even at a time so close to the commencement of the Holocaust, on 24 April 1940, the Reich Central Security Department issued a decree in which the Reich government did not prevent emigration to Palestine—even though it tightened the supervision of arrangements and declared "the expansion of the Palestine travel . . . undesirable" (p. 320).

A similar but not identical attitude to Jewish emigration to other countries was displayed by the judicial system. Here, too, various tendencies operated simultaneously: on the one hand, the encouragement of Jewish emigration and, on the other, the attempt to gain financial and economic benefit from both those emigrating and from those remaining. The Jews themselves felt simultaneously the encouragement to emigrate and the increasing difficulty of leaving. In both cases they were subject to Gestapo directions, such as that of 8 February 1938: "Even when no facts are known that indicate earlier activity hostile to the state . . . or punishable deeds, the Jews are in all cases enemies of the state . . ." (p. 215). Nevertheless, the chronological evolution of the juridical status shows a tendency to get rid of the Jews through emigration.

On 18 February 1935, the Reich Ministry of Economics and the Prussian Secretary of Economics and Labor issued a decree providing that "the training of Jews who wish to emigrate should not be impeded, and the admission of Jews in such courses should not be made difficult" (p. 106). In the same spirit, on 13 July 1936 the Reich Ministry of Science, Education and Popular Education issued a decree approving the establishment of vocational schools for training in various trades and agriculture for Jews preparing to leave Germany. The approval was subject to various technical and formal limitations (p. 167f.). Later, on 17 June 1936 and 12 December 1938 (pp. 165, 177, 266), the emigrationist trend was still in force, but at the same time, on 28 September 1938, for instance, apparently due to the preparations for war, restrictions were placed on emigration to neighboring countries (p. 242) which the regime was planning to annex. In 1939, too, the judicial policy of encouraging emigration—through administrative procedures, the issuance of passports, help to the needy, special conditions for young people, an attempt at administrative concentration of emigration matters—was maintained, while in general restrictions became harsher and harsher. On 25 February 1939 the Reich Ministry of the Interior stipulated in an unpublished decree that ". . . all efforts must be made to further promote the emigration of Jews" (p. 284; cf. pp. 276, 278), and on 31 January 1939 an order of the Reich SS leader and Chief of the German Police stated that even administrative detainees who were not classified as criminal or political prisoners were permitted to emigrate (p. 278).

However, the interest of the Reich authorities and perhaps of the local authorities as well to prevent the removal of property, gems, and other precious objects led to a series of decrees that severely diminished the holdings of well-to-do Jews who sought to emigrate. In addition, the unpredictable, inconsistent frequent alterations in government policy placed severe obstacles in the path of wealthier people and the leadership of Jewish organizations in all matters connected with emigration (pp. 225, 285, 288, 291, 313).

A significant change in emigration policy became discernible primarily in the spring of 1940. On 24 April of that year, the Reich Central Security Department decreed that while Jewish emigration out of the Reich was to be increasingly promoted, the emigration of Jews capable of working to European countries and especially enemy countries was forbidden. The emigration of Polish (or formerly Polish) Jews who were in concentration camps and the voluntary evacuation of Jews to the Government-General were likewise prohibited. And on 20 May 1941 the Reich Central Security Department, in a secret decree, stipulated that restrictions should be placed on Jewish emigration "in view of the very imminent final solution of the Jewish question" (p. 341). And finally, on 23 October 1941 the same department, again in a secret provision, decreed that "the emigration of Jews from Germany is absolutely forbidden for the duration of the war" (p. 353; cf. pp. 361, 363), thus closing the circle.

Another crucial subject in the book is the legal status of the Jews in the economic sphere. Here, too, is a long, variegated series—marked by inner contradictions—of laws, regulations, decrees. In 1938 General Keitel said of the regime that the social and economic structure of Nazism was such that all were in a constant state of internal war. And within that tangled web perhaps one of the greatest conflicts was the opposition between a rational economic policy in regard to the Jews based on the effective exploitation of their property, international connections, knowledge, skills, talents and even manpower, on the one hand, and an irrational policy that was based on the political myth of Nazism even at the expense of economic profit, on the other hand. The impact of the latter, so it would seem, grew stronger after 1936 and even more so during the war. The rich documentation in the book indeed supports the conclusion reached by political and economic historians, such as T. W. Mason, that "the fundamental irrationality had in part its origin and found its concrete expression in the specific irrationality of the National Socialist ideology" (in S. J. Woolf [ed.], *The Nature of Fascism*, New York, 1969 p. 194). Indeed, soon after the establishment of the Third Reich, it became necessary to restrain local political forces (with their own economic interests) which were seeking to deprecate Jewish property, enterprises and economic activity (e.g. p. 17). More than once it turned out that the removal of Jews from key positions in commerce or finance, without careful advance planning, and the arbitrary policy of "Aryanization" of the economy were having deleterious effects on the German economy and state.

At times anti-Jewish economic policy was inspired by local factors which did not always accord with the general Reich policy. Thus, for instance, in October 1933 the Reich Ministry for Economics issued a decree cancelling the prohibitions ordered by municipal bodies against buying in Jewish-owned stores or maintaining business relations with Jewish agencies (p. 58). Similarly, a series of decrees were published in the years 1938–41 which sought to prevent the total waste of Jewish manpower, while nonetheless complying with the policy of segregation dictated by Nazi ideology.

Until the end of 1937, Hjalmar Schacht as Minister of Economics may have had a restraining influence, for a measured policy could make use of the Jews as a vital economic and financial factor much more effectively than one of sporadic violence. In the course of 1938, however, and especially after the conference (held on 12 November 1938) of the heads of the Reich economy including Walter Funk, the Economics Minister, and Schwerin von Krosigk, the Finance Minister, the racist policy came to the fore, elevating the Nazi messianic political vision above economic expediency. As Hermann Goering summarized it, the aim was not simply to exploit Jews, their possessions and gifts; but rather, to "implore the competent agencies to take all measures to eliminate the Jews from the German economy" (Noakes & Pridhaim, p. 477). And still on 19 December 1941 the Reich Ministry of Labor could issue a circular letter to the presidents of regional labor offices stating that "Jews in forced labor units are to be protected from Gestapo interference" (p. 360). Raul Hilberg in his monumental study, *The Destruction of the European Jews,* indicates that similar instructions were issued on 4 and 27 March 1942.

From mid-1941 on, this tension between the rational exploitation of Jews as a source of finance and manpower and the total destruction of the Jews as a mythic or even magical object of Nazi politics even extended to the actual Holocaust in Eastern Europe, and thus beyond the scope of Walk's book. A typical example of the continued conflict between rational utilization and the political myth is the secret instruction issued on 18 December 1941 by Otto Brautigam, deputy to Leibrandt of the Ministry for Eastern Occupied Territories, to the Political Division for Occupied *Ostland,* that "economic interests in the regulation of the problem are not to be taken into account on principle." Similarly, a report by Heinrich Seraphim indicated that the solution of the Jewish problem as implemented in the Ukraine was based on ideological theories and not on economic considerations (Hilberg, p. 247).

It may appear out of place to criticize omissions in this book, because it cites so many primary sources and detailed references, and provides so rich, precise and illuminating a picture of Nazi law on the Jews. What is missing, however, is an indication of the context of the texts quoted. This could have been done with a minimum of supplementary information and detail, and without enlarging the volume very much.

The detachment of the laws applying to Jews from those applying to non-Jews makes it difficult to study the peculiar nature of the former and thus perhaps it may diminish the contribution made by this study to the understanding of Nazism and the history of its juridical and moral problems. Naturally, a collection of this kind cannot include complete parallel documentation of the measures applying to non-Jews. However, some reference to basic concepts, albeit selective, is needed to exemplify the nature of Nazi law and judicial philosophy. For the special law for the Jews did not stand alone; its basic concepts were quarried from the rock of the general Nazi culture. Not a single one of these concepts was other than a product of Nazi ideology, a reflection of Nazi semantics, and an expression of practical Nazi policy. Thus, comparative analytic and bibliographical references, even though restricted in scope, seem essential to grasp the historical significance of the subject of this important book. Furthermore, the legal framework for the Jews reflected aspects of the Nazi judicial system in general and of its social and political morality in particular. Thus, the total separation of the history of Jews from that of non-Jews severely impedes the understanding of the subject.

The institutional history of the reciprocal relations between the law on Jews and Nazism, including its judicial, moral and political philosophy, was manifested years before the final solution, for example, in the activity of both the Academy for German Law (founded on 26 June 1933 and headed by Hans Frank) and also of the University Instructors' Group of the National Socialist Jurists' Union after 1934. While the former helped shape the law in practice, the latter developed the cognitive and ideological foundation for the particular law that applied to the Jews.

On 3 and 4 October 1936 a national conference held on the subject of "Jewry in Jurisprudence" was attended by scholars from the Universities of, *inter alia,* Berlin, Göttingen, Freiburg, Marburg, and Munich. One of the main theses in which most of the professors concurred was that the Jews were divested of the status of man and citizen in the Third Reich and that this was significant testimony to the fact that German law had entered a new historical phase. In this new phase the concept of blood became both a legal and moral category and the Führer's will became the expression of the general will, that is, of all those of pure German blood.

In this light, it would have sufficed for the editor to indicate selected examples of basic concepts in the special law for the Jews which would illustrate this historical background. Thus, the notion of "popular instinct" *(Volksempfinden)* was borrowed from anthropology and political ideology and used as a legal term. For example, an interesting regulation of 8 May 1939 (which was not allowed to be published) permitted the continued operation of Jewish or mixed welfare foundations, on condition that the foundation "agreed with the dogmas of the National Socialist state leadership," such as the encouragement of Jewish emigration. On the other hand, the regulation forbade German citizens to establish new foundations which catered to Jews on the grounds that "they contradict the German popular instinct" (p. 293f.). In this case, a reference to even a few sample sources would have shown that this notion aroused great interest and even serious controversy among intellectuals, attorneys and educators during the Nazi era, for "Volksempfinden" was a central concept in National Socialist ideology and policy.

In 1935 the official law register *(R.G.Bl.)* stipulated that "healthy popular instinct" was a legal category and whoever acted contrary to it should be punished. Indeed, even before the Nazis' actual rise to power and in their early years, judicial philosophy as evolved by its best theoreticians, among them Carl Schmitt, developed the notion of racially pure jurisprudence into a school of thought with binding authority. Accordingly, it was decided that the only source for determining the nature of a "healthy popular instinct" was the Führer. The same view guided the thought and actions of Roland Freisler, State Secretary in the Reich Ministry of Justice, President of the People's Court, and one of the participants in the Wannsee Conference of 20 January 1942. Other jurists, too, writing in the official journal *Deutsche Justiz,* asserted that the value criteria for justice and injustice had to be derived from the "healthy popular instinct" *(gesundes Volksempfinden)* as expressed in the *völkisch* law and order. The source of authority for this folk way of life was the general will as defined, dictated and carried out by the Führer.

Just as the context of such key concepts should have been indicated, certainly there should have been an indication of the context of the double notion of *Sonderrecht*—the special or exceptional law upon which the entire book rests. The notion of *sonder* in the context under discussion developed through the misconstrual and reversal of the original meaning of paragraph 48 in the constitution of the Weimar Republic. That provision, which was already problematical under Weimar, empowered the Reich president to suspend temporarily the fundamental rights established in various articles of the constitution: freedom of the individual; freedom of residence; secrecy in public communication facilities; freedom of expression; freedom of assembly; freedom of organization; the security of personal property.

Through a radical perversion of the original meaning of paragraph 48, the Third Reich produced a series of judicial notions around the term *sonder,* so that years ago Walther Hofer had already noted that "exceptional legal status is a typical feature of the National Socialist states." Applied to the Jews the term became a key concept, as was noted by Joseph Wulf in *Sonderbehandlung und verwandte Worte in national-sozialistischen Dokumenten* (Gütersloh, 1963). Thus, the concept the whole book revolves around, *sonder,* and its meaning for Jewish history cannot be understood without reference to its general semantic and legal roots; while its significance for German and universal history is illuminated in the light of the special status of the Jews. Here, too, Hofer aptly indicated this contextual interdependence when he noted that "special courts that are not felt to be bound by any positive law . . . became the pure embodiment of the Führer's judicial authority." Those courts acquired a broader historical significance because to them was assigned the treatment of the Jewish population.

A contextual view is needed as well for *Recht,* the second concept in the title of the book. This word embodies the essence of the book, for *Recht* means basically law, justice, right, and in many phrases has added connotations. Thanks to its semantic richness, the historic significance of the term has acquired vast importance. What are the criteria for determining whether a legal decree is just or unjust; whether a law is legitimate or illegitimate, in the sense of *Recht* and *Gerechtigheit;* whether a law is or is not lawful; whether an established ethical code can be immoral?

As already noted, Walk's book could not be expected to treat these problems in their entirety, but it should have made the reader aware of this rich and variegated context.

This critical note, the main import of which is methodological and historiographical, cannot detract from the great esteem that will be accorded the book by anyone desiring to study the history of the Jews in Germany under the Third Reich, the history of anti-Semitism, Nazism and even the history of Germany and Central Europe in the twentieth century. Thus, what we have here is an excellent study and a scholarly contribution of the first rank, and it is to be hoped that Hebrew and English translations will appear in the near future.

URIEL TAL
Tel-Aviv University

Short Reviews

Shmuel Almog, *Ziyonut vehistoriah* (Zionism and History) Jerusalem: J. L. Magnes Press, The Hebrew University, 1982.

Shmuel Almog's *Zionism and History* is a valuable addition to the growing body of literature dealing with the intellectual and ideological roots of the Jewish national movement. The book is a study of the ways in which different groups and individuals within the Zionist movement viewed the Jewish past in relation to the Jewish future. Based on the author's doctoral dissertation, the book grew out of a wish to answer the perennial question: Does Zionism constitute a break or a continuity in Jewish history? That wish (as the author predictably admits) was frustrated, but the examination of how the early Zionists viewed Jewish history proved to be fruitful nonetheless. For their varying attitudes towards the past provided important clues for understanding their positions on the burning issues of the present.

The "present" for Almog is the ten-year period between the publication of Herzl's *The Jewish State* in 1896 and the Helsingfors Conference of the Russian Zionist movement in 1906. Three important debates raged within the Zionist movement during that time: the debate over "cultural work," intended to modernize Jewish culture; the debate over "present-day work" *(Gegenwartsarbeit),* designed to improve the economic and political situation of the Jews while still in the Diaspora; and most important of all, the debate over the Uganda project.

The different positions adopted by the participants in these debates reflected, in one way or another, their feelings on the crucial issue of the relationship between Zionism and what the author calls *"yahadut."* The latter is a broad and rather vague concept (which can be rendered in English in at least two ways—Judaism and Jewry), and Almog does not seem to be sensitive enough to its haziness. Thus he does not always make explicit the sense in which he uses the term in any given context. Broadly speaking, a thinker's attitude towards *"yahadut"* can be seen as involving his or her opinion on four distinct issues: the pre-Exilic past and its relevance for the Jewish renaissance; the social and psychological traits of contemporary Diaspora Jews; contemporary Jewish culture, whether religious or secular; and the place *erez yisrael* should occupy in the project of Jewish renewal.

Almog's analysis of the various combinations of views held on these issues by "representative" (rather than "brilliant or profound") Zionist thinkers is cogent and thought-provoking. He points out, for example, that the concern to restore Jewish honor and redeem the Jews from their present contemptible state—a concern inherited from the Haskalah and common to all streams within Zionism, with the possible exception of the Mizrachi—involved an acceptance of the Jewish stereotypes promoted by anti-Semites. This is an important issue for Almog, since he believes (inaccurately, I would argue) that the restoration of Jewish honor, rather than the rescue of the Jews from persecution, was the *primary* concern of Zionism, at least in the period before its crystallization into a coherent political movement. The pre-Exilic past was used in that context, Almog argues, to portray an "honorable" Jewish existence, as an antithesis to the miserable present, and as a model for its transformation.

Another use of the pre-Exilic past was to legitimize the aims of the Zionist movement itself. All national movements use the myth of the glorious past, whether real or imaginary, as a keystone in their ideologies. In contrast to most of them, however, the Zionist movement had to use that myth for reinforcing its claim that a Jewish nation actually existed at all. The idea of Jewish nationality, Almog points out, was disputed at the time not only by non-Jews, but by two important elements within the body of Jewry as well—the emancipated Jews of the West and the Orthodox Jews of the East. Both groups considered Judaism primarily a religion and, each for its own reasons, objected to it being redefined in strictly national terms.

I am unable to discuss here some of the other facets of the debates analyzed by Almog, which were conducted both within the Zionist movement and also between it and other groups within the Jewish world. One point that should be mentioned, however, is the author's keen sense of paradox, manifested in his discussion, for example, of the positions taken by the Mizrachi and by Eliezer Ben-Yehuda on the Uganda question (both were in favor of Uganda); by Ahad Ha'am on the question of "present-day work" (he opposed it); and by the "political" Zionists on assimilation (while they counteracted it in practice, they still argued that one of the merits of Zionism was that its success would facilitate the assimilation of those Jews who would remain in the Diaspora). Overall, *Zionism and History* is an interesting and important study which does a great deal to enrich and enliven our view of the Zionist movement in its formative years.

YOAV PELED
Hebrew University

Mordecai Altshuler, *Hayevsekziah bivrit hamo'azot, 1918–1930: bein leumiut vekomunizm*. (The Evsektsiia in the Soviet Union, 1918–1930: Between Nationalism and Communism) Tel Aviv: Sifriat Poalim, 1981.

Mordecai Altshuler's research on the Evsektsiia (the Jewish Sections of the CPSU) from its inception up to its abolition in 1930 represents a painstaking scholarly effort to rescue a significant episode in Russian Jewish history from the grip of the ideological and political controversy that has agitated the Jewish public ever since 1918, through the 1930s and 1940s when the Soviet Jewish establishment was in the process of liquidation, right up to and beyond the openly anti-Jewish twilight of the Stalinist regime. It is hardly surprising that the administrative and ideological assault by the Soviet regime on the Jewish communal structure—creative, rich in values, the intellectual, political and organizational mainstay of world Jewry—should be a sensitive and emotion-laden topic. It is no wonder that those who have written in the past on this development were in general not inclined to examine the many manifestations of Jewish loyalty and devotion that were expressed within the confines of the Evsektsiia and its activities. Moreover, this disinclination characterized both ideological extremes—on the one hand, the opponents of the Evsektsiia who bitterly condemned the regime and, on the other, those who admired it to the point of losing virtually all their critical faculties.

The confrontation between Zionism and anti-Zionism, between assimilationism and an embattled Jewish nationalism, cannot leave the historian completely untouched. Awareness of this problem undoubtedly dictated Altshuler's exceedingly cautious approach, his methodological precision. The difficulty is compounded by the almost total lack of archival sources and by the necessity to rely on Soviet printed material.

There are two important lessons that in my judgment Altshuler wishes to impress on his readers. First, even though the rule of the Evsektsiia represented a profound break in the history of the Jews in Russia, it nonetheless retained elements of continuity and revealed the power exerted by the Jewish heritage. What happened to the Jews in Soviet Russia in the 1920s was not just one unbroken sequence of liquidation, alienation and destruction but also a stubborn effort to establish, develop and advance a secular Jewish national way of life. That is to say, the ideological battle which the Evsektsiia saw itself bound to wage was not assimilatory in principle or intent, although that was its effect.

The Evsektsiia did in fact strike at consecrated values of the Jewish heritage and even worked deliberately to undermine traditional structures, but at the same time with stubborn determination went to great pains to try and reconstruct Jewish life on a secular, but nonetheless national and even territorial, basis. Moreover, and perhaps even paradoxically, the more the Evsektsiia stuck to these aims, the more its Party and ideological obligations dictated ever harsher measures against traditional Jewry and against the Zionist movements. This caused it to be much hated, and in the last analysis finally and irrevocably cut off from the very public that constituted its only potential reservoir of at least limited support.

The second main point Altshuler makes is that the Soviet leadership could not rely on abstract principles when it had to cope with real conditions in Soviet society as a whole and the Jewish sector in particular. Theory had to be laid aside and "theoretical" legitimization had to be improvised which would permit the governmental and economic machinery to function and keep the wheels of society turning. For all its determination to overthrow the *ancien régime,* the Soviet revolution had no choice but to make certain concessions to the old order. Thus, despite the theories of Lenin and Stalin on the nationalities question, which explicitly excluded the Jews from nationality status, when it came to implementation of policy, the Soviet state had to come to terms with the parameters of Jewish reality. Denial of this reality could only obstruct the fulfillment of the regime's practical and political priorities among the Jewish population, and lead Soviet policy dangerously close to the anti-Semitic measures of the Tsars.

The deep-rooted aspiration of the Jews for a regime of "personal autonomy," however, dovetailed with the strong desire of the territorial minorities to preserve some degree of self-rule. For, after all, an autonomy for the Jews based on Yiddish would act as a barrier to their russification in the border republics and would thus indirectly bolster the status of the predominant nationalities (the Ukrainians and White Russians) relative to the cultural and numerical weight of the Russians. Thus it would run counter to the Russian nationalist aspiration, inherited almost intact by the Soviet regime, to swallow up the minorities. In sum, to recognize fully the national interests of the territorial minority peoples would have meant to legitimize Jewish nationalism. And by the same token to work (whether openly or surreptitiously) against the national interests of the territorial minority peoples called first and foremost for the annihilation of Jewish nationalism, which because of its unique ("extra-territorial") status was bound to inspire other "deviational" national demands. The fourth chapter in Altshuler's book which deals with the Evsektsiia at its peak, and especially the sub-section on the interrelationship between the Evsektsiia and the policies of "Ukrainization" and "Belorussization," make an outstanding contribution to our understanding of the confrontation between the opposing trends within the Soviet establishment.

The Evsektsiia relied increasingly on the plan for the large-scale settlement of Jews on the land, which was often seen as preliminary to their territorialization. It was also of course a product of the belief that there was no future for Bundist (i.e. Austro-Marxist) solutions to the Jewish problem and that an attempt had therefore to be made to carry through territorial solutions. But here too the Evsektsiia in the twenties was not on solid Party ground, the more so as this issue was not in its sole province. The higher echelons in the government and Party (the Central Committee) grappled with the Jewish question in all its aspects.

In this connection, I do not share Altshuler's opinion that one should accept as given the explanation regarding the term "Temporary," appended to the title of the Commissariat for Jewish National Affairs (p. 23)—an adjective not appended to other nationality commissariats. The reason given was that the team which founded the Commissariat saw its appointment as temporary and valid only until a more representative forum convened to set up an official Commissariat. If there were any truth in this explanation, it should also have applied to the other nationality commissariats, which were established in the same, usurpatory way. The Commissariat for Jewish National Affairs was called "temporary," in fact, as a compromise between the traditional Bolshevik position, which was fundamentally opposed to "Jewish national affairs," and the realistic policy that sought solid ground underfoot.

A lengthier consideration might have been given to the Jewish autonomous institutions established in the Ukraine from mid-1917. The Jewish community in the Ukraine was, at the time, the largest unit within the Soviet Jewish population. Altshuler himself is very much aware of the parallel between the Soviet organizational framework for the nationalities and the forms of national organization that preceded the Revolution (see his remarks on the Moslem Commissariat, p. 20).

In this context, too, I do not think that one should try to belittle the importance of Kalinin's speech to the OZET Congress in 1926. Altshuler states (p. 20) that Kalinin "appeared unexpectedly at the Congress and his speech, which contained many contradictions, was not prepared beforehand but given *extempore* and should therefore not be regarded as a programmatic announcement." This contention does not bear critical scrutiny, in my view, because if the speech had been the improvised, uncontrolled outburst of a single individual, it could not conceivably have been printed in the pages of *Der emes* and republished in the official reports. There is no sign of censorship in the speech as published. It is clear to me that Kalinin simply came with the deliberate intention of saying what he had to say; the form of the speech was not spontaneous in the main, and his opponents were not yet sufficiently powerful to demand that the speech be suppressed.

Despite these points, Altshuler's book fully elucidates the two contradictory trends in the top Soviet leadership (and not only in 1926): the one gave its backing to the territorialization of the Jews in southern Russia, while the other was determined to stamp out this scheme directly—or indirectly (by relocating it in Birobidzhan). The latter school was concentrated in Stalin's entourage, which was adept at the manipulation of opinion within the Party. Thus the attempt by Esther Frumkin to resist this trend by theoretical argument represented a significant effort by the Evsektsiia to win "ideological" legitimization for territorialism as a solution to the cultural and national problems of the Jewish people.

Altshuler's work is not just a learned account of yet another chapter in Jewish history; nor is it an essay in archivism, bombarding us with detail and yet more detail. It is an achievement for Jewish historiography in Israel, which has until now lacked such an account of a critical episode in the life of Soviet Jewry.

MATITYAHU MINTZ
Tel-Aviv University

Robert Attal and Yosef Tobi, *Yehudei hamizraḥ uẓefon afrikah: bibliografiah mu'eret, 5734–5736* (Oriental and North African Jewry: An Annotated Bibliography, 1974–1976). Jerusalem: Ben-Zvi Institute, 1980. 95 pp. (467 entries). Offprint from *Sefunot* n.s. I (-Vol. 16).

At first sight this bibliography seems intended as a supplement to Attal's *Les Juifs d'Afrique du Nord,* published by the Ben-Zvi Institute in 1973. To some extent this is so in practice but not in theory. In the earlier work the selection criteria are less clear, the geographic scope is limited to the Maghreb, and the arrangement is inconvenient: author lists under country, with subject indexing of varying adequacy. The new bibliography is classified by subject categories under region and country, with author indexes. Selection this time is generally limited to research, both books and articles, with some popular material of wider interest included. The geographic scope now takes in the entire non-Ashkenazic Jewish Dispersion—the word "Oriental" in the title evidently means the Near *and* Far East, taking in such groups as the now defunct community of native Chinese Jews. It was decided to include the Karaites and to give them a special section because of their geographic dispersion. Western-language articles and books—mostly in English and French—are listed, but all the generously provided annotations are in Hebrew.

If this bibliography realizes its ambition to become an annual survey, it will be a welcome addition to existing Judaica bibliographies in spite of its partially duplicating the Jewish National and University Library's *Index of Articles on Jewish Studies*. The authors would be well advised to adopt the latter's practice of providing a subject index at least for personal and geographic names.

A. A. GREENBAUM
Haifa University

Shlomo Avineri, *The Making of Modern Zionism: the Intellectual Origins of the Jewish State*. New York: Basic Books, 1981. x + 287 pp. $15.50.
Arthur Hertzberg, *Being Jewish in America: The Modern Experience*. New York: Schocken, 1979. xx + 287 pp. $7.95

Arthur Hertzberg's book is a collection of essays about the situation of American Jewry; but since it is written from a Zionist angle of vision, it is broadly concerned with Jewish history and above all with the historic functions and current problems of the state of Israel. Avineri's volume of essays on seventeen Zionist and pre-Zionist thinkers focuses on the origins of the Jewish state; but the past and future condition of world Jewry, the context out of which Zionism arose, is a constant point of reference in this discussion.

This convergence is reinforced by the parallel personal backgrounds of these two authors, and serves to highlight the points of divergence between them. Both are scholars, political activists, and practicing intellectuals, all at once. As teachers, they seek to be detached; as politicians, pragmatic and flexible, while involved; and as intellectuals, both involved and principled, independent. The Zionist issues to which these books are devoted are the very arena in which all these qualities are most immediately called forth.

Avineri began work on his book when he returned to full-time teaching in 1977 upon resigning from the director-generalship of the Israeli Foreign Ministry. It is based on the lecture series on Zionist intellectual history that he began at the Hebrew University and presumably continued at La Jolla as a visiting professor at the University of California; and Hertzberg's well-known anthology, *The Zionist Idea,* frequently cited by Avineri in his new book, could well have been the major text assigned for the readings in primary sources in such a course. At the same time, the new book allows Avineri to define his own individual Zionist position, which he does particularly in relatively full reconsiderations of such figures as Jabotinsky and Ben-Gurion, Ahad Ha'am and Rabbi Kook.

In Hertzberg's case the collected essays primarily document his record as an independent Jewish intellectual. But they also clearly reflect his continuing activity as a practicing American rabbi, a scholar and professor of history, and a semi-detached member of the "Jewish establishment"—having served as president of the American Jewish Congress as well as a "non-party" member of the Executive of the American Section of the Jewish Agency. Thus, included in the collection are proposals which he drew up in anticipation of the Twenty-eighth World Zionist Congress as well as studies of the American rabbinate, and more strictly ideological essays.

Compared to Hertzberg, Avineri has a more well-defined political and party orientation in Zionism, though he, too, typically functions as a free-floating intellectual. His stance is both Israel-centered and Labor-oriented, and this is reflected in the reconstruction of Zionist history implied in these essays. Anyone who specializes in intellectual history is likely to impose the logic of ideas on his subject; and if Avineri is continually hearing echoes of Hegel wherever he turns, it is not surprising in one whose Hegelian studies are known internationally. The basic Zionist idea, according to Avineri, is the decision, or resolve, to *take action* in order to end the Jewish Exile; and its basic method is to reconstruct the whole social-economic as well as political structure of Jewish life, as conducted in the Diaspora in a way appropriate to independence.

In consequence, he tends to leave out of the history of Zionist ideas those figures who were active in the movement, but belonged to a different tradition of ideas; and he includes in its history others who foreshadowed some of its ideas before the movement arose. Thus, even though the Zionist movement arose as a shaky coalition between certain modernizing elements within traditional Jewry, committed to something other than the Zionism Avineri projects, and the young, rebellious secularists who first became its authentic bearers; and even though traditional Jews supplied the movement with most of its membership for many of its early years, and conducted a not unsuccessful fight to impose their demands on others—Avineri does not include Orthodox Zionists in the intellectual history of the movement, until he reaches the highly exceptional figure of Rabbi Kook.

One may cavil at other implications of Avineri's historical approach, but some perceptions are both penetrating and important. He traces the rise of Labor hegemony to the fact that the workers were personally committed to the tasks which formed the core of the World Zionist strategy in Mandatory Palestine (and, of course, the polity of Israel arose from the political structure of the WZO and of the Va'ad Leumi). He is also on the mark in his excellent comments on the role of Israel in defining the identity and shaping the self-image of Diaspora Jews; and he is correct in noting that Israel performs this function best in presenting an ideal in sharp contrast to the life of Diaspora Jewry. But he is overly optimistic in assuming that a *single* (Labor Zionist) ideal of Israel could perfectly suit the Diaspora—or that a Jewry unwilling to see itself in Exile can be actively inspired by any Zionist vision, no matter what its political content.

Hertzberg's essays are more directly related to value preferences than Avineri's historical sketches, since the former are reflections on current topics. But there are some underlying assumptions here, too, that are implied, rather than explicitly stated. Hertzberg knows himself to be the scion of an elitist Jewish tradition—that of the rabbinical aristocracy of *sheyne yidn*—even though he is required to function in a milieu dominated by the children of *proste yidn,* the "plutodemocracy" of American Jewry. His repeated studies of the American rabbinate are rooted in this awareness; and it is behind his interest in class as a factor in Zionist history. He, like Avineri, has a lively awareness of the cardinal role played by Israel in the self-awareness of American Jewry and on several occasions he has expressed this by noting that imputed hostility to Israel would constitute the only grounds on which an American Jew might be excommunicated by his community today.

In a way rather unusual among American Zionists, Hertzberg shares the view of Avineri and most Israelis that the rejection of Exile is the cardinal element of Zionism—so that the beginning of Zionism is seen as a rebellion against the condition of Diaspora Jewry and the quietist tradition that sustains it. But unlike Avineri, Hertzberg is committed to a community and its situation rather than to an ideal principle; and in the community of Zionists he recognizes all those who have accepted that name in spite of the logical complications which this allegiance involves. He thus has to leave room within the camp for the large contingent of Zionists whose concern is to perpetuate or revitalize, rather than overturn, the traditions by which Diaspora Jewry has survived. His description of the history of Zionist thought includes both the rebellious "neo-Messianists" and the defensive "survivalists;" and his implicit plea is for a flexibility that will tolerate both in the same ideological community.

At the same time, there is ample evidence of Hertzberg's sensitivity to the strains involved. His awareness of the price of Exile and the compromises entailed in the style of Diaspora life is sharply expressed. But however strongly drawn he is by the appeal of a purist, revolutionary solution to the Jewish problem, his commitment to the whole community overbears it. And since the current balance of values in world Jewry, in its scattered parts, precludes a radical Zionist solution to the problem through an imminent "in-gathering," Hertzberg has concluded that we (still) live in a time of "waiting"—and must resort to a "defensive" Zionism.

BEN HALPERN
Brandeis University

Yehuda Bauer. *American Jewry and the Holocaust: The American Jewish Joint Distribution Committee, 1939–1945.* Detroit: Wayne State University Press, 1981. 504 pp. $25.00.

The Joint Distribution Committee has been by far the most formidable of the American organizations engaged in the relief and rescue of beleaguered Jews overseas. Differing from other defense agencies in its emphasis on helping other Diaspora communities, the JDC has seemed to embody the spirit of Jewish internationalism. That sense of *klal yisrael* may also be why the coerced confessions during the purge trials that swept Eastern Europe three decades ago falsely implicated the "Joint." Its impact has probably made it the most studied of American Jewish organizations, the subject of previous books by Herbert Agar and Oscar Handlin. In *My Brother's Keeper* (1974), Yehuda Bauer brought the story of the JDC to the eve of the Holocaust; this volume is its sequel. It is a gripping and disconsolate work.

The title of *American Jewry and the Holocaust* is somewhat misleading, however. The JDC raised and spent $73 million between 1939 and 1945, and the food and other aid it provided was very often a matter of life and death. But the JDC did not represent American Jewry itself, and its organizational imperatives sometimes clashed with, say, the World Jewish Congress. No voice of American Jewry had an exclusive claim to authenticity. Nor does Bauer focus on the American matrix itself; indeed the scope of his book is amazingly comprehensive. Wherever the Nazis persecuted the Jews, wherever the refugees fled, the author follows them—from the Pyrenees to Lithuania to Transnistria, from Santo Domingo to Shanghai and even to Kobe, Japan. Global in its range, drawing upon primary and secondary sources in six languages, *American Jewry and the Holocaust* is both more and less than its title implies. But its density of detail, synthetic power and moral thoughtfulness are commensurate with the drama of an organization that Bauer describes as "a symbol of Jewish unity and Jewish compassion" (p. 457).

Relying primarily on the JDC archives in New York, he has located among its emissaries some authentic heroes, no villains and mostly communal leaders of varied abilities and frailties who were overwhelmed by the unprecedented terror that engulfed European Jewry. While sympathetic, Bauer's account lacks the consolations of romance; nor does it reveal much disturbing complicity among the local agencies under German rule which the JDC assisted. Above all this book is blessed with a sense of proportion, for the intensity of the Nazi desire to murder the Jewish people almost invariably outstripped the capacity of that people and its pitifully few friends to avert that design. A small and defenseless minority lacked weapons and political independence, and the organization's leadership in New York accepted the assumption of the Roosevelt administration that a quick military victory over the Axis was the only way to save the Jews. Even when the U.S. created the War Refugee Board early in 1944, its funding came almost entirely from the JDC itself, as though underscoring the disparity of resources between the killers of the Jewish people and its friends.

Much of the failure, Bauer notes, was cognitive: not even the Jews themselves could grasp the full dimensions of a policy of genocide or could understand the Judeocentrism of the Nazi mind. Hitler attacked the Soviet Union largely to strike at the sources of "Jewish power", and Himmler was later willing to spare some camp inmates as a peace gesture to a Western Alliance he believed was ruled by Jews. Tragically short of funds, JDC volunteers like the legendary Saly Mayer of Switzerland permitted his trapped co-religionists to cling to the hope that a wealthy and influential American Jewry would not allow the catastrophe to continue. One of the unsparing themes of Bauer's book is its demonstration of how illusory the idea of Jewish power actually was.

American Jewry and the Holocaust is institutional history at its best, for the story of the JDC is connected to the larger history of the Diaspora during its most terrible ordeal. Personalities are not ignored; and the tangled relationships between the JDC and local Jewish agencies and movements are sorted out, even though the American background itself is rather sketchily treated. This impressively erudite account adds to our knowledge of how poorly the Jews fared by appealing to the consciences of Allied and neutral powers and by bribing their racist tormentors. Without polemical stridency, Bauer arranges the historical facts so that they add up to a terrible indictment of brutality, which the civilized intelligence must somehow strengthen itself to confront.

STEPHEN J. WHITFIELD
Brandeis University

R. Bilski, I. Galnoor, D. Inbar, Y. Manor, G. Shefer (eds.), *Can Planning Replace Politics? The Israeli Experience*. The Hague: Martinus Nijhoff, 1980.

This volume, the product of the Research Team of the Jerusalem Group for National Planning, consists of five theoretical studies on planning and four case studies of national planning in Israel. Discussing the experiences of planning in water utilization; in the public health services; urban and regional government; and in the mobilization of capital, the authors conclude that in spite of various factors in Israel favorable to the concept, such as a favorable ideology and central government intervention in the economy and society, there exists in fact no system of national planning in the country. They rather identify a system of "partial planning" in which plans are consistent with the parochial goals of sub-units in the system and are designed essentially to solve operational rather than fundamental problems. The political confrontations inherent in comprehensive planning are thus largely avoided. According to the authors, there has been no real conflict between the autonomy of such partial planning and the centralizing attempts to coordinate planning because the government has not been ready to pay the political costs involved.

Galnoor's case study on water planning stands out in the insights it provides on the dynamics of planning in Israel. Galnoor differentiates between two sets of problems faced by policymakers in the field. The first is to manage available water resources and provide "access" for potential users. The second is to cope with an overall shortage of water in the system. In 1964, with the completion of the National Water Carrier, Israel's water planning machinery, designed to cope with the first problem, had begun to face a severe problem of shortage and the fascinating question asked by the author is how it adapted to the new conditions. Galnoor's study reveals that water planning from 1965 on had continued to be oriented mainly toward solving the problem of accessibility: the construction of regional schemes and the utilization of the existing potential.

No long-term or basic organizational reforms were introduced and instead of new policies to cope with the problem of shortage, the ambitious and unfeasible Desalination Plan was designed in an attempt to hold on to the "accessibility orientation." The large scale desalination plan, writes Galnoor, would serve as a kind of new "National Carrier" and it attracted the planners precisely because it required no drastic changes in the composition and management of the system. The uncritical assumption that the previous normative objectives had retained their validity acted to inhibit any reexamination of goals, and planners were effectively prevented from presenting the policymakers with the normative repercussions of the solutions they had adopted.

This brings up the question expressed in the title of the book. To what extent can the planner overcome constraints imposed by political ideology, structure and entrenched behavior and be more effective in the determination of societal objectives? What levers will allow him to intervene in the formulation and reformulation of normative assumptions and what role should he play in the societal dialogue over ways and means? Unfortunately, the theoretical studies in this volume do not point the way towards an answer. This is so not only because the questions are never spelled out beyond the simplistic title, but because of an inbuilt "fear of politics" haunting this volume and preventing serious analysis of the interaction between planning and politics.

Although defined in the preface as the interaction between ongoing political transactions and "the more abstract processes of policy formulation" (p. 2), "planning" is seen repeatedly in this book as an abstract, technical, apolitical process which impinges on politics as a disturbance rather than as a constraint. This is nicely expressed by Manor to whom national planning "is not in the least natural; it strives to replace certain rules of the game with others" (p. 40). Thus, planning, the establishment of priorities in society, is not conceived as a dimension of political life but as external to it. Lip service is paid to planning as a "social process" (p. 11), but it is hardly considered part of the process of societal regulation; planning remains a distinct sphere conceptualized as "preregulation, that is to say, as predispositions, actions, preceding effective steering and guidance of effective regulation" (p. 52).

Even when authors such as Bilski and Galnoor aim at shifting attention away from the document—the plan—to the political arena, the actual process is described in terms whereby "intentions are translated into action in a more or less systematic way" (p. 81). Political conflict, the condition with which every plan must cope in reality, is placed beyond the scope of planning; and it is defined as a condition where sectors in public administration seek to attain objectives "outside their legitimate spheres" (p. 14).

This volume is representative of an academic tradition which approaches planning without true consideration of its political setting. It considers pluralist political behavior a hindrance to "the needs of the national system" (p. 329) and partial planning as disfunctional by definition. This tradition, flourishing in Israeli academia, has made an important contribution by taking up the cause of comprehensive planning in Israel. It is time, however, to go beyond such advocacy and search for the ways to integrate notions of planning with the real, empirical constraints of the highly politicized society it is intended to serve.

MICHAEL KEREN
Tel-Aviv University

Max P. Birnbaum, *Staat und Synagoge 1918–1938; Eine Geschichte des Preussischen Landesverbandes jüdischer Gemeinden. (Schriftenreihe wissenschaftlicher Abhandlungen des Leo Baeck Instituts)*. Tübingen, Mohr 1981. xii + 298 pp.

The pluralistic character of German Jewry in the last generation before its destruction was expressed not only in a wide range of opinions and modes of life but also in the multiplicity of associations and institutions, all of them acting side by side, without any central coordination. The present work by Max Birnbaum discusses the problem of this array of organizations, and constitutes the first comprehensive research on the subject. Most publications about the Jews of Germany deal with their cultural achievements; with the problem of their integration into the surrounding society; with their political activity; or with anti-Semitism and their ways of reacting to it. The volume before us, a superlative piece of research based on thorough examination of many sources, therefore fills a historiographical gap. It distinguishes between the period of the Weimar Republic, which takes up two-thirds of the volume, and the period of the Third Reich, in the years 1933 to 1939, during which the various Jewish organizations tried to centralize their planning and in great measure increased or altered the range of their tasks.

The book concentrates on two subjects: one—the founding and activities of the Preussischer Landesverband jüdischer Gemeinden—PLV (Prussian Association of Jewish Communities) which functioned from 1922 to 1938, comprising some three-quarters of the entire Jewish population in Germany; and the other—the question of the establishment of an overall organization of German Jews.

The efforts to set up a nationwide association of all the Jewish communities, efforts which had begun as early as the mid-nineteenth century, intensified with the creation of the Weimar Republic. Its constitution of 1919 seemed to offer the legal basis for such an association to gain for Jewish congregations a status under public law similar to that of the Christian churches. The chief initiative came from Ismar Freund, a rabbi and a senior official of the Jewish community in Berlin, an outstanding and complex personality well delineated in this book. Freund's plan for the establishment of a comprehensive Jewish organization was accepted at the Assembly *(Gemeindetag)* of the Deutsch-Israelitischer Gemeindebund (The German-Jewish Union of Communities) in January 1921. Its realization, however, was postponed over and over again due to opposition from within and without.

Birnbaum does not belong to the school, whose adherents have become more numerous of late, which decries the importance of the differences of opinion and the schisms in German Jewry, and seeks to depict its life as harmonious. It emerges from what he has to say that the efforts to bring about organizational unity actually heightened factional and personal animosities. The book deals fully with the complex internal Jewish relationships, including the problem of relations between the Zionist camp, the "liberal" assimilationist sector, and the separatist Orthodoxy, all fiercely involved in their controversies. Jewish leaders in southern Germany, who had their own regional associations, feared that in a nationwide framework they would become a permanent minority and therefore advocated a mere "roof" organization with limited powers.

There was also outside opposition—from the Prussian ministries and from the Reich government. Birnbaum systematically examines the policies of these authorities which exploited the antagonism among the different Jewish groups in order to prevent the creation of a nationwide Jewish organization with a legal status equal to that of the churches. When it became clear that the authorities had no intention of changing their methods, Ismar Freund initiated a different plan, and with unmatched alacrity and speed, brought about the foundation of the Preussischer Landesverband jüdischer Gemeinden on 25 June 1922—one day after the murder of Walter Rathenau, the German minister of foreign affairs.

Birnbaum combines the history of this organization with a discussion of the problems of the wider Jewish public and the political and economic development of the Prussian state. The reader is thus provided with a broad view of the Jewish predicament in Germany.

From Birnbaum's research it emerges that as long as the reins of power in Prussia remained in the hands of the so-called Weimar Coalition (Socialists, Democrats and Catholic Centre), the PLV enjoyed equal rights with the churches at least in principle if not in extent. This involved, for example, state budget allocations for Jewish religious education and for the salaries of rabbis in needy communities. As the influence of the right-wing forces increased in the ruling establishment, the attitude of the officials in the ministries of Education and Religion and of Finance hardened, reverting to the pre-Republican pattern.

The author describes the fierce debates between the liberals and the Zionists which characterized most of the annual conferences of the PLV. These assemblies of some one hundred and thirty deputies were elected in the first strictly democratic elections of comparable size ever to have taken place in the Jewish world. Thus, they were truly representative, and the published records of the discussions in this "Jewish parliament" offer a rich source for the historian.

There were not only parliamentary fights and dissensions however, but also numerous instances of fruitful co-operative endeavors which prepared the ground for later measures of self-help under Nazi rule. Constant co-operation was already established, in fact, at the time of the economic crisis from 1929 to 1932, in the activities of the Wirtschaftsausschuss (Economic Commission). Here the anti-Zionist Bruno Woyda worked side by side with Max Kreutzberger and Adler-Rudel of Poalei-Zion. As against this, the PLV did not concern itself with the large political problems governing the fate of the Jewish population, and failed to formulate any policy in reaction to the growth of the National-Socialist Party.

Not until January 1932, when a serious political and economic crisis already gripped the country, was the Reichsvertretung der Jüdischen Landesverbaende Deutschlands (the National Board of Representatives of the Jewish State Associations in Germany) established, in order to confront the dangerous increase in anti-Semitic incidents, and act as official spokesman for German Jewry. Surprisingly enough, this body was not convened for a whole year to discuss the critical situation and to frame a plan of action. The author puts the blame for this failure mainly on the weakness of Leo Wolff, the organization's chairman. It would be of interest to carry out some complementary research into the degree of vigilance and awareness displayed by other persons and organizations and how they responded to the growing threat of Nazism in the final years of the Weimar Republic. Were they really any more alive to what was happening than Leo Wolff?

The change came in 1933. The shock of Hitler's appointment as Chancellor of the Reich spurred the Jews of Germany to close ranks, and set up central institutions for the entire community. The author's account of this matter is clearer and more convincing than the accepted version given in the historical literature. He gives the credit for taking the initiative firstly to the "young guard" in the Zionist and non-Zionist camp (men like Ludwig Tietz, Wilfried Israel and Georg Lubinski [Giora Lotan]); secondly to a group of senior officials and jurists, who were forced out of government and into service in Jewish institutions; and thirdly to the Jewish aid societies and associations in the USA and Britain, which kept close track of what was happening in the Third Reich. All three groups joined forces to create the Central Committee for Aid and Reconstruction and—in the fall of 1933—to replace the "old" organization run by Leo Wolff by the "new" Reichsvertretung der deutschen Juden (The National Board of Representatives of German Jews), headed by Leo Baeck and Otto Hirsch. Involved here was not a political volte-face nor the uninterrupted continuation of existing organizations but a combination of the old and the new. A central authority was created that acted without break for the next five years, maintaining the unity of its diverse components despite certain strains and controversies. The Reichsvertretung acted as a voluntary body, and could work by means of persuasion, because its authority was greatly strengthened by the financial backing of the international Jewish aid organizations (the Joint, HIAS, ICA, the Central British Fund).

The author stresses that the central institutions set up in 1933—the Reichsvertretung and the "Central Committee"—overshadowed the PLV and took over part of its functions. But the problems of the hour presented new challenges, and from then on the PLV had to devote considerable effort to easing the isolation of small communities and to alleviating the spiritual and economic distress of their members. Hundreds of small communities had to be reorganized in wider administrative units that received religious and social services from the regional teacher and rabbi. With the creation of the "National Union of the Jews in Germany" (Reichsvereinigung der Juden in Deutschland) by order of the authorities in July 1939, the PLV was swallowed up together with all the other Jewish bodies.

This excellent work by Birnbaum is based on a wealth of archival documentation and on the press of the period, on his experience as a senior official in the PLV service and on his personal acquaintance with most of the Jewish activists. Writing a chapter of history when one has taken part oneself in what happened is rightly considered a problematic undertaking that raises the question of the writer's impartiality. However, the volume before us proves that in this case the author has succeeded in producing a scholarly piece of research. The book is marked by the same virtues that characterized Birnbaum's earlier publications—his extraordinarily wide knowledge of Jewish life in Germany, the statistical basis of his findings in the social and demographic sphere, and his clear and exact language. Special importance attaches to the eighty-three biographical notes in the book, which contain a rich mine of information. There is also an index of names, a bibliography, and an appendix on sources relevant to the legal and political aspects of the Jewish communal life in Prussia.

ABRAHAM MARGALIOT
Hebrew University

John W. Boyer, *Political Radicalism in Late Imperial Vienna. Origins of the Christian Social Movement 1848–1897.* Chicago: University of Chicago Press, 1981. 577 pp. $35.00

The resurgence of interest in fin-de-siècle Vienna during recent years has been very much connected with the belief that it was one of the cradles of twentieth-century modernism. A number of scholars, Professor Carl Schorske foremost among them, have also argued that the retreat from liberal culture and politics took a particularly sharp form in Vienna, expressing itself in such diverse phenomena as the birth of psychoanalysis, Austro-Marxism, Zionism, anti-Semitic mass movements and the kind of aesthetic innovations associated with Klimt, Schoenberg, Kokoschka and the Vienna Secession; not to speak of the critique of language pioneered by Karl Kraus and Ludwig Wittgenstein.

What has been conspicuously lacking, however, in such fascinating attempts to show the interplay between politics and culture, has been a solid examination of the Viennese social background and the more mundane processes at work in shaping the anti-liberal movement that triumphed in the Habsburg capital at the end of the nineteenth century. The book under review, the work of a young American social historian, is especially welcome as a pioneering contribution to our understanding of the Christian social movement under Karl Lueger and its emergence as a major political force in Vienna. It is at one and the same time a model exercise in urban, and political history, in exposing the social class bases of ideological polarization, and in tracing the dialectical interaction between liberalism and anti-liberal politics in the half-century following the abortive 1848 revolution in Austria.

In contrast to the Schorske school of cultural history, Boyer stresses the continuities in the *Bürger* political culture and social structure of 19th century Vienna as well as the elements of radical change. He is primarily concerned with that middle section of Viennese society, the *Bürgertum,* which for all its diversity and subtle internal class distinctions, remained remarkably faithful to traditional, pre-industrial values and indifferent to new ideas, whether in politics or the arts. This social class came to reject the liberal order and a liberal outlook, not so much in favor of a "post-rational politics" (as the current fashion would have it) as out of a desire to restore its fragmented unity and its traditional ideals, threatened by modernization. One of Boyer's main theses, indeed, is the contention that the Christian-Socials, in spite of their manipulation of political clericalism and anti-Semitism, did not repudiate the liberal *Rechtstaat;* though attacking liberal political pieties they borrowed a great deal, on the technical and organizational level, from their antagonists and like them sought essentially to represent bourgeois social interests.

While not denying the clerical input, especially the role of the lower clergy in mobilizing cadres into the Christian Social Party and the importance of the Church as a legitimizing cultural factor, Boyer argues against exaggerating the Catholic nature of the movement; similarly, though he stresses the effectiveness of anti-Semitism as a political lever, particularly for the economically depressed Viennese artisans, the author rejects any attempt to see Christian Socialism as purely and simply an anti-Semitic movement. Nor, he argues, can it properly be viewed as a proto-fascist outburst of irrationalism, a harbinger of the twentieth-century politics of the Radical Right, even if Karl Lueger was one of Adolf Hitler's political mentors. The roots of Christian Socialism as a movement of bourgeois social protest lie much more in the desire of the Austro-Viennese *Bürgertum* to enhance its endangered material security and social status by gaining control of privileged political resources.

Boyer skilfully demonstrates how Lueger and his Party managed to transform and adapt an old pre-1848 political language to a new social class situation; to blend cultural traditionalism with a desire for change, notable with mass politics, *Vormärz* conservatism with modern techniques of political mobilization. Lueger, in this account, was less the paradigm for Nazi-style, *déclassé* desperadoes rousing atomized masses, than he was a patrimonial, patriarchal and quintessentially Habsburg political leader in the Baroque mode, seeking to stabilize and reunite bourgeois society around interest-politics and the defense of its privileges.

Boyer's book, which takes the story up to 1897, the year of Lueger's capture of Vienna, is illuminating not only on the social composition of the Christian Social Party and the cultural roots of its ideology (there are good sections on Vogelsang, Scheicher, Schindler and Austrian Catholicism) but also on the history of Austro-Viennese liberalism. With a frequent side-glance at parallel developments in Germany (the study is indebted to a number of recent works on German social history), he reveals many of the historical factors that explain the weakness and timidity of Central European liberalism and the absence of a strong left bourgeois democratic tradition in Austria. Into this vacuum it was easier for a third force, secular, anti-liberal yet no less bourgeois than its adversaries, to emerge—especially in view of the unique curial system developed in Vienna.

Perhaps the one unsatisfactory aspect of this remarkably documented and well-organized piece of research, full as it is of insights into Viennese social history, lies in the author's treatment of the difficult subject of anti-Semitism. Much of what Boyer has to say about the economic base of the antipathy to Jews in certain Viennese social strata is certainly correct and there is no attempt to disguise how this hostility was exploited demagogically to bring about the demise of Austro-liberalism. Indeed, the author plausibly argues, Christian Social anti-Semitism provided the legitimating principle and political answer to liberal anti-clericalism, and thus became the integrating ideology which made possible the unification of previously fragmented strata within the Austrian *Bürgertum*.

His quasi-sociological explanation does not, however, account for the extraordinary receptivity of such widely different strata of the Austrian population to anti-Semitic rhetoric, its particular resonance in fin-de-siècle Vienna as a political slogan, and the deeper historical roots of the phenomenon in Austria. Boyer is right to insist that Christian Socialism was more than just a Jew-baiting party, yet the flavor and the violence of this component in its rise to power is somehow missing from his book. Unlike nationalism, anti-Semitism was the very stuff of political radicalism in the late nineteenth-century Viennese politics so exhaustively analyzed by the author—even if Karl Lueger later dismissed it as the sport of the rabble necessary for winning power but useless as a constructive program. Economic explanations of its appeal, while certainly central to any understanding of the phenomenon, do not tell the whole story. This is one of the few lacunae in an otherwise most illuminating and superbly researched example of the new school of urban history.

ROBERT S. WISTRICH
Hebrew University

Randolph L. Braham, *The Politics of Genocide, The Holocaust in Hungary*. New York: Columbia University Press, 1981. 2 vols., 1269 pp. $90.00

Nathaniel Katzburg, *Hungary and the Jews: Policy and Legislation 1920–1943*. Ramat-Gan, Israel: Bar-Ilan University Press, 1981. 299 pp.

Extra Hungariam non est vita, et si est vita, non est ita, (outside Hungary nothing exists, or if anything exists, it is inferior). This slogan encapsulated the world-outlook of the Magyar gentry, its haughtiness, arrogance, and snobbery. It epitomized, in a comparable degree, also the world-outlook, haughtiness, arrogance, and snobbery of many Hungarian Jews. While the close attachment of German Jewry to its fatherland is well known and often discussed, less attention has been paid to the parallel trends in the Kingdom of Hungary.

Magyars, latecomers to the ethnic composition of Europe, felt themselves isolated within the continental family of nations. In particular, the sea of Slav humanity to the north and south was the source of deep anxiety among the Magyars. Hungarian nationalism was defensive in nature; it was a nationalism fired by fear of national eclipse. Therefore, any addition to the national body politic was welcomed—be it even the Jew. As long as a Jew defined himself as a Magyar of Mosaic persuasion—and he was mostly ready to do so—even a convinced anti-Semite would reconsider his stand. The Jews appreciated the Magyar hospitality. In fact, Hungary witnessed the emergence of a sui generis type of Jew, marked off by both manners and *Weltanschauung*. His nationalism was "more Catholic than the Pope" and he gladly served as a vanguard of Magyarization among other ethnic groups. Slovak anti-Semitic nationalists before World War I dubbed the Danubian kingdom *Júdaország* (instead of *Magyarország*), and its capital *Judapest*. The Slovak abuse had its roots in socio-political realities.

The Jewish delusion terminated in 1918. Once the Trianon Peace Treaty squeezed the lands of St. Stephan's Crown into a fraction of the pre-war area, making Hungary almost monolithic ethnically, the Magyars no longer had cause to fear for their internal dominance and no longer needed their Jewish compatriots. Instead, Magyar nationalists—including the higher nobility—started to cherish racial purity. Now the Hungarian elite felt free to vent its deep-seated contempt for, and scorn of, Jews. The onslaught was led not by the broad masses, however much they were inculcated with hatred, but by the gentry, the nobility and the clergy. These were almost the same elements which in the past had opened the doors of Magyar life to the Jews. Naturally, the competing bourgeoisie happily lent its hand. Yet many a Jew failed to comprehend the change. Katzburg and Braham both document well the blindness of Magyar Jewry.

Given such a background, one may easily understand the modus operandi of Jewish leadership during the war. In its servility, docility, cowardice and smoke-screening it surpassed the behavior of Jewish Councils elsewhere in Eastern Europe. Perhaps the particular mentality outlined above goes at least some way to explain the extent and rapid success of the "Final Solution" in Hungary. It is enough to note the high proportion of Jewish refugees from Slovakia and Poland in the Hehalutz underground in Hungary.

Another outstanding feature of the tragedy was the refusal of the Western Allies to help the Jews being decimated in Hungary. The Hungarian Holocaust took place in 1944, when neither the aims nor the methods of the Nazis were a secret anymore. Nevertheless, Jewish lamentation fell on deaf ears. It seems that the Allies deemed it less costly to sacrifice the Jews than to try to save them. Unfortunately, in his long list of those culpable by omission, Braham does not include the United States Army and Air Force, which together with the British generals searched for reasons why not to bomb the railroads leading to Auschwitz (and the camp itself). The officers took refuge in an earlier decision of the US Deputy Chief of Staff, reached in concurrence with the British military, which read as follows: "We must constantly bear in mind however that the most effective relief which can be given to victims of enemy persecution is to insure the speedy defeat of the Axis."[1] Accordingly, American and British armed forces were willing neither to bomb the railroad centers nor to deploy parachute troops to impede the deportation of Jews to Poland.[2]

However, Braham does devote space to another side of the coin: the conduct of the Hungarian gentile population, including the depravity and extremism of the gendarmerie, which carried through the Jewish expulsion. The gendarmes are worthy of particular exploration; after all, this professional police equaled and occasionally surpassed the SS in the brutality of their conduct. Perhaps they, too, would provide us with another cue to the Magyar enigma. Ever since this force was created in Austria-Hungary, the gendarmes were trained to mistreat their victims, be they political or criminal. The very mention of their nick-name (the "cock-feathered") was enough to make a Romanian, a Slovak, or a Croatian patriot tremble. Now they brutalized Jews as they had the other minorities in the past. Furthermore, in Hungary, as elsewhere throughout Europe, the radical Right had found fertile ground within the security forces.

Braham has designed his study as a chronicle of the entire Jewish-Hungarian drama. Subsequent students may still reinterpret particular topics; they will not have much new information to add. Katzburg has chosen to work within narrower limits, but even so he has hardly exhausted his topic: a review of anti-Jewish legislation in the inter-war period. We would like to learn more about the laws relating to the Jews in the outlying areas of the state. His pages on the Jews of Carpathian Rus' demonstrate that central institutions left the door open for local authorities to act on their own initiative and to introduce variations on general themes. The Jewish response to persecutions in that region likewise followed its own pattern. Again, one wonders why Katzburg neglected to inspect German documentation. True, he has made good use of hitherto untapped sources in British and American archives; but these sources are of relatively less importance than the German materials.

The books under review relieve the urgency of the need for general studies of the Holocaust in Hungary. The emphasis in the scholarly agenda can now shift away from over-all description to the elaboration of detail, and this is the unquestionable achievement of these two books.

YESHAYAHU JELINEK
Ben-Gurion University of the Negev

Notes

1. See US National Archives, Washington, D.C., OPD 334.8, War Refugee Board, 28 January 1944.
2. See USNA, OPD 383.7, Memo for record, 23 June 1944. Cf. OPD 383.7, Proposed Air Action to Impede Deportation of Hungarian and Slovak Jews, 23 June 1944.

Arthur A. Cohen, *The Tremendum: A Theological Interpretation of the Holocaust*. New York: Crossroad, 1981. xvii + 110 pp. $9.95

Günther Ginzel (ed.), *Auschwitz als Herausforderung für Juden und Christen*. Heidelberg: Lambert Schneider, 1980. 671 pp.

A. Roy Eckardt with Alice Eckardt, *Long Night's Journey into Day*. Detroit: Wayne State University Press, 1982. 206 pp. $16.50

The Tremendum asserts that the Holocaust is a radical caesura in Jewish history (and, consequently, also for Jewish theology) and poses as the fundamental task of thought to produce—if such a thing is possible—a "bridge across the abyss." Clear and indeed pioneering in general conception, the slim volume is, however, unclear and faltering in execution. Thus, the author rightly seeks new linguistic depths (p. 37) but all too often finds mere obscurity. Thus, too, he confronts an abyss barring the way to thought—the horror of Auschwitz "exceeds the category of horror" (p. 31)—yet, in the attempt to bridge the abyss, incongruously resorts to writings that lie on the other side, e.g. those of Schelling, Rosenzweig and the Kabbalah. Such unclarity reflects less on the work of the author than on the extreme and indeed unprecedented difficulty of his task. The Holocaust "paralyzes the metaphysical capacity" (T. Adorno). It surely paralyzes the theological as well. The question thus is: is there a third alternative for thought, other than paralysis or, as against this, the denial of reality?

That the Holocaust is a caesura for Christian thought also is the chief, though often hidden, subject of *Auschwitz als Herausforderung*. One contributor writes that "whether an anti-Semitism that in the last analysis denies Jews the right to exist may not be rooted in the Christian tradition itself is a question that is not yet asked seriously by German theology and the German church" (p. 553 ff.). Others demonstrate some of the consequences that follow if the question is not asked. Thus in 1948 a German church council wrote that "it is a sign of

God's patience that His judgment pursues Israel in her rejection to this day," and that the "silent sermon of the Jewish fate is that God is not mocked" (p. 541). Worse still, in 1963 a German Lutheran theologian wrote that mission to the Jews was "the only possibility of a genuine and meaningful *Wiedergutmachung* on the part of German Christendom" (p. 566). Rarely in history have there been such samples of *odium theologicum*—or so eloquent a proof of Bonhoeffer's admission that, after Nazism, Christian missionizing of Jews must come to an end. On this fundamental thesis the Christian contributors to this volume are all agreed; and since these include such well-known fighters for Jewish-Christian understanding as W.P. Eckert, F. Heer, R. Rendtorff and the editor, the volume may be said to be a substantial contribution to Jewish-Christian dialogue.

Nevertheless, to judge by this book, the Jewish-Christian conference on which it was based must have had its limitations. This, moreover, is only to be expected. In dialogue with each other, Jews and Christians do not seek the same thing. Christians primarily seek theological legitimation. Jews seek, and after Auschwitz must seek, primarily safety for their children. For this reason virtually every Jewish contributor stressed the importance of a Jewish state—its existence, prosperity and, above all, its safety. Yet their message to this effect fell largely on deaf Christian ears.

That this reflects on their theology but not on their humanity comes to light in what must have been the most moving moment of the whole conference. Y. Amir reported how as a post-war Israeli *ulpan* teacher he had received many survivors as language students, and had wondered how he could celebrate Hannukah with them. At length he had told them that now, at last, they were where they were wanted, loved, at home, and that, after what had occurred, this was perhaps a miracle. This account shook the delegates so deeply that they were unable to conduct a theological discussion—a fact the more remarkable because most of them were young Germans born after 1945.

Is there hope, then, that Christian theology might rise to the challenge of Christian humanity? Hope comes from the outstanding contribution of J.B. Metz. Heeding his own warning against Christian "excuse mechanisms," Metz suggests that Jews in history may have suffered the fate intended by the New Testament for Christians; that after Auschwitz God is accessible to Christians, if at all, only together with Jews; and that any theology which supposedly is equally valid before and after Auschwitz is worthless (pp. 196, 183, 193, 175 ff.).

These are radical programmatic assertions. That it is possible to abide by them is shown by no Christian theologian's work more powerfully than by that of A. Roy Eckardt. For a whole lifetime, Eckardt has struggled singlemindedly for a theology of the "older" (Jewish) brother, in which every trace of Christian supersessionism over Judaism—in his view the deepest source of anti-Semitism—is overcome. Assisted by his wife Alice (an able theologian in her own right), he has not flinched from his task even though in the "long night" of Auschwitz it must have been so excruciatingly painful that a resort to "excuse mechanisms" would have been understandable. And the reward in this book is that any Jew can find in it a "brother," i.e. one who accepts and loves him by his own self-understanding, with all theological ifs and buts left behind.

It is not for a Jew to say whether *Long Night's Journey into Day* provides a post-Holocaust theology adequate for Christians. (The crucial thesis is that "No past event, however holy or divine, can ever redeem the terror of the present. Only a future event can do this" p. 150.) What a Jew can say, however, is by no means insignificant: this book gives unique grounds for some hope that, after a night far too long, the older and the younger brother may, because of all and despite all, be reconciled.

EMIL FACKENHEIM
Hebrew University

Gary B. Cohen, *The Politics of Ethnic Survival: Germans in Prague, 1861–1914*. Princeton, N.J.: Princeton University Press, 1981. xvii, 344 pp. $36.00.

For several years now Gary B. Cohen has been engaged in an effort to introduce quantitative precision and analytical rigor to the study of Prague German society. In a 1977 article published in *Central European History,* he took issue with the impressionistic accounts of Jewish life in Prague by such contemporaries as Felix Weltsch and Max Brod. Their oft-quoted remarks, he argued, that Jews felt excluded not only from the Czech majority in the city but also from German society as well, could not stand up to scrutiny. Jews comprised a crucial element in German public life throughout the second half of the nineteenth century and the first decade of the twentieth. They suffered relatively little in the way of social discrimination at the hands of a German establishment which remained steadfast in its commitment to liberalism. By any formal measure, the Jewish community as a whole displayed no great dissatisfaction with (and certainly no disloyalty toward) the Prague German community.

With *The Politics of Ethnic Survival,* Cohen offers a full-length study of the social composition and political mobilization of the German community. Based on detailed use of organization archives, police reports, communal records, and census data, the work stands out as a major contribution to the social history of multi-ethnic Central Europe. In it Cohen not only elaborates on the theme of German-Jewish social interaction and cooperation, but offers a cohesive account of the process by which Prague Germans organized and delineated their social life and defended their collective interests. He highlights the tightly-knit associational network which emerged in the public sphere in the 1860's and 1870's—at the head of which stood the venerable German Casino—analyzes its social composition, traces its political affiliations, and examines its effectiveness in defending the social and cultural interests of a dwindling elite.

The overall picture that emerges is one of longstanding commitment to the ideals of European liberalism and religious tolerance, an effective alliance of German and Jewish middle class interests even in the face of growing political and ethnic radicalism at the turn of the century. In the end, Cohen's book serves to remind us that despite the increased vociferousness of nationalist politics, despite the emerging Czech-Jewish movement, the infant Prague Zionist groupings, and the anti-Semitic pan-German phenomenon, Jews and non-Jews effectively combined forces in promoting German culture and politics. The fact that as many as 47 percent of the "German" residents of Prague's inner city as late as 1900 were Jews is basic and irrefutable. For the Prague Germans, ethnic defense required that public life in all its forms be open to Jews of the upper and middle classes. Theirs was a marriage of interest and necessity which breathed life into political liberalism long after it had expired elsewhere on the European continent.

I have two substantive criticisms of the book. The first concerns the author's theoretical approach to the question of ethnicity. Cohen argues that an ethnic group cannot be said to have emerged until it has developed organized social relations in the public sphere and self-consciously promotes its particular social and cultural interests. Consequently, he denies the existence of unreflective ethnic feeling among the Prague Germans before the 1860's and belittles the significance of informal or subjective expressions of ethnic attachment. Accordingly, the Prague Germans "essentially created an identity *de novo* after 1848" as an "upper-strata" minority facing social, economic, and political challenges from a Czech-speaking, lower-middle and working class population. This approach is based in large part on Michael Hecter's work on the "political economy" of ethnic affiliations. It is overly determined by economic factors and tends to confuse the phenomenon of ethnicity on the one hand and ethnic—or cultural—nationalism on the other. One remains unconvinced that there was no Czech or German "ethnicity" in Bohemia before 1848 simply because the German Casino had not yet been organized or because specific programs for national advancement had not yet been articulated.

My second criticism concerns the book's handling of the Jews of Prague. This is not a study of Jewish society or even of Jewish group feeling, and, hence, what Cohen has to say about Jews is expressed in the context of German or Czech public life. Jews are seen as constituting a "swing population" which in theory could lend its weight as a religious minority to either of the two contending nationalities, but in practice, because of long-standing cultural propensities and recent historical conditioning, tended to identify solidly with the Prague Germans. The author's "working definition" of ethnicity invariably leads to a general submersion of Jewish distinctiveness. He refuses to speak of Jewish ethnicity in Prague before 1900 because only with the advent of organized Zionism in Prague did Jews begin to agitate for the official recognition of the Jewish nationality in the monarchy. Likewise, he views with suspicion any suggestion that Jews sought to distance themselves from an exclusive identification with Austro-German liberalism since public indications of Jewish support for the Czech national movement toward the end of the nineteenth century were contradicted by other formal indicators, such as school attendance.

Cohen's insistence on the use of quantifiable indicators of national allegiance necessarily creates a limited and static picture of social and cultural life in Prague. He conveys a good sense of the public manifestations of everyday social values but few indications of the critical situations out of which change was likely to emerge. And we know that considerable cultural reorientation and adjustment did take place, after all; witness the remarkable vitality of three very different cultural enterprises during the short life of the Czechoslovak Republic: Czech-Jewish assimilation, the Jewish national movement, and the flowering of Prague German literature.

Given Cohen's methodological approach, one is puzzled by the fact that he did not choose to consider Jewish public life and voluntary associations as vehicles for the promotion of group identity and interests parallel to the German Casino or the *Matice česká*. Is one to assume that in an age of increasing secularization and religious indifference the network of communal institutions constituted purely religious entities? What of the *Centralverein zur Pflege jüdischer Angelegenheiten,* founded in 1885, in which the fathers of Robert

Weltsch, Max Brod, Willy Haas, and Franz Kafka were all active? Or the various B'nai B'rith lodges of the turn of the century which provided hundreds of Prague Jews with a secular, non-Zionist forum for social and cultural development? Ought not even overtly assimilationist endeavors, such as the Association of Czech Jewish Academics or the Jewish-dominated *Lese- und Redehalle,* be considered areas of Jewish public life and not merely subsets of the Czech and German communities?

In closing, I would reiterate my preliminary remarks that Gary Cohen's book is a major achievement in social history which goes a long way toward reopening—in a serious manner—the field of ethnic and national studies. The rigor of his approach has yielded tremendous rewards, but its formalism has also produced a rigid, if at times imaginative, framework for analysis. What is lacking, I believe, is the concept of post-emancipatory Jewish ethnicity. In the context of Prague, it would have complemented the Czech and German phenomena and also have served as a theoretical bridge between the pre-modern community, which was unabashedly national in its own estimation, and the post-liberal period of cultural experimentation and national reorientation.

HILLEL J. KIEVAL
Brandeis University

Stuart A. Cohen, *English Zionists and British Jews: The Communal Politics of Anglo-Jewry, 1895–1920.* Princeton: Princeton University Press, 1982. $32.50

Stuart Cohen's *English Zionists and British Jews* is an important contribution to the historiography not only of the Anglo-Jewish community but also of Zionism in general. It belongs to the long overdue, but recently growing, genre of historical research which submits the phenomenon of Zionism to close scrutiny within the context of particular societal and Jewish communal frameworks; an approach aptly described by Cohen as "a complementary, second-tier approach, one that might focus specifically on the mechanics of the process whereby what was universal in the appeal of political Zionism was welded to what was singular in the circumstances of particular Jewish communities." Cohen's book is the product of comprehensive and thorough research into a wide variety of archival and other contemporary sources in an area which has until now received but scant scholarly treatment. (Notable exceptions are provided by the chapters on intra-communal controversy in the books on the Balfour Declaration by Leonard Stein and Isaiah Friedman.) Furthermore, it innovatively probes the inner dimensions of the Jewish communal polity—the fascinating relationship between considerations of ideology and those of "power" or influence in the community institutions.

To be sure, the description of Anglo-Jewish Zionism which emerges from this work is far from flattering. Cohen depicts a Zionism which was both organizationally weak and intellectually arid. As late as 1917 the nominal membership of the various Zionist groups was no more than four thousand and it was far weaker than other Anglo-Jewish associations, for example than the United Council of Friendly Societies which had a membership in excess of thirty-one thousand. Indeed, according to Cohen, it even "suffered from a comparison with such equally small, but more robust, advocates of social and political reform as the Jewish Social Democratic Organization." This weakness of the English Zionist Federation was in part the result of a strategy which gave priority to the enlistment of support from the more acculturated elite of the community rather than to the mobilization of immigrant masses from Eastern Europe. Hence, "the spokesmen of Anglo-Jewry's immigrant and proletarian classes were not noticeably and actively supportive of organized Zionism in Britain before 1917." It was only in the wake of Weizmann's diplomatic achievement in gaining the Balfour Declaration that Zionist membership rose to about thirty thousand by 1921.

In a chapter displaying adroit, almost Namierian, use of detail, the author argues that even the celebrated decision by the Board of Deputies to censure the publication by the Conjoint Foreign Committee of an anti-Zionist manifesto in the *Times* of 24th May 1917, was not quite a Zionist victory. Rather, it was the result of a largely fortuitous alignment between the Zionist minority and some other groups of deputies who were, in essence, seeking "a larger share in the management of communal affairs."

Least complimentary of all is Cohen's depiction of the intellectual calibre of the Zionists. "From an ideological perspective," he states, "Anglo-Jewish Zionists were a barren assemblage." They were uninformative as polemicists, unimaginative, "made virtually no independent contribution to Zionist theory," and "made no concerted attempt to construct a cohesive theory of Jewish nationalism consistent with local conditions."

In contrast to this distinctly uncomplimentary characterization of the Zionists, the author offers a generous evaluation of their anti-Zionist antagonists. "In the main," he says, "the clearest and most intellectually aggressive home-grown expositions of doctrine emanated from the anti-Zionists." One cannot help wondering whether Cohen has not overstated the case in consequence of his obvious penchant for revisionist historiography. He appears to be at pains to redress a putative historiographical wrong—the wronged party being the Jewish anti-Zionists who have, Cohen suggests, been left "in a state of oblivion." He likens this to "a conscious or unconscious type of Whig history." It is not clear, however, to which "histories" Cohen refers. The fact of the matter seems to be that neither side has hitherto benefited from serious historiographical inquiry of the kind which Cohen himself has so admirably provided. At most, it has been memoirs and publicistic writing, which have given the anti-Zionist, Anglo-Jewish elite a bad press.

While the English Zionists may not have been as ideologically inventive as their counterparts in Germany or even in the United States, they were not entirely arid. Harry Sacher, for example, demonstrated considerable intellectual prowess in countering the "Contract Theory" propounded by anti-Zionists like B. L. Abrahams and Israel Abrahams. This theory argued that having won emancipation in the nineteenth century as a religion rather than a nation, the Jews could not now unilaterally alter those terms. Thus what the Zionists wanted not only corroborated the charge of anti-Semites that Jews were unassimilable, but was also injurious to Jewish self-respect. Sacher rather ingeniously turned the tables on this theory by arguing that emancipation had been granted to the British Jews at a time when Parliament was fully cognizant of the national dimension inherent in Judaism. Hence if emanciption in England was indeed based upon an implicit "contract," it was one which "set the seal of approval upon Judaism as the national-religion of the Jews with all that it implies, while it could not have approved the anti-nationalistic form of Judaism, of which it knew nothing." (See Harry Sacher, *Jewish Emancipation: The Contract Myth,* London, 1917.)

By the same token, one senses a certain imbalance in Cohen's attempt—commendable and impressive in itself—to expose the dimension of intra-communal power seeking which underlay the ideological rhetoric of the Zionists. "The Zionists (and especially the leaders of the E.Z.F.) were by and large an overly ambitious group of men," he writes. By contrast, he is markedly more generous in his depiction of the elite ("Cousinhood") anti-Zionists, who regarded it as their natural right to direct the affairs of the community and who generally treated the immigrant generation with paternalism and condescension.

Likewise, if it be true that the Zionists sometimes engaged in excessive denigration of their adversaries (imputing to them selfish motives, insensibility to Jewish distress, and "assimilationism"), the anti-Zionists were no less guilty of rhetorical excesses. One of the ugliest charges was that the Zionists "were all foreign Jews, bearing no quality to speak for the native Jews of the United Kingdom" (as Lucien Wolf and his associates put it in an effort to dissuade governmental authorities from lending their support to the Zionists).

This is not to deny, however, that Cohen has probed the anti-Zionist position with great perception. He shows that far from displaying what Isaiah Friedman has considered "an inept understanding of the British mind and of the British political and social make up," the anti-Zionists were in fact "attuned to the traditional British values of honesty and fair play." Their opposition to Zionism was both sincere and intellectually rational. Indeed, they persevered in their opposition to Zionism even when it was evident that gentile political figures like Lord Milner were outspokenly out of sympathy with their attitude.

Comprehended as a whole, the impressiveness of Stuart Cohen's work is but little impaired by the imbalance which we have noted. Elegantly written, thoroughly researched and incisively analytical, it is a pioneering work which places all students of the history of Anglo-Jewry, as well as of Zionism as a whole, in debt to its author.

GIDEON SHIMONI
Hebrew University

Scott Cummings (ed.), *Self-Help in Urban America*. New York: Kennikat Press, 1980. $23.95

Most visitors to American cities will note that the spatial distribution of people is not random. That is, there are neighborhoods which are largely white, black, Puerto Rican, Italian, Jewish, etc., etc. The more observant visitor will note that there are economic as well as geographic "neighborhoods" or "turfs." Ethnic groups tend to predominate in certain industries, jobs, skills. Stereotypically, one thinks of the Jewish tailor, the Italian shoemaker, the Irish saloon keeper. Three generations after the period of mass migration to the United States ethnic turfs continue to exist along with ethnic-specific modes of capital formation and styles of entrepreneurship. The essays in this volume describe and attempt to explain the enduring fact of ethnic economic behavior.

Ethnicity works in various ways to shape economic life. In some instances migrating ethnic groups come to their new land with profitable old-country skills. Surprisingly, this most obvious sort of ethnic economics tends to be quite uncommon (and least interesting). More frequently, the migrating ethnic group is frozen out of mainstream jobs by virtue of limited facility in the host country's language or out-and-out discrimination. Somewhere during the early period of the group's migration some pioneering ethnics enter a low capitalization business. As their compatriots arrive, the pioneers either employ them or in some other way teach them the business. In other words, the predominance of Chinese in the hand laundry business tells nothing about indigenous Chinese skills; rather it tells us something about the American urban opportunity structure. The same holds true of Greeks in the short-order restaurant business and many other ethnic businesses. The newcomers follow in the path blazed for them by the pioneering compatriots.

Some ethnic groups have devised ways of accumulating investment capital. They create the functional equivalent of banks in the form of rotating credit associations based on village ties, blood ties or even group-wide ties. Some have developed particular styles of entrepreneurship which may or may not have anything directly to do with their home country. These and other issues are discussed in the context of describing the economic behavior of a wide variety of ethnic groups including various Slavic groups, Finns, Koreans, Irish, Mormons (!) and Jews. Sad to say, the essay on the Jews strikes me as the weakest chapter in the book. The authors show little knowledge of either the history or sociology of modern Jewish life. In addition to their limited knowledge of Jewish materials the authors elaborate the obvious and then make major logical and methodological errors. Putting that essay aside, the book could be useful to the readers of this journal.

There are interesting theoretical models presented with applicability to Jewish materials. There are helpful reviews of the empirical and theoretical literature. Many a book is made valuable by its index and bibliography. Finally, the comparative material could be used to help identify Jewish particularity or, alternatively, to demonstrate that that which we thought was peculiarly Jewish was in fact more generally ethnic or immigrant behavior.

PAUL RITTERBAND
City University of New York

Moshe Davis (ed.), *Zionism in Transition*. New York: Herzl Press/ Institute of Contemporary Jewry of the Hebrew University, 1980. xv + 377 pp. $18.00

This book is the product of an institution that is uniquely Israeli—the seminar that is held at the residence of the President of the State of Israel which brings together well-known thinkers and leading personalities from the Jewish world. The working sessions constitute a high level "think tank" operation, at which many well-informed and sharp minds are focused on a single topic. The seminar brings together intellectuals from all over the world. Participants whose contributions comprise this volume came from Argentina, South Africa, France, Brazil, England, Canada and Sweden; but the majority, as might be expected, are from Israel and the United States. When persons with such diverse backgrounds discuss Zionism, it is quite natural, as Moshe Davis points out in his Introduction, that we should find that what is being discussed is not Zionism but Zionisms. If the participants had been asked to agree on a definition *before* they could contribute to the discussion, there would have been no meeting of the seminar. In this respect, Zionism is no worse off than is, for example, Judaism, or Christianity, or Marxism, or Americanism. Yet, as this volume clearly illustrates, though there be many tongues, and many varieties of Zionism, one soul is in them, and somehow all speak of the same subject.

The book is the product of forty-six contributors, whose papers are placed in four different sections: (I) Ideological Perspectives; (II) Diaspora Zionism—Achievements and Problems; (III) Zionism and the State of Israel; (IV) Reformulations. A work of such wide-ranging scope cannot of course, be reviewed in detail. But without hesitation one can readily recommend the book as a whole for its high quality of serious thought, for the honesty and sincerity of its authors, and for its comprehensive coverage of a complicated idea and movement. The book can readily serve as a basis for a seminar or a course in the history and meaning of Zionism, and it can be profitably read by any mature person, though it would be a more useful book if it were the subject of group study, so that the issues it raises could be critically analyzed and discussed. For, after all is said and done, the book provokes rather than answers questions.

Zionism, howsoever defined, whether by its proponents or its enemies, is a living force. It consoles or troubles the mind and conscience. A Jew can pretend to be indifferent to it, but he knows that he cannot ignore it, and openly or covertly must try to come to terms with it.

The forty-page essay on the ideological developments in Zionism by Gideon Shimoni, of the Hebrew University, is a masterly summary of its subject. It is encyclopedic in scope, yet written not only to convey factual information but to interpret and critically evaluate the contributions of the great Zionist thinkers from Moses Hess to Ben-Gurion.

Many of the papers throughout the book consider the question whether the Diaspora should be negated or affirmed; whether Diaspora Jewry has a future; whether a Jewish culture can be expected to develop anywhere outside of Israel; whether Israeli Jews have a Jewish culture or are likely to develop one; what should be the Zionist agenda for Jews in the Diaspora; what should Israel do for non-Israeli Jewish life and culture? Each contributor has his own answer to these and other challenging questions. There was no attempt at the President's seminar to reach a consensus on such issues. I do not believe that such an attempt would have been productive. Each thinker is a soloist; the contributors could not possibly have been made into an orchestra.

The impression one is left with is that ideological pluralism is an inescapable aspect of Zionism. Yet despite the great diversity in points of view on important issues, there is one point on which there is no dissent; that is, the first proposition of the Jerusalem Program as formulated at the Zionist Congress in 1968: "The aims of Zionism are: the unity of the Jewish people . . ." As this book amply manifests, there may still be disagreements on everything else in the Jerusalem program, but from this proposition there is no deviation. For the rediscovery of this all-important fact alone, a reading of the book is eminently worthwhile.

MILTON R. KONVITZ
Cornell University

Shlomo Deshen and Walter P. Zenner (eds.), *Jewish Societies in the Middle East—Community, Culture and Authority.* Washington, DC: University Press of America, 1982. $12.25

The migration to Israel of large collectivities of Jews who previously lived in the Moslem world has thrown into relief the need for broader and more thorough-going research of these Jewish communities. At the present time this research is focused on two main fields: first, the historical processes and social systems that molded the communities in the past; and, second, the specific characteristics of these groups in the process of modernization and of social integration into the frame of Israeli society.

Two scholars working in this field, Shlomo Deshen and Walter Zenner, have edited a collection of articles oriented along these two lines, with the main stress on the transition of the communities in question from the traditional to the modern. In the preface, the editors state that their aim is to give an overall picture of the Jewish social and cultural system in the countries of Islam. "We are interested in relating our work to general conceptualizations of cultural development. Therefore we use general models . . . in relation to specific communities" (p. 5). Their underlying assumptions are presented in the preface, which in fact constitutes a summing up. It discusses themes to be found both in the articles collected here and also in the bibliography which they cite. In it, they seek to define the principal traits common to the Jewish communities in these countries. The preface is joined by two introductory articles. In his "Traditional Society and Modern Society," J. Katz delineates the general characteristics of a traditional Jewish society, while S. Sharot ("Judaism in 'Pre-Modern' Societies") focuses on the connection between the Jewish community and the wider society.

The rest of the articles involve specific studies which, the editors consider, provide affirmation of the theses presented in the introductory articles. The title of the collection indicates the three main subjects to be discussed—community, authority, and culture—but the articles deal in fact with a whole series of sub-issues: education, family, occupations, leaders and intermediaries, inter-group relations, and patterns of stratification. Despite this wide range, the articles can be grouped according to the various subjects dealt with; for example, the family is analyzed in articles by W. P. Zenner, S. D. Goitein, D. Feitelson, D. Shai and M. Glazer; education in those by W. P. Zenner, Goitein, and Feitelson; interaction between groups as well as stratification in the articles by S. Deshen, W. P. Zenner, L. D. Loeb and Glazer.

Nonetheless, despite these shared areas of interest, it is hard to find common ground between the articles in a given group, because each article discusses a different aspect of authority or a different sphere of family relations. This lack of unity is also due to the wide geographical range—from the Maghreb to the Yemen and from Kurdistan to Turkey; to the variations in historical depth (Y. Tobi begins his review with the seventeenth century); to the inclusion of some articles which deal with the composition of communities in the Diaspora and of others which discuss the process of integration in Israel, without necessarily focusing on the continuity between the two; and to the separate treatment of traditional social systems and of processes of modernization. All this represents a mixture of differing treatments and it is hard to find any connecting thread linking the articles to each other. Thus instead of an overall picture and a perception of uniformity, the reader is made more aware of what differentiates than of what unites the communities.

Nevertheless, when one scrutinizes the specific articles chosen for the collection, one finds a number of important contributions. It is well known that research into the Jewish communities of the Islamic world is faced with major difficulties. Because tradition in these countries was handed down verbally, there is relatively little written material, and this problem is compounded by the fact that most of these communities have been uprooted and transplanted. The scholar is often obliged to adopt the method of reconstruction when analyzing past events and processes. However, the fact that the editors bring together in one volume articles from different disciplines—history, sociology, anthropology and folklore—enables the reader to observe these communities from different angles, thus permitting him to theorize about those areas where information is lacking.

Moreover, many of the articles illustrate what methods those working in this field can use to overcome the lack of documents or evidence. From this point of view, the articles of S. D. Goitein, M. Shokeid, and H. Goldberg, are noteworthy. When Goitein described the educational system characteristic of the Yemenite Jews, he drew the greater part of his information from interviews with Yemenites soon after their arrival in Israel. This exploration of virgin territory has, nonetheless, become the classic source for research in this sphere. The article by Shokeid is an interesting attempt to build from recent testimonies a hypothesis on patterns of social mediation in the country of origin and it demonstrates effectively how folklore material can provide the basis for sociological interpretations. And the article by Goldberg, which sets out to study the present-day conduct of the secretary of a moshav in the light of the traditional behavior patterns of a sheikh, completes another link in the same methodological chain.

The greater part of the collection is made up of articles already published in the past, although four articles are published for the first time. Of these, most noteworthy, perhaps, is the article of A. R. Meyers, which examines Jewish social status in Morocco. The status of Jews in Islamic countries was generally defined as that of "protected" persons. Various scholars have sought to ascertain the legal and social meaning of this general conception which was grounded in the patronage afforded the Jewish subject by the Muslim ruler. Meyers contributes to our understanding of this conception, stripping off its general characteristics and showing the complexity of the phenomenon of spelling out the patterns of interaction between the ruler and the ruled, between the grant of protection and its acceptance—in accord with different specific data the power relations between them underwent significant variations. In this way more light is thrown on the conception of *dhimma*; a new approach to Jewish status in the Islamic world is suggested; and conceptions hitherto prevailing in this field have been importantly modified.

To sum up, this collection is indeed very welcome, for even if it does not give us an inclusive, overall picture of the Jewish communities that were part of the tissue of Moslem culture, it sharpens our insight, opening up important new paths for further reflection and comparison.

PNINA MORAG-TALMON
Hebrew University

Leonard Dinnerstein, *America and the Survivors of the Holocaust*. New York: Columbia University Press, 1982. 409 pp. $19.95.

For the first three centuries of their existence, the North American colonies—later the United States—eagerly welcomed millions of immigrants to their shores. As early as the eighteenth century, Hector de St. John Crevecoeur saw the diversity of the many peoples making up the new nation as the wellspring of American strength. But, throughout, a darker strain—a fear of and hostility towards those who were different—was also present.

Americans enslaved Blacks and extirpated the Indians; Puritans hanged Quakers on the Boston Common. In the nineteenth century nativism emerged and it attained its greatest triumph with the passage of the Johnson Act of 1924, which not only sharply curtailed the number of immigrants allowed each year, but also set up a quota system to discriminate against South and East Europeans calculated to keep out Jews and Catholics.

As Nazism gained power in Germany and then after 1938 spread across Europe, Jews attempting to flee found that they were shut in. The gates of Palestine were closed and Jews looking westward discovered, in David Wyman's phrase, that "paper walls" effectively blocked the way. As the terrible news of the "final solution" leaked out, American attitudes barely changed. Even when the War Refugee Board was established in 1944, it proved, as Henry Feingold has shown, to be too little and too late.

When the full extent of the slaughter became known in the spring and summer of 1945, one might have expected a more sympathetic approach toward the pitiful remnant that had survived the death camps. But as Leonard Dinnerstein shows in this important and well-constructed study, the darker forces still held sway in post-war America. Traditional attitudes of generosity ran smack into an open and blatant anti-Semitism.

The end of the war found some twenty to thirty million Europeans uprooted, including refugees, prisoners of war, camp inmates and others. Facing the Allied armies was the immediate problem of dealing with some seven million displaced persons. By September 1945, the army had repatriated some six million of them, but there were still hundreds of thousands who either had no home to return to or no desire to go back to lands in which they had been so cruelly persecuted. Among these were the Jewish survivors of the death camps, and neither the army nor the civilian agencies knew what to do with them. Nothing in human experience had prepared the Allies to deal with the men, women and children who had stumbled out of hell.

Amidst persistent reports of ill-treatment of the survivors, Harry Truman dispatched Earl Harrison as his personal emissary to find out the extent of the problem. In a scathing indictment, Harrison wrote:

> With a few notable exceptions, nothing in the way of a program of activity or organized effort toward rehabilitation has been inaugurated and the internees, for they are literally such, have little to do except to dwell upon their plight, the uncertainty of their future and, what is more unfortunate, to draw comparisons between their treatment "under the Germans" and "in liberation." Beyond knowing that they are no longer in danger of the gas chambers, torture and other forms of violent death, they see—and there is—little change.

The Harrison Report galvanized the American government into action, and Dinnerstein gives high marks to Dwight Eisenhower for implementing a more humane policy. He ordered the camp inmates resettled, and told field officers to appropriate German homes, hotels and apartment buildings if necessary to do so.

The American army itself, however, reflected the same attitudes and biases as people did at home, and Dinnerstein bluntly documents the widespread anti-Semitism among officers in charge of the DP's. One Jewish chaplain noted that as far as the army was concerned, the problems of the DP's constituted "just one grand nuisance." General George S. Patton, Jr., insisted that the detainees be treated like prisoners, and wrote in his diary that other people "believe that the Displaced Person is a human being, which he is not, and this applies particularly to the Jews who are lower than animals."

In contradistinction, the army gave quite good treatment to the Balts (many of whom spoke English, were relatively clean, well-fed and orderly, and had migrated westward with considerable possessions), despite the fact that this group counted among its number some of the most vicious and active collaborators of the Nazis.

Eventually, domestic political pressure by outraged Jewish organizations as well as the innate decency of Truman, Eisenhower and others led to a general improvement in the camps. Social workers set up schools and rehabilitation programs, and the survivors began to recover some of their physical health. Now the problem was what to do with them. Few wanted to be repatriated to Germany or other Central or East European countries; their goal was Palestine, but Britain steadfastly refused to open the gates. Even when the Anglo-American Committee of 1946 recommended the grant of 100,000 visas for entry to Palestine, Attlee and Bevin refused to give way, and their delaying tactics only served to anger an already irate Harry Truman.

While the Zionist groups headed by Abba Hillel Silver and Stephen S. Wise now intensified their push for a Jewish commonwealth in Palestine, the non-Zionist American Jewish Committee and the anti-Zionist American Council for Judaism worked to bring 100,000 Jewish refugees into the United States. To effect this end, they created the non-denominational Citizens Committee on Displaced Persons. Irving Engel of the Committee directed the operation, while Lessing Rosenwald of the Council supplied most of the funds. Rosenwald has been the object of much criticism, from Zionists and scholars, for his anti-Zionist activities. Yet his generosity and insistence on securing entry visas to the United States for the survivors should certainly alter the "self-hating Jew" tag with which he has been labelled. In fact there was no inconsistency in his work. He was a proud American who believed Jews constituted a religious group and not a separate nation. America had been, and would remain, a land of refuge and opportunity, and what group deserved that chance more than those who had suffered so much? Despite attacks from Zionists, who saw the work of the Citizens Committee as undermining their efforts to achieve a Jewish state, the Committee worked, with ultimate success, to liberalize American immigration laws and thus to bring in some 400,000 DP's between 1945 and 1952, of whom 137,450 were Jews. In the same period, 136,000 settled in Israel.

Approximately half the book is devoted to the work of the Citizens Committee, which had to overcome enormous obstacles, especially in Congress, where anti-immigrationists such as Senator Pat McCarren of Nevada held pivotal committee posts. Based on the extensive use of manuscript sources, government documents and interviews, Dinnerstein's work will be the definitive study on this phase of American immigration policy for years to come. Despite the success of the Committee, its efforts highlighted the failure of a nation built by refugees to help the survivors of the Holocaust. As Dinnerstein somberly concludes: "Although in the long run the DP acts of 1949 and 1950 established fine precedents, and in the long run benefited refugees the world over, they failed to meet the needs of the majority of the Jewish DP's in Europe." The America which had turned its back on Jews in the thirties did so after the war as well. Should there ever be another conflagration in the world, its survivors may find the United States again denying its heritage, again mocking the noble words of Emma Lazarus inscribed on the Statue of Liberty.

MELVIN I. UROFSKY
Virginia Commonwealth University

Ulrich Dunker, *Der Reichsbund jüdischer Frontsoldaten 1919–1938. Geschichte eines jüdischen Abwehrvereins.* Düsseldorf: Droste Verlag, 1977. DM 52.

This study of the National League of Jewish Front Line Veterans is a useful addition to the growing number of histories devoted to German-Jewish organizations between the two World Wars. The League, formed in 1919 to counteract the anti-Semitic charges that the Jews had shirked in the Great War, grew to become the second largest organization of German Jews, second only to the *Centralverein*. Dunker convincingly portrays the veterans as assimilationists for whom self-defense involved documenting Jewish rootedness in, and service to, the Fatherland. However, his analysis of League activities during the years of the Weimar Republic shows that they were by no means limited to the refutation of racist propaganda. They formed armed defensive squads to protect their coreligionists from physical attacks, built agricultural settlements for Jews who wished to break away from traditional Jewish occupations, and established sport groups to involve the younger generation of Jews in traditional martial values of discipline and physical fitness. The author is somewhat critical of the two latter categories as implicitly endorsing anti-Semitic stereotypes of Jews as unproductive weaklings.

Dunker devotes as much attention to the first two years of the Hitler regime as to the entire Weimar period, an emphasis dictated largely by his sources, but nonetheless fortunate in view of the extremely interesting material he brings to light about the Jewish response to the Nazi state. In the hope of reaching some sort of accommodation with the new order, the veterans adopted the Führer principle and tried repeatedly to convince the Nazis that most German Jews were eager to go on serving their country under the direction of former frontline soldiers. This brought them into sharp conflict with the Zionists, for whom emigration alone offered any hope.

Dunker maintains that the new position adopted by the League amounted to the abandonment of self-defense, although it probably is better viewed as a radical revision of defensive strategy. That it survived even the exclusion of Jews from military conscription and the Nuremberg Laws in 1935 says a great deal about the veterans' lack of flexibility and realism. And yet, Dunker argues, they were able to influence the authorities to exempt Jewish veterans from the purge of the civil service in 1933 and to secure the release of League members from concentration camps following the Crystal Night pogroms five years later.

Occasionally Dunker reaches tenuous conclusions. He does not convincingly demonstrate that the level of anti-Semitic violence was fairly constant throughout the Weimar period, rather than concentrated in its early and late years. Nor do statements published after 1933 in an effort to deflect Nazi racism constitute proof of sympathy for some aspects of fascism on the part of League leaders. But in most respects his study is both balanced in its judgments and firmly grounded in archival research in Germany and Israel and in interviews with a few surviving League members. Without doubt his greatest achievement is the sympathetic understanding he brings to most aspects of his subject. In eschewing fatalistic condemnations based on hindsight, Dunker presents a generally convincing portrayal of German-Jewish patriots battling for their honor against what were to prove hopeless odds.

DONALD L. NIEWYK
Southern Methodist University

Daniel J. Elazar (ed.), *Kinship and Consent: The Jewish Political Tradition and Its Contemporary Uses*. Washington, DC: University Press of America, 1983 (Ramat Gan: Turtledove, 1981). 397 pp. $24.00

This collection of essays is an effort to retrieve a lost tradition—or better, it is an effort to demonstrate that there is a lost tradition of Jewish political thought that is worth retrieving. The word tradition implies coherence and continuity, and in the opening essay, Daniel Elazar, who convened the conference where the essays were first read and then edited the volume in which they now appear, provides a heroic argument for both. From the days of Sinai until the early days of the Yishuv, Elazar claims, the idea of the covenant has been at the center of Jewish thinking about politics (and of Jewish political practice too).

The idea is rarely articulated in philosophical terms—philosophy is not central to the tradition—and sometimes it is not articulated at all. But it is so deeply ingrained in Jewish religion and culture that it conditions or shapes every political venture. And it is plainly visible at the four great moments of foundation: at the time of the Exodus and conquest, after the return from Babylonia, in the reiterated foundings that constituted the classic *kehillah,* and at the beginnings of the Zionist movement. The emerging "polity" in each of these cases is non-hierarchical, consensual, decentralized, federal, republican, anti-monarchical and anti-statist. The argument is attractive and it clearly takes in a great deal, but Elazar has some difficulty with the House of David—and then with its religious continuation in the Babylonian exilarchate and with its long-expected return in the messianic kingdom (which may well have none at all of the convenantal characteristics). And he has problems, too, with the contemporary State of Israel, for while Israel is certainly a republic, it is also a centralized state, "superimposed," as Elazar writes, "on a network of cooperative associations."

Indeed, Elazar's argument works best (leaving aside the tribal confederacy about which we don't really know a great deal) for the medieval period. It is not surprising, then, that the finest essays in this collection, the most assured, enlightening, and persuasive, are those that deal with the autonomous communities of North Africa and Europe between roughly the tenth and seventeenth centuries. The pieces by Shlomo D. Goitein on political conflict in the days of the *genizah,* by Menachem Elon on halachic conceptions of authority, and by Gerald Blidstein on the individual and the community truly open up a new world for Western political theorists—"an enormously flexible, decentralized polity," in the words of Dan Segre—which deserves to stand alongside the city-state, the empire, the feudal regime, the absolute monarchy, and the modern republic as a significant human alternative.

Here indeed there is a coherent tradition, rooted in the idea of the covenant as Elazar evokes it, consensual and republican. But this tradition arises out of a non-territorial politics, and it is probably crucial to both its existence and its character that the communities in which it was developed were autonomous but never sovereign. Hence it is by no means clear how to connect this tradition to the various experiences of statehood in Biblical times and to the reborn state of our own time.

Segre's essay and another by David Hartman are centrally concerned with the second half of this problem: the value of halachic politics, that is, of a politics shaped by halachic understandings, for Israel today. These are probing, nuanced, ultimately uneasy essays—morally appealing in their very uncertainty. Similarly, the prolegomena to Jewish political thought, written by Bernard Susser and Eliezer Don Yihyeh, is intellectually and professionally appealing because of its own uncertainty. All these writers share Elazar's project, without fully committing themselves to his central argument. So there is an internal discourse in this book, which itself reflects the deep meaning of its subject matter and does credit to the editor and the authors.

MICHAEL WALZER
The Institute for Advanced Study
Princeton

M. Eliav (ed.), *Sefer ha'aliyah harishonah* (The Book of the First Aliyah). Jerusalem: Ben-Zvi Institute/ Defense Ministry, 1982.

Shulamit Laskov, *Ha-Biluim* (The Bilu). Tel Aviv University/ Institute of Zionist Research; Jerusalem: Hasifriyah haẓionit, 1979/80.

In *Sefer ha'aliyah harishonah* we have a new addition to the shelf of compilations on the history of the Yishuv, a work which in part follows and in part deviates from its direct predecessors. The books on the Aliyot (the "Second Aliyah," the "Third Aliyah") or on the pre-state para-military organizations (Hashomer, Palmaḥ) were published either on the initiative of those who themselves had participated in the movements described or else on that of their political disciples and heirs. They sought to preserve and to glorify the receding past.

The *Book of the First Aliyah* has been published for somewhat similar reasons. Its raison d'être is the importance of that Aliyah as the first, but not less important, there is the belief that hitherto the First Aliyah has suffered from "discrimination" by historians, who have memorialized the Second Aliyah at length and on a grand scale. This collection is thus meant to atone for a "historical wrong." However, the innovation here is that the source materials—memoirs, documents—are prefaced by twenty articles by historians (neither participants nor direct disciples) who set out to analyze the importance of the First Aliyah from different angles and (in the article by Ettinger and Bartal) to put it in historical perspective.

The aspects covered are social and economic life (Druyan, Avitzur, Salmon, Kolatt, Krack); culture (Walk, Haramati, Berlovitz, Sidorsky); the history and geography of the new farming colonies, *moshavot* (Aaronson, Ben-Aryeh); the self-image of the colonies (Kellner); their relations with their supporters and benefactors (Laskov, Giladi, Harel); with their Arab neighbors (Ro'i); with the "old Yishuv" (Kaniel); and with the authorities (Carmel). The findings are already in large part familiar (for example, those of Salmon, Laskov and Ro'i), but their appearance together imparts a fresh viewpoint and a new dimension. The high quality of the articles, taken individually, ensures that the book is without question largely successful. It certainly provides a more or less even-handed and reliable picture of the way of life and the hopes of the people of the First Aliyah.

Nevertheless, the collection suffers from a major shortcoming. There is a one-sided concentration in the articles on the activities and influence of the First Aliyah on the Yishuv in Palestine. This Palestine-centered focus distorts the account of both the origins and the impact of the First Aliyah.

In the excellent article by Ettinger and Bartal—and to some extent in the important contribution of Kolatt—there is, it is true, a general evaluation of the First Aliyah, its membership and its impact. Shulamit Laskov, too, recounts the organization of Hibat Zion in her article, which in fact summarizes Y. Klausner's book-length study *B'hitorer 'am* (A People Awakes). These articles are not sufficient, however, to fill what is a very large gap. By this we mean that there is not one single analysis either of the motivation and organization that produced this group of settlers; or of the overall influence exerted on Diaspora Jewry by the farming colonies in Palestine.

Harel's article does describe the reaction within the *moshavot* to Herzl and the Zionist Organization, but again this is in the local context, on the spot, which simply underscores the Palestinocentrist thrust of the book. Furthermore, this attitude is apparent in the selection of the source material presented here, most of which refers to specific problems in the day-to-day experience of the immigrants in their new country. There is much to be learned from the material about their lives, their way of thinking, their attitude to religion and to their benefactors. One will not find out, however, why they went to Palestine nor why those they left behind so often saw them as a ray of light.

Many Jewish agricultural colonies were established in the period 1882–1903 in places as far apart as the Argentine and the United States. Nevertheless, the Jewish national myth was woven around the unsuccessful *moshavot* in Palestine, which were simply poor imitations of French villages and which reached a total population no larger than that of a small town in the Pale of Settlement. The mystique surrounding them emerged and burgeoned in Eastern Europe. It was an image which at times had no connection at all with reality, but which was a unique factor in the development of the Jewish national movement, and made a decisive contribution to the success of Herzl and the Zionist organization.

The book under review is not unique in its Palestine-centered trend. In recent years we have witnessed a flood of books on the history of Palestine. Every field cleared of stones since 1878 in any part of Palestine (in the Jewish settlements, of course) has had—or no doubt will have—an article, a book or a piece of research devoted to it. Acting as pioneers in this matter have been the editors of the quarterly *Kathedra* who, for example, decided to put out two entire issues on the jubilee of Petaḥ Tikvah. These researches are certainly of value in themselves. But one cannot overlook the political implications of this bias for the Israel of today (1983) with its territorial dilemmas and with its officially-sponsored efforts to undermine the historiographical hegemony of the Second Aliyah.

The subject of the First Aliyah is analyzed from a different angle in Shulamit Laskov's book on the Biluim. This history of the student group which came into being in Kharkov in order to serve as "pioneers of the great Jewish national movement" (p. 39) looks, at first glance, like another example of the restricted trend criticized above, but this is not the case. In her thorough and penetrating analysis, the author makes the distinction between the pathetically meager results actually achieved by the Biluim in Palestine and the mystique which was woven around the group and which became "the corner-stone of the settlement enterprise in the country" (p. 363). Even if this incisive, unqualified view remains controversial, nevertheless the way in which she presents the issue, her analysis and her conclusions all represent a great advance beyond most traditional Zionist historiography. No more high-flown phraseology without factual support (as for example in the books on the same subject by Zitron and Dinaburg), no more dry details strung together without sufficient background or analysis (as in the works of Yisrael Klausner), but a coherent synthesis of narrative and analysis, firmly based on primary sources, some of them previously unknown. She gives an unadorned account of the growth of the movement, what came of it in Russia, Constantinople and Palestine and its effect on the following generations, successfully mastering the great amount of material she had at hand.

Laskov's book on the Biluim is a fine example of how to maintain a just balance between Palestine and the Diaspora while writing on the First Aliyah. As she demonstrates so ably, the point of origin was after all the crisis in the Pale of Settlement (most immediately, the pogroms of 1881–1882).

Shulamit Laskov has thus succeeded where *Sefer ha'aliyah harishonah* failed. Her achievement is that she has written a dynamic account embracing both origins and development, both the Diaspora and the Yishuv, both reality and myth. Her book is a fundamental contribution to Zionist historiography.

YOSSI GOLDSTEIN
Hebrew University

Sidra D. Ezrahi, *By Words Alone: The Holocaust in Literature.* Chicago: University of Chicago Press, 1980. $15.00

There was a time, not so long ago, when it was feared by some and argued by others that nothing could ever be said about Hitler's Holocaust of the Jews, or that nothing ought to be said. That time is now past. Virtually each week new books appear, with the result that the literature on the Nazi destruction, while still very much in progress, has already grown beyond the point of mastery. Because of the size, range, variety, and quality of these writings, it is imperative that we have a secondary literature to sort through the vast quantity of books that have appeared and make some discriminating judgments about them. This need is especially acute in the United States, where interest in the Holocaust remains very high and courses on the subject are being offered with increasing frequency at schools, colleges, and universities across the country.

Who will teach the teachers, one wonders, or otherwise guide them through the unmanageable bibliographies that are in circulation? Particularly in the realm of imaginative literature, how will they know which novels and stories begin to approach the truth of the history, which poems evoke an authentic pain, which plays reproduce events in anything like a credible manner? Hundreds of literary works now exist, among which a teacher is typically forced to choose less than a dozen. Which are these to be, and what will determine the choice?

Anyone beset by such questions as these could hardly do better than turn to Sidra Ezrahi's *By Words Alone*. Serious-minded, well informed, and highly reliable in its critical judgments, this book is as comprehensive a taxonomy of Holocaust literature as we have been given to date. Ezrahi has read very widely and has managed to think her way successfully through a remarkably large and diverse body of literature. All of the major authors are taken up in her pages, and consideration is given as well to dozens of lesser figures. She has been able to sort these out in some useful critical categories, which define writing about the Jewish tragedy on a historical and literary spectrum that begins with documentation and ends in myth-making. Ezrahi is fully alert to the theoretical implications of reading imaginative writings against actual events and defines her critical terms carefully and convincingly. One comes away from her discussions of documentary art and "concentrationary realism" for instance, persuaded by the rightness of her aesthetic insights and appreciative of the kinds of problems that authors who wrote in these modes had to face. The same can generally be said for her discussions of most other authors.

If there are weaknesses or limitations here they derive from the fact that Ezrahi has cast her critical net very widely and attempted to encompass an unusually large number of writers. Inevitably, this means that some authors will be described cursorily and in summary fashion. Poetry suffers more than prose from such a procedure, and certain very complex figures, such as Paul Celan, are not given their due as a result. Nevertheless, there are more virtues than defects to Ezrahi's encyclopedic ambitions, and most readers in search of a guide to the whole range of writings on the Holocaust will profit greatly from her efforts. *By Words Alone* has already won for itself a respected place in the small but growing body of critical studies of Holocaust literature and ought to be welcomed by all who read, teach, and write about the subject.

ALVIN H. ROSENFELD
Indiana University

Egal Feldman, *The Dreyfus Affair and the American Conscience, 1895–1906*. Detroit: Wayne State University Press, 1981 ix + 187 pp. $17.95.

Three studies have now appeared on the American reaction to the Dreyfus affair: Rose A. Halpern's 1941 M.A. thesis at Columbia University, Ronald A. Urquhart's 1972 Ph.D. dissertation at the same university, and now Egal Feldman's volume, the only one of the three to be published commercially. That so much attention has been focused on so narrow a subject would seem to indicate that the subject possesses vast importance, perhaps as a turning point in American or American Jewish life. Such, however, is not the case. The most that the Dreyfus affair by itself really offers an American historian, as Feldman candidly admits in his preface, is "an occasion to monitor and evaluate American observations of the legal, political, and social customs of France during a very critical period."

Given these limited possibilities, Egal Feldman acquits himself well. He surveys an immense amount of literature, organizes it sensibly, and presents it, with copious quotations, in fair-minded fashion. The views of Protestants, Catholics and Jews, Anglophiles and Francophiles, militarists and anti-militarists, lawyers, ministers and others all find expression in these pages, and where diversity of opinion exists, Feldman gives all sides a fair hearing. Few will question or express surprise at his general conclusion: "Except for American Catholics, there was general support in the United States for Captain Alfred Dreyfus and those Frenchmen who fought for justice on his behalf. However, not all Americans supported Dreyfus or were disturbed by events in France for the same reasons, nor did they draw the same practical lessons from the case." Native-born American Jews and Central European Jewish immigrants of longstanding residence spoke out less vigorously for Dreyfus and against French anti-Semitism than did more recent East European Jewish immigrants; the latter protested as vigorously as they could.

If Feldman's conclusion might have been anticipated, his interpretation happily provides deeper insight. He convincingly argues that responses to the Dreyfus affair reveal more about America and its internal conflicts than about France. He shows how different groups exploited the widespread interest in the affair to advance independently formulated positions on foreign affairs, militarism, social morality, Catholicism and jurisprudence. The affair, in other words, provided prooftexts for sermons already written. In similar fashion, he shows how it served as a barometer for measuring Jewish attitudes toward anti-Semitism and American exceptionalism, as well as Catholic attitudes toward liberalism and Church discipline. Since the affair did not intrude on many critical areas of public life, particularly domestic politics (William Jennings Bryan does not figure in these pages) and economics, Feldman cannot quite live up to his promise to use responses to the Dreyfus affair to "tell us about American estimates of their own life and institutions." But many of his observations are nevertheless suggestive.

Yet by focusing so narrowly on responses to the Dreyfus affair, he misses opportunities to shed light on important broader issues. The discussion of Jews and Catholics, for example, would have benefited from a retrospective glance back to the Mortara affair, the outcry following Church seizure of a forcibly converted Jewish child in Italy in 1858, when similar questions of liberalism versus Catholicism arose. A few paragraphs on Jewish responses to anti-Catholicism in America, and sidelong glances at Jewish-Catholic cooperation on issues related to immigration, Americanization and opposition to Protestant evangelicalism would also have added perspective. Similarly, comparisons might have been made to the two so-called "American Dreyfus cases," and the reactions to them: the Lauchheimer Controversy of 1910–1912 (see Wayne Wiegand in *Military Affairs* XL [1976] 54–59) and the better known case of Robert Rosenbluth, 1921–1924 (see Rosemary Davis, *The Rosenbluth Case: Federal Justice on Trial,* 1970). Finally, the whole subject of American government and popular concern with human rights violations in other nations deserves a more substantial analysis than this brief volume provides.

In short, what Feldman has done, he has done well. But this is a limited study.

JONATHAN D. SARNA
Hebrew Union College-Jewish
Institute of Religion (Cincinnati)

Geoffrey Field, *Evangelist of Race: The Germanic Vision of Houston Stewart Chamberlain.* New York: Columbia University Press, 1981. xi + 565 pp. $25.00.

Geoffrey G. Field's book, *Evangelist of Race: The Germanic Vision of Houston Stewart Chamberlain,* is a fine work, and certainly represents a significant contribution to the field of European cultural history. Methodologically, the work is sound. There are a few lapses of accuracy, e.g., Alfred Waldersee is rendered Alfred Waldensee, Otto Boeckel comes out as August Boeckel, Arthur Moeller van den Bruck as Ernst Moeller van den Bruck, and Erich von Falkenhayn as Erich von Falkenhaym. Furthermore, I question Field's statement regarding German casualties on the Somme and at Verdun (p. 386), and his assertion that the German Verdun offensive collapsed as late as 1917 (p. 387). On the whole, though, such errors are rare.

New information on Houston Stewart Chamberlain has been brought to bear, and, as never before, both man and career have been placed within their historical context. Chamberlain's racism can be seen as part and parcel of general German—and, to some extent, European—developments. If understanding the sources, methods, and consequences of Western racism is important to the humanistic tradition (and I believe it is), this work will prove of extraordinary value to layman and specialist alike.

Field's book is quite innovative, most particularly when he focuses upon Chamberlain's career after 1900. Even, however, when the author focuses upon earlier concerns, as, for example, the relationship between Chamberlain and Cosima Wagner, much new material (at least for Americans) has been provided.

Of great interest to any student of the history of ideas is the enthusiasm with which Chamberlain's magnum opus, *Foundations of the Nineteenth Century,* was received, not only in Germany but throughout the West. Perhaps one should not be surprised that George Bernard Shaw who, despite his adherence to Fabian Socialism, had a strong anti-egalitarian streak in him, received it with enthusiasm. The same holds true for D. H. Lawrence, a proto-fascist in so many ways. In America, Senator Albert T. Beveridge, one of the nation's most prominent colonialists (and an adherent of racist thought in various permutations), "professed to be strongly influenced by the book; so did the Immigration Restriction League, at that time engaged in a campaign to curb the free entry of 'non-Aryan' elements into the country" (p. 465). Naturally, the American racist thinker Madison Grant, a vice-president of the League, "was especially impressed with it." Theodore Roosevelt, while finding some fault with *Foundations of the Nineteenth Century,* found it to be "a beneficial antidote to 'well-meaning and feebleminded sentimentalists'" (p. 466).

As Field points out, enthusiasm for Chamberlain's work was not confined to recognized exponents of right-wing or racist principles. The Progressive historian Carl Becker praised the book. Indeed, in the years immediately preceding World War I, *Foundations of the Nineteenth Century* enjoyed a widespread appeal which, while largely to be found on the right, cut across recognized ideological lines. The term "cultural despair" coined by Fritz Stern would appear to be particularly apposite in this regard.

With the exception of Field's excursion into historiography—not, it would seem, an area of expertise for him—he argues his points very well and, at times, in a most eloquent fashion. Regarding the issue of German racism and Chamberlain's own singular contribution to this tradition, Field is impressively articulate. It is rare to come across a work that is both so extremely informative and well-written. These qualities combined with Field's extraordinary ability to synthesize so vast and complex a tradition as European racism, will ensure that this work will have a lasting impact. It is a work that will remain vital for purposes of historical interpretation for the foreseeable future, and it can certainly be highly recommended for both undergraduate and graduate reading courses.

ROBERT A. POIS
University of Colorado

Gerald Fleming, *Hitler und die Endlösung*. Wiesbaden and Munich, 1982. 214 pp.

Dr. Fleming, of the University of Surrey, has made an important contribution to the debate about who exactly was responsible for what in the mass murder of the Jewish people. In a sense, the fact that this book is really a reply to the so-called Revisionist "historians", or at least to some of them, shows that there is some value even in lunatic writing by people who claim that the earth is flat: the Holocaust never happened, they say, or at least if it did happen, Hitler was not responsible. This kind of writing has unfortunately gained some respectability, to the point where one of the authors referred to directly by Dr. Fleming, the notorious Mr. David Irving, even made an appearance following the repeat showing of "Holocaust" on German television recently. Dr. Fleming's book does not take the Revisionist arguments lightly; he follows the career of the Führer very carefully and shows, using an extensive array of sources, how the deep-seated anti-Semitic prejudices of the young Hitler became a tremendous spur to a career of destruction in the wake of personal and social crises. Dr. Fleming details something that many historians, especially German historians, have said only in general terms—that Hitler's anti-Semitism was not an incidental part of his mental make-up or just one of the issues that occupied his mind, but, rather, a central pillar of the *Weltanschauung* of a manichean power maniac.

Dr. Fleming bases himself, in part, on completely new or unknown materials, such as his analysis of the testimonies of Friedrich Jeckeln and of two German officers at Riga. He shows convincingly that Hitler was not only predisposed ideologically to provide the general direction of policy leading to the murder of Jews, but that he also gave the orders—orally—and then received the reports on their execution. The two—predisposition and action—are not at all the same thing, but Dr. Fleming shows that both can safely be attributed to Hitler. Skilfully using both oral testimonies and documentary evidence, he shows how all the instructions ultimately emanated from the general directives of the Führer, and how then, once they had been translated into murderous practice, they returned to the Führerhauptquartier as statistics (the quantitative reports on those murdered).

Very importantly, Gerald Fleming's book demonstrates the reasons behind the secrecy enjoined upon the murderers in their actions, and the ways this was accomplished. Dr. Fleming's book is thus not only an important addition to our knowledge of the Holocaust generally, but also an important contribution to the fight for historical truth.

YEHUDA BAUER
Hebrew University

Maurice Friedman, *Martin Buber's Life and Work: The Early Years 1878–1923*. New York: E. P. Dutton, 1981. 455 pp. $25.75.

There is a "Buber paradox" familiar to many of his readers: the philosopher of dialogue rarely draws his audience into a dialogue. He either spellbinds with his breathless, enraptured prose, seducing readers into a state of wide-eyed reverence and piety or, alternately, he leaves them sceptical and distant, refusing to be dazzled by what they see as overheated, swollen prose, or, worse still, as intellectual dandyism. Dialogue—the encounter of two responsible, autonomous individuals, relating yet withstanding, striving mightily to understand but not necessarily to agree—is strangely absent. Buber fathered disciples and detractors but, paradoxically, very few who are prepared to be neither obedient nor recalcitrant, i.e., to enter into an authentic dialogue.

Maurice Friedman stands at the head of the camp of disciples. For some three decades he has worked to make Buber accessible to the English-speaking public through translations, anthologies, essays and books. A bibliography of Buber-related material in English would repeat the name Friedman nearly as often as Buber. Indeed, the rise of a Buber "vogue" in the United States in recent years probably owes more to his efforts than those of Buber himself. And now, after years in preparation, Friedman has published his major work on Buber, a two-volume intellectual biography, the first of which is under review here.

Covering the period from his birth to the *I and Thou* years, Friedman reviews every grain of information, every crumb of anecdote and, of course, every snippet of written word, to present what is doubtless the most comprehensive study of Buber available. Of Buberiana one could scarcely want more—from human interest details (e.g., Buber grew his beard to cover a hare-lip) to an exhaustive study of the intellectual roots of *I and Thou*—it is all there. In Friedman, Buber has found his Boswell.

The tone is unabashedly hagiographical. Friedman approaches the master with shoes doffed, as if he were leading a cultural pilgrimage. Nary a word of criticism intrudes into the four hundred some odd pages of text and Friedman takes on all comers in defending Buber from blame. The work is more in the nature of a monument erected to Buber and a preaching to the yet-unconverted than an attempt to assess his life and thought critically.

The Buber who emerges from Friedman's pages is a cult figure, a personality about whom legend and hushed voices are more appropriate than careful, controlled discussion. From his earliest essays and activities onward, Friedman consistently finds hints and foreshadowings, encounters pregnant with destiny, stages of spiritual ripening that seem virtually ordained. Intimations of glory shine through even Buber's most turgid youthful excesses and the urgency of the oracular mission hovers about his every turn.

If it is true that Buber needs to be saved from his own canonizers, it is ironically Friedman's work that will be an irreplaceable source for those who undertake to comprehend the complicated, intensely self-conscious, restless, very human and uncannily inspired personality that was Martin Buber. For Friedman's work is an encyclopedic labor of love that is unlikely to be surpassed as a standard reference for all who seek entrance into the world of Buber. Nor yet is it likely to be surpassed as an act of fealty to the master.

BERNARD SUSSER
Tel-Aviv University

Lloyd P. Gartner, *History of the Jews of Cleveland (1836–1945)*. Cleveland: Western Reserve Historical Society, 1978.

Judged by the standards of ten years ago, this is an exemplary local history. "Playing together the social and cultural with the communal (xiv)," Lloyd Gartner examines Cleveland Jewry within the context of both the changing midwestern metropolis and the evolving national Jewish scene. The use of narrative primary sources is thorough and the analysis is trenchant. There is no hint of filiopietism or apologetica. The chapters dealing with the growth of religious institutions, the limits of social acceptance and the dynamics of economic life are especially well done. Indeed, in almost every respect the volume is superior not only to Gartner's earlier co-authored studies of Milwaukee and Los Angeles, but also to the vast majority of local Jewish histories published prior to 1975.

If this volume represents traditional local history at its best, one must note that the field has changed tremendously in recent years and that some traditional approaches have become outdated. Part of the problem is rooted in a matter of definition; Gartner has written less a history of the Jews of Cleveland—as his title suggests—than a communal and institutional history. Consequently, he has failed to address such crucial concerns as economic mobility, geographic persistence, social structures, family organization and interaction between Jews and their ethnic neighbors—issues which are increasingly commanding the attention of younger practitioners. A related problem is the author's avoidance of the quantitative and sampling techniques that would have enabled him to address these and other questions. Without constructing a representative sample of the population, it is also difficult to distinguish between the representative and the exceptional. The bias of Gartner's narrative sources is reflected in his almost exclusive focus on the communally prominent, economically successful and civically involved; we learn little about the experience of more ordinary people.

Caveats aside, members of the Cleveland Jewish community are well served by this book which they may read and understand with profit. Professor Gartner's fellow historians are somewhat less richly rewarded.

STEVEN G. HERTZBERG
Institute for Research in History
(New York)

Martin Gilbert, *Atlas of the Holocaust*. London and Tel Aviv, 1982. 256 pp. £7.50

This is a monumental work indeed—an effort to put into visual form (maps accompanied by some photographs) and a very brief text—the whole history of the Holocaust. Ranging from some brief introductory sketches of pre-1933 Jewish life (mainly maps 3 and 5) to the aftermath of the Holocaust, the 316 maps present a novel approach to the subject. The purpose appears to be chiefly didactic: to depict in dramatic form something which is so difficult to comprehend. Maps, of course, are Martin Gilbert's specialty (not the only one, by any means); but these maps are really special. They try—I think they succeed—to bring the life and death of millions to the reader not only by showing him or her the places and the numbers, but also by making it come alive through the introduction of the fates of individuals picked out almost at random by the author from among the multitudes of victims.

Almost, because of course there is a design in choosing the names: children, who might have grown into wonderful human beings; persons who were born in places that were not engulfed by the Holocaust but who happened to be in places hit by the whirlwind; oldsters, who were denied the right to end their life in peace among their loved ones. The second category is especially poignant—Martin Gilbert shows how accidental it all was: the Nazis intended to strike at the Jews of New York, Moscow or Jerusalem no less than at those of Wlodawa or Amsterdam. Ignatz Baum, for instance, was deported to Auschwitz from Paris on 27 March 1942. He was, however, not a French Jew or a Polish Jew. He had been born in Haifa in 1901. Berthe Francfort, deported to Auschwitz on 3 November 1942 hailed from Texarkana, born in 1894; and Susanne Marx had been born in Mexico City in 1908. The fates of individuals bring out the basic problem much clearer than the big and horrible figures—they of course have to be there, too.

The *Atlas* is strictly chronological. Year by year, month by month, and in 1942 week by week, the maps follow the unfolding of the "Final Solution." The element of repetition, which would be tedious in an ordinary historical description, becomes itself an expression of the uniqueness of the situation. The death marches at the end of the *Atlas,* describing the last period of the war, graphically present the irrational element in the mass murder of the Jews, again with that terrible repetition, which in this case is an essential part of the story.

Some of the elements that made up the Holocaust situation are missing—one cannot do everything: the story of Shanghai with the only non-European ghetto (but what a difference), established by the Japanese; the rescue attempts via Lisbon, when thousands were shipped on Portuguese ships, mostly to the Americas (and in two instances, to Palestine); the Brandt mission and the Istanbul outpost; illegal immigration to Palestine up to the Struma incident, and in 1943–44 from Romania and from Greece; the actions and nonactions of the Allies (but it is difficult perhaps to present this in maps); the arguments about bombing Auschwitz and the railways, on which Martin Gilbert is of course an expert—and other items. The *Atlas* concentrates on Europe and the "Final Solution," though it does deal with North Africa, which the Wannsee conference included in the plans for the annihilation of the Jews.

There are of course mistakes here and there—hardly avoidable in a work like this; but these can be corrected in future editions. What the *Atlas* does is to deal with the Holocaust directly, with the mass murder and the victims' reactions. It does not deal with the perpetrators and the bystanders, except in passing, and then almost only in the text. Within its self-imposed limits, it is a most important and valuable addition to the teaching of the Holocaust, a tool for dissemination of information. The general conclusions are not stated but very forcefully and convincingly implied: the Nazis' irrational rationality of murderous intent; the trap that the victims found themselves in; the impossibility of resistance, yet resistance nonetheless; the senselessness of this mass dying, and the possible beauty of its alternative—the life of the victims. One can only hope that Gilbert will supplement this work, enlarge it and continue on this path.

YEHUDA BAUER
Hebrew University

Morris Goldman (ed.), *Society in Israel 1980—Statistical Highlights*. Jerusalem: Central Bureau of Statistics, 1980. 26 + 254 + 62 pp. (Hebrew and English)

The lively interest in social matters in modern welfare-oriented states has led to the "social indicators" movement, propounded and developed especially by academic theoreticians. Another outcome of the tendency for improved and conveniently accessible documentation in these respects are compendia of judiciously selected data in social statistics, compiled by official statistics bureaus. An increasing number of countries have published such compendia, and recommendations for their contents and methodology have been issued by the United Nations and other international bodies.

Israel's Central Bureau of Statistics published its first compendium in 1976 under the title *Society in Israel—Selected Statistics* (edited by this reviewer). The 1980 edition essentially follows the earlier one, obviously with updates as well as with improvements in content and presentation.

The present volume is divided into eleven chapters, each of which presents concise data on the development and current situation with regard to: population; households; immigration and absorption; income, expenditure and savings; employment; social security and welfare; health; education; housing; crime and justice; leisure.

The basic data are presented in time series showing the evolution that has taken place with regard to various topics. Cross-classifications are generally provided, with standard variables such as sex, age, years of schooling, region of birth—Israel-born by father's region of birth and period of immigration (for Jews), and religion (for non-Jews). Specific aspects of Israel's socio-demographic scene are reflected, inter alia by the last-named classifications as well as by the chapter on immigration and immigrant absorption.

A methodological introduction and a recent bibliography is provided for each chapter as well as a subject index for the whole book. Numerous graphs illustrate the information in the statistical tables.

While not presenting any hitherto unpublished data, *Society in Israel* is a well-organized and extremely useful repertory of the key information available in the various fields of social statistics. By grouping together in one comprehensive volume the principal statistics on so many social phenomena and trends—a great deal of which can otherwise only be found scattered in specialized publications—this volume greatly facilitates the integration of statistical information.

Besides its function as a convenient reference book, *Society in Israel 1980* is an illuminating inventory of the available types of social statistics in Israel. To the thoughtful reader it can be a source of stimulating reflections on the evolution and current status of a great many social phenomena and trends in Israel.

U. O. SCHMELZ
Hebrew University

Sherry Gorelick, *City College and the Jewish Poor: Education in New York 1880–1924*. New Brunswick: Rutgers University Press, 1981. $7.95.

The late 1960's and early 1970's were years of turmoil and transformation at the City College of New York. Black and Hispanic students demanded that the student body of this municipally-funded institution accurately reflect the racial composition of New York City high schools. When the Open Admissions struggle succeeded and the number of "minority" students rose dramatically, strident undergraduate voices were raised with increasing vehemence to demand significant curricular changes. Black and Hispanic studies programs ultimately resulted from the student complaints that Third World cultures had been ignored in the previously Western-oriented curriculum.

Opponents of this academic revolution mourned the "demise" of City's commitment to educational excellence. The new generation of students was characterized as a breed apart from the meritorious aspirants of the past. The new disciplines were declared intellectually vacuous. And it is Sherry Gorelick's claim that the enemies of change now extolled a mythological history of CCNY which told of generations of poor Jewish students who "with brilliant intellectual preparation and docile, grateful demeanor inspired an appreciative faculty" (p. 194).

Not so, argues Gorelick's revisionist and highly polemical history. City College, in her view, has long tended to denigrate the cultural traditions of its predominantly immigrant and (or) working class student body. And, likewise, a considerable proportion of the students receiving a "free" education have throughout sought to resist the destruction of their ethnic, racial or religious heritage. In short, Gorelick's heavily didactic message informs those of her fellow City University alumni who opposed the changes of the 1970's that it is they and not the students who have broken with the real past of the College.

City College, Gorelick argues, was until almost the turn of the century a school for the children of the prosperous, pervaded with the classics and resistant to the commercial or technical disciplines. Twenty years later, it housed a predominantly Jewish working class student body and was training an elite segment of the immigrant youth both as general participants in the capitalist system and, more particularly, as educators, expected to Americanize their fellow (new) citizens. This far-reaching change, Gorelick suggested, was pioneered by members—and under the influence—of the Jewish socialist and labor movement. It was organized labor, after all, which created the conditions of social unrest that made reform attractive and even essential in the eyes of those Progressive leaders of American business who supported higher education.

But the influence of the left on the City College establishment did not touch the curriculum. On campus, the Jewish student was bombarded with racist and pro-capitalist ideas and values. They were instructed to abandon their "inferior" Jewish socialist and religious cultures. Gorelick implies that only the most ideologically committed socialist students survived the assimilatory pressures to surrender their working class heritage.

Unfortunately, the volume offers little evidence that Jewish students were anything other than "co-conspirators" in their absorption of majority cultural traits and values. While many were undeniably troubled by the criticisms of their heritage, it is also certain that few came to the College to read—as Gorelick suggests they should have—Yiddish poetry. That was the world they were willing to leave behind. And to suggest otherwise is to put unsubstantiated words into their mouths. But the "minority" students of today are different. They come to City College in search of both personal mobility and their own cultural heritage. This change may well explain the communication gap which separates City College students, past and present.

JEFFREY S. GUROCK
Yeshiva University

Arthur Goren (ed. and intro.), *Dissenter in Zion*. Cambridge: Harvard University Press, 1982. vxi + 554 pp. $30.00.

This selection from the writings of Judah L. Magnes adds significantly to the published material on recent Jewish history from a particularly illuminating angle: that of a centrally important participant who was a perennial outsider and "dissenter." No one shared more intimately than Magnes the crucial experiences of so wide a range of Jewish circles in his time—and no one remained as detached and independent as he did. He was the "uptown" German Jew who alone could speak for "downtown" East European immigrants in New York; he was the American Jewish leader who, together with Henrietta Szold, shared the whole travail of the Yishuv in Palestine throughout the

Mandate period. His life story, documented in his own words, illuminates the period in a peculiarly revealing light.

Yet what is revealed about the times is almost incidental to the purpose of this book, in which Arthur Goren presents a striking portrait of a truly extraordinary man. This documentary collection does not seek to overwhelm us by the massive coverage of its subject. It achieves its aim, an understanding of a man and his times, by a selection that focuses with unerring accuracy on the essential events and crucial personal dilemmas of a life revealed with unusual candor and eloquence. The broad development and decisive moments of that biography, lucidly documented, are solidly grounded in the editor's introduction, which sets the scene with economy, judgment and a lightly sketched critical perspective.

John Haynes Holmes once wrote that "Magnes is the greatest prophetic spirit in the world of Jewry today." A prophet, among other qualifications, must hold fast to principle in the face of certain, immediate defeat, and in the face of the facts as commonly perceived. Magnes obviously took a prophetic role, in this sense, as his model; but Goren makes it clear that commitment was far from a simple or superficial matter for him. In spite of the "innocent," unquestioning faith that some saw in his dedication to the absolute demands of his chosen role, he experienced with considerable anguish the crisis of belief; and, moreover, he was often given to rationalizations more suitable to a politician and a negotiator than to a prophet.

Magnes was a rabbi unable to attain theological conviction. In a telling passage that Goren highlights, Magnes' "journal" quotes from an article by Karl Barth, "Paradox ethical: 'To seek God's will zealously, with the foregone conclusion that God's will cannot be found . . . This is not discovering God's will, but it is, after all, acknowledging it.'" This, however, is the attitude of a pietist, not a prophet. In the context of this reflection, Magnes describes his own life as a Zionist: "to seek the fullness of Judaism zealously, with the conclusion foregone that this cannot be found . . ." But none of his own doubt was allowed to invade his messages to the Jewish people—except on the occasion of his sermons delivered to the Hebrew University during the years of war and Holocaust. At other times he spoke to the Jews, or for the Jewish people, in the tones of a veritable prophet indeed.

A prophet speaks with authority; and Magnes spoke with authority—if not with that of a divine message, then with that which came to him as the voice both of "the fullness of Judaism" and also of the authentic will of the Jewish people in his time. To do so in the face of contradictory evidence, sometimes overwhelming; required not only faith but a considerable skill in rationalization. Magnes made his first indelible impression upon the Jewish public by his unrivalled rapport, as a leader of "uptown" German Jewish Americans, with the Russian Jewish immigrant "masses" downtown. But in the battle over the creation of the American Jewish Congress in World War I he broke with the "common" Jews to side with the establishment of wealth and notability—not, however, without arguing that his own position represented the only possible, authentic consensus of American, and world, Jewry.

The same course was traced in his relations with the Jews of Palestine. He lived the better part of his active life among them, and he shared all their most uplifting and most tragic experiences. Yet a moment came when he felt that, in the name of the "fullness of Judaism," Palestinian Jewry—or at least the leaders they had chosen (for he claimed to know that in their deepest hearts the majority would side with him)—should have imposed upon them from the outside, by Britain and America, the form of their future relations with their Arab neighbors.

To achieve this end, he lent himself to the anti-Zionist, if not anti-Jewish, designs of diplomats who sought at the eleventh hour to abort the birth of the Jewish state. But on the morrow of Israel's birth, Magnes came to Dr. Weizmann to congratulate him on the event. This was in one way, a characteristic act of American, or "Anglo-Saxon" sportsmanship. It had a deeper significance, for Magnes was utterly committed to sharing the destiny of the Jewish state he had so staunchly opposed. He died soon after, in the midst of a gallant effort to achieve the peaceable integration of the sovereign Jewish state into a regional federation with its Arab neighbors.

It was a truly exemplary, an epic life. The portrait presented to us by Dr. Goren is in every way worthy of its subject.

BEN HALPERN
Brandeis University

Moshe R. Gottlieb, *American Anti-Nazi Resistance, 1933–1941*. New York: Ktav Publishing House, Inc., 1982, xxi + 426 pp. n.p.

This book is organized in a rather uncommon way: thirty-eight chapters (each chapter with sub-chapters), each one dealing with a different aspect or organization connected with the efforts made in the United States against Nazi Germany, mainly on the economic level.

The title gives too general an idea of the theme. It turns out that what happened hardly added up to "resistance." The term "boycott" would have been more appropriate, especially considering that most of the efforts were on the economic level. Furthermore, the whole matter cannot be considered widely "American," but rather American Jewish: all the outstanding figures, most of the organizations, almost all of the meager financial resources were Jewish. Indeed, the one major problem of the boycott movement was not so much that larger segments of American society did not participate in it, but that a significant segment of the American Jewish leadership or leading organizations kept aloof from it. And the few non-Jewish associations formed—like the Volunteer Christian Committee to Boycott Nazi Germany—did so late (at the end of 1938) and remained small and ineffective.

On a more general level, the whole theme of "anti-Nazi boycott" raises again the old but significant question of how to evaluate the effectiveness of "public opinion" and "public pressure." The obvious answer—through its results—has the not less obvious limitation that it is exceedingly difficult to differentiate between the diverse components of a change of policy—the public, political, economic, ideological, military. Another useful gauge of the strength of "public opinion" is to verify how much its spokesmen are ready to sacrifice, in terms of personal, public or national interests, for the sake of their goals. Considering the plight of German Jewry during the thirties, one sure answer to their difficulties would have been to promote their emigration from Germany. At that stage, this was also the aim of the Nazis. Jewish immigration to the United States could also conceivably have become a major goal of American Jewry. But as Feingold *(The Politics of Rescue)*, Kubowsky *(Unity and Dispersion)*, Neuringer *(American Jews and United States Immigration Policy, 1881–1953)* and others have more than convincingly shown, to act for such a solution was beyond either the capacity, or the strength of will or the conviction of American Jewry and its representative figures.

In other words, considered by these (or any reasonable) criteria, it seems that American Jewish activity during the thirties on behalf of German Jewry or against Nazi Germany accomplished very little. Gottlieb's book, although detailed and soberly written (even if less soberly titled), strives unfortunately in the wrong direction. By trying to transform a non-theme into a theme, it misses the point that at least from the perspective of American Jewish history would have been the important one—why did American Jewry do so little during the thirties for German Jewry.

The fact is that during the first two decades of the century American Jewry and its leadership had been much more active in the defense of their European brethren's rights. They had stood in the vanguard of the effort against limitation of free immigration into the United States, even when it meant acting against the swelling tide of sentiment in the WASP establishment and in other important sectors of American society. Later on, during the forties, American Jewry mobilized again, and quite successfully so, in the cause of a Jewish state in Palestine.

The twenties and thirties, on the other hand, were years of relative inactivity, as far as the external interests of American Jewry were concerned. The question is how to explain that behavior of the Jewish community during these years. What were the internal developments which had made it possible; who were the leaders and what forces in the community did they represent; and what were the patterns of relationship between Jews and non-Jews influencing the community?

These are questions Gottlieb has not addressed. Nevertheless, because of the wealth of information the book contains, it represents a positive contribution towards a history of American Jewry during the twenties and thirties, still to be written.

EVYATAR FRIESEL
Hebrew University

Alfred Abraham Greenbaum, *Jewish Scholarship and Scholarly Institutions in Soviet Russia 1918–1953*. Jerusalem: The Hebrew University of Jerusalem, Center for Research and Documentation of East European Jewry, 1978.

The publication of this survey reflects Professor A. A. Greenbaum's continued interest in the organization and the categorization of scholarly writings on Jewish topics produced by Jews and non-Jews in the Soviet Union since the Revolution. In this work, the author does not confine himself to the historical field only, but also catalogs the research and publication of works in the fields of literature, philology, sociology and demography. Professor Greenbaum's effort represents the result of a meticulous search of the literature in order to uncover not only the publications from the period but also to identify manuscripts that were in the process of being prepared but still remain unpublished.

As is to be expected, the work concentrates on the official, state-sponsored, scholarly activities generally associated with the government-supported institutes at Kiev and Minsk and with the circle of writers gathered about the publicist M. Litvakov in Moscow in the late 1920's and 1930's. In addition, Professor Greenbaum also reviews the work of such independent scholars as Saul Ginsburg, Israel Zinberg, Iulii Gessen and even Simon Dubnov as they tried to continue the pre-revolutionary traditions of Jewish scholarship promoted by the Society for the Dissemination of Culture Among Jews and by the Jewish Historical-Ethnographic Society, both of which functioned through the first decade of Soviet rule.

However, a truly complete analysis of Jewish scholarship in this period should also shed light on the manner in which the Soviet Revolution served to alter the traditions and the methodologies employed in scholarly circles in Imperial Russia. In doing so, such a study would also provide us with another perspective on Soviet policies toward the nationality question in general and the Jewish community in particular. While Professor Greenbaum's work does touch on some of these concerns, notably the ideological twists and turns taken in the aftermath of the Revolution by historians when dealing with Jewish history, the truth is that his work does not furnish us with that broader, more comprehensive analysis called for by this topic and by the title of the work.

What we have here is much more of a bibliographic essay with comments about particular publications rather than an analytical assessment of the material. Professor Greenbaum does make the effort to offer such an analysis, but his assessment rarely goes beyond the identification of author, title and date of publication, and a summary of the topics covered by that particular work. There is no discussion here of the argumentation or the methodologies employed by the Soviet scholars, nor is there any effort made to compare Jewish scholarship with either the scholarship of other ethnic groups produced in the same period, or with the general Soviet scholarly orientations at the time. These omissions, together with the overall character of the work suggest that the study was intended for a very narrow audience—that is, one already familiar with the general tendencies of the period and so only in need of the titles and other source material made available here.

While we are in Professor Greenbaum's debt for this very valuable bibliographical resource, we are still very much in need of the kind of analysis of Jewish scholarship hinted at but not developed in these pages. With this guide in hand, such a study can now be undertaken more readily.

ALEXANDER ORBACH
University of Pittsburgh

Jeffrey S. Gurock, *When Harlem was Jewish*. New York: Columbia University Press, 1979. $22.50.

Jeffrey Gurock's history of Harlem applies the methods of social history to the study of an urban Jewish community. Relying upon census data, city directories, housing reports, and atlases, Gurock paints a portrait of a thriving New York City Jewish neighborhood. In fact, during the first two decades of the twentieth century two Jewish Harlems flourished side by side: a working-class settlement located in the densely populated tenements east of Lexington Avenue and a prosperous quarter of successful Jewish immigrants living in the brownstones and modern apartments north of Central Park.

Despite their class differences, both sections of the Harlem Jewish community responded similarly to the critical issue of assimilation that confronted all immigrant groups in the United States. Both working and middle-class Jews in Harlem created innovative communal institutions designed to combat the anarchic pressures of urban life that uprooted Jewish immigrants from their ethnic and religious heritage. The former built a model Jewish socialist school under Workmen's Circle auspices and hired American-born public school teachers sympathetic to radicalism to serve the needs of a new generation of American Jews. The latter turned to the Uptown Talmud Torah, a community-sponsored afternoon Hebrew school, and transformed it into a leading modern Jewish educational institution.

This desire to reach the American-educated generation also fueled the beginnings of Conservative Judaism and the synagogue center movement. Harlem's modern Orthodox synagogues, especially Israel Goldstein's Institutional Synagogue, which was established in 1917 in the comfortable section of Harlem, catered to the second generation and served as a prototype for future American synagogues. The development of these organizations brought together Jews of German and East European background. The rapprochement of these two segments of New York Jewry in the educational and religious endeavors of Harlem also presaged changing patterns in American Jewish life.

Gurock portrays this institutional activity against a rich backdrop of urban growth and intra-city migration. He guides the reader through Harlem's tumultuous early years of real estate boom and bust. He skillfully analyzes how the real estate cycle intersected with the growing demand for housing on the part of Jewish immigrants crowded into the Lower East Side and led to the establishment of the Jewish community in Harlem. While Gurock discusses sociological theories of immigrant succession in neighborhoods and the movement from the inner city slum to areas of second settlement, his detailed narrative of the process in Harlem suggests that models may be too simple an explanatory tool to account for the complexities of intra-city migration, even of one immigrant group. The vitality of Harlem's Jewish community, numbering over 100,000 at its peak in 1910, and especially its vibrant working-class culture, leads Gurock to argue that areas of first and second settlement "do not refer to static geographic localities but to differing types of settler behavior" (p. 56); physical mobility does not necessarily imply social mobility. Similarly, in explaining the rapid decline of Jewish Harlem in the 1920s, he shows how the expected pattern of intra-city migration did not materialize, because the real estate market was drastically influenced by the desperate need of Blacks for housing. This demand forced up Harlem rents and encouraged immigrant Jews to leapfrog over West Harlem and move to the Bronx.

Because it addresses issues concerning the Jewish community as it was structured in institutions and examines theories relevant to the nature of urban Jewish life in its ecological setting, *When Harlem Was Jewish* makes an important contribution to the study of modern Jewry. Its quantified social data encourages comparisons with other Jewish communities; its challenge to social science theories of immigrant mobility and assimilation reveals the need for new constructs; and its attention to the economic underpinnings of migration prompts a fresh look at assumptions regarding the immigrant experience.

DEBORAH DASH MOORE
Vassar College

Zeev Hadari and Zeev Tzahor, *Oniot o medinah? Korot oniot hama'apilim "Pan York" u-"Pan Crescent"* (Ships or a State? The Story of the Underground Immigrant Ships "Pan York" and "Pan Crescent"). Tel Aviv: Ha-kibbutz ha-meuhad and Ben-Gurion University of the Negev.

Ships or a State? tells the story of the largest and most complicated illegal immigration effort undertaken after the Second World War. Two cargo ships, the "Pan York" and the "Pan Crescent," were bought in the United States and converted for the transport of illegal immigrants to Palestine. This single trip of 15,000 immigrants from

Romania accounted for 20 percent of all illegal immigration to Palestine after the war.

The journey to Palestine started on 27 December 1947, almost a month after the UN partition resolution which, *inter alia,* called for the opening of a free port for Jewish immigrants by 1 February 1948. The voyage was preceded by a fierce dispute between the political leadership of the Zionist movement and the head of the Mossad le-aliyah (underground immigration organization) as to whether to send the ships to Palestine, thus risking newly-won political achievements, or to delay the journey and thereby risk not only this operation but also future immigration from Communist Romania. The ships sailed and the immigrants were caught by British forces. They were sent to Cyprus, having offered no resistance as was agreed beforehand between the Mossad activists and the political leaders.

The large Jewish community in Romania survived the Holocaust and gave shelter to many refugees. A great proportion of Romanian Jewry was ready to emigrate. Some of them were Zionists; some did not want to live under a communist regime; and some did not want to live in a gentile and hostile society. The Romanian government was favorably disposed to Jewish emigration, which would rid the country of a lower middle class whose integration into a communist system was difficult; it would provide the country—in poor shape after the war—with the benefits deriving from the property the Jews left behind, and from the foreign currency it received for each emigrant. Last but not least, Soviet interest in obstructing British policy in the Middle East favored such emigration.

Transporting 15,000 people in a few days was a complicated business involving a considerable amount of paperwork and checking with the interior office and the police. The emigrants went by train to Burgas and from there boarded the ships. An additional three thousand people not on the official lists had smuggled themselves on board. It was extremely difficult to handle so many people in two crowded boats, to maintain order and to create as little confusion as possible. Much discipline, efficiency and trust were needed to complete the task in only a few days. Misunderstandings and sometimes even mistreatment by the Israeli escorts are not overlooked in this account. The gap between different worlds of the emigrants on the one hand and the young Mossad people on the other is depicted with insight. We have here in microcosm an illustration of the confrontation between the world of the Diaspora and that of the Palestinian-Israeli.

The climax of the drama of the two "Pans" was reached in the debate between the Mossad le-aliyah and the political leadership, which the authors describe meticulously. The objection of the politicians to the voyage rested on the pressure of the US government to stop illegal immigration and in particular to halt the voyage of the "Pan York" and "Pan Crescent." American objections weighed heavily in Zionist political considerations: a change in US policy toward partition could prove disastrous. Moshe Shertok (later Sharett) took the position that the ships' voyage should be postponed or even cancelled, and he was supported by both Ben-Gurion and Golda Meir.

The Mossad people appreciated the delicacy of the political situation, but could not agree to halt the immigrants' departure. Here were people who believed strongly in the importance of action in achieving the goals of national rebirth. They could not accept that illegal immigration was to be regarded merely as a political tool. The conflict between them and the Zionist leadership also entailed tensions between established leaders and a new, young social group.

Although the Mossad le-aliyah could not work except under the authority of the Haganah—and above it, the Jewish Agency—the activists opted to go ahead with the "Pans" operation, evading the clear intent of the political leadership if not openly disobeying.

The questions raised here are basic to any understanding of the illegal immigration: Was it a national movement of the masses, or a political tactic used by politicians? How important was the Mossad le-aliyah in giving the movement impetus and how did the Mossad evolve along the way? Was it only a branch of the Haganah, or did it develop its own "vested interests" and try to become as independent as possible? What were the relations between the activists in the field and the leaders in Jerusalem, New York and London? What was the importance of the immigration to the immigrants themselves, to the Yishuv in general and to Zionist policy?

Some of these questions are raised in the book, while some are only hinted at. A full and thorough discussion can take place only within the framework of a comparative analysis of illegal immigration vis-à-vis Jewish needs and Jewish politics at various points in the history of the immigration movement. Research is still in the early stages in this regard, and we need to know more about specific operations before we can generalize. The importance of the story of the two "Pans" lies in its contribution to the understanding of illegal immigration as a phenomenon in Jewish history. We have now reached an in-between stage in the research—between case studies and an integrated approach. This book therefore has intrinsic limitations, but is an important and interesting study.

DALIA OFER
Hebrew University

Janet R. Hadda, *Yankev Glatshteyn*. Boston: Twayne Publishers, 1980. $13.50.

To live in *goles (galut)* [exile], he was fond of saying, Glatshteyn had to know who Auden was, but Auden didn't have to know who Glatshteyn was. Implied in this witty phrase was a world where poetry mattered; more craftily, where he, the American-Yiddish poet, was equal in stature to Auden (Glatshteyn never sold himself short) and finally, where even the most urbane and modern of Yiddish poets was still confined to living in exile. To the extent that Glatshteyn and his contemporaries defied the pressures of *goles*, refused to be pigeonholed, parochialized, rendered obsolete and insisted on their rightful place in the culture of nations, they broke new ground both as Jews and as poets. Once they gave up trying, they guaranteed a future in which their own grandchildren would join with Auden in a conspiracy of indifference.

As Janet Hadda shows in this first full-length study of Glatshteyn's poetry in any language, there was no harsher critic of his own work and that of others than Glatshteyn himself. At the height of his popularity, he was able to recognize the price he had had to pay to assume the mantle of a "national poet": it had meant abandoning the internal discipline of free verse, his natural medium, for the easy recourse of rhyme (pp. 17, 113); addressing the Great Issues of the day, not as experienced and filtered through his individual psyche, but as garnered second-hand, and perhaps most damaging of all—it meant covering his tracks. If we are now in a position to uncover the true extent of his rebellion and to look back in sober reevaluation, it is due in no small measure to the relentless introspection and sophisticated irony that accompanied Glatshteyn's best efforts throughout fifty years of extraordinary productivity.

But when we ask: Will the real Jacob Glatshteyn please stand up, two very different candidates vie for that position. In the view which Glatshteyn himself favored, as shown in his retrospective anthology of 1956 and which the majority of his critics support, the "real" Glatshteyn was the poet of the Holocaust and the one who chose Rabbi Nahman of Bratslav as his poetic mouthpiece. The minority opinion is that Glatshteyn's lasting achievement rests with his first four books of verse, his two novels and his uncollected short stories; in other words, that his period of greatness is identical to the lifespan of the Introspectivist movement which he spearheaded, the years 1920–1940, the heyday of Yiddish modernism. After 1940 he thrived primarily as a critic, a journalist and public figure.

The question, it seems to me, extends beyond conferring grades on this book or that, to a more fundamental question of the limits of Yiddish literature itself. Glatshteyn was by no means the only Jewish writer traumatized by history, nor the only Jewish modernist to adopt a public voice in the face of catastrophe. Natan Alterman's name readily comes to mind in this context. The crucial difference is that Alterman, who made himself over from the most esoteric to the most accessible Hebrew poet, was rediscovered as the pioneer of Hebrew modernism by a generation of native-born Israeli poets, critics and readers, while the audience for Yiddish modernism, as small as it was to begin with, vanished altogether after the Holocaust. No postwar Yiddish poet could afford the luxury of pure introspection if he wanted to see his books published, let alone read.

There are those, moreover, who argue that it couldn't have been otherwise, that a Yiddish culture divorced from its traditional sources was doomed to begin with; that a purely secular, cosmopolitan form of expression could not have thrived in Yiddish and that the Holocaust merely drove the final nail into the coffin. This was I. B. Singer's position as far back as 1943, before the full extent of the Holocaust became known. Glatshteyn had always belonged to the other camp, to those like his mentor Moyshe Leyb Halpern, whose rebellion against Jewish tradition and against traditional poetics was part of an effort to make Yiddish culture self-sufficient. The genius of a poet like Glatshteyn, I would argue, was that he nearly succeeded, and that up until the mid-sixties, he didn't give up trying.

His rebellion, as I said, was total, which made his return that much more tortuous. Hadda is at her best when she documents the impossibility for a man of Glatshteyn's worldliness to do a complete about-face: how he admitted to being the unwilling mouthpiece of his people (p. 94); how he treated God with a mixture of compassion and deprecation (103); how he struggled for simplicity through the figure of Rabbi Nahman (96–98) and used the Hasidic master to ask whether one had the right to exploit the Holocaust for poetic purpose (125); how he lamented the fate of Yiddish after the Holocaust when too much meaning was now being forced into the language and when the poets were reduced to patting each other on the back (146–48).

Alas, this self-knowledge on Glatshteyn's part was partially offset by lapses of self-delusion. To further his public image, he felt compelled to write pro-Zionist poems which were as clichéd in their praise of Israel as they had earlier been in their condemnation. To end an otherwise penetrating self-portrait, he had the urbane Jewish narrator retire—to a Hasidic *shtibl,* there to recite *kaddish* (152). What began in 1938 as a brilliant protest against Western ideas of progress, against the myth of an open society, in his celebrated poem "Good Night, World," became, by the 1960's, a convenient fall-back, a way to avoid staking new ground as a poet. Glatshteyn even went so far as to deny that he and his fellow modernists had ever intended to reject Jewish tradition (pp. 157–58, 167, 173)!

The poet doth protest too much. If anything, such a blatant misrepresentation of the past, offered late in life, suggests that Glatshteyn never really renounced his modernism, that his two attempts at "reconciliation" may never have actually happened, for the poet never fully rejected his self for the sake of the collective or allowed the public agenda to displace his poetic commitment. This is where the novels, as Dan Miron has taught, come in.

Based on a visit to Poland in 1934, the novels *Ven Yash iz geforn* (1938) and *Ven Yash iz gekumen* (1940) show Glatshteyn moving towards a synthesis of self and society while insisting on the formal requirements of literature in rendering that society. Though the Holocaust intervened, all but submerging the poet's individual voice for a while, he managed, even then, to find the perfect complement of form for the content of unfolding terror, especially in such early poems as "Ghetto song" with its heart-rending use of diminutive verb forms and "Wagons" (1938), an understated vision of death and mass expulsion. The final reconciliation in *Gezangen fun rekhts tsu links* ("Songs from Right to Left," 1971)—with womankind, with his Jewishness, with Israel, Yiddish and his own rebellious past—was sooner a capitulation, a pathetic attempt to recant for the sins of his youth. Hadda admits as much, try as she might to bring the book—and Glatshteyn's life—to a happier end (p. 179).

Every great poet lives in exile. That Glatshteyn tried to escape from his own state of *goles* by seeking the embrace of a putative Tradition was an ironic, if understandable choice, because his eventual redemption will come, I believe, when a Yiddish poet is no longer valued solely for what he has to say about *yidishkeyt*. When that day comes, Glatshteyn's rehabilitation will be swift and resounding. "Glatshteyn we know," they will say. "But who was Auden?"

DAVID G. ROSKIES
The Jewish Theological Seminary
of America

Colin Holmes, *Anti-Semitism in British Society 1876–1939*. London: Edward Arnold, 1979, viii + 328 pp. £ 15.

A modern historian trying to use background knowledge about the Anglo-Jewish community to enable him to understand fully the development of anti-Semitism in Britain, during his selected period, is entitled to complain that information is scarce, as does the author of this work. It is not clear, however, why the complaint is directed solely against Anglo-Jewish sociologists, who are criticized for over-concentration on the questions of Jewish identity and cohesiveness, and for ignoring matters such as statistics about Jewish economic life. Surely, historians themselves and other social scientists are at least equally to blame for the lacunae.

If Holmes feels that his analysis was hampered by this lack of information, the deficiency is less than obvious—no doubt due to the masterly manner in which he recounts and analyzes the by-ways of British anti-Semitism. He covers the entire ground step by step: from the xenophobic sentiments of "Britain for the British" to the accusation that "genuine Jews" could not be patriotic; from conspiratorial theories of world domination expressed even in respected journalistic and literary circles to the unfounded fears expressed by medical men and scientists, such as Karl Pearson, regarding the dangers to health that alien immigrants, synonymous with Jewish immigrants in the late 19th century, posed to the British population; from secularized versions of the medieval view that Jews would bring about the spiritual and physical ruin of Christendom to the irrational claims that Jews either personified capitalism and materialism or that they were all Bolsheviks.

These are the well-known elements that make up the fabric of modern anti-Semitism, but innovation is to be found in the way Colin Holmes focuses on the interaction between these ideas and the personal psyche of the men holding them or utilizing them second-hand (*The Protocols,* for example). Thus we come across the leading British anti-Semites active both in dissemination of anti-Semitic literature and the organization of such movements as the Militant Christian Patriots or the British Union of Fascists.

Anti-Semitism in Britain was influenced first by the anti-Semitism of the Tsars in Russia and later by the Hitlerite version in Germany, although their excesses militated against the movements in Britain. Holmes holds, however, that the social disruption caused by the First World War and by the economic collapse of the 1930s was a more potent force aiding the enemies of the Jews. Yet, in comparison with other European countries, anti-Semitic thought was relatively little translated into action in Britain. A strong liberalism was rooted in British society and its political structure was able to withstand the crises and tensions. And the Jewish community itself was not slow in organizing its own defense. As a result, "although Jews in Britain faced a wider challenge than other racial and ethnic minorities," there were strong forces in Britain which opposed anti-Semitism. But the author warns that it would be a deception to think that anti-Semitism was insignificant in Britain and sees the continuance of such a hostile tradition and the fear of Jewish power as especially potent in situations of economic and social dislocation.

Incidentally, one is prompted by Holmes' conclusions to speculate that the anti-Israeli stance of Britain and other European countries, in the era following the period scrutinized by him, might stem from an irrational fear of Jewish power symbolized by a strong Israel, especially in military terms. But only further research will lift such ideas out of the realm of speculation. Can it be, though, that the hostile tradition in this earlier period, uncovered by Holmes, is now maintaining itself in a modern guise?

ERNEST KRAUSZ
Bar-Ilan University

Alfred Jospe (ed. and intro.), *Studies in Jewish Thought: An Anthology of German Jewish Scholarship*. A Publication of the Leo Baeck Institute. Detroit: Wayne State University Press, 1981. 434 pp. $25.00.

It continues to be true in Jewish studies that knowledge of the German language is indispensable for the scholar whatever his or her field of specialization. Yet students in the United States and in Israel rarely master the language unless or until they embark on doctoral studies. The most significant writings of *Wissenschaft des Judentums* nearly all remain inaccessible to them and to general readers, although the best of these studies retain not only specific scholarly value but also broader interest.

Alfred Jospe's anthology of German Jewish scholarship in the area of Jewish thought, translated into English, thus serves a useful purpose. He has selected those essays which were either themselves epoch making, such as Leopold Zunz's "On Rabbinic Literature," or made a scholarly contribution which has stood the test of time. Most of the writers who appear as authors of the seventeen selections are twentieth-century scholars. Represented more than once are Julius Guttmann, Max Wiener, Isaak Heinemann, and Alexander Altmann. Their subjects range from mysticism to philosophy, the periods discussed from antiquity to modernity. Two essays are devoted to Maimonides, no less than four to Moses Mendelssohn. In a few instances the notes of the original have been omitted.

Jospe has provided a brief—perhaps too brief—introduction and some background information on each of the scholars represented. The translations, which were done by Jospe himself and five others, seem competent and fluent, the addition of an index quite helpful. At a time when progressively fewer Jews claim German as their mother tongue, this volume comes to transplant some of the most vigorous shoots of German Jewish scholarship into a new linguistic soil.

                      MICHAEL A. MEYER
                      Hebrew Union College-Jewish Institute
                      of Religion (Cincinnati)

Nathan M. Kaganoff (ed.), *Guide to America-Holy Land Studies.* Vol. 1: American Presence. Introd. by Moshe Davis. New York: Arno Press, 1980. 127 pp. $20.00.

Nathan M. Kaganoff (ed.), *Guide to America-Holy Land Studies, 1620–1948.* Vol. 2: Political Relations and American Zionism. Introd. by Moshe Davis. New York: Praeger Publications, 1982. 214 pp.

These two volumes constitute a descriptive guide to archival holdings in which material pertaining to ties between America and Palestine "from the early nineteenth century to 1948" is to be found. They form part of the "America-Holy Land Studies" series co-sponsored by the American Jewish Historical Society and the Institute of Contemporary Jewry in Jerusalem. In the first volume, based on some fifty repositories, the emphasis is on unofficial ties. Among the topics covered are travelers' reports, problems of immigrants, colonization schemes, some diplomatic correspondence, and the missionary presence. The emphasis in the second volume is on political ties, and it covers fewer repositories but more collections of organizational and personal papers, including those of Presidents Roosevelt and Truman. The backward extension of the time span is not borne out by the volume in hand and may be intended for future volumes.

Coverage is limited to archives in the USA and Israel. The editors admit that it would have been desirable to include repositories in other countries as well, but the project is based on personal inspection rather than correspondence, and preference has been given to detail of description rather than to extensiveness of coverage. This detail, much greater than in most similar publications, seems excessive in some instances and may reflect the interests of the participants in the project more than the anticipated needs of the user.

Another point on which this work can be criticized is the lack of sequential item numbering, today almost de rigueur in such publications (a reference to item rather than page number saves the reader's time). Furthermore, while the index of personal and organizational names is good as far as it goes, the editors should have risked limited subject entries (e.g. medicine) in spite of the ensuing complications in their files. However, such technical points aside, this is a very useful and well-written publication.

ALFRED A. GREENBAUM
Haifa University

Yehoshua Kaniel, *Hemshekh utemurah: Hayishuv hayashan vehayishuv heḥadash bitkufat ha'aliyah harishonah vehashniyah* (Continuity and Change, the Old Yishuv and the New Yishuv during the Period of the First and Second Aliyah). Jerusalem: Yad Ben-Zvi, 1981.

This work by Yehoshua Kaniel is an account of the relations between the "old" Yishuv and the "new" as they developed in Palestine in the years 1880–1914. It is divided into two parts, one dealing with the period known as the First Aliyah, from 1882 to 1903, and the other with the period of the Second Aliyah, 1904–1914. The author has had recourse to much material not utilized previously, an astonishing profusion of sources in archives and the press. He explains the distinction between the two parts of the book in his foreword, where he defines the first period as that of the struggle between the "old" and the "new" Yishuv and the second as marking the withdrawal of the former camp from the contest. This is the first scholarly attempt from within to analyze the social life of the "old" Yishuv and to trace its response to the challenge of the post-1881 immigration.

In the introductory chapter the author sketches a profile of the Yishuv in the nineteenth century from the social and organizational points of view. His description centers around the Ashkenazi urban Yishuv only—thus neglecting the Sephardi and Oriental Jews—a fact he does not sufficiently emphasize. In terms of the organizational side of the "old" Yishuv, the author sees the *halukah* (charitable distribution system) not only as the economic basis of the Yishuv but also as the lynchpin of its social structure. In cultural terms, he contends that the period was marked by the losing battle of the "old" Yishuv to prevent the successful introduction of "modern" education.

The author in his foreword explains the confrontation between the "old" Yishuv and the "new" as a clash between religious and secular-national values. He states that the polarization between the "old" and the "new" became so sharply defined during the 1880's as to be irreconcilable. In presenting his conclusions so unequivocally before he offers any precise analysis, the author obscures the dynamic relationship between the "old" and the "new," which was perhaps the most interesting phenomenon concealed behind the declared attitudes of both sides.

Even though these terms—the "old" and the "new" Yishuv—date from the 1890's, Kaniel applies the term "old" to the Yishuv as far back as the end of the eighteenth century. In general, the more he enters into a detailed analysis, the harder it becomes to retain any clear-cut distinction between the two camps. Certainly they were not divided by a neat line running between rural and urban settlement, a productive and non-productive society, or between a national and a religious ideology. It cannot even be said that members of the new Yishuv arrived later than those in the old Yishuv, since most of the Ashkenazi population of the old Yishuv were actually newcomers of the 1870's, 1880's, and 1890's.

Eventually, Kaniel falls back on three criteria for defining membership in the older community: attachment to the values of its founders; an organizational link to the *halukah* system (particularly via the *kolelim*); and an identification with the way of life as it had taken shape by 1881 in the Jewish communities of the four "holy cities." Whoever did not fit this definition belonged either to the Sephardi community or to the "new" Yishuv. In his urge to distinguish the different camps typologically, the author misses the dynamism revealed in the many instances of inter-group relations; fails to give an account of the relative size and geographic distribution of the groups; and neglects the concrete socio-economic picture. Moreover, he himself later shows that in many instances members of the "new" Yishuv, in the farm colonies, benefited from the *ḥalukah*, either as individuals or collectively; and that most of them retained an attachment to the traditional East European way of life. If this was the case, then clearly to a great extent, at least, the proposed typologies break down.

Kaniel cites an 1898 issue of *Ḥavaẓelet*, in which Frumkin contended that, "The nationality of Israel is the Torah," and that terms such as "motherland," "rebirth" and "soil" were not to be found in the lexicon of the "old" Yishuv (pp. 40–41). The author pays no heed to the fact this was put forward in the course of the polemics of the 1890's and that Frumkin himself had expressed far-reaching nationalist ideas in the early 1880's. If modern nationalism is identified with secularism, then we are faced with an a priori exclusion of religious Zionism—a hypothesis that the author himself rejects (p. 42). And yet he fails, in practice, to distinguish clearly between opposition to secular nationalism and opposition to religious nationalism.

The author's account of the deepening inroads made by secularism does not succeed in evaluating its precise scope. In examining the controversy over Hebrew, he comes to the interesting conclusion that opposition to its use as a vernacular did not start as a matter of principle but developed because the "re-birth" of Hebrew became a slogan of the modernizing, nationalist *maskilim*. The attitude of the "old" Yishuv to modern education lay in fact at the heart of the struggle and the author enumerates a number of foci of tension involving pedagogy. But he does not explain how they actually differed regarding the values and the content of education, nor does he make clear how far the new ideas were actually incorporated into the schooling of the "old" Yishuv.

The author considers that the *ḥalukah* was also a focus of strained relations between the two sides, and he is very successful in describing the *ḥalukah* institutions and their place in the social network of the Yishuv. However, he does not discriminate between objective and polemical sources and as a result produces contradictory data. For example, on p. 62, the number of those receiving *ḥalukah* funds is given once as 27,170 (p. 62), and elsewhere as 19,000 (p. 66). The former figure is for 1909 and the latter for 1913. What happened in these four years to reduce the number so drastically? Or is one of the sources unreliable?

As regards the attitude to agricultural settlement, the author shows that the opposition by the "old" Yishuv was not primarily a matter of principle. It was, in part, the result of objective circumstances such as the endemic insecurity in the country and, in part, a reaction to the development of the "new" Yishuv—fear of secularization and fear for the loss of hegemony in the Yishuv. As regards practical settlement activity, the "old" Yishuv had a large share in the initiatives of the "new" (pp. 112–115). Here the author nullifies his own previous definition connecting the "new" Yishuv with secularization, since he shows that observant Jews were the predominant element in many of the farming colonies (p. 122).

The second part of the book deals with the "old" Yishuv in the period when, according to the author, it withdrew from confrontation with the "new". Here the author points to the extreme elements such as the Hungarian *kolel* which provoked intellectual ferment and splits within the "old" Yishuv. Among the groups which now drew closer to the "new" Yishuv he includes the founders of Agudat Israel in Palestine and the coterie that formed around the newspaper *Hamoriah* (pp. 198–200); the "Shomrei-Torah" League (which established an educational network for strictly observant Jews in the *moshavot*); and the successor to this league, the German Hitahdut haharedim. On the other hand, he shows how extreme traditional elements in the "old" Yishuv supported the pro-German against the pro-Hebrew camp in the language conflict, and not merely in order to enrage the nationalists (p. 207). This is undoubtedly one of the most illuminating chapters in the book.

Elsewhere the author shows the spiritual-religious tie between the "old" Yishuv and the agricultural colonies *(moshavot)*, and describes the initiatives it took to increase its influence in them (p. 236). This to some extent contradicts his basic contention that in the period of the Second Aliyah the "old" Yishuv withdrew in face of the "new". Similarly, his contention that World War I disrupted cooperation between the two camps likewise undermines the thesis that the "old" had retreated into itself long before 1914.

The complex realities described by the author likewise undermine his schematization when it comes to the chapter on the labor movement. Workers from the "old" Yishuv were on occasion drawn to the trade unions established by the socialists of the Second Aliyah. Against this threat to the established order, leaders of both the "old" and the "new" Yishuv were ready to make common cause—at least on an ad hoc (strike-breaking) basis.

In sum, it is correct to say that the institutions of the "old" Yishuv were weakened in the first decades of the twentieth century, but this led not to its retreat but rather to its cooperation with the generation of the First Aliyah in the face of the challenge from the next wave of immigrants.

In spite of meanderings to and fro in the narrative and inconsistencies in the conclusions drawn, Kaniel's book unquestionably opens a new phase in the study of the beginnings of the "new" Yishuv and its relations with the "old." It also forms an excellent complement to Menahem Friedman's *Society and Religion: Non-Zionist Orthodoxy in Palestine, 1918–1936* (published in Hebrew in 1978). Kaniel sheds new light on the complex phenomenon called the Jewish Yishuv in Palestine at the close of the Ottoman period and for this he deserves the warmest praise.

YOSSI SALMON
Ben-Gurion University of the Negev

Marion A. Kaplan, *Die jüdische Frauenbewegung in Deutschland: Organisation und Ziele des jüdischen Frauenbundes 1904–1938.* (Hamburger Beiträge zur Geschichte der deutsche Juden, Band VII) Hamburg: Hans Christians Verlag, 1981. English edition: *The Jewish Feminist Movement in Germany* Westport, CT: Greenwood Press, 1981. $19.95.

The historiography of German Jewry has been for years the prerogative of German Jewish emigrant scholars. Above all, it has been the Leo Baeck Institute which has collected and published the writings of these men and women about their lost community. It was the task of a generation, a kind of memorial to past glory. One had good reason to fear that with the gradual passing away of those who had grown up in Germany, enjoyed mastery of its language and cherished its heritage, this work would come to an end. Such, however, has not been the case. Everywhere, especially, but not exclusively, in the United States, a new generation of scholars has taken over. The product of a different language, education and culture, they have brought to the task a fresh energy, combined with the advantages of perspective and professionalism. They write a different kind of history, of course, but it is none the less valuable.

Marion Kaplan is one of these historians. Combining her training in general German history with her dedication to the cause of feminism, she has written an interesting and useful book. Like all good works of history, this one too makes one wonder why it had not been written earlier. It is a book about the Jüdischer Frauenbund (JFB), from its inception in the early years of this century until its final dissolution by the Nazis late in 1938. Characteristically, it had been first written and published in English (in a series of works in women's studies), and only later translated and published in German (in a series of works on German Jewish history). The German version before us is somewhat less readable, the result of an only partially successful translation, but it is somewhat enlarged at crucial junctures, and has been revised, lending more precision to a number of the earlier formulations. As it now stands it is a model for the monographic work on German Jewry that we need—a social history, which vigorously applies new perspectives and poses new questions, while at the same time relying on the study of a single organization in order to keep within the bounds of manageable research and in order to end up with modest but firmly based results.

The Jüdischer Frauenbund, a unique organization, encompassing even during its early years over one-quarter of all eligible Jewish women in Germany, is in itself significant enough, and well worth an investigation. But for Marion Kaplan this is but an opportunity to pose new questions in the fields of German Jewish history, of German women's history, and even of general German history. She begins by arguing for an additional dimension in the study of German Jews. One must go beyond the Berlin-oriented and the elite-centered studies, she argues. Furthermore, one must add the perspective of gender to the familiar divisions of religion (or ethnicity) and of class. Her book proves the validity of these assertions. Throughout the nineteenth century, and into the twentieth, Kaplan explains, Jewish women carried the double jeopardy of an identity determined by both their religious or ethnic situation (never defined as national by Kaplan) and their sex. Their emancipation both as Jews and as women had to be continuously reasserted, but the burden of their sex, she argues convincingly, was for them often the more problematic.

We are thus confronted with the double story of Jewish and women's emancipation. In the history of European social change these have often gone hand in hand, from the latter part of the eighteenth century onward. Interestingly enough, it was Jewish emancipation which was first formally achieved, while the emancipation of women, especially in Germany, evolved more slowly, suffering repeated setbacks until well into the Weimar period. Jewish women, therefore, shared with the men the burden of anti-Semitism, and many—though, I would add, by no means all—of the concrete manifestations of discrimination and exclusion. As women they probably were often protected from some of the more crass manifestations of anti-Jewishness. But at the same time, they shared in full measure the disadvantages— and, one is again tempted to add, the advantages—of German women.

They shared with them, above all, the class-specific role of the "höhere Töchter," brought up to serve the needs and the wishes of her future husband, as his subordinate, fulfilling honorably her sacred role of "Hausfrau" and "Mutter."

On the Jewish side, most interesting are the efforts of the JFB to strengthen Jewish self-awareness among its members. Studies of German Jewish history, Kaplan notes rightly, have over-emphasized the drive to assimilation, and neglected to pay due attention to the impressive care with which Jews in Germany, especially after 1890, treated their unique Jewish identity. It is socially and psychologically interesting that the JFB, striving to raise the consciousness of its members as women, also contributed to their growing awareness as Jews. (Note the link between present-day American feminism and the re-emergence of ethnic identity there.)

As a Jewish organization, the JFB took up the tradition of pre-emancipation Jewish women's groups, and became primarily engaged in social work. The class and gender attributes of its members predictably led them to work among less-fortunate Jewish women, victims of moral and material deprivation. In addition, their religious (or ethnic) situation made entry into the professions acceptable to women particularly difficult, so that voluntary social work became almost the single practical outlet. The Jewish women's organization thus developed a special kind of "social-feminism," less political, less outward-oriented and less radical than that prevalent in the general German women's movement. Only after World War I did the JFB begin to pay more attention to women's occupational and political rights. It carried on a prolonged fight for voting rights in the Jewish community, where male opposition proved no less intransigent than in German society as a whole. Under the pressure of growing anti-Semitism, however, Jewish issues became increasingly more important, and during its last years the JFB was primarily concerned with the preservation of Jewish dignity in the face of Nazism, and with preparing its members for emigration.

It is perhaps only of contemporary interest to note that the author, throughout her book, is quite unable to conceal a measure of disappointment at the inability of the JFB and its leadership to develop a more militant and comprehensive Jewish feminism. The disappointment for me, however, has been to find out that they too did not see the dangers facing Jewish existence in Germany and failed to rethink its history, even on the very eve of the catastrophe.

SHULAMIT VOLKOV
Tel-Aviv University

Yosef Kermish and Israel Bialostotski (eds.), *'Itonut hamaḥteret hayehudit begeto varshah* (The Jewish Underground Press in the Warsaw Ghetto). Jerusalem: Yad Vashem, 1979, 2 vols.

These two volumes, covering the period from May 1940 to June 1941, represent part of a larger project (six volumes in all) which is to republish the entire underground press from the Warsaw Ghetto under the Nazi occupation. The underground papers in the Ghetto were put together and distributed under the hardest imaginable conditions, with constant difficulties and complications. Except for one edition of the Betar paper, *Hamedinah*, they were all typed and duplicated by mimeograph in a limited number of copies; they were given out to trusted people and were passed from hand to hand. Great efforts were made to give the papers an aesthetic appearance by means of illustrations and decorative lettering, but they still look primitive enough compared with ordinary newspapers today and even with the Warsaw Jewish newspapers of the period between the two World Wars. Nevertheless, this press fulfilled a most important function, far more indispensable than that of the so-called "fourth estate" in normal times. Under the occupation, the Jews were forbidden to own radios and no papers from the outside reached the Ghetto—even the regular German press was forbidden reading. The only paper intended for the Jews in the Ghetto was the weekly *Gazeta Zydowska* (Jewish Newspaper), which was put out at the instance of the authorities and under their control, the hated General-Gouvernement. In these conditions, the underground press was the only window to the world and the only forum for free expression and for the exchange of opinions in different spheres.

The underground press published reliable surveys of the situation on the fighting fronts, news from the world political arena, broad and courageous political commentaries, wide-ranging discussion of the different trends of thought, news of the situation of the Jews under the occupation, and items on the problems within the Ghetto itself.

The papers were published by the political bodies active in the underground. The overall number of issues in the archives of Yad Vashem is 52 and the number of pages 2,933. Of these ten were published by the Bund; eight by Hashomer Hatzair; five each by Dror and the Left Poalei Zion; three each by the Right Poalei-Zion (TSS), Gordonia and the Communist movement; two by Betar; one each by the General Zionists, the Noar Zioni and Agudat Israel; and others by smaller political groups. In this wide range, the share of the Zionist trends, especially of the pioneer youth movements, is conspicuous.

Papers published in Warsaw were passed into the Ghetto in spite of the serious danger involved as well as to other Jewish centers across the length and breadth of occupied Poland. Many paid with their lives for preparing, printing and distributing the underground press. At one stage the Nazi authorities threatened that if clandestine newspapers continued to appear, the entire Ghetto would be harmed, and Adam Cherniakov, head of the Warsaw Ghetto Judenrat, tried to persuade the political bodies to stop publishing. The proposals and the threats were duly weighed up—this is not the place to expatiate on the complex issues involved—and it was decided not only to continue the publication of the newspapers but to sharpen their tone. More and more news was given on the destruction being visited on the Jews of Poland, and the call went out for resistance and the organization of armed struggle.

Practically the entire underground press was preserved in the secret archives of Ringelblum, which were buried in the earth in the Ghetto and for the greater part retrieved after the war. All the originals are today kept in the Jewish Historical Institute in Warsaw. Isolated issues are to be found in other archives, and in the opinion of the specialists the material that has reached us constitutes an almost complete collection of all the papers that were brought out in the Warsaw Ghetto.

Dr. Y. Kermish, director of the Yad Vashem Archives for many years, has edited the series and has devoted lengthy, painstaking labor to the collection of the material and to the deciphering of partly damaged issues. The assistant editor, Mr. Israel Bialostotski, prepared the notes, throwing light on the many obscure points in the texts. All the material has been translated into Hebrew from the Yiddish and the Polish originals (except in the case of one paper, *Shaviv* of the Noar Hazioni which appeared entirely in Hebrew). Part if not all the material ought certainly to be translated into English.

This undertaking is impressive testimony to the strength and the scope of the Jewish underground in Warsaw and is an extremely important document for the study of the period as a whole and the underground in particular.

YISRAEL GUTMAN
Hebrew University

Anny Latour, *The Jewish Resistance in France (1940–1944)*. New York: Holocaust Library, 1981. 287 pp. $6.95.

This is not the first major book about Jewish resistance in occupied France during World War II,[1] nor is it the most recent,[2] the French edition having appeared in 1970. But it is among the most comprehensive, and surely the most vivid. A veteran of underground activity, Mme. Latour has supplemented her own knowledge and official records with gripping quotations from interviews and personal papers gathered in France and Israel.

Any historian of the Jewish resistance to Hitler must contend with two contradictory myths: the myth of passive submission, and the myth of decisive military impact. The first has effectively disappeared from resistance scholarship.[3] As for the second, common to all resistance history written from personal experience, Mme. Latour has not really asked what material difference the Jewish resistance made in France. An answer to that question would have required extensive research in German military and intelligence archives as well as a more cold-bloodedly analytical approach than most resistance veterans would find congenial. The most authoritative historian of the European resistance reminds us that though resistance helped, conventional armies determined the war's outcome; as for France, the leading student of German army archives finds that the resistance did not affect German strategic deployment until 1944.[4] Not that Mme. Latour makes the fulsome claims of some.[5] She takes a wiser path, suggesting that the main impact of resistance was upon those who resisted. In particular, from her Zionist viewpoint, resistance helped many French and foreign Jews to discover or affirm their Jewish identity.

A large proportion of Jewish resisters in France were, in fact, non-French. A three-way tension runs through the history of Jewish resistance in France: between French and foreign Jews; between legal organizations that emphasized relief (where French Jews predominated) and illegal organizations that committed assassinations and sabotage (where foreign Jews predominated); and between Zionists and Communists on the ultimate significance of the fight. Mme. Latour is more frank about these divisions than most, but her best efforts to be comprehensive cannot quite overcome a bias toward organizations she knew personally, a bias endemic to resistance history where security requirements kept any participant from having a view of the whole. Mme. Latour was closest to the Zionist Scouts and the *Armée juive*, later the *Organisation juive de combat* (O.J.C.), and to those who worked clandestinely within the "Sixth Section" of the official *Union*

Générale des Israélites de France (U.G.I.F.). This puts her at odds with Ravine, for example, who writes from experience within Communist-organized refugee groups such as *Main-d'oeuvre immigrée* (M.O.I.). For him, U.G.I.F. cost more lives than the resisters within it saved, and the Zionist organizations erred by cultivating a "certain isolationist ideology" that underestimated the need for cooperation with other "democratic forces."[6] It should also be noted that Mme. Latour rules out of her account those many French Jews in Free France and the internal resistance who resisted as Frenchmen rather than as Jews.

Another tension divides participants in an experience as intense as underground resistance from professional historians who come later to dissect it. Professional historians have been slow to deal effectively with resistance in general, and no monograph has explored in a fully scholarly fashion the social and intellectual roots of the French Jewish resistance, or its impact then or later. The most penetrating scholarly study of any aspect of resistance so far is H. R. Kedward's *Resistance in Vichy France* (Oxford, 1978), which explores how resistance began and among what sorts of people. Mme. Latour's work corroborates Kedward's analysis on several points: that resistance began among groups which Vichy had already excluded from the national community (e.g. foreign Jews), and that it helped to have some kind of network in which contact could be made and trust established, a function served for foreign Jews in France by Zionist and Communist organizations.

It was not Mme. Latour's intention to exhaust this kind of scholarly enquiry, however. She wanted to tell a story. Her book is organized dramatically rather than chronologically, beginning with the more mundane resistance tasks such as fabricating ID and ration cards, and ascending through armed resistance to the harshest test of all, withstanding torture in the cellars of the Gestapo and the Milice. This is a powerful and committed account that can not be read without emotion.

ROBERT O. PAXTON
Columbia University

Notes

1. *Activité des organisations juives en France sous l'occupation*, a study of legal relief activities, and David Knout, *Contribution à l'histoire de la résistance juive*, a companion study of military resistance, both published by the Centre de Documentation Juive Contemporaine in Paris, in 1947.

2. David Diamant, *Les Juifs dans la Résistance française, 1940–44* (Paris, 1971) Jacqúes Ravine, *La Résistance organisée des Juifs en France* (Paris, 1973), and Adam Rutkowski, *La Lutte des Juifs en France à l'époque de l'occupation* (Paris, 1975).

3. Henri Michel, *The Shadow War: The European Resistance, 1939–45* (New York, 1972), pp. 177–80; cf. also Yehuda Bauer, *The Jewish Emergence from Powerlessness* (Toronto, 1979), p. 33.

4. Michel, p. 358; Hans Umbreit, "La Stratégie défensive de l'Allemagne," in *La Libération de la France,* actes du colloque international tenu à Paris du 28 au 31 octobre 1974 (Paris, 1976), p. 258.

5. Ravine, pp. 90ff, says the Jewish partisans had an impact of "importance colossale" on German forces.

6. Ravine, pp. 292ff. Maurice Rajsfus, *Des Juifs dans la collaboration: l'UGIF, 1941–44* (Paris, 1980) is even more uncompromising, refusing any excuses of good faith under impossible conditions to UGIF as well as the possibility of resistance within its ranks.

R.F. Leslie (ed.), *The History of Poland since 1863.* Cambridge University Press, 1980. £25. ($49.50)

Norman Davies, *God's Playground—A History of Poland.* Vol. I, From Origin to 1795, 606 pp.; Vol. II, 1795 to the Present, 726 pp. Clarendon Press: Oxford University Press, 1981. £27.50 each volume ($60.00 for set)

In the last several years the two most prestigious university presses in Britain have each published a survey of Polish history. Both are valuable additions to the growing number of English language studies on East European countries. The first continues the tradition of *The Cambridge History of Poland* published in 1941–50 (reprinted in 1978 by the Octagon Books, New York) and is made up of essays solicited from different scholars; Davies's opus is a remarkable single-handed tour de force, spanning the entire course of Polish history from the legendary Piast the Wheelwright to Lech Walesa.

Leslie has done splendid work as an editor. Collective volumes usually display a lack of coherence and a great deal of overlap. There is none of this in the new Cambridge volume. Chapters on consecutive periods, 1864–1914 by Leslie himself; 1914–1939 by Antony Polonsky; 1939–1945 by Jan M. Chiechanowski; and 1945–1975 by Z. A. Pelczynski, run smoothly into one another, thus permitting the reader to follow various themes throughout, while retaining the individuality of the authors. Moreover, there is no noticeable differences due to the nationality of the respective contributors—Leslie and Polonsky share the immense factual knowledge of the Poles, who in turn demonstrate as much objectivity as their western colleagues. If anything, political sympathies and predilections are perhaps most pronounced in Leslie's own contribution.

Within the territories of pre-partition Poland, Jews constituted about ten per cent of the population, but they formed a substantial percentage of the urban population, and in some market towns they were in fact a majority. Because of religious and legal restrictions imposed over the centuries they were concentrated primarily in handicrafts and retail trades. Most of them followed strictly the religious precepts and mores of Judaism, and spoke Yiddish. Very few chose to identify themselves with Polish (or Russian) society, and by the late nineteenth century various autonomous Jewish political movements had emerged. By then, too, mass migration to the New World had begun. These developments are succinctly described by Leslie. The rise of the National Democrats under the leadership of Roman Dmowski and Zygmunt Bielicki, who stressed the principle of national exclusiveness and egoism and who appealed to the déclassé nobility and petty bourgeoisie, as well as to the *lumpenproletariat,* led to pogroms (in Czestochowa in 1902, in Lodz in 1905 and elsewhere). Relations between Poles and Jews now involved a bitter estrangement which (as Polonsky demonstrates) did not abate in the inter-war years.

Jews tended to be extremely poor and their advancement was retarded by the slow economic progress of the country. They were concentrated in the less modern sectors of the economy and during the inter-war period the traditional outlets of emigration were closed to them. Anti-Semitism was widespread. The majority of the Jews still adhered to orthodoxy though there were some stirrings in the stifling atmosphere of the shtetl, and many were drawn to the freedom of the big city—a step which marked an internal upheaval in the closed world of traditional Judaism. There were a few important Jewish-owned industrial enterprises in Lodz and elsewhere, but the typical Jewish capitalist was either the owner of a small factory or a master craftsman with a large workshop. However, a growing number of Jews were found among writers, artists and scholars.

The position deteriorated even more seriously on the eve of World War II. Anti-Semitism, held somewhat in check under the benevolent semi-dictatorial regime of Pilsudski (1926–1935), began to play an ever-increasing role under his successors as they sought to win over the younger nationalists and divert attention from pressing social problems. There were violent incidents in 1936–37, and although the government condemned anti-Jewish excesses, it saw nothing objectionable in the economic boycott as such (hence the notorious "owszem" [by all means] of the then Prime Minister Felicjan Slawoj-Skladkowski). Infamous "ghetto benches" were established in most of the institutions of higher learning in October 1937, but it must be stressed that no mass populist anti-Semitic movement emerged, as it did at the time in Romania and Hungary. (This period has been examined in depth by Edward O. Wynot, Jr. in his excellent paper, "A Necessary Cruelty: the Emergence of Official Anti-Semitism in Poland, 1938–1939," *American Historical Review* CLXXVI, no. 4 [1971] not cited by Polonsky.) The government saw the solution to the Jewish problem in large-scale emigration (despite the fact that the world was closed to refugees); supported Zionism; and propounded chimeric schemes, such as the Jewish colonization of Madagascar or some other territory. By 1939 perhaps one-third of Polish Jews were almost entirely dependent on relief provided by charitable Jewish organizations, for the most part American.

However, the climacteric period in the history of Polish Jews and the Polish-Jewish relations are the years 1939–45. Jews were assigned by the German occupation regime to immediate, or imminent, extermination. Close to three million Polish Jews perished, and a mere forty or fifty thousand, including only five thousand children, escaped the massacre. Many Poles bravely risked their lives to protect their Jewish fellow citizens, but Chiechanowski's claim, that "all Poles but a few extremists of the near-fascist elements of the extreme right responded stoutly to the protection of the Jews," seems somewhat exaggerated. More should perhaps have been said about the uprising in the Warsaw Ghetto, which the author describes as "heroic, but hopeless." Hopeless it certainly was, but as Chiechanowski himself admits, it had "a deep effect on other Poles . . . [as] a clear indication of the length to which the Nazis would go in their pursuit . . . of . . . German racial superiority, and consequently stiffened the Polish determination to fight." There was probably a direct link to the Warsaw uprising of 1 August 1944. Both taught noble lessons of how to lose and how to die with honor and dignity.

The developments in Communist-dominated Poland since 1945 are dealt with by Pelczynski. Not many Jews remained; most of those who had survived, or who now returned from the USSR, left the country, especially after 1948 when the state of Israel was established. But the seemingly perennial "Jewish question" did not fade away and persisted in the form of inter-factional quarrels within the PZPR (Polish United Workers Party). This came out into the open in 1956 with Gomulka's return to power; in 1967 in the aftermath of the June War; and in 1973 after the Yom Kippur War. Pelczynski's *terminus ad quem* is 1975, well before the rise and fall of the Solidarity movement and the military coup of General Wojciech Jaruzelski who makes only a shadowy appearance as deputy member, later member of the Politburo and Minister of Defense; nothing much is said about him (even his initial is given as "P"). Oddly enough, in a book published much earlier, in 1969 (Hans Roos, *A History of Modern Poland*), Jaruzelski is firmly placed as one of the "Partisans" group, who were marked, as Roos puts it, by "an almost military severity, even brutality, in their mode of governing and by a decided hostility to discussion and culture which was aimed particularly against liberals" (meaning of course, the Jews).*

Davies' *God's Playground* is an admirable piece of historical writing and certainly the most lively and entertaining survey of Polish history ever written in any language. The title seems to me a bit contrived; it is lifted from Jan Kochanowski's epigram *Czlowiek—Igrzysko Boże* (Man—God's bauble) which in context seems to mean no more than man's fate is in God's hands. Davies uses it as an epithet for Poland "where fate has frequently played mischievous tricks and where a lively sense of humour has always formed an essential item in the equipment for the national survival." This can equally well be applied to any country or to any group of people, with or without the accompanying *Galgenhumor*. Disciple of the indomitable A. J. P. Taylor, Davies shares his master's high spirits, epigrammatic style, and his penchant for recondite information and comparisons. Where else would one learn that Michal Korybut Wisniowiecki, who reigned briefly between 1669–1673, died from a surfeit of gherkins, and that Augustus the Strong of the Saxon Wettin dynasty (1673–1697) justified his cognomen by fathering some three hundred children? What other historian illustrates his narrative by apt quotations from Polish, Latin, French, German, Russian and Italian poems, from Bach's cantata and oratorios, and from Baedecker? And who else would commit to paper the following exercise in alliteration:

> The proliferating profusion of possible political permutations among the pullulating peoples and parties of the Polish provinces in this period palpably prevented the propagation of permanent pacts between potential partners.

Davies writes about the Jews with knowledge, understanding and sympathy. He sees the Jews of Poland not only as "a question" or "a problem" to be solved either by total emigration or by total assimilation, but also in their positive role in furthering the economic life of the

---

*I am grateful to my friend Mr. Bohdan Brzerinski from London for drawing my attention to this passage.

country from the earliest times. (It was indeed a Moorish Jew from Spain who left the first documentary evidence of the existence of Poland in 965/66; and Judaism, as preserved by the descendants of the Khazar kingdom in eastern Galicia, actually antedated Christianity in Poland.) Illuminating references to the Jews are scattered throughout the two volumes. Thus, for example, his description of the structure of Jewish autonomy (I, 440–44) is accompanied by a very clear schematic diagram. And a lengthy chapter (II, 240–66) deals specifically with the political, socio-economic and cultural evolution of the Jewish population from the beginning of the nineteenth century until 1945. Recriminatory asides by Jewish scholars and writers about the conduct of the non-Jewish population towards the Nazis' Final Solution, Davies dismisses as "one of the meanest of modern historical controversies" (pp. 264–65). Both sides overlook the realities of life under the Nazi Terror. "To ask why the Poles did little to help the Jews is rather like asking why the Jews did nothing to assist the Poles . . . Both were victims to the Terror, and were conditioned by it."

There are a few easily avoidable minor mistakes and inaccuracies: Marceli Handelsman was not the "younger disciple in diplomatic history in Warsaw" of Szymon Askenazy (I, 13). He was not a disciple of Askenazy; his chair was in general and not in diplomatic history; and apart from their Jewish origin, the two distinguished historians had very little in common with, and heartily disliked, each other. The General Charter of Jewish Liberties, the famous Kalisz Statute, was granted to the Jews in 1264 not by Boleslaus the Modest (1226–79), Prince of Cracow (I, 79) but by his contemporary, Boleslaus the Pious (1221–79), the Prince of Kalisz. Jakob Frank settled at the end of his life in Offenbach and not in Oberrad (I, 195). The mysterious *Das* of his teaching means *daat* (knowledge) and not *It*. Davies writes that "not a few [Jews] were formally ennobled" (I, 218). In fact only one practicing Jew was ennobled in pre-partition Poland—Michael Ezofowicz in 1525, though of course a number of others entered the ranks of nobility after conversion. The editor of *Jutrzenka* was Daniel Neufeld and not Ludwig Gumplowicz (III, 248). Slobodka, the seat of the famous yeshiva, is situated near Kovno and not Odessa (II, 249). The Jewish flyweight champion in 1938 was Shapsio Rotholc and not Lazar Rundstein (II, 408).

Both volumes are full of printing errors and mistakes: Nakowski for Nalkowski, Kronenburg for Kronenberg, Hawelburg for Wawelberg, Shore for Schorr, etc. One would expect a higher standard of proofreading from the Clarendon Press. But I am not pointing them out to in any way denigrate Davies' splendid achievement. All are minor blemishes which can be easily corrected in future editions. Michelangelo remarked somewhere that one should never take mean details lightly; they are the basis of perfection, and perfection is not a mean detail.

PAUL GLIKSON
Hebrew University

Rosemarie Leuschen-Seppel, *Sozialdemokratie und Antisemitismus im Kaiserreich. Die Auseinandersetzungen der Partei mit den Konservativen und Völkischen Strömungen des Antisemitismus 1871–1914*. Bonn: Verlag Neue Gesellschaft GmbH, 1978.

In this scholarly, though unnecessarily convoluted, monograph Dr. Rosemarie Leuschen-Seppel takes issue with two interpretations often encountered in historical literature of the attitude towards anti-Semitism prevailing in the Social Democratic movement. According to one interpretation, anti-Jewish prejudice was so deeply rooted among the leaders and rank and file of the movement that it is appropriate to speak of "socialist anti-Semitism." According to the second, the German working class was the "only large sector of the population that was almost completely immune to anti-Semitism." Dr. Leuschen-Seppel demonstrates convincingly the inadequacy of both interpretations and shows that the record of the party was not as clear-cut as previous scholars have indicated.

With few exceptions, the leaders of the German socialist movement and the editors of its main publications repudiated anti-Semitism. They denounced the political movements that after the 1880s made anti-Semitism the centerpiece of their program and they favored the emancipation of the Jews and their integration into German society. In stressing these points Dr. Leuschen-Seppel does not break new ground. Indeed, her long discussions of the anti-Semites, Adolf Stoecker and Hermann Ahlwardt, among others, are based largely on well-known secondary sources.

But her detailed analysis of the "family magazines" *(Unterhaltungspresse)* published by the German Social Democratic Party is interesting, revealing, and original. Dr. Leuschen-Seppel points out that in socialist magazines and periodicals devoted to satire, quite extensive after 1890, the dominant stereotype of the Jew was distinctly unflattering. In caricatures and jokes the Jew was depicted as unscrupulous in business, interested above all in making money, devoid of humanity, and even dirty and sexually perverted. It is not possible to measure the impact of the family magazines on working-class thinking, but the conclusion reached by the Jewish socialist, Fritz Naphtali, seems persuasive. The "socialist ethic," he declared, was "alarmingly superficial" in "our movement" and socialists had not at all succeeded in solving in their own minds "the problem of Jews living in a non-Jewish world." As Leuschen-Seppel emphasizes, by 1914 there was a "gulf" between the political orientation of German Social Democracy, which repudiated anti-Semitism, and its cultural orientation, in which the notion of the Jew as an alien and corrosive element in German civilization was deeply rooted.

Unfortunately, the study covers only the period from 1871 to 1914. It would be interesting to know whether the "gulf" in the socialist movement persisted in the years from 1914 to 1933, when anti-Semitism became so critical an issue in German politics. A study of the later period might contribute even more than the book under review to an understanding of the success of National Socialist propaganda in attracting mass support, and Dr. Leuschen-Seppel is eminently qualified to undertake it.

ABRAHAM ASCHER
City University of New York

Ladislav Lipscher, *Die Juden im Slowakischen Staat 1939–1945*. Munich, Vienna: Oldenbourg Press, 1980. 210 pp.

The fate of Slovak Jews during the Second World War was reviewed in minute detail during the trials of Nazi collaborators held before the National Tribunal in 1946–48 at Bratislava. Thus, the earliest works of Leon Poliakov and Gerald Reitlinger on the "Final Solution" in occupied Europe could already assert that "Slovakia occupied a special place on the map of Nazi genocide." The abrupt halt called in the fall of 1942 to the deportation of Jews, and the circumstances that led to this halt—the intervention of the Vatican and the activities of the clandestine Bratislava "Working Group"—certainly suggest that there is much validity in this statement.

Research and memoirs subsequently published in Israel have expanded the range of our knowledge, especially with regard to the various rescue attempts: the so-called "Europa Plan;" the stand of the churches and of the Vatican vis-à-vis the Jewish question in Slovakia; and the active Jewish participation in the Slovak National Uprising.

In his recent contribution to this literature, Dr. Lipscher has consulted Slovak archival sources as well as research dealing with Slovak domestic affairs. The work is divided into seven chapters that present a systematic account of events but do not, however, offer any original conceptualization. The author, a lawyer by training, has naturally paid special attention to legislative and parliamentary procedure. He has also interviewed a number of the *dramatis personae,* former members of Parliament belonging to Hlinka's Slovak People's Party and who enjoyed behind-the-scenes knowledge of events.

Thus we learn—according to Carnogursky's communication of November 1969—that when the infamous deportation law was put to the vote on 15 May 1942, he himself and five additional members of Parliament (Moravcik, Mora, Tvrdy and the Fathers Ferencik and Filkorn) quietly left the plenum (p. 112). These were signs of noncompliance, albeit timid, which must be added to the overt protest of Janos Esterhazy, the Hungarian Minority representative.

One of the lacunae in Lipscher's work occurs in his references to research published outside of Slovakia in the last decade. The main omission is the documentary series (especially volumes IV, 1967; VIII 1974; IX, 1975) published by the Holy See and covering the war years, which contain a wealth of material on Slovak-Vatican relations in general and on the Jewish question in particular.

Another shortcoming is to be found in Lipscher's assessment of the degree to which the Slovak government was aware of the Nazi policy of extermination. That the government had knowledge of the Nazis' intentions has been demonstrated beyond any doubt by the Bratislava Tribunal and by subsequent research. However, in referring to the first group of Jewish youngsters deported to Auschwitz and Lublin-Maidanek in the spring of 1942 (numbering twenty thousand), Dr. Lipscher categorically asserts that "the Slovak authorities surely had no inkling *(ahnten sicher nicht)* that by taking this fatal decision they would embark on the extermination of Slovak Jewry" (p. 188).

The unique case of the Slovak Jews has now been held up to examination in a German language publication for the first time. Appended to this work is a most useful annotated index of persons and a bibliography of published and unpublished source material.

LIVIA ROTHKIRCHEN
Yad Vashem

Laurence D. Loeb, *Outcaste: Jewish Life in Southern Iran*. New York/London/Paris: Gordon and Breach, 1977. xxv + 328 pp., n.p.

The author, an anthropologist born in the United States, spent over a year in Shiraz from August 1967 to December 1968, conducting research. In 1970 he submitted the results as a doctoral thesis to Columbia University under the title: "The Jews of Southwest Iran: A Study of Cultural Persistance." The book before us, based for the most part on the doctorate, does not (despite its title) deal with the Jews of Southern Iran as a whole, but only with what is specific to the Jews of Shiraz.

The book is divided into separate historical and anthropological sections. The historical outline, as the author acknowledges, is based mainly on secondary sources, but even as such it could have been better researched. Stressing in particular the persecutions to which the Jews of Persia have been subjected, it presents disconnected items of information taken from the writings of Walter Fischel, Wilhelm Bacher, Jacob A. Brawer, Yitzhak Ben-Zvi and Moshe Yishai, as well as passages from the accounts of travellers (mostly as quoted in the works of the above authors). It is difficult to get any sort of adequate critical notion from this patchwork. However, the greater part of the book is anthropological research, with a running commentary of a personal-subjective nature by the author on his observations. Though one may have reservations about not a few of his judgments, this part does constitute an original contribution.

The book opens with an account of a pogrom against the Jews of Shiraz in the autumn of 1910. In the author's words: "Murder, pillage, rape and extensive vandalism were reported to have left the entire community of six thousand virtually homeless and terrorized" (p. 1). This description is based on information given the author by members of the community (although it emerges later (p. 33) that the pogrom was also reported at the time in the publications of the *Alliance israelite universelle*. Apparently this opening is meant to prepare the ground for the author's contention that this community is nothing but "outcaste." Holding this theory, the author follows in the footsteps of G. Sjoberg, (*The Pre-Industrial City*, 1960) but while the latter argues that the Jews belong in general to the upper social level of the "outcaste" because of their control of strategic economic positions, the author makes the proviso that "this was not true for Shirazi Jews, who were truly the lowest of the low" (p. 3).

The facts presented in his book, however, contradict this thesis.

The history of the Jews of Iran and not just the Jews of Shiraz was marked by frequent persecution and humiliating legal restrictions; yet each and every community developed set patterns of life, imbibing culture from without and developing it from within. After all, at the time, the Shiraz community numbered among its members nineteen doctors, which constituted a relatively high percentage of the total (p. 83). The community members paid city taxes like all the other citizens and were not subject to any special poll-tax *(jaziyeh)* as they used to be in the past (p. 100). They owned much property, and many of them were partners in business and real estate dealings with Muslims (p. 270). They were permitted to send their children to government schools since 1925, and when the author was there, half the pupils were enrolled in non-Jewish schools. Jewish students then formed a higher proportion (relative to total population) at the local university than did the non-Jews (p. 148).

In the author's view, the Jews were generally able to conduct their cultural life without interference. "The Shirazi Jew," he states, "is proud of being Jewish. He considers himself superior in every way to non-Jews," and his "identification with Jews all over the world and particularly with those in Israel is very strong" (pp. 174–75). Can a well-established community with so impressive a sense of its own identity and such varied relations with the environment be properly called "outcaste"? The author's final conclusion in this matter is that Shirazi Jews could easily have found a way out of their special situation by converting to Islam but they chose to hold their ground (p. 272).

What are the qualities and the values that the author assigns to the Jews of Shiraz and sometimes to the Jews of Iran as a whole? "The Shirazi Jew is exceedingly penurious," he writes (p. 101). He agrees with the "non-Jew" he cites not only on the Jews of Shiraz but on the Jews of Iran as such: "For the non-Jew, the Iranian Jew is stereotyped as niggardly. One who haggles tenaciously over the price of an item is said to be engaged in *jud baazi* (the Jew game). This characterization, however unfortunate its implications, seems to be well deserved" (pp. 168–69). And yet on the same page (p. 169), in a marginal comment in small print, the author can write that "Jews generally give large sums to Israel with minimal coaxing."

The author writes that, "The Shirazi Jew readily admits to being lazy" (p. 101) and he himself accepts this characterization; but elsewhere he writes that those who have acquired a certain wealth—about one hundred-and-twenty rich families and about one thousand middle class families out of the total fifteen hundred—achieved this through "struggle" (p. 169). The author remarks: "The Shirazi Jew is concerned with the present and the immediate future . . . The future beyond two or three months is not even considered" (p. 166). The chapter on education proves the opposite.

About two and a half years after the author left Shiraz, I went there to do research on the life of the community and I visited the city thereafter every year up to April 1978. In my humble opinion the Jews there are not found to be "liars, lazy and niggardly." Though it is true that the Jewish quarter is very dirty, and that the level of education in general and the state of religious observance is far from satisfactory, the root causes of these problems require far more searching analysis than that provided by the author.

Be it said to the credit of the Jews of Shiraz, together with those of Yazd and Mashhad, that they have demonstrated a fierce determination to keep the Jewish spark alive—to a greater extent, indeed, than have all the other Jewish communities in Iran. Shirazi Jews were the first and perhaps the only ones to dismiss the teachers of the *Alliance israelite*—for example—because what they taught was far from Jewish in content.

It was in the Shirazi Jewish community that I found the largest number of Judeo-Persian manuscripts, including very valuable works like *Sefer hamelizah*. Is it not rather remarkable that Dr. Loeb, who is supposedly dealing with the socio-cultural aspects of Jewish community life, did not devote even a short sub-section to this culture in all the eleven chapters of his book, which include subjects like homosexuality, prostitution and begging?

Again, the author ignores the fact that the Jews of Shiraz were among the first immigrants from Persia to Palestine and contributed to the construction of Jerusalem outside the Old City walls. In proportion to their numbers and given the hard living conditions, the community in Shiraz produced outstanding personalities in the fields of academic research, teaching, the rabbinate, publishing, music and public service as well as skilled artisans in the building and other crafts. The book by Rav Raphael Haim Hacohen, *Avanim behomah* (Jerusalem, 1970), is to be found in the bibliography, but the author does not seem to have studied it very attentively.

To sum up, there is no doubt that a scholar is bound to record the truth however unpalatable and unacceptable it may be, but this duty imposes a great responsibility on him to weigh his words carefully before going to print. After spending a year and a half among the Jews of Shiraz, the author ends his research with a chapter entitled "Redemption," the last sentence of which reads: "But for the moment it appears as if the future of Shirazi Jewry is to be left again to 'the hand of God'" (p. 273). This is the conclusion of the research of Dr. Laurence Loeb, anthropologist.

AMNON NETZER
Hebrew University

Heinz-Dietrich Löwe, *Antisemitismus und reaktionäre Utopie-Russischer Konservatismus im Kampf gegen den Wandel von Staat und Gesellschaft 1890–1917*. Hamburg: Hoffman und Campe Verlag, 1978. Reihe: "Historische Perspektiven" Band 13. 304 pp. DM 58.

At the present, the last quarter of a century preceding the revolutions of 1917 is perhaps the period most intensively studied in the Soviet Union as well as in the West. The flow of monographs is accompanied by the gushing stream of doctoral dissertations that bring into circulation new documentation and suggest novel explanations. As a result, received notions are the object of revision or qualification, while new perspectives are opened on heretofore neglected problems of social and political history. More specifically, we now have a better picture of the workings of the imperial government, of the character of political parties and professional associations, as well as more information on the structure and dynamics of social groups or the pattern of economic modernization. Under the circumstances all attempts at dealing comprehensively with any specific aspect of Russian life in that period are, perforce, in the nature of interim reports, subject to modification and qualification as new evidence and monographic studies become available.

These observations should be kept in mind in assessing the limits and limitations of the book under review. In spite of their crucial importance, the problems and policies with respect to the non-Russian nationalities of the empire have not received the attention they deserve. More particularly, the monographs that have addressed one or the other aspect of these issues have but rarely considered it within the context of the social and political (not to mention intellectual or cultural) developments of the empire as a whole. In the book under review, H.-D. Löwe has had the daring not only to tackle a large, difficult, and controversial question, namely that of policies and attitudes towards the Jews on the part of the government and conservative parties. But he has also attempted to locate attitudes and policies in relation to the socio-economic and political happenings in the empire. It is not surprising, however, that (with very minor exceptions) he has done so on the basis of published sources and secondary literature, and that in many particulars additional and more reliable information has become available since he completed his manuscript in 1977 (although it is odd that he has not availed himself of Roberta T. Manning's dissertation on the nobility 1905–1907, available since 1975 which touches directly on some crucial aspects of this book): *Crisis of the Old Order in Russia* (Princeton University Press, 1982).

The present study provides a comprehensive overview of the imperial government's and the conservative social establishment's attitudes with respect to the Jewish question. The story is fairly well known in its outline, but Dr. Löwe chronicles it with much useful detail and he is also successful in his effort at relating the Jewish problem to the broader context of domestic policies. He focuses on two major aspects. Chronologically (ca. 1890 to 1905) and in terms of importance, the first is an account of the conflicting policies advocated by the "modernizing" Witte, and his successors in the ministry of finance, on the one hand, and the repressive Pleve and his followers in the ministry of internal affairs, on the other. The former were ready to respond, however cautiously and gradually, to the Jews' demands for legal equality and an end to the discriminatory legislation that fettered them in the empire (i.e. pale of settlement, numerus clausus, prohibitions against acquistion of cultivated land and participation in local administrative institutions). The latter, concerned with preserving law and order and averting popular movements, opposed liberalization; eventually they came to regard anti-Semitic legislation as one of the cornerstones of the social and political status quo. This picture, however accurate, is not very original and Dr. Löwe tends to overdraw the contrast between the "modernizers" and the conservatives. As he admits himself, even conservative bureaucrats and dignitaries favored Russia's rapid industrialization.

The second major aspect relates to the emergence, after 1905, of "right wing" political movements, more particularly the conservative nobility organized in the Soviet of the United Nobility—and the ancillary Union of the Russian People and the Black Hundreds. A crass, but not racial, anti-Semitism was a major ingredient of these movements' *Weltanschauung* and the most visible and vocal aspect of their political activities. Countenanced by the most conservative members of the government, they also enjoyed the Court's tacit sympathy and approbation for their violent actions (e.g. pogroms). The combined efforts of this right wing element of society and its conservative supporters or advocates in the government, not only prevented the emancipation of the Jews, but succeeded in preserving and even reintroducing most of the restrictive and discriminatory legislation. Finally, during World War I, the Jews became the object of most callous repressive measures, in spite of their loyalty and the pleas made on their behalf by the Western powers and the more progressive elements of the political establishment.

Dr. Löwe views the attitudes and policies with respect to the Jews as a most significant and tale-telling indicator of the government's legislation and of the political movements' programs. Time and again, in his view, did the Jewish question (or more precisely, the issue of an officially condoned and implemented anti-Semitism) prove to be crucial in the struggle between liberal "modernizers" and progressives on the one hand, and conservative traditionalists on the other. Many a social or economic question and policy became entangled in the issue of antisemitism. After 1906 the position taken on anti-Semitism frequently provided a litmus test for the willingness, or ability, of either the tsarist regime (e.g. Stolypin) or the political spokesmen of public opinion *(obshchestvennost')*—e.g. the Octobrists—to bring about a reform of the imperial system. Practically none of the historians working in this period (with the signal exception of Professor Hans Rogger) has given this aspect its due attention or assessed its significance. Dr. Löwe is to be congratulated and thanked for having done so—albeit in a preliminary, general and not unassailably professional manner. (Thus he refers to secondary literature when citing legislative sources; there are garbled titles—*Poslednie Vedomosti* for *Poslednie Novosti;* incomplete bibliographical entries, etc.)

So far so good. Unfortunately Dr. Löwe seems mesmerized—as so many younger German historians—by the trappings and claims of social and political "science." He feels under compulsion to relate the events he chronicles to a "model" and to explain them in esoteric language. The model is that of enforced and belated modernization. Such a modernization implies rapid industrialization and the introduction—with the help of the government—of capitalist economic institutions and norms. But the backwardness of Russia produced a heterogeneity of development, with the traditional agrarian, rural sector still providing the dominant cultural values and social framework. Modernization was advocated by the progressive bureaucracy centered in the ministry of finance and it was opposed by the conservative, landowning nobility whose traditionalist ideology (a "reactionary utopia") drew its inspiration from Slavophilism (of which our author has but a shadowy idea) and chauvinism. According to this "analysis" the Jewish question was a manifestation and instance of the conflict between the several sectors (levels of development) in Russia, between "capitalists" and agrarian "traditionalists." And anti-Semitism was shaped into a symbol (as well as instrument) of the rural reactionary utopia. For all this Dr. Löwe supplies neither evidence nor proofs; he only repeatedly asserts that this was indeed the case by referring back to the model itself. This is not only methodologically untenable but also disturbing on more general, historical grounds. In the first place, such an "analysis" totally neglects the religious, cultural, and intellectual dimensions. Anticapitalism, for instance, was not only the hallmark of the rural conservative (whoever he may have been); it permeated all of Russia's intellectual, political and ethical tradition. Discussion of and comparison with Austria-Hungary, Germany or France would have been most apposite here. In the second place, and more surprisingly, Dr. Löwe disregards nationalism. But in view of the fact that both the Jewish pale and the home base of the "rural reactionaries" lay in the western provinces with their Polish past and complex mixture of national, cultural, and religious traditions, such disregard is inexcusable. In spite of his obvious sympathy for the plight of the Jewish population, Dr. Löwe's deterministic model leads to the conclusion (or, at any rate, strong implication) that both the excessive anti-Semitism and the inability to bring about the emancipation of the Jews in Russia were preordained and unavoidable once "capitalist modernization" was introduced. This is questionable to say the least. Moreover, recent studies have well shown the hopelessly contradictory views held and conflicting policies pursued by both the imperial regime and *"obshchestvennost";* thus any interpretation of the predetermined character of the tsarist regime's evolution becomes completely untenable. There were no visible and coherently held alternatives to solve the many crises confronted by the imperial system, thus leaving options open. This was equally true of the anti-Semitic, conservative, landowning nobility whose opposition to a "capitalist" or modern development was by no means as total and consistent as Dr. Löwe would have us believe.

Anti-Semitism was not the making of the Jews, of course; but in any discussion of it attention should also be paid to Jewish—as well as other non-Russian—attitudes and reactions to the imperial system. Dr. Löwe deals with this facet very perfunctorily and only as it pertains to the organization of self-defense following the pogroms of 1905–1906. A last word: some of the chapter and section headings—fortunately not developed or justified in the text itself—are arrant nonsense, e.g.

"feudaler Antikapitalismus," "Antisemitismus im Dienst feudaler Restauration." Such phrases, wherever placed, impart an unhistorical and disturbing tone to the book and strain the reader's confidence.

MARC RAEFF
Columbia University

Michael R. Marrus and Robert O. Paxton, *Vichy France and the Jews.* New York: Basic Books, 1981. 432 pp. $20.00

Historical research on the history of Vichy France has shied away from delving into an essential issue—Vichy's treatment of the "Jewish Question." Robert Paxton stands among those few historians who have attempted to view this issue within the prism of the New Order and in his *Vichy France—Old Guard and New Order, 1940–1944* (1972, 1982) went so far as to designate the anti-Semitism of Vichy as the darkest stain in its entire history. But Paxton's major concern there was with general ideology and policy and room was thus left for a full-length study of this issue. Hence, the volume under review, *Vichy France and the Jews,* was clearly a historical desideratum.

The basic orientation of the previous book also characterizes the new work. Paxton presented the Vichy regime as an integral element in French history and as a logical continuation of the turbulent thirties. Vichy inherited the xenophobic ideology from the Daladier regime, which had undermined the "influence" of foreigners, Jews and refugees on French society by curbing their rights. Its implementation of anti-republican and anti-liberal principles thus resulted from the growing disenchantment with republican ideals during the thirties rather than from the German occupation. This portrayal of Vichy as a sovereign regime with its own autonomous ideology and policy, independent of German pressure, again forms the backbone of the present book. And within this framework, the energies expended by the authors to isolate French from German initiatives on the "Jewish Question", become all the more logical. For the major thesis of the book—the voluntary complicity of the Vichy government in the actions against the Jews—stands or falls on whether the authors prove the existence of its independent anti-Semitic course.

The authors have judiciously chosen a narrative-chronological approach. They rightly point to the mass deportations of the summer of

1942 as the turning point in the developments under review, having arrived at their conclusion not only from the specific Jewish point of view, but also from the vantage point of French-German collaboration and of French public opinion on the "Jewish Question."

The major claims of the authors relating to the period prior to the summer of 1942 are sharp and unequivocal. The first anti-Jewish regulations of August and October 1940 were indeed Vichy-inspired, although public opinion at the time was highly unconcerned with the Jews. These laws rested upon "a reservoir of antipathy to Jews in France often stagnant and scarcely visible" (p. 26) which was reactivated by the xenophobic atmosphere that permeated France in the closing years of the Third Republic. One of the major architects of these policies was the self-proclaimed anti-Semite, Xavier Vallat, whose activities as head of the Commissariat for Jewish Affairs (March 1941–May 1942) are masterfully described. Vallat's "state anti-Semitism" merged with his concern for French sovereignty and disdain for the Germans to produce an active policy against the Jews. The economic organization of Jewish property, which nimbly avoided any German economic gains, was a case in point. As for the reception of these anti-Semitic policies, the authors claim that the Commissariat scarcely faced any objections—either from within the French civil service or from the French public at large.

Their rich and pioneering analysis of French public opinion results in several provocative conclusions. In the free zone, popular anti-Semitism grew extensively during 1941–42, and by the summer of 1942, it had reached such a peak that French officials were being prodded by the populace to find a remedy to the "Jewish Question." The authors intimate that a predisposition for collaboration with Germany in the Final Solution was thereby establishing itself. With regard to the Christian churches until 1942, the authors present a dismal picture, one in which silence was the predominant mode of response. Finally, somewhat contradicting their previous contentions, the authors conclude that "Vichy's anti-Jewish program still met with the indifference of most French people" (p. 214).

The authors' wholehearted condemnation of Vichy policy takes on still more serious overtones in their important discussion of the deportations of the summer of 1942. French collaboration is seen as a precondition for the successful operation of the Final Solution in France and as a salient factor in determining the number of deportees. Moreover, the authors dismiss the commonplace apologia of French leaders that their efforts to protect French Jews necessitated the surrender of foreign Jews, showing that they had no basis to believe that the Germans would in fact refrain from the deportation of French Jews.

Although much of the documentary material supporting these conclusions is known, the emphasis placed upon French responsibility is given a louder hearing. The only source for optimism was the behavior of the French public and churches which broke their silence and advocated a more humane attitude to the Jews. But even here the authors are troubled by the fleeting nature of this change of heart and by the speed with which Church leaders returned to their original support of Vichy.

In their treatment of the last two years of the German occupation, the authors deal with the pressure that Germany exerted on Vichy to rescind its naturalization laws in order to widen the web of those eligible for deportation. They convincingly show that even in their steadfast attempts to avoid German pressure, the Vichy leaders did not reassess their Jewish policy but rather reappraised their relationship with Germany and began to consider their political future at war's end. In this regard, as in others, Laval's policy is seen as outright cynicism.

The Manichean portrayal by Marrus and Paxton of Vichy's Jewish policy overstates their case. It appears that in each stage of this historical development one can find certain contradictory sources which would by no means overturn their thesis but would give it a somewhat different tilt. For example, a complete discussion of Vallat must take into consideration the Jewish sources, as well, which give us a different image: one of a Frenchman bent on carrying out his policy of "state anti-Semitism" but attempting to safeguard the status of French Jews by trying to drive a wedge between them and the more extreme designs of the Germans. But seemingly this was true not only of Vallat. Reports from a policy arm of the Commissariat constantly decry the fact that the Commissariat's anti-Jewish policies find little support among the French public and local *prefets,* while French bureaucrats do little to strengthen the Commissariat's hand.

This brings us to the general appraisal of French public opinion prior to 1942. Here I would rely on various monthly reports of an investigatory arm of the Commissariat in conjunction with the *prefet* reports utilized extensively by the authors. The trend seems to have been in the direction of indifference to the "Jewish Question" as to all other issues beyond daily concerns—an analysis which would confirm the authors' overall conclusion but not their specific findings. Moreover, there is probably room for a more positive assessment of the Church's activity after the summer of 1942. Many Church groups, inspired by their leaders' public pronouncements, played an active role in aiding Jews to escape deportation. Clearly, the authors' well-supported thesis that were it not for Vichy fewer Jews would have been deported does not cancel out contrary evidence that many Jews were saved by the active assistance of the French public. As for German-Vichy relations, even if the authors have at times underrated the implications of German pressure on Vichy (with regard, for example, to the deportation of Jews, the creation of the UGIF, the deportations of 1942), no attempt has been made to whitewash Germany or to absolve it of the ultimate responsibility for the Final Solution in France. Although certain implications regarding the nature of Vichy collaboration seem to be unjustified, the authors have brought to bear irrefutable evidence to prove fundamental complicity.

Vichy France and the Jews is an exhaustive historical study which constitutes a seminal contribution to our understanding of this tragic period. Superbly written, with a deep moral perspective, the study clearly fills what has hitherto remained a major historical vacuum.

RICHARD COHEN
Hebrew University

Ezra Mendelsohn, *Zionism in Poland: The Formative Years, 1915–1926*. New Haven and London: Yale University Press, 1981. 416 pp. $35

Based on a rich variety of archival sources, Ezra Mendelsohn has produced an exhaustive, detailed description and analysis of the complex development of Zionism and Zionist parties in Poland in the years between the First World War and the Pilsudski *coup d'état*. Following a general introduction on "Polish Jewry and Its Political Heritage," there are seven chapters. The first is devoted to the time of German and Austrian occupation; the subsequent years are divided into three periods, 1918–1921, 1921–1923, 1924–1926, and two chapters are devoted to each period. There is a "Conclusion" which is largely a prosopographic essay based on the YIVO collection of autobiographies by young Polish Jews. There are also two appendices, one on "Polish Nationalism and Zionism," and another on "Polish Zionism and the Arab Question."

In discussions of political organization, cultural institutions and ideological points of view, the differences in the patterns of development in Galicia (East and West), Congress Poland and (Jewish)

Lithuania and the border regions emerge repeatedly throughout the work. For example, Mendelsohn ascribes "the extremism of Jewish politics in Congress Poland" and the relative moderation of the Galicians to the differing legacies of pre-World War I Russian and Austrian administrations. And after describing the four separate Zionist federations (Congress Poland, East Galicia, West Galicia and Silesia, Vilna-Lithuania), the author concludes that despite the inescapable duplication, "the artificial concentration of all Zionist work in Warsaw, given the very real and substantial [regional] differences . . . would have done more harm than good" (p. 179).

As the First World War drew to a close Zionism became a "great and powerful mass movement" in Poland. This occurred not only because of the removal of Tsarist repression but because of a variety of new currents unleashed by the war itself—new nations emerging as empires crumbled, the accelerated modernization of Polish Jewry, the deepening crisis of the established Jewish leadership, the emergence of Polish nationalism. Thus, "the Balfour Declaration followed the Zionist boom in Poland—it did not cause it" (p. 45).

In the new democratic state of Poland the Parliament became an arena in which the Jewish parties could test their strategies for serving Jewish interests. Mendelsohn's analyses of the failures of these strategies are probably the strongest parts of his book. The disintegration of the Minorities Bloc and the embarrassing failure of the Ugoda are clearly described and carefully analyzed. Yitzhak Grünbaum, the Zionist leader from Congress Poland, and his confrontational style proved as ineffective as the "realistic" compromises of the Galicians, Yehoshua Thon and Leon Reich. Still, in a final "balance sheet" Mendelsohn does conclude that although the Polish Zionist politicians failed to achieve "Jewish equality, national autonomy and an end to anti-Semitism, without their activities things would surely have been much worse" (p. 337).

The divisions in the Polish Zionist movement were not only regional, but also ideological, generational, linguistic and psychological. The fragmentation of the movement bewildered the rank and file and enfuriated Jews in Palestine who demanded unified support. In those years, however, the Marxist Socialist Zionists (Poalei Zion) split, the non-Marxist socialist Zionists (Zeirei Zion) split, Ha-Shomer split, even the General Zionists split. The major issues included the attitude to Yiddish which was taken as an indication of attitudes toward the Jewish working class; the question of work in the Diaspora *(Gegenwartsarbeit)* as opposed to a strictly Palestinian orientation; and advocacy of mass as against elitist emigration to Palestine. In relation to this last issue Mendelsohn makes the following observation in the course of his description of events connected with the Fourth Aliyah when many middle class Polish Jews went to Palestine: "[T]here is no better illustration of the extreme ideological character of Grünbaum's thought and of the Zionist Left's near fanatic belief that only pioneers were worthy of going to Palestine than their ferocious attacks on the middle class Jews who wanted to go to Palestine at a time of mounting anti-Semitism and Jewish economic crisis" in Poland (p. 268f.).

Ideological disputes among Polish Jews were not limited to members of the Zionist movement alone. There was a certain parallel between the dilemmas faced by the parties at two edges of the movement. "Indeed, the ideological predicament of Poale Zion is reminiscent of the dilemma of Mizrachi, with the role of the anti-Zionist Orthodox played in this case by the anti-Zionist Marxists" (p. 139). Mendelsohn attributes the tendency toward fragmentation of the Zionist parties to Jewish powerlessness. This powerlessness freed them from the necessity of compromise and enabled them to pursue ideological purity.

In the course of his work the author stresses the distinction between pro-Zionist sentiment on the part of most Polish Jews and actual membership in the movement. In this regard there were not only regional differences but a dramatic contrast between towns and cities. In Lodz in 1923 there were about 200,000 Jews but only 8,562 *shekel* payers (i.e., official members). For most of the book Mendelsohn concentrates on parties and their leaders and their institutions. In an all too brief but brilliant synthetic conclusion he portrays the rank and file and identifies their motives in affiliating with Zionism. It was "an alternative to the old Jewish world that was helpless in the face of the new realities of the modern anti-Semitic nation-state" (p. 344).

Finally, it may be worth noting that this major monograph contains no explicit criticism of earlier work in the field. Still, to take one clear example, few readers will fail to catch the rejection of recent sociological writing in the following passage: "[E]nough Jews rose to prominence in Polish cultural, economic and political life to rule out any meaningful comparisons with Indian untouchables, American blacks or Southeast Asian Chinese" (p. 15). Mendelsohn's book, by contrast is characterized by rich detail, clear-sighted, objective and balanced description, and careful analysis undistorted by sterile, inexact analogies. This volume, together with the sequel promised by the author, will become, undoubtedly, the definitive history of Zionism in Poland between the wars.

GERSHON DAVID HUNDERT
McGill University

Gabrielle Michalski, *Der Antisemitismus im deutschen akademischen Leben in der Zeit nach dem I Weltkrieg*. (Europäische Hochschulschriften, Series III: "Geschichte und ihre Hilfswissenschaften," Vol. 128) Frankfurt am Main, Bern, & Cirencester/U.K.: Peter D. Lang. 1980. 245 pp.

This anthology of documents and introductory essays casts its net wider than the title suggests. On the questionable assumption that the universities were the principal transmitters of anti-Jewish ideas, it attempts to survey the entire history of German anti-Semitism and to show how it influenced scholarship in the various academic fields. Unfortunately, the issue is confused in that most of the figures represented are politicians and journalists rather than scholars. Nor is the material always introduced with precision. The identification of Hans F. K. Günther, author of racist studies published in the 1920's, as a professor of anthropology years *before* the Nazis forced him upon the faculty at Jena, is typical of the errors that all too frequently mar this work.

DONALD L. NIEWYK
Southern Methodist University

Deborah Dash Moore, *B'nai B'rith and the Challenge of Ethnic Leadership*. Albany: State University of New York Press, 1981. xvi + 288 pp. $19.95.

There are two ways of writing an organizational history. One is to illuminate significant historical issues, as through a prism, by the experience of one organization. Naomi Cohen's study of the American Jewish Committee and Yehuda Bauer's work on the Joint Distribution Committee come to mind in this connection. The other approach focuses on the organization itself, its achievements and great leaders, against a backdrop of contemporary events.

Deborah Dash Moore's study of B'nai B'rith attempts to steer a middle course, to study the nature of Jewish institutional response to social and historical change. Thus, the organization is the historical issue as well. The author's analysis of B'nai B'rith as an agent of resocialization for upwardly mobile German Jewish immigrants as well as her account of how it responded to the East European mass immigration, Zionism and the Holocaust successfully blend a social-historical perspective with a chronicle of organizational adaptation and change.

This balance is sustained to a lesser degree in her treatment of the last thirty-five years. There is a tendency here to slip over into a straightforward organizational history, at the expense of analysis and interpretation. Why, for example, is it important to know that when in 1959 the B'nai B'rith covered the last debts on its new, $1.6 million Washington, D.C. headquarters, it celebrated by burning the mortgage (p. 223)?

The author refers to B'nai B'rith as a "secular synagogue." The content of the term "secular" is never made clear, however, and there remains some confusion about its application. In some contexts, it appears to be used as a substitute term for a Jewish form of ecumenism or non-denominationalism (which would not usually be considered secular); while in other contexts it is used to signify an ethnic or cultural approach to Jewishness.

The study takes as its sub-theme the quest for "ethnic leadership" pursued by the leaders of B'nai B'rith for over a century. The author concludes that "the question of who speaks for American Jews remains unanswered" (p. 255). One would have liked to see a fuller discussion of the implied inconsistency of a drive to create a "cohesive community" based on the ethnic principle with a commitment to voluntarism based on service (p. 252).

While Moore skilfully places B'nai B'rith within the context of national American Jewish politics, there is no attempt in her book at placing the B'nai B'rith lodge in its local context. As a "secular synagogue," where does the lodge stand in relation to the rivalry for local leadership between the synagogue *per se* and the "secular" federations? We get no inkling of whether the B'nai B'rith lodges now, or ever did, serve some Jews as their primary communal identification. In her preface the author notes that writing the history of B'nai B'rith from the vantage point of the national leadership may "slight the Order's mass membership." A choice has certainly been made here, but one wonders if it had to be one of either-or.

Because B'nai B'rith epitomizes the American Jewish experience in so many ways, this book raises important and disturbing questions about the content of Jewish life in the United States. Moore writes of a "culture of organizations," characterized by what Harold Weisberg of the B'nai B'rith has called "an ideology . . . of belonging and conforming" (p. 225). Rejecting political ideologies, B'nai B'rith claims that "serving is believing" and "believing is belonging." In this culture of "serving and belonging," fund-raising becomes what Moore calls "a necessary obsession," blurring the distinction between means and ends (p. 248). "Fund-raising itself became a program," she writes, echoing a former president of the organization, Philip Klutznick.

A full discussion of these issues of contemporary Jewish life in America clearly lies outside the scope of this study. The fact that Moore has raised them at all, however, indicates the objectivity with which she has treated her material and vindicates her attempt to make an organizational history serve a wider purpose.

ELI LEDERHENDLER
Jewish Theological Seminary
Hebrew University

George Mosse, *Masses and Man: Nationalist and Fascist Perceptions of Reality*. New York: Howard Fertig, 1980. 362 pp. $28.50.

George Mosse is the *doyen* of American students of Nazi Germany and of its cultural origins. This collection groups some of his major essays on a common theme: "the mobilization of private discontent into collectivities that promised to transcend the anxieties of the modern age." The most effective of these collectivities was the nation, and—despite powerful competition—nationalism appears as the most effective ideological force of the last 150 years. The nationalism that interests Mosse is of the radical sort: what he calls the bourgeois anti-bourgeois revolution. He pursues this, under various guises, among French, Italians, Jews but, above all, as manifested among the Germans. Mosse nods briefly in the direction of humanistic nationalism, interested in human dignity and the unity of all mankind—and, given the effects of such aspirations, it is just as well the nod is brief. He looks much harder at the contrast between the high-minded, moderate and relatively tolerant literary fare of ordinary Germans—including Hitler with his addiction to the virtuous Karl May—and the dictatorship which contradicted all the values such books carried.

The bloody-mindedness and brutality of the Nazis cannot be attributed to cultural fodder of this sort, but rather to the shadow that falls between the idea and the act, to compartmented standards and values, to the discrepancy between historical reality and human perceptions of it. Of course, historical reality is what the historian says it is, and

Mosse does not escape (or ignore) the problems posed when a rational mind examines irrational phenomena. But he handles them coolly and adroitly, and does not press speculation too far.

Inevitably, when dealing with mass phenomena, myths, symbols, stereotypes rear their seductive heads. Did their rule really increase in the 20th century, as Mosse believes, or did their incidence and sway simply vary, as folklorists and students of popular culture might argue? Symbols make ideas concrete, stereotypes make them more soothing. How else are abstractions to take shape? All ages have embodied their abstractions, or abstracted harsh realities, by such recourse to audio-visual aids. Ours is just more blatant about it.

It is always interesting to seek out some of the origins of great events, and reading Mosse the interest seldom flags. But his forays also demonstrate that an attempt to reconcile innocuous sources and poisonous growths can fall beside the point. History accomodates all (apparent) contradictions. Wars of religion embody the easy passage from high-minded ends to horrendous means. There is no necessary conflict between a fancy for Beethoven and efficient functioning in a slaughterhouse. As Eichmann found, a leather coat can easily be wiped clean of spattered babies' brains. And, while surveying literary sources, a glance at Wilhelm Busch reminds us that those whom decent folk regard as a public nuisance may well end up as chicken food or fertilizer.

EUGEN WEBER
University of California, Los Angeles

Donald L. Niewyk, *The Jews in Weimar Germany*. Baton Rouge and London: Louisiana State University Press, 1980. 229 pp. $17.50.

The Jews in Weimar Germany is an important contribution to the field of German history as well as to the study of German Jewry. Donald Niewyk has uncovered much unknown material and overturned some commonly held assumptions in a work which places the economic, political and cultural history of German Jews within the framework of the economic crises, political turmoil and cultural ferment of the Weimar Republic. Moreover, he has examined the Jewish community from inside, devoting separate chapters to its responses to anti-Semitism; its debates over Jewish identity (both the assimilationist and Zionist perspectives); its approaches to patriotism; and its loyalty to German liberalism.

A careful discussion of the political and social roots of anti-Semitism is one of the strongest chapters. The author examines the earliest, *völkisch* bands, including the most important and active one, the Deutsch-Völkischer Schutz und Trutz Bund. With the generous support of German industry, this group grew to 250 locals and 110,000 members by 1920 and exceeded 200,000 by 1922. Germans content with a less fanatical brand of racism, however, did not have to look to one of the dozen small organizations. They could join the German Nationalists (Deutschnationale Volkspartei), whose principles called for the elimination of "every destructive, un-German spirit" and the rejection of "the predominance of Jewry in government and public life . . . [and] the influx of aliens . . ." (p. 49).

Niewyk is discerning in his approach to the prominent social groups in German society and to the nature of the anti-Semitism that existed among them. He focuses on antipathy toward Jews in churches, universities, political parties and government and introduces the novel concept of "moderate anti-Semitism." For example, even when condemning the right-wing, anti-Christian radicals, church spokesmen often endorsed a more limited version of anti-Semitism. Similarly, but in contrast to the students, ("no group of Germans was more susceptible to anti-Semitism", p. 61), university faculties, while repudiating right-wing extremism, still showed patience for "cultivated" attitudes which connected Jewry to materialism, modernity, Marxism, and cultural decadence. Further, his survey of the political parties opposed to anti-Semitism like that of the government branches (the judiciary comes out looking better than—the army, as bad as—generally thought) reveals an anti-Semitism which was uneven, sporadic, and rarely of the extremist variety. Here, I would have added that even *friends* of Jews often shared with the anti-Semites an impatience with Jewish distinctiveness. Mirroring German liberalism, they invited Jewish integration at the price of Jewish identity and were decidedly uncomfortable in the face of Jews who resisted homogenization.

By distinguishing between the radicals (outright hatred) and the "moderates" (mere distaste), Niewyk offers an important lesson in the history of anti-Semitism: we should pay as much attention to the "silent majority" as to the rabid ideologues. He concludes, correctly, that: "More common and widespread than outright hatred or sympathy for the Jews was . . . moderate anti-Semitism, that vague sense of unease about Jews that stopped far short of wanting to harm them but that may have helped to neutralize whatever aversion Germans might otherwise have felt for the Nazis. . . . Hence the Nazis were able to attract hard core anti-Semites with racialist appeals without having to fear that this would drive away an equal or greater number of potential followers" (pp. 80, 81). Niewyk's discussion of moderate anti-Semitism suggests not only why Germans may not have been so averse to the Nazis, but also why Jews, no matter how much they insisted that they were integrated—and there were many who did "protest too much"—never felt completely at ease in German society. Despite unprecedented achievements in the professions, culture, and business, and despite the fact that "in most cases anti-Semitism was as abstract to the Jews as Jews were to anti-Semites" (p. 86). Jews viewed anti-Semitism as a "fact of life" (p. 112).

Niewyk adds new information on the economic position of Jews in Weimar and challenges a central assumption about the wealth of the Jewish community. He notes that the inflation and Depression heightened an economic decline already present before World War I. Popular stereotypes of rich Jews notwithstanding, the age of Jewish prosperity had not survived the structural changes in the German economy. Fears of creeping proletarianization made middle-class Jews look toward radical occupational reorientation in agriculture and the skilled trades for men and in home economics (an omission in the book) for women. While the Zionists saw this as a way of preparing Jews for the practical trades needed in Palestine, others hoped to make the Jewish occupational profile similar enough to the German one to do away with that anti-Semitism which focused on the Jews' "unrepresentative" job distribution in mercantile and professional vocations. Niewyk suggests that the latter were "far-sighted" (p. 21) and that had their mission succeeded, "the plausibility of attacks on the Jews for their role in the economy would have declined" (p. 25).

It is surprising that the author accepts the rationale of these Jewish leaders who themselves demonstrated a common characteristic of oppressed minorities, absorbing much of what was the worst in German political culture: an intolerance of (their own) diversity; a strong preference for conformity; and a readiness to take the blame on themselves for their victimization. One wonders whether it would not have made more sense to have examined the folly and class interests of these leaders: men and women whose vision ran counter to the historical development of Jewish employment and to the basic tendencies of advanced, capitalist economies in which commerce and industry rather than agriculture, crafts, and domestic service offer opportunities for profitable employment; who deluded themselves as to the possibility of mitigating the hatred of their detractors by rational action; and who never intended this kind of retraining for themselves or their offspring, but only for their poorer, East European, immigrant co-religionists.

As a first comprehensive study of Weimar Jews within Weimar society, this book will be indispensable reading for historians of the period and, because of its accessible and fluid style, will also engage interested lay readers. In the future, I would expect a more differentiated gender analysis equal in sophistication to the analyses here of the class, geographical, ethnic and political factors. For the history of German-Jewish women is not subsumed under the history of German-Jewish men: their experiences were distinct. Even though their educational, professional and occupational profiles showed marked disparities from those of Jewish males, and they maintained separate social service, feminist, social and kin networks, these are nowhere highlighted in this book. In recent years our understanding of German history has benefited from the contributions of German-Jewish history, which is, needless to say, of intrinsic value. Comparably, the women's dimension can add much to Jewish history.

MARION A. KAPLAN
Leo Baeck Institute

Miriam Novitch, Lucy Dawidowicz, Tom L. Freudenheim, *Spiritual Resistance: Art from Concentration Camps, 1940–1945.* Philadelphia: The Jewish Publication Society of America, 1981.

Janet Blatter and Sybil Milton, *Art of the Holocaust.* New York: The Rutledge Press, 1981 and London: Pan Books and Orbis Publishing Ltd., 1982.

In 1981, two books were published which made important, albeit different, contributions to research on Holocaust Art. The first, *Spiritual Resistance: Art from Concentration Camps, 1940–1945* by Miriam Novitch, Lucy Dawidowicz and Tom L. Freudenheim, is a selection of works from the Holocaust Museum of Kibbutz Lohamei Hagettaot. This is the second book on the museum's collection. The first—written by Novitch alone—bore a similar title: *Resistenza Spirituale 1940–1945* (Comune of Milan, 1979). Each book contains over one hundred different works done in the camps, most of them hitherto unavailable in reproduction. Novitch apparently planned the two books to complement each other: there is almost no duplication of illustrations and, with the exception of Malvina Schalkova, artists who were well-represented in the first book, are given limited space in, or excluded from, the second.

In her introductions to both books, Novitch deals with the museum's collection and with the importance of the camp drawings as documentary evidence. In *Spiritual Resistance,* this is supplemented by a short but illuminating essay by Lucy Dawidowicz on the reasons for camp art and the types of subjects that were represented, and by an unsuccessful attempt by Tom Freudenheim to deal with the style of this art. Both books provide short biographies on each artist, set alongside his works, and histories of the camps. The latter are grouped together with maps at the end of *Spiritual Resistance,* in which the illustrations are organized alphabetically according to artist, and piecemeal throughout *Resistenza Spirituale,* where the material is grouped by the camp in which it was produced, without any discernible order. As these books lack both an index and a table of contents, the reader will have difficulty finding cross-references or even whole sections. In *Spiritual Resistance,* Novitch adds a list of artists killed in the camps, but not illustrated in the book, and a short incomplete bibliography and list of exhibitions on Holocaust art.

One of the main problems in the new book involves the plates, which form the body of the work. In *Resistenza Spirituale,* all the works—even the black and white drawings—were reproduced in color. In *Spiritual Resistance,* most of the reproductions are in black and white, and the color plates are grouped together in two sections. Unfortunately this layout posed a problem which was not resolved and results in massive confusion. First of all, no information is provided on most of the color plates, and the only reference to them appears elsewhere under the artist's name. This is helpful when the reader is referred in the section on Yehuda Bacon on p. 48 to the color plate of his work on p. 131, but woe betide the reader who arrives at p. 131 without having memorized that information—no hint of the artist's identity greets his eye!

Secondly, the editors had a problem with six artists who appear only in a single color plate and their solution is devastating. They pulled these artists out of alphabetical order and put the information on them opposite the color plate. The result is that one follows the alphabet from Accatino to Mellé-Oldeboerrigter, to be suddenly confronted by Abraham Berline, six unidentified color plates, Jindrich Flutter (set logically after Aizik Feder who fortunately signed his works), and six more unidentified plates, before returning to the alphabetical order with Jacques Ochs. The situation is even worse in the second color section which includes three artists whose names appear in the alphabetical sequence *following* the plates!

These defects do not, however, detract from the real value of the books which give excellent, clear reproductions of works which have been carefully selected for quality, theme and interest, and provide a good introduction to Holocaust art. Novitch succeeds in forcing us to remember the past and in giving the artists who worked in the camps fitting, beautifully produced memorials.

Art of the Holocaust by Janet Blatter and Sybil Milton is a work of an entirely different nature, and it will undoubtedly become a necessary sourcebook for anyone dealing with the subject. It is well-thought out, well-documented, and well-produced. It has none of the defects of Novitch's books, although there are occasional mistakes, such as the assignment of Marcel Janco's drawing on p. 97 to "Ernst Janko." The book contains 359 works culled in part from books such as Novitch's (full credit to the sources is given in the notes), and adds a large number of unpublished works assembled from museums all over the world. The plates, both black and white and color, are well reproduced, and although the page design is often crowded, the wealth and choice of the material makes up for this.

The book is divided into clear sections. It begins with Henry Friedlander's concise historical essay on the camps, giving important dates and documentary descriptions which present the reader with a picture of the Holocaust as a whole. This is followed by an often brilliant analysis by Janet Blatter on the various types of camp art and the reasons they were created. This long essay is a valuable, objective contribution to a field too often dominated by sentimental or politically-motivated outpourings. It is followed by an interesting analysis by Sybil Milton on the ways in which the remnants of Holocaust art were saved during and after the war, and on their preservation in museums and archives. This last section, reinforced at the end of the book by a list giving the addresses of museums and research centers dealing with Holocaust art, will be particularly valuable for young researchers who are often unaware of the extent and location of the available resources.

The main section of the book is divided into eight chapters, chosen for the different kinds of experiences and artistic responses involved. Starting with a brief chapter on pre-war anti-Fascist art, the authors move with increasing drama from the ghettoes, to the transit and POW camps, to artists in hiding and partisans, to the concentration camps, ending with the Death March. Following this are two short chapters on post-liberation depictions of the Holocaust. The last chapter, on post-war works by former camp inmates, is particularly interesting, as it shows an increase in anger and in expressionism after the war.

Each chapter has an introduction which explains conditions at each stage of this Via Dolorosa. Quotations from artists and writers are scattered among the illustrations to reinforce their impact.

The book ends with a full documentation of the works, including concise biographies of each artist, complete with bibliographical notes, and cross-references to the plates. The only fault here is that too much space is given to famous artists such as Käthe Kollwitz, whose work is reproduced only once in the first chapter. At the end, there is a bibliography which is more complete than Novitch's, and it is divided with the same methodological care that is discernible in the rest of the book.

Art of the Holocaust is a must for every reader and scholar interested in this field. It will undoubtedly become a classic on this subject and remain so for years to come.

ZIVA AMISHAI-MAISELS
Hebrew University

Yisrael Oppenheim, *Tnu'at hehaluz befolin (1917–1929)*. (The Halutz Movement in Poland, 1917–1929). Jerusalem: Magnes Press, 1982.

The Halutz (Pioneer) movement in interwar Poland has been relatively fortunate in the amount of attention it has received in the historical literature. Indeed, we possess a real historiography of the Halutz, something which cannot be said for other Jewish political movements of the period. The historiographical tradition commences with various surveys published by the movement itself, continues with a number of scholarly and semi-scholarly works of the post-war era, and reaches a new level of achievement with the appearance of the massive volume under review.[1] The fact that more has been written about the Polish Halutz than about all other Polish Jewish movements is probably a function of the highly developed historical consciousness of its members, who believed that they represented the avantgarde of the new Jewish nation-in-the-making. It may also derive from the success of the movement. Many of its members did in fact go to Palestine, drain the swamps, and play a crucial role in the establishment of the Jewish state. And historians tend to favor the winners rather than the losers.

Professor Oppenheim's work, the first of a promised two-volume study, will doubtless serve for many years as our chief source of knowledge of the Polish Pioneer. It commences with a detailed examination of the sources of the pioneering idea in Zionist history, from the First Aliya on, and then settles down to a meticulous examination of the development of the Pioneer's ideology, its relations with the General Zionist organization and with the various youth movements, and its establishment of numerous vocational training *(hakhshara)* institutions. Professor Oppenheim explains how an ideologically vague, romantic organization of youth seeking to flee from Poland to Palestine was transformed, as a result of external influences (the Russian Pioneer, the Dror group, Palestinian emissaries) and internal dynamics (the need to keep the movement going in times of virtually no aliya), into a socialist, collectivist organization closely identified with the Palestinian Kibbutz Hameuhad and the Ahdut Haavoda party. This is done in an objective, clear way, and the narrative is firmly grounded on the extensive documentation, much of it archival in nature, to be found in Israel.

This said, certain aspects of the book are open to criticism. For one thing, it is far too long. Is it not an exaggeration to write a volume of close to 700 pages on eleven years in the history of a fairly small (though important) movement? Professor Oppenheim does not even write about the Pioneer in all of Poland, omitting (for unconvincing reasons) Galicia, where the movement took a different course from that in former Congress Poland and the eastern borderlands. There are innumerable repetitions, and in general, the hand of a good editor is missing. Its exaggerated length is one reason why this book might not find as many readers as it deserves. Potential readers may also be put off by the dry style of the book and by its tendency to devote all too many pages to summaries of innumerable conferences and meetings. Too little attention, on the other hand, is paid to the dynamics of Polish Jewish society. There is no systematic treatment of the general Polish and Polish-Jewish context within which the Pioneer movement grew, and too little space is devoted to demographic and regional factors which exerted a considerable impact on the fortunes of the Pioneer. I feel, also, that too little emphasis is placed on the human dimension of this most vibrant form of Polish Zionism. The pioneering movement was, after all, a remarkable expression of revolt on the part of mostly poor youths from traditional homes who found Polish anti-Semitism and the conservative Jewish milieu insufferable and who dreamed of creating a new society in Palestine. Who were these pioneers? Why did some members of the new generation join, and others not? What kind of sacrifices were involved? What was it like to work at the stone quarries and kibbutzim of the movement? These questions are scarcely raised. Professor Oppenheim's wish to be the wholly objective, unemotional recorder of the Pioneer's history can be understood in light of previous (romanticizing) tendencies in the historical literature, but he has gone too far in his reaction, and in general his book is characterized by an extremely conservative approach which takes little account of new methods in social and political historiography. I must add that the book ends without any effort at summing up its findings, which is most unfortunate.

Professor Oppenheim has written a formidable book which sets high standards of scrupulous scholarship and which amply reveals his unrivalled knowledge of the subject. No one interested in the history of Zionism and of Polish Jewry can afford to ignore it. Is it possible to hope that his second volume, on the crucial 1930's, will be shorter, more readable, and more ready to deal with the social and human aspects of what is, in the last analysis, a dramatic and very moving chapter in modern Jewish history?

EZRA MENDELSOHN
Hebrew University

Note

1. See, for example, *Measef letnu'at hehaluz,* Warsaw, 1930; Leib Shpeizman (ed.), *Halutsim in Poyln,* New York, 1959; Yisrael Otiker, *Tnu'at HeHaluz befolin* 1932–1935, (Tel-Aviv, 1972); L. A. Sarid, *Hehaluz utnu'ot hano'ar befolin,* 2 vols, Tel-Aviv, 1979.

Esther L. Panitz, *The Alien in Their Midst: Images of Jews in English Literature.* E. Brunswick, NJ: Fairleigh Dickinson University Press, 1981. 197 pp.

The thesis of Esther Panitz's book is suggested by its title and repeatedly emphasized in its seven chapters: Christian writers of English literature have consistently seen the Jew as a stranger, an alien distinguished by his connection with money and power but forever separate from English life. The argument is not new, but the author's focus on its Christian as well as Jewish implications offers an unusual vantage point. Her insistence on the inability of writers to portray individualized Jewish characters suggests the extent to which specifically Christian views of the Jew (rather than less clearly definable British views or even sociological and historical realities) may have determined the literary presentation of Jews. The Christian context of her book, however, tends to overwhelm the literary analysis and is often emphasized at the expense of a broader cultural perspective. The most successful discussions in the book are precisely those in which some wider context is glimpsed.

Beginning, as do virtually all such studies, with Chaucer's *Prioress' Tale* and ending with twentieth-century fiction, the book attempts to illustrate the underlying uniformity with which Jews are depicted while also accounting for the surface differences in these presentations. The latter is accomplished by a brief, sweeping social history of each period, placing writers within some social framework and explaining their Jewish characters in terms of that changing framework and its effect on consistently maintained Christian themes. Thus, the Renaissance gives rise to Barabas and Shylock because Marlow and Shakespeare, products of their time with its emphasis on power and manipulation, add these contemporary concerns to the traditional image of Jew as moneylender and outcast. Similarly, the Victorians (with Browning as the one exception) are charged with depicting Jewish characters only in terms of wealth and race, these, indeed, being central issues of the period.

Such explanations accurately highlight major currents of thought, but they place unwarranted stress on the significance of Jewish characters in the works of most English writers and obscure the need to analyze such characters in terms of each author's own literary methods and productions. Ms. Panitz is quite correct to warn us against judging Chaucer by modern standards of character presentation, but she then goes on to judge other writers by similarly inappropriate measures. It is very much stretching the point to argue, as she does, that Defoe's anti-Semitism reveals itself in Robinson Crusoe's explanation to Friday of original sin and salvation—non-Jewish concepts which see the Jew as "lost."

Dickens may also be accused of using highly unflattering Jewish stereotypes, but we need not go to the length of seeing Harthouse in *Hard Times* as a caricature of Disraeli, or the nouveaux riches in *Our Mutual Friend* as parodies of the wealthy Anglo-Jewish community. Nor is Dickens' indifference to a Jewish view of evil in *Oliver Twist* a particularly salient point. Dickens is, indeed, disdainful of the dandy figure and of the idle rich; in all his works he is virtually obsessed with money and the existence of evil. To link such issues with Jewish themes, however, is to largely ignore the writer in indefensible favor of the Christian, anti-Semitic man of his age. The argument about Dickens can be extended to virtually all the authors discussed in the book.

The Alien in Their Midst should not be read as a work of literary history or analysis. It is more convincing as a series of essays on varying social myths, always united by what Ms. Panitz insists is the Christian myth of the Jew as outsider.

ANITA NORICH
Lady Davis Fellow, Hebrew University
University of Michigan

Leonard Prager, *Yiddish Literary and Linguistic Periodicals and Miscellanies: A Selective Annotated Bibliography*. Darby, PA/Haifa: Norwood Editions, for the Association for the Study of Jewish Languages, 1982.

Existing bibliographies of Yiddish periodical publications are almost exclusively arranged according to geographical criteria. Leonard Prager's bibliography presents, for the first time, an array of Yiddish literary and linguistic periodicals and miscellanies ("zaml-bikher") from the initial such publication (*Kol mevaser,* Odessa 1862–1873) to the present. This new criterion of selection and presentation is in itself a significant contribution to Yiddish literary research. As the compiler states in his acknowledgements, the present bibliography is part of what was once planned as a larger (but as yet unexecuted) "Guide to Yiddish Literature" (p. 28), which, among its various other functions, was to have served also as a guidebook to literary periodical publications.

It is the vital connection between the rise of the Yiddish press and the development of Yiddish literature that is the focal concern of Prager's succinct, but perhaps too short, introduction. Given the quantity and diffusion of the material involved, the scope of such a bibliography is bound to be selective, and thus somewhat personal. Prager defines his intended audience at the start. His work "aims to serve students of Yiddish language and literature as well as of related disciplines" (p. 9). It is surprising and somewhat disturbing that Hebrew literature is not included in the subsequent short list of related disciplines, for such a work as this can do much to advance the study of bilingual (Hebrew-Yiddish) authors.

The selection of entries encompasses "1) the most important Yiddish literary and linguistic periodicals and miscellanies . . . 2) a representative body of periodicals, including amateur efforts, short-lived experiments, bibliophilic rarities and . . . [journals] of partly literary character." Prager goes on to declare that he has assigned priority to the "general user's needs," has exercised "selectivity," and has focused on Eastern Europe and North America. There subsequently follows a list of twenty categories which were *"for the most part"* (his emphasis) excluded from the bibliography. These include, among others, dailies, general weeklies, and provincial literary journals, as well, for example, as party and organizational periodicals, journals purely about literature, and theatrical periodicals. Each of these categories is described with mention of its potential importance to the study of Yiddish, at times with a sample listing of the periodicals excluded from the bibliography; and often with mention of significant publications in a specific excluded category which are nevertheless included. Thus we read, for instance, that "Most of the serious theatrical journals have been included here . . . But I have omitted a great many items which do have some literary relevance" (p. 17).

The result is that the user is left with a feeling of uncertainty about just when it is advisable to consult this particular reference work and this impairs its effectiveness as a research tool. Had the compiler presented it either as a purely personal, though educated, selection, or else presented strict guidelines and adhered to them, the user would have been able to make better use of the volume. Given the dearth of bibliographical guidebooks to Yiddish literary material and the relative unavailability of the primary material itself, perhaps it would have been preferable to present a selection more limited in size but still more detailed in annotation.

This flaw in the bibliography nonetheless stems from virtues. One can debate the seminal importance of such an entry as *Naye vintn* (No. 202) of which six issues were published in Radom by "a poet butcher whose stories of butcher's life appear here," but its existence did reflect the vitality of the Yiddish literary press. And this is the overall impression left by Prager's selection—he is a bibliographer very much captivated by his material and he has attempted to transmit its excitement and flavor to the general public. Whether this goal is not more appropriate to a descriptive essay than to a bibliography—where it can deter from its scholarly effectiveness—must remain an open question.

For the student of Yiddish literature the inclusion of minor items at the expense of significant literary efforts is to be regretted. Publications such as the following, to name a few, definitely have a place in a bibliography of this kind: *Amol in a yoyvl; zamlbukh far beletristik* (Warsaw 1929, 1931), which included for example contributions by A. Tseytlin, I. Bashevis Singer, K. Molodovski, M. Ravitch and Y. Perle; *Os: Lid, novele, esey, bild* (Lodz-Warsaw 1936–39), edited by Yisroel Rabon, with contributions by A. Sutskever, M. Ulinover, M. Broderzon and I.M. Vaysnberg; and *Lebn un visnshaft* (Vilna 1909–12). Also helpful in such a guidebook would have been the inclusion of journals that regularly listed Yiddish literary works as they were published. Contemporary examples are *Kiryat sefer* and the *Jewish Book Annual*.

The bibliography contains 386 entries arranged alphabetically by the romanized original title (given in the YIVO transcription system). Each entry also includes an idiomatic translation of the title and subtitle; the place of publication; the publisher (primarily in the case of the miscellanies); the collation of issues; and the editors; as well as annotations in which the compiler has "not strained to achieve detached objectivity. My intention is to stimulate the user's interest in the materials described" (p. 20). In his description, Prager often characterizes the journal, describes connections to other publications, mentions a few sample topics covered and most importantly, offers a selective list of notable or frequent contributors (deciphering the pseudonyms). He states when he has not seen a work. Following the annotations are a bibliography relevant to the item, at times including contemporary reviews; a selection of previous reference sources which list the item; and finally, repositories where the item can be located.

Here too in terms of presentation, one feels that Prager is seeking, in the main, to address the general, at the expense of the specialist, user. By arranging the material according to the romanized title, he seems to be catering to the widest possible audience. But this creates its own problems. For example, Prager enters items beginning with the preposition "oyf" as "af", as it is usually pronounced, and those with the adverbial complement as "oyf" (e.g., "Oyfgang"), though this is usually pronounced "uf". Is the general user assumed not to be able to read a Yiddish title in the original, yet to be well versed in the intricacies of the transcription system? Or does the present arrangement stem rather from budgetary limitations and the costs of using Hebrew typeface in the computer print-out? At this juncture, when an increasing amount of work can be best undertaken with computers, it is more efficient to use the original Yiddish title entries for such reference works. It should be noted that a majority of libraries have Hebrew-character catalogs for their Yiddish holdings.

On the whole the bibliography would have greatly benefited from a network of cross-references—be it in the case of the transcribed titles ("oyf see af") or, still more, in that of titles with non-standard orthography (we find the use of "Idish", "Yidish", "Yudish" in separate places). Even the criteria used for entries can cause confusion. *"S'feld"* for whatever reason is not entered under F and should at least have a cross-reference. Also, given the fact that the editor has done quite a lot of genealogical research, it would have been helpful to have this consistently reflected in the bibliography in the form of cross-references (e.g., the special relationship between *Literatur un lebn*— #180—and *Di yudishe velt*—#363).

The numerous valuable indices also lack cross-references. Thus the joint place of publication of *Heftn* appears in the index as "Detroit/Montreal" but there is no entry under Montreal. In the same vein, cross-references are lacking in the contributors index for "Abramovits [Mendele Moykher-Sforim (pseud.)], Sh.Y"; "Ish (pseud.) - [Mendele Moykher-Sforim]" and "Mendele Moykher-Sforim (pseud.)." Again, a significant number of journals mentioned in the introduction or the annotations are not recorded in the index (e.g., the Tel Aviv publication *Shtamen,* described in the annotations to *Eyns*).

Another point that is somewhat perplexing is the matter of repositories. This is a most welcome feature of the bibliography and can help libraries to complete sets and scholars to locate rare items. But a random check revealed, for example, that if the Jewish National and University Library is not listed as a repository (e.g., in the case of *Tint und feder* or *Tsuzamen*), it does not necessarily mean that the item is not found there. In a few cases no repository is given (nos. 318, 341). This too leads to the feeling of uncertainty about just when the present volume is sufficient for a specific bibliographical search.

The extensive bibliography at the back of the volume is particularly useful. For the sake of completeness we shall mention two important items that have been omitted: Naygreshl, M., "Der letster dor yidishe poetn in galitsye," *Tsukunft* LV (Dec 1950) 460–464; LVI (Jan. 1951) 25–28 (this precedes the more extensive article by Naygreshl that does appear in the bibliography); Tsinberg, S.L. (I), *Istoriia evreiskoi pechati v Rossii v svyazi s obshchestvennymi techeniiami* (Petrograd, 1915: this is the pioneering book on the Jewish press in Russia).

Generally, these are all minor flaws which do, however, detract from the usefulness of an otherwise important, readable and well researched bibliography. Hopefully much can be improved in a second edition. The very existence of this bibliography, with its intrinsic problem of selectivity for a wide ranging audience, only underlines the need for further bibliographical tools which can provide students of Yiddish with a sound, fundamental "Guide to Yiddish Literature." Once such basic groundwork is laid, scholars and bibliographers will be able to progress more freely in presenting the rich and varied material that constitutes the Yiddish literary edifice.

CHONE SHMERUK and
AGNES ROMER-SEGAL
Hebrew University

Jehuda Reinharz (ed.), *Dokumente zur Geschichte des deutschen Zionismus 1882–1933*. Tübingen: Mohr, 1981. (Schriftenreihe wissenshaftlicher Abhandlungen des Leo Baeck Instituts). li + 580 pp., with introduction.

The Zionist idea emerged in Germany towards the end of the nineteenth century when the process of Jewish integration into German society was at its height. Unlike the Jewish national awakening in Eastern Europe, German Zionism was a post-assimilationist creation and this was what made it singularly problematic. Most of the German Zionists did not arrive at Zionism by way of a deep-rooted Jewish heritage as happened among Zionists in Russia and Poland, but under the influence of European nationalist ideas and by way of German literature and philosophy. They believed that Zionism would transform their Judaism, so impoverished and meager in content, into a source of vitality and inspiration, but within the framework of European culture.

The documents which Jehuda Reinharz has expertly selected and edited—the great majority of them published here for the first time—provide a detailed picture of the development of Zionism in Germany, until Hitler's accession to power. In his scholarly, polished introduction, a broad survey, he divides the history of German Zionism into three stages. The first generation, men of the Herzl period and attracted to his ideas, was deeply disturbed by the question of double loyalty—to Jewish nationality on the one hand and to Germany and her laws on the other. They viewed the idea of a national home in Palestine as a solution to the distressed condition of East European Jewry, and for this purpose they were prepared to extend generous assistance. As for themselves, they envisaged the continuation of Jewish life in the region between the Rhine and the Oder, under conditions of full emancipation. They sought to cultivate a consciousness of their own Jewish heritage and historic destiny, but at the same time emphasized their integral link to German civilization.

Shortly before World War I, however, the new generation challenged the German-patriotic and Jewish-philanthropic attitudes of its predecessor. The change was marked by the decision of the Posen Conference in 1912 that members of the Zionist movement were duty bound to include Palestine in their personal plans for the future. This focus on Palestine was accompanied by the call to develop an independent Jewish culture. It was the view of the Conference that as a quintessential difference existed between the Jews and German society, it was incumbent on them inwardly to preserve their distance and to refrain from involvement in German politics, to demonstrate "restraint."

In the aftermath of the war and the Balfour Declaration, German Zionism began a transition to a third stage. Its outstanding characteristic was the activity of the "youth" movements—Blauweiss, He-Halutz, Bahad and others—and there was a growing call for "Zionist self-fulfillment:" training for physical labor and settlement in Palestine. A synthesis of socialism and Zionism on the model of the Labor movement in Palestine, and the figure of the Hebrew pioneer, were increasingly presented as the ideal. For their part, the heads of the Zionist Federation (Zionistische Vereinigung für Deutschland) identified themselves with the principles and policy of Weizmann, supporting a gradualist development of the Yishuv; the quest for an understanding with the Arab sector; and the rejection of extremist political demands that could only sharpen the conflict with the British.

Thus far the Introduction. Even if one does not agree with Reinharz on every point, there is no question that he has provided an excellent summing up of the main trends.

In the wealth of documents in this collection, certain themes stand out. Among them is the recurring question of how the Zionists—as such—regarded their Jewishness on the one hand and their Germanness on the other. What was the significance of their support for the Jewish national idea in the reality of their everyday lives? As it appears from the documentation before us, there was endless debate on the subject both among the Zionists themselves and also between them and their political adversaries in the Jewish community.

"We were of course Germans devoted enthusiastically to our Fatherland," writes Rachel Strauss in her memoirs, and she goes on to say that her circle of friends was at the same time imbued with Jewish consciousness both in the religious and the national sense. This double existence hardly permitted internal fulfillment and wholeness, but the Zionist idea was nonetheless a constant source of inspiration.

The "Janus-faced" ambiguity described here also finds expression in the documents which reveal the attitudes to the War of 1914–18. The major Zionist organizations (the Zionist Federation, Blauweiss, the KjV) called on young Jews to volunteer for the German military and fight enthusiastically for the German fatherland, all this out of pride in their Jewishness, as befitted the scions of the Maccabees and Bar Kokhba. They openly affirmed that by fighting for Germany they wished to serve Jewish aims: to contribute towards liberating the Jewish masses in Russia from the yoke of Tsarist oppression, ensure the freedom of the Jews of Galicia, and entrench their own standing as German citizens with equal rights. It was not only "Germany's war," wrote a well-known Zionist leader in 1914, but also "the war of the Jews." When it ended the Jewish national idea, so they hoped, would earn recognition from the nations of the world. Only isolated individuals were to be found who resolutely opposed the war and army service, in witness whereof Reinharz includes the forceful passages written by Gershon Scholem.

The great sensitivity of the German Zionists to the Arab question is reflected in a considerable number of the documents. They contended that moral considerations and willingness to make concessions to the Arab side had to serve as the guidelines for a Jewish national movement based on humane principles as well as on political realism. However, the proceedings of the Jena Conference of 1929 as well as other documents published here suggest the need to revise the accepted notion that the German Zionists held a uniform position on the central political questions. True, the Zionist Federation as a roof organization exerted itself to coordinate the work of its constituent elements, secure their self-restraint at times of internal dispute, and represent them jointly at Zionist Congresses. Yet, all through the years German Zionism comprised a wide gamut of opinions. (For example, at the Jena Conference Nahum Goldmann and others opposed the majority's doveish approach to the Arab question.)

The heads of the Zionist Federation, who thus correctly discerned the central importance of the Arab question in Palestine, did not realize in time the gravity of the danger inherent in the growing strength of the National-Socialist Party. A vast amount of attention was devoted to the significance of anti-Semitism in principle, but as against this, current events in Germany, including anti-Jewish outrages, received only limited treatment in the Zionist newspapers and other publications. The Zionists believed that anti-Semitism was an inescapable part of exilic life, and that Jewish existence in Exile was bound to collapse sooner or later. It therefore seemed futile to try and stop the course of history or to invest a great deal of energy in the fight against anti-Semitism.

The Zionists were absolutely opposed to the defense tactics against the anti-Semitic parties adopted by the Central-Verein (CV) and criticized its apologetic-patriotic tone fiercely. Except for one instance (in 1930), they rejected proposals all through the years for a common struggle against the extreme Right, but they did not propose any action of their own to bar its way. The main reaction to what was going on was to strengthen the Palestine-centered trend—but without planning for mass emigration. As against this, the Jewish People's Party (Jüdische Volkspartei), which was in the main Zionist, was better able—thanks to its support for action in the here and now *(Gegenwartsarbeit)*—to meet the challenge of the hour. In order to strengthen Jewish life in Germany, they demanded that the leaders restore the local *kehillot* to their central position in Jewish society; broaden the network of autonomous institutions, including Jewish schools; and foster Jewish culture in all its forms.

A group of optimists was found in the Zionist Federation who believed it was possible to reach an arrangement with the National-Socialists. As members of the Jewish national movement, they hoped to meet with understanding from the "representatives of the new German nationalism," as they called them. Room could be found for different nationalities, and it would be possible for an autonomous Jewish collectivity to exist, separate from German society. What was said by those who objected to this line appears only in fragmentary form in this collection. Various opinions were put forward at the National Executive meeting of 8 January 1933, but nobody voiced the view that they must prepare for mass emigration because time was getting short.

These, then, are only some of the principal themes of this superb volume, which is packed with much instructive documentary material. Use of the collection is facilitated by Reinharz's excellent introduction; by the hundreds of instructive notes appended to the documents; and by an index of place-names, persons and subjects that covers no less than twenty-three pages, prepared with scrupulous precision by Eli Rothschild. (One can, however, regret that place-names and subjects mentioned in the introduction have not also been included.) The notes also supply, inter alia, important bibliographical information on a variety of subjects, and place the documents in their wider historical context. The documents themselves appear with headings indicating their main content, and with full indications of the source for each entry.

The archives of the Zionist Federation in Germany have unfortunately been lost, but Reinharz has succeeded in producing an exemplary documentary collection. The book includes sources from twenty-two archives and, all in all, represents a veritable encyclopedic source for German Zionist and Jewish affairs. The documents can serve as a good starting point for further research into questions that have not yet been dealt with. It is to be hoped that the appearance of this collection will encourage the publication of documentary collections of similar high quality on the development of Zionism in other countries, too.

ABRAHAM MARGALIOT
Hebrew University

Paul Ritterband (ed.), *Modern Jewish Fertility*. Leiden: E. J. Brill, 1981. 293 pp.

This book contains a series of essays by different authors on research into various manifestations of the transition from "traditional" to "modern" fertility patterns in Jewish populations.

Besides the central theme of fertility, other topics of the natural movement of Jewish populations were investigated in some of these studies: frequency of marriage and age at first marriage; mixed marriage; mortality and especially child mortality; family life cycle. Through cross-classification with fertility variables, some information is also provided on the structural characteristics of Jewish populations: urban-rural distribution, occupation, education. In the Introduction, the editor outlines some of the problems of interpreting the early timing and the intensity with which family limitation was adopted by many Diaspora Jewries.

Traditional and early transitional fertility patterns of the Jews form the subject of the following studies: Andrejs Plakans and M. Halpern, on household structure in Kurland (Latvia) towards the end of the eighteenth century; Robert Cohen, on eighteenth century Jews in what became the United States; Paula Hyman, on nineteenth century France; Steven M. Lowenstein, on four localities in northern Bavaria in the nineteenth century; Alice Goldstein, on the Jews of a village in Baden during the nineteenth century and the beginning of the twentieth.

Zvi Gitelman summarizes the demographic evolution of the Jews in Russia from the end of the nineteenth century until our times. Sidney Goldstein analyzes Jewish fertility in the United States as compared to that of the other principal religious groups there. Most of his analysis relates to the 1960's and is based on the records of Jewish women from a general survey of women currently giving birth. Steven Martin Cohen and Paul Ritterband have studied college graduates in the United States of the 1960's with a view toward interreligious comparison of fertility targets and of the processes giving rise to their differentiation.

This enumeration shows both the thematic contributions and the lacunae of the collected essays: many of the later stages of the fertility transition among the Jews are missing, as is the contemporary Diaspora outside the United States; the book touches only marginally on the implications of the present very low fertility in the Diaspora, including the United States, for the demographic future of the Jews there. Various types of sources and various methods of analysis have been used in reported studies. Some of the historical investigations have meritoriously employed the laborious technique of family reconstitution, but for very small groups and under the handicap of partly incomplete records, due to the geographical mobility of the Jews.

Even so, this book constitutes a valuable addition to the literature on Jewish fertility in particular and on the demography of the Jews in general. It is a mine of factual information for specialists in this field. It should prove a welcome spur both to them and to the less specialized reader to ponder the trends of Jewish demographic evolution; the determinants and correlates of modernization among the Jews; and the differences in the demographic and other processes of modernization which distinguish the Jews from the corresponding general populations and the various geo-culturally distinct Jewish groups from each other.

U. O. SCHMELZ
Hebrew University

Dov Sadan, *Toyern un tirn: Eseyen un etyudn* (Gates and Portals: Essays and Studies) Tel-Aviv: Yisroel-bukh, 1979.

It is somehow characteristic that Professor Dov Sadan, who has recently been feted on the occasion of his eightieth birthday, should refer to *Toyern un tirn,* his thirteenth book about Yiddish, as "a kind of *bar-mitsve.*" For there is a freshness emanating from this collection of reprinted essays, a sense of the author's youthful enthusiasm about his subject, that declares itself almost in defiance of the reminiscent and sometimes memorial quality of the articles themselves.

The book is divided into four sections, each one devoted to a different aspect of Yiddish: prose, poetry, criticism, and the world of Yiddish itself. A glance at the table of contents provides evidence of Professor Sadan's eclectic tastes and, equally, of his independence: such familiar artists as Uri Zvi Greenberg, Y. Y. Shvartz, and Der Nister share his attention with authors and critics who are far less well-known and celebrated. But a closer reading reveals that there is actually no disharmony. Whatever the topic, Sadan's major focus is always on people (as the book's lengthy index of names confirms)—people he has encountered, heard of, read about. His procedure for introducing them is unabashedly personal, epitomizing his unique style and underscoring his vast and unusual knowledge.

In a selection originally written as the introduction to a collection of essays by Shloyme Grodzenski, for example, Sadan comes to discuss the talents of Grodzenski's Hebrew translater, Shloyme Shvaytser. The latter's gift, he explains, runs in the family: shared by "(his cousin, Shloyme Dikman—both are named after the same grandfather—and their uncle, Avrom Frank)" (p. 186). Similarly, in an article devoted to the centenary of Sholem-Aleykhem's birth, he arrives at an experiment in translating Sholem-Aleykhem conducted by three students (all mentioned by name) in a course headed by Professor Khone Shmeruk of the Hebrew University.

Sadan's passionate interest in—and phenomenal memory for—people and their names may be seen as a counterpart of his consuming interest in Yiddish sayings, a "romance," as he puts it in one of the essays reprinted here, that has enchanted him almost since childhood. The Yiddish saying, Sadan observes, "condenses thought and feeling, prudence and temptation, naiveté and shrewdness, belief and travesty, all the nuances of human contradictions" (p. 310). This formulation is, at the same time, a clue to the philological method, for Sadan is a master at unraveling condensations, employing a fascinating mixture of fact and intuition, perspective and experience.

I have heard Professor Sadan speculate that, in the future, his efforts to collect and record may be achieved by computers. This is inconceivable, precisely because of his free-associative critical style which, in turn, often encompasses explicit statements of implicit and condensed connections. Sadan's means of expressing his remarkable cultural possession thus resembles the essential process of classical psychoanalysis. And, in fact, he speaks of himself as a pioneering psychoanalytic critic in Yiddish. In typical fashion—for both Sadan and psychoanalysis—this revelation occurs almost as an aside, in an evaluation of his colleague Gershon Sapozhnikov's psychoanalytically-oriented writings. Sadan comments that he has left this method behind, yet its imprint, or his innate affinity for it, is evident throughout his work.

Although *Toyern un tirn* is an amalgam of essays spanning a diversity of topics and composed at different times, it ultimately achieves a balance based on the intellect and heart of Professor Sadan. He himself proves the best summary of its underlying force: "With the book *Toyern un tirn,* we come to thirteen, the gematria of which is—*ahava.*" (p. 309).

JANET HADDA
University of California, Los Angeles

Anita Shapira, *Berl: Biografia* (Berl [Katznelson]: A Biography). Tel Aviv: Am Oved, 1980. 2 vols. 796 pp.

The biography of Berl Katznelson is the third major work published by Anita Shapira on the Jewish labor movement in the pre-state days of the Yishuv. Her writing, with its sharp cutting edge, has throughout aroused unusual interest and is evidently inspired by a deep conviction that in telling the story of the founding fathers the narrator not only can but also should unearth the historical truth buried beneath the layers of historiographical myth.

Her study of the Gedud Ha'avodah (Labor Battalion)—originally an M.A. thesis, published as a multi-part article in *Baderekh* in the late 1960's—was a powerful work of unabashed demythologizing. For the first time the story of the Gedud was told from the vantage point of the losers, many of whom felt that they had been forced by the Histadrut to leave Palestine for the Soviet Union. Next came her book on the attitude of the Left to Arab labor in the Yishuv in which she demonstrated that, rhetoric aside, the application of ideological principle had been largely dependent on the economics of supply and demand.

And now we have this two-volume biography which seeks out the man behind the persona, the politician behind the icon—the widely reproduced photo which hangs in so many Histadrut offices showing Berl with an open and benevolent smile. However, this time no gauntlet has been thrown down. This is biography pure and simple, eschewing alike hagiography and inconoclasm; neither "Life and Letters" nor *Eminent Victorians*.

Berl Katznelson, as he emerges here, was extraordinarily gifted, but also highly complex and, in certain crucial respects, flawed. True, his basic political strategy ("constructivism") took shape very early, in the years 1909–1914, and he held true to it until his death in 1944: only if the Yishuv were built up from the first along socialist and cooperative lines would it be possible, given the Arab competition, to entrench a large Jewish working class and so prepare the way for millions of Jews to come from Europe.

But beyond this hard granite-like core of belief, his thinking and reactions remained unpredictable. As a historian and man of letters he himself sought out the dialectical, the paradoxical, profoundly admiring Dostoevsky, Kafka, Berdichevsky and Brenner. And as portrayed so faithfully here, he constantly surprises, inspiring admiration, anger, disappointment, but never boredom.

The paradoxes abound, fascinate, perplex. A man who was seen by the public (in many ways rightly so) as possessed of unbending will would frequently resign his post in anger only to return sheepishly, nothing gained. He believed strongly in the primacy of the agricultural sector (the cooperative and collective settlements); took little interest in the wage-earning urban proletariat; and yet dwelled for most of his active life in the city (Jaffa-Tel Aviv).

No other labor leader in the Yishuv denounced the Bolshevik dictatorship so early, so consistently or with such acute insight. But for all his passionate belief in democracy, when it came to his own movement he was impatient of constitutional safeguards, parliamentary procedures, accountability by the leadership. (It was he, we read, who acted "as the secret appointments committee of the party.")

He utterly rejected the dictum that ends justify means, and took up the theme of Ivan Karamazov that it would be morally unacceptable to buy well-being for all mankind if the price were the torture of even one child. Thus, he opposed the use of terror as a political weapon whether in Russia or Palestine. And yet nobody else in the top leadership of the labor movement showed himself so willing to reach an accomodation with the Revisionists, who frequently had resort to terror in retaliation against Arab blood-letting.

Throughout his life he was a socialist, humanist, and internationalist. He identified strongly with the Social Democrats in Germany and Austria, and with Labour in Britain. But he refused even to try to understand the opponents of the Yishuv and was quick to lump the British and the Arabs in Palestine together with the long line of Hamans and Chmielnickis. ("It was as if he had transferred . . . the bitterness felt by the Jews in the Pale generation after generation for the Russian and Ukrainian pogromists to the Arab peasant. In general, he did not care for non-Jews.")

Finally, there was the paradox of the political leader, a member (together with Ben-Gurion and Tabenkin) of the dominant troika—perhaps the most authoritative for long periods—who nonetheless held no major political office. This unusual modus operandi is to be explained, in the view of Anita Shapira, by the fact that he was preeminently a charismatic leader. Indeed, the entire book can best be understood, perhaps, as a study of charisma and its limitations in the formative years of a new movement. His political life is seen as falling into three distinct periods: the apprenticeship (1905–1919); the years of charismatic dominance (1919–1930); and the decline as his style of leadership became increasingly anachronistic.

He was the driving force behind the establishment of the new party, Ahdut Ha'avodah, which held sway in the labor movement throughout the 1920's. Led almost entirely by the few veterans of the pre-war period (the Second Aliyah), the party drew its rank and file from the newcomers (the Third Aliyah). But the movement was still small in size and Berl with his decade of experience as a pioneer, his single-minded concentration on a few crucial issues, and his undemonstrative but persuasive (almost hypnotic) oratorical power was able to command majority support with an apparently casual ease.

In the thirties as the movement grew by leaps and bounds; divided into numerous, largely autonomous sub-groups; developed a paid bureaucracy—in short, was institutionalized—the face-to-face society of the early years atrophied. For all his prestige, he felt himself excluded, frustrated. Long before his early death, the mantle of leadership was passing to Ben-Gurion, a leader who knew how to draw power from organizations, bureaucracies and formal political office. A personal tragedy was thus immanent within the public triumph.

When faced by a work so masterly and authoritative, a reviewer is naturally reluctant to look too closely at the blueprints used to produce it. Nonetheless, the choice of priorities here is occasionally puzzling. Why, one wonders, is Ben-Gurion kept so firmly in the wings, leaving Tabenkin, the lesser figure, to share the limelight with Katznelson? Again, more space could perhaps have been set aside to analyze Berl's historiographical and ideological writings. He, after all, saw himself above all as an educator, the Socratic guide to the younger generation. He was a friend of, and could hold his own with, Brenner, Agnon, S. H. Bergman, and Scholem. True, his collected works in twelve volumes are readily available; but his role as historian and thinker, his breadth and sweep of knowledge, his dry humor, his delight in the idiosyncratic, deserved a full chapter of their own. (Among other things, a close analysis of his thought would probably have suggested that it was not created de novo in Palestine to the extent that he argued and that the ideology, for example, of Syrkin, who makes only the briefest of appearances here, exerted a deep and abiding influence.)

It is almost cavalier, however, to raise such issues when commenting on a book of this caliber. Anita Shapira has brought to this work great erudition which is worn lightly; a style of epigrammatic but unpretentious elegance; a powerful intelligence ever critical but not self-important. Her achievement is all the more remarkable because the world of Jewish scholarship in Israel has hitherto produced few major biographies and those that there are (Scholem's *Sabbetai Ṣevi*, for example) have almost always dealt with the pre-modern period. It required courage to break out of the monographic mold and the result is immensely rewarding. Anyone seeking the key to the rise of the labor movement in the Yishuv and its fall in Israel could not do better than to take up this biography.

JONATHAN FRANKEL
Hebrew University

R. Shapira, H. Adler, M. Lerner, R. Peles, *Hulzah k'hulah vezavaron lavan: Mehkar al 'olamam hahevrati shel bogrei tnu'ot no'ar beyisrael*. (Blue Shirt and White Collar: Research on the Social World of Graduates of Israeli Youth Movements). Tel Aviv: Am Oved, 1979.

The research reported in this book, carried out in the early seventies, investigates the function of the youth movements in Israeli society, as agents of socialization, primarily political. The basic theses of the book are, in brief, as follows:

First, Israeli youth movement members today are homogeneously derived from middle class, white collar families with aspirations to serve in the "volunteer" units of Army service, and to higher education, followed by a white collar professional career. They usually join with parental encouragement the same movement as that to which their parents had belonged; stay active about four years; engage in leadership role-playing; and thus become socialized into the movements' attitudes which in the main, reinforce those at home. The movements, therefore, act as agents not of social change but of social continuity and conformism to the mainstream ideology at any given time.

Second, the movements tend to succeed in this task more with those members who are activist than with those who are passive, activism tending to influence behavior in terms (for example) of volunteering for elite military units. Further, those movements which are more radical are more successful in socializing their attitudes than the "moderate" movements, because they possess more developed mechanisms of social control.

It can be observed from the study, which examined three age cohorts (twenty-nine, twenty-four and eighteen-year-olds), that judging by the younger, most recent, graduates, the religious movements have moved (in relation to the establishment) from a moderate to an extreme position, from the ideological center to the right. At the same time Hashomer Hatzair moved from an extreme to moderate posture vis-à-vis the establishment and from left to center in terms of political attitudes. Thus we find that the religious movements have become more successful in socializing their members (as has the right-wing Betar movement) while the left-wing movements (including Mahanot Haolim, Hanoar Haoved, Hatzofim) have become less successful.

The left-wing movements failed to mobilize a large proportion of members to settle in kibbutzim (and those who did make this choice were strangely excluded from the research sample). At the same time, these movements failed to generate new challenges which would reassert their radicalism—and thence their influence—by distancing themselves from the establishment (from which, it may now be added, they have since become somewhat estranged by force of circumstance).

Within its own terms of reference this book is very informative and popularly written, without burdensome statistical analyses; yet it fails to spell out the structural reasons for the change in the role of the movements in the post-revolutionary epoch of the Zionist movement. It is necessary to shed light on this matter to understand both the character of contemporary Israeli Zionism and its future direction. We could perhaps here be better served by a theoretical approach different from the (too) convenient functionalist, teleological model used by the authors.

The fate of revolutionary movements was best expressed in Weber's classic analysis of the tension between the forces of rationalization and charisma in every social movement. To understand contemporary Israeli Zionism one needs to analyze its charismatic bases and the character of their rationalization. The possibility of any future change is inextricably linked to the possibility of a charismatic renaissance within Israeli society and the consequent structural transformation of practical Zionism in the everyday life of the Zionist movement and first and foremost in the Zionist youth movements. Thus if the "left"-oriented youth movements derived their charisma from the kibbutz movement while the state was still a programmatic goal, the establishment of Israel with its consequent ideology of *mamlakhtiut* (statism) deprived the movements, in time, of this base. The form and future character of the state-in-the-making was henceforth taken for granted as a technocratic and not an ideological question. Rationalization was as inevitable for the youth movements as for the kibbutzim which inspired them.

The Six Day War, in reopening historical options about the type of state which Israel could become, can, in retrospect, be seen to have broken the spell of *mamlakhtiut* but, ironically, not for the movements of the left. The religious movements generated their charismatic anti-establishment focus from their yeshivas, and translated the new historical option into a messianic imperative and the messianic goal into an historical possibility. *Hagshamah 'azmit** acquired the force of a historically transcendent, divinely inspired act, buttressed by rabbinical sanction. This force, then, joined politically with the mainstream charismatic populism of Beginism, which in its turn aggressively asserted what should never have been taken for granted in the first place, namely the demand for integration of all Israelis, regardless of ethnic

---

*"Self-fulfillment"—a slogan of the youth movements denoting personal realization of ideological goals.

and social origin, into the Zionist dream, not only in theory but also in practice.

The authors criticize the youth movements in general for being middle class, closed, elitist and ethnically homogeneous, as well as too dependant on their respective political patrons and reluctant to express generational revolt.

In the final analysis all the youth movements need to be measured by a more serious socio-historical yardstick than by their determinate socio-economic base or by the political socialization and mobility of their members. The point is, after all, not whether movement members can fulfill the goals given by contemporary Israeli society, but whether they can create goals of their own. This research betrays its functional standpoint by often begging this cardinal question rather than asking it. Its answer is not only a matter of sociological research, but a key challenge to the future of contemporary Zionism. Whether the Israeli youth movements and their respective legitimate patrons can rise to this challenge yet remains to be seen.

DAVID MITTELBERG
Kibbutz Yizreel
University of Haifa

Gideon Shimoni, *Jews and Zionism: The South African Experience (1910–1967).* Cape Town: Oxford University Press, 1980.

Doubtless startling, the idea of reflecting the history of a Jewish community through the examination of a particular ideology and its development within a social-political movement, is nevertheless impressively achieved by Gideon Shimoni in what has become widely acclaimed as an exemplary modern history, quite the most authoritative description of the history and contemporary state of South African Jewry yet published.

While Shimoni's real competence as an historian is apparent throughout, his perspective is the most inspired of choices. The clear risk and daring of choosing such a perspective would make the reader wary at first, but Shimoni is nothing if not a most disarming author. He has marshalled his facts with such care, selected and arranged them with such precision and writes with attractive directness that very soon all seems so obviously apt that there would plainly appear to be no other way to have done it.

A question: is it possible, having due regard to Shimoni's persuasive chapters, to examine the doings of a whole community during a relatively long period—certainly tempestuous times and in a tempestuous place—through the glass of an ideology or even an ideological movement? In the South African Jewish community, Zionism is an almost universal ideology. And the community is remarkably monolithic, on the surface uniquely, almost peculiarly so. But Zionism is not altogether universal and questions about the intensity of the wider community's commitment to the Zionist banner do arise. In fact, the plaint about communal apathy is ubiquitous, most especially within the Zionist organizations themselves. Even while so monolithic on the surface, and a deal beyond the surface, much of Jewish life in South Africa is more influenced by a variety of societal, political, historical and cultural—even regional—differences than it is influenced by its own inner communal life, well organized and widespread communal organizations, notwithstanding. The book can well answer for itself in that it purports to be a study of the Zionist idea and the movements which congealed about that idea in South Africa. That it is much more than that, that it is inexorably more than that, rather more reflects the South African reality than it is a fault of the book.

Indeed, Shimoni is so openly aware of this and so diligent in pointing it out that he is finally his own most convincing advocate. But most convincing of all, are the factual details of South African Jewish history. Here page after page yields the picture of a community overwhelmed by the centrifugal force of the Zionist idea which has been so widely pervasive as to make it possible, through observing the course of Zionism, to watch the community acting and reacting, responding to events and developing structurally.

Quite naturally, the relationship between Jew and Afrikaner is a major theme of the book as it has been a major factor in the South African Jewish experience. That is a relationship which has undergone many changes ranging from a deep sympathy by the Afrikaner for the Jews, to open hostility and anti-Semitism within the Afrikaner national movement, particularly during the 1930's and 1940's and a complex, by no means steady rapprochement after 1948 with the political ascendence of Afrikaner nationalism and the establishment of the state of Israel.

Going further than an examination and exploration of the whole complex nature of the Jew's interaction with the other races and nations of South Africa, Shimoni has dared an explanation of the Jewish reaction to the peculiar South African situation with its racist society and politics. And this explanation emerges as one of the most profoundly plausible descriptions yet formulated of a community of individuals on the one hand, many of whom have given vociferous and often courageous voice to their moral outrage and on the other hand, a community which sees itself as vulnerable and therefore, through its official organizations, emphasizes its strict neutrality and non-involvement in the major political issues of the nation.

While never openly moralizing, Shimoni's careful documentation of the community policy speaks for itself about the relative wisdom or self-deception of the policy of political non-involvement. We are shown this policy evolving, in the first instance as an instinctive response to the communal sense of vulnerability and in the second, as a means of realizing the desire for a relationship which was at least stable and at best cordial, with the Afrikaner power establishment.

In a remarkable epilogue, the book takes its story to the 1970's, and notes the striking change in South African public tolerance of a more progressive and liberalized socio-political climate. Within what Shimoni calls the extended "boundaries of public moral criticism permitted by the Afrikaner consensus," it became "possible for Jewish communal leaders, speaking from official communal platforms such as the Jewish Board of Deputies, outspokenly to vent views which the Afrikaner consensus would have regarded as disloyal and treacherous only ten years earlier."

South Africa's hypersensitive responses to Israeli foreign policy in regard to apartheid and African affairs over the years have had consequences for South African Jewry which have often been decidedly disproportionate, undeserved, puzzling and vexatious. Having dealt with this matter at length and in careful detail during the course of his book, Shimoni writes in his concluding paragraph: "Few if any, communities of the Jewish Diaspora have been so deeply affected by the fluctuations of Israel's foreign policy. In the eventuality of a new constellation of circumstances such as might alter Israel's present relations with South Africa, there can be little doubt that this would again carry grave consequences for South African Jewry. . . . While there can be no doubt that, in the final analysis, Jews are fully committed to the survivalist interests of the Whites, their historical record in South African society, and particularly the Jewish community's recent official statements, indicate that Jews may be counted upon to support change, liberalization, and accommodation to greater sharing of power with all of South Africa's peoples."

In the contemporary international climate, Shimoni's book becomes impressive even beyond itself as it remorselessly examines, on the one hand, a Jewish community, impeccably, if rather too uncritically, loyal to Israel and Zionism over many years, when that loyalty was often among its greatest risks and on the other hand, a community which, despite accommodation of attitudes and views through public pressure has retained a sense of moral rectitude and resilience which binds it to the Jewish ethic and the broader Jewish family.

But everything else aside, the book is also remarkable in itself—an important contribution to historical writing in general and Jewish historical writing in particular. Certainly it is one of the more important studies of Zionism written for many years and its added bonus is that it was written by a firm and careful but fine hand.

DENNIS DIAMOND
Jerusalem

Marshall Sklare (ed.), *Understanding American Jewry*. Center for Modern Jewish Studies, Brandeis University/New Brunswick: Transaction Books, 1982, xiv + 310 pp.

In October 1979 a conference to discuss the idea of a Center for Modern Jewish Studies, and more specifically on American Jewish Studies, was convened at Brandeis University. The need for a center was perceived by many both within and outside the academic world who, having witnessed the recent rapid growth of Jewish studies at American universities, lamented the absence in the United States of a central research facility in the field. With a view toward assessing the feasibility of such a center, the conference organizers selected seven major research areas for consideration: demography; Jewish identity; religion and religious life; Jewish education; the family; the Jewish community; anti-Semitism and intergroup relations. Experts were asked to prepare statements on the current and projected status of research in each of these areas. The twelve papers collected in this volume constitute an outgrowth of the Brandeis conference.

Calvin Goldscheider's essay on demography is the longest and one of the most thorough in the book, and population issues are frequently referred to by other authors—which may reflect the particular importance of demographic research for the study of American Jewry. Demography (in comparison to the other areas) has the advantage of employing more structured and less controversial methods for the study of a community. Further, other, more qualitative processes can often, it seems, benefit by being studied in relation to trends and changes in population size and structure.

The two papers on the Jewish family, by Sheila Kamerman and Chaim Waxman, draw heavily on demographic materials and utilize them in the discussion of possible family policies for American Jewry. The paper on recent Jewish immigration to the United States, by Drora Kass and Seymour Martin Lipset, also deals with a process of primary importance to American Jewish population trends. Indeed, immigration has been the counterbalancing factor offsetting numerical losses that would have otherwise occurred due to a negative balance of Jewish births and deaths as well as losses attributable to assimilation. The paper is mainly concerned with changes in the attitudes of the absorbing community toward immigrants—mainly toward Israelis and Russian Jews—and with the changes affecting the immigrants themselves as they become "Americanized."

The centrality of the debate about Jewish population processes also emerges in the two papers which express the "user" perspective of the organized Jewish community. Ira Silverman assesses research needs from the national policymaking point of view, and Bruce Phillips reports on the kind of research required on the local level.

Definitional and methodological problems appear to be much greater in other areas, such as in Jewish identity research or in the study of Jewish education. Here, the great diversity of conceptual perspectives and methodologies has often prevented a consistent build-up of cumulative knowledge to be exploited for comparative analysis. This has left certain areas either virtually unexplored, or else confused because of unclear perceptions of the dynamics of identificational and educational processes in relation to age, life cycle and generation. Harold Himmelfarb notes at the outset of his systematic review that the shifting disciplinary focus of various studies on identity and identification—at times more sociological, at others more psychological—has affected the very nature of such studies. While the central point of concern has gradually shifted from Jewish integration to Jewish survival, Jewish *identification* studies have often been taken—wrongly—for studies of Jewish *identity* (as Simon Herman has remarked elsewhere).

In Jewish education research, the difficulty in mapping out the boundaries of the field of investigation and choosing pertinent research tools emerges even more sharply, as David Resnick's paper points out. Resnick emphasizes the relatively underdeveloped state of research literature in the field and indicates the dilemmas and obstacles encountered in establishing an agenda for research in Jewish education.

Charles Liebman is perhaps even more critical when pointing to the dearth of studies on American Jews making use of the conceptual approach of the sociology of religion. This appears to be a momentous shortcoming since the religious behavior of American Jews is presumably important in understanding other aspects of their behavior—even in a highly secularized societal context.

The research agenda in the field of Jewish political studies is presented by Daniel J. Elazar. Elazar, after distinguishing between the three major areas of Jewish political institutions and behavior; Jewish political thought; and Jewish public affairs, presents a detailed typology of Jewish institutions and organizations. He concludes with a word of caution on the very preliminary status of the field, in terms of the available tools, bibliographies and facilities for training and research. Elazar's internal perspective is complemented by Earl Raab's paper on the perception of the Jewish minority by other segments of American society.

The editor's essay occupies a place of its own in this collection. Marshall Sklare offers the professional reader some of his own thinking on how an original work of synthesis and interpretation on the sociology of American Jewry might be undertaken. Of special interest, and wider applicability, are his reflections on the respective merits of using an internal, special framework or alternatively, a general, larger theoretical framework for the study of Jewish life.

This is a book about the "state of the art," but it also reveals a great deal about the (perceived) "state of the nation." American Jewry has grown to such a degree of complexity that its study requires scientific, multidisciplinary efforts of conceptualization, data collection and analysis. The endemic preoccupation with Jewish survival, evident in several of these essays, may surprise the non-American reader who would expect fewer feelings of uneasiness within the community that, more than any other in the Diaspora, has achieved public recognition and social prestige, material well-being and, perhaps, physical security. But this uncertainty about the future serves here as a powerful incentive toward more abundant and better research.

In this regard, it is encouraging that a broad consensus seems to emerge here despite the diversity of disciplinary perspectives and individual priorities. The need to develop standardized concepts and measures—especially in the more qualitative and value laden areas—is strongly expressed. Similarly, survey techniques should be improved, with emphasis on repeated monitoring over time. Crucial analytical questions should be tackled through direct research efforts rather than—as has often been the case in the past—as a by-product of less focused investigations. Studies have to be sufficiently comprehensive to reveal the impact of processes at the national level, and yet allow for comparisons within and between regional, socio-demographic, institutional and ideological sub-settings. This approach might well be complemented by a consideration of parallel developments in other Jewish communities, particularly in Israel.

This book issues a tremendous intellectual and institutional challenge. It is to be hoped that the appropriate talent, tools and means will be brought together to meet it, at least in part.

SERGIO DELLAPERGOLA
Hebrew University

Yehuda Slutzky, *Ha-itonut ha-yehudit russit ba-meah ha-esrim* (The Russian-Language Jewish Press in the Twentieth Century). Tel Aviv: Tel-Aviv University, 1978. 511 pp.

Yehuda Slutzky's earlier volume dealing with the Russian-Jewish press of the nineteenth century (*Ha-itonut ha-yehudit russit ba-meah ha-tesha esreh,* 1970) was a meticulous exploration of a phenomenon concentrated for the most part in two cities (first Odessa and later St. Petersburg); dominated by one editor and publisher (Adolph Landau); and ultimately reduced to one extraordinary "thick journal," the monthly *Voskhod*. The period covered by the present study, 1900–1917, witnessed, in contrast, a proliferation of Russian-language Jewish periodicals (seventy between 1900 and 1917, as compared with ten in the nineteenth century as a whole) and the emergence of a much larger readership. Bundists and Zionists—in addition to the exponents of Jewish russification—now developed their own Russian-language press. (The Zionist *Razsvet* had ten thousand readers by 1914 while its Hebrew counterpart *Ha-Olam* had a mere three thousand.) A sufficiently substantial readership emerged to make possible the publication of specialized journals devoted to the study of East European Jewish history or to educational problems. Even magazines catering to Jewish children appeared in Russian.

In some settings, especially in the cities of New Russia, the Jewish intelligentsia in this period consisted of a second generation of Russian readers increasingly estranged from the particularist preoccupations of their parents. Elsewhere, even in the smallest, most culturally remote communities, the local *batei midrash* were attracting fewer young Jews. They were being supplanted by the *gymnazii* and to a lesser extent (as Shaul Stampfer points out in his recent Hebrew University dissertation) by the large Lithuanian yeshivas, thus producing a new generation of aspiring intellectuals and "half-intellectuals" eager to participate in the modern age. The Russian-Jewish press helped open the window on to this otherwise largely inaccessible world.

Slutzky devotes chapters to the different kinds of periodicals: Bundist, Zionist, Territorialist and the like, with special attention to the last seven years of *Voskhod* (now under a new editorship), as well as *Budushchnost'* and *Razsvet*. In each case he reviews the way in which the given journal treated specific issues: its perspective on, for instance, the social and economic problems of East European Jewry, educational issues, emigration, the Yishuv in Palestine, and the preferred Jewish language. Most interesting, in fact, is Slutzky's analysis of the response (as reflected in these periodicals) to the challenge of Yiddish, now taken more seriously by intellectuals in the wake of the 1897 census which had found that ninety-seven percent of the Jews in Russia declared it as their mother tongue. Moreover, the flowering of Yiddish literature in this same period; the appearance of the first Yiddish daily, *Der fraynd,* in 1902; and the increasingly potent threat of assimilationism (especially between 1906 and 1914), encouraged even cultural Zionists to look toward the entrenchment of Yiddish as a way to bolster Jewish solidarity. Indeed, russified Jewish intellectuals could not help but be aware that while Yiddish had produced masters like Abramovitch, Sholem Aleichem and Peretz, Russian-Jewish literature in the first decades of the twentieth century could not even replicate the modest achievements of Bogrov, Levanda, and Osip Rabinovich.

This richly documented volume has, unfortunately, some rather serious flaws. First, its structure encourages a certain repetitiveness since Slutzky insists on separate treatment of the periodicals (whether individually or in groups), evaluating in each particular case their attitude toward more or less the same set of issues and concerns. More effective, perhaps, would have been a thematic approach whereby chapters would have been built around certain salient themes (such as language, Zionism or emigration). In addition, Slutzky pays relatively little attention to the analysis of major articles, and potentially absorbing questions are often treated, if at all, in too cursory a fashion.

The author observes that the Russian-Jewish literature produced in this period was distinctly inferior to that published earlier but he does not examine why this might have been so. More might have been said about the evolution of Russian-Jewish historiography, given the absence of a scholary journal devoted to this field prior to 1909 and the consequent publication of historical articles before then in *Voskhod*. A comparison between the images of Western and Central Europe in the periodicals of this period and those dominant in the nineteenth century might have been intriguing, especially in view of the fact that the world-outlook of the liberal Haskalah was now increasingly being supplanted by "post-liberal" ideologies. While Slutzky pays close attention to the degree to which economic concerns preoccupied the various journals, he does not evaluate what impact, if any, the growth in the number of secondary school and university graduates might have had on the quality of the articles written on this theme (or on other rather technical themes for that matter) in comparison to those written in previous decades. In general, it would have been valuable to explore the relationship between the increasingly sophisticated Russian-Jewish reading public and the journals catering to it (or perhaps increasingly to the "half-intellectuals" since the acculturated Jewish intelligentsia no longer had the same need for specifically Jewish journals). Indeed, the typology of the readership—provincials eager to gain some foothold in the larger cultural milieu, the nearly assimilated bruised by the openly anti-Semitic tenor of much of Russian society in this period, students caught between the narrow sectarianism of the Jewish street and the apparent xenophobia manifest beyond it—could have been examined on the basis of memoir literature. Slutzky shows some interest in the character of the *Voskhod* readership in his previous volume, but here such questions are left largely unasked.

As long as archival materials in the Soviet Union relevant to Russian-Jewish history remain inaccessible, students of the subject will no doubt continue to utilize the press as a primary research source. Slutzky's new volume is a useful introduction to this body of hitherto largely unmined material, its value enhanced by the absence of a comprehensive index comparable to the *Sistematicheskii ukazatel' literatury o evreiakh na ruskom iazyke so vremeni vvedeniia grazhdanskogo shrifta (1708–1889)* for the subsequent period. The reputation of the late Professor Slutzky, however, will rest on the considerable achievements of his *Toldot ha-Haganah* and his fine study of the Russian-Jewish press in the nineteenth century. In these works he combined an extraordinary command of sources (which, to be sure, is no less evident in this, his last book) with a readiness to shape and evaluate his data. It is this fortunate combination, missing for the most part in the present volume, which makes these earlier studies historical works of unquestioned eminence and originality.

STEVE J. ZIPPERSTEIN
Oxford University

Roderick Stackelberg, *Idealism Debased: From Völkisch Ideology to National Socialism*. Kent, Ohio: Kent State University Press, 1981. 202 pp. $18.00

There is a recognized genre of modern German intellectual history. It consists of searching the recent (and not so recent) German past for ideas which bear apparent similarities to the ideas of the Nazis. The commonest way of doing this has been to identify precursors, either individuals or movements whose thinking anticipates, in the spirit or the letter, the salient features of National Socialist ideology. Fritz Stern and George Mosse exemplify the two main approaches.

In *The Politics of Cultural Despair* (Berkeley, 1961) Stern drew our attention to three literati—Paul de Lagarde, Julius Langbehn, Arthur Moeller van den Bruck—whose overlapping careers provided a sequence of cultural pessimism between the period of German unification and the 1920s, which prepared the way for the Nazis. Moreover, he generalized his argument, convicting the German *Bildungsbürgertum* of "civic nonage," "vulgar idealism," and a general retreat from the healthy "Western" virtues of citizenship and responsibility.

Likewise, Mosse's *Crisis of German Ideology* (New York, 1964) extended a similar sort of argument to an entire intellectual culture (that of the predominantly Protestant sections of the educated middle classes) in a veritable Cook's tour of a survey, encompassing everything from mainstream nationalist associations to youth movements, experimental education, exotic leadership philosophies, nature worship, sectarian pseudo-religion and all manner of intellectual and literary currents. The titles of Mosse's more recent books—*The Nationalization of the Masses* (New York, 1975), and *Toward the Final Solution* (New York, 1978)—accurately express the main thrust of Mosse's intellectual commitment: heavily teleological, and powerfully concentrated on the cultural patterning which is thought to have increased popular receptivity to different kinds of Social Darwinist, elitist, and racist ideology.

Many others have traced this path, exploring the ideas of this or that *völkisch* thinker or organized current of opinion. Among the best are Herman Lebovics, *Social Conservatism and the Middle Classes in Germany, 1914–1933* (Princeton, 1969), and Walter Struve, *Elites Against Democracy. Leadership Ideals in Bourgeois Political Thought in Germany, 1890–1933* (Princeton, 1973).

In the circumstances of Wilhelmine Germany, when capitalism was visibly transforming the country into an urban, industrial society in which the presence of the working masses was raised to a central cultural fact of the time, *völkisch* ideology carried a conservative political charge. Old certainties, amongst them a firm sense of social place and the associated cultural values, were rendered sensitive and vulnerable. Many intellectuals responded to this fragility (and not just in Germany) with various kinds of romanticism and organicism, lamenting a loss of integrity, authenticity, and much else too. They contrasted wholeness, inner freedom, self-cultivation and a German spiritual essence, with the degeneration caused by liberalism and industry.

Stackelberg applies this theme in a study of three "representative" intellectuals, two of them minor, one of them major. Heinrich von Stein (1857–1887), a young academic philosopher and key member of the Bayreuth Circle between Richard Wagner's death in 1883 and his own four years later, is presented as an example of an other-worldly idealism whose consistency and integrity remained largely intact—"the most admirable side of the *völkisch* mentality" (p. 19), "the incorruptible conscience of an incipient *völkisch* movement, whose excesses he would hardly have sanctioned." (p. 26)

The second, Friedrich Lienhard (1865–1929) was a popular novelist and dramatist, most known for his associations with the *Heimatkunst* movement. In Stackelberg's framework Lienhard marks the beginnings of a sordid descent into "political reaction," preaching "a pseudo-religious doctrine designed primarily to prevent social and political change" (p. 158). Finally, for Houston Stewart Chamberlain (1855–1927), who unlike the others needs little introduction, "*völkisch* idealism" acquired an altogether uglier ring. "He carried to an extreme the idealist equation of freedom with submission to a higher authority" (p. 158). In this sense Chamberlain provided a direct bridge to the Nazis, "a further stage in the developing counterrevolution" (p. 158).

On the whole this makes good sense as a selection of cases. Although the treatment of Chamberlain inevitably suffers by comparison with Geoffrey Field's new full-length biographical study, *Evangelist of Race. The Germanic Vision of Houston Stewart Chamberlain* (New York, 1981), it is still an excellent introduction to its subject. Similarly, while the section on Stein is too kind to its protagonist—a humorless young prig of opaquely second-rate ideas, who found his rightful niche amongst the cultural *apparatchiki* of Bayreuth—it does a good job in placing him in the 1880s ambience of academic middlebrow philosophy. Lienhard is the least known of the three figures (e.g. neither Stern, Mosse, Lebovics nor Struve include him in their index), and this is the most useful of the three sections.

At another level Stackelberg makes a good case for seeing the three writers as part of the same generation of conservative intellectuals, preoccupied with trying "to salvage a culture that would buttress authoritarian politics in a traditional social order."

In a way this was just the specifically German form of the general reaction to the "rise of the masses" and the specter of "mass culture," a radicalized version of the cultural criticism already familiar across the North Sea. As one of Lienhard's readers asked him: "Has prosperity, the cultural blessing, as it is called, ennobled England or America? Have the achievements of the 1870's, the immense increases in prosperity, been a blessing for us?" (p. 11f.).

On this basis Stackelberg has made a useful addition to the literature on pre-1914 *völkisch* thought. But at the same time one cannot help feeling that "the biographical method used by Fritz Stern," as Stackelberg calls it (p. ix), has reached the point of diminishing returns. After all, we are asked to take the "representative" status of the three individuals very much on trust. This is easier to do in the case of Chamberlain, whose cultural and political impact is well attested, than it is for the others. We have reached the point where studies of Wahnfried's cultural influence or the sociology of *Heimatkunst* would be more useful than the critical exegesis of another individual's ideas, however careful and sensitive. As Geoffrey Barraclough remarked ten years ago (in the *New York Review of Books,* 19 October 1972), "Search the libraries and you will find hundreds of obscure Germans who scribbled obscure and incriminating thoughts." What we really need is some imaginative sociology of knowledge—studies of genres rather than individuals, reception studies rather than exegesis, studies of intellectual networks, cultural institutions, and the process of literary production. What we really need, in other words, is an imaginative historical sociology of the German literary intelligentsia.

We have advanced much further in this direction recently—e.g. in work on the *Heimatkunstbewegung* with Klaus Bergmann's *Agrarromantik und Grosstadtfeindschaft* (Meisenheim, 1970), Karl-Heinz Rossbacher's *Heimatkunstbewegung und Heimatroman* (Stuttgart, 1975), and Peter Zimmermann's *Der Bauernroman* (Stuttgart, 1975), and more generally in the work of Rolf Engelsing and Rudolf Schenda on popular reading—and it is a pity that Stackelberg did not spread his wings to undertake this kind of analysis.

Moreover, it is always unclear precisely what kind of causal relationship is being postulated between the exponents of *völkisch* ideology before 1914 and the rise of the Nazis. On the one hand, Stackelberg is careful to disclaim any simple intentions, often with a forthrightness which belies the actual thrust of the detailed exposition in the book (e.g. "there is no attempt here to establish a causal link between *völkisch* thought and Nazism," p. x). On the other hand, the whole point of writing the book was presumably to suggest that connection, and Stackelberg's arguments are explicitly concerned with "the ideological antecedents of National Socialism" (p. 159). I suspect that this problem—that of specifying adequately the concept of causality which underlies the search for precursors—can only be resolved by leaving the terrain of conventional intellectual history. If the object of analysis is to be certain deep cultural patterns or ideological structures, then we have to think very carefully about how such things are to be studied.

But beyond a certain point this is not a terribly fair criticism of the book. Within the limits of an established genre Stackelberg has produced three valuable essays, which are combined intelligently together within a persuasively argued general thesis regarding certain aspects of German intellectual culture before 1914.

GEOFF ELEY
University of Michigan

Herbert A. Strauss (ed.), *Jewish Immigrants of the Nazi Period in the U.S.A.* Munich; K.G. Saur, 1978–1982. Sponsored by the Research Foundation for Jewish Immigration, New York.
Vol. 1. Archival Resources. 1978. 279 pp.
Vol. 2. Classified and Annotated Bibliography of Books and Articles on the Immigration and Acculturation of Jews from Central Europe to the U.S.A. since 1933. 1981. 286 pp.
Vol. 3/1. Guide to the Oral History Collection of the Research Fund. 1982. 152 pp.
Vol. 3/2. Classified List of Articles Concerning Emigration in Germany. 1982. 177 pp.

The above work gives intensive bibliographic coverage to the topic of Jewish emigration from Central Europe (here defined as Germany, Austria and Czechoslovakia) to the U.S. during the Nazi period and a little beyond. If some subjects can be said to have attracted too much bibliographical attention—relative to the coverage of Jewish historical topics in general—this is probably one of them. Not that we have a right to complain. The decision to compile and publish bibliographies is a function not only of public interest but also of available funds and of individual initiative.

We find the coverage in the work under review somewhat broader than the title pages indicate, and therefore of use to a wider audience than the one directly addressed. Thus, the first volume gives a history, with bibliographic references where possible, of the many archives listed, as well as biographical sketches in the case of personal papers. In the following two volumes the countries of "intermediate settlement" are covered, since a number of emigrants stopped elsewhere before reemigration to the U.S. One of the countries thus covered is Palestine, and here we disagree with the editor's statement in his preface to Volume Two that the number of Central European reemigrants from Mandatory Palestine ("yordim" in local parlance) was "apparently miniscule." The area index to Volume Three (Part One) in itself seems to indicate the opposite.

In our opinion the most valuable volume is the second, a well-classified list of over 2,400 books, articles and some unpublished works on different aspects of the emigration movement. Topics include, inter alia, the legal, psychological and medical aspects of the subject, postwar reparations, and, as noted, countries of intermediate settlement. Annotations are provided for works not self-explanatory. Material is in Western languages, largely English and German, with a sprinkling of Hebrew in the "Palestine" section. Our only criticism is that the net was cast too widely, taking in general works on immigration and the Holocaust in which the specific subject under review here is tangential at best.

Volume Three is evidently intended for the specialist. Part One consists of a descriptive listing of some two hundred and fifty informants, who provided material for the oral history collection. Part Two is in our opinion ill conceived, being not only limited to the emigration and resettlement question as seen by the major German-Jewish weeklies (1933–1938) but so arranged that its value even for the specialist is limited. If, for example, the *CV-Zeitung* has material on Palestine and the Palestine emigration question in nearly every issue, what point is there in listing these hundreds of issues in simple chronological order under "Palestine/Zionism"?

With these three volumes, the bibliographical part of the project has been completed. Three volumes of documents are planned.

ALFRED A. GREENBAUM
Haifa University

Walter Strauss (ed.), *Signs of Life: Jews From Württemberg. Reports for the Period after 1933 in Letters and Descriptions.* New York: Ktav Publishing House, 1982. xvii + 389 pp.

This is a compilation of a special kind: it is not a collection of autobiographical pieces nor is it one of the "memorial books" for perpetuating the memory of Jewish communities in Central and Eastern Europe that were destroyed; but nevertheless it is in some measure both of these things. Its character was dictated by the way it was produced from hundreds of questionnaires that the Organization of the Jews from Wuerttemberg sent out to its members. Many accounts were received from people living today in the USA, England, Israel, Argentina and elsewhere. They belong to different age groups and social strata: some had achieved position and influence in Germany in their day, and others left Germany while they were still school children. As regards their political opinions, too, they are a very varied lot. According to their own statements, some have been active as liberals or as Communists or as Zionists, or were members of associations of German patriots of Jewish origin. Many have not been active in any political circle.

The replies to the questionnaires were printed just as they were written (apart from cuts made for reasons of space limitations) and without any comment by the editor. Thus, the personal nature of the accounts is preserved without blurring their original stamp; but as a result, there is no unity of style and scope or even of stress in the matters dealt with, all of which change from one account to the next. Contrary to the usual custom, moreover, the reader is not given a selection of the material received by the editor but rather a pile of unclassified testimonies, with the addition of short biographical notes. As a result of this sort of editing, it was impossible to eliminate duplication (as, for instance, in the case of details recounted by various members of the same family).

The questionnaire asked the Wuerttembergers to describe their personal and family background; their past occupations; what happened to them during the racial persecutions; their migration and problems of economic, social and cultural integration encountered in their countries of refuge; their public activity there and the positions of their children and relatives. The hundreds of narratives assembled in this way come together to form a varied human document, but the treatment of many subjects is quite superficial. Astonishingly, the respondents were not asked to describe their attitude to Germany or their level of Jewish consciousness—matters which, one would have thought, necessarily arise precisely with such a group. Nor is enough light thrown on the stages of acculturation that the emigrants went through in their new countries.

As against this, the narratives do record instructive details on what happened to the writers during the racial persecutions in Germany and on their experiences along the path of wandering. One's curiosity is especially aroused by testimony recording help afforded by Germans in rescuing Jews. In this context, we draw attention to the account of the systematic rescue action carried out by Hans Walz, one of the directors of the Bosch enterprise, and also to the story of the young Jew, Otto S. Adler, who in 1940 received assistance from the Lufthansa people in Spain and even from a member of the German Consulate in Madrid—enabling him to reach the USA.

What emerges quite clearly in most testimonies is the emigres' ability to survive and to live on, their firm determination to go on fighting and rebuild their lives.

The book has an index of place names, a detailed map of the Jewish communities in Wuerttemberg and ten photographs to complement the written word. One could have wished for a detailed preface on the history of the Wuertemberg Jewish communities, including their social and demographic circumstances in earlier generations.

Despite the lack of proper editing, the collection does bring to light an important new body of source material on the experience of a large group of emigrants from Germany.

ABRAHAM MARGALIOT
Hebrew University

Shabbetai Tevet, *Kinat David: Hayei David Ben-Gurion* (David's Passion: The Life of David Ben-Gurion). Jerusalem/Tel Aviv: Schocken, 1980. Vol. 2.

The role of Ben-Gurion as *accoucheur* at the birth of the state of Israel has secured him a unique place in Zionist historiography. More biographies and research have been devoted to him than to any other personality in the movement. The biographies published prior to Tevet's, however, dealt with Ben-Gurion's activity in select spheres only, without exploring his motives, methods and personality structure—factors which have their place in any complete biography but which in the nature of things are neglected in partial studies.

Shabbetai Tevet has undertaken a monumental enterprise—to write a complete biography of Ben-Gurion based on extensive archival material. One can only admire the firmness of his resolution to make this his life-work, when one considers the enormous quantity of documentation that he has to master, as well as the multiplicity of themes and the tremendous range of activity that characterized Ben-Gurion's life. Moreover, the task of the biographer is as much complicated as facilitated by Ben-Gurion's own passion for documentation, which made him keep copies of the letters he wrote in the early days and write a detailed diary all through the years. And the diary, of course, provides its own problems as a historical source.

According to Tevet's original plan, as he presented it in his introduction to the first volume, he intended to publish three volumes, each of which would cover one political period in his hero's life: the Ottoman period, the British Mandate and then finally the state. He soon realized, however, that this division according to the political systems within which Ben-Gurion acted did not match the needs of the biography. He could be content with one volume for the Ottoman period when the character of the young Ben-Gurion was still being formed into the mold of the rising labor leader. However, in order to keep up the same level of detail for the later periods, Tevet clearly had no choice except to write not two but more and still more volumes. Today one can say with certainty that the series will be at least twice the size initially envisaged by the author.

It is difficult to criticize a biography that has not yet been published in full and which is in fact still in its gestation—some of the things criticized may well be corrected in the later volumes. This review should therefore be considered an interim report.

The two volumes published so far contain a wealth of new historical material. In Volume One there is a very interesting account of Ben-Gurion's "American period" when he was exiled from Palestine during World War I. This is the first time that a full account has been published of this chapter in his life, which was not without its importance in forming his personality and shaping his methods of action. Volume Two—where Tevet reconstructs the rise of the Executive of the Histadrut with clarity and devotion to the facts—constitutes an important contribution to the institutional history of the labor movement in Palestine, its uniqueness and the sources of its success. There is, moreover, an acerbic, sharp-eyed account of the bankruptcy of Solel Boneh and the accompanying scandals in the economic crisis of 1927. Here the author not only describes the strengths of his protagonist but also mercilessly reveals his weaknesses.

The central theme of the volume is Ben-Gurion's activity as Secretary of the Histadrut when he shaped this institution into an effective instrument for the labor movement's struggle for power against its Zionist rivals. It describes how the Executive secured domination over particularist institutions within the Histadrut and over workers' organizations that sought to compete with it from outside. And, parallel with this, it gives an account of the struggles waged by the Histadrut against various categories of employers.

What is clearly depicted here, therefore, is Ben-Gurion's complete dedication to his goal and his unwavering view of the importance of establishing the Histadrut Executive's authority over the Workers' Movement. Paradoxically, however, what emerges from the story is not the conversion of the Histadrut into a unified, centralist body, imposing its ascendancy over its rivals by the strength of its organization—in almost diabolical fashion as it seemed to right-wing rivals—but the dedication of Ben-Gurion to securing his own ascendancy within the Histadrut. It was not so much that Ben-Gurion built a power base for the institution he headed; rather, he exerted himself to build up his own image as a "strong," forceful leader. This may provide a key to understanding the weakness at later periods of this conglomeration, loosely grouped together in the Histadrut.

Since the leitmotif of this volume is the build-up of control, the author has excluded everything that had any relation to Ben-Gurion's intellectual life and the development of his social and political thinking. The author is entitled to assert that Ben-Gurion's socialist ideology was in the nature of a thin, superficial varnish and not something deeply-rooted in his political psyche, but surely this issue deserved to be fully discussed. It is impossible, however, not to give due weight to this issue. The Ben-Gurion of the twenties tried again and again to construct a rationale for his actions in terms drawn from the world of socialist thought in order to secure legitimacy and a reference point. In this volume you won't find the Ben-Gurion of *From Class to Nation,* his well-known collection of articles written in this period, but only the militant trade union leader.

So too as regards his political outlook: from the beginning of the Mandatory period at least, Ben-Gurion had a clear conception of the way to build up the country and put Zionism into practice. His outlook underwent changes in the course of the twenties, paralleling changes in his view of the Arab question. If there is one sphere where Ben-Gurion's greatness stands out clearly it is in his transformation, maturation, from labor leader to statesman. If this volume had given an account of the interaction and the tension between his Zionist conception, which remained firmly founded and unchanging, and his perception of the Jewish-Arab-British triangle, which changed beyond recognition, the reader would have had revealed to him a much deeper, more interesting, multi-faceted personality.

This weakness of the second volume stems from the author's apparent decision to break up the chronological order which he followed in the previous volume and to concentrate on a single theme (the central one in Tevet's judgement) in Ben-Gurion's life during this period. As a consequence, what we get is a flat, one-dimensional figure, guided by a sole ambition—the will to rule. The dynamic development of the politician and the statesman is not reflected in this volume.

The author's decision to break up the chronological sequence was the result, it would seem, of the wealth of material at his disposal. He avoided a major task of the historian and biographer, selection. A genre exists of the "official" biography, which records absolutely everything its subject ever did, leaving the reader in the final analysis without a clue to the riddle of his personality. Tevet has fortunately avoided falling into this trap, but there are quite a few chapters in this book where some passages could certainly have been excised. This refers especially to the first chapters and to those dealing with various labor disputes. The burden of detail hinders the reader from grasping the author's intentions. Since Shabbetai Tevet's talent as a writer is well known, it follows that he has deliberately subjugated his talent in order to detail the facts. In the places in the book—and there are quite a few of these too—where Tevet writes in his own style, freeing himself from official records and documents, the reader reaps the benefit.

As we said at the outset, we offer all these reservations with "limited liability." We have yet to read the biography in full, and perhaps when the time comes to review the great undertaking as a completed work, these remarks will have lost their relevance. At all events, one thing is clear already. Anyone who wants to follow in Tevet's footsteps and write a biography of Ben-Gurion cannot ignore this work, which will serve for many years to come as a basic work in research on Ben-Gurion, the history of the Yishuv and of the Zionist movement in this country.

ANITA SHAPIRA
Tel-Aviv University

Yosef Tobi, Jacob Barnai and Shalom Bar-Asher, *Toldot hayehudim be-arzot ha-islam,* 2 (History of the Jews in Islamic Countries). Edited by Shmuel Ettinger. Jerusalem: Zalman Shazar Center, 1981. 326 pp.

The Shazar Center has brought out another useful textbook on Jewish history aimed at the general Hebrew-reading public. Its publication was aided by the Center for the Integration of the Oriental Jewish

Heritage of the Israel Ministry of Education and Culture which in recent years has done a significant service by sponsoring books and educational projects that deal with the rich, but neglected, patrimony of Sefardi and Oriental Jewry.

The book is divided into two principal parts. The first comprises three historical chapters, each by a different author. The second part contains apposite sources from published works and is divided in parallel manner to the chapters in part one. The chapters are, respectively: "The Jewish Centers in Asia" (Yemen, Iraq, Kurdistan, Iran and Central Asia) by Yosef Tobi; "The Jews in the Ottoman Empire" (Asia Minor, the Balkans, Syria-Palestine) by Jacob Barnai; and "The Jews in North Africa and Egypt" by Shalom Bar-Asher. Each chapter opens with a brief review of earlier history. This is followed by a discussion of the political framework within which the Jews lived, their legal status, economic activities, and internal communal structure. Due attention is also paid to spiritual trends and intellectual creativity. Each of the chapters is written in a straightforward, textbook style. There are no footnotes or annotations of any kind in the historical chapters. However, the fairly variegated sources in part two are well annotated with simple clarifications of names, places, dates, and unusual terms or phrases.

The sources are followed by a very skimpy "Selected Bibliography" that includes only six items in languages other than Hebrew (five in English and one in French). Although there is always room for debate in matters of bibliographical selection, the bibliography here seems particularly idiosyncratic with regard to both its inclusions and omissions. Thus, for example, works by Ch.-A. Julien and Stanford Shaw that do not specifically deal with Jews are included, while S. D. Goitein's *Jews and Arabs* and *From the Land of Sheba;* Jacob Landau's *The Jews in Nineteenth-Century Egypt* (which exists in a Hebrew edition); or the present reviewer's *The Jews of Arab Lands* are not.

The bibliography is followed by a helpful glossary of technical and foreign terms; a valuable, but somewhat thin, comparative table of events in Europe, the Ottoman Empire, North Africa, and Asia from the fifteenth to mid-nineteenth century; and four very good fold-out maps. Unfortunately, there is only an index of names and places. Since one of the stated aims of the book (as stated by Shmuel Ettinger in his Introduction) is a comparison of elements of unity and variety, the lack of a subject index is all the more to be regretted.

These minor and mainly technical criticisms aside, this book is a welcome addition to the advanced high school or introductory college reading list.

NORMAN A. STILLMAN
State University of New York
at Binghamton

Zeev Tzahor, *Baderekh lehanhagat hayishuv* (On the road to Yishuv Leadership). Jerusalem: Yad Ben-Zvi Publications, 1981. 321 pp.

In this account of the origins and foundation of the Histadrut and its organizational and political development until the mid-twenties, Zeev Tzahor attempts to avoid the extremes of some former historians of the Yishuv, and gives a balanced picture which will "embrace . . . both ideology and organization."

Beginning with a brief sketch of the development of the labor movement in Palestine during the Second Aliyah, and the abortive attempt to create a unified framework with the establishment of Ahdut Ha'avoda, he shows that the leaders of both major parties expected this episode to be repeated in the founding conference of the Histadrut at the end of 1920; and indeed, that this very nearly happened. It was only under pressure from the newly arrived *haluzim* of the Third Aliyah that the founding conference was called at all and that the plenary sessions then took on a momentum of their own, which swept aside the objections and antagonisms of the party veterans on both sides.

The new organization was based on a compromise between the centralistic tendencies of Ahdut Ha'avoda and the insistence of Hapoel Hatzair on its ideological and educational independence. The Histadrut was to deal with constructive and "professional" work, while the two parties would continue to engage in political and educational activity. But, as Tzahor shows, the parties—or, more accurately, their leaders and administrative workers—played a vital part in the work of the new organization. Its structure was centralistic. Although workers' councils, local trade unions, and workers' cooperatives chose their own leadership, overall policy was decided by the nationally elected conference and council, which appointed a central executive. And, all of the central positions were filled by veterans of the Second Aliyah, members of the two parties appointed according to a strict party key.

But, at the same time, there began a centrifugal process, with the development of the major economic and social institutions—the Sick Fund (Kupat Holim); the agricultural marketing organization (Hamashbir); absorption and employment offices; and, above all, the Public Works Office, which became the chief agent for contracting work from the Mandatory Government and the Zionist movement. Each of these institutions had been founded under the two-party regime. Within the Histadrut framework, they gradually gained a strength and independence of their own; whereas the central institutions—elected and appointed alike—and the local workers' councils found themselves in increasing organizational and financial difficulties.

The author emphasizes that, with all the enthusiasm, experience, and faith of its members, the Histadrut was beset, from its earliest days, by crises of organization and policy: a chronic lack of funds to accomplish its "historic tasks" of absorption and settlement; the immanent tension between Zionist constructivism and its social and trade-union functions; and the basic commitment to defend its members from physical attack and economic need. Six months after the founding conference its future seemed in doubt, its leadership amateurish, unwilling, and inefficient.

The riots of May 1921, and the traumatic effect of the death of Yosef Chaim Brenner, were, in the author's view, the "last straw" which led to reform and recovery. In the field of broad policy, the Histadrut established a "political committee," whose function was to represent the working class (and, to no small extent, the whole of the Yishuv) as against the Mandatory Government and the Zionist movement; in terms of self-defense, the Haganah was reorganized; and, above all, Ben-Gurion, who now became Secretary of the Executive, initiated a series of reforms which increased the efficiency of the Histadrut machinery, tightened up the centralist tendencies which already existed, and defeated any possible rivals for leadership (principally Gedud Ha'avodah).

Tzahor shows how, despite the influence of the traditional parties in determining the make-up of the administrative machinery, even political appointees quickly identified with their new tasks, creating "Histadrut consciousness," and a loyalty which sometimes even conflicted with their party allegiance. This was partly the result of their economic dependence on the Histadrut, partly of the feeling that they were dealing with the real work of constructive Zionism, as against the "empty ideologies" of the parties. The attitude of the leaders of the Histadrut to the Zionist movement also changed, but in a different way. From a very early stage, they realized that they could not achieve the lofty aims they set for themselves without outside aid—political, and even more, financial. Equally, the leaders of the Zionist movement (and particularly Weizmann and Ruppin) recognized the working class organized in the Histadrut as the only body in the Yishuv which could take on the constructive tasks (such as settlement of the Jezreel Valley) without which Zionism would lose its internal momentum. The appointment of Sprinzak to the Zionist Executive in 1921 was not only a symbol of this symbiosis; it was also a very tangible asset to the constructive work of the Histadrut. The exclusion of the labor movement from the Zionist Executive in the wake of the Fourth Aliyah led to the campaign to "conquer the Zionist movement," and its eventual success in 1935.

All of this is important, and much is new. The author has used archival material well, and uncovered facts and discussions which cast new light on the relationships between the groups which created the Histadrut and turned it into a dominant force in the Yishuv. But, to use his own categorization, the focus on organization has led to the neglect of ideology. Thus, of 304 pages of the text, he devotes 16 (Chapter 1) to a systematic account of the ideological background of the founders of the Histadrut. In the rest of the book, ideological matters as such are discussed only in their relation to the organizational difficulties and power struggles of the time.

This is surely a mistake. For if one thing is clear about the men of the Second and Third Aliyot alike, it is that they took their ideology seriously, and any historian would be advised to take this into account. In his account of the foundation of the Histadrut, the author seems to assume that the differences between the two major parties were trivial, or the result of differences in style, personality, or institutional interest alone. In this he is, of course, adopting another ideological stance, largely accepted in the historiography of the Labour movement (following Berl Katznelson and Ben-Gurion, among others). But is it true? Even by the author's own account, there were serious differences of opinion between them. To take two examples: had Hapoel Hatzair not maintained its separate existence, Sprinzak would not have joined the Zionist Executive in 1921; and had Ahdut Ha'avoda not had its way, the moshav would have been given preference over the kibbutz. These were not issues which were invented in order to justify the separate existence of the parties, as Tzahor seems to maintain (p. 243). To dismiss them as such is to distort the nature of the people, the period, and the issues themselves.

It was not only the men of the Second Aliyah who took their ideology seriously. Tzahor proves convincingly that men of the Second Aliyah took control of the Histadrut machinery at top levels from the very earliest days. But his remark that "It is hard not to feel that the matter was arranged . . . purposely by the men of the Second Aliyah" (p. 144) reveals an underlying assumption that, behind all the ideological discussions of the time, the leaders of the Histadrut were waging a conscious struggle for power. Such an assumption is surely anachronistic. In this case, for instance, it seems more likely that the men of the Third Aliyah really believed what they said: that they preferred physical work to administration, that they found their political expression in existing parties, and that they were opposed to political parties based on sectoral or generational interests. In this and in many other instances, ideology played a more important part than Tzahor is prepared to admit.

An exhaustive treatment of the subject would treat this and other similar themes with more subtlety and more attention to the beliefs and words of the protagonists. As it is, the author has certainly redressed the historiographical balance of our view of the Histadrut in its formative period, though at the expense of the balance between ideology and organization which he promises in his introduction. Nonetheless, it is no faint praise to say that this book adds considerably to our knowledge and understanding of the subject.

HENRY NEAR
Oranim
Harvard University

David Vital, *Zionism: The Formative Years*. New York and London: Oxford University Press, 1982. xviii + 514 pp. £22.50.

This second volume of David Vital's projected three-volume study of early Zionism brings the story from the point where his first volume *(The Origins of Zionism)* ended, at the conclusion of the First Zionist Congress, to the turbulent readjustment which the movement made after Herzl's death, at the Seventh Congress and at the Helsingfors Conference of the Russian Zionists. When the third volume is published, Vital will have given us a history of Zionism up to or even beyond World War I in which the recent major accumulation of scholarly studies will be comprehensively organized and illuminated with bold judgment and penetrating understanding.

As Vital has noted (in the bibliographical notes to the first volume), Zionist historiography has been blessed with many detailed accounts of various aspects of the past, but these have often also been largely "undigested." The first great virtue of Vital's work is that he has thoroughly digested the vast amount of material he has used, and done so with what one can only call magisterial judgment. His history is completely devoid of pedantry—he is firm in telling us nothing not necessary to know; and by avoiding the morass of trivia, he succeeds in telling us lucidly all that is necessary to be known in order to follow readily the complex history of Zionism as he sees it.

It is a general truth about historical accounts, especially those that compose a tight, comprehensible story, that by selecting some matters to be stressed they discount others. This is a problem inherent in any reconstruction of a history; yet the history of Zionism must certainly be a particularly hard case. The sheer geographical spread of the Jews, for whom Zionism was meant and who produced it or responded to it, brings a vast number of chance conditions into play. Vital's study differs from much else written on Zionist history, for the periods he covers, by dealing with the *whole subject* rather than with some local or partial aspect of it. In his first volume he touched, however lightly in some respects, on every significant area, from Bulgaria to the Shavei Zion in the United States. In this volume, he concentrates more narrowly on two major arenas—the personal activities and problems of Herzl and the developments, occurring in counterpoint to the former, of the semi-legal Russian Zionist organization. There is a certain faded quality to what is said about other aspects of Zionist history occurring simultaneously, such as the affairs of the Yishuv, to name the most notable matter.

Nevertheless, Vital's approach allows him to give the most comprehensive account of the whole range of the Zionist-related developments in this period yet written, and nonetheless to hold a clear story line. This combination of comprehensiveness and selection is an effect of the principles which he applies to his work. His perspective, that of a historian working primarily from an academic and practical base in politics, highlights two elements in history—that of leadership and that of organization. In this volume (unlike the first, where neither element is clearly delineated) both the leader, Herzl, and the bulk of the organization represented by Russian Zionism, are unmistakably evident to an objective eye; and concentrating on them, Vital is able to deal with almost everything. (Some developments belonging to the period of this book, like the rise and splintering of socialist Zionism, may perhaps be dealt with more specifically in the third volume, yet to appear.)

If Vital's principle of selection will raise some controversial questions, it is less in what he underplays (for example, Romanian Zionists may feel slighted) than in such matters as periodization and the definition of historic phenomena. In the first volume, Vital dealt with pre-1880 religious "precursor" Zionism in a way that suggested (rather than asserted) that—in relation to it—real Zionism was essentially discontinuous. In this volume he remarks, here and there in passing, that real Zionism in effect began with Herzl, calling what came before, the Hovevei Zion, by the name of "proto-Zionists." Such verbal preferences stem largely from the focus imposed by the story Vital intends to tell, the emergence of Jewish nationalism as a political force—and he himself does not make a great point of such issues of nomenclature.

They have, nevertheless, more than a merely verbal significance. If more attention had been paid to the continuity between the precursors and Hibbat Zion, the story of the religious-secular clash in Zionism could have been written more completely. Vital's story of the relations between Herzl and the Hovevei Zion, so admirably and usefully told in the first volume, could have been more enlightening on the development of Zionist leftism, among other themes, if attention had been devoted not only to the (then) central figures confronting Herzl in official rivalry, but also to peripheral developments in Russian Zionism, later to become important.

But to ask this would be to demand a "Cambridge History of Zionism"—properly the work of many hands, such as is now being prepared in Israel. And it would also be to deprive us of the grace and illumination of a historical construction expressing the irreplaceable insight of one extremely able and highly gifted man.

BEN HALPERN
Brandeis University

Stephen J. Whitfield, *Into the Dark: Hannah Arendt and Totalitarianism.* Philadelphia: Temple University Press, 1980, 338 pp.

Hannah Arendt's writings on totalitarianism remain as fresh and provocative as they are problematic. Never intended solely as an exercise in comparative political analysis and political theory, *The Origins of Totalitarianism* sought to confront what its author viewed as "the burden of our times." She discerned this burden in the very breadth and depth of what Hitlerism and Stalinism wrought. *Eichmann in Jerusalem,* published a dozen years after *The Origins,* still arouses controversy today both because of the various arguments it makes and because of its often cavalier marshalling of historical materials. As Stephen J. Whitfield astutely notes in *Into the Dark: Hannah Arendt and Totalitarianism,* "Given a choice, Arendt would rather have been original than right. Had she merely been right, she could not have had such an impact, nor could she have teased so many stunning perceptions from the stuff of history."

What was odd—or perhaps remarkable—about Arendt's work was that it retained its power despite her lapses and errors. One is still perplexed when reading her claim that the late 19th century was marked by the decline of the nation-state; or when one realizes that over five hundred pages dedicated to the origins of totalitarianism in Germany and Russia omit virtually any analysis of Tsarism, Leninism, and the peculiarities of Russian historical development. Arendt's comparative study of Nazi and Stalinist domination in the last third of her tome sustains itself best on the level of structure rather than that of genesis, despite the volume's title.

Whitfield's intelligent study sets out to demonstrate that despite the many forceful challenges to the very concept of totalitarianism in the last quarter of a century, Arendt's interpretation, as developed in *The Origins* and extended and amended in *Eichmann,* constitutes the most convincing single effort to grasp the meaning of the Hitler and Stalin regimes. Strangely enough, however, most of *Into the Dark* is a critical analysis demonstrating the many problems inherent in Arendt's work, and its author never really carries through the argument to the avowed conclusion. What we do have is an illuminating and interesting, if sometimes arguable, exegesis; we clearly see the importance and multi-dimensionality of Arendt's endeavor, but not what makes it (in Whitfield's view) the single most convincing exploration of its subject nor why the fundamental points of criticism should be ultimately discounted.

Arendt's oeuvre was that of a European—a German Jew—in America. Whitfield is, in his words, "an historian of American political culture, not of modern Germany or of the Soviet Union." His book clearly reflects his background. It is strongest when placing Arendt within the American intellectual milieu and tracing her impact there. Whitfield provides a good overview of the Eichmann controversy and pursues various illuminating side issues. He contrasts Arendt's approach to that prevailing in American political science and demonstrates how her analysis of statelessness in *The Origins* has influenced American legal thinking. However, since adoration of Hellas was an important theme in German Romanticism, one is surprised to read that "Arendt was called a Romantic, and yet she was irresistably drawn to the classic ages of Greece and Rome" (p. 248).

Again, the author begins his book with a survey of the American literature on totalitarianism and largely passes over relevant works from Europe, particularly from the Left (e.g., Medvedev, Ayçoberry, Ellenstein, Poulantzis). The Frankfurt School, with the exception of Franz Neumann and a brief reference to Theodor Adorno, is ignored. This is a significant lacuna. Max Horkheimer's famous remark that "Anyone who does not wish to discuss capitalism should stay silent on the subject of Fascism" is representative of a substantial literature— much of it by German emigrés—whose approach is contrary to that of

Arendt (e.g., the writings of Pollock, Kirschheimer, and Reich in the 1930's and 1940's).

One suspects that Whitfield's strong and evident anti-Marxist bias is the source of this gap. It also leads him occasionally to misleading assertions such as a comment that Arendt learned "very little" from Marx. While her writings engage in an ongoing and vigorous critique of Marx—Arendt saw the foundations of Marx's thought as antithetical to her own—this hardly means that she found no value in him. The beginning of *The Human Condition* makes explicit reference to "the great wealth of Marxian ideas and insights . . . ." Whitfield, referring to a comment Arendt made in that same book, states that she "suppressed" her criticisms of Marx so as to avoid abetting McCarthyism in the 1950's. This self-denial, he says, displayed dubious judgment because it is "incongruent with a sense of intellectual honor to curtail one's service to truth lest political primitives accidentally find themselves in agreement." In fact, Arendt did not "suppress" her views—she began working on a study of what she saw as the totalitarian elements in Marxism in the early 1950's (the project was later reconceived as *The Human Condition*). However, having been compelled to flee political primitives once in her life, she did not want to help them, even accidentally, elsewhere. This is hardly blameworthy. Arendt remained equally opposed to Marxism and to hysterical anti-communism which she believed was, fundamentally, a threat to freedom. (See in particular her essay "The Ex-Communists," *Commonweal* March 20, 1953.)

Whitfield's book, as such, is not the final word on its subject matter. It is, however, a valuable and worthwhile contribution to the literature on the question of totalitarianism in general, and to the rapidly emerging literature on Hannah Arendt.

MITCHELL COHEN
Baruch College, CUNY

Evan Wilson, *Decision on Palestine*. Stanford: Hoover Institution, 1979. 244 pp.

Kenneth Ray Bain, *The March to Zion*. Austin: Texas University Press, 1979. 235 pp.

Both of these books criticize the American policy which contributed to the establishment of the State of Israel. However, despite this common ground, there is no identity of approach here. Wilson's book reflects the conception of the career officers in the Foreign Service who see themselves as the true defenders of American interests. Loy Henderson, Gordon Merriam, Frazer Wilkins and Robert McClintock were consulted by the author, and according to him, "The resulting book is really a joint effort." Wilson hints that he and his colleagues agreed with the position taken by Wallace Murray (who headed the Office of Near Eastern and African Affairs—the NEA—before Henderson) which viewed the Zionists as "intruders" in the Middle East. He himself claims that in 1946 he came to the conclusion that American support for the establishment of a Jewish state, contrary to the position taken by the Arab majority, would cause the United States considerable damage and might endanger the peace. He saw the struggle as "a conflict between legitimate rights, the right of the Jews to a national home and the right of the Arabs to self-determination," but nonetheless felt that American interests dictated support for the latter cause against the former.

The views held by Kenneth Ray Bain are far more radical than those of Wilson. He writes: "Events of the twentieth century produced a tragic sequence: Zionism grew from the bigotry and jingoism of Christendom; Jewish leaders sought revenge for the Holocaust and found targets in the hapless Arabs." He sees Palestine as Arab territory; he accepts the viewpoint of W. T. Stace and Kermit Roosevelt that large-scale Jewish immigration constituted aggression against the Arab people. And, in his opinion, the Arabs objected rightly to any Jewish immigration at all, since "the country could not absorb the arrivals from Europe without displacing its own inhabitants."

While Wilson's book is generally documented with care, Bain's claim to be an objective historian must be seriously questioned. He relies on such books as Fred J. Khouri's *The Arab-Israeli Dilemma* for information on the 1948 refugees. In Bain's opinion, the Zionists employed Nazi methods of terror. They distorted the Balfour Declaration. He holds that the British White Paper of 1939 was correct and just, lamenting that if the British had "enforced the document, there would be no Jewish state." Bain further states that the Zionists used the Holocaust for political gain, and created an artificial connection between the problem of the displaced persons and the establishment of a Jewish state. The United States, he feels, should have immediately rejected the claim "that only through the establishment of a Jewish state could the seed of Abraham find peace."

Evan Wilson, on the other hand, drawing on the experience gained during his four years at the Palestine desk of the State Department, concludes that under the conditions created by the Second World War, it would have been difficult to prevent the United States from supporting the Jewish cause in Palestine. He points to two factors, the humanitarian and the domestic political imperatives that decisively influenced Truman's policy. In Wilson's opinion, Truman did not assign sufficient weight to the views of the State Department experts, who alone were capable of perceiving the Palestine issue in the broader context of the overall American interest. His opinion is that later events justified the approach taken by the career diplomats. Furthermore, Truman's pro-Zionist steps (partially prompted by the fact that the "American Jews enjoyed an influence on politics out of proportion to their numbers") actually gained him no tangible advantage in his election campaign.

Wilson tries to justify the positions taken by him and his colleagues in the years 1944–48, but admits that they did make miscalculations. He discloses that, above all, they were stunned by the convincing Jewish victory in the War of Independence. Similarly, they hadn't taken into consideration the possibility that the Soviet Union might support the establishment of a Jewish state. Still, he does not view the rise of Israel as the failure of his group at the State Department and their friends in the British Foreign Office. He believes that it was mainly the UN that failed by not being able to propose an acceptable solution when the Palestine problem was brought before it in 1947. The attempts of the UN to defuse the "struggle between the rights" were in vain.

Wilson's reading of American Jewry is close to the mark when he recognizes that "its mood between 1939 and Pearl Harbor was ostrich-like;" but his knowlege is more limited concerning the Jewish Yishuv in Palestine. Thus his conclusion that "a substantial minority favored a binational state" is somewhat surprising.

The steps taken by President Roosevelt with regard to the Palestine question are reviewed favorably in the book. The author takes pride in having performed a "very valuable service" for the President in his position at the time, by formulating the explanatory letters to the Arabs after the publication of the President's pro-Zionist declarations. In Wilson's opinion, Roosevelt really did favor Zionism, but he was also aware of the serious damage that support for the establishment of a Jewish state might cause. He explains that Roosevelt believed that his considerable prestige would assist him in realizing, once the war was over, a trusteeship plan based on the three monotheistic religions. Roosevelt, he claims, was deeply impressed by Ibn Saud and therefore much disturbed by his own failure to influence the desert king during their famous meeting at Bitter Lake. Roosevelt was persuaded there that only by means of considerable outside force would it be possible to set up a Jewish state, and that should many Jews immigrate to Palestine, the Arabs would do everything possible "to cut their throats."

Wilson is certain that Roosevelt, had he lived, would have acted according to the recommendations of the NEA rather than ignore them as Truman did.

According to Wilson, Truman was naive in contrast to the more experienced Roosevelt. The professional diplomats did, in fact, immediately warn the new President about the Zionists; but the Jewish advisors in the White House, David Niles and Sam Rosenman, succeeded in acquiring decisive influence on the subject of Palestine and the State Department lost control of this issue in the summer of 1946. Thus it happened that after the Harrison report on the displaced persons, Truman—without consulting the State Department—faced Atlee with the demand to issue one hundred thousand Palestine immigration permits.

The chapter dealing with the Anglo-American Committee of Inquiry is interesting. Wilson was one of the secretaries of the Committee and thus relates first-hand information. He reports that the NEA recommended a trusteeship plan to the Committee. Wilson quotes extensively from the testimony of Azzam Pasha, the Secretary of the Arab League, while he considers that of Judah Magnes to have been the best moderate testimony received.

He describes the Jews as aggressors, against whom the Arabs had to defend themselves (this in 1946). Similarly, he holds that the Jews did nothing to improve the economic and educational situation of the Arabs. In Wilson's opinion, the report of the Anglo-American Committee was the last opportunity to reach an arrangement short of a Jewish state. He blames Truman for the fact that the recommendations of the Committee were not carried out.

Kenneth Bain's conclusions resemble Wilson's, but Bain tends to embellish the facts. His narrative begins with a romantic description of the Roosevelt-Ibn Saud meeting. Bain claims that the President "pledged that the United States would not aid the Jewish nationalists in the fight against the Arabs," although Roosevelt's promise to Ibn Saud was actually worded in a less decisive fashion. However, even interpreted thus, the meeting was not totally satisfactory from Bain's point of view: the President should have made it clear to the Jews that there was no chance of establishing a state. According to Bain, Roosevelt's inability to abandon Zionism completely proved ultimately disastrous. Roosevelt left Truman "fictions, half-truths and self-contradictions." But this criticism pales in comparison with that levelled at Truman. "Truman was a beleaguered and accidental president who found it impossible to understand complex situations."

While Wilson demonstrates a great deal of knowledge about American Jewry, Bain does not. He is not aware, for example, that the NZO was the Revisionist "New Zionist Organization," and not a "National Zionist Organization." He errs again when noting that the American Council for Judaism was a "major group."

In reviewing the report of the Anglo-American Committee, Bain permits himself to edit and adjust it to his own views. The Committee's conclusion that neither an Arab nor a Jewish state should be established in Palestine is reformulated by the author: "It had rejected the creating of a New Israel." According to Bain, the Committee recommended that "education must cease to be a process of inculcating youth with Zionist propaganda." Phrases of this sort do not appear in the report. Finally, he dismisses the American team on the Committee as "too biased to conduct an impartial and disinterested investigation."

His account of the events of 1947/48 is full of distortions. A large part of Bain's statements concerning the opinions of the Secretary of State and the people of the State Department are incorrect, as can be proven by even a superficial glance at the documentation. His claim, for example, that George Marshall opposed the partition plan in October 1947—arguing that the Arabs had proposed a compromise plan—is baseless. The proposal was in fact presented by Charles Malik twenty-four hours before the vote on partition on 29 November 1947.

Bain has Kfar Etzion conquered by the Arabs as early as January 1948; it actually fell to the Arab Legion only in May. Bain has Truman willing to assign American forces to enforce the ceasefire; but it is well known that Truman was at no time ready for such a step. Bain writes of the Jewish struggle for the possession of Haifa as if the Jews had never been in the city: "Haganah and Irgun forces took the initiative on 2 April . . . *they drove* (my italics-MK) into Haifa."

Both Bain and Wilson claim that serious mistakes made by the Truman administration contributed to the establishment of the state of Israel. The difference between the two is that Wilson tries to prove that the establishment of the Jewish state was against American interests; Bain, on the other hand, merely asserts that Zionism was an aggressive nationalism seeking to rob the Palestinian nation of its land; to expel the Arab population as far as possible; and to deny political rights to those Arabs remaining in Jewish Palestine. Wilson's book commands respect; Bain's is simply pseudo-scientific.

MENAHEM KAUFMAN
Hebrew University

Y. Zilberscheid and A. Pielkov (eds.), *Tel-ḥai: kibbuẓ hakhsharah befolin al shem ḥalalei Tel-ḥai* (Kibbutz Tel-Hai in Poland). Tel Aviv: Beit Lohamei Hagettaot and Ha-Kibbutz Ha-Meuhad, 1980.

Beit Lohamei Hagettaot (Ghetto Fighters House—an institute dedicated to the memory of the poet Yitzḥak Katznelson) is well known as an important center for the documentation and research of Jewish history during the Holocaust and in particular of Jewish resistance under Nazi rule. Apart from this, however, the institute specializes in the history of the Hehalutz (Pioneer) movement in Eastern Europe and more especially in Poland between the two world wars.

One important undertaking consists in publishing documentary material on the history of the kibbutz training system *(hakhsharah)* of Hehalutz in Poland. Four of these compilations have appeared so far: on the Lodz training kibbutz;[1] on Grokhov;[2] on Klosova;[3] and now the book under review. The specific characteristic of these books is that they comprise both documents from the period concerned and also secondary material.

The Hehalutz movement in Poland between the two world wars numbered thousands of members. It was the largest of the pioneer organizations and served as the main source of young immigrants to Palestine.

The collection before us relates the story of one of these training kibbutzim from the day it was started till its liquidation by the Nazis. Kibbutz Tel-Hai did not distinguish itself like Klosova and Shaharia in the ideological sphere, nor did it carve out new paths in the pioneer movement generally, nor in agricultural specialization like Grokhov, nor in industry like Lodz. It was founded at the very nadir of the Fourth Aliyah, and its members moved from place to place far from the pulsating centers of Jewish life, isolated in the forests and in remote localities for years on end. Nevertheless, it made a name for itself in the variegated mosaic of pioneer training in Poland, both because (unlike the other training kibbutzim) it was set up not in the east but in the center of the country, and also because in the years 1932–35, with the great upsurge of Hehalutz in Poland, it expanded to some twenty units or detachments, comprising more than eight hundred members—a significant percentage of the total.

The history of the kibbutz was a long sequence of moves from place to place in search of work and permanency. It was founded in 1927 near the town of Helm in central Poland; from there it moved to the north-east of the country in the environs of Vilna and Lida, until it finally settled down in the city of Bialystok in the early 1930's. In the course of wandering from one place to another and changing over from one kind of work to another—in agriculture, in the timber section and the wood-working industry—it had a hard struggle to maintain the collective way of life. As regards its social composition, it comprised people from towns and villages across the length and breadth of the country, from Hasidic as well as secular families, some with, some without a formal education, some of them from the youth movements and others who joined the training collectives when they were older—in short it reflected the whole spectrum of Polish Jewry. Together with the rest of the pioneer movement, it created a patterned way of life for itself. In Palestine, its members joined the Kibbutz Hameuhad.

As we have said, the last stop in their wandering was in Bialystok and its surrounding area. On the face of it new economic perspectives opened up for the kibbutz in this city, a textile center second in importance only to Lodz. In fact, however, the members did not gain a foothold in industry and most of them were employed in ill-paid, seasonal, unskilled work. This exclusion from the industrial enterprises is laid at the door of the Communists and the Bund, who dominated the trade unions and were against employing the Zionists of the kibbutz.

The book describes the wide range of activities undertaken by the kibbutz within the Jewish community as well as the complex problems it faced as a pioneer movement that consistently negated the legitimacy of the Diaspora (anti-Galut).

When aliyah to Palestine was stopped in the second half of the thirties, the kibbutz found itself facing grave difficulties. Instead of a short stay in the training centers prior to emigration, the members now had to spend from three to five years there. The kibbutz was thereby confronted with complicated social problems, and the attempts to solve them repeatedly created severe tensions.

With the outbreak of war and the Soviet occupation of the city, the kibbutz members had to disperse and hide their activities. The last tragic chapter in the story opens with their organizing themselves anew in Bialystok ghetto, which soon became one of the most important centers of the pioneer underground in Poland. The kibbutz was led by Mordekhai Tennenbaum-Tamaroff, later to be the commander of the ghetto underground.

The minutes of the deliberations at the general meeting of the kibbutz on 27 February 1943 are a terrible and moving document. They show how the arguments went back and forth among the young men fully aware that their fate was sealed; their main concern how to go to their deaths without betraying the principles of their movement and their honor as Jews and human beings. The attempted rising in the last days of the deportation of the Jews of Bialystok closes the annals of the kibbutz.

This collection is arranged chronologically, like its predecessors. The introduction gives an overall historical sketch of the kibbutz, a map of its lengthy and prolonged wanderings, and an index of place names and persons.

Like its predecessors, too, this is the work of many hands (one hundred and seventy people were involved), and naturally it is not all on the same level. The disparities are particularly marked with regard to testimonies and memoirs written specially for this book. It would perhaps have been better to apply stricter criteria in the choice of material. On the other hand, the documents and other material contemporaneous with the events described are of great importance. In spite of a few shortcomings, the collection is a valuable addition to the historiography of the largest Zionist pioneer movement in Europe.

ISRAEL OPPENHEIM
Ben-Gurion University of the Negev

Notes

1. *The Story of the Training Kibbutz in Lodz* (named in memory of B. Grukhov).
2. *Grokhov* (in "Skhemot Grokhov").
3. *The Book of Klosova* (in memory of Yosef Trumpeldor).

Gebhard Zwerenz, *Kurt Tucholsky: Biographie eines guten Deutschen*. Munich: C. Bertelsmann, 1979. 335 pp.

This book is a labor of love: the author, a political writer of Federal Germany, finds himself in full agreement with Tucholsky, a political writer of Weimar Germany. Both are men of great passion who adore polemics, satire, the *bon mot,* the elegant turn of phrase, the quick repartee, peace, democracy, and socialism, and both hate hypocrisy, capitalism, soldiers, reactionary judges, bureaucrats, nationalism, wishy-washy Social Democrats, dogmatic Communists, and many of their fellow-writers. At a distance of 50 years from one another, both Zwerenz and Tucholsky see Germany in mortal danger from an international arms race and from the ruthlessness, stupidity, and corruption of its own leaders. In short, both are left-wing intellectuals.

This, then, is a book with a message, though not an unscholarly book. Zwerenz seems to have read everything that has appeared in Germany on or by Tucholsky, and he has tried to interview everyone able to recall the master, an attempt that got him into trouble with a number of dedicated female guardians of Tucholsky's hallowed memory. He has not, however, consulted works in other languages, particularly in English, a language with which he does not appear to be familiar, judging from his repeated use of such English phrases as "much to high" and "head eggs."

Zwerenz very correctly divides his study into three major sections: *Sprechen, Schreiben,* and *Schweigen,* a take-off on Tucholsky's own periodization of his career. "Talking" (1) refers vaguely to Tucholsky's pre-Weimar days (he was born in 1890 in Berlin), when he was still largely un-political but already known as the author of the popular *Rheinsberg,* a delightful love story. "Writing" (2) refers to the period 1918–1932, when Tucholsky was a militant political journalist, poet, song-writer, and orator, as well as the chief collaborator and, for a while, the editor of *Die Weltbühne,* the greatest of all the left-wing intellectual journals. "Silence" (3) was the fate of the exiled Tucholsky, who refused to write publicly because "the Germans deserved Hitler."

Within the framework of each of these time periods, the text is organized topically, a most fitting approach, in view of Tucholsky's life-long preoccupation with such subjects as German justice, public morality, prison reform, and pacifism, but one that unavoidably leads to some repetition. Zwerenz's evaluation of Tucholsky's career is ambiguous: he sees him as the conscience of Germany, a true republican who criticized the Republic only because it was not really one. He was not a Communist, but he worked for and with Communists in the late 20's and early 30's because the Communists alone seemed prepared to stop the reactionaries and nationalists. When the Communists, too, failed—and quite dismally—against Hitler, Tucholsky moved away from them as well. Toward the end of his life, he again became a liberal. Finally, Zwerenz insists, the Jewish Tucholsky was unjustly accused of anti-Semitism: his critique of the Jews was really a critique of capitalism.

All this is fundamentally appealing. One must also agree with Zwerenz that Tucholsky's journalism and that of *Die Weltbühne* had an "American" flavor, in that it was extremely outspoken, and would have been perfectly at home in the United States. And yet, there is also much to disagree with. First of all, one would have expected a profound analysis of Weimar society and politics, rather than a simple repetition of Tucholsky's own arguments. Secondly, Zwerenz might well have borne in mind that the Weimar Republic was much less firmly established than was the United States, and consequently was more in need of support than of "purifying" criticism. Tucholsky's idea of an effective defense of German democracy and of the European idea was to portray the Social Democratic leaders as sorry lower-class buffoons; to proclaim repeatedly that "there is [in Germany] no state worth dying for"; and, in his *Deutschland, Deutschland über alles* (1929), to equate Stresemann with Krupp and war-mongering. The same book included a photo-montage of some old soldiers, with the caption "Animals Looking at You": this in a country desperately preoccupied with the honor of its military and the memory of millions of war dead. Zwerenz rightly hates generalizations, and yet, in his fierce defense of Tucholsky's politics, he lumps into the same enemy camp the conservative nationalists who object to Tucholsky because "he has dirtied our German national nest," and those who say that it was a grave error to give so much ammunition to the mortal enemies of the Weimar constitution. For, after all is said and done, it was not the democrats and republicans who profited most from Tucholsky's brilliance and idealism, but the Communists, the Nationalists, and the Nazis.

ISTVAN DEAK
Columbia University

Partial List of Recently Completed Doctoral Dissertations

Compiled from *American Jewish History, Dissertations Abstracts International*, "Reshimat talmidei meḥkar befakultaot ha'iyuniot" (Hebrew University), and other sources.

Victoria Aarons University of California, Berkeley, 1981
"Audience and Intention in the Works of Sholom Aleichem"

Edna Aizenberg Columbia University, 1981
"Religious Ideas/Eternal Metaphors: The Jewish Presence in Borges"

James D. Armstrong University of California, Riverside, 1982
"Life Among Friends: Interpersonal Relations and Social Processes in Tel Aviv, Israel"

Asi Morad Osman Ohio University, 1981
"Arabs, Israelis and US Television Networks"

Yitzhak Avneri Tel-Aviv University, 1981
"Hahistadrut haẓionit veha'aliyah habilti legalit le-ereẓ yisrael" (The Zionist Organization and Illegal Immigration to Palestine)

Gershon Bacon Columbia University, 1979
"Agudath Israel in Poland, 1916–1939: An Orthodox Response to the Challenge of Modernity"

Avraham Balaban Tel-Aviv University, 1980
"Mashma'ut ẓurot veretorikah be "Kokhavim baḥuẓ" me-et Natan Alterman" (Meaning of Structure and Rhetoric in Natan Alterman's "Kokhavim baḥuẓ")

Moshe Ben-Eliezer New York University, 1981
"Political Metaphors and Behavior: The Dominant Metaphors Used By a Selected Sample of American Jews for the State of Israel and Their Relationship to Activities Performed by American Jews on Behalf of the State of Israel"

Avner Ben-ner State University of New York, Stony Brook, 1981
"On the Economics of Self-management and Communalism: the Israeli Kibbutz"

Arthur K. Berliner — North Texas State University, 1982
"The Social Thought of Sigmund Freud"

Sylvain Boni — Bryn Mawr College, 1981
"The Self and the Other in the Ontologies of Sartre and Buber"

Karin Brinkmann Brown — City University of New York, 1982
"Karl Lueger as Liberal: Democracy, Municipal Reform and the Struggle for Power in the Vienna City Council 1875–1881"

Stanley C. Brubaker — University of Virginia, 1979
"Benjamin Nathan Cardozo: An Intellectual Biography"

Barbara A. Kalin Bundt — University of Minnesota, 1981
"Leisure and Religion: A Contemporary Jewish Sabbath Paradigm"

Michael T. Burns — Yale University, 1981
"Politics Face to Face: Rural Reactions to Boulangism and the Dreyfus Affair in France 1886–1900"

Kitty Calavita — University of Delaware, 1980
"A Sociological Analysis of United States Immigration Policy, 1820–1924"

William D. Camp — Carnegie-Mellon University, 1981
"Religion and Horror: the American Religious Press Views Nazi Death Camps and Holocaust Survivors"

Gayle Meyer Coolick — Georgia State University, 1981
"The Public Career of Cyrus Adler"

Stephen David Corrsin — University of Michigan, 1981
"Political and Social Change in Warsaw from the January 1863 Insurrection to the First World War: Polish Politics and the 'Jewish Question'"

Mark Cowett — University of Cincinnati, 1982
"Rabbi Morris Newfield of Birmingham: A Study in Ethnic Leadership"

James D. Cunningham — University of Toronto, 1981
"National Identity—National Unity. The Integrational Aspect of Adult Education in the Development of the Modern State of Israel, 1948–1973"

Charles Cutter — Ohio State University, 1979
"The American Yiddish Daily Press Reaction to the Rise of Nazism, 1930–1933"

Barry D. Cytron — Iowa State University, 1982
"A Rationale and Proposed Curriculum for Jewish-Christian Dialogue"

D. Delmaire — Université de Lille, 1980
"L'Antisemitisme de la Croix du Nord à l'epoque de l'affaire Dreyfus"

Herbert C. Dobrinsky   Yeshiva University, 1980
"Selected Laws and Customs of Sephardic Jews in the United States"

Yehoiakim Doron   Tel-Aviv University, 1979
"Haziyonut hamerkaz-eirope-it mul ideologiot germaniot bein hashanim 1885–1914" (Central European Zionism and German Ideologies, 1885–1914)

Rita B. Dravich   University of Oregon, 1980
"A Comparison of the Leisure Attitudes of Elderly Jews and non-Jews"

Yigal Drori   Tel-Aviv University, 1981
"'Hahugim haezrahiim' be-yishuv haerezyisraeli bishnot ha-20" (The Bourgeoisie in the Palestine Yishuv in the Twenties)

Marsha Bryan Edelman Columbia University—Teachers College, 1982
"Music Education in the Jewish Schools of Metropolitan New York"

Samuel Martin Edelman   University of Arizona, 1981
"Hermeneutics of Ethnic Rediscovery: Rhetorical, Sociolinguistic Analysis of Selected Works of Twentieth Century American Jewish Fiction"

David Marvin Elcott   Columbia University, 1981
"The Political Resocialization of German Jews in Palestine, 1933–1939"

Dan Eldar   Tel-Aviv University, 1979
"Hamediniyut hazarfatit balevant ve-yahasah laleumiyut ha'aravit uleziyonut bein hashanim 1914–1920" (French Policy in the Levant and its Attitude to Arab Nationalism and Zionism, 1914–1920)

Norbert Louis Elliot   University of Tennessee, 1981
"Allegory in the Novels of Isaac Bashevis Singer"

Naomi Fejgin   University of Chicago, 1982
"The Reform in Education in Israel: Integration, Academic Aspirations and Student Morale"

Lanora L. Field   University of Toronto, 1980
"Immunoglobulin Allotypes in the American and Canadian Jewish Population"

Irene A. Fine   The Union for Experimenting Colleges and Universities, 1980
"Developing a Jewish Studies Program for Women: A Springboard to History"

Ivan Cecil Frank   University of Pittsburgh, 1981
"A Study of the Degree to Which an Israeli Educational Youth Encampment Program, the Youth Aliyah Remedial Program in Kibbutz, Influences Attitudes Toward Social Integration"

Sylvia H. W. Frankel — University of Oregon, 1981
"Jewish Sources in Elie Wiesel's Work"

Ruth Gruber Fredman — Temple University, 1982
"Cosmopolitans at Home: An Anthropological View of the Sephardic Jews of Washington, DC"

Joseph L. Freedman — Columbia University, 1980
"A Life Coping Skills Approach to Guiding College-bound Jewish Students"

William J. Freiburger — University of Cincinnati, 1980
"The Lone Socialist Vote: A Political Study of Meyer London"

Ellen M. Brown French — Middle Tennessee State University, 1981
"Archetype and Metaphor: An Approach to the Early Novels of Elie Wiesel"

Melvin A. Friedlander — The American University, 1982
"The Management of Peace-Making in Egypt and Israel, 1977–79"

Patricia Ann Farrant Gartland — University of Iowa, 1981
"Out of the Burning: Response to the Holocaust"

Arieh Gelbard — Tel-Aviv University, 1981
"Ha'Bund' harusi bishnat 1917" (The Russian Bund in 1917)

Mitchell Brian Gelfand — Carnegie-Mellon University, 1982
"Chutzpah in El Dorado: Social Mobility of Jews in Los Angeles 1900–1920"

Ruth S. Geller — State University of New York, Buffalo, 1980
"The American Labor Novel 1871–1884"

Yaakov Geller — Tel-Aviv University, 1981
"Hakehillah hayehudit beromaniah hayeshanah (Regat) bein shtei milḥamot ha'olam (1919–1941)" (The Jewish Community of Old-Regime Romania [Regat] Between the Two World Wars [1919–1941])

Larry G. Gerber — University of California, Berkeley, 1979
"The Limits of Liberalism: A Study of the Careers and Ideological Development of Josephus Daniels, Henry Stimson, Bernard Baruch, Donald Richberg and Felix Frankfurter"

Baruch Gitlis — University of Southern California, 1981
"The Nazi Anti-Semitic Film: A Study of its Productional Rhetoric"

Marjorie Salgado Gordon — University of Maryland, 1981
"Alberto Gerschunoff and Samuel Eichelbaum: Two Literary Reflections on *Judeo-Argentinidad*"

Shmuel Herzl Govreen-Yehudaeen — University of Massachusetts, 1982
"The Challenge of Transculturation in a Westernized Technological Society: Reconstructing Jewish Values in Israel Through a Dialogical Approach to Education"

Nancy L. Green University of Chicago, 1980
"Class Struggle in the Pletzl: Jewish Immigrant Workers in Paris, 1881–1914"
William Norman Greenbaum Harvard University, 1978
"The Idea of Cultural Pluralism in the United States 1915–1975"
Ezra Greenspan Brown University, 1981
"The Schlemiel Comes to America: A Reading of Jewish-American Literature"
Richard E. Hanley State University of New York, Binghamton, 1981
"Place to Place: A Study of the Movement Between the City and the Country in Selected 20th Century American Fiction (Bernard Malamud, Saul Bellow, Norman Mailer, Bruce Jay Friedman, Philip Roth)"
Sheila Zarb Harper United States International University, 1982
"A Comparison of the Academic Achievement of Jewish and Non-Jewish Children After Parental Separation"
Donald Harvey University of Texas at Austin, 1982
"British Imperialism in the Middle East of World War I: A Psychosocial History of the Arab Revolt"
Marlene Eve Heinemann Indiana University, 1981
"Women Prose Writers of the Nazi Holocaust"
Kathryn A. Hellerstein Stanford University, 1980
"Moyshe Leyb Halpern's *In New York:* A Modern Yiddish Narrative"
Myrna L. Hewitt University of Massachusetts, 1980
". . . but they're still Jews. Jewish Identity, Assimilation, and the Ethnogenesis Model"
Azriel Hildesheimer Hebrew University, 1982
"Ha-irgun hamerkazi shel yehudei germaniah bashanim 1933–1945" (The Central Organization of German Jews 1933–1945)
Deanne Honeyman-Goodman University of Southern California, 1982
"An Exploration of the Communication Patterns of an Aged Ethnic Population in a Modern Urban Setting: The Old Jews of Venice, California"
S. Katunarich Pontificia Universitas Gregoriana, 1981
"Lo spirito del dialogo ebraico-cristiano in Samuel Sandmel"
Ziona Kopelovich University of Michigan, 1982
"Modality in Hebrew Literature"
Blaine P. Lamb Arizona State University, 1982
"Jewish Pioneers in Arizona, 1850–1920"
Shlomo Lambroza Rutgers University, New Brunswick, 1981
"The Pogrom Movement in Tsarist Russia 1903–06"
Margaret Landenberger St. Johns University, 1981

"United States Diplomatic Efforts on Behalf of Moroccan Jews, 1880–1906"
Pearl David Laufer University of Maryland, 1981
"Between Two Worlds: The Fiction of Anzia Yezierska"
Robert Laurentz State University of New York, Binghamton, 1980
"Racial/Ethnic Conflict in the New York City Garment Industry 1933–1980"
George Lebovitz University of Cincinnati, 1981
"Satisfaction and Dissatisfaction Among Judaic Studies Teachers in Midwestern Jewish Day Schools"
Mary J. Leddy University of Toronto, 1980
"The Event of the Holocaust and the Philosophical Reflections of Hannah Arendt"
Diana Lieb New York University, 1982
"Conflict Resolution—Theory and Practice: A Case Study of The Egyptian-Israeli Peace Treaty (1973–1979)"
Paul J. Lopatto Florida State University, 1982
"Religion and Politics in America"
Matthew Maibaum Claremont College, 1980
"The New Student and Youth Movement, 1965–1972: A Perspective View on Some Social and Political Developments in American Jews as a Religio-national Group"
Morton L. Manilla University of Toronto, 1980
"Identity and Loss: An Historical Critique of American-Jewish Literature"
Judith A. Freiman Mastai University of British Columbia, 1981
"Adaptation Tasks of Israeli Immigrants to Vancouver"
George M. Mobley Emory University, 1980
"American Civil Religion: Religion or Politics? (Protestants, Catholics and Jews)
Stephen Gross Mostov Brandeis University, 1981
"A 'Jerusalem' On the Ohio: The Social and Economic History of Cincinnati's Jewish Community, 1840–1875"
John A. Muresianu Harvard University, 1982
"War of Ideas: American Intellectuals and the World Crisis, 1938–1945"
Sipo Elijah Mzimela New York University, 1981
"Nazism and Apartheid: The Role of the Christian Churches in Nazi Germany and Apartheid South Africa"
Pamela S. Nadell Ohio State University, 1982
"The Journey to America by Steam: The Jews of Eastern Europe in Transition"
Levi Ness Yeshiva University, 1980

"Jewish Attitudes of the 1979 Graduates of Suffolk Conservative Afternoon Schools"

Kalman Nusbaum Tel-Aviv University, 1982
"Ḥelkam shel hayehudim be-irgun ufe'ulot haleḥimah shel haẓava hapolani bivrit hamo'aẓot" (Jewish Role in the Organization and Combat Activity of the Polish Army in the Soviet Union)

Dalia Ofer Hebrew University, 1982
"'Aliyah bilti legalit le-ereẓ yisrael bitkufat milḥemet ha'olam hashniyah (Illegal Immigration to Palestine During the Second World War) 1939–1942"

Michele Helane Pavin Ohio State University, 1981
"Sports and Leisure of the American Jewish Community 1848–1976"

Elad Peled Columbia University, 1979
"The Hidden Agenda of Educational Policy in Israel: the Interrelationship Between the Political System and the Educational System"

Yoav Peled University of California, Los Angeles, 1982
"Class, Nation and Culture: The Debate Over Jewish Nationality in the Russian Revolutionary Movement, 1893–1906"

Paul F. Peri Columbia University, 1980
"Education for Piety: An Investigation of the Works of Abraham J. Heschel"

Francis M. Perko Stanford University, 1981
"A Time to Favor Zion: A Case Study of Religion as a Force in American Educational Development"

Rivka Perlis Hebrew University, 1982
"Tnu'ot hano'ar haḥaluẓiyot befolin hakevushah biyedei hanaẓim bitkufat hashoah" (The Halutzic Youth Movements in Nazi-occupied Poland in the Holocaust Period)

Edward D. Pinsky New York University, 1980
"Cooperation Among American Jewish Organizations In Their Effort to Rescue European Jewry During the Holocaust"

Marcia J. Posner New York University, 1980
"A Search for Jewish Content in American Children's Fiction"

Judith Ann Press University of Connecticut, 1982
"An Ethnographic and Phenomenological Study of Students' Perceptions about Hebrew School"

Ronald L. Reynolds University of California, Los Angeles, 1982
"Organizational Goals and Effectiveness: The Function of Goal-Ambiguity in Jewish Congregational Afternoon Schools"

Timothy S. Roach Duke University, 1981
"Appearance in History: Hannah Arendt's Metaphorical Logic of the Person"

Marc Lyle Robbins — Princeton University, 1981
"The Strategy of Innocence: Political Resocialization of Oriental Jews in Israel"

Anna Halberstam Rubin — Kent State University, 1982
"Sholom Aleichem: The Author as Social Historian"

John W. Rumble — Vanderbilt University, 1980
"Fred Rose and the Development of the Nashville Music Industry 1942–1954"

Nancy Ellen Rupprecht — University of Michigan, 1982
"Ideology and Socialization in the Pre-War Hitler Youth"

Shlomo M. Russ — City University of New York, 1981
"The 'Zionist Hooligans': the Jewish Defense League"

Muhammed Sadiq — University of California, Berkeley, 1981
"Patterns of Identity in the Hebrew and Arabic Novel"

Nana Sagi — Hebrew University, 1982
"Teguvat haziburiyut hayehudit bebritaniah lirdifat hayehudim baraikh hashlishi (The Response of British Jewry to the Persecution of Jews in the Third Reich) 1930–1939"

W. Sauer — Universität Wien, 1979
"Viennese Catholic Associations: History of the Christian-Social/Conservative Party Until 1914"

Jeffrey Lee Schein — Temple University, 1981
"*Genesis* and *In Their Footsteps:* An Evaluation of Two Programs in Moral Education Designed for Jewish Schools"

Sidney H. Schwarz — Temple University, 1982
"Law and Legitimacy: An Intellectual History of Conservative Judaism, 1902–1973"

Bernard A. Segall — University of Colorado, Boulder, 1981
"Language and Self-identity Among A Sample of Jewish Families"

Baila Round Shargel — Jewish Theological Seminary of America, 1982
"Israel Friedlander and the Transformation of European Jewish Thought in America"

Uri Sharvit — Columbia University, 1982
"The Role of Music in the Jewish Yemenite Ritual: A Study of Ethnic Persistance"

Zohar Shavit — Tel-Aviv University, 1979
"'Aliyat eskolah beshirah: 'aliyat hamodernizm bashirah ha'ivrit saviv kvuzat 'Ktuvim'" (The Emergence of a Poetic School: The Rise of Modernism in Hebrew Poetry in the *Ktuvim* Circle)

Menahem Shelach — Tel-Aviv University, 1981
"Rezah yehudei kroaziah al-yedei hagermanim ve'ozreihem bemilhemet ha'olam hashniyah" (The Murder of the Jews of Croatia by the Germans and Their Collaborators During the Second World War)

Judith E. Smith Brown University, 1980
"Remaking Their Lives: Italian and Jewish Immigrant Family, Work and Community in Providence, RI, 1900-1940"

Sidney Solomon Jewish Theological Seminary of America, 1982
"The Conservative Congregational School as a Response to the American Scene"

Morris Sosevsky Yeshiva University, 1980
"Incorporating Moral Education Into the Jewish Secondary School Curriculum"

Shmuel Spektor Hebrew University, 1982
"Shoat yehudei volhin" (The Holocaust of Volhynian Jewry)

Howard Jerry Stanislawski Brandeis University, 1981
"Elites, Domestic Interest Groups, and International Interests in the Canadian Foreign Policy Decision-Making Process: The Arab Economic Boycott of Canadians and Canadian Companies Doing Business With Israel"

Theodore Steinberg New York University, 1980
"Max Kadushin, Scholar of Rabbinic Judaism"

Charles W. Stephenson University of Wisconsin, 1980
"Migration and Mobility in Late 19th Century and Early 20th Century America"

Leah Tovav Hebrew University, 1982
"Po'alah shel Leah Goldberg beshirat hayeladim" (Leah Goldberg's Oeuvre in Children's Poetry)

Yosef Te-eni Hebrew University, 1982
"'Aliyat Hitler lashilton vehashpa'atah shel ha-antishemiyut hapolanit al mazavam shel yehudei polin bashanim 1933-1939" (The Rise of Hitler and the Impact of Polish Anti-Semitism on the Status of Polish Jewry, 1933-1939)

Jane Hegge Thompson University of North Carolina, Chapel Hill, 1980
"The Theme of Rebirth in Five Dramas of Nelly Sachs"

Avraham Tzivyon Hebrew University, 1982
"Hamorashah hayehudit be'izuv 'olamo haruḥani shel Berl Katznelson" (The Judaic Tradition in the Shaping of Berl Katznelson's Worldview)

Yogev Tzuk Concordia University, 1981
"A Jewish Communal Welfare Institution in a Changing Society: Montreal 1920-1980"

Ellen M. Umansky Columbia University, 1981
"Lily H. Montagu and the Development of Liberal Judaism in England"

Rina Vaisman Hebrew University, 1982
"Aspects de l'identité juive et representations de l'état d'Israel—le cas des juifs français"

Yaakov Vaitzner   Hebrew University, 1982
"Shalom Aleikhem bateatron hayehudi" (Sholem Aleichem in Jewish Theater)
Robert S. Wechsler   Columbia University, 1979
"The Jewish Garment Trade in East London, 1875–1914"
Schlomo Weissblueth   University of Witwatersrand (SA), 1981
"Rabbi Nachman Krochmal and His Approach to the Interpretation of the Bible and Jewish History, His Language and Style"
Jack Wertheimer   Columbia University, 1979
"German Policy and Jewish Politics: The Absorption of East European Jews in Germany"
Bruce C. Westrate   University of Michigan, 1982
"Imperialists All: The Arab Bureau and the Evolution of British Policy in the Middle East, 1916–1920"
Gary P. William   Ohio State University, 1980
"Sacred Commitment in a Jewish Community: A Study of Religiosity, Secularized Humanism and Uncommitment"
Alan Bernard Wolf   University of Akron, 1982
"Responding to Transition: A Study of the Taylor Road Jewish Community"
Michael L. Yoder   University of Wisconsin, Milwaukee, 1980
"Religion as a Determinant of Fertility Among White Americans, 1965"
Arieh Zaidman   Tel-Aviv University, 1982
"Ha-otonomiah haleumit hayehudit be-ukrainah ha'azmait bashanim 1917–1919" (Jewish National Autonomy in Independent Ukraine, 1917–1919)

Paul Glikson: In Memoriam

Paul Glikson passed away in Jerusalem on 5 January 1983.

He was born in Warsaw in 1921 in a middle class family, and concluded high school studies at the "Gimnasia Hinukh" in 1939. Upon the German invasion of Poland, his parents and their children succeeded in escaping to Italy and after a long overland journey via Turkey eventually reached Palestine. Paul enlisted in the Free Polish forces of General Anders. At the end of the war he began to study economics in Italy. He obtained his B.Sc. degree in statistics at the London School of Economics in 1951. He served as Secretary of the Cultural Department of the World Jewish Congress in London, then directed by Professor Aaron Steinberg, from 1953 to 1963. On the founding of the *Jewish Journal of Sociology* he assisted the late Professor Maurice Freedman as editorial secretary and advisory reader from 1959 to 1963, and regularly contributed the "Chronicle" to that journal. He immigrated to Israel in 1963 and joined the Institute of Contemporary Jewry at the Hebrew University.

Throughout the period from his aliyah until his untimely death, Paul Glikson was a senior staff member of the Division for Jewish Demography and Statistics of the Institute of Contemporary Jewry. His work extended over the entire field of modern and historical demography of the Jews, covering a wide range both thematically and geographically. He also took upon himself many practical tasks for the promotion of studies in Jewish demography. In particular he accomplished the exacting work of monitoring current research and publications in Jewish demography worldwide. His great knowledge of both facts and languages and his persistent reading well fitted him for this painstaking task.

The results were a series of bibliographies, some of them thoroughly annotated, as well as special compendia of recent data, publications and studies, which have proved of great value to researchers in this field. He took an active part in the publication of all the volumes in the series, *Jewish Population Studies,* which is issued by the Institute of Contemporary Jewry. Altogether thirteen volumes appeared in this series from 1971 until his death; two more that bear his name as co-editor are to be published shortly.

Among his various posts was that of Honorary Treasurer of the International Association for Jewish Demography and Statistics.

Towards the end of his life he was engaged in preparing a systematic documentary compilation on the demographic history of the Jews in Poland, a task for which he would have been eminently suited. He passed away suddenly, the day after putting the finishing touches to the proofs of *Studies in Jewish Demography: Survey for 1972–1980,* on which he had bestowed the devoted labor of years.

Paul was of a scholarly disposition, widely interested in intellectual and cultural matters—both historical and contemporary—a keen reader and lover of books. He was deeply attached to the Jewish people, an untiring student of Jewish history and of the socio-demographic evolution of modern Jewry throughout the world. Partly because of his work at the Institute, but still more because of his own intellectual inclinations, he was one of the few persons thoroughly conversant with the state of the art in Jewish demography. His vast knowledge of the literature in the field provided him with a sure critical sense of the respective merits and shortcomings of new research work being published. Yet, in his bibliographical compilations and annotations, one could always detect those traits of fairness and equanimity that mark good scholarship.

Paul Glikson was a modest and unassuming person, always ready to help his fellows. In particular he assisted many colleagues in Jerusalem with the translation, or editing in English, of their writings. His wide knowledge and intellectual interests, and his great perseverence despite the physical difficulties which afflicted him, earned him the respect and affection of those who knew him. Faithful to the ideals of scholarship and ever willing to help colleagues unselfishly in their scholarly endeavors, he represented the best in the tradition of public service.

SERGIO DELLAPERGOLA and U. O. SCHMELZ

STUDIES IN CONTEMPORARY JEWRY

II

1985

Edited by Peter Medding

will include a symposium on

Orthodoxy's Responses to the Challenge of Modernity

with essays by

MENAHEM FRIEDMAN, on recent polarizing trends in the Orthodox community

ELIEZER GOLDMAN, on responses to modernity in religious philosophy

ZVI ZOHAR, on the halakhic responses of rabbis in Syria and Egypt to social and technological change in the early twentieth century

GERSHON BACON, on the political response of Agudath Israel in interwar Poland

ARYEI FISHMAN, on modernizing trends in religious Zionism

GIDEON ARAN, on the crisis within religious Zionism after 1948 and the precursors of Gush Emunim

STEVEN M. COHEN and SAMUEL HEILMAN, on the observance of ritual and its relation to internal differentiation among Orthodox Jews of New York